THE OXFORD
ILLUSTRATED DICKENS

MARTIN CHUZZLEWIT

THE OXFORD ILLUSTRATED DICKENS

Charles John Huffham Dickens was born on 7 February 1812 at Landport near Portsmouth, where his father was a Navy pay clerk. His family moved to London in 1815 and in 1817 to Chatham, where Dickens spent the happiest time of his boyhood. This was followed by a period of misery during which his father was imprisoned for debt in the Marshalsea and Dickens was withdrawn from school and, at the age of 12, sent to work in a blacking warehouse. These experiences deeply affected him and his future work. He returned to school, and left at 15 to become a clerk, a shorthand reporter in the law courts, and a reporter of debates in the Commons. In 1833 he began contributing articles to periodicals, which were later reprinted as *Sketches by Boz* (1836–7); these led to an approach from publishers, resulting in the creation of Mr Pickwick and the publication in monthly numbers of *The Posthumous Papers of the Pickwick Club* (1836–7). In 1836 he married Catherine Hogarth; they had ten children over the next 16 years. Dickens began to publish *Oliver Twist* in 1837 in *Bentley's Miscellany*, a periodical of which he was the first editor. *Nicholas Nickleby* followed in 1838–9. *The Old Curiosity Shop* (1840–1) and *Barnaby Rudge* (1841) were intended for *Master Humphrey's Clock*, a weekly written by Dickens, but he eventually abandoned 'Master Humphrey'.

Dickens's visit to America in 1842 resulted in *American Notes* (1842) and an American section in *Martin Chuzzlewit* (1843–4). He lost readership with the latter but regained it with 'A Christmas Carol' (1843), the first of his five *Christmas Books*. In 1844 he visited Italy, and contributed 'Pictures from Italy' (1846) to the *Daily News*, a paper he founded. *Dombey and Son* appeared in 1846–8 and *David Copperfield* in 1849–50. In 1850 Dickens began the weekly journal *Household Words*, incorporated in 1859 into *All The Year Round*, which he edited until his death. In these appeared essays later issued as *Reprinted Pieces* (1858) and *The Uncommercial Traveller* (1861), and his *Christmas Stories*. *A Child's History of England* was published in 1851–3, *Bleak House* in 1852–3, *Hard Times* in 1854, *Little Dorrit* in 1855–7, *A Tale of Two Cities* in 1859, *Great Expectations* in 1860–1, and *Our Mutual Friend* in 1864–5. In 1856 Dickens bought a country house, Gad's Hill Place, near Rochester, and in 1858 he and his wife separated. He threw himself into public readings of his works, which were greatly successful but draining. His last work, *The Mystery of Edwin Drood*, was left unfinished when he died suddenly on 9 June 1870.

THE LIFE AND ADVENTURES

OF

MARTIN CHUZZLEWIT

By
CHARLES DICKENS

With Forty Illustrations by 'Phiz'
and an Introduction by GEOFFREY RUSSELL

OXFORD   NEW YORK   TORONTO   MELBOURNE
OXFORD UNIVERSITY PRESS

Oxford University Press, Walton Street, Oxford OX2 6DP
Oxford New York Toronto
Delhi Bombay Calcutta Madras Karachi
Petaling Jaya Singapore Hong Kong Tokyo
Nairobi Dar es Salaam Cape Town
Melbourne Auckland
and associated companies in
Berlin Ibadan

Oxford is a trade mark of Oxford University Press

Martin Chuzzlewit was published in serial form, the first part appearing in January 1843, and then as a novel in July 1844, with illustrations by 'Phiz' (Hablot K. Browne).

In the Oxford Illustrated Dickens (known before 1966 as the New Oxford Illustrated Dickens) it was first published in 1951, and reprinted in 1959, 1966, 1968, 1971, 1975, 1981, 1987, 1989, 1989, 1991.

Published in the United States by Oxford University Press, USA

This volume: ISBN 0 19 254509 4
21-volume set: ISBN 0 19 254522 1

Printed in the United States of America

INTRODUCTION

GEOFFREY RUSSELL

DICKENS began to write *Martin Chuzzlewit* in 1842. Publication was begun (in parts) in January 1843 and it was published by Chapman & Hall in full in July 1844—with a dedication to Miss Burdett Coutts.

While the book was in the making Dickens was at outs with his publishers (as he had been before with Bentley) not only about money but, chiefly, because in his mind it was he and not the publishers who had put him where he was and, in effect, they wanted him more than he wanted them. All this is described fully and fairly by Forster who was engaged in both quarrels as a sort of arbitrator or amiable compositeur. There is no doubt that at the time Dickens was worried and flustered about all this. But it is no longer a matter of consideration. In addition, there was the worry that, to quote Forster, 'Chuzzlewit had fallen short of all the expectations formed of it in regard to sale, unaccompanied by any falling off either in his writing or in the writer's reputation: it was very temporary but it was present and to be dealt with accordingly'.

Dickens wrote to Forster, early in the composition of the book, 'You know as well as I that I think "Chuzzlewit" in a hundred points immeasurably the best of my stories, that I feel my power more than I ever did; that I have a greater confidence in myself than I ever had; that I *know* that if I have health I could sustain myself in the minds of thinking men though fifty writers started up to-morrow.' And in Forster's view *Martin Chuzzlewit* was the 'turning point' of Dickens's career and he gives his reasons for agreeing with what Dickens had said: 'Martin Chuzzlewit' was 'less upon the surface, going deeper into springs of character. . . . The persons in former books had been more agreeable but never so interpenetrated with meanings. . . . Dickens had scrutinised as keenly, but he had never shewn the imaginative insight in which he now sent his humour and his art into the core of the vices of the time.' And they were right. *Martin Chuzzlewit* is something other and better in tone and quality and goes deeper than anything Dickens had written before.

Charles Dickens was first and foremost a social reformer. Chesterton once wrote of him that, like Arabella Allen who 'didn't know what she did like but did know what she didn't like', Dickens did know what he didn't like and if he thought that it wanted hitting he hit it hard—very often for reasons that he could not have explained. Greed and selfishness even to murder are the theme of *Martin Chuzzlewit*. That greed and selfishness are social evils is not difficult to discover nor to understand—and Dickens hit them hard in this book.

He had put into the first chapter of the book, a chapter not generally admired and indeed for the most part very silly and worse than silly but filling a place, the character of the Chuzzlewit family as 'remarkable for taking uncommon good care of themselves'. But for the *type* of selfishness and greed he uses Pecksniff. Pecksniff is the first-mentioned character in the story and Forster tells us (when writing of Dickens's excitement about the first number and Sydney Smith's comment 'Pecksniff and his daughters are admirable—such as no one but yourself can execute') that 'the notion of taking Pecksniff for a type of character was really the origin of the book, the design being to show more or less by every person introduced, the number and variety of humours and vices that have their root in selfishness'. And this grew to flower as the production went on. Dickens wrote to Forster 'of two of the most prominent figures as soon as all their capabilities were revealed to him', 'as to the way in which these characters have opened out, that is, to me, one of the most surprising processes of the mind in this sort of invention. Given what one knows, what one does not know springs up; and I am as absolutely certain of its being true as I am of the law of gravitation—if such a thing be possible more so.' Of 'the two most prominent characters' one must have been Pecksniff and, I think, the other Jonas Chuzzlewit.

Pecksniff, set forth in satire perhaps unmatched in Dickens's work, is abomination and is drawn consistently as abomination. There is rarely savagery but even when Dickens, writing of Pecksniff, is at his most 'amusing' there is always the sting of bitter mockery. Other people have taken a different view and argue that Dickens's sense of comedy prevented the success of the satire.

I cannot read Pecksniff as burlesque. He is drawn, and most skilfully drawn, to be hated by the reader and everything written about him, even when it is most 'amusing', makes the reader hate him worse. He is hated by every other character in the book except Tom Pinch—and in the end Tom Pinch's heart is nearly broken by the discovery of Pecksniff's vileness.

Tom and Ruth Pinch are good as Pecksniff is wicked. Tom is introduced in the second chapter of the book, as Pecksniff and his daughters are, and from that chapter we begin to know Tom as we begin to know Pecksniff. He is consistent all through the book. As Pecksniff is hateful, so Tom is lovable, to every-body. Think of his departure from the village for London when Pecksniff turned him out, the kindness of Mrs. Lupin, the astonishment and regrets of the tollman. Think of the love that Westlock and young Martin had for him. And think of the love his sister had for him and the way she showed it: read Chapters L and LII and then, in choosing among Dickens's heroines not one to be amusedly read about but one to be a mother to your children, consider Ruth Pinch.

Mrs. Gamp is perhaps the best of all Dickens's clowns and one of the greatest clowns in literature: not, indeed, greater than Falstaff, but then Falstaff was far more than a clown. Mrs. Gamp is in the book because she typifies one of the dis-graces that Dickens, the social reformer, would sweep away. He made her, as he sets out in his preface, a fair representation of the hired attendant of the poor in sickness but, to follow Forster, he might have added that the rich were no better off, for Mrs. Gamp's original was in reality a person hired by a lady who was quite well off. And in the novel most of the people who suffered under this foul woman did not suffer because they or their friends were poor: they suffered because there was no proper nursing to be had.

'Mrs. Gamp was a lady of that happy temperament which can be ecstatic without any other stimulating cause than a general desire to establish a large and profitable connection.' For her marvellous lingo (which Dickens warned Forster that he would have difficulty in understanding) the original Dickens must be consulted. 'No one would be so rash as to abridge or paraphrase' Mrs. Gamp (as a distinguished his-torian once wrote about John Henry Newman). Forster says that by the additional invention of Mrs. Harris the comic invention is all reproduced, acted over with renewed spirit and doubled and quadrupled in her favour, and that this on the whole is the happiest stroke of humorous art in all the writings of Dickens. To many people *Martin Chuzzlewit* is primarily 'the book with Mrs. Gamp in it'.

For others the most Dickensy part of all the book is Todgers's. It was so to me as a boy and I think that I knew it almost by heart before I began to care about the plot of the book. For one thing, and the most important thing in those days, it was the part that my father used to read aloud to us when we were little and there have been with me ever since such things as 'Mr. Pecksniff, looking out of window (of the night coach that took them there) said it was to-morrow morning and they were there'; the inscription 'Commercial Boarding House. M. Todgers'; Bailey Junior who at the festival dinner to Pecksniff and his daughters 'with his hands in his pockets and his legs pretty wide apart led the laughter and enjoyed the conversation'; and his remark when he was put in charge of Pecksniff, very drunk, that 'he hoped he knowed wot o'clock it wos in gineral and didn't date his letters to his friends from Todgers's for nothing'.

Other matters of Todgers's interest reached me later. Mr. Pecksniff and his daughters 'present Mr. Bailey with a gratuity so liberal that he could hardly do enough to show his gratitude'. What in the 1840's would be a liberal tip in those circumstances? I should guess ten shillings from the three of them at the most.

And, but not for about twenty chapters later, we hear of Todgers's again. That was when Charity Pecksniff left her father and was conducted by M. Todgers to 'her peaceful home beneath the shadow of the Monument'. Mr. Bailey was gone and '(such is the decay of human greatness)' was succeeded by an old woman whose name 'was reported to be Tamaroo—which seemed an impossibility'. (Cf. Orlick in *Great Expectations*: 'He pretended that his christian name was Dolge—a clear impossibility.') That chapter is devoted to the wooing by Charity of the gloomy man (in the earlier chapters 'the youngest gentleman in company')—Moddle.

In Chapter XXXVII Tom Pinch caught by Charity straying near the Monument, after he had parted from Pecksniff, is taken into Todgers's and there meets Mercy who, in her misery with Jonas, had 'found the secret door in Mrs. Todgers's breast with "Woman" written on the spring which at a touch from Mercy's hand had flown wide open and admitted her for shelter'.

We see Todgers's once more; and this time not with Dickens at his best. The chapter is headed 'Gives the Author great concern. For it is the last in the book'. It begins 'Todgers's was in high feather' and deals mainly with the preparation for the wedding of Charity and Moddle all broken up by Moddle's jilting of her and his flight from her. Clever—but it seems somehow wrong that the book should end (except for a few artificial paragraphs of apostrophe to Tom Pinch) on a note of cruelty to Charity not at all needed for the story—and we leave Charity 'fainted away in earnest'.

There must be a word about Mark Tapley. We find his formula of the credit, or lack of credit, in being jolly a little tiresome, and it is artificial and forced to an unusual extent. But, after all, it is this, and not his estimable qualities, that got his name into common speech as the symbol of resilient gaiety under difficulties just as the name Pecksniff is the symbol of hypocrisy. The best in Mark Tapley is his tenderness to Martin in America and his faithfulness to Martin after.

In point of construction the inclusion in the book of 'the American part', as it is always called, has been the subject of controversy and, I think, the balance of opinion is that it was unfortunate. That is my own opinion. It is not a novel within a novel, still less a mere interpolated story like those in *Pickwick*, but a separate story. Both stories are injured. The reader's attention is from time to time switched off by the American part from the main story and often for so long at a time that he has to look back to find out where he is. Both Dickens and Forster saw this while the book was in the writing. Dickens wrote to Forster, 'It is against the grain with me to go back to America when my interest is strong in the other parts of the tale.' Forster, in one passage in the *Life*, says that 'what is lost as a story by the American episode' (and episode is the right word) 'is gained in the other direction; young Martin by happy use of a bitter experience, casting off his slough of selfishness in the poisonous swamp of Eden'. This is half-hearted. I believe that the true reason why Dickens and Forster decided to include the American part is to be found in another passage in the *Life* where Forster, dealing with 'the undeniable fact of a grave depreciation of sale in his writings' says, 'They rose somewhat on Martin's ominous announcement, at the end of the fourth number, that he'd *go to America*; but though it was believed that this resolve, which Dickens adopted as suddenly as his hero, might increase the number of his readers, that reason influenced him less than the challenge to make good his *Notes* ("American Notes for General Circulation" published just before "Martin Chuzzlewit" was begun) which every mail had been bringing him from unsparing assailants across the Atlantic. The substantial effect of the American episode upon the sale was yet by no means great. A couple of thousand additional purchasers were added.'

It will be found that it is very well worth while reading the two parts separately. Only a year or two ago, when I last went to America, I had taken with me a pocket edition of the book to read on the voyage so that I might not be found, among old friends with whom I was going to stay, forgetful of such people as Elijah Pogram, Jefferson Brick, The Watertoast Association, and Mrs. Hominy. I re-read the American part and found it most exciting. For there again is found Charles Dickens's wonderful power of rousing by mockery detestation of wickedness. I should have been rewarded, if only by the description of the storm as seen from the ship. Dickens always did storms well and two of the best of them are in *Martin Chuzzlewit*.

In a Preface to a later edition of *Martin Chuzzlewit* he wrote: 'the American portion of this story is in no other respect a caricature, than as it is an exhibition, for the most part (Mr. Bevan excepted) of a ludicrous side, *only*, of the American character—of that side which was four-and-twenty years ago, from its nature the most obtrusive, and the most likely to be seen by such travellers as young Martin and Mark Tapley.' And in 1868 when he was again in America he made a speech 'At a Public Dinner given to me on Saturday the 18th of April 1868 in the City of New York by two hundred representatives of the Press of the United States of America' and at the end of the speech said 'So long as this book shall last, I hope that what I have said will form a part of it, and will be fairly read as inseparable from my experiences and impressions of America'.

An important part of the progress of the main plot of the book is the story of Montague Tigg's Insurance Company, the Anglo-Bengalee Disinterested Loan and Life Insurance Company. A note on this is appended at the end of the book.

Much unkind comment has been made of Dickens's use of blank verse. *Martin Chuzzlewit* has many instances of this and

some people ascribe its frequency in that book to the disturbed
state of his mind; partly over the quarrels with the publishers
and partly by the fact that he was tired and worn out with
overwork. Robert Louis Stevenson said that fatigue showed
itself by a tendency to drop into blank verse. Dickens himself
was aware of the habit in himself and disliked it.

I do not believe that it is true that in Dickens's case this
was the result of fatigue or, at any rate, always true. It may
be true about such things as:

> and it was sealed with Mr. Pecksniff's seal.
>
> and so it ought to seem to you, you dog.
>
> until the rising of another sun
> proclaimed the advent of another post.
>
> No idle Pecksniff lingered far inland,
> unmindful of the changes of the stream.

but not about such things as:

> Look round and round upon this bare bleak plain,
> and see even here, upon a winter's day,
> how beautiful the shadows are.
>
> in other days might have survived the rack,
> and had its strongest life in weakest death.
>
> who dreamed of Freedom in a slave's embrace,
> and waking sold her offspring and his own
> in public markets.
>
> this was the realm of Hope through which they moved.
>
> and the red light
> used them as foils to set its brightness off,
> and aid the lustre of the dying day.

Just about this time Dickens's friendship for, and great
admiration of, Tennyson had begun, and in 1842 he had sent
a copy of his works to the man 'whose writings enlist my whole
heart and nature in admiration of their truth and beauty', and
it is not difficult, at any rate for me, to believe that in some
of these passages of blank verse Dickens was, perhaps unconsciously, perhaps deliberately, trying to write like Tennyson.
And here is another noticeable thing. Read the murder of
Montague by Jonas in Chapter XLVII and then read the first
three stanzas of *Maud* published in 1854. Is there no reflection
from Dickens to Tennyson?

Martin Chuzzlewit is not Dickens's longest novel (*Bleak House*,

David Copperfield, Little Dorrit, and *Our Mutual Friend* are a few pages longer), but many people find it in parts long-winded. I still do myself, but it is dangerous to skip, for, in some of the parts most tempting to skip (e.g. some of Ruth and Tom Pinch and Mark Tapley's 'jollity') there are bits of fact necessary to the full understanding of the main plot. Plots were not Dickens's strong point, but he took a great deal of trouble about this one and it works—and it holds us in that suspense for which we read novels.

Devout Dickensians have differed over *Martin Chuzzlewit.* But we may decide that Dickens was great first as a creator of character and then as a moralist and only less great as an artist because he could not be severe with himself. He could not see that if his morality was strong (as it was) there was no need of moralizing; that if his characters were strong (as they were) there was no need for these apostrophes in the second person singular to Tom Pinch. (That apostrophe trick is irritating; just about the time of this book Dickens was much under the influence of Carlyle and his 'style'.)

For Dickens's characters, we need never discuss whether they are caricatures, exaggerations, unreal; they are real in Dickens's world. Dickens himself, in a Preface to a later edition of the book wrote: 'What is exaggeration to one class of minds and perceptions is plain truth to another.' 'All the Pecksniff family upon earth are quite agreed, I believe, that Mr. Pecksniff is an exaggeration, and that no such character ever existed. I will not offer any plea on his behalf to so powerful and genteel a body.'

And the story must be rounded off with the punishment of the wicked. Pecksniff cannot be a humbug and wrong everyone around him without undergoing the consequences—lying and begging for his bread. Slyme who is purely contemptible is allowed to live in ignominy: Montague Tigg, who is unscrupulous, is murdered; Jonas, his murderer, and only by accident not the murderer of his father, commits suicide.

Forster, in the *Life,* 1874, says 'its sale has ranked next after *Pickwick Papers* and *Copperfield*' and it is still, as it deserves to be, one of the most widely read novels of its author, for truly in this novel we have that incomparable Dickens, his inventive powers producing every possible creature and no two quite alike; every one of them a little larger than life.

Note: From careful re-readings of the book for the purposes of this introduction I have got much that I did not know before and much that I had forgotten. And I owe much to discussions with friends. From one of these friends, more learned in Dickens's novels than I am, I have had so much light and leading that he would certainly have been mentioned by name had he not strongly wished otherwise.

PREFACE

WHAT is exaggeration to one class of minds and perceptions, is plain truth to another. That which is commonly called a long-sight, perceives in a prospect innumerable features and bearings non-existent to a short-sighted person. I sometimes ask myself whether there may occasionally be a difference of this kind between some writers and some readers; whether it is *always* the writer who colours highly, or whether it is now and then the reader whose eye for colour is a little dull?

On this head of exaggeration I have a positive experience, more curious than the speculation I have just set down. It is this:—I have never touched a character precisely from the life, but some counterpart of that character has incredulously asked me: 'Now really, did I ever really, see one like it?'

All the Pecksniff family upon earth are quite agreed, I believe, that Mr. Pecksniff is an exaggeration, and that no such character ever existed. I will not offer any plea on his behalf to so powerful and genteel a body, but will make a remark on the character of Jonas Chuzzlewit.

I conceive that the sordid coarseness and brutality of Jonas would be unnatural, if there had been nothing in his early education, and in the precept and example always before him, to engender and develop the vices that make him odious. But so born and so bred; admired for that which made him hateful, and justified from his cradle in cunning, treachery, and avarice; I claim him as the legitimate issue of the father upon whom those vices are seen to recoil. And I submit that their recoil upon that old man, in his unhonoured age, is not a mere piece of poetical justice, but is the extreme exposition of a direct truth.

I make this comment and solicit the reader's attention to it in his or her consideration of this tale, because nothing is more common in real life than a want of profitable reflection on the causes of many vices and crimes that awaken general horror. What is substantially true of families in this respect, is true of a whole commonwealth. As we sow, we reap. Let the reader go into the children's side of any prison in England, or, I grieve to add, of many workhouses, and judge whether those are monsters who disgrace our streets, people our hulks and penitentiaries, and overcrowd our penal colonies, or are creatures whom we have deliberately suffered to be bred for misery and ruin.

The American portion of this story is in no other respect a caricature, than as it is an exhibition, for the most part, (Mr. Bevan excepted) of a ludicrous side, *only*, of the American character—of that side which was, four-and-twenty years ago, from its nature, the most obtrusive, and the most likely to be seen by such travellers as Young Martin and Mark Tapley. As I had never, in writing fiction, had any disposition to soften what is ridiculous or wrong at home, so I then hoped that the good-humoured people of the United States would not be generally disposed to quarrel with me for carrying the same usage abroad. I am happy to believe that my confidence in that great nation was not misplaced.

When this book was first published, I was given to understand, by some authorities, that the Watertoast Association and eloquence were beyond all bounds of belief. Therefore I record the fact that all that portion of Martin Chuzzlewit's experiences is a literal paraphrase of some reports of public proceedings in the United States (especially of the proceedings of a certain Brandywine Association), which were printed in the Times Newspaper in June and July 1843, at about the time when I was engaged in writing those parts of the book; and which remain on the file of *The Times* Newspaper, of course.

In all my writings, I hope I have taken every available opportunity of showing the want of sanitary improvements in the neglected dwellings of the poor. Mrs. Sarah Gamp was, four-and-twenty years ago, a fair representation of the hired attendant on the poor in sickness. The Hospitals of London were, in many respects, noble Institutions; in others, very defective. I think it not the least among the instances of their mismanagement, that Mrs. Betsey Prig was a fair specimen of a Hospital Nurse; and that the Hospitals, with their means and funds, should have left it to private humanity and enterprise to enter on an attempt to improve that class of persons—since, greatly improved through the agency of good women.

CONTENTS

LIST OF ILLUSTRATIONS

CHARACTERS

BAILEY JUNIOR, *boots at Mrs. Todgers's Commercial Boarding-house, afterwards 'tiger' to Tigg Montague.*

MR. BEVAN, *a warm-hearted Massachusetts physician.*

JEFFERSON BRICK, *war correspondent of* The New York Rowdy Journal.

MR. CHUFFEY, *a weazen-faced old man; clerk to Anthony Chuzzlewit.*

GENERAL CYRUS CHOKE, *an American militia officer.*

MAJOR HANNIBAL CHOLLOP, *a 'worshipper of Freedom'.*

ANTHONY CHUZZLEWIT, *father of Jonas, and brother of the elder Martin.*

JONAS CHUZZLEWIT, *his son; a sly, cunning, scheming man.*

MARTIN CHUZZLEWIT, SENIOR, *a rich and eccentric old gentleman.*

MARTIN CHUZZLEWIT, THE YOUNGER, *the hero of the story; grandson of the preceding, by whom he is brought up.*

DAVID CRIMPLE, *a pawnbroker; afterwards Secretary to the Anglo-Bengalee Assurance Company.*

COLONEL DIVER, *editor of* The New York Rowdy Journal.

MR. FIPS, *a lawyer.*

GENERAL FLADDOCK, *a starched and punctilious American militia officer.*

DOCTOR JOHN JOBLING, *medical officer to the Anglo-Bengalee Assurance Company.*

MR. LA FAYETTE KETTLE, *an inquisitive, bombastic American.*

MR. LEWSOME, *a degraded assistant to a London general medical practitioner.*

MR. AUGUSTUS MODDLE, *the 'youngest gentleman' at Mrs. Todgers's.*

MR. MOULD, *an undertaker.*

MR. NADGETT, *Tom Pinch's landlord, and a secret inquiry agent.*

SETH PECKSNIFF, *a resident near Salisbury, ostensibly an architect and land surveyor, who receives Martin Chuzzlewit as a pupil.*

TOM PINCH, *an unpretentious but high-souled man; assistant to Mr. Pecksniff.*

THE HONOURABLE ELIJAH POGRAM, *a Member of Congress.*

ZEPHANIAH SCADDER, *agent of the Eden Land Corporation.*

CHEVY SLYME, *a poor and shiftless relative of old Martin Chuzzlewit.*

MR. SPOTTLETOE, *a designing relative of old Martin Chuzzlewit.*

PAUL SWEEDLEPIPE ('Poll'), *a bird-fancier and hairdresser.*

MARK TAPLEY, *hostler at the Blue Dragon Inn; afterwards manservant to young Martin Chuzzlewit.*

CHAPTER I

Introductory, concerning the pedigree of the Chuzzlewit family

AS no lady or gentleman, with any claims to polite breeding, can possibly sympathise with the Chuzzlewit Family without being first assured of the extreme antiquity of the race, it is a great satisfaction to know that it undoubtedly descended in a direct line from Adam and Eve; and was, in the very earliest times, closely connected with the agricultural interest. If it should ever be urged by grudging and malicious persons, that a Chuzzlewit, in any period of the family history, displayed an overweening amount of family pride, surely the weakness will be considered not only pardonable but laudable, when the immense superiority of the house to the rest of mankind, in respect of this its ancient origin, is taken into account.

It is remarkable that as there was, in the oldest family of which we have any record, a murderer and a vagabond, so we never fail to meet, in the records of all old families, with innumerable repetitions of the same phase of character. Indeed, it may be laid down as a general principle, that the more extended the ancestry, the greater the amount of violence and vagabondism; for in ancient days those two amusements, combining a wholesome excitement with a promising means of repairing shattered fortunes, were at once the ennobling pursuit and the healthful recreation of the Quality of this land.

Consequently, it is a source of inexpressible comfort and happiness to find, that in various periods of our history, the Chuzzlewits were actively connected with divers slaughterous conspiracies and bloody frays. It is further recorded of them, that being clad from head to heel in steel of proof, they did on many occasions lead their leather-jerkined soldiers to the death with invincible courage, and afterwards return home gracefully to their relations and friends.

There can be no doubt that at least one Chuzzlewit came over with William the Conqueror. It does not appear that this illustrious ancestor 'came over' that monarch, to employ the vulgar phrase, at any subsequent period: inasmuch as the Family do not seem to have been ever greatly distinguished by the possession of landed estate. And it is well known that for the bestowal of that kind of property upon his favourites, the liberality and gratitude of the Norman were as remarkable as those virtues are usually found to be in great men when they give away what belongs to other people.

Perhaps in this place the history may pause to congratulate itself upon the enormous amount of bravery, wisdom, eloquence, virtue, gentle birth, and true nobility, that appears to have come into England with the Norman Invasion: an amount which the genealogy of every ancient family lends its aid to swell, and which would beyond all question have been found to be just as great, and to the full as prolific in giving birth to long lines of chivalrous descendants, boastful of their origin, even though William the Conqueror had been William the Conquered; a change of circumstances which, it is quite certain, would have made no manner of difference in this respect.

There was unquestionably a Chuzzlewit in the Gunpowder Plot, if indeed the arch-traitor, Fawkes himself, were not a scion of this remarkable stock; as he might easily have been, supposing another Chuzzlewit to have emigrated to Spain in the previous generation, and there intermarried with a Spanish lady, by whom he had issue, one olive-complexioned son. This probable conjecture is strengthened, if not absolutely confirmed, by a fact which cannot fail to be interesting to those who are curious in tracing the progress of hereditary tastes through the lives of their unconscious inheritors. It is a notable circumstance that in these later times, many Chuzzlewits, being unsuccessful in other pursuits, have, without the smallest rational hope of enriching themselves, or any conceivable reason, set up as coal-merchants; and have, month after month, continued gloomily to watch a small stock of coals, without in any one instance, negotiating with a purchaser. The remarkable similarity between this course of proceeding and that adopted by their Great Ancestor beneath the vaults of the Parliament House at Westminster, is too obvious and too full of interest, to stand in need of comment.

It is also clearly proved by the oral traditions of the Family, that there existed, at some one period of its history which is not distinctly stated, a matron of such destructive principles, and so familiarised to the use and composition of inflammatory and combustible engines, that she was called 'The Match Maker': by which nickname and byword she is recognised in the

Family legends to this day. Surely there can be no reasonable
doubt that this was the Spanish lady, the mother of Chuzzlewit
Fawkes.

But there is one other piece of evidence, bearing immediate
reference to their close connexion with this memorable event
in English History, which must carry conviction, even to a
mind (if such a mind there be) remaining unconvinced by these
presumptive proofs.

There was, within a few years, in the possession of a highly
respectable and in every way credible and unimpeachable
member of the Chuzzlewit Family (for his bitterest enemy
never dared to hint at his being otherwise than a wealthy man),
a dark lantern of undoubted antiquity; rendered still more
interesting by being, in shape and pattern, extremely like such
as are in use at the present day. Now this gentleman, since
deceased, was at all times ready to make oath, and did again
and again set forth upon his solemn asseveration, that he had
frequently heard his grandmother say, when contemplating
this venerable relic, 'Aye, aye! This was carried by my fourth
son on the fifth of November, when he was a Guy Fawkes.'
These remarkable words wrought (as well they might) a strong
impression on his mind, and he was in the habit of repeating
them very often. The just interpretation which they bear, and
the conclusion to which they lead, are triumphant and irresistible. The old lady, naturally strong-minded, was nevertheless
frail and fading; she was notoriously subject to that confusion
of ideas, or, to say the least, of speech, to which age and garrulity
are liable. The slight, the very slight, confusion apparent in
these expressions is manifest, and is ludicrously easy of correction. 'Aye, aye,' quoth she, and it will be observed that no
emendation whatever is necessary to be made in these two
initiative remarks, 'Aye, aye! This lantern was carried by my
forefather'—not fourth son, which is preposterous—'on the
fifth of November. And *he* was Guy Fawkes.' Here we have a
remark at once consistent, clear, natural, and in strict accordance with the character of the speaker. Indeed the anecdote is
so plainly susceptible of this meaning, and no other, that it
would be hardly worth recording in its original state, were it
not a proof of what may be (and very often is) effected not only
in historical prose but in imaginative poetry, by the exercise
of a little ingenious labour on the part of a commentator.

It has been said that there is no instance, in modern times,

of a Chuzzlewit having been found on terms of intimacy with
the Great. But here again the sneering detractors who weave such
miserable figments from their malicious brains, are stricken
dumb by evidence. For letters are yet in the possession of
various branches of the family, from which it distinctly appears,
being stated in so many words, that one Diggory Chuzzlewit
was in the habit of perpetually dining with Duke Humphrey.
So constantly was he a guest at that nobleman's table, indeed;
and so unceasingly were His Grace's hospitality and companionship forced, as it were, upon him; that we find him
uneasy, and full of constraint and reluctance: writing his
friends to the effect that if they fail to do so and so by bearer,
he will have no choice but to dine again with Duke Humphrey:
and expressing himself in a very marked and extraordinary
manner as one surfeited of High Life and Gracious Company.

It has been rumoured, and it is needless to say the rumour
originated in the same base quarters, that a certain male
Chuzzlewit, whose birth must be admitted to be involved in
some obscurity, was of very mean and low descent. How stands
the proof? When the son of that individual, to whom the secret
of his father's birth was supposed to have been communicated
by his father in his lifetime, lay upon his deathbed, this question was put to him in a distinct, solemn, and formal way:
'Toby Chuzzlewit, who was your grandfather?' To which he,
with his last breath, no less distinctly, solemnly, and formally
replied: and his words were taken down at the time, and signed
by six witnesses, each with his name and address in full: 'The
Lord No Zoo.' It may be said—it *has* been said, for human
wickedness has no limits—that there is no Lord of that name,
and that among the titles which have become extinct, none at
all resembling this, in sound even, is to be discovered. But what
is the irresistible inference?—Rejecting a theory broached by
some well-meaning but mistaken persons, that this Mr. Toby
Chuzzlewit's grandfather, to judge from his name, must surely
have been a Mandarin (which is wholly insupportable, for
there is no pretence of his grandmother ever having been out
of this country, or of any Mandarin having been in it within
some years of his father's birth; except those in the tea-shops,
which cannot for a moment be regarded as having any bearing
on the question, one way or other), rejecting this hypothesis,
is it not manifest that Mr. Toby Chuzzlewit had either received
the name imperfectly from his father, or that he had forgotten

it, or that he had mispronounced it? and that even at the recent period in question, the Chuzzlewits were connected by a bend sinister, or kind of heraldic over-the-left, with some unknown noble and illustrious House?

From documentary evidence, yet preserved in the family, the fact is clearly established that in the comparatively modern days of the Diggory Chuzzlewit before mentioned, one of its members had attained to very great wealth and influence. Throughout such fragments of his correspondence as have escaped the ravages of the moths (who, in right of their extensive absorption of the contents of deeds and papers, may be called the general registers of the Insect World), we find him making constant reference to an uncle, in respect of whom he would seem to have entertained great expectations, as he was in the habit of seeking to propitiate his favour by presents of plate, jewels, books, watches, and other valuable articles. Thus, he writes on one occasion to his brother in reference to a gravy-spoon, the brother's property, which he (Diggory) would appear to have borrowed or otherwise possessed himself of: 'Do not be angry, I have parted with it—to my uncle.' On another occasion he expresses himself in a similar manner with regard to a child's mug which had been entrusted to him to get repaired. On another occasion he says, 'I have bestowed upon that irresistible uncle of mine everything I ever possessed.' And that he was in the habit of paying long and constant visits to this gentleman at his mansion, if, indeed, he did not wholly reside there, is manifest from the following sentence: 'With the exception of the suit of clothes I carry about with me, the whole of my wearing apparel is at present at my uncle's.' This gentleman's patronage and influence must have been very extensive, for his nephew writes, 'His interest is too high'—'It is too much' —'It is tremendous'—and the like. Still it does not appear (which is strange) to have procured for him any lucrative post at court or elsewhere, or to have conferred upon him any other distinction than that which was necessarily included in the countenance of so great a man, and the being invited by him to certain entertainments, so splendid and costly in their nature, that he calls them 'Golden Balls'.

It is needless to multiply instances of the high and lofty station, and the vast importance of the Chuzzlewits, at different periods. If it came within the scope of reasonable probability that further proofs were required, they might be heaped upon each other until they formed an Alps of testimony, beneath which the boldest scepticism should be crushed and beaten flat. As a goodly tumulus is already collected, and decently battened up above the Family grave, the present chapter is content to leave it as it is: merely adding, by way of a final spadeful, that many Chuzzlewits, both male and female, are proved to demonstration, on the faith of letters written by their own mothers, to have had chiselled noses, undeniable chins, forms that might have served the sculptor for a model, exquisitely-turned limbs, and polished foreheads of so transparent a texture that the blue veins might be seen branching off in various directions, like so many roads on an ethereal map. This fact in itself, though it had been a solitary one, would have utterly settled and clenched the business in hand; for it is well known, on the authority of all the books which treat of such matters, that every one of these phenomena, but especially that of the chiselling, are invariably peculiar to, and only make themselves apparent in, persons of the very best condition.

This history having, to its own perfect satisfaction, (and, consequently, to the full contentment of all its readers,) proved the Chuzzlewits to have had an origin, and to have been at one time or other of an importance which cannot fail to render them highly improving and acceptable acquaintance to all right-minded individuals, may now proceed in earnest with its task. And having shown that they must have had, by reason of their ancient birth, a pretty large share in the foundation and increase of the human family, it will one day become its province to submit, that such of its members as shall be introduced in these pages, have still many counterparts and prototypes in the Great World about us. At present it contents itself with remarking, in a general way, on this head: Firstly, that it may be safely asserted, and yet without implying any direct participation in the Monboddo doctrine touching the probability of the human race having once been monkeys, that men do play very strange and extraordinary tricks. Secondly, and yet without trenching on the Blumenbach theory as to the descendants of Adam having a vast number of qualities which belong more particularly to swine than to any other class of animals in the creation, that some men certainly are remarkable for taking uncommon good care of themselves.

CHAPTER II

Wherein certain persons are presented to the reader, with whom he may, if he please, become better acquainted

IT was pretty late in the autumn of the year, when the declining sun, struggling through the mist which had obscured it all day, looked brightly down upon a little Wiltshire village, within an easy journey of the fair old town of Salisbury.

Like a sudden flash of memory or spirit kindling up the mind of an old man, it shed a glory upon the scene, in which its departed youth and freshness seemed to live again. The wet grass sparkled in the light; the scanty patches of verdure in the hedges—where a few green twigs yet stood together bravely, resisting to the last the tyranny of nipping winds and early frosts—took heart and brightened up; the stream which had been dull and sullen all day long, broke out into a cheerful smile; the birds began to chirp and twitter on the naked boughs, as though the hopeful creatures half believed that winter had gone by, and spring had come already. The vane upon the tapering spire of the old church glistened from its lofty station in sympathy with the general gladness; and from the ivy-shaded windows such gleams of light shone back upon the glowing sky, that it seemed as if the quiet buildings were the hoarding-place of twenty summers, and all their ruddiness and warmth were stored within.

Even those tokens of the season which emphatically whispered of the coming winter, graced the landscape, and, for the moment, tinged its livelier features with no oppressive air of sadness. The fallen leaves, with which the ground was strewn, gave forth a pleasant fragrance, and subduing all harsh sounds of distant feet and wheels, created a repose in gentle unison with the light scattering of seed hither and thither by the distant husbandman, and with the noiseless passage of the plough as it turned up the rich brown earth, and wrought a graceful pattern in the stubbled fields. On the motionless branches of some trees, autumn berries hung like clusters of coral beads, as in those fabled orchards where the fruits were jewels; others, stripped of all their garniture, stood, each the centre of its little heap of bright red leaves, watching their slow decay; others again, still wearing theirs, had them all crunched

B

and crackled up, as though they had been burnt; about the stems of some were piled, in ruddy mounds, the apples they had borne that year; while others (hardy evergreens this class) showed somewhat stern and gloomy in their vigour, as charged by nature with the admonition that it is not to her more sensitive and joyous favourites she grants the longest term of life. Still athwart their darker boughs, the sunbeams struck out paths of deeper gold; and the red light, mantling in among their swarthy branches, used them as foils to set its brightness off, and aid the lustre of the dying day.

A moment, and its glory was no more. The sun went down beneath the long dark lines of hill and cloud which piled up in the west an airy city, wall heaped on wall, and battlement on battlement; the light was all withdrawn; the shining church turned cold and dark; the stream forgot to smile; the birds were silent; and the gloom of winter dwelt on everything.

An evening wind uprose too, and the slighter branches cracked and rattled as they moved, in skeleton dances, to its moaning music. The withering leaves no longer quiet, hurried to and fro in search of shelter from its chill pursuit; the labourer unyoked his horses, and with head bent down, trudged briskly home beside them; and from the cottage windows lights began to glance and wink upon the darkening fields.

Then the village forge came out in all its bright importance. The lusty bellows roared Ha ha! to the clear fire, which roared in turn, and bade the shining sparks dance gaily to the merry clinking of the hammers on the anvil. The gleaming iron, in its emulation, sparkled too, and shed its red-hot gems around profusely. The strong smith and his men dealt such strokes upon their work, as made even the melancholy night rejoice, and brought a glow into its dark face as it hovered about the door and windows, peeping curiously in above the shoulders of a dozen loungers. As to this idle company, there they stood, spell-bound by the place, and, casting now and then a glance upon the darkness in their rear, settled their lazy elbows more at ease upon the sill, and leaned a little further in: no more disposed to tear themselves away than if they had been born to cluster round the blazing hearth like so many crickets.

Out upon the angry wind! how from sighing, it began to bluster round the merry forge, banging at the wicket, and grumbling in the chimney, as if it bullied the jolly bellows for doing anything to order. And what an impotent swaggerer it was too, for all its noise: for if it had any influence on that hoarse companion, it was but to make him roar his cheerful song the louder, and by consequence to make the fire burn the brighter, and the sparks to dance more gaily yet: at length, they whizzed 'so madly round and round, that it was too much for such a surly wind to bear: so off it flew with a howl: giving the old sign before the ale-house door such a cuff as it went, that the Blue Dragon was more rampant than usual ever afterwards, and indeed, before Christmas, reared clean out of its crazy frame.

It was small tyranny for a respectable wind to go wreaking its vengeance on such poor creatures as the fallen leaves, but this wind happening to come up with a great heap of them just after venting its humour on the insulted Dragon, did so disperse and scatter them that they fled away, pell-mell, some here, some there, rolling over each other, whirling round and round upon their thin edges, taking frantic flights into the air, and playing all manner of extraordinary gambols in the extremity of their distress. Nor was this enough for its malicious fury: for not content with driving them abroad, it charged small parties of them and hunted them into the wheelwright's saw-pit, and below the planks and timbers in the yard, and, scattering the sawdust in the air, it looked for them underneath, and when it did meet with any, whew! how it drove them on and followed at their heels!

The scared leaves only flew the faster for all this, and a giddy chase it was: for they got into unfrequented places, where there was no outlet, and where their pursuer kept them eddying round and round at his pleasure; and they crept under the eaves of houses, and clung tightly to the sides of hay-ricks, like bats; and tore in at open chamber windows, and cowered close to hedges; and in short went anywhere for safety. But the oddest feat they achieved was, to take advantage of the sudden opening of Mr. Pecksniff's front-door, to dash wildly into his passage; whither the wind following close upon them, and finding the back-door open, incontinently blew out the lighted candle held by Miss Pecksniff, and slammed the front door against Mr. Pecksniff who was at that moment entering, with such violence, that in the twinkling of an eye he lay on his back at the bottom of the steps. Being by this time weary of such trifling performances, the boisterous rover hurried away rejoicing, roaring over moor and meadow, hill and flat, until it got out to sea, where it met with other winds similarly disposed, and made a night of it.

In the meantime Mr. Pecksniff, having received from a sharp angle in the bottom step but one, that sort of knock on the head which lights up, for the patient's entertainment, an imaginary general illumination of very bright short-sixes, lay placidly staring at his own street-door. And it would seem to have been more suggestive in its aspect than street-doors usually are; for he continued to lie there, rather a lengthy and unreasonable time, without so much as wondering whether he was hurt or no: neither, when Miss Pecksniff inquired through the key-hole in a shrill voice, which might have belonged to a wind in its teens, 'Who's there?' did he make any reply: nor, when Miss Pecksniff opened the door again, and shading the candle with her hand, peered out, and looked provokingly round him, and about him, and over him, and everywhere but at him, did he offer any remark, or indicate in any manner the least hint of a desire to be picked up.

'*I* see you,' cried Miss Pecksniff, to the ideal inflicter of a runaway knock. 'You'll catch it, sir!'

Still Mr. Pecksniff, perhaps from having caught it already, said nothing.

'You're round the corner now,' cried Miss Pecksniff. She said it at a venture, but there was appropriate matter in it too; for Mr. Pecksniff, being in the act of extinguishing the candles before mentioned pretty rapidly, and of reducing the number of brass knobs on his street-door from four or five hundred (which had previously been juggling of their own accord before his eyes in a very novel manner) to a dozen or so, might in one sense have been said to be coming round the corner, and just turning it.

With a sharply-delivered warning relative to the cage and the constable, and the stocks and the gallows, Miss Pecksniff was about to close the door again, when Mr. Pecksniff (being still at the bottom of the steps) raised himself on one elbow, and sneezed.

'That voice!' cried Miss Pecksniff. 'My parent!'

At this exclamation, another Miss Pecksniff bounced out of the parlour: and the two Miss Pecksniffs, with many incoherent expressions, dragged Mr. Pecksniff into an upright posture.

'Pa!' they cried in concert. 'Pa! Speak, Pa! Do not look so wild, my dearest Pa!'

But as a gentleman's looks, in such a case of all others, are by no means under his own control, Mr. Pecksniff continued to keep his mouth and his eyes very wide open, and to drop his lower jaw, somewhat after the manner of a toy nut-cracker: and as his hat had fallen off, and his face was pale, and his hair erect, and his coat muddy, the spectacle he presented was so very doleful, that neither of the Miss Pecksniffs could repress an involuntary screech.

'That'll do,' said Mr. Pecksniff. 'I'm better.'

'He's come to himself!' cried the youngest Miss Pecksniff.

'He speaks again!' exclaimed the eldest.

With these joyful words they kissed Mr. Pecksniff on either cheek; and bore him into the house. Presently, the youngest Miss Pecksniff ran out again to pick up his hat, his brown paper parcel, his umbrella, his gloves, and other small articles: and that done, and the door closed, both young ladies applied themselves to tending Mr. Pecksniff's wounds in the back parlour.

They were not very serious in their nature: being limited to abrasions on what the eldest Miss Pecksniff called 'the knobby parts' of her parent's anatomy, such as his knees and elbows, and to the development of an entirely new organ, unknown to phrenologists, on the back of his head. These injuries having been comforted externally, with patches of pickled brown paper, and Mr. Pecksniff having been comforted internally, with some stiff brandy-and-water, the eldest Miss Pecksniff sat down to make the tea, which was all ready. In the meantime the youngest Miss Pecksniff brought from the kitchen a smoking dish of ham and eggs, and, setting the same before her father, took up her station on a low stool at his feet: thereby bringing her eyes on a level with the teaboard.

It must not be inferred from this position of humility, that the youngest Miss Pecksniff was so young as to be, as one may say, forced to sit upon a stool, by reason of the shortness of her legs. Miss Pecksniff sat upon a stool because of her simplicity and innocence, which were very great: very great. Miss Pecksniff sat upon a stool because she was all girlishness, and playfulness, and wildness, and kittenish buoyancy. She was the most arch and at the same time the most artless creature, was the youngest Miss Pecksniff, that you can possibly imagine. It was her great charm. She was too fresh and guileless, and too full of child-like vivacity, was the youngest Miss Pecksniff, to wear combs in her hair, or to turn it up, or to frizzle it, or braid it. She wore it in a crop, a loosely flowing crop, which had so many rows of curls in it, that the top row was only one curl. Moderately buxom was her shape, and quite womanly too; but sometimes—yes, sometimes—she even wore a pinafore; and how charming *that* was! Oh! she was indeed 'a gushing thing' (as a young gentleman had observed in verse, in the Poet's Corner of a provincial newspaper), was the youngest Miss Pecksniff!

Mr. Pecksniff was a moral man: a grave man, a man of noble sentiments and speech: and he had had her christened Mercy. Mercy! oh, what a charming name for such a pure-souled being as the youngest Miss Pecksniff! Her sister's name was Charity. There was a good thing! Mercy and Charity! And Charity, with her fine strong sense, and her mild, yet not reproachful gravity, was so well named, and did so well set off and illustrate her sister! What a pleasant sight was that, the contrast they presented: to see each loved and loving one sympathising with, and devoted to, and leaning on, and yet correcting and counter-checking, and, as it were, antidoting, the other! To behold each damsel, in her very admiration of her sister, setting up in business for herself on an entirely different principle, and announcing no connexion with over-the-way, and if the quality of goods at that extablishment don't please you, you are respectfully invited to favour ME with a call! And the crowning circumstance of the whole delightful catalogue was, that both the fair creatures were so utterly unconscious of all this! They had no idea of it. They no more thought or dreamed of it than Mr. Pecksniff did. Nature played them off against each other: *they* had no hand in it, the two Miss Pecksniffs.

It has been remarked that Mr. Pecksniff was a moral man. So he was. Perhaps there never was a more moral man than Mr. Pecksniff: especially in his conversation and correspondence. It was once said of him by a homely admirer, that he had a Fortunatus's purse of good sentiments in his inside. In this particular he was like the girl in the fairy tale, except that if they were not actual diamonds which fell from his lips, they were the very brightest paste, and shone prodigiously. He was a most exemplary man: fuller of virtuous precept than a copy-book. Some people likened him to a direction-post, which is always telling the way to a place, and never goes there: but

A New Pupil

these were his enemies; the shadows cast by his brightness; that was all. His very throat was moral. You saw a good deal of it. You looked over a very low fence of white cravat (whereof no man had ever beheld the tie, for he fastened it behind), and there it lay, a valley between two jutting heights of collar, serene and whiskerless before you. It seemed to say, on the part of Mr. Pecksniff, 'There is no deception, ladies and gentlemen, all is peace, a holy calm pervades me.' So did his hair, just grizzled with an iron-grey, which was all brushed off his forehead, and stood bolt upright, or slightly drooped in kindred action with his heavy eyelids. So did his person, which was sleek though free from corpulency. So did his manner, which was soft and oily. In a word, even his plain black suit, and state of widower, and dangling double eyeglass, all tended to the same purpose, and cried aloud, 'Behold the moral Pecksniff!'

The brazen plate upon the door (which being Mr. Pecksniff's, could not lie) bore this inscription, 'PECKSNIFF, ARCHITECT,' to which Mr. Pecksniff, on his cards of business, added, 'AND LAND SURVEYOR.' In one sense, and only one, he may be said to have been a Land Surveyor on a pretty large scale, as an extensive prospect lay stretched out before the windows of his house. Of his architectural doings, nothing was clearly known, except that he had never designed or built anything; but it was generally understood that his knowledge of the science was almost awful in its profundity.

Mr. Pecksniff's professional engagements, indeed, were almost, if not entirely, confined to the reception of pupils; for the collection of rents, with which pursuit he occasionally varied and relieved his graver toils, can hardly be said to be a strictly architectural employment. His genius lay in ensnaring parents and guardians, and pocketing premiums. A young gentleman's premium being paid, and the young gentleman come to Mr. Pecksniff's house, Mr. Pecksniff borrowed his case of mathematical instruments (if silver-mounted or otherwise valuable); entreated him, from that moment, to consider himself one of the family; complimented him highly on his parents or guardians, as the case might be; and turned him loose in a spacious room on the two-pair front; where, in the company of certain drawing-boards, parallel rulers, very stiff-legged compasses, and two, or perhaps three, other young gentlemen, he improved himself, for three or five years, according to his articles, in making elevations of Salisbury Cathedral from every possible point of sight; and in constructing in the air a vast quantity of Castles, Houses of Parliament, and other Public Buildings. Perhaps in no place in the world were so many gorgeous edifices of this class erected as under Mr. Pecksniff's auspices; and if but one-twentieth part of the churches which were built in that front room, with one or other of the Miss Pecksniffs at the altar in the act of marrying the architect, could only be made available by the parliamentary commissioners, no more churches would be wanted for at least five centuries.

'Even the worldly goods of which we have just disposed,' said Mr. Pecksniff, glancing round the table when he had finished, 'even cream, sugar, tea, toast, ham,—'

'And eggs,' suggested Charity in a low voice.

'And eggs,' said Mr. Pecksniff, 'even they have their moral. See how they come and go! Every pleasure is transitory. We can't even eat, long. If we indulge in harmless fluids, we get the dropsy; if in exciting liquids, we get drunk. What a soothing reflection is that!'

'Don't say we get drunk, Pa,' urged the eldest Miss Pecksniff.

'When I say we, my dear,' returned her father, 'I mean mankind in general; the human race, considered as a body, and not as individuals. There is nothing personal in morality, my love. Even such a thing as this,' said Mr. Pecksniff, laying the forefinger of his left hand upon the brown paper patch on the top of his head, 'slight casual baldness though it be, reminds us that we are but'—he was going to say 'worms', but recollecting that worms were not remarkable for heads of hair, he substituted 'flesh and blood'.

'Which,' cried Mr. Pecksniff after a pause, during which he seemed to have been casting about for a new moral, and not quite successfully, 'which is also very soothing. Mercy, my dear, stir the fire and throw up the cinders.'

The young lady obeyed, and having done so, resumed her stool, reposed one arm upon her father's knee, and laid her blooming cheek upon it. Miss Charity drew her chair nearer the fire, as one prepared for conversation, and looked towards her father.

'Yes,' said Mr. Pecksniff, after a short pause, during which he had been silently smiling, and shaking his head at the fire: 'I have again been fortunate in the attainment of my object. A new inmate will very shortly come among us.'

'A youth, papa?' asked Charity.

'Ye-es, a youth,' said Mr. Pecksniff. 'He will avail himself of the eligible opportunity which now offers, for uniting the advantages of the best practical architectural education with the comforts of a home, and the constant association with some who (however humble their sphere, and limited their capacity) are not unmindful of their moral responsibilities.'

'Oh Pa!' cried Mercy, holding up her finger archly. 'See advertisement!'

'Playful—playful warbler,' said Mr. Pecksniff. It may be observed in connexion with his calling his daughter a 'warbler', that she was not at all vocal, but that Mr. Pecksniff was in the frequent habit of using any word that occurred to him as having a good sound, and rounding a sentence well, without much care for its meaning. And he did this so boldly, and in such an imposing manner, that he would sometimes stagger the wisest people with his eloquence, and make them gasp again.

His enemies asserted, by the way, that a strong trustfulness in sounds and forms was the master-key to Mr. Pecksniff's character.

'Is he handsome, Pa?' inquired the younger daughter.

'Silly Merry!' said the eldest: Merry being fond for Mercy. 'What is the premium, Pa? tell us that.'

'Oh, good gracious, Cherry!' cried Miss Mercy, holding up her hands with the most winning giggle in the world, 'what a mercenary girl you are! oh you naughty, thoughtful, prudent thing!'

It was perfectly charming, and worthy of the Pastoral age, to see how the two Miss Pecksniffs slapped each other after this, and then subsided into an embrace expressive of their different dispositions.

'He is well looking,' said Mr. Pecksniff, slowly and distinctly: 'well looking enough. I do not positively expect any immediate premium with him.'

Notwithstanding their different natures, both Charity and Mercy concurred in opening their eyes uncommonly wide at this announcement, and in looking for the moment as blank as if their thoughts had actually had a direct bearing on the main chance.

'But what of that!' said Mr. Pecksniff, still smiling at the fire. 'There is disinterestedness in the world, I hope? We are not all

arrayed in two opposite ranks: the *off*ensive and the *def*ensive.
Some few there are who walk between; who help the needy as
they go; and take no part with either side. Umph!'

There was something in these morsels of philanthropy which
reassured the sisters. They exchanged glances, and brightened
very much.

'Oh! let us not be for ever calculating, devising, and plotting
for the future,' said Mr. Pecksniff, smiling more and more, and
looking at the fire as a man might, who was cracking a joke
with it: 'I am weary of such arts. If our inclinations are but
good and open-hearted, let us gratify them boldly, though they
bring upon us Loss instead of Profit. Eh, Charity?'

Glancing towards his daughters for the first time since he had
begun these reflections, and seeing that they both smiled, Mr.
Pecksniff eyed them for an instant so jocosely (though still with
a kind of saintly waggishness) that the younger one was moved
to sit upon his knee forthwith, put her fair arms round his neck,
and kiss him twenty times. During the whole of this affectionate
display she laughed to a most immoderate extent: in which
hilarious indulgence even the prudent Cherry joined.

'Tut, tut,' said Mr. Pecksniff, pushing his latest-born away
and running his fingers through his hair, as he resumed his
tranquil face. 'What folly is this! Let us take heed how we laugh
without reason, lest we cry with it. What is the domestic news
since yesterday? John Westlock is gone, I hope?'

'Indeed, no,' said Charity.

'And why not?' returned her father. 'His term expired
yesterday. And his box was packed, I know; for I saw it, in the
morning, standing in the hall.'

'He slept last night at the Dragon,' returned the young lady,
'and had Mr. Pinch to dine with him. They spent the evening
together, and Mr. Pinch was not home till very late.'

'And when I saw him on the stairs this morning, Pa,' said
Mercy with her usual sprightliness, 'he looked, oh goodness,
such a monster! with his face all manner of colours, and his eyes
as dull as if they had been boiled, and his head aching dreadfully, I am sure from the look of it, and his clothes smelling, oh
it's impossible to say how strong, of'—here the young lady
shuddered—'of smoke and punch.'

'Now I think,' said Mr. Pecksniff with his accustomed gentleness, though still with the air of one who suffered under injury
without complaint, 'I think Mr. Pinch might have done better

than choose for his companion one who, at the close of a long intercourse, had endeavoured, as he knew, to wound my feelings. I am not quite sure that this was delicate in Mr. Pinch. I am not quite sure that this was kind in Mr. Pinch. I will go further and say, I am not quite sure that this was even ordinarily grateful in Mr. Pinch.'

'But what can anyone expect from Mr. Pinch!' cried Charity, with as strong and scornful an emphasis on the name as if it would have given her unspeakable pleasure to express it, in an acted charade, on the calf of that gentleman's leg.

'Aye, aye,' returned her father, raising his hand mildly: 'it is very well to say what can we expect from Mr. Pinch, but Mr. Pinch is a fellow-creature, my dear; Mr. Pinch is an item in the vast total of humanity, my love; and we have a right, it is our duty, to expect in Mr. Pinch some development of those better qualities, the possession of which in our own persons inspires our humble self-respect. No,' continued Mr. Pecksniff. 'No! Heaven forbid that I should say, nothing can be expected from Mr. Pinch; or that I should say, nothing can be expected from any man alive (even the most degraded, which Mr. Pinch is not, no really); but Mr. Pinch has disappointed me: he has hurt me: I think a little the worse of him on this account, but not of human nature. Oh no, no!'

'Hark!' said Miss Charity, holding up her finger, as a gentle rap was heard at the street-door. 'There is the creature! Now mark my words, he has come back with John Westlock for his box, and is going to help him to take it to the mail. Only mark my words, if that isn't his intention!'

Even as she spoke, the box appeared to be in progress of conveyance from the house, but after a brief murmuring of question and answer, it was put down again, and somebody knocked at the parlour door.

'Come in!' cried Mr. Pecksniff—not severely; only virtuously. 'Come in!'

An ungainly, awkward-looking man, extremely short-sighted, and prematurely bald, availed himself of this permission; and seeing that Mr. Pecksniff sat with his back towards him, gazing at the fire, stood hesitating, with the door in his hand. He was far from handsome certainly; and was drest in a snuff-coloured suit, of an uncouth make at the best, which, being shrunk with long wear, was twisted and tortured into all kinds of odd shapes; but notwithstanding his attire, and his

clumsy figure, which a great stoop in his shoulders, and a
ludicrous habit he had of thrusting his head forward, by no
means redeemed, one would not have been disposed (unless
Mr. Pecksniff said so) to consider him a bad fellow by any
means. He was perhaps about thirty, but he might have been
almost any age between sixteen and sixty: being one of those
strange creatures who never decline into an ancient appearance,
but look their oldest when they are very young, and get it over
at once.

Keeping his hand upon the lock of the door, he glanced
from Mr. Pecksniff to Mercy, from Mercy to Charity, and from
Charity to Mr. Pecksniff again, several times; but the young
ladies being as intent upon the fire as their father was, and
neither of the three taking any notice of him, he was fain to say,
at last,

'Oh! I beg your pardon, Mr. Pecksniff: I beg your pardon
for intruding; but—'

'No intrusion, Mr. Pinch,' said that gentleman very sweetly,
but without looking round. 'Pray be seated, Mr. Pinch. Have
the goodness to shut the door, Mr. Pinch, if you please.'

'Certainly, sir,' said Pinch: not doing so, however, but holding it rather wider open than before, and beckoning nervously
to somebody without: 'Mr. Westlock, sir, hearing that you
were come home—'

'Mr. Pinch, Mr. Pinch!' said Pecksniff, wheeling his chair
about, and looking at him with an aspect of the deepest melancholy, 'I did not expect this from you. I have not deserved this
from you!'

'No, but upon my word, sir'—urged Pinch.

'The less you say, Mr. Pinch,' interposed the other, 'the
better. I utter no complaint. Make no defence.'

'No, but do have the goodness, sir,' cried Pinch, with great
earnestness, 'if you please. Mr. Westlock, sir, going away for
good and all, wishes to leave none but friends behind him. Mr.
Westlock and you, sir, had a little difference the other day; you
have had many little differences.'

'Little differences!' cried Charity.

'Little differences!' echoed Mercy.

'My loves!' said Mr. Pecksniff, with the same serene uprais-
ing of his hand; 'My dears!' After a solemn pause he meekly
bowed to Mr. Pinch, as who should say, 'Proceed;' but Mr.
Pinch was so very much at a loss how to resume, and looked so

helplessly at the two Miss Pecksniffs, that the conversation would most probably have terminated there, if a good-looking youth, newly arrived at man's estate, had not stepped forward from the doorway and taken up the thread of the discourse.

'Come, Mr. Pecksniff,' he said, with a smile, 'don't let there be any ill-blood between us, pray. I am sorry we have ever differed, and extremely sorry I have ever given you offence. Bear me no ill-will at parting, sir.'

'I bear,' answered Mr. Pecksniff, mildly, 'no ill-will to any man on earth.'

'I told you he didn't,' said Pinch, in an under-tone; 'I knew he didn't! He always says he don't.'

'Then you will shake hands, sir?' cried Westlock, advancing a step or two, and bespeaking Mr. Pinch's close attention by a glance.

'Umph!' said Mr. Pecksniff, in his most winning tone.

'You will shake hands, sir.'

'No, John,' said Mr. Pecksniff, with a calmness quite ethereal; 'no, I will not shake hands, John. I have forgiven you. I had already forgiven you, even before you ceased to reproach and taunt me. I have embraced you in the spirit, John, which is better than shaking hands.'

'Pinch,' said the youth, turning towards him, with a hearty disgust of his late master, 'what did I tell you?'

Poor Pinch looked down uneasily at Mr. Pecksniff, whose eye was fixed upon him as it had been from the first: and looking up at the ceiling again, made no reply.

'As to your forgiveness, Mr. Pecksniff,' said the youth, 'I'll not have it upon such terms. I won't be forgiven.'

'Won't you, John?' retorted Mr. Pecksniff, with a smile. 'You must. You can't help it. Forgiveness is a high quality; an exalted virtue; far above *your* control or influence, John. I *will* forgive you. You cannot move me to remember any wrong you have ever done me, John.'

'Wrong!' cried the other, with all the heat and impetuosity of his age. 'Here's a pretty fellow! Wrong! Wrong I have done him! He'll not even remember the five hundred pounds he had with me under false pretences; or the seventy pounds a year for board and lodging that would have been dear at seventeen! Here's a martyr!'

'Money, John,' said Mr. Pecksniff, 'is the root of all evil. I grieve to see that it is already bearing evil fruit in you. But

I will not remember its existence. I will not even remember the conduct of that misguided person'—and here, although he spoke like one at peace with all the world, he used an emphasis that plainly said 'I have my eye upon the rascal now'—'that misguided person who has brought you here to-night, seeking to disturb (it is a happiness to say, in vain) the heart's repose and peace of one who would have shed his dearest blood to serve him.'

The voice of Mr. Pecksniff trembled as he spoke, and sobs were heard from his daughters. Sounds floated on the air, moreover, as if two spirit voices had exclaimed: one, 'Beast!' the other, 'Savage!'

'Forgiveness,' said Mr. Pecksniff, 'entire and pure forgiveness is not incompatible with a wounded heart; perchance when the heart *is* wounded, it becomes a greater virtue. With my breast still wrung and grieved to its inmost core, by the ingratitude of that person, I am proud and glad to say that I forgive him. Nay! I beg,' cried Mr. Pecksniff, raising his voice, as Pinch appeared about to speak, 'I beg that individual not to offer a remark: he will truly oblige me by not uttering one word, just now. I am not sure that I am equal to the trial. In a very short space of time, I shall have sufficient fortitude, I trust, to converse with him as if these events had never happened. But not,' said Mr. Pecksniff, turning round again towards the fire, and waving his hand in the direction of the door, 'not now.'

'Bah!' cried John Westlock, with the utmost disgust and disdain the monosyllable is capable of expressing. 'Ladies, good evening. Come, Pinch, it's not worth thinking of. I was right and you were wrong. That's a small matter; you'll be wiser another time.'

So saying, he clapped that dejected companion on the shoulder, turned upon his heel, and walked out into the passage, whither poor Mr. Pinch, after lingering irresolutely in the parlour for a few seconds, expressing in his countenance the deepest mental misery and gloom, followed him. Then they took up the box between them, and sallied out to meet the mail.

That fleet conveyance passed, every night, the corner of a lane at some distance; towards which point they bent their steps. For some minutes they walked along in silence, until at length young Westlock burst into a loud laugh, and at intervals

Meekness of Mr. Pecksniff and his Charming Daughters
(p. 18)

into another, and another. Still there was no response from his companion.

'I'll tell you what, Pinch!' he said abruptly, after another lengthened silence—'You haven't half enough of the devil in you. Half enough! You haven't any.'

'Well!' said Pinch with a sigh, 'I don't know, I'm sure. It's a compliment to say so. If I haven't, I suppose, I'm all the better for it.'

'All the better!' repeated his companion tartly: 'All the worse, you mean to say.'

'And yet,' said Pinch, pursuing his own thoughts and not this last remark on the part of his friend, 'I must have a good deal of what you call the devil in me, too, or how could I make Pecksniff so uncomfortable? I wouldn't have occasioned him so much distress—don't laugh, please—for a mine of money: and Heaven knows I could find good use for it too, John. How grieved he was!'

'*He* grieved!' returned the other.

'Why didn't you observe that the tears were almost starting out of his eyes!' cried Pinch. 'Bless my soul, John, is it nothing to see a man moved to that extent and know one's self to be the cause! And did you hear him say that he could have shed his blood for me?'

'Do you *want* any blood shed for you?' returned his friend, with considerable irritation. 'Does he shed anything for you that you *do* want? Does he shed employment for you, instruction for you, pocket-money for you? Does he shed even legs of mutton for you in any decent proportion to potatoes and garden stuff?'

'I am afraid,' said Pinch, sighing again, 'that I am a great eater: I can't disguise from myself that I'm a great eater. Now, you know that, John.'

'*You* a great eater!' retorted his companion, with no less indignation than before. 'How do you know you are?'

There appeared to be forcible matter in this inquiry, for Mr. Pinch only repeated in an under-tone that he had a strong misgiving on the subject, and that he greatly feared he was.

'Besides, whether I am or no,' he added, 'that has little or nothing to do with his thinking me ungrateful. John, there is scarcely a sin in the world that is in my eyes such a crying one as ingratitude: and when he taxes me with that, and believes me to be guilty of it, he makes me miserable and wretched.'

'Do you think he don't know that?' returned the other scornfully. 'But come, Pinch, before I say anything more to you, just run over the reasons you have for being grateful to him at all, will you? change hands first, for the box is heavy. That'll do. Now, go on.'

'In the first place,' said Pinch, 'he took me as his pupil for much less than he asked.'

'Well,' rejoined his friend, perfectly unmoved by this instance of generosity. 'What in the second place?'

'What in the second place?' cried Pinch, in a sort of desperation, 'why, everything in the second place. My poor old grandmother died happy to think that she had put me with such an excellent man. I have grown up in his house, I am in his confidence, I am his assistant, he allows me a salary: when his business improves, my prospects are to improve too. All this, and a great deal more, is in the second place. And in the very prologue and preface to the first place, John, you must consider this, which nobody knows better than I: that I was born for much plainer and poorer things, that I am not a good hand for his kind of business, and have no talent for it, or indeed for anything else but odds and ends that are of no use or service to anybody.'

He said this with so much earnestness, and in a tone so full of feeling, that his companion instinctively changed his manner as he sat down on the box (they had by this time reached the finger-post at the end of the lane); motioned him to sit down beside him; and laid his hand upon his shoulder.

'I believe you are one of the best fellows in the world,' he said, 'Tom Pinch.'

'Not at all,' rejoined Tom. 'If you only knew Pecksniff as well as I do, you might say it of him, indeed, and say it truly.'

'I'll say anything of him, you like,' returned the other, 'and not another word to his disparagement.'

'It's for my sake, then; not his, I am afraid,' said Pinch, shaking his head gravely.

'For whose you please, Tom, so that it does please you. Oh! He's a famous fellow! *He* never scraped and clawed into his pouch all your poor grandmother's hard savings—she was a housekeeper, wasn't she, Tom?'

'Yes,' said Mr. Pinch, nursing one of his large knees, and nodding his head: 'a gentleman's housekeeper.'

'*He* never scraped and clawed into his pouch all her hard

savings; dazzling her with prospects of your happiness and advancement, which he knew (and no man better) never would be realised! *He* never speculated and traded on her pride in you, and her having educated you, and on her desire that you at least should live to be a gentleman. Not he, Tom!'

'No,' said Tom, looking into his friend's face, as if he were a little doubtful of his meaning; 'of course not.'

'So I say,' returned the youth, 'of course he never did. *He* didn't take less than he had asked, because that less was all she had, and more than he expected: not he, Tom! He doesn't keep you as his assistant because you are of any use to him; because your wonderful faith in his pretensions is of inestimable service in all his mean disputes; because your honesty reflects honesty on him; because your wandering about this little place all your spare hours, reading in ancient books and foreign tongues, gets noised abroad, even as far as Salisbury, making of him, Pecksniff the master, a man of learning and of vast importance. *He* gets no credit from you, Tom, not he.'

'Why, of course he don't,' said Pinch, gazing at his friend with a more troubled aspect than before. 'Pecksniff get credit from *me!* Well!'

'Don't I say that it's ridiculous,' rejoined the other, 'even to think of such a thing?'

'Why, it's madness,' said Tom.

'Madness!' returned young Westlock. 'Certainly it's madness. Who but a madman would suppose he cares to hear it said on Sundays, that the volunteer who plays the organ in the church, and practises on summer evenings in the dark, is Mr. Pecksniff's young man, eh, Tom? Who but a madman would suppose it is the game of such a man as he, to have his name in everybody's mouth, connected with the thousand useless odds and ends you do (and which, of course, he taught you), eh, Tom? Who but a madman would suppose you advertised him hereabouts, much cheaper and much better than a chalker on the walls could, eh, Tom? As well might one suppose that he doesn't on all occasions pour out his whole heart and soul to you; that he doesn't make you a very liberal and indeed rather an extravagant allowance; or, to be more wild and monstrous still, if that be possible, as well might one suppose,' and here, at every word, he struck him lightly on the breast, 'that Pecksniff traded in your nature, and that your nature was to be timid and distrustful of yourself, and trustful of all other men, but most of all, of him who least deserves it. There would be madness, Tom!'

Mr. Pinch had listened to all this with looks of bewilderment, which seemed to be in part occasioned by the matter of his companion's speech, and in part by his rapid and vehement manner. Now that he had come to a close, he drew a very long breath; and gazing wistfully in his face as if he were unable to settle in his own mind what expression it wore, and were desirous to draw from it as good a clue to his real meaning as it was possible to obtain in the dark, was about to answer, when the sound of the mail guard's horn came cheerily upon their ears, putting an immediate end to the conference: greatly as it seemed to the satisfaction of the younger man, who jumped up briskly, and gave his hand to his companion.

'Both hands, Tom. I shall write to you from London, mind!'

'Yes,' said Pinch. 'Yes. Do, please. Good-bye. Good-bye. I can hardly believe you're going. It seems, now, but yesterday that you came. Good-bye! my dear old fellow!'

John Westlock returned his parting words with no less heartiness of manner, and sprung up to his seat upon the roof. Off went the mail at a canter down the dark road: the lamps gleaming brightly, and the horn awakening all the echoes, far and wide.

'Go your ways,' said Pinch, apostrophising the coach: 'I can hardly persuade myself but you're alive, and are some great monster who visits this place at certain intervals, to bear my friends away into the world. You're more exulting and rampant than usual to-night, I think: and you may well crow over your prize; for he is a fine lad, an ingenuous lad, and has but one fault that I know of: he don't mean it, but he is most cruelly unjust to Pecksniff!'

CHAPTER III

In which certain other persons are introduced; on the same terms as in the last chapter

MENTION has been already made more than once, of a certain Dragon who swung and creaked complainingly before the village ale-house door. A faded and an ancient dragon he was; and many a wintry storm of rain, snow, sleet, and hail, had changed his colour from a gaudy blue to a faint lack-lustre shade of grey. But there he hung; rearing, in a state of monstrous imbecility, on his hind legs; waxing, with every month that passed, so much more dim and shapeless, that as you gazed at him on one side of the sign-board it seemed as if he must be gradually melting through it, and coming out upon the other.

He was a courteous and considerate dragon, too; or had been in his distincter days; for in the midst of his rampant feebleness, he kept one of his fore paws near his nose, as though he would say, 'Don't mind me—it's only my fun;' while he held out the other in polite and hospitable entreaty. Indeed it must be conceded to the whole brood of dragons of modern times, that they have made a great advance in civilisation and refinement. They no longer demand a beautiful virgin for breakfast every morning, with as much regularity as any tame single gentleman expects his hot roll, but rest content with the society of idle bachelors and roving married men: and they are now remarkable rather for holding aloof from the softer sex and discouraging their visits (especially on Saturday nights), than for rudely insisting on their company without any reference to their inclinations, as they are known to have done in days of yore.

Nor is this tribute to the reclaimed animals in question so wide a digression into the realms of Natural History as it may, at first sight, appear to be: for the present business of these pages is with the dragon who had his retreat in Mr. Pecksniff's neighbourhood, and that courteous animal being already on the carpet, there is nothing in the way of its immediate transaction.

For many years, then, he had swung and creaked, and flapped himself about, before the two windows of the best bedroom in that house of entertainment to which he lent his name: but never in all his swinging, creaking, and flapping, had there been such a stir within its dingy precincts, as on the evening next after that upon which the incidents, detailed in the last chapter, occurred; when there was such a hurrying up and down stairs of feet, such a glancing of lights, such a whispering of voices, such a smoking and sputtering of wood newly lighted in a damp chimney, such an airing of linen, such a scorching smell of hot warming-pans, such a domestic bustle and to-do, in short, as never dragon, griffin, unicorn, or other animal of that species presided over, since they first began to interest themselves in household affairs.

An old gentleman and a young lady, travelling, unattended, in a rusty old chariot with post-horses; coming nobody knew whence, and going nobody knew whither; had turned out of the high road, and driven unexpectedly to the Blue Dragon: and here was the old gentleman, who had taken this step by reason of his sudden illness in the carriage, suffering the most horrible cramps and spasms, yet protesting and vowing in the very midst of his pain, that he wouldn't have a doctor sent for, and wouldn't take any remedies but those which the young lady administered from a small medicine-chest, and wouldn't, in a word, do anything but terrify the landlady out of her five wits, and obstinately refuse compliance with every suggestion that was made to him.

Of all the five hundred proposals for his relief which the good woman poured out in less than half-an-hour, he would entertain but one. That was, that he should go to bed. And it was in the preparation of his bed, and the arrangement of his chamber, that all the stir was made in the room behind the Dragon.

He was, beyond all question, very ill, and suffered exceedingly: not the less, perhaps, because he was a strong and vigorous old man, with a will of iron, and a voice of brass. But neither the apprehensions which he plainly entertained, at times, for his life, nor the great pain he underwent, influenced his resolution in the least degree. He would have no person sent for. The worse he grew, the more rigid and inflexible he became in his determination. If they sent for any person to attend him, man, woman, or child, he would leave the house directly (so he told them), though he quitted it on foot, and died upon the threshold of the door.

Now, there being no medical practitioner actually resident

in the village, but a poor apothecary who was also a grocer and general dealer, the landlady had, upon her own responsibility, sent for him, in the very first burst and outset of the disaster. Of course it followed, as a necessary result of his being wanted, that he was not at home. He had gone some miles away, and was not expected home until late at night; so the landlady, being by this time pretty well beside herself, dispatched the same messenger in all haste for Mr. Pecksniff, as a learned man who could bear a deal of responsibility, and a moral man who could administer a world of comfort to a troubled mind. That her guest had need of some efficient services under the latter head was obvious enough from the restless expressions, importing, however, rather a worldly than a spiritual anxiety, to which he gave frequent utterance.

From this last-mentioned secret errand, the messenger returned with no better news than from the first; Mr. Pecksniff was not at home. However, they got the patient into bed without him; and in the course of two hours, he gradually became so far better that there were much longer intervals than at first between his terms of suffering. By degrees, he ceased to suffer at all: though his exhaustion was occasionally so great that it suggested hardly less alarm than his actual endurance had done.

It was in one of his intervals of repose, when, looking round with great caution, and reaching uneasily out of his nest of pillows, he endeavoured, with a strange air of secrecy and distrust, to make use of the writing materials which he had ordered to be placed on a table beside him, that the young lady and the mistress of the Blue Dragon found themselves sitting side by side before the fire in the sick chamber.

The mistress of the Blue Dragon was in outward appearance just what a landlady should be: broad, buxom, comfortable, and good-looking, with a face of clear red and white, which, by its jovial aspect, at once bore testimony to her hearty participation in the good things of the larder and cellar, and to their thriving and healthful influences. She was a widow, but years ago had passed through her state of weeds, and burst into flower again; and in full bloom she had continued ever since; and in full bloom she was now; with roses on her ample skirts, and roses on her bodice, roses in her cap, roses in her cheeks,—aye, and roses, worth the gathering too, on her lips, for that matter. She had still a bright black eye, and jet black hair; was comely, dimpled, plump, and tight as a gooseberry;

and though she was not exactly what the world calls young, you may make an affidavit, on trust, before any mayor or magistrate in Christendom, that there are a great many young ladies in the world (blessings on them, one and all!) whom you wouldn't like half as well, or admire half as much, as the beaming hostess of the Blue Dragon.

As this fair matron sat beside the fire, she glanced occasionally, with all the pride of ownership, about the room; which was a large apartment, such as one may see in country places, with a low roof and a sunken flooring, all down-hill from the door, and a descent of two steps on the inside so exquisitely unexpected, that strangers, despite the most elaborate cautioning, usually dived in head first, as into a plunging-bath. It was none of your frivolous and preposterously bright bedrooms, where nobody can close an eye with any kind of propriety or decent regard to the association of ideas; but it was a good, dull, leaden, drowsy place, where every article of furniture reminded you that you came there to sleep, and that you were expected to go to sleep. There was no wakeful reflection of the fire there, as in your modern chambers, which upon the darkest nights have a watchful consciousness of French polish; the old Spanish mahogany winked at it now and then, as a dozing cat or dog might, nothing more. The very size and shape, and hopeless immovability of the bedstead, and wardrobe, and in a minor degree of even the chairs and tables, provoked sleep; they were plainly apoplectic and disposed to snore. There were no staring portraits to remonstrate with you for being lazy; no round-eyed birds upon the curtains, disgustingly wide awake, and insufferably prying. The thick neutral hangings, and the dark blinds, and the heavy heap of bed-clothes, were all designed to hold in sleep, and act as non-conductors to the day and getting up. Even the old stuffed fox upon the top of the wardrobe was devoid of any spark of vigilance, for his glass eye had fallen out, and he slumbered as he stood.

The wandering attention of the mistress of the Blue Dragon roved to these things but twice or thrice, and then for but an instant at a time. It soon deserted them, and even the distant bed with its strange burden, for the young creature immediately before her, who, with her downcast eyes intently fixed upon the fire, sat wrapped in silent meditation.

She was very young; apparently no more than seventeen; timid and shrinking in her manner, and yet with a greater share of self-possession and control over her emotions than usually belongs to a far more advanced period of female life. This she had abundantly shown, but now, in her tending of the sick gentleman. She was short in stature; and her figure was slight, as became her years; but all the charms of youth and maidenhood set it off, and clustered on her gentle brow. Her face was very pale, in part no doubt from recent agitation. Her dark brown hair, disordered from the same cause, had fallen negligently from its bonds, and hung upon her neck: for which instance of its waywardness no male observer would have had the heart to blame it.

Her attire was that of a lady, but extremely plain; and in her manner, even when she sat as still as she did then, there was an indefinable something which appeared to be in kindred with her scrupulously unpretending dress. She had sat, at first looking anxiously towards the bed; but seeing that the patient remained quiet, and was busy with his writing, she had softly moved her chair into its present place: partly, as it seemed, from an instinctive consciousness that he desired to avoid observation: and partly that she might, unseen by him, give some vent to the natural feelings she had hitherto suppressed.

Of all this, and much more, the rosy landlady of the Blue Dragon took as accurate note and observation as only woman can take of woman. And at length she said, in a voice too low, she knew, to reach the bed:

'You have seen the gentleman in this way before, miss? Is he used to these attacks?'

'I have seen him very ill before, but not so ill as he has been to-night.'

'What a Providence!' said the landlady of the Dragon, 'that you had the prescriptions and the medicines with you, miss!'

'They are intended for such an emergency. We never travel without them.'

'Oh!' thought the hostess, 'then we are in the habit of travelling, and of travelling together.'

She was so conscious of expressing this in her face, that meeting the young lady's eyes immediately afterwards, and being a very honest hostess, she was rather confused.

'The gentleman—your grandpapa'—she resumed, after a short pause, 'being so bent on having no assistance, must terrify you very much, miss?'

'I have been very much alarmed to-night. He—he is not my grandfather.'

'Father, I should have said,' returned the hostess, sensible of having made an awkward mistake.

'Nor my father,' said the young lady. 'Nor,' she added, slightly smiling with a quick perception of what the landlady was going to add, 'Nor my uncle. We are not related.'

'Oh dear me!' returned the landlady, still more embarrassed than before: 'how could I be so very much mistaken; knowing, as anybody in their proper senses might, that when a gentleman is ill, he looks so much older than he really is? That I should have called you "Miss," too, Ma'am!' But when she had proceeded thus far, she glanced involuntarily at the third finger of the young lady's left hand, and faltered again: for there was no ring upon it.

'When I told you we were not related,' said the other mildly, but not without confusion on her own part, 'I meant not in any way. Not even by marriage. Did you call me, Martin?'

'Call you?' cried the old man, looking quickly up, and hurriedly drawing beneath the coverlet the paper on which he had been writing. 'No.'

She had moved a pace or two towards the bed, but stopped immediately, and went no farther.

'No,' he repeated, with a petulant emphasis. 'Why do you ask me? If I had called you, what need for such a question?'

'It was the creaking of the sign outside, sir, I dare say,' observed the landlady: a suggestion by the way (as she felt a moment after she had made it), not at all complimentary to the voice of the old gentleman.

'No matter what, ma'am,' he rejoined: 'it wasn't I. Why how you stand there, Mary, as if I had the plague! But they're all afraid of me,' he added, leaning helplessly backward on his pillow; 'even she! There is a curse upon me. What else have I to look for?'

'Oh dear, no. Oh no, I'm sure,' said the good-tempered landlady, rising, and going towards him. 'Be of better cheer, sir. These are only sick fancies.'

'What are only sick fancies?' he retorted. 'What do you know about fancies? Who told *you* about fancies? The old story! Fancies!'

'Only see again there, how you take one up!' said the mistress of the Blue Dragon, with unimpaired good humour. 'Dear heart alive, there is no harm in the word, sir, if it is an old one. Folks in good health have their fancies, too, and strange ones, every day.'

Harmless as this speech appeared to be, it acted on the traveller's distrust, like oil on fire. He raised his head up in the bed, and, fixing on her two dark eyes whose brightness was exaggerated by the paleness of his hollow cheeks, as they in turn, together with his straggling locks of long grey hair, were rendered whiter by the tight black velvet skull-cap which he wore, he searched her face intently.

'Ah! you begin too soon,' he said, in so low a voice that he seemed to be thinking it, rather than addressing her. 'But you lose no time. You do your errand, and you earn your fee. Now, who may be *your* client?'

The landlady looked in great astonishment at her whom he called Mary, and finding no rejoinder in the drooping face, looked back again at him. At first she had recoiled involuntarily, supposing him disordered in his mind; but the slow composure of his manner, and the settled purpose announced in his strong features, and gathering, most of all, about his puckered mouth, forbade the supposition.

'Come,' he said, 'tell me who is it? Being here, it is not very hard for me to guess, you may suppose.'

'Martin,' interposed the young lady, laying her hand upon his arm; 'reflect how short a time we have been in this house, and that even your name is unknown here.'

'Unless,' he said, 'you—' He was evidently tempted to express a suspicion of her having broken his confidence in favour of the landlady, but either remembering her tender nursing, or being moved in some sort by her face, he checked himself, and changing his uneasy posture in the bed, was silent.

'There!' said Mrs. Lupin: for in that name the Blue Dragon was licensed to furnish entertainment, both to man and beast. 'Now, you will be well again, sir. You forgot, for the moment, that there were none but friends here.'

'Oh!' cried the old man, moaning impatiently, as he tossed one restless arm upon the coverlet; 'why do you talk to me of friends! Can you or anybody teach me to know who are my friends, and who my enemies?'

'At least,' urged Mrs. Lupin, gently, 'this young lady is your friend, I am sure.'

'She has no temptation to be otherwise,' cried the old man,

like one whose hope and confidence were utterly exhausted. 'I suppose she is. Heaven knows. There: let me try to sleep. Leave the candle where it is.'

As they retired from the bed, he drew forth the writing which had occupied him so long, and holding it in the flame of the taper burnt it to ashes. That done, he extinguished the light, and turning his face away with a heavy sigh, drew the coverlet about his head, and lay quite still.

This destruction of the paper, both as being strangely inconsistent with the labour he had devoted to it and as involving considerable danger of fire to the Dragon, occasioned Mrs. Lupin not a little consternation. But the young lady evincing no surprise, curiosity, or alarm, whispered her, with many thanks for her solicitude and company, that she would remain there some time longer; and that she begged her not to share her watch, as she was well used to being alone, and would pass the time in reading.

Mrs. Lupin had her full share and dividend of that large capital of curiosity which is inherited by her sex, and at another time it might have been difficult so to impress this hint upon her as to induce her to take it. But now, in sheer wonder and amazement at these mysteries, she withdrew at once, and repairing straightway to her own little parlour below stairs, sat down in her easy-chair with unnatural composure. At this very crisis, a step was heard in the entry, and Mr. Pecksniff, looking sweetly over the half-door of the bar, and into the vista of snug privacy beyond, murmured:

'Good evening, Mrs. Lupin!'

'Oh dear me, sir!' she cried, advancing to receive him, 'I am so very glad you have come.'

'And *I* am very glad I have come,' said Mr. Pecksniff, 'if I can be of service. I am very glad I have come. What is the matter, Mrs. Lupin?'

'A gentleman taken ill upon the road, has been so very bad up-stairs, sir,' said the tearful hostess.

'A gentleman taken ill upon the road, has been so very bad up-stairs, has he?' repeated Mr. Pecksniff. 'Well, well!'

Now there was nothing that one may call decidedly original in this remark, nor can it be exactly said to have contained any wise precept theretofore unknown to mankind, or to have opened any hidden source of consolation: but Mr. Pecksniff's manner was so bland, and he nodded his head so soothingly,

Martin Chuzzlewit Suspects the Landlady
without any Reason
(p. 30)

and showed in everything such an affable sense of his own excellence, that anybody would have been, as Mrs. Lupin was, comforted by the mere voice and presence of such a man; and, though he had merely said 'a verb must agree with its nominative case in number and person, my good friend,' or 'eight times eight are sixty-four, my worthy soul,' must have felt deeply grateful to him for his humanity and wisdom.

'And how,' asked Mr. Pecksniff, drawing off his gloves and warming his hands before the fire, as benevolently as if they were somebody else's, not his: 'and how is he now?'

'He is better, and quite tranquil,' answered Mrs. Lupin.

'He is better, and quite tranquil,' said Mr. Pecksniff. 'Very well! ve-ry well!'

Here again, though the statement was Mrs. Lupin's and not Mr. Pecksniff's, Mr. Pecksniff made it his own and consoled her with it. It was not much when Mrs. Lupin said it, but it was a whole book when Mr. Pecksniff said it. '*I* observe,' he seemed to say, 'and through me, morality in general remarks, that he is better and quite tranquil.'

'There must be weighty matters on his mind, though,' said the hostess, shaking her head, 'for he talks, sir, in the strangest way you ever heard. He is far from easy in his thoughts, and wants some proper advice from those whose goodness makes it worth his having.'

'Then,' said Mr. Pecksniff, 'he is the sort of customer for me.' But though he said this in the plainest language, he didn't speak a word. He only shook his head: disparagingly of himself too.

'I am afraid, sir,' continued the landlady, first looking round to assure herself that there was nobody within hearing, and then looking down upon the floor. 'I am very much afraid, sir, that his conscience is troubled by his not being related to—or—or even married to—a very young lady—'

'Mrs. Lupin!' said Mr. Pecksniff, holding up his hand with something in his manner as nearly approaching to severity, as any expression of his, mild being that he was, could ever do. 'Person! Young person?'

'A very young person,' said Mrs. Lupin, curtseying and blushing: '—I beg your pardon, sir, but I have been so hurried to-night, that I don't know what I say—who is with him now.'

'Who is with him now,' ruminated Mr. Pecksniff, warming his back (as he had warmed his hands) as if it were a widow's

back, or an orphan's back, or an enemy's back, or a back that
any less excellent man would have suffered to be cold: 'Oh
dear me, dear me!'

'At the same time I am bound to say, and I do say with all
my heart,' observed the hostess, earnestly, 'that her looks and
manner almost disarm suspicion.'

'Your suspicion, Mrs. Lupin,' said Mr. Pecksniff gravely, 'is
very natural.'

Touching which remark, let it be written down to their confusion, that the enemies of this worthy man unblushingly maintained that he always said of what was very bad, that it was
very natural; and that he unconsciously betrayed his own
nature in doing so.

'Your suspicion, Mrs. Lupin,' he repeated, 'is very natural,
and I have no doubt correct. I will wait upon these travellers.'

With that he took off his great-coat, and having run his
fingers through his hair, thrust one hand gently in the bosom
of his waistcoat and meekly signed to her to lead the way.

'Shall I knock?' asked Mrs. Lupin, when they reached the
chamber door.

'No,' said Mr. Pecksniff, 'enter if you please.'

They went in on tiptoe: or rather the hostess took that precaution, for Mr. Pecksniff always walked softly. The old gentleman was still asleep, and his young companion still sat reading
by the fire.

'I am afraid,' said Mr. Pecksniff, pausing at the door, and
giving his head a melancholy roll, 'I am afraid that this looks
artful. I am afraid, Mrs. Lupin, do you know, that this looks
very artful!'

As he finished this whisper, he advanced before the hostess;
and at the same time the young lady, hearing footsteps, rose.
Mr. Pecksniff glanced at the volume she held, and whispered
Mrs. Lupin again: if possible, with increased despondency.

'Yes, ma'am,' he said, 'it is a good book. I was fearful of that
beforehand I am apprehensive that this is a very deep thing
indeed!'

'What gentleman is this?' inquired the object of his virtuous
doubts.

'Hush! don't trouble yourself, ma'am,' said Mr. Pecksniff,
as the landlady was about to answer. 'This young'—in spite of
himself he hesitated when 'person' rose to his lips, and substituted another word: 'this young stranger, Mrs. Lupin, will

excuse me for replying briefly, that I reside in this village; it may be in an influential manner, however undeserved; and that I have been summoned here by you. I am here, as I am everywhere, I hope, in sympathy for the sick and sorry.'

With these impressive words, Mr. Pecksniff passed over to the bedside, where, after patting the counterpane once or twice in a very solemn manner, as if by that means he gained a clear insight into the patient's disorder, he took his seat in a large armchair, and in an attitude of some thoughtfulness and much comfort, waited for his waking. Whatever objection the young lady urged to Mrs. Lupin went no further, for nothing more was said to Mr. Pecksniff, and Mr. Pecksniff said nothing more to anybody else.

Full half-an-hour elapsed before the old man stirred, but at length he turned himself in bed, and, though not yet awake, gave tokens that his sleep was drawing to an end. By little and little he removed the bed-clothes from about his head, and turned still more towards the side where Mr. Pecksniff sat. In course of time his eyes opened; and he lay for a few moments as people newly roused sometimes will, gazing indolently at his visitor, without any distinct consciousness of his presence.

There was nothing remarkable in these proceedings, except the influence they worked on Mr. Pecksniff, which could hardly have been surpassed by the most marvellous of natural phenomena. Gradually his hands became tightly clasped upon the elbows of the chair, his eyes dilated with surprise, his mouth opened, his hair stood more erect upon his forehead than its custom was, until, at length, when the old man rose in bed, and stared at him with scarcely less emotion than he showed himself, the Pecksniff doubts were all resolved, and he exclaimed aloud:

'You *are* Martin Chuzzlewit!'

His consternation of surprise was so genuine, that the old man, with all the disposition that he clearly entertained to believe it assumed, was convinced of its reality.

'I *am* Martin Chuzzlewit,' he said, bitterly: 'and Martin Chuzzlewit wishes you had been hanged, before you had come here to disturb him in his sleep. Why, I dreamed of this fellow!' he said, lying down again, and turning away his face, 'before I knew that he was near me!'

'My good cousin—' said Mr. Pecksniff.

'There! His very first words!' cried the old man, shaking his grey head to and fro upon the pillow, and throwing up his hands. 'In his very first words he asserts his relationship! I knew he would: they all do it! Near or distant, blood or water, it's all one. Ugh! What a calendar of deceit, and lying, and false-witnessing, the sound of any word of kindred opens before me!'

'Pray do not be hasty, Mr. Chuzzlewit,' said Pecksniff, in a tone that was at once in the sublimest degree compassionate and dispassionate; for he had by this time recovered from his surprise, and was in full possession of his virtuous self. 'You will regret being hasty, I know you will.'

'*You* know!' said Martin, contemptuously.

'Yes,' retorted Mr. Pecksniff. 'Aye, aye, Mr. Chuzzlewit: and don't imagine that I mean to court or flatter you: for nothing is further from my intention. Neither, sir, need you entertain the least misgiving that I shall repeat that obnoxious word which has given you so much offence already. Why should I? What do I expect or want from you? There is nothing in your possession that *I* know of, Mr. Chuzzlewit, which is much to be coveted for the happiness it brings you.'

'That's true enough,' muttered the old man.

'Apart from that consideration,' said Mr. Pecksniff, watchful of the effect he made, 'it must be plain to you (I am sure) by this time, that if I had wished to insinuate myself into your good opinion, I should have been, of all things, careful not to address you as a relative: knowing your humour, and being quite certain beforehand that I could not have a worse letter of recommendation.'

Martin made not any verbal answer; but he as clearly implied, though only by a motion of his legs beneath the bed-clothes, that there was reason in this, and that he could not dispute it, as if he had said as much in good set terms.

'No,' said Mr. Pecksniff, keeping his hand in his waistcoat as though he were ready, on the shortest notice, to produce his heart for Martin Chuzzlewit's inspection, 'I came here to offer my services to a stranger. I make no offer of them to you, because I know you would distrust me if I did. But lying on that bed, sir, I regard you as a stranger, and I have just that amount of interest in you which I hope I should feel in any stranger, circumstanced as you are. Beyond that, I am quite as indifferent to you, Mr. Chuzzlewit, as you are to me.'

Having said which, Mr. Pecksniff threw himself back in the easy-chair: so radiant with ingenuous honesty, that Mrs. Lupin almost wondered not to see a stained-glass Glory, such as the Saint wore in the church, shining about his head.

A long pause succeeded. The old man, with increased restlessness, changed his posture several times. Mrs. Lupin and the young lady gazed in silence at the counterpane. Mr. Pecksniff toyed abstractedly with his eye-glass, and kept his eyes shut, that he might ruminate the better.

'Eh?' he said at last: opening them suddenly, and looking towards the bed. 'I beg your pardon. I thought you spoke. Mrs. Lupin,' he continued, slowly rising. 'I am not aware that I can be of any service to you here. The gentleman is better, and you are as good a nurse as he can have. Eh?'

This last note of interrogation bore reference to another change of posture on the old man's part, which brought his face towards Mr. Pecksniff for the first time since he had turned away from him.

'If you desire to speak to me before I go, sir,' continued that gentleman, after another pause, 'you may command my leisure; but I must stipulate, in justice to myself, that you do so as to a stranger: strictly as to a stranger.'

Now if Mr. Pecksniff knew, from anything Martin Chuzzlewit had expressed in gestures, that he wanted to speak to him, he could only have found it out on some such principle as prevails in melodramas, and in virtue of which the elderly farmer with the comic son always knows what the dumb girl means when she takes refuge in his garden, and relates her personal memoirs in incomprehensible pantomime. But without stopping to make any inquiry on this point, Martin Chuzzlewit signed to his young companion to withdraw, which she immediately did, along with the landlady: leaving him and Mr. Pecksniff alone together. For some time they looked at each other in silence; or rather the old man looked at Mr. Pecksniff, and Mr. Pecksniff, again closing his eyes on all outward objects, took an inward survey of his own breast. That it amply repaid him for his trouble, and afforded a delicious and enchanting prospect, was clear from the expression of his face.

'You wish me to speak to you as to a total stranger,' said the old man, 'do you?'

Mr. Pecksniff replied, by a shrug of his shoulders and an apparent turning-round of his eyes in their sockets before he

opened them, that he was still reduced to the necessity of entertaining that desire.

'You shall be gratified,' said Martin. 'Sir, I am a rich man.
Not so rich as some suppose, perhaps, but yet wealthy. I am
not a miser, sir, though even that charge is made against me,
as I hear, and currently believed. I have no pleasure in hoarding. I have no pleasure in the possession of money. The devil
that we call by that name can give me nothing but unhappiness.'

It would be no description of Mr. Pecksniff's gentleness of
manner to adopt the common parlance, and say that he looked
at this moment as if butter wouldn't melt in his mouth. He
rather looked as if any quantity of butter might have been
made out of him, by churning the milk of human kindness, as
it spouted upwards from his heart.

'For the same reason that I am not a hoarder of money,' said
the old man, 'I am not lavish of it. Some people find their
gratification in storing it up; and others theirs in parting with
it; but I have no gratification connected with the thing. Pain
and bitterness are the only goods it ever could procure for me.
I hate it. It is a spectre walking before me through the world,
and making every social pleasure hideous.'

A thought arose in Mr. Pecksniff's mind, which must have
instantly mounted to his face, or Martin Chuzzlewit would not
have resumed as quickly and as sternly as he did:

'You would advise me for my peace of mind, to get rid of
this source of misery, and transfer it to some one who could
bear it better. Even you, perhaps, would rid me of a burden
under which I suffer so grievously. But, kind stranger,' said the
old man, whose every feature darkened as he spoke, 'good
Christian stranger, that is a main part of my trouble. In other
hands, I have known money do good: in other hands I have
known it triumphed in, and boasted of with reason, as the
master-key to all the brazen gates that close upon the paths to
worldly honour, fortune, and enjoyment. To what man or
woman; to what worthy, honest, incorruptible creature; shall
I confide such a talisman, either now or when I die? Do you
know any such person? *Your* virtues are of course inestimable,
but can you tell me of any other living creature who will bear
the test of contact with myself?'

'Of contact with yourself, sir?' echoed Mr. Pecksniff.

'Aye,' returned the old man, 'the test of contact with me—
with me. You have heard of him whose misery (the gratifica-

tion of his own foolish wish) was, that he turned every thing he touched into gold. The curse of my existence, and the realisation of my own mad desire, is that by the golden standard which I bear about me, I am doomed to try the metal of all other men, and find it false and hollow.'

Mr. Pecksniff shook his head, and said, 'You think so.'

'Oh yes,' cried the old man, 'I think so! and in your telling me "I think so," I recognise the true unworldly ring of *your* metal. I tell you, man,' he added, with increasing bitterness, 'that I have gone, a rich man, among people of all grades and kinds; relatives, friends, and strangers; among people in whom, when I was poor, I had confidence, and justly, for they never once deceived me then, or, to me, wronged each other. But I have never found one nature, no, not one, in which, being wealthy and alone, I was not forced to detect the latent corruption that lay hid within it, waiting for such as I to bring it forth. Treachery, deceit, and low design; hatred of competitors, real or fancied, for my favour; meanness, falsehood, baseness, and servility; or,' and here he looked closely in his cousin's eyes, 'or an assumption of honest independence, almost worse than all; these are the beauties which my wealth has brought to light. Brother against brother, child against parent, friends treading on the faces of friends, this is the social company by whom my way has been attended. There are stories told—they may be true or false—of rich men who, in the garb of poverty, have found out virtue and rewarded it. They were dolts and idiots for their pains. They should have made the search in their own characters. They should have shown themselves fit objects to be robbed and preyed upon and plotted against and adulated by any knaves, who, but for joy, would have spat upon their coffins when they died their dupes; and then their search would have ended as mine has done, and they would be what I am.'

Mr. Pecksniff, not at all knowing what it might be best to say in the momentary pause which ensued upon these remarks, made an elaborate demonstration of intending to deliver something very oracular indeed: trusting to the certainty of the old man interrupting him, before he should utter a word. Nor was he mistaken, for Martin Chuzzlewit having taken breath, went on to say:

'Hear me to an end; judge what profit you are like to gain from any repetition of this visit; and leave me. I have so corrupted and changed the nature of all those who have ever attended on me, by breeding avaricious plots and hopes within them; I have engendered such domestic strife and discord, by tarrying even with members of my own family; I have been such a lighted torch in peaceful homes, kindling up all the inflammable gases and vapours in their moral atmosphere, which, but for me, might have proved harmless to the end; that I have, I may say, fled from all who knew me, and taking refuge in secret places have lived, of late, the life of one who is hunted. The young girl whom you just now saw—what! your eye lightens when I talk of her! You hate her already, do you?'

'Upon my word, sir!' said Mr. Pecksniff, laying his hand upon his breast, and dropping his eyelids.

'I forgot,' cried the old man, looking at him with a keenness which the other seemed to feel, although he did not raise his eyes so as to see it. 'I ask your pardon. I forgot you were a stranger. For the moment you reminded me of one Pecksniff, a cousin of mine. As I was saying—the young girl whom you just now saw, is an orphan child, whom, with one steady purpose, I have bred and educated, or, if you prefer the word, adopted. For a year or more she has been my constant companion, and she is my only one. I have taken, as she knows, a solemn oath never to leave her sixpence when I die, but while I live, I make her an annual allowance: not extravagant in its amount and yet not stinted. There is a compact between us that no term of affectionate cajolery shall ever be addressed by either to the other, but that she shall call me always by my Christian name: I her, by hers. She is bound to me in life by ties of interest, and losing by my death, and having no expectation disappointed, will mourn it, perhaps: though for that I care little. This is the only kind of friend I have or will have. Judge from such premises what a profitable hour you have spent in coming here, and leave me: to return no more.'

With these words, the old man fell slowly back upon his pillow. Mr. Pecksniff as slowly rose, and, with a prefatory hem, began as follows:

'Mr. Chuzzlewit.'

'There. Go!' interposed the other. 'Enough of this. I am weary of you.'

'I am sorry for that, sir,' rejoined Mr. Pecksniff, 'because I have a duty to discharge, from which, depend upon it, I shall not shrink. No, sir, I shall not shrink.'

It is a lamentable fact, that as Mr. Pecksniff stood erect beside the bed, in all the dignity of Goodness, and addressed him thus, the old man cast an angry glance towards the candlestick, as if he were possessed by a strong inclination to launch it at his cousin's head. But he constrained himself, and pointing with his finger to the door, informed him that his road lay there.

'Thank you,' said Mr. Pecksniff, 'I am aware of that; I am going. But before I go, I crave your leave to speak, and more than that, Mr. Chuzzlewit, I must and will—yes indeed, I repeat it, must and will—be heard. I am not surprised, sir, at anything you have told me to-night. It is natural, very natural, and the greater part of it was known to me before. I will not say,' continued Mr. Pecksniff, drawing out his pocket-handkerchief, and winking with both eyes at once, as it were, against his will, 'I will not say that you are mistaken in me. While you are in your present mood I would not say so for the world. I almost wish, indeed, that I had a different nature, that I might repress even this slight confession of weakness: which I cannot disguise from you: which I feel is humiliating: but which you will have the goodness to excuse. We will say, if you please,' added Mr. Pecksniff, with great tenderness of manner, 'that it arises from a cold in the head, or is attributable to snuff, or smelling-salts, or onions, or anything but the real cause.'

Here he paused for an instant, and concealed his face behind his pocket-handkerchief. Then, smiling faintly, and holding the bed-furniture with one hand, he resumed:

'But, Mr. Chuzzlewit, while I am forgetful of myself, I owe it to myself, and to my character—aye, sir, and I *have* a character which is very dear to me, and will be the best inheritance of my two daughters—to tell you, on behalf of another, that your conduct is wrong, unnatural, indefensible, monstrous. And I tell you, sir,' said Mr. Pecksniff, towering on tiptoe among the curtains, as if he were literally rising above all worldly considerations, and were fain to hold on tight, to keep himself from darting skyward like a rocket, 'I tell you without fear or favour, that it will not do for you to be unmindful of your grandson, young Martin, who has the strongest natural claim upon you. It will not do, sir,' repeated Mr. Pecksniff, shaking his head. 'You may think it will do, but it won't. You must provide for that young man; you shall provide for him;

you *will* provide for him. I believe,' said Mr. Pecksniff, glanc-ing at the pen-and-ink, 'that in secret you have already done so. Bless you for doing so. Bless you for doing right, sir. Bless you for hating me. And good night!'

So saying, Mr. Pecksniff waved his right hand with much solemnity; and once more inserting it in his waistcoat, de-parted. There was emotion in his manner, but his step was firm. Subject to human weaknesses, he was upheld by con-science.

Martin lay for some time, with an expression on his face of silent wonder, not unmixed with rage: at length he muttered in a whisper:

'What does this mean? Can the false-hearted boy have chosen such a tool as yonder fellow who has just gone out? Why not! He has conspired against me, like the rest, and they are but birds of one feather. A new plot; a new plot! Oh self, self, self! At every turn nothing but self!'

He fell to trifling, as he ceased to speak, with the ashes of the burnt paper in the candlestick. He did so, at first, in pure abstraction, but they presently became the subject of his thoughts.

'Another will made and destroyed,' he said, 'nothing deter-mined on, nothing done, and I might have died to-night! I plainly see to what foul uses all this money will be put at last,' he cried, almost writhing in the bed: 'after filling me with cares and miseries all my life, it will perpetuate discord and bad passions when I am dead. So it always is. What lawsuits grow out of the graves of rich men, every day: sowing perjury, hatred, and lies among near kindred, where there should be nothing but love! Heaven help us, we have much to answer for! Oh self, self, self! Every man for himself, and no creature for me!'

Universal self! Was there nothing of its shadow in these reflections, and in the history of Martin Chuzzlewit, on his own showing?

CHAPTER IV

From which it will appear that if union be strength, and family affection be pleasant to contemplate, the Chuzzlewits were the strongest and most agreeable family in the world

THAT worthy man Mr. Pecksniff having taken leave of his cousin in the solemn terms recited in the last chapter, withdrew to his own home, and remained there three whole days: not so much as going out for a walk beyond the boundaries of his own garden, lest he should be hastily summoned to the bedside of his penitent and remorseful relative, whom, in his ample benevolence, he had made up his mind to forgive unconditionally, and to love on any terms. But such was the obstinacy and such the bitter nature of that stern old man, that no repentant summons came; and the fourth day found Mr. Pecksniff apparently much farther from his Christian object than the first.

During the whole of this interval, he haunted the Dragon at all times and seasons in the day and night, and, returning good for evil, evinced the deepest solicitude in the progress of the obdurate invalid; insomuch that Mrs. Lupin was fairly melted by his disinterested anxiety (for he often particularly required her to take notice that he would do the same by any stranger or pauper in the like condition), and shed many tears of admiration and delight.

Meantime, old Martin Chuzzlewit remained shut up in his own chamber, and saw no person but his young companion, saving the hostess of the Blue Dragon, who was, at certain times, admitted to his presence. So surely as she came into the room, however, Martin feigned to fall asleep. It was only when he and the young lady were alone, that he would utter a word, even in answer to the simplest inquiry; though Mr. Pecksniff could make out, by hard listening at the door, that they two being left together, he was talkative enough.

It happened on the fourth evening, that Mr. Pecksniff walking, as usual, into the bar of the Dragon and finding no Mrs. Lupin there, went straight up-stairs; purposing, in the fervour of his affectionate zeal, to apply his ear once more to the keyhole, and quiet his mind by assuring himself that the hardhearted patient was going on well. It happened that Mr.

Pecksniff, coming softly upon the dark passage into which a spiral ray of light usually darted through the same keyhole, was astonished to find no such ray visible; and it happened that Mr. Pecksniff, when he had felt his way to the chamber-door, stooping hurriedly down to ascertain by personal inspection whether the jealousy of the old man had caused this keyhole to be stopped on the inside, brought his head into such violent contact with another head, that he could not help uttering in an audible voice the monosyllable 'Oh!' which was, as it were, sharply unscrewed and jerked out of him by very anguish. It happened then, and lastly, that Mr. Pecksniff found himself immediately collared by something which smelt like several damp umbrellas, a barrel of beer, a cask of warm brandy-and-water, and a small parlour-full of stale tobacco smoke, mixed; and was straightway led down-stairs into the bar from which he had lately come, where he found himself standing opposite to, and in the grasp of, a perfectly strange gentleman of still stranger appearance, who, with his disengaged hand, rubbed his own head very hard, and looked at him, Pecksniff, with an evil countenance.

The gentleman was of that order of appearance which is currently termed shabby-genteel, though in respect of his dress he can hardly be said to have been in any extremities, as his fingers were a long way out of his gloves, and the soles of his feet were at an inconvenient distance from the upper leather of his boots. His nether garments were of a bluish grey—violent in its colours once, but sobered now by age and dinginess—and were so stretched and strained in a tough conflict between his braces and his straps, that they appeared every moment in danger of flying asunder at the knees. His coat, in colour blue and of a military cut, was buttoned and frogged up to his chin. His cravat was, in hue and pattern, like one of those mantles which hairdressers are accustomed to wrap about their clients, during the progress of the professional mysteries. His hat had arrived at such a pass that it would have been hard to determine whether it was originally white or black. But he wore a moustache—a shaggy moustache too: nothing in the meek and merciful way, but quite in the fierce and scornful style: the regular Satanic sort of thing—and he wore, besides, a vast quantity of unbrushed hair. He was very dirty and very jaunty; very bold and very mean; very swaggering and very slinking; very much like a man who might have been something better, and unspeakably like a man who deserved to be something worse.

'You were eaves-dropping at that door, you vagabond!' said this gentleman.

Mr. Pecksniff cast him off, as Saint George might have repudiated the Dragon in that animal's last moments, and said:

'Where is Mrs. Lupin, I wonder! can the good woman possibly be aware that there is a person here who—'

'Stay!' said the gentleman. 'Wait a bit. She *does* know. What then?'

'What then, sir?' cried Mr. Pecksniff. 'What then? Do you know, sir, that I am the friend and relative of that sick gentleman? That I am his protector, his guardian, his—'

'Not his niece's husband,' interposed the stranger, 'I'll be sworn; for he was there before you.'

'What do you mean?' said Mr. Pecksniff, with indignant surprise. 'What do you tell me, sir?'

'Wait a bit!' cried the other. 'Perhaps you are a cousin—the cousin who lives in this place?'

'I *am* the cousin who lives in this place,' replied the man of worth.

'Your name is Pecksniff?' said the gentleman.

'It is.'

'I am proud to know you, and I ask your pardon,' said the gentleman, touching his hat, and subsequently diving behind his cravat for a shirt-collar, which however he did not succeed in bringing to the surface. 'You behold in me, sir, one who has also an interest in that gentleman up-stairs. Wait a bit.'

As he said this, he touched the tip of his high nose, by way of intimation that he would let Mr. Pecksniff into a secret presently; and pulling off his hat, began to search inside the crown among a mass of crumpled documents and small pieces of what may be called the bark of broken cigars: whence he presently selected the cover of an old letter, begrimed with dirt and redolent of tobacco.

'Read that,' he cried, giving it to Mr. Pecksniff.

'This is addressed to Chevy Slyme, Esquire,' said that gentleman.

'You know Chevy Slyme, Esquire, I believe?' returned the stranger.

Mr. Pecksniff shrugged his shoulders as though he would say 'I know there is such a person, and I am sorry for it.'

'Very good,' remarked the gentleman. 'That is my interest and business here.' With that he made another dive for his shirt-collar, and brought up a string.

'Now this is very distressing, my friend,' said Mr. Pecksniff, shaking his head and smiling composedly. 'It is very distressing to me, to be compelled to say that you are not the person you claim to be. I know Mr. Slyme, my friend: this will not do: honesty is the best policy: you had better not; you had indeed.'

'Stop!' cried the gentleman, stretching forth his right arm, which was so tightly wedged into his threadbare sleeve that it looked like a cloth sausage. 'Wait a bit!'

He paused to establish himself immediately in front of the fire, with his back towards it. Then gathering the skirts of his coat under his left arm, and smoothing his moustache with his right thumb and forefinger, he resumed:

'I understand your mistake, and I am not offended. Why? Because it's complimentary. You suppose I would set myself up for Chevy Slyme. Sir, if there is a man on earth whom a gentleman would feel proud and honoured to be mistaken for, that man is my friend Slyme. For he is, without an exception, the highest-minded, the most independent-spirited, most original, spiritual, classical, talented, the most thoroughly Shakspearian, if not Miltonic, and at the same time the most disgustingly-unappreciated dog I know. But, sir, I have not the vanity to attempt to pass for Slyme. Any other man in the wide world, I am equal to; but Slyme is, I frankly confess, a great many cuts above me. Therefore you are wrong.'

'I judged from this,' said Mr. Pecksniff, holding out the cover of the letter.

'No doubt you did,' returned the gentleman. 'But, Mr. Pecksniff, the whole thing resolves itself into an instance of the peculiarities of genius. Every man of true genius has his peculiarity. Sir, the peculiarity of my friend Slyme is, that he is always waiting round the corner. He is perpetually round the corner, sir. He is round the corner at this instant. Now,' said the gentleman, shaking his forefinger before his nose, and planting his legs wider apart as he looked attentively in Mr. Pecksniff's face, 'that is a remarkably curious and interesting trait in Mr. Slyme's character; and whenever Slyme's life comes to be written, that trait must be thoroughly worked out by his biographer, or society will not be satisfied. Observe me, society will not be satisfied!'

Mr. Pecksniff coughed.

'Slyme's biographer, sir, whoever he may be,' resumed the gentleman, 'must apply to me; or, if I am gone to that what's-his-name from which no thingumbob comes back, he must apply to my executors for leave to search among my papers. I have taken a few notes in my poor way, of some of that man's proceedings—my adopted brother, sir,—which would amaze you. He made use of an expression, sir, only on the fifteenth of last month when he couldn't meet a little bill and the other party wouldn't renew, which would have done honour to Napoleon Bonaparte in addressing the French army.'

'And pray,' asked Mr. Pecksniff, obviously not quite at his ease, 'what may be Mr. Slyme's business here, if I may be permitted to inquire, who am compelled by a regard for my own character to disavow all interest in his proceedings?'

'In the first place,' returned the gentleman, 'you will permit me to say, that I object to that remark, and that I strongly and indignantly protest against it on behalf of my friend Slyme. In the next place, you will give me leave to introduce myself. My name, sir, is Tigg. The name of Montague Tigg will perhaps be familiar to you, in connexion with the most remarkable events of the Peninsular War?'

Mr. Pecksniff gently shook his head.

'No matter,' said the gentleman. 'That man was my father, and I bear his name. I am consequently proud—proud as Lucifer. Excuse me one moment. I desire my friend Slyme to be present at the remainder of this conference.'

With this announcement he hurried away to the outer door of the Blue Dragon, and almost immediately returned with a companion shorter than himself, who was wrapped in an old blue camlet cloak with a lining of faded scarlet. His sharp features being much pinched and nipped by long waiting in the cold, and his straggling red whiskers and frowzy hair being more than usually dishevelled from the same cause, he certainly looked rather unwholesome and uncomfortable than Shakspearian or Miltonic.

'Now,' said Mr. Tigg, clapping one hand on the shoulder of his prepossessing friend, and calling Mr. Pecksniff's attention to him with the other, 'you two are related; and relations never did agree, and never will: which is a wise dispensation and an inevitable thing, or there would be none but family parties, and everybody in the world would bore everybody else to death. If you were on good terms, I should consider you a most confoundedly unnatural pair; but standing towards each other as you do, I look upon you as a couple of devilish deep-thoughted fellows, who may be reasoned with to any extent.'

Here Mr. Chevy Slyme, whose great abilities seemed one and all to point towards the sneaking quarter of the moral compass, nudged his friend stealthily with his elbow, and whispered in his ear.

'Chiv,' said Mr. Tigg aloud, in the high tone of one who was not to be tampered with. 'I shall come to that presently. I act upon my own responsibility, or not at all. To the extent of such a trifling loan as a crownpiece to a man of your talents, I look upon Mr. Pecksniff as certain:' and seeing at this juncture that the expression of Mr. Pecksniff's face by no means betokened that he shared this certainty, Mr. Tigg laid his finger on his nose again for that gentleman's private and especial behoof: calling upon him thereby to take notice, that the requisition of small loans was another instance of the peculiarities of genius as developed in his friend Slyme; that he, Tigg, winked at the same, because of the strong metaphysical interest which these weaknesses possessed; and that in reference to his own personal advocacy of such small advances, he merely consulted the humour of his friend, without the least regard to his own advantage or necessities.

'Oh, Chiv, Chiv!' added Mr. Tigg, surveying his adopted brother with an air of profound contemplation after dismissing this piece of pantomime. 'You are, upon my life, a strange instance of the little frailities that beset a mighty mind. If there had never been a telescope in the world, I should have been quite certain from my observation of you, Chiv, that there were spots on the sun! I wish I may die, if this isn't the queerest state of existence that we find ourselves forced into, without knowing why or wherefore, Mr. Pecksniff! Well, never mind! Moralise as we will, the world goes on. As Hamlet says, Hercules may lay about him with his club in every possible direction, but he can't prevent the cats from making a most intolerable row on the roofs of the houses, or the dogs from being shot in the hot weather if they run about the streets unmuzzled. Life's a riddle: a most infernally hard riddle to guess, Mr. Pecksniff. My own opinion is, that like that cele-brated conundrum, "Why's a man in jail like a man out of jail?" there's no answer to it. Upon my soul and body, it's the queerest sort of thing altogether—but there's no use in talk-ing about it. Ha! ha!'

With which consolatory deduction from the gloomy pre-mises recited, Mr. Tigg roused himself by a great effort, and proceeded in his former strain.

'Now I'll tell you what it is. I'm a most confoundedly soft-hearted kind of fellow in my way, and I cannot stand by, and see you two blades cutting each other's throats when there's nothing to be got by it. Mr. Pecksniff, you're the cousin of the testator up-stairs and we're the nephew—I say we, meaning Chiv. Perhaps in all essential points, you are more nearly related to him than we are. Very good. If so, so be it. But you can't get at him, neither can we. I give you my brightest word of honour, sir, that I've been looking through that keyhole, with short intervals of rest, ever since nine o'clock this morning, in expectation of receiving an answer to one of the most moderate and gentlemanly applications for a little temporary assistance—only fifteen pounds, and *my* security—that the mind of man can conceive. In the meantime, sir, he is per-petually closeted with, and pouring his whole confidence into the bosom of, a stranger. Now I say decisively, with regard to this state of circumstances, that it won't do; that it won't act; that it can't be; and that it must not be suffered to con-tinue.'

'Every man,' said Mr. Pecksniff, 'has a right, an undoubted right, (which I, for one, would not call in question for any earthly consideration: oh no!) to regulate his own proceedings by his own likings and dislikings, supposing they are not im-moral and not irreligious. I may feel in my own breast, that Mr. Chuzzlewit does not regard—me, for instance: say me—with exactly that amount of Christian love which should sub-sist between us; I may feel grieved and hurt at the circum-stance; still I may not rush to the conclusion that Mr. Chuzzle-wit is wholly without a 'justification in all his coldnesses; Heaven forbid! Besides; how, Mr. Tigg,' continued Pecksniff even more gravely and impressively than he had spoken yet, 'how could Mr. Chuzzlewit be prevented from having these peculiar and most extraordinary confidences of which you speak; the existence of which I must admit; and which I cannot but deplore—for his sake? Consider, my good sir—' and here Mr. Pecksniff eyed him wistfully—'how very much at random you are talking.'

'Why, as to that,' rejoined Tigg, 'it certainly is a difficult question.'

'Undoubtedly it is a difficult question,' Mr. Pecksniff answered. As he spoke he drew himself aloft, and seemed to grow more mindful, suddenly, of the moral gulf between himself and the creature he addressed. 'Undoubtedly it is a very difficult question. And I am far from feeling sure that it is a question any one is authorised to discuss. Good evening to you.'

'You don't know that the Spottletoes are here, I suppose?' said Mr. Tigg.

'What do you mean, sir? what Spottletoes?' asked Pecksniff, stopping abruptly on his way to the door.

'Mr. and Mrs. Spottletoe,' said Chevy Slyme, Esquire, speaking aloud for the first time, and speaking very sulkily: shambling with his legs the while. 'Spottletoe married my father's brother's child, didn't he? And Mrs. Spottletoe is Chuzzlewit's own niece, isn't she? She was his favourite once. You may well ask what Spottletoes.'

'Now, upon my sacred word!' cried Mr. Pecksniff, looking upwards. 'This is dreadful. The rapacity of these people is absolutely frightful!'

'It's not only the Spottletoes either, Tigg,' said Slyme, looking at that gentleman and speaking at Mr. Pecksniff. 'Anthony Chuzzlewit and his son have got wind of it, and have come down this afternoon. I saw 'em not five minutes ago, when I was waiting round the corner.'

'Oh, Mammon, Mammon!' cried Mr. Pecksniff, smiting his forehead.

'So there,' said Slyme, regardless of the interruption, 'are his brother and another nephew for you, already.'

'This is the whole thing, sir,' said Mr. Tigg; 'this is the point and purpose at which I was gradually arriving, when my friend Slyme here, with six words, hit it full. Mr. Pecksniff, now that your cousin (and Chiv's uncle) has turned up, some steps must be taken to prevent his disappearing again; and, if possible, to counteract the influence which is exercised over him now, by this designing favourite. Everybody who is interested feels it, sir. The whole family is pouring down to this place. The time has come when individual jealousies and interests must be forgotten for a time, sir, and union must be made against the common enemy. When the common enemy is routed, you will all set up for yourselves again; every lady and gentleman who

has a part in the game, will go in on their own account and
bowl away, to the best of their ability, at the testator's wicket;
and nobody will be in a worse position than before. Think of it.
Don't commit yourself now. You'll find us at the Half Moon
and Seven Stars in this village, at any time, and open to any
reasonable proposition. Hem! Chiv, my dear fellow, go out and
see what sort of a night it is.'

Mr. Slyme lost no time in disappearing, and, it is to be presumed, in going round the corner. Mr. Tigg, planting his legs
as wide apart as he could be reasonably expected by the most
sanguine man to keep them, shook his head at Mr. Pecksniff
and smiled.

'We must not be too hard,' he said, 'upon the little eccentri-
cities of our friend Slyme. You saw him whisper me?'

Mr. Pecksniff had seen him.

'You heard my answer, I think?'

Mr. Pecksniff had heard it.

'Five shillings, eh?' said Mr. Tigg, thoughtfully. 'Ah! what
an extraordinary fellow! Very moderate too!'

Mr. Pecksniff made no answer.

'Five shillings!' pursued Mr. Tigg, musing: 'and to be
punctually repaid next week; that's the best of it. You
heard that?'

Mr. Pecksniff had not heard that.

'No! You surprise me!' cried Tigg. 'That's the cream of the
thing, sir. I never knew that man fail to redeem a promise, in
my life. You're not in want of change, are you?'

'No,' said Mr. Pecksniff, 'thank you. Not at all.'

'Just so,' returned Mr. Tigg. 'If you had been, I'd have got
it for you.' With that he began to whistle; but a dozen seconds
had not elapsed when he stopped short, and, looking earnestly
at Mr. Pecksniff, said:

'Perhaps you'd rather not lend Slyme five shillings?'

'I would much rather not,' Mr. Pecksniff rejoined.

'Egad!' cried Tigg, gravely nodding his head as if some
ground of objection occurred to him at that moment for the
first time, 'it's very possible you may be right. Would you
entertain the same sort of objection to lending *me* five shillings,
now?'

'Yes, I couldn't do it, indeed,' said Mr. Pecksniff.

'Not even half-a-crown, perhaps?' urged Mr. Tigg.

'Not even half-a-crown.'

'Why, then we come,' said Mr. Tigg, 'to the ridiculously small amount of eighteenpence. Ha! ha!'

'And that,' said Mr. Pecksniff, 'would be equally objectionable.'

On receipt of this assurance, Mr. Tigg shook him heartily by both hands, protesting with much earnestness, that he was one of the most consistent and remarkable men he had ever met, and that he desired the honour of his better acquaintance. He moreover observed that there were many little characteristics about his friend Slyme, of which he could by no means, as a man of strict honour, approve; but that he was prepared to forgive him all these slight drawbacks, and much more, in consideration of the great pleasure he himself had that day enjoyed in his social intercourse with Mr. Pecksniff, which had given him a far higher and more enduring delight than the successful negotiation of any small loan on the part of his friend could possibly have imparted. With which remarks he would beg leave, he said, to wish Mr. Pecksniff a very good evening. And so he took himself off: as little abashed by his recent failure as any gentleman would desire to be.

The meditations of Mr. Pecksniff that evening at the bar of the Dragon, and that night in his own house, were very serious and grave indeed; the more especially as the intelligence he had received from Messrs. Tigg and Slyme touching the arrival of other members of the family, were fully confirmed on more particular inquiry. For the Spottletoes had actually gone straight to the Dragon, where they were at that moment housed and mounting guard, and where their appearance had occasioned such a vast sensation that Mrs. Lupin, scenting their errand before they had been under her roof half-an-hour, carried the news herself with all possible secrecy straight to Mr. Pecksniff's house: indeed it was her great caution in doing so which occasioned her to miss that gentleman, who entered at the front door of the Dragon just as she emerged from the back one. Moreover, Mr. Anthony Chuzzlewit and his son Jonas were economically quartered at the Half Moon and Seven Stars, which was an obscure ale-house; and by the very next coach there came posting to the scene of action, so many other affectionate members of the family (who quarrelled with each other, inside and out, all the way down, to the utter distraction of the coachman), that in less than four-and-twenty hours the scanty tavern accommodation was at a premium, and all the private lodgings in the place, amounting to full four beds and a sofa, rose cent. per cent. in the market.

In a word, things came to that pass that nearly the whole family sat down before the Blue Dragon, and formally invested it; and Martin Chuzzlewit was in a state of siege. But he resisted bravely; refusing to receive all letters, messages, and parcels; obstinately declining to treat with anybody; and holding out no hope or promise of capitulation. Meantime the family forces were perpetually encountering each other in divers parts of the neighbourhood: and, as no one branch of the Chuzzlewit tree had ever been known to agree with another within the memory of man, there was such a skirmishing, and flouting, and snapping off of heads, in the metaphorical sense of that expression; such a bandying of words and calling of names; such an upturning of noses and wrinkling of brows; such a formal interment of good feelings and violent resurrection of ancient grievances; as had never been known in those quiet parts since the earliest record of their civilised existence.

At length, in utter despair and hopelessness, some few of the belligerents began to speak to each other in only moderate terms of mutual aggravation; and nearly all addressed themselves with a show of tolerable decency to Mr. Pecksniff, in recognition of his high character and influential position. Thus by little and little they made common cause of Martin Chuzzlewit's obduracy, until it was agreed (if such a word can be used in connexion with the Chuzzlewits) that there should be a general council and conference held at Mr. Pecksniff's house upon a certain day at noon: which all members of the family who had brought themselves within reach of the summons, were forthwith bidden and invited, solemnly, to attend.

If ever Mr. Pecksniff wore an apostolic look, he wore it on this memorable day. If ever his unruffled smile proclaimed the words, 'I am a messenger of peace!' that was its mission now. If ever man combined within himself all the mild qualities of the lamb with a considerable touch of the dove, and not a dash of the crocodile, or the least possible suggestion of the very mildest seasoning of the serpent, that man was he. And, oh, the two Miss Pecksniffs! Oh, the serene expression on the face of Charity, which seemed to say, 'I know that all my family have injured me beyond the possibility of reparation, but I forgive them, for it is my duty so to do!' And, oh, the gay simplicity of Mercy: so charming, innocent, and infant-like, that if she had gone out walking by herself, and it had been a little earlier in the season, the robin-redbreasts might have covered her with leaves against her will, believing her to be one of the sweet children in the wood, come out of it, and issuing forth once more to look for blackberries in the young freshness of her heart! What words can paint the Pecksniffs in that trying hour? Oh, none: for words have naughty company among them, and the Pecksniffs were all goodness.

But when the company arrived! That was the time. When Mr. Pecksniff, rising from his seat at the table's head, with a daughter on either hand, received his guests in the best parlour and motioned them to chairs, with eyes so overflowing and countenance so damp with gracious perspiration, that he may be said to have been in a kind of moist meakness! And the company: the jealous, stony-hearted, distrustful company, who were all shut up in themselves, and had no faith in anybody, and wouldn't believe anything, and would no more allow themselves to be softened or lulled asleep by the Pecksniffs than if they had been so many hedgehogs or porcupines!

First, there was Mr. Spottletoe, who was so bald and had such big whiskers, that he seemed to have stopped his hair, by the sudden application of some powerful remedy, in the very act of falling off his head, and to have fastened it irrevocably on his face. Then there was Mrs. Spottletoe, who being much too slim for her years, and of a poetical constitution, was accustomed to inform her more intimate friends that the said whiskers were 'the lodestar of her existence;' and who could now, by reason of her strong affection for her uncle Chuzzlewit, and the shock it gave her to be suspected of testamentary designs upon him, do nothing but cry—except moan. Then there were Anthony Chuzzlewit, and his son Jonas: the face of the old man so sharpened by the wariness and cunning of his life, that it seemed to cut him a passage through the crowded room, as he edged away behind the remotest chairs; while the son had so well profited by the precept and example of the father, that he looked a year or two the elder of the twain, as they stood winking their red eyes, side by side, and whispering to each other softly. Then there was the widow of a deceased brother of Mr. Martin Chuzzlewit, who being almost supernaturally disagreeable, and having a dreary face and a bony figure and a masculine voice, was, in right of these qualities, what is commonly called a strong-minded woman; and who, if she could, would have established her claim to the title, and have shown herself, mentally speaking, a perfect Samson, by shutting up her brother-in-law in a private mad-house, until he proved his complete sanity by loving her very much. Beside her sat her spinster daughters, three in number, and of gentlemanly deportment, who had so mortified themselves with tight stays, that their tempers were reduced to something less than their waists, and sharp lacing was expressed in their very noses. Then there was a young gentleman, grand-nephew of Mr. Martin Chuzzlewit, very dark and very hairy, and apparently born for no particular purpose but to save looking-glasses the trouble of reflecting more than just the first idea and sketchy notion of a face, which had never been carried out. Then there was a solitary female cousin who was remarkable for nothing but being very deaf, and living by herself, and always having the tooth-ache. Then there was George Chuzzlewit, a gay bachelor cousin, who claimed to be young but had been younger, and was inclined to corpulency, and rather over-fed himself: to that extent, indeed, that his eyes were strained in their sockets, as if with constant surprise; and he had such an obvious disposition to pimples, that the bright spots on his cravat, the rich pattern on his waistcoat, and even his glittering trinkets, seemed to have broken out upon him, and not to have come into existence comfortably. Last of all there were present Mr. Chevy Slyme and his friend Tigg. And it is worthy of remark, that although each person present disliked the other, mainly because he or she *did* belong to the family, they one and all concurred in hating Mr. Tigg because he didn't.

Such was the pleasant little family circle now assembled in Mr. Pecksniff's best parlour, agreeably prepared to fall foul of Mr. Pecksniff or anybody else who might venture to say anything whatever upon any subject.

'This,' said Mr. Pecksniff, rising and looking round upon them with folded hands, 'does me good. It does my daughters good. We thank you for assembling here. We are grateful to you with our whole hearts. It is a blessed distinction that you have conferred upon us, and believe me:' it is impossible to conceive how he smiled here: 'we shall not easily forget it.'

'I am sorry to interrupt you, Pecksniff,' remarked Mr. Spottletoe, with his whiskers in a very portentous state; 'but you are assuming too much to yourself, sir. Who do you imagine has it in contemplation to confer a distinction upon *you*, sir?'

A general murmur echoed this inquiry, and applauded it.

'If you are about to pursue the course with which you have begun, sir,' pursued Mr. Spottletoe in a great heat, and giving a violent rap on the table with his knuckles, 'the sooner you desist, and this assembly separates, the better. I am no stranger, sir, to your preposterous desire to be regarded as the head of this family, but I can tell *you*, sir—'

Oh yes, indeed! *He* tell. *He!* What? He was the head, was he? From the strong-minded woman downwards everybody fell, that instant, upon Mr. Spottletoe, who after vainly attempting to be heard in silence was fain to sit down again, folding his arms and shaking his head most wrathfully, and giving Mrs. Spottletoe to understand in dumb show, that that scoundrel Pecksniff might go on for the present, but he would cut in presently, and annihilate him.

'I am not sorry,' said Mr. Pecksniff in resumption of his address, 'I am really not sorry that this little incident has happened. It is good to feel that we are met here without disguise. It is good to know that we have no reserve before each other, but are appearing freely in our own characters.'

Here, the eldest daughter of the strong-minded woman rose a little way from her seat, and trembling violently from head to foot, more as it seemed with passion than timidity, expressed a general hope that some people *would* appear in their own characters, if it were only for such a proceeding having the attraction of novelty to recommend it: and that when they (meaning the some people before mentioned) talked about their relations, they would be careful to observe who was present in company at the time; otherwise it might come round to those relations' ears, in a way they little expected; and as to red noses (she observed) she had yet to learn that a red nose was any disgrace, inasmuch as people neither made nor coloured their own noses, but had that feature provided for them without being first consulted; though even upon that branch of the subject she had great doubts whether certain noses were redder than other noses, or indeed half as red as some. This remark being received with a shrill titter by the two sisters of the speaker, Miss Charity Pecksniff begged with much politeness to be informed whether any of those very low observations were levelled at her; and receiving no more explanatory answer than was conveyed in the adage 'Those the cap fits, let them wear it,' immediately commenced a somewhat acrimonious and personal retort, wherein she was much comforted and abetted by her sister Mercy, who laughed at the same with great heartiness: indeed far more naturally than life. And it being quite impossible that any difference of opinion can take place among women without every woman who is within hearing taking active part in it, the strong-minded lady and her two daughters, and Mrs. Spottletoe, and the deaf cousin (who was not at all disqualified from joining in the dispute by reason of being perfectly unacquainted with its merits), one and all plunged into the quarrel directly.

The two Miss Pecksniffs being a pretty good match for the three Miss Chuzzlewits, and all five young ladies having, in the figurative language of the day, a great amount of steam to dispose of, the altercation would no doubt have been a long one but for the high valour and prowess of the strong-minded woman, who, in right of her reputation for powers of sarcasm, did so belabour and pummel Mrs. Spottletoe with taunting words that that poor lady, before the engagement was two minutes old, had no refuge but in tears. These she shed so plentifully, and so much to the agitation and grief of Mr. Spottletoe, that that gentleman, after holding his clenched fist close to Mr. Pecksniff's eyes, as if it were some natural curiosity from the near inspection whereof he was likely to derive high gratification and improvement, and after offering (for no particular reason that anybody could discover) to kick Mr. George Chuzzlewit for, and in consideration of, the trifling sum of sixpence, took his wife under his arm, and indignantly withdrew. This diversion, by distracting the attention of the combatants, put an end to the strife, which, after breaking out afresh some twice or thrice in certain inconsiderable spirts and dashes, died away in silence.

It was then that Mr. Pecksniff once more rose from his chair. It was then that the two Miss Pecksniffs composed themselves to look as if there were no such beings—not to say present, but in the whole compass of the world—as the three Miss Chuzzlewits: while the three Miss Chuzzlewits became equally unconscious of the existence of the two Miss Pecksniffs.

'It is to be lamented,' said Mr. Pecksniff, with a forgiving recollection of Mr. Spottletoe's fist, 'that our friend should have withdrawn himself so very hastily, though we have cause for mutual congratulation. even in that, since we are assured that he is not distrustful of us in regard to anything we may say or do while he is absent. Now that is very soothing, is it not?'

'Pecksniff,' said Anthony, who had been watching the whole party with peculiar keenness from the first: 'don't you be a hypocrite.'

'A what, my good sir?' demanded Mr. Pecksniff.

'A hypocrite.'

'Charity, my dear,' said Mr. Pecksniff, 'when I take my chamber candlestick to-night, remind me to be more than usually particular in praying for Mr. Anthony Chuzzlewit; who has done me an injustice.'

This was said in a very bland voice, and aside, as being addressed to his daughter's private ear. With a cheerfulness of conscience, prompting almost a sprightly demeanour, he then resumed:

'All our thoughts centring in our very dear but unkind relative, and he being as it were beyond our reach, we are met to-day, really as if we were a funeral party, except—a blessed exception—that there is no Body in the house.'

The strong-minded lady was not at all sure that this was a blessed exception. Quite the contrary.

'Well, my dear madam!' said Mr. Pecksniff. 'Be that as it may, here we are; and being here, we are to consider whether it is possible by any justifiable means—'

'Why, you know as well as I,' said the strong-minded lady, 'that any means are justifiable in such a case, don't you?'

'Very good, my dear madam, very good; whether it is possible by *any* means, we will say by *any* means, to open the eyes of our valued relative to his present infatuation. Whether it is possible to make him acquainted by any means with the real character and purpose of that young female whose strange, whose very strange position, in reference to himself,' here Mr. Pecksniff sunk his voice to an impressive whisper, 'really casts a shadow of disgrace and shame upon this family; and who, we know,' here he raised his voice again, 'else why is she his companion? harbours the very basest designs upon his weakness and his property.'

In their strong feeling on this point, they, who agreed in nothing else, all concurred as one mind. Good Heaven, that she should harbour designs upon his property! The strong-minded lady was for poison, her three daughters were for

Bridewell and bread-and-water, the cousin with the tooth-ache advocated Botany Bay, the two Miss Pecksniffs suggested flogging. Nobody but Mr. Tigg, who, notwithstanding his extreme shabbiness, was still understood to be in some sort a lady's man, in right of his upper lip and his frogs, indicated a doubt of the justifiable nature of these measures; and he only ogled the three Miss Chuzzlewits with the least admixture of banter in his admiration, as though he would observe, 'You are positively down upon her to too great an extent, my sweet creatures, upon my soul you are!'

'Now,' said Mr. Pecksniff, crossing his two fore-fingers in a manner which was at once conciliatory and argumentative: 'I will not, upon the one hand, go so far as to say that she deserves all the inflictions which have been so very forcibly and hilariously suggested;' one of his ornamental sentences; 'nor will I, upon the other, on any account compromise my common understanding as a man, by making the assertion that she does not. What I would observe is, that I think some practical means might be devised of inducing our respected, shall I say our revered—?'

'No!' interposed the strong-minded woman in a loud voice.

'Then I will not,' said Mr. Pecksniff. 'You are quite right, my dear madam, and I appreciate and thank you for your discriminating objection—our respected relative to dispose himself to listen to the promptings of nature, and not to the—'

'Go on, pa!' cried Mercy.

'Why, the truth is, my dear,' said Mr. Pecksniff, smiling upon his assembled kindred, 'that I am at a loss for a word. The name of those fabulous animals (pagan, I regret to say) who used to sing in the water, has quite escaped me.'

Mr. George Chuzzlewit suggested 'Swans.'

'No,' said Mr. Pecksniff. 'Not swans. Very like swans, too. Thank you.'

The nephew with the outline of a countenance, speaking for the first and last time on that occasion, propounded 'Oysters.'

'No,' said Mr. Pecksniff, with his own peculiar urbanity, 'nor oysters. But by no means unlike oysters; a very excellent idea; thank you, my dear sir, very much. Wait! Sirens. Dear me! sirens, of course. I think, I say, that means might be devised of disposing our respected relative to listen to the promptings of nature, and not to the siren-like delusions of art. Now we must not lose sight of the fact that our esteemed friend has a grandson, to whom he was, until lately, very much attached, and whom I could have wished to see here to-day, for I have a real and deep regard for him. A fine young man: a very fine young man! I would submit to you, whether we might not remove Mr. Chuzzlewit's distrust of us, and vindicate our own disinterestedness by—'

'If Mr. George Chuzzlewit has anything to say to *me*,' interposed the strong-minded woman, sternly, 'I beg him to speak out like a man; and not to look at me and my daughters as if he could eat us.'

'As to looking, I have heard it said, Mrs. Ned,' returned Mr. George, angrily, 'that a cat is free to contemplate a monarch; and therefore I hope I have some right, having been born a member of this family, to look at a person who only came into it by marriage. As to eating, I beg to say, whatever bitterness your jealousies and disappointed expectations may suggest to you, that I am not a cannibal, ma'am.'

'I don't know that!' cried the strong-minded woman.

'At all events, if I was a cannibal,' said Mr. George Chuzzlewit, greatly stimulated by this retort, 'I think it would occur to me that a lady who had outlived three husbands, and suffered so very little from their loss, must be most uncommonly tough.'

The strong-minded woman immediately rose.

'And I will further add,' said Mr. George, nodding his head violently at every second syllable; 'naming no names, and therefore hurting nobody but those whose consciences tell them they are alluded to, that I think it would be much more decent and becoming, if those who hooked and crooked themselves into this family by getting on the blind side of some of its members before marriage, and manslaughtering them afterwards by crowing over them to that strong pitch that they were glad to die, would refrain from acting the part of vultures in regard to other members of this family who are living. I think it would be full as well, if not better, if those individuals would keep at home, contenting themselves with what they have got (luckily for them) already; instead of hovering about, and thrusting their fingers into, a family pie, which they flavour much more than enough, I can tell them, when they are fifty miles away.'

'I might have been prepared for this!' cried the strong-minded woman, looking about her with a disdainful smile as

she moved towards the door, followed by her three daughters:
'indeed I was fully prepared for it from the first. What else
could I expect in such an atmosphere as this!'

'Don't direct your half-pay-officer's gaze at me, ma'am, if
you please,' interposed Miss Charity; 'for I won't bear it.'

This was a smart stab at a pension enjoyed by the strong-
minded woman, during her second widowhood and before her
last coverture. It told immensely.

'I passed from the memory of a grateful country, you very
miserable minx,' said Mrs. Ned, 'when I entered this family;
and I feel now, though I did not feel then, that it served me
right, and that I lost my claim upon the United Kingdom of
Great Britain and Ireland when I so degraded myself. Now,
my dears, if you're quite ready, and have sufficiently improved
yourselves by taking to heart the genteel example of these two
young ladies, I think we'll go. Mr. Pecksniff, we are very much
obliged to you, really. We came to be entertained, and you
have far surpassed our utmost expectations, in the amusement
you have provided for us. Thank you. Good-bye!'

With such departing words, did this strong-minded female
paralyse the Pecksniffian energies; and so she swept out of the
room, and out of the house, attended by her daughters, who,
as with one accord, elevated their three noses in the air, and
joined in a contemptuous titter. As they passed the parlour
window on the outside, they were seen to counterfeit a perfect
transport of delight among themselves; and with this final
blow and great discouragement for those within, they vanished.

Before Mr. Pecksniff or any of his remaining visitors could
offer a remark, another figure passed this window, coming, at
a great rate, in the opposite direction: and immediately afterwards, Mr. Spottletoe burst into the chamber. Compared with
his present state of heat, he had gone out a man of snow or ice.
His head distilled such oil upon his whiskers, that they were
rich and clogged with unctuous drops; his face was violently in-
flamed, his limbs trembled; and he gasped and strove for breath.

'My good sir!' cried Mr. Pecksniff.

'Oh yes!' returned the other: 'Oh yes, certainly! Oh to be
sure! Oh, of course! You hear him? You hear him? all of you!'

'What's the matter?' cried several voices.

'Oh nothing!' cried Spottletoe, still gasping. 'Nothing at all!
It's of no consequence! Ask him! *He*'ll tell you!'

'I do not understand our friend,' said Mr. Pecksniff, looking about him in utter amazement. 'I assure you that he is quite unintelligible to me.'

'Unintelligible, sir!' cried the other. 'Unintelligible! Do you mean to say, sir, that you don't know what has happened! That you haven't decoyed us here, and laid a plot and a plan against us! Will you venture to say that you didn't know Mr. Chuzzlewit was going, sir, and that you don't know he's gone, sir?'

'Gone!' was the general cry.

'Gone,' echoed Mr. Spottletoe. 'Gone while we were sitting here. Gone. Nobody knows where he's gone. Oh, of course not! Nobody knew he was going. Oh, of course not! The landlady thought up to the very last moment that they were merely going for a ride; she had no other suspicion. Oh, of course not! She's not this fellow's creature. Oh, of course not!'

Adding to these exclamations a kind of ironical howl, and gazing upon the company for one brief instant afterwards, in a sudden silence, the irritated gentleman started off again at the same tremendous pace, and was seen no more.

It was in vain for Mr. Pecksniff to assure them that this new and opportune evasion of the family was at least as great a shock and surprise to him as to anybody else. Of all the bullyings and denunciations that were ever heaped on one unlucky head, none can ever have exceeded in energy and heartiness those with which he was complimented by each of his remaining relatives, singly, upon bidding him farewell.

The moral position taken by Mr. Tigg was something quite tremendous; and the deaf cousin, who had the complicated aggravation of seeing all the proceedings and hearing nothing but the catastrophe, actually scraped her shoes upon the scraper, and afterwards distributed impressions of them all over the top step, in token that she shook the dust from her feet before quitting that dissembling and perfidious mansion.

Mr. Pecksniff had, in short, but one comfort, and that was the knowledge that all these his relations and friends had hated him to the very utmost extent before; and that he, for his part, had not distributed among them any more love than, with his ample capital in that respect, he could comfortably afford to part with. This view of his affairs yielded him great consolation; and the fact deserves to be noted, as showing with what ease a good man may be consoled under circumstances of failure and disappointment.

CHAPTER V

Containing a full account of the installation of Mr. Pecksniff's new pupil into the bosom of Mr. Pecksniff's family. With all the festivities held on that occasion, and the great enjoyment of Mr. Pinch

THE best of architects and land surveyors kept a horse, in whom the enemies already mentioned more than once in these pages pretended to detect a fanciful resemblance to his master. Not in his outward person, for he was a raw-boned, haggard horse, always on a much shorter allowance of corn than Mr. Pecksniff; but in his moral character, wherein, said they, he was full of promise, but of no performance. He was always, in a manner, going to go, and never going. When at his slowest rate of travelling, he would sometimes lift up his legs so high, and display such mighty action, that it was difficult to believe he was doing less than fourteen miles an hour; and he was for ever so perfectly satisfied with his own speed, and so little disconcerted by opportunities of comparing himself with the fastest trotters, that the illusion was the more difficult of resistance. He was a kind of animal who infused into the breasts of strangers a lively sense of hope, and possessed all those who knew him better with a grim despair. In what respect, having these points of character, he might be fairly likened to his master, that good man's slanderers only can explain. But it is a melancholy truth, and a deplorable instance of the uncharitableness of the world, that they made the comparison.

In this horse, and the hooded vehicle, whatever its proper name might be, to which he was usually harnessed—it was more like a gig with a tumour, than anything else—all Mr. Pinch's thoughts and wishes centred, one bright frosty morning: for with this gallant equipage he was about to drive to Salisbury alone, there to meet with the new pupil, and thence to bring him home in triumph.

Blessings on thy simple heart, Tom Pinch, how proudly dost thou button up that scanty coat, called by a sad misnomer, for these many years, a 'great' one; and how thoroughly, as with thy cheerful voice thou pleasantly adjurest Sam the hostler 'not to let him go yet,' dost thou believe that quadruped desires to go, and would go if he might! Who could repress a smile—

of love for thee, Tom Pinch, and not in jest at thy expense, for thou art poor enough already, Heaven knows—to think that such a holiday as lies before thee, should awaken that quick flow and hurry of the spirits, in which thou settest down again, almost untasted, on the kitchen window-sill, that great white mug (put by, by thy own hands, last night, that breakfast might not hold thee late), and layest yonder crust upon the seat beside thee, to be eaten on the road, when thou art calmer in thy high rejoicing! Who, as thou drivest off, a happy man, and noddest with a grateful lovingness to Pecksniff in his night-cap at his chamber-window, would not cry: 'Heaven speed thee, Tom, and send that thou wert going off for ever to some quiet home where thou mightst live at peace, and sorrow should not touch thee!'

What better time for driving, riding, walking, moving through the air by any means, than a fresh, frosty morning, when hope runs cheerily through the veins with the brisk blood, and tingles in the frame from head to foot! This was the glad commencement of a bracing day in early winter, such as may put the languid summer season (speaking of it when it can't be had) to the blush, and shame the spring for being sometimes cold by halves. The sheep-bells rang as clearly in the vigorous air, as if they felt its wholesome influence like living creatures; the trees, in lieu of leaves or blossoms, shed upon the ground a frosty rime that sparkled as it fell, and might have been the dust of diamonds. So it was to Tom. From cottage chimneys, smoke went streaming up high, high, as if the earth had lost its grossness, being so fair, and must not be oppressed by heavy vapour. The crust of ice on the else rippling brook was so transparent and so thin in texture, that the lively water might of its own free will have stopped—in Tom's glad mind it had—to look upon the lovely morning. And lest the sun should break this charm too eagerly, there moved between him and the ground, a mist like that which waits upon the moon on summer nights—the very same to Tom—and wooed him to dissolve it gently.

Tom Pinch went on; not fast, but with a sense of rapid motion, which did just as well; and as he went, all kinds of things occurred to keep him happy. Thus when he came within sight of the turnpike, and was—Oh a long way off!—he saw the tollman's wife, who had that moment checked a waggon, run back into the little house again like mad, to say

Pleasant little Family Party at Mr. Pecksniff's

(p. 57)

(she knew) that Mr. Pinch was coming up. And she was right, for when he drew within hail of the gate, forth rushed the toll-man's children, shrieking in tiny chorus, 'Mr. Pinch!' to Tom's intense delight. The very tollman, though an ugly chap in general, and one whom folks were rather shy of handling, came out himself to take the toll, and give him rough good morning: and that with all this, and a glimpse of the family breakfast on a little round table before the fire, the crust Tom Pinch had brought away with him acquired as rich a flavour as though it had been cut from a fairy loaf.

But there was more than this. It was not only the married people and the children who gave Tom Pinch a welcome as he passed. No, no. Sparkling eyes and snowy breasts came hur-riedly to many an upper casement as he clattered by, and gave him back his greeting: not stinted either, but sevenfold, good measure. They were all merry. They all laughed. And some of the wickedest among them even kissed their hands as Tom looked back. For who minded poor Mr. Pinch? There was no harm in *him*.

And now the morning grew so fair, and all things were so wide awake and gay, that the sun seeming to say—Tom had no doubt he said—'I can't stand it any longer: I must have a look,' streamed out in radiant majesty. The mist, too shy and gentle for such lusty company, fled off, quite scared, before it; and as it swept away, the hills and mounds and distant pasture lands, teeming with placid sheep and noisy crows, came out as bright as though they were unrolled bran new for the occasion. In compliment to which discovery, the brook stood still no longer, but ran briskly off to bear the tidings to the water-mill, three miles away.

Mr. Pinch was jogging along, full of pleasant thoughts and cheerful influences, when he saw, upon the path before him, going in the same direction with himself, a traveller on foot, who walked with a light quick step, and sang as he went: for certain in a very loud voice, but not unmusically. He was a young fellow, of some five or six-and-twenty perhaps, and was dressed in such a free and fly-away fashion, that the long ends of his loose red neckcloth were streaming out behind him quite as often as before; and the bunch of bright winter berries in the buttonhole of his velveteen coat was as visible to Mr. Pinch's rearward observation, as if he had worn that garment wrong side foremost. He continued to sing with so much energy, that he did not hear the sound of wheels until it was close behind him; when he turned a whimsical face and a very merry pair of blue eyes on Mr. Pinch, and checked himself directly.

'Why, Mark!' said Tom Pinch, stopping. 'Who'd have thought of seeing you here? Well! this is surprising!'

Mark touched his hat, and said, with a very sudden decrease of vivacity, that he was going to Salisbury.

'And how spruce you are, too!' said Mr. Pinch, surveying him with great pleasure. 'Really, I didn't think you were half such a tight-made fellow, Mark!'

'Thankee, Mr. Pinch. Pretty well for that, I believe. It's not my fault, you know. With regard to being spruce, sir, that's where it is, you see.' And here he looked particularly gloomy.

'Where what is?' Mr. Pinch demanded.

'Where the aggravation of it is. Any man may be in good spirits and good temper when he's well dressed. There an't much credit in that. If I was very ragged and very jolly, then I should begin to feel I had gained a point, Mr. Pinch.'

'So you were singing just now, to bear up, as it were, against being well dressed, eh, Mark?' said Pinch.

'Your conversation's always equal to print, sir,' rejoined Mark, with a broad grin. 'That was it.'

'Well!' cried Pinch, 'you are the strangest young man, Mark, I ever knew in my life. I always thought so; but now I am quite certain of it. I am going to Salisbury, too. Will you get in? I shall be very glad of your company.'

The young fellow made his acknowledgments and accepted the offer; stepping into the carriage directly, and seating himself on the very edge of the seat with his body half out of it, to express his being there on sufferance, and by the politeness of Mr. Pinch. As they went along, the conversation proceeded after this manner.

'I more than half believed, just now, seeing you so very smart,' said Pinch, 'that you must be going to be married, Mark.'

'Well, sir, I've thought of that, too,' he replied. 'There might be some credit in being jolly with a wife, 'specially if the children had the measles and that, and was very fractious indeed. But I'm a'most afraid to try it. I don't see my way clear.'

'You're not very fond of anybody, perhaps?' said Pinch.

'Not particular, sir, I think.'

'But the way would be, you know, Mark, according to your views of things,' said Mr. Pinch, 'to marry somebody you didn't like, and who was very disagreeable.'

'So it would, sir; but that might be carrying out a principle a little too far, mightn't it?'

'Perhaps it might,' said Mr. Pinch. At which they both laughed gaily.

'Lord bless you, sir,' said Mark, 'you don't half know me, though. I don't believe there ever was a man as could come out so strong under circumstances that would make other men miserable, as I could, if I could only get a chance. But I can't get a chance. It's my opinion that nobody never will know half of what's in me, unless something very unexpected turns up. And I don't see any prospect of that. I'm a-going to leave the Dragon, sir.'

. 'Going to leave the Dragon!' cried Mr. Pinch, looking at him with great astonishment. 'Why, Mark, you take my breath away!'

'Yes, sir,' he rejoined, looking straight before him and a long way off, as men do sometimes when they cogitate profoundly. 'What's the use of my stopping at the Dragon? It an't at all the sort of place for *me*. When I left London (I'm a Kentish man by birth, though), and took that sitivation here, I quite made up my mind that it was the dullest little out-of-the-way corner in England, and that there would be some credit in being jolly under such circumstances. But, Lord, there's no dulness at the Dragon! Skittles, cricket, quoits, nine-pins, comic songs, choruses, company round the chimney corner every winter's evening. Any man could be jolly at the Dragon. There's no credit in *that*.'

'But if common report be true for once, Mark, as I think it is, being able to confirm it by what I know myself,' said Mr. Pinch, 'you are the cause of half this merriment, and set it going.'

'There may be something in that, too, sir,' answered Mark. 'But that's no consolation.'

'Well!' said Mr. Pinch, after a short silence, his usually subdued tone being even more subdued than ever. 'I can hardly think enough of what you tell me. Why, what will become of Mrs. Lupin, Mark?'

Mark looked more fixedly before him, and further off still, as he answered that he didn't suppose it would be much of an object to her. There were plenty of smart young fellows as would be glad of the place. He knew a dozen himself.

'That's probable enough,' said Mr. Pinch, 'but I am not at all sure that Mrs. Lupin would be glad of them. Why, I always supposed that Mrs. Lupin and you would make a match of it, Mark; and so did every one, as far as I know.'

'I never,' Mark replied, in some confusion, 'said nothing as was in a direct way courting-like to her, nor she to me, but I don't know what I mightn't do one of these odd times, and what she mightn't say in answer. Well, sir, *that* wouldn't suit.'

'Not to be landlord of the Dragon, Mark?' cried Mr. Pinch.

'No, sir, certainly not,' returned the other, withdrawing his gaze from the horizon, and looking at his fellow-traveller. 'Why, that would be the ruin of a man like me. I go and sit down comfortably for life, and no man never finds me out. What would be the credit of the landlord of the Dragon's being jolly? Why, he couldn't help it, if he tried.'

'Does Mrs. Lupin know you are going to leave her?' Mr. Pinch inquired.

'I haven't broke it to her yet, sir, but I must. I'm looking out this morning for something new and suitable,' he said, nodding towards the city.

'What kind of thing now?' Mr. Pinch demanded.

'I was thinking,' Mark replied, 'of something in the grave-digging way.'

'Good gracious, Mark!' cried Mr. Pinch.

'It's a good damp, wormy sort of business, sir,' said Mark, shaking his head argumentatively, 'and there might be some credit in being jolly, with one's mind in that pursuit, unless grave-diggers is usually given that way; which would be a drawback. You don't happen to know how that is in general, do you, sir?'

'No,' said Mr. Pinch, 'I don't indeed. I never thought upon the subject.'

'In case of that not turning out as well as one could wish, you know,' said Mark, musing again, 'there's other businesses. Undertaking now. That's gloomy. There might be credit to be gained there. A broker's man in a poor neighbourhood wouldn't be bad perhaps. A jailor sees a deal of misery. A doctor's man is in the very midst of murder. A bailiff's an't a lively office nat'rally. Even a tax-gatherer must find his feelings

Pinch starts Homeward with the New Pupil
(*p. 76*)

rather worked upon, at times. There's lots of trades in which I should have an opportunity, I think.'

Mr. Pinch was so perfectly overwhelmed by these remarks that he could do nothing but occasionally exchange a word or two on some indifferent subject, and cast sidelong glances at the bright face of his odd friend (who seemed quite unconscious of his observation), until they reached a certain corner of the road, close upon the outskirts of the city, when Mark said he would jump down there, if he pleased.

'But bless my soul, Mark,' said Mr. Pinch, who in the progress of his observation just then made the discovery that the bosom of his companion's shirt was as much exposed as if it was Midsummer, and was ruffled by every breath of air, 'why don't you wear a waistcoat?'

'What's the good of one, sir?' asked Mark.

'Good of one?' said Mr. Pinch. 'Why, to keep your chest warm.'

'Lord love you, sir!' cried Mark, 'you don't know me. *My* chest don't want no warming. Even if it did, what would no waistcoat bring it to? Inflammation of the lungs, perhaps? Well, there'd be some credit in being jolly, with a inflammation of the lungs.'

As Mr. Pinch returned no other answer than such as was conveyed in his breathing very hard, and opening his eyes very wide, and nodding his head very much, Mark thanked him for his ride, and without troubling him to stop, jumped lightly down. And away he fluttered, with his red neckerchief, and his open coat, down a cross-lane: turning back from time to time to nod to Mr. Pinch, and looking one of the most careless, good-humoured, comical fellows in life. His late companion, with a thoughtful face, pursued his way to Salisbury.

Mr. Pinch had a shrewd notion that Salisbury was a very desperate sort of place; an exceeding wild and dissipated city: and when he had put up the horse, and given the hostler to understand that he would look in again in the course of an hour or two to see him take his corn, he set forth on a stroll about the streets with a vague and not unpleasant idea that they teemed with all kinds of mystery and bedevilment. To one of his quiet habits this little delusion was greatly assisted by the circumstance of its being market-day, and the thoroughfares about the market-place being filled with carts, horses, donkeys, baskets, waggons, garden-stuff, meat, tripe, pies, poultry, and huckster's wares of every opposite description and possible variety of character. Then there were young farmers and old farmers, with smock-frocks, brown great-coats, drab great-coats, red worsted comforters, leather-leggings, wonderful shaped hats, hunting-whips, and rough sticks, standing about in groups, or talking noisily together on the tavern steps, or paying and receiving huge amounts of greasy wealth, with the assistance of such bulky pocket-books that when they were in their pockets it was apoplexy to get them out, and when they were out it was spasms to get them in again. Also there were farmers' wives in beaver bonnets and red cloaks, riding shaggy horses purged of all earthly passions, who went soberly into all manner of places without desiring to know why, and who, if required, would have stood stock still in a china-shop, with a complete dinner-service at each hoof. Also a great many dogs, who were strongly interested in the state of the market and the bargains of their masters; and a great confusion of tongues, both brute and human.

Mr. Pinch regarded everything exposed for sale with great delight, and was particularly struck by the itinerant cutlery, which he considered of the very keenest kind, insomuch that he purchased a pocket knife with seven blades in it, and not a cut (as he afterwards found out) among them. When he had exhausted the market-place, and watched the farmers safe into the market dinner, he went back to look after the horse. Having seen him eat unto his heart's content, he issued forth again, to wander round the town and regale himself with the shop windows: previously taking a long stare at the bank, and wondering in what direction underground the caverns might be, where they kept the money; and turning to look back at one or two young men who passed him, whom he knew to be articled to solicitors in the town; and who had a sort of fearful interest in his eyes, as jolly dogs who knew a thing or two, and kept it up tremendously.

But the shops. First of all there were the jewellers' shops, with all the treasures of the earth displayed therein, and such large silver watches hanging up in every pane of glass, that if they were anything but first-rate goers it certainly was not because the works could decently complain of want of room. In good sooth they were big enough, and perhaps, as the saying is, ugly enough, to be the most correct of all mechanical performers; in Mr. Pinch's eyes, however, they were smaller than

Geneva ware; and when he saw one very bloated watch announced as a repeater, gifted with the uncommon power of striking every quarter of an hour inside the pocket of its happy owner, he almost wished that he were rich enough to buy it.

But what were even gold and silver, precious stones and clockwork, to the bookshops, whence a pleasant smell of paper freshly pressed came issuing forth, awakening instant recollections of some new grammar had at school, long time ago, with 'Master Pinch, Grove House Academy,' inscribed in faultless writing on the fly-leaf! That whiff of russia leather, too, and all those rows on rows of volumes, neatly ranged within: what happiness did they suggest! And in the window were the spick-and-span new works from London, with the title-pages, and sometimes even the first page of the first chapter, laid wide open: tempting unwary men to begin to read the book, and then, in the impossibility of turning over, to rush blindly in, and buy it! Here too were the dainty frontispiece and trim vignette, pointing like handposts on the outskirts of great cities, to the rich stock of incident beyond; and store of books, with many a grave portrait and time-honoured name, whose matter he knew well, and would have given mines to have, in any form, upon the narrow shelf beside his bed at Mr. Pecksniff's. What a heart-breaking shop it was!

There was another; not quite so bad at first, but still a trying shop; where children's books were sold, and where poor Robinson Crusoe stood alone in his might, with dog and hatchet, goat-skin cap and fowling-pieces; calmly surveying Philip Quarll and the host of imitators round him, and calling Mr. Pinch to witness that he, of all the crowd, impressed one solitary foot-print on the shore of boyish memory, whereof the tread of generations should not stir the lightest grain of sand. And there too were the Persian tales, with flying chests and students of enchanted books shut up for years in caverns: and there too was Abudah, the merchant, with the terrible little old woman hobbling out of the box in his bedroom: and there the mighty talisman, the rare Arabian Nights, with Cassim Baba, divided by four, like the ghost of a dreadful sum, hanging up, all gory, in the robbers' cave. Which matchless wonders, coming fast on Mr. Pinch's mind, did so rub up and chafe that wonderful lamp within him, that when he turned his face towards the busy street, a crowd of phantoms waited on his pleasure, and he lived again, with new delight, the happy days before the Pecksniff era.

He had less interest now in the chemists' shops, with their great glowing bottles (with smaller repositories of brightness in their very stoppers); and in their agreeable compromises between medicine and perfumery, in the shape of toothsome lozenges and virgin honey. Neither had he the least regard (but he never had much) for the tailors', where the newest metropolitan waistcoat patterns were hanging up, which by some strange transformation always looked amazing there, and never appeared at all like the same thing anywhere else. But he stopped to read the playbill at the theatre, and surveyed the doorway with a kind of awe, which was not diminished when a sallow gentleman with long dark hair came out, and told a boy to run home to his lodgings and bring down his broadsword. Mr. Pinch stood rooted to the spot on hearing this, and might have stood there until dark, but that the old cathedral bell began to ring for vesper service, on which he tore himself away.

Now, the organist's assistant was a friend of Mr. Pinch's, which was a good thing, for he too was a very quiet gentle soul, and had been, like Tom, a kind of old-fashioned boy at school, though well-liked by the noisy fellows too. As good luck would have it (Tom always said he had great good luck) the assistant chanced that very afternoon to be on duty by himself, with no one in the dusty organ-loft but Tom: so while he played, Tom helped him with the stops; and finally, the service being just over, Tom took the organ himself. It was then turning dark, and the yellow light that streamed in through the ancient windows in the choir was mingled with a murky red. As the grand tones resounded through the church, they seemed, to Tom, to find an echo in the depth of every ancient tomb, no less than in the deep mystery of his own heart. Great thoughts and hopes came crowding on his mind as the rich music rolled upon the air, and yet among them—something more grave and solemn in their purpose, but the same—were all the images of that day, down to its very lightest recollection of childhood. The feeling that the sounds awakened, in the moment of their existence, seemed to include his whole life and being; and as the surrounding realities of stone and wood and glass grew dimmer in the darkness, these visions grew so much the brighter that Tom might have forgotten the new pupil and the expectant master, and have sat there pouring out his grateful heart till midnight, but for a very earthy old verger insisting on locking up the cathedral forthwith. So he took leave of his friend, with many thanks, groped his way out, as well as he could, into the now lamp-lighted streets, and hurried off to get his dinner.

All the farmers being by this time jogging homewards, there was nobody in the sanded parlour of the tavern where he had left the horse; so he had his little table drawn out close before the fire, and fell to work upon a well-cooked steak and smoking hot potatoes, with a strong appreciation of their excellence, and a very keen sense of enjoyment. Beside him, too, there stood a jug of most stupendous Wiltshire beer; and the effect of the whole was so transcendent, that he was obliged every now and then to lay down his knife and fork, rub his hands, and think about it. By the time the cheese and celery came, Mr. Pinch had taken a book out of his pocket, and could afford to trifle with the viands; now eating a little, now drinking a little, now reading a little, and now stopping to wonder what sort of a young man the new pupil would turn out to be. He had passed from this latter theme and was deep in his book again, when the door opened, and another guest came in, bringing with him such a quantity of cold air, that he positively seemed at first to put the fire out.

'Very hard frost to-night, sir,' said the new-comer, courteously acknowledging Mr. Pinch's withdrawal of the little table, that he might have place. 'Don't disturb yourself, I beg.'

Though he said this with a vast amount of consideration for Mr. Pinch's comfort, he dragged one of the great leather-bottomed chairs to the very centre of the hearth, notwithstanding; and sat down in front of the fire, with a foot on each hob.

'My feet are quite numbed. Ah! Bitter cold to be sure.'

'You have been in the air some considerable time, I dare say?' said Mr. Pinch.

'All day. Outside a coach, too.'

'That accounts for his making the room so cool,' thought Mr. Pinch. 'Poor fellow! How thoroughly chilled he must be!'

The stranger became thoughtful likewise, and sat for five or ten minutes looking at the fire in silence. At length he rose and divested himself of his shawl and great-coat, which (far different from Mr. Pinch's) was a very warm and thick one; but he was not a whit more conversational out of his great-coat than in it, for he sat down again in the same place and attitude, and leaning back in his chair, began to bite his nails. He was young —one-and-twenty, perhaps—and handsome; with a keen dark eye, and a quickness of look and manner which made Tom sensible of a great contrast in his own bearing, and caused him to feel even more shy than usual.

There was a clock in the room, which the stranger often turned to look at. Tom made frequent reference to it also: partly from a nervous sympathy with its taciturn companion; and partly because the new pupil was to inquire for him at half after six, and the hands were getting on towards that hour. Whenever the stranger caught him looking at this clock, a kind of confusion came upon Tom as if he had been found out in something; and it was a perception of his uneasiness which caused the younger man to say, perhaps, with a smile:

'We both appear to be rather particular about the time. The fact is, I have an engagement to meet a gentleman here.'

'So have I,' said Mr. Pinch.

"At half-past six,' said the stranger.

'At half-past six,' said Tom in the very same breath; whereupon the other looked at him with some surprise.

'The young gentleman, I expect,' remarked Tom, timidly, 'was to inquire at that time for a person by the name of Pinch.'

'Dear me!' cried the other, jumping up. 'And I have been keeping the fire from you all this while! I had no idea you were Mr. Pinch. I am the Mr. Martin for whom you were to inquire. Pray excuse me. How do you do? Oh, do draw nearer, pray!'

'Thank you,' said Tom, 'thank you. I am not at all cold, and you are: and we have a cold ride before us. Well, if you wish it, I will. I—I am very glad,' said Tom, smiling with an embarrassed frankness peculiarly his, and which was as plainly a confession of his own imperfections, and an appeal to the kindness of the person he addressed, as if he had drawn one up in simple language and committed it to paper: 'I am very glad indeed that you turn out to be the party I expected. I was thinking, but a minute ago, that I could wish him to be like you.'

'I am very glad to hear it,' returned Martin, shaking hands with him again; 'for I assure you, I was thinking there could be no such luck as Mr. Pinch's turning out like *you*.'

'No, really!' said Tom, with great pleasure. 'Are you serious?'

'Upon my word I am,' replied his new acquaintance. 'You

and I will get on excellently well, I know: which it's no small relief to me to feel, for to tell you the truth, I am not at all the sort of fellow who could get on with everybody, and that's the point on which I had the greatest doubts. But they're quite relieved now.—Do me the favour to ring the bell, will you?'

Mr. Pinch rose, and complied with great alacrity—the handle hung just over Martin's head, as he warmed himself—and listened with a smiling face to what his friend went on to say. It was:

'If you like punch, you'll allow me to order a glass a-piece, as hot as it can be made, that we may usher in our friendship in a becoming manner. To let you into a secret, Mr. Pinch, I never was so much in want of something warm and cheering in my life; but I didn't like to run the chance of being found drinking it, without knowing what kind of person you were; for first impressions, you know, often go a long way, and last a long time.'

Mr. Pinch assented, and the punch was ordered. In due course it came: hot and strong. After drinking to each other in the steaming mixture, they became quite confidential.

'I'm a sort of relation of Pecksniff's, you know,' said the young man.

'Indeed!' cried Mr. Pinch.

'Yes. My grandfather is his cousin, so he's kith and kin to me, somehow, if you can make that out. I can't.'

'Then Martin is your Christian name?' said Mr. Pinch, thoughtfully. 'Oh!'

'Of course it is,' returned his friend: 'I wish it was my surname, for my own is not a very pretty one, and it takes a long time to sign. Chuzzlewit is my name.'

'Dear me!' cried Mr. Pinch, with an involuntary start.

'You're not surprised at my having two names, I suppose?' returned the other, setting his glass to his lips. 'Most people have.'

'Oh, no,' said Mr. Pinch, 'not at all. Oh dear no! Well!' And then remembering that Mr. Pecksniff had privately cautioned him to say nothing in reference to the old gentleman of the same name who had lodged at the Dragon, but to reserve all mention of that person for him, he had no better means of hiding his confusion than by raising his own glass to his mouth. They looked at each other out of their respective tumblers for a few seconds, and then put them down empty.

'I told them in the stable to be ready for us ten minutes ago,' said Mr. Pinch, glancing at the clock again. 'Shall we go?'

'If you please,' returned the other.

'Would you like to drive?' said Mr. Pinch; his whole face beaming with a consciousness of the splendour of his offer. 'You shall, if you wish.'

'Why, that depends, Mr. Pinch,' said Martin, laughing, 'upon what sort of a horse you have. Because if he's a bad one, I would rather keep my hands warm by holding them comfortably in my great-coat pockets.'

He appeared to think this such a good joke, that Mr. Pinch was quite sure it must be a capital one. Accordingly, he laughed too, and was fully persuaded that he enjoyed it very much. Then he settled his bill, and Mr. Chuzzlewit paid for the punch; and having wrapped themselves up, to the extent of their respective means, they went out together to the front door, where Mr. Pecksniff's property stopped the way.

'I won't drive, thank you, Mr. Pinch,' said Martin, getting into the sitter's place. 'By-the-bye, there's a box of mine. Can we manage to take it?'

'Oh, certainly,' said Tom. 'Put it in, Dick, anywhere!'

It was not precisely of that convenient size which would admit of its being squeezed into any odd corner, but Dick the hostler got it in somehow, and Mr. Chuzzlewit helped him. It was all on Mr. Pinch's side, and Mr. Chuzzlewit said he was very much afraid it would encumber him; to which Tom said, 'Not at all;' though it forced him into such an awkward position, that he had much ado to see anything but his own knees. But it is an ill wind that blows nobody any good; and the wisdom of the saying was verified in this instance; for the cold air came from Mr. Pinch's side of the carriage, and by interposing a perfect wall of box and man between it and the new pupil, he shielded that young gentleman effectually: which was a great comfort.

It was a clear evening, with a bright moon. The whole landscape was silvered by its light and by the hoar-frost; and everything looked exquisitely beautiful. At first, the great serenity and peace through which they travelled, disposed them both to silence; but in a very short time the punch within them and the healthful air without, made them loquacious, and they talked incessantly. When they were half-way home, and stopped to give the horse some water, Martin (who was very generous with his money) ordered another glass of punch, which they drank between them, and which had not the effect of making them less conversational than before. Their principal topic of discourse was naturally Mr. Pecksniff and his family; of whom, and of the great obligations they had heaped upon him, Tom Pinch, with the tears standing in his eyes, drew such a picture as would have inclined any one of common feeling almost to revere them: and of which Mr. Pecksniff had not the slightest foresight or preconceived idea, or he certainly (being very humble) would not have sent Tom Pinch to bring the pupil home.

In this way they went on, and on, and on—in the language of the story-books—until at last the village lights appeared before them, and the church spire cast a long reflection on the grave-yard grass: as if it were a dial (alas, the truest in the world!) marking, whatever light shone out of Heaven, the flight of days and weeks and years, by some new shadow on that solemn ground.

'A pretty church!' said Martin, observing that his companion slackened the slack pace of the horse, as they approached.

'Is it not?' cried Tom, with great pride. 'There's the sweetest little organ there you ever heard. I play it for them.'

'Indeed?' said Martin. 'It is hardly worth the trouble, I should think. What do you get for that, now?'

'Nothing,' answered Tom.

'Well,' returned his friend, 'you *are* a very strange fellow!'

To which remark there succeeded a brief silence.

'When I say nothing,' observed Mr. Pinch, cheerfully, 'I am wrong, and don't say what I mean, because I get a great deal of pleasure from it, and the means of passing some of the happiest hours I know. It led to something else the other day; but you will not care to hear about that, I dare say?'

'Oh yes, I shall. What?'

'It led to my seeing,' said Tom, in a lower voice, 'one of the loveliest and most beautiful faces you can possibly picture to yourself.'

'And yet I am able to picture a beautiful one,' said his friend, thoughtfully, 'or should be, if I have any memory.'

'She came,' said Tom, laying his hand upon the other's arm, 'for the first time, very early in the morning, when it was hardly light; and when I saw her, over my shoulder, standing just within the porch, I turned quite cold, almost believing her to be a spirit. A moment's reflection got the better of that, of course, and fortunately it came to my relief so soon, that I didn't leave off playing.'

'Why fortunately?'

'Why? Because she stood there, listening. I had my spectacles on, and saw her through the chinks in the curtains as plainly as I see you; and she was beautiful. After a while she glided off, and I continued to play until she was out of hearing.'

'Why did you do that?'

'Don't you see?' responded Tom. 'Because she might suppose I hadn't seen her; and might return.'

'And did she?'

'Certainly she did. Next morning, and next evening too: but always when there were no people about, and always alone. I rose earlier and sat there later, that when she came, she might find the church door open, and the organ playing, and might not be disappointed. She strolled that way for some days, and always stayed to listen. But she is gone now, and of all unlikely things in this wide world, it is perhaps the most improbable that I shall ever look upon her face again.'

'You don't know anything more about her?'

'No.'

'And you never followed her when she went away?'

'Why should I distress her by doing that?' said Tom Pinch. 'Is it likely that she wanted *my* company? She came to hear the organ, not to see me; and would you have had me scare her from a place she seemed to grow quite fond of? Now, Heaven bless her!' cried Tom, 'to have given her but a minute's pleasure every day, I would have gone on playing the organ at those times until I was an old man: quite contented if she sometimes thought of a poor fellow like me, as a part of the music; and more than recompensed if she ever mixed me up with anything she liked as well as she liked that!'

The new pupil was clearly very much amazed by Mr. Pinch's weakness, and would probably have told him so, and given him some good advice, but for their opportune arrival at Mr. Pecksniff's door: the front door this time, on account of the occasion being one of ceremony and rejoicing. The same man was in waiting for the horse who had been adjured by Mr. Pinch in the morning not to yield to his rabid desire to start; and after delivering the animal into his charge, and beseeching Mr. Chuzzlewit in a whisper never to reveal a syllable of what he had just told him in the fulness of his heart, Tom led the pupil in, for instant presentation.

Mr. Pecksniff had clearly not expected them for hours to come: for he was surrounded by open books, and was glancing from volume to volume, with a black-lead pencil in his mouth, and a pair of compasses in his hand, at a vast number of mathematical diagrams, of such extraordinary shapes that they looked like designs for fireworks. Neither had Miss Charity expected them, for she was busied, with a capacious wicker basket before her, in making impracticable nightcaps for the poor. Neither had Miss Mercy expected them, for she was sitting upon her stool, tying on the—oh good gracious!—the petticoat of a large doll that she was dressing for a neighbour's child: really, quite a grown-up doll, which made it more confusing: and had its little bonnet dangling by the ribbon from one of her fair curls, to which she had fastened it, lest it should be lost or sat upon. It would be difficult, if not impossible, to conceive a family so thoroughly taken by surprise as the Pecksniffs were, on this occasion.

'Bless my life!' said Mr. Pecksniff, looking up, and gradually exchanging his abstracted face for one of joyful recognition. 'Here already! Martin, my dear boy, I am delighted to welcome you to my poor house!'

With this kind greeting, Mr. Pecksniff fairly took him to his arms, and patted him several times upon the back with his right hand the while, as if to express that his feelings during the embrace were too much for utterance.

'But here,' he said, recovering, 'are my daughters, Martin: my two only children, whom (if you ever saw them) you have not beheld—ah, these sad family divisions!—since you were infants together. Nay, my dears, why blush at being detected in your everyday pursuits? We had prepared to give you the reception of a visitor, Martin, in our little room of state,' said Mr. Pecksniff, smiling, 'but I like this better, I like this better!'

Oh blessed star of Innocence, wherever you may be, how did you glitter in your home of ether, when the two Miss Pecksniffs put forth each her lily hand, and gave the same, with mantling cheeks, to Martin! How did you twinkle, as if fluttering with sympathy, when Mercy, reminded of the bonnet in her hair, hid her fair face and turned her head aside: the while her gentle sister plucked it out, and smote her, with a sister's soft reproof, upon her buxom shoulder!

'And how,' said Mr. Pecksniff, turning round after the contemplation of these passages, and taking Mr. Pinch in a friendly manner by the elbow, 'how has our friend here used you, Martin?'

'Very well indeed, sir. We are on the best terms, I assure you.'

'Old Tom Pinch!' said Mr. Pecksniff, looking on him with affectionate sadness. 'Ah! It seems but yesterday that Thomas was a boy, fresh from a scholastic course. Yet years have passed, I think, since Thomas Pinch and I first walked the world together!'

Mr. Pinch could say nothing. He was too much moved. But he pressed his master's hand, and tried to thank him.

'And Thomas Pinch and I,' said Mr. Pecksniff, in a deeper voice, 'will walk it yet, in mutual faithfulness and friendship! And if it comes to pass that either of us be run over, in any of those busy crossings which divide the streets of life, the other will convey him to the hospital in Hope, and sit beside his bed in Bounty!'

'Well, well, well!' he added in a happier tone, as he shook Mr. Pinch's elbow hard. 'No more of this! Martin, my dear friend, that you may be at home within these walls, let me show you how we live, and where. Come!'

With that he took up a lighted candle, and, attended by his young relative, prepared to leave the room. At the door, he stopped.

'You'll bear us company, Tom Pinch?'

Aye, cheerfully, though it had been to death, would Tom have followed him: glad to lay down his life for such a man!

'This,' said Mr. Pecksniff, opening the door of an opposite parlour, 'is the little room of state, I mentioned to you. My girls have pride in it, Martin! This,' opening another door, 'is the little chamber in which my works (slight things at best) have been concocted. Portrait of myself by Spiller. Bust by Spoker. The latter is considered a good likeness. I seem to recognise something about the left-hand corner of the nose, myself.'

Martin thought it was very like, but scarcely intellectual enough. Mr. Pecksniff observed that the same fault had been found with it before. It was remarkable it should have struck his young relation too. He was glad to see he had an eye for art.

'Various books you observe,' said Mr. Pecksniff, waving his

hand towards the wall, 'connected with our pursuit. I have scribbled myself, but have not yet published. Be careful how you come up-stairs. This,' opening another door, 'is my chamber. I read here when the family suppose I have retired to rest. Sometimes I injure my health, rather more than I can quite justify to myself, by doing so: but art is long and time is short. Every facility you see for jotting down crude notions, even here.'

These latter words were explained by his pointing to a small round table on which were a lamp, divers sheets of paper, a piece of India rubber, and a case of instruments: all put ready, in case an architectural idea should come into Mr. Pecksniff's head in the night; in which event he would instantly leap out of bed, and fix it for ever.

Mr. Pecksniff opened another door on the same floor, and shut it again, all at once, as if it were a Blue Chamber. But before he had well done so, he looked smilingly round, and said, 'Why not?'

Martin couldn't say why not, because he didn't know anything at all about it. So Mr. Pecksniff answered himself, by throwing open the door, and saying:

'My daughters' room. A poor first-floor to us, but a bower to them. Very neat. Very airy. Plants you observe; hyacinths; books again; birds.' These birds, by-the-bye, comprised, in all, one staggering old sparrow without a tail, which had been borrowed expressly from the kitchen. 'Such trifles as girls love are here. Nothing more. Those who seek heartless splendour, would seek here in vain.'

With that he led them to the floor above.

'This,' said Mr. Pecksniff, throwing wide the door of the memorable two-pair front; 'is a room where some talent has been developed, I believe. This is a room in which an idea for a steeple occurred to me, that I may one day give to the world. We work here, my dear Martin. Some architects have been bred in this room: a few, I think, Mr. Pinch?'

Tom fully assented; and, what is more, fully believed it.

'You see,' said Mr. Pecksniff, passing the candle rapidly from roll to roll of paper, 'some traces of our doings here. Salisbury Cathedral from the north. From the south. From the east. From the west. From the south-east. From the nor'-west. A bridge. An alms-house. A jail. A church. A powder-magazine. A wine-cellar. A portico. A summer-house. An ice-house.

Plans, elevations, sections, every kind of thing. And this,' he added, having by this time reached another large chamber on the same story, with four little beds in it, 'this is your room, of which Mr. Pinch here is the quiet sharer. A southern aspect; a charming prospect; Mr. Pinch's little library, you perceive; everything agreeable and appropriate. If there is any additional comfort you would desire to have here at any time, pray mention it. Even to strangers, far less to you, my dear Martin, there is no restriction on that point.'

It was undoubtedly true, and may be stated in corroboration of Mr. Pecksniff, that any pupil had the most liberal permission to mention anything in this way that suggested itself to his fancy. Some young gentlemen had gone on mentioning the very same thing for five years without ever being stopped.

'The domestic assistants,' said Mr. Pecksniff, 'sleep above; and that is all.' After which, and listening complacently as he went, to the encomiums passed by his young friend on the arrangements generally, he led the way to the parlour again.

Here a great change had taken place; for festive preparations on a rather extensive scale were already completed, and the two Miss Pecksniffs were awaiting their return with hospitable looks. There were two bottles of currant wine, white and red; a dish of sandwiches (very long and very slim); another of apples; another of captain's biscuits (which are always a moist and jovial sort of viand); a plate of oranges cut up small and gritty; with powdered sugar, and a highly geological home-made cake. The magnitude of these preparations quite took away Tom Pinch's breath: for though the new pupils were usually let down softly, as one may say, particularly in the wine department, which had so many stages of declension, that sometimes a young gentleman was a whole fortnight in getting to the pump; still this was a banquet; a sort of Lord Mayor's feast in private life; a something to think of, and hold on by, afterwards.

To this entertainment, which apart from its own intrinsic merits, had the additional choice quality, that it was in strict keeping with the night, being both light and cool, Mr. Pecksniff besought the company to do full justice.

'Martin,' he said, 'will seat himself between you two, my dears, and Mr. Pinch will come by me. Let us drink to our new inmate, and may we be happy together! Martin, my dear friend, my love to you! Mr. Pinch, if you spare the bottle we shall quarrel.'

And trying (in his regard for the feelings of the rest) to look as if the wine were not acid and didn't make him wink, Mr. Pecksniff did honour to his own toast.

'This,' he said, in allusion to the party, not the wine, 'is a Mingling that repays one for much disappointment and vexation. Let us be merry.' Here he took a captain's biscuit. 'It is a poor heart that never rejoices; and our hearts are not poor. No!'

With such stimulants to merriment did he beguile the time, and do the honours of the table; while Mr. Pinch, perhaps to assure himself that what he saw and heard was holiday reality, and not a charming dream, ate of everything, and in particular disposed of the slim sandwiches to a surprising extent. Nor was he stinted in his draughts of wine; but on the contrary, remembering Mr. Pecksniff's speech, attacked the bottle with such vigour, that every time he filled his glass anew, Miss Charity, despite her amiable resolves, could not repress a fixed and stony glare, as if her eyes had rested on a ghost. Mr. Pecksniff also became thoughtful at those moments, not to say dejected: but as he knew the vintage, it is very likely he may have been speculating on the probable condition of Mr. Pinch upon the morrow, and discussing within himself the best remedies for colic.

Martin and the young ladies were excellent friends already, and compared recollections of their childish days, to their mutual liveliness and entertainment. Miss Mercy laughed immensely at everything that was said; and sometimes, after glancing at the happy face of Mr. Pinch, was seized with such fits of mirth as brought her to the very confines of hysterics. But for these bursts of gaiety her sister, in her better sense, reproved her; observing, in an angry whisper, that it was far from being a theme for jest; and that she had no patience with the creature; though it generally ended in her laughing too— but much more moderately—and saying that indeed it was a little too ridiculous and intolerable to be serious about.

At length it became high time to remember the first clause of that great discovery made by the ancient philosopher, for securing health, riches, and wisdom; the infallibility of which has been for generations verified by the enormous fortunes constantly amassed by chimney-sweepers and other persons who get up early and go to bed betimes. The young ladies accordingly rose, and having taken leave of Mr. Chuzzlewit with much sweetness, and of their father with much duty, and of Mr. Pinch with much condescension, retired to their bower. Mr. Pecksniff insisted on accompanying his young friend up-stairs, for personal superintendence of his comforts; and taking him by the arm, conducted him once more to his bed-room, followed by Mr. Pinch, who bore the light.

'Mr. Pinch,' said Pecksniff, seating himself with folded arms on one of the spare beds. 'I don't see any snuffers in that candlestick. Will you oblige me by going down, and asking for a pair?'

Mr. Pinch, only too happy to be useful, went off directly.

'You will excuse Thomas Pinch's want of polish, Martin,' said Mr. Pecksniff, with a smile of patronage and pity, as soon as he had left the room. 'He means well.'

'He is a very good fellow, sir.'

'Oh, yes,' said Mr. Pecksniff. 'Yes. Thomas Pinch means well. He is very grateful. I have never regretted having be-friended Thomas Pinch.'

'I should think you never would, sir.'

'No,' said Mr. Pecksniff. 'No. I hope not. Poor fellow, he is always disposed to do his best; but he is not gifted. You will make him useful to you, Martin, if you please. If Thomas has a fault, it is that he is sometimes a little apt to forget his position. But that is soon checked. Worthy soul! You will find him easy to manage. Good night!'

'Good night, sir.'

By this time Mr. Pinch had returned with the snuffers.

'And good night to *you*, Mr. Pinch,' said Pecksniff. 'And sound sleep to you both. Bless you! Bless you!'

Invoking this benediction on the heads of his young friends with great fervour, he withdrew to his own room; while they, being tired, soon fell asleep. If Martin dreamed at all, some clue to the matter of his visions may possibly be gathered from the after-pages of this history. Those of Thomas Pinch were all of holidays, church organs, and seraphic Pecksniffs. It was some time before Mr. Pecksniff dreamed at all, or even sought his pillow, as he sat for full two hours before the fire in his own chamber, looking at the coals and thinking deeply. But he, too, slept and dreamed at last. Thus in the quiet hours of the night, one house shuts in as many incoherent and incongruous fancies as a madman's head.

CHAPTER VI

Comprises, among other important matters, Pecksniffian and architectural, an exact relation of the progress made by Mr. Pinch in the confidence and friendship of the new pupil

IT was morning; and the beautiful Aurora, of whom so much hath been written, said, and sung, did, with her rosy fingers, nip and tweak Miss Pecksniff's nose. It was the frolicsome custom of the Goddess, in her intercourse with the fair Cherry, so to do; or in more prosaic phrase, the tip of that feature in the sweet girl's countenance was always very red at breakfast-time. For the most part, indeed, it wore, at that season of the day, a scraped and frosty look, as if it had been rasped; while a similar phenomenon developed itself in her humour, which was then observed to be of a sharp and acid quality, as though an extra lemon (figuratively speaking) had been squeezed into the nectar of her disposition, and had rather damaged its flavour.

This additional pungency on the part of the fair young creature led, on ordinary occasions, to such slight consequences as the copious dilution of Mr. Pinch's tea, or to his coming off uncommonly short in respect of butter, or to other the like results. But on the morning after the Installation Banquet, she suffered him to wander to and fro among the eatables and drinkables, a perfectly free and unchecked man; so utterly to Mr. Pinch's wonder and confusion, that like the wretched captive who recovered his liberty in his old age, he could make but little use of his enlargement, and fell into a strange kind of flutter for want of some kind hand to scrape his bread, and cut him off in the article of sugar with a lump, and pay him those other little attentions to which he was accustomed. There was something almost awful, too, about the self-possession of the new pupil; who 'troubled' Mr. Pecksniff for the loaf, and helped himself to a rasher of that gentleman's own particular and private bacon, with all the coolness in life. He even seemed to think that he was doing quite a regular thing, and to expect that Mr. Pinch would follow his example, since he took occasion to observe of that young man 'that he didn't get on:' a speech of so tremendous a character, that Tom cast down his eyes involuntarily, and felt as if he himself had committed some horrible deed and heinous breach of Mr. Pecksniff's confidence. Indeed, the agony of having such an indiscreet remark addressed to him before the assembled family, was breakfast enough in itself, and would, without any other matter of reflection, have settled Mr. Pinch's business and quenched his appetite, for one meal, though he had been never so hungry.

The young ladies, however, and Mr. Pecksniff likewise, remained in the very best of spirits in spite of these severe trials, though with something of a mysterious understanding among themselves. When the meal was nearly over, Mr. Pecksniff smilingly explained the cause of their common satisfaction.

'It is not often,' he said, 'Martin, that my daughters and I desert our quiet home to pursue the giddy round of pleasures that revolves abroad. But we think of doing so to-day.'

'Indeed, sir!' cried the new pupil.

'Yes,' said Mr. Pecksniff, tapping his left hand with a letter which he held in his right. 'I have a summons here to repair to London; on professional business, my dear Martin; strictly on professional business; and I promised my girls, long ago, that whenever that happened again, they should accompany me. We shall go forth to-night by the heavy coach—like the dove of old, my dear Martin—and it will be a week before we again deposit our olive-branches in the passage. When I say olive-branches,' observed Mr. Pecksniff, in explanation, 'I mean, our unpretending luggage.'

'I hope the young ladies will enjoy their trip,' said Martin.

'Oh! that I'm sure we shall!' cried Mercy, clapping her hands. 'Good gracious, Cherry, my darling, the idea of London!'

'Ardent child!' said Mr. Pecksniff, gazing on her in a dreamy way. 'And yet there is a melancholy sweetness in these youthful hopes! It is pleasant to know that they never can be realised. I remember thinking once myself, in the days of my childhood, that pickled onions grew on trees, and that every elephant was born with an impregnable castle on his back. I have not found the fact to be so; far from it; and yet those visions have comforted me under circumstances of trial. Even when I have had the anguish of discovering that I have nourished in my breast an ostrich, and not a human pupil: even in that hour of agony, they have soothed me.'

At this dread allusion to John Westlock, Mr. Pinch precipitately choked in his tea; for he had that very morning received a letter from him, as Mr. Pecksniff very well knew.

'You will take care, my dear Martin,' said Mr. Pecksniff, resuming his former cheerfulness, 'that the house does not run away in our absence. We leave you in charge of everything. There is no mystery; all is free and open. Unlike the young man in the Eastern tale—who is described as a one-eyed almanack, if I am not mistaken, Mr. Pinch?'

'A one-eyed calender, I think, sir,' faltered Tom.

'They are pretty nearly the same thing, I believe,' said Mr. Pecksniff, smiling compassionately; 'or they used to be in my time. Unlike that young man, my dear Martin, you are forbidden to enter no corner of this house; but are requested to make yourself perfectly at home in every part of it. You will be jovial, my dear Martin, and will kill the fatted calf if you please!'

There was not the least objection, doubtless, to the young man's slaughtering and appropriating to his own use any calf, fat or lean, that he might happen to find upon the premises; but as no such animal chanced at that time to be grazing on Mr. Pecksniff's estate, this request must be considered rather as a polite compliment than a substantial hospitality. It was the finishing ornament of the conversation; for when he had delivered it, Mr. Pecksniff rose, and led the way to that hotbed of architectural genius, the two-pair front.

'Let me see,' he said, searching among the papers, 'how you can best employ yourself, Martin, while I am absent. Suppose you were to give me your idea of a monument to a Lord Mayor of London; or a tomb for a sheriff; or your notion of a cowhouse to be erected in a nobleman's park. Do you know, now,' said Mr. Pecksniff, folding his hands, and looking at his young relation with an air of pensive interest, 'that I should very much like to see your notion of a cow-house?'

But Martin by no means appeared to relish this suggestion.

'A pump,' said Mr. Pecksniff, 'is very chaste practice. I have found that a lamp-post is calculated to refine the mind and give it a classical tendency. An ornamental turnpike has a remarkable effect upon the imagination. What do you say to beginning with an ornamental turnpike?'

'Whatever Mr. Pecksniff pleased,' said Martin, doubtfully.

'Stay,' said that gentleman. 'Come! as you're ambitious, and are a very neat draughtsman, you shall—ha ha!—you shall try your hand on these proposals for a grammar-school: regulating your plan, of course, by the printed particulars. Upon my word, now,' said Mr. Pecksniff, merrily, 'I shall be very curious to see what you make of the grammar-school. Who knows but a young man of your taste might hit upon something, impracticable and unlikely in itself, but which I could put into shape? For it really is, my dear Martin, it really is in the finishing touches alone, that great experience and long study in these matters tell. Ha, ha, ha! Now it really will be,' continued Mr. Pecksniff, clapping his young friend on the back in his droll humour, 'an amusement to me, to see what you make of the grammar-school.'

Martin readily undertook this task, and Mr. Pecksniff forthwith proceeded to entrust him with the materials necessary for its execution: dwelling meanwhile on the magical effect of a few finishing touches from the hand of a master; which, indeed, as some people said (and these were the old enemies again!) was unquestionably very surprising, and almost miraculous; as there were cases on record in which the masterly introduction of an additional back window, or a kitchen door, or half-a-dozen steps, or even a water-spout, had made the design of a pupil Mr. Pecksniff's own work, and had brought substantial rewards into that gentleman's pocket. But such is the magic of genius, which changes all it handles into gold!

'When your mind requires to be refreshed by change of occupation,' said Mr. Pecksniff, 'Thomas Pinch will instruct you in the art of surveying the back garden, or in ascertaining the dead level of the road between this house and the finger-post, or in any other practical and pleasing pursuit. There are a cart-load of loose bricks, and a score or two of old flower-pots, in the back yard. If you could pile them up, my dear Martin, into any form which would remind me on my return, say of St. Peter's at Rome, or the Mosque of St. Sophia at Constantinople, it would be at once improving to you and agreeable to my feelings. And now,' said Mr. Pecksniff, in conclusion, 'to drop, for the present, our professional relations and advert to private matters, I shall be glad to talk with you in my own room, while I pack up my portmanteau.'

Martin attended him; and they remained in secret conference together for an hour or more; leaving Tom Pinch alone. When the young man returned, he was very taciturn and dull, in which state he remained all day; so that Tom, after trying him once or twice with indifferent conversation, felt a delicacy in obtruding himself upon his thoughts, and said no more.

He would not have had leisure to say much, had his new friend been ever so loquacious: for first of all Mr. Pecksniff called him down to stand upon the top of his portmanteau and represent ancient statues there, until such time as it would consent to be locked; and then Miss Charity called him to come and cord her trunk; and then Miss Mercy sent for him to come and mend her box; and then he wrote the fullest possible cards for all the luggage; and then he volunteered to carry it all down-stairs; and after that to see it safely carried on a couple of barrows to the old finger-post at the end of the lane; and then to mind it till the coach came up. In short, his day's work would have been a pretty heavy one for a porter, but his thorough good-will made nothing of it; and as he sat upon the luggage at last, waiting for the Pecksniffs, escorted by the new pupil, to come down the lane, his heart was light with the hope of having pleased his benefactor.

'I was almost afraid,' said Tom, taking a letter from his pocket, and wiping his face, for he was hot with bustling about though it was a cold day, 'that I shouldn't have had time to write it, and that would have been a thousand pities: postage from such a distance being a serious consideration, when one's not rich. She will be glad to see my hand, poor girl, and to hear that Pecksniff is as kind as ever. I would have asked John Westlock to call and see her, and tell her all about me by word of mouth, but I was afraid he might speak against Pecksniff to her, and make her uneasy. Besides, they are particular people where she is, and it might have rendered her situation uncomfortable if she had had a visit from a young man like John. Poor Ruth!'

Tom Pinch seemed a little disposed to be melancholy for half a minute or so, but he found comfort very soon, and pursued his ruminations thus:

'I'm a nice man, I don't think, as John used to say (John was a kind, merry-hearted fellow: I wish he had liked Pecksniff better), to be feeling low, on account of the distance between us, when I ought to be thinking, instead, of my extraordinary good luck in having ever got here. I must have been born with a silver spoon in my mouth, I am sure, to have ever come across Pecksniff. And here have I fallen again into my usual good luck with the new pupil! Such an affable, generous, free fellow, as he is, I never saw. Why, we were companions directly! and he a relation of Pecksniff's too, and a clever, dashing youth who might cut his way through the world as if it were a cheese! Here he comes while the words are on my lips,' said Tom: 'walking down the lane as if the lane belonged to him.'

In truth, the new pupil, not at all disconcerted by the honour of having Miss Mercy Pecksniff on his arm, or by the affectionate adieux of that young lady, approached as Mr. Pinch spoke, followed by Miss Charity and Mr. Pecksniff. As the coach appeared at the same moment, Tom lost no time in entreating the gentleman last mentioned, to undertake the delivery of his letter.

'Oh!' said Mr. Pecksniff, glancing at the superscription. 'For your sister, Thomas. Yes, oh yes, it shall be delivered, Mr. Pinch. Make your mind easy upon that score. She shall certainly have it, Mr. Pinch.'

He made the promise with so much condescension and patronage, that Tom felt he had asked a great deal (this had not occurred to his mind before), and thanked him earnestly. The Miss Pecksniffs, according to a custom they had, were amused beyond description at the mention of Mr. Pinch's sister. Oh the fright! The bare idea of a Miss Pinch! Good heavens!

Tom was greatly pleased to see them so merry, for he took it as a token of their favour, and good-humoured regard. Therefore he laughed too and rubbed his hands, and wished them a pleasant journey and safe return, and was quite brisk. Even when the coach had rolled away with the olive-branches in the boot and the family of doves inside, he stood waving his hand and bowing: so much gratified by the unusually courteous demeanour of the young ladies, that he was quite regardless, for the moment, of Martin Chuzzlewit, who stood leaning thoughtfully against the finger-post, and who after disposing of his fair charge had hardly lifted his eyes from the ground.

The perfect silence which ensued upon the bustle and departure of the coach, together with the sharp air of the wintry afternoon, roused them both at the same time. They turned, as by mutual consent, and moved off arm-in-arm.

'How melancholy you are!' said Tom; 'what is the matter?'

'Nothing worth speaking of,' said Martin. 'Very little more than was the matter yesterday, and much more, I hope, than will be the matter to-morrow. I'm out of spirits, Pinch.'

'Well,' cried Tom, 'now do you know I am in capital spirits to-day, and scarcely ever felt more disposed to be good company. It was a very kind thing in your predecessor, John, to write to me, was it not?'

'Why, yes,' said Martin carelessly; 'I should have thought he would have had enough to do to enjoy himself, without thinking of you, Pinch.'

'Just what I felt to be so very likely,' Tom rejoined; 'but no, he keeps his word, and says, "My dear Pinch, I often think of you," and all sorts of kind and considerate things of that description.'

'He must be a devilish good-natured fellow,' said Martin, somewhat peevishly: 'because he can't mean that, you know.'

'I don't suppose he can, eh?' said Tom, looking wistfully in his companion's face. 'He says so to please me, you think?'

'Why, is it likely,' rejoined Martin, with greater earnestness, 'that a young man newly escaped from this kennel of a place, and fresh to all the delights of being his own master in London, can have much leisure or inclination to think favourably of anything or anybody he has left behind him here? I put it to you, Pinch, is it natural?'

After a short reflection, Mr. Pinch replied, in a more subdued tone, that to be sure it was unreasonable to expect any such thing, and that he had no doubt Martin knew best.

'Of course I know best,' Martin observed.

'Yes, I feel that,' said Mr. Pinch, mildly. 'I said so.' And when he had made this rejoinder, they fell into a blank silence again, which lasted until they reached home: by which time it was dark.

Now, Miss Charity Pecksniff, in consideration of the inconvenience of carrying them with her in the coach, and the impossibility of preserving them by artificial means until the family's return, had set forth, in a couple of plates, the fragments of yesterday's feast. In virtue of which liberal arrangement, they had the happiness to find awaiting them in the parlour two chaotic heaps of the remains of last night's pleasure, consisting of certain filmy bits of oranges, some mummied sandwiches, various disrupted masses of the geological cake, and several entire captain's biscuits. That choice liquor in which to steep these dainties might not be wanting, the remains of the two bottles of currant wine had been poured together and corked with a curl-paper; so that every material was at hand for making quite a heavy night of it.

Martin Chuzzlewit beheld these roystering preparations

with infinite contempt, and stirring the fire into a blaze (to the great destruction of Mr. Pecksniff's coals), sat moodily down before it, in the most comfortable chair he could find. That he might the better squeeze himself into the small corner that was left for him, Mr. Pinch took up his position on Miss Mercy Pecksniff's stool, and setting his glass down upon the hearth-rug and putting his plate upon his knees, began to enjoy himself.

If Diogenes coming to life again could have rolled himself, tub and all, into Mr. Pecksniff's parlour, and could have seen Tom Pinch as he sat on Mercy Pecksniff's stool, with his plate and glass before him, he could not have faced it out, though in his surliest mood, but must have smiled good-temperedly. The perfect and entire satisfaction of Tom; his surpassing apprecia-tion of the husky sandwiches, which crumbled in his mouth like saw-dust; the unspeakable relish with which he swallowed the thin wine by drops, and smacked his lips, as though it were so rich and generous that to lose an atom of its fruity flavour were a sin; the look with which he paused sometimes, with his glass in his hand, proposing silent toasts to himself; and the anxious shade that came upon his contented face when, after wandering round the room, exulting in its uninvaded snugness, his glance encountered the dull brow of his companion; no cynic in the world, though in his hatred of its men a very griffin, could have withstood these things in Thomas Pinch.

Some men would have slapped him on the back, and pledged him in a bumper of the currant wine, though it had been the sharpest vinegar—aye, and liked its flavour too; some would have seized him by his honest hand, and thanked him for the lesson that his simple nature taught them. Some would have laughed with, and others would have laughed at him; of which last class was Martin Chuzzlewit, who, unable to restrain him-self, at last laughed loud and long.

'That's right,' said Tom, nodding approvingly. 'Cheer up! That's capital!'

At which encouragement young Martin laughed again; and said, as soon as he had breath and gravity enough:

'I never saw such a fellow as you are, Pinch.'

'Didn't you though?' said Tom. 'Well, it's very likely you do find me strange, because I have hardly seen anything of the world, and you have seen a good deal I dare say?'

'Pretty well for my time of life,' rejoined Martin, drawing his chair still nearer to the fire, and spreading his feet out on

Mr. Pinch and the New Pupil on a Social Occasion

the fender. 'Deuce take it, I must talk openly to somebody. I'll talk openly to you, Pinch.'

'Do!' said Tom. 'I shall take it as being very friendly of you.'

'I'm not in your way, am I?' inquired Martin, glancing down at Mr. Pinch, who was by this time looking at the fire over his leg.

'Not at all!' cried Tom.

'You must know then, to make short of a long story,' said Martin, beginning with a kind of effort, as if the revelation were not agreeable to him: 'that I have been bred up from childhood with great expectations, and have always been taught to believe that I should be, one day, very rich. So I should have been, but for certain brief reasons which I am going to tell you, and which have led to my being disinherited.'

'By your father?' inquired Mr. Pinch, with open eyes.

'By my grandfather. I have had no parents these many years. Scarcely within my remembrance.'

'Neither have I,' said Tom, touching the young man's hand with his own and timidly withdrawing it again. 'Dear me!'

'Why, as to that, you know, Pinch,' pursued the other, stirring the fire again, and speaking in his rapid, off-hand way: 'it's all very right and proper to be fond of parents when we have them, and to bear them in remembrance after they're dead, if you have ever known anything of them. But as I never did know anything about mine personally, you know, why, I can't be expected to be very sentimental about 'em. And I am not: that's the truth.'

Mr. Pinch was just then looking thoughtfully at the bars. But on his companion pausing in this place, he started, and said 'Oh! of course,' and composed himself to listen again.

'In a word,' said Martin, 'I have been bred and reared all my life by this grandfather of whom I have just spoken. Now, he has a great many good points; there is no doubt about that; I'll not disguise the fact from you; but he has two very great faults, which are the staple of his bad side. In the first place, he has the most confirmed obstinacy of character you ever met with in any human creature. In the second, he is most abominably selfish.'

'Is he indeed?' cried Tom.

'In those two respects,' returned the other, 'there never was such a man. I have often heard from those who know, that they have been, time out of mind, the failings of our family; and I believe there's some truth in it. But I can't say of my own knowledge. All I have to do, you know, is to be very thankful that they haven't descended to me, and to be very careful that I don't contract 'em.'

'To be sure,' said Mr. Pinch. 'Very proper.'

'Well, sir,' resumed Martin, stirring the fire once more, and drawing his chair still closer to it, 'his selfishness makes him exacting, you see; and his obstinacy makes him resolute in his exactions. The consequence is that he has always exacted a great deal from me in the way of respect, and submission, and self-denial when his wishes were in question, and so forth. I have borne a great deal from him, because I have been under obligations to him (if one can ever be said to be under obligations to one's own grandfather), and because I have been really attached to him; but we have had a great many quarrels for all that, for I could not accommodate myself to his ways very often—not out of the least reference to myself, you understand, but because——' he stammered here, and was rather at a loss.

Mr. Pinch being about the worst man in the world to help anybody out of a difficulty of this sort, said nothing.

'Well! as you understand me,' resumed Martin, quickly, 'I needn't hunt for the precise expression I want. Now I come to the cream of my story, and the occasion of my being here. I am in love, Pinch.'

Mr. Pinch looked up into his face with increased interest.

'I say I am in love. I am in love with one of the most beautiful girls the sun ever shone upon. But she is wholly and entirely dependent upon the pleasure of my grandfather; and if he were to know that she favoured my passion, she would lose her home and everything she possesses in the world. There is nothing very selfish in *that* love, I think?'

'Selfish!' cried Tom. 'You have acted nobly. To love her as I am sure you do, and yet in consideration for her state of dependence, are you not even to disclose——'

'What are you talking about, Pinch?' said Martin pettishly: 'don't make yourself ridiculous, my good fellow! What do you mean by not disclosing?'

'I beg your pardon,' answered Tom. 'I thought you meant that, or I wouldn't have said it.'

'If I didn't tell her I loved her, where would be the use of my being in love?' said Martin: 'unless to keep myself in a perpetual state of worry and vexation?'

'That's true,' Tom answered. 'Well! I can guess what *she* said when you told her,' he added, glancing at Martin's handsome face.

'Why, not exactly, Pinch,' he rejoined, with a slight frown: 'because she has some girlish notions about duty and gratitude, and all the rest of it, which are rather hard to fathom; but in the main you are right. Her heart was mine, I found.'

'Just what I supposed,' said Tom. 'Quite natural!' and, in his great satisfaction, he took a long sip out of his wineglass.

'Although I had conducted myself from the first with the utmost circumspection,' pursued Martin, 'I had not managed matters so well but that my grandfather, who is full of jealousy and distrust, suspected me of loving her. He said nothing to her, but straightway attacked me in private, and charged me with designing to corrupt the fidelity to himself (there you observe his selfishness), of a young creature whom he had trained and educated to be his only disinterested and faithful companion, when he should have disposed of me in marriage to his heart's content. Upon that, I took fire immediately, and told him that with his good leave I would dispose of myself in marriage, and would rather not be knocked down by him or any other auctioneer to any bidder whomsoever.'

Mr. Pinch opened his eyes wider, and looked at the fire harder than he had done yet.

'You may be sure,' said Martin, 'that this nettled him, and that he began to be the very reverse of complimentary to myself. Interview succeeded interview; words engendered words, as they always do; and the upshot of it was, that I was to renounce her, or be renounced by him. Now you must bear in mind, Pinch, that I am not only desperately fond of her (for though she is poor, her beauty and intellect would reflect great credit on anybody, I don't care of what pretensions, who might become her husband), but that a chief ingredient in my composition is a most determined—'

'Obstinacy,' suggested Tom in perfect good faith. But the suggestion was not so well received as he had expected; for the young man immediately rejoined, with some irritation,

'What a fellow you are, Pinch!'

'I beg your pardon,' said Tom, 'I thought you wanted a word.'

'I didn't want that word,' he rejoined. 'I told you obstinacy was no part of my character, did I not? I was going to say, if you had given me leave, that a chief ingredient in my composition is a most determined firmness.'

'Oh!' cried Tom, screwing up his mouth, and nodding. 'Yes, yes; I see!'

'And being firm,' pursued Martin, 'of course I was not going to yield to him, or give way by so much as the thousandth part of an inch.'

'No, no,' said Tom.

'On the contrary, the more he urged, the more I was determined to oppose him.'

'To be sure!' said Tom.

'Very well,' rejoined Martin, throwing himself back in his chair, with a careless wave of both hands, as if the subject were quite settled, and nothing more could be said about it: 'There is an end of the matter, and here am I!'

Mr. Pinch sat staring at the fire for some minutes with a puzzled look, such as he might have assumed if some uncommonly difficult conundrum had been proposed, which he found it impossible to guess. At length he said:

'Pecksniff, of course, you had known before?'

'Only by name. No, I had never seen him, for my grandfather kept not only himself but me, aloof from all his relations. But our separation took place in a town in the adjoining county. From that place I came to Salisbury, and there I saw Pecksniff's advertisement, which I answered, having always had some natural taste, I believe, in the matters to which it referred, and thinking it might suit me. As soon as I found it to be his, I was doubly bent on coming to him if possible, on account of his being—'

'Such an excellent man,' interposed Tom, rubbing his hands: 'so he is. You were quite right.'

'Why, not so much on that account, if the truth must be spoken,' returned Martin, 'as because my grandfather has an inveterate dislike to him, and after the old man's arbitrary treatment of me, I had a natural desire to run as directly counter to all his opinions as I could. Well! As I said before, here I am. My engagement with the young lady I have been telling you about is likely to be a tolerably long one; for neither her prospects nor mine are very bright; and of course I shall not think of marrying until I am well able to do so. It would never do, you know, for me to be plunging myself into poverty and shabbiness and love in one room up three pair of stairs, and all that sort of thing.'

'To say nothing of her,' remarked Tom Pinch, in a low voice.

'Exactly so,' rejoined Martin, rising to warm his back, and leaning against the chimney-piece. 'To say nothing of her. At the same time, of course it's not very hard upon her to be obliged to yield to the necessity of the case: first, because she loves me very much; and secondly, because I have sacrificed a great deal on her account, and might have done much better, you know.'

It was a very long time before Tom said 'Certainly;' so long, that he might have taken a nap in the interval, but he did say it at last.

'Now, there is one odd coincidence connected with this love-story,' said Martin, 'which brings it to an end. You remember what you told me last night as we were coming here, about your pretty visitor in the church?'

'Surely I do,' said Tom, rising from his stool, and seating himself in the chair from which the other had lately risen, that he might see his face. 'Undoubtedly.'

'That was she.'

'I knew what you were going to say,' cried Tom, looking fixedly at him, and speaking very softly. 'You don't tell me so?'

'That was she,' repeated the young man. 'After what I have heard from Pecksniff, I have no doubt that she came and went with my grandfather. Don't you drink too much of that sour wine, or you'll have a fit of some sort, Pinch, I see.'

'It is not very wholesome, I am afraid,' said Tom, setting down the empty glass he had for some time held. 'So that was she, was it?'

Martin nodded assent: and adding, with a restless impatience, that if he had been a few days earlier he would have seen her; and that now she might be, for anything he knew, hundreds of miles away; threw himself, after a few turns across the room, into a chair, and chafed like a spoilt child.

Tom Pinch's heart was very tender, and he could not bear to see the most indifferent person in distress; still less one who had awakened an interest in him, and who regarded him (either in fact, or as he supposed) with kindness, and in a spirit of lenient construction. Whatever his own thoughts had been a few moments before—and to judge from his face they must have been pretty serious—he dismissed them instantly, and gave his young friend the best counsel and comfort that occurred to him.

'All will be well in time,' said Tom, 'I have no doubt; and some trial and adversity just now will only serve to make you more attached to each other in better days. I have always read that the truth is so, and I have a feeling within me, which tells me how natural and right it is that it should be. What never ran smooth yet,' said Tom, with a smile which, despite the homeliness of his face, was pleasanter to see than many a proud beauty's brightest glance: 'what never ran smooth yet, can hardly be expected to change its character for us; so we must take it as we find it, and fashion it into the very best shape we can, by patience and good-humour. I have no power at all; I needn't tell you that; but I have an excellent will; and if I could ever be of use to you, in any way whatever, how very glad I should be!'

'Thank you,' said Martin, shaking his hand. 'You're a good fellow, upon my word, and speak very kindly. Of course you know,' he added, after a moment's pause, as he drew his chair towards the fire again, 'I should not hesitate to avail myself of your services if you could help me at all; but mercy on us!' Here he rumpled his hair impatiently with his hand, and looked at Tom as if he took it rather ill that he was not somebody else: 'you might as well be a toasting-fork or a frying-pan, Pinch, for any help you can render me.'

'Except in the inclination,' said Tom, gently.

'Oh! to be sure. I meant that, of course. If inclination went for anything, I shouldn't want help. I tell you what you may do, though, if you will, and at the present moment too.'

'What is that?' demanded Tom.

'Read to me.'

'I shall be delighted,' cried Tom, catching up the candle with enthusiasm. 'Excuse my leaving you in the dark a moment, and I'll fetch a book directly. What will you like? Shakspeare?'

'Aye!' replied his friend, yawning and stretching himself. 'He'll do. I am tired with the bustle of to-day, and the novelty of everything about me; and in such a case, there's no greater luxury in the world, I think, than being read to sleep. You won't mind my going to sleep, if I can?'

'Not at all?' cried Tom.

'Then begin as soon as you like. You needn't leave off when you see me getting drowsy (unless you feel tired), for it's pleasant to wake gradually to the sounds again. Did you ever try that?'

'No, I never tried that,' said Tom.

'Well! You can, you know, one of these days when we're both in the right humour. Don't mind leaving me in the dark. Look sharp!'

Mr. Pinch lost no time in moving away; and in a minute or two returned with one of the precious volumes from the shelf beside his bed. Martin had in the meantime made himself as comfortable as circumstances would permit, by constructing before the fire a temporary sofa of three chairs with Mercy's stool for a pillow, and lying down at full-length upon it.

'Don't be too loud, please,' he said to Pinch.

'No, no,' said Tom.

'You're sure you're not cold?'

'Not at all!' cried Tom.

'I am quite ready, then.'

Mr. Pinch accordingly, after turning over the leaves of his book with as much care as if they were living and highly cherished creatures, made his own selection, and began to read. Before he had completed fifty lines his friend was snoring.

'Poor fellow!' said Tom, softly, as he stretched out his head to peep at him over the backs of the chairs. 'He is very young to have so much trouble. How trustful and generous in him to bestow all this confidence in me. And that was she, was it?'

But suddenly remembering their compact, he took up the poem at the place where he had left off, and went on reading; always forgetting to snuff the candle, until its wick looked like a mushroom. He gradually became so much interested, that he quite forgot to replenish the fire; and was only reminded of his neglect by Martin Chuzzlewit starting up after the lapse of an hour or so, and crying with a shiver:

'Why, it's nearly out, I declare! No wonder I dreamed of being frozen. Do call for some coals. What a fellow you are, Pinch!'

CHAPTER VII

In which Mr. Chevy Slyme asserts the independence of his spirit; and the Blue Dragon loses a limb

MARTIN began to work at the grammar-school next morning, with so much vigour and expedition, that Mr. Pinch had new reason to do homage to the natural endowments of that young gentleman, and to acknowledge his infinite superiority to himself. The new pupil received Tom's compliments very graciously; and having by this time conceived a real regard for him, in his own peculiar way, predicted that they would always be the very best of friends, and that neither of them, he was certain (but particularly Tom), would ever have reason to regret the day on which they became acquainted. Mr. Pinch was delighted to hear him say this, and felt so much flattered by his kind assurances of friendship and protection, that he was at a loss how to express the pleasure they afforded him. And indeed it may be observed of this friendship, such as it was, that it had within it more likely materials of endurance than many a sworn brotherhood that has been rich in promise; for so long as the one party found a pleasure in patronising, and the other in being patronised (which was in the very essence of their respective characters), it was of all possible events among the least probable, that the twin demons, Envy and Pride, would ever arise between them. So in very many cases of friendship, or what passes for it, the old axiom is reversed, and like clings to unlike more than to like.

They were both very busy on the afternoon succeeding the family's departure: Martin with the grammar-school: and Tom in balancing certain receipts of rents, and deducting Mr. Pecksniff's commission from the same; in which abstruse employment he was much distracted by a habit his new friend had of whistling aloud while he was drawing. They were not a little startled by the unexpected obtrusion into that sanctuary of genius, of a human head which, although a shaggy and somewhat alarming head in appearance, smiled affably upon them from the doorway, in a manner that was at once waggish, conciliatory, and expressive of approbation.

'I am not industrious myself, gents both,' said the head, 'but I know how to appreciate that quality in others, I wish I may

turn grey and ugly, if it isn't, in my opinion, next to genius, one
of the very charmingest qualities of the human mind. Upon
my soul, I am grateful to my friend Pecksniff for helping me to
the contemplation of such a delicious picture as you present.
You remind me of Whittington, afterwards thrice Lord Mayor
of London. I give you my unsullied word of honour, that you
very strongly remind me of that historical character. You are
a pair of Whittingtons, gents, without the cat; which is a most
agreeable and blessed exception to me, for I am not attached
to the feline species. My name is Tigg; how do you do?'

Martin looked to Mr. Pinch for an explanation; and Tom,
who had never in his life set eyes on Mr. Tigg before, looked
to that gentleman himself.

'Chevy Slyme?' said Mr. Tigg, interrogatively, and kissing
his left hand in token of friendship. 'You will understand me
when I say that I am the accredited agent of Chevy Slyme;
that I am the ambassador from the court of Chiv? Ha ha!'

'Heyday!' asked Martin, starting at the mention of a name
he knew. 'Pray, what does he want with me?'

'If your name is Pinch,' Mr. Tigg began.

'It is not,' said Martin, checking himself. 'That is Mr. Pinch.'

'If that is Mr. Pinch,' cried Tigg, kissing his hand again, and
beginning to follow his head into the room, 'he will permit me
to say that I greatly esteem and respect his character, which
has been most highly commended to me by my friend Pecksniff; and that I deeply appreciate his talent for the organ,
notwithstanding that I do not, if I may use the expression,
grind myself. If that is Mr. Pinch, I will venture to express a
hope that I see him well, and that he is suffering no inconvenience from the easterly wind?'

'Thank you,' said Tom. 'I am very well.'

'That is a comfort,' Mr. Tigg rejoined. 'Then,' he added,
shielding his lips with the palm of his hand, and applying them
close to Mr. Pinch's ear, 'I have come for the letter.'

'For the letter,' said Tom, aloud. 'What letter?'

'The letter,' whispered Tigg, in the same cautious manner
as before, 'which my friend Pecksniff addressed to Chevy
Slyme, Esquire, and left with you.'

'He didn't leave any letter with me,' said Tom.

'Hush!' cried the other. 'It's all the same thing, though not
so delicately done by my friend Pecksniff as I could have
wished. The money.'

'The money!' cried Tom, quite scared.

'Exactly so,' said Mr. Tigg. With which he rapped Tom twice or thrice upon the breast and nodded several times, as though he would say that he saw they understood each other; that it was unnecessary to mention the circumstance before a third person; and that he would take it as a particular favour if Tom would slip the amount into his hand, as quietly as possible.

Mr. Pinch, however, was so very much astounded by this (to him) inexplicable deportment, that he at once openly declared there must be some mistake, and that he had been entrusted with no commission whatever having any reference to Mr. Tigg or to his friend either. Mr. Tigg received this declaration with a grave request that Mr. Pinch would have the goodness to make it again; and on Tom's repeating it in a still more emphatic and unmistakable manner, checked it off, sentence for sentence, by nodding his head solemnly at the end of each. When it had come to a close for the second time, Mr. Tigg sat himself down in a chair and addressed the young men as follows:

'Then I tell you what it is, gents both. There is at this present moment in this very place, a perfect constellation of talent and genius, who is involved, through what I cannot but designate as the culpable negligence of my friend Pecksniff, in a situation as tremendous, perhaps, as the social intercourse of the nineteenth century will readily admit of. There is actually at this instant, at the Blue Dragon in this village, an ale-house observe; a common, paltry, low-minded, clodhopping, pipe-smoking ale-house; an individual, of whom it may be said, in the language of the Poet, that nobody but himself can in any way come up to him; who is detained there for his bill. Ha! ha! For his bill. I repeat it. For his bill. Now,' said Mr. Tigg, 'we have heard of Fox's Book of Martyrs, I believe, and we have heard of the Court of Requests, and the Star Chamber; but I fear the contradiction of no man alive or dead, when I assert that my friend Chevy Slyme being held in pawn for a bill, beats any amount of cock-fighting with which I am acquainted.'

Martin and Mr. Pinch looked, first at each other, and afterwards at Mr. Tigg, who with his arms folded on his breast surveyed them, half in despondency and half in bitterness.

'Don't mistake me, gents both,' he said, stretching forth his right hand. 'If it had been for anything but a bill, I could have borne it, and could still have looked upon mankind with some feeling of respect: but when such a man as my friend Slyme is detained for a score—a thing in itself essentially mean; a low performance on a slate, or possibly chalked upon the back of a door—I do feel that there is a screw of such magnitude loose somewhere, that the whole framework of society is shaken, and the very first principles of things can no longer be trusted. In short, gents both,' said Mr. Tigg with a passionate flourish of his hands and head, 'when a man like Slyme is detained for such a thing as a bill, I reject the superstitions of ages, and believe nothing. I don't even believe that I *don't* believe, curse me if I do!'

'I am very sorry, I am sure,' said Tom after a pause, 'but Mr. Pecksniff said nothing to me about it, and I couldn't act without his instructions. Wouldn't it be better, sir, if you were to go to—to wherever you came from—yourself, and remit the money to your friend?'

'How can that be done, when I am detained also?' said Mr. Tigg; 'and when moreover, owing to the astounding, and I must add, guilty negligence of my friend Pecksniff, I have no money for coach-hire?'

Tom thought of reminding the gentleman (who, no doubt in his agitation had forgotten it) that there was a post-office in the land; and that possibly if he wrote to some friend or agent for a remittance it might not be lost upon the road; or at all events that the chance, however desperate, was worth trusting to. But, as his good-nature presently suggested to him certain reasons for abstaining from this hint, he paused again, and then asked:

'Did you say, sir, that you were detained also?'

'Come here,' said Mr. Tigg, rising. 'You have no objection to my opening this window for a moment?'

'Certainly not,' said Tom.

'Very good,' said Mr. Tigg, lifting the sash. 'You see a fellow down there in a red neckcloth and no waistcoat?'

'Of course I do,' cried Tom. 'That's Mark Tapley.'

'Mark Tapley is it?' said the gentleman. 'Then Mark Tapley had not only the great politeness to follow me to this house, but is waiting now, to see me home again. And for that attention, sir,' added Mr. Tigg, stroking his moustache, 'I can tell you, that Mark Tapley had better in his infancy have been fed to suffocation by Mrs. Tapley, than preserved to this time.'

Mr. Pinch was not so dismayed by this terrible threat, but that he had voice enough to call to Mark to come in, and up-stairs; a summons which he so speedily obeyed, that almost as soon as Tom and Mr. Tigg had drawn in their heads and closed the window again, he, the denounced, appeared before them.

'Come here, Mark!' said Mr. Pinch. 'Good gracious me! what's the matter between Mrs. Lupin and this gentleman?'

'What gentleman, sir?' said Mark. 'I don't see no gentleman here, sir, excepting you and the new gentleman,' to whom he made a rough kind of bow: 'and there's nothing wrong between Mrs. Lupin and either of you, Mr. Pinch, I am sure.'

'Nonsense, Mark!' cried Tom. 'You see Mr.—'

'Tigg,' interposed that gentleman. 'Wait a bit. I shall crush him soon. All in good time!'

'Oh *him!*' rejoined Mark, with an air of careless defiance. 'Yes, I see *him.* I could see him a little better, if he'd shave himself, and get his hair cut.'

Mr. Tigg shook his head with a ferocious look, and smote himself once upon the breast.

'It's no use,' said Mark. 'If you knock ever so much in that quarter, you'll get no answer. I know better. There's nothing there but padding; and a greasy sort it is.'

'Nay, Mark,' urged Mr. Pinch, interposing to prevent hostilities, 'tell me what I ask you. You're not out of temper, I hope?'

'Out of temper, sir!' cried Mark, with a grin; 'why no, sir. There's a little credit—not much—in being jolly, when such fellows as him is a-going about like roaring lions: if there *is* any breed of lions, at least, as is all roar and mane. What is there between him and Mrs. Lupin, sir? Why, there's a score between him and Mrs. Lupin. And I think Mrs. Lupin lets him and his friend off very easy in not charging 'em double prices for being a disgrace to the Dragon. That's my opinion. I wouldn't have any such Peter the Wild Boy as him in my house, sir, not if I was paid race-week prices for it. He's enough to turn the very beer in the casks sour with his looks: he is! So he would, if it had judgment enough.'

'You're not answering my question, you know, Mark,' observed Mr. Pinch.

'Well, sir,' said Mark, 'I don't know as there's much to answer further than that. Him and his friend goes and stops at the Moon and Stars till they've run a bill there; and then comes and stops with us and does the same. The running of bills is common enough, Mr. Pinch; it an't that as we object to; it's the ways of this chap. Nothing's good enough for him; all the women is dying for him he thinks, and is over-paid if he winks at 'em; and all the men was made to be ordered about by him. This not being aggravation enough, he says this morning to me, in his usual captivating way, "We're going to-night, my man." "Are you, sir?" says I. "Perhaps you'd like the bill got ready, sir?" "Oh no, my man," he says; "you needn't mind that. I'll give Pecksniff orders to see to that." In reply to which, the Dragon makes answer, "Thankee, sir, you're very kind to honour us so far, but as we don't know any particular good of you, and you don't travel with luggage, and Mr. Pecksniff an't at home (which perhaps you mayn't happen to be aware of, sir), we should prefer something more satisfactory;" and that's where the matter stands. And I ask,' said Mr. Tapley, pointing, in conclusion, to Mr. Tigg, with his hat, 'any lady or gentleman, possessing ordinary strength of mind, to say whether he's a disagreeable-looking chap or not!'

'Let me inquire,' said Martin, interposing between this candid speech and the delivery of some blighting anathema by Mr. Tigg, 'what the amount of this debt may be?'

'In point of money, sir, very little,' answered Mark. 'Only just turned of three pounds. But it an't that; it's the——'

'Yes, yes, you told us so before,' said Martin. 'Pinch, a word with you.'

'What is it?' asked Tom, retiring with him to a corner of the room.

'Why, simply—I am ashamed to say—that this Mr. Slyme is a relation of mine, of whom I never heard anything pleasant; and that I don't want him here just now, and think he would be cheaply got rid of, perhaps, for three or four pounds. You haven't enough money to pay this bill, I suppose?'

Tom shook his head to an extent that left no doubt of his entire sincerity.

'That's unfortunate, for I am poor too; and in case you had had it, I'd have borrowed it of you. But if we told this landlady we would see her paid, I suppose that would answer the same purpose?'

'Oh dear, yes!' said Tom. 'She knows me, bless you!'

'Then let us go down at once and tell her so; for the sooner we are rid of their company the better. As you have conducted the conversation with this gentleman hitherto, perhaps you'll tell him what we purpose doing; will you?'

Mr. Pinch complying, at once imparted the intelligence to Mr. Tigg, who shook him warmly by the hand in return, assuring him that his faith in anything and everything was again restored. It was not so much, he said, for the temporary relief of this assistance that he prized it, as for its vindication of the high principle that Nature's Nobs felt with Nature's Nobs, and that true greatness of soul sympathised with true greatness of soul, all the world over. It proved to him, he said, that like him they admired genius, even when it was coupled with the alloy occasionally visible in the metal of his friend Slyme; and on behalf of that friend, he thanked them; as warmly and heartily as if the cause were his own. Being cut short in these speeches by a general move towards the stairs, he took possession at the street-door of the lapel of Mr. Pinch's coat, as a security against further interruption; and entertained that gentleman with some highly improving discourse until they reached the Dragon, whither they were closely followed by Mark and the new pupil.

The rosy hostess scarcely needed Mr. Pinch's word as a preliminary to the release of her two visitors, of whom she was glad to be rid on any terms: indeed, their brief detention had originated mainly with Mr. Tapley, who entertained a constitutional dislike to gentlemen out-at-elbows who flourished on false pretences; and had conceived a particular aversion to Mr. Tigg and his friend, as choice specimens of the species. The business in hand thus easily settled, Mr. Pinch and Martin would have withdrawn immediately, but for the urgent entreaties of Mr. Tigg that they would allow him the honour of presenting them to his friend Slyme, which were so very difficult of resistance that, yielding partly to these persuasions and partly to their own curiosity, they suffered themselves to be ushered into the presence of that distinguished gentleman.

He was brooding over the remains of yesterday's decanter of brandy, and was engaged in the thoughtful occupation of making a chain of rings on the top of the table with the wet foot of his drinking-glass. Wretched and forlorn as he looked, Mr. Slyme had once been, in his way, the choicest of swaggerers: putting forth his pretensions, boldly, as a man of infinite taste and most undoubted promise. The stock-in-trade requisite to set up an amateur in this department of business is very slight, and easily got together; a trick of the nose and a curl of the lip sufficient to compound a tolerable sneer, being ample provision for any exigency. But, in an evil hour, this off-shoot of the Chuzzlewit trunk, being lazy, and ill qualified for any regular pursuit, and having dissipated such means as he ever possessed, had formally established himself as a professor of Taste for a livelihood; and finding, too late, that something more than his old amount of qualifications was necessary to sustain him in this calling, had quickly fallen to his present level, where he retained nothing of his old self but his boastfulness and his bile, and seemed to have no existence separate or apart from his friend Tigg. And now so abject and so pitiful was he—at once so maudlin, insolent, beggarly, and proud—that even his friend and parasite, standing erect beside him, swelled into a Man by contrast.

'Chiv,' said Mr. Tigg, clapping him on the back, 'my friend Pecksniff not being at home, I have arranged our trifling piece of business with Mr. Pinch and friend. Mr. Pinch and friend, Mr. Chevy Slyme! Chiv, Mr. Pinch and friend!'

'These are agreeable circumstances in which to be introduced to strangers,' said Chevy Slyme, turning his bloodshot eyes towards Tom Pinch. 'I am the most miserable man in the world, I believe!'

Tom begged he wouldn't mention it; and finding him in this condition, retired, after an awkward pause, followed by Martin. But Mr. Tigg so urgently conjured them, by coughs and signs, to remain in the shadow of the door, that they stopped there.

'I swear,' cried Mr. Slyme, giving the table an imbecile blow with his fist, and then feebly leaning his head upon his hand, while some drunken drops oozed from his eyes, 'that I am the wretchedest creature on record. Society is in a conspiracy against me. I'm the most literary man alive. I'm full of scholarship; I'm full of genius; I'm full of information; I'm full of novel views on every subject; yet look at my condition! I'm at this moment obliged to two strangers for a tavern bill!'

Mr. Tigg replenished his friend's glass, pressed it into his hand, and nodded an intimation to the visitors that they would see him in a better aspect immediately.

'Obliged to two strangers for a tavern bill, eh!' repeated

Mr. Slyme, after a sulky application to his glass. 'Very pretty! And crowds of impostors, the while, becoming famous: men who are no more on a level with me than—Tigg, I take you to witness that I am the most persecuted hound on the face of the earth.'

With a whine, not unlike the cry of the animal he named, in its lowest state of humiliation, he raised his glass to his mouth again. He found some encouragement in it; for when he set it down he laughed scornfully. Upon that Mr. Tigg gesticulated to the visitors once more, and with great expression: implying that now the time was come when they would see Chiv in his greatness.

'Ha, ha, ha,' laughed Mr. Slyme. 'Obliged to two strangers for a tavern bill! Yet I think I've a rich uncle, Tigg, who could buy up the uncles of fifty strangers! Have I, or have I not? I come of a good family, I believe! Do I, or do I not? I'm not a man of common capacity or accomplishments, I think! Am I, or am I not?'

'You are the American aloe of the human race, my dear Chiv,' said Mr. Tigg, 'which only blooms once in a hundred years!'

'Ha, ha, ha!' laughed Mr. Slyme again. 'Obliged to two strangers for a tavern bill! I! Obliged to two architect's apprentices. Fellows who measure earth with iron chains, and build houses like bricklayers. Give me the names of those two apprentices. How dare they oblige me!'

Mr. Tigg was quite lost in admiration of this noble trait in his friend's character; as he made known to Mr. Pinch in a neat little ballet of action, spontaneously invented for the purpose.

'I'll let 'em know, and I'll let all men know,' cried Chevy Slyme, 'that I'm none of the mean, grovelling, tame characters they meet with commonly. I have an independent spirit. I have a heart that swells in my bosom. I have a soul that rises superior to base considerations.'

'Oh Chiv, Chiv,' murmured Mr. Tigg, 'you have a nobly independent nature, Chiv!'

'You go and do your duty, sir,' said Mr. Slyme, angrily, 'and borrow money for travelling expenses; and whoever you borrow it of, let 'em know that I possess a haughty spirit, and a proud spirit, and have infernally finely-touched chords in my nature, which won't brook patronage. Do you hear? Tell 'em I hate 'em, and that that's the way I preserve my self-respect;

and tell 'em that no man ever respected himself more than I do!'

He might have added that he hated two sorts of men; all those who did him favours, and all those who were better off than himself; as in either case their position was an insult to a man of his stupendous merits. But he did not; for with the apt closing words above recited, Mr. Slyme; of too haughty a stomach to work, to beg, to borrow, or to steal; yet mean enough to be worked or borrowed, begged or stolen for, by any catspaw that would serve his turn; too insolent to lick the hand that fed him in his need, yet cur enough to bite and tear it in the dark; with these apt closing words Mr. Slyme fell forward with his head upon the table, and so declined into a sodden sleep.

'Was there ever,' cried Mr. Tigg, joining the young men at the door, and shutting it carefully behind him, 'such an independent spirit as is possessed by that extraordinary creature? Was there ever such a Roman as our friend Chiv? Was there ever a man of such a purely classical turn of thought, and of such a toga-like simplicity of nature? Was there ever a man with such a flow of eloquence? Might he not, gents both, I ask, have sat upon a tripod in the ancient times, and prophesied to a perfectly unlimited extent, if previously supplied with gin-and-water at the public cost?'

Mr. Pinch was about to contest this latter position with his usual mildness, when, observing that his companion had already gone down-stairs, he prepared to follow him.

'You are not going, Mr. Pinch?' said Tigg.

'Thank you,' answered Tom. 'Yes. Don't come down.'

'Do you know that I should like one little word in private with you, Mr. Pinch?' said Tigg, following him. 'One minute of your company in the skittle-ground would very much relieve my mind. Might I beseech that favour?'

'Oh, certainly,' replied Tom, 'if you really wish it.' So he accompanied Mr. Tigg to the retreat in question: on arriving at which place that gentleman took from his hat what seemed to be the fossil remains of an antediluvian pocket-handkerchief, and wiped his eyes therewith.

'You have not beheld me this day,' said Mr. Tigg, 'in a favourable light.'

'Don't mention that,' said Tom, 'I beg.'

'But you have *not*,' cried Tigg. 'I must persist in that opinion.

If you could have seen me, Mr. Pinch, at the head of my regiment on the coast of Africa, charging in the form of a hollow square, with the women and children and the regimental plate-chest in the centre, you would not have known me for the same man. You would have respected me, sir.'

Tom had certain ideas of his own upon the subject of glory; and consequently he was not quite so much excited by this picture as Mr. Tigg could have desired.

'But no matter!' said that gentleman. 'The school-boy writing home to his parents and describing the milk-and-water, said "This is indeed weakness." I repeat that assertion in reference to myself at the present moment: and I ask your pardon. Sir, you have seen my friend Slyme?'

'No doubt,' said Mr. Pinch.

'Sir, you have been impressed by my friend Slyme?'

'Not very pleasantly, I must say,' answered Tom, after a little hesitation.

'I am grieved but not surprised,' cried Mr. Tigg, detaining him with both hands, 'to hear that you have come to that conclusion; for it is my own. But, Mr. Pinch, though I am a rough and thoughtless man, I can honour Mind. I honour Mind in following my friend. To you of all men, Mr. Pinch, I have a right to make appeal on Mind's behalf, when it has not the art to push its fortune in the world. And so, sir—not for myself, who have no claim upon you, but for my crushed, my sensitive and independent friend, who has—I ask the loan of three half-crowns. I ask you for the loan of three half-crowns, distinctly, and without a blush. I ask it, almost as a right. And when I add that they will be returned by post, this week, I feel that you will blame me for that sordid stipulation.'

Mr. Pinch took from his pocket an old-fashioned red-leather purse with a steel clasp, which had probably once belonged to his deceased grandmother. It held one half-sovereign and no more. All Tom's worldly wealth until next quarter-day.

'Stay!' cried Mr. Tigg, who had watched this proceeding keenly. 'I was just about to say, that for the convenience of posting you had better make it gold. Thank you. A general direction, I suppose, to Mr. Pinch, at Mr. Pecksniff's, will find you?'

'That'll find me,' said Tom. 'You had better put Esquire to Mr. Pecksniff's name, if you please. Direct to me, you know, at Seth Pecksniff's, Esquire.'

'At Seth Pecksniff's, Esquire,' repeated Mr. Tigg, taking an exact note of it with a stump of pencil. 'We said this week, I believe?'

'Yes: or Monday will do,' observed Tom.

'No, no, I beg your pardon. Monday will *not* do,' said Mr. Tigg. 'If we stipulated for this week, Saturday is the latest day. Did we stipulate for this week?'

'Since you are so particular about it,' said Tom, 'I think we did.'

Mr. Tigg added this condition to his memorandum; read the entry over to himself with a severe frown; and that the transaction might be the more correct and business-like, appended his initials to the whole. That done, he assured Mr. Pinch that everything was now perfectly regular; and, after squeezing his hand with great fervour, departed.

Tom entertained enough suspicion that Martin might possibly turn this interview into a jest, to render him desirous to avoid the company of that young gentleman for the present. With this view he took a few turns up and down the skittle-ground, and did not re-enter the house until Mr. Tigg and his friend had quitted it, and the new pupil and Mark were watching their departure from one of the windows.

'I was just a-saying, sir, that if one could live by it,' observed Mark, pointing after their late guests, 'that would be the sort of service for me. Waiting on such individuals as them would be better than grave-digging, sir.'

'And staying here would be better than either, Mark,' replied Tom. 'So take my advice, and continue to swim easily in smooth water.'

'It's too late to take it now, sir,' said Mark. 'I have broke it to her, sir. I am off to-morrow morning.'

'Off!' cried Mr. Pinch, 'where to?'

'I shall go up to London, sir.'

'What to be?' asked Mr. Pinch.

'Well! I don't know yet, sir. Nothing turned up that day I opened my mind to you, as was at all likely to suit me. All them trades I thought of was a deal too jolly; there was no credit at all to be got in any of 'em. I must look for a private service, I suppose, sir. I might be brought out strong, perhaps, in a serious family, Mr. Pinch.'

'Perhaps you might come out rather too strong for a serious family's taste, Mark.'

'That's possible, sir. If I could get into a wicked family, I might do myself justice: but the difficulty is to make sure of one's ground, because a young man can't very well advertise that he wants a place, and wages an't so much an object as a wicked sitivation; can he, sir?'

'Why, no,' said Mr. Pinch, 'I don't think he can.'

'An envious family,' pursued Mark, with a thoughtful face; 'or a quarrelsome family, or a malicious family, or even a good out-and-out mean family, would open a field of action as I might do something in. The man as would have suited me of all other men was that old gentleman as was took ill here, for he really was a trying customer. Howsever, I must wait and see what turns up, sir; and hope for the worst.'

'You are determined to go then?' said Mr. Pinch.

'My box is gone already, sir, by the waggon, and I'm going to walk on to-morrow morning, and get a lift by the day coach when it overtakes me. So I wish you good-bye, Mr. Pinch— and you too, sir,—and all good luck and happiness!'

They both returned his greeting laughingly, and walked home arm-in-arm; Mr. Pinch imparting to his new friend, as they went, such further particulars of Mark Tapley's whimsical restlessness as the reader is already acquainted with.

In the mean time Mark, having a shrewd notion that his mistress was in very low spirits, and that he could not exactly answer for the consequences of any lengthened *tête-à-tête* in the bar, kept himself obstinately out of her way all the afternoon and evening. In this piece of generalship he was very much assisted by the great influx of company into the taproom; for the news of his intention having gone abroad, there was a perfect throng there all the evening, and much drinking of healths and clinking of mugs. At length the house was closed for the night; and there being now no help for it, Mark put the best face he could upon the matter, and walked doggedly to the bar-door.

'If I look at her,' said Mark to himself, 'I'm done. I feel that I'm a-going fast.'

'You have come at last,' said Mrs. Lupin.

Aye, Mark said: There he was.

'And you are determined to leave us, Mark?' cried Mrs. Lupin.

'Why, yes; I am,' said Mark; keeping his eyes hard upon the floor.

'I thought,' pursued the landlady, with a most engaging hesitation, 'that you had been—fond—of the Dragon?'

'So I am,' said Mark.

'Then,' pursued the hostess: and it really was not an unnatural inquiry: 'why do you desert it?'

But as he gave no manner of answer to this question; not even on its being repeated; Mrs. Lupin put his money into his hand, and asked him—not unkindly, quite the contrary—what he would take?

It is proverbial that there are certain things which flesh and blood cannot bear. Such a question as this, propounded in such a manner, at such a time, and by such a person, proved (at least, as far as Mark's flesh and blood were concerned) to be one of them. He looked up in spite of himself directly; and having once looked up, there was no looking down again; for of all the tight, plump, buxom, bright-eyed, dimple-faced landladies that ever shone on earth, there stood before him then, bodily in that bar, the very pink and pineapple.

'Why, I tell you what,' said Mark, throwing off all his constraint in an instant, and seizing the hostess round the waist: at which she was not at all alarmed, for she knew what a good young man he was: 'if I took what I liked most, I should take you. If I only thought what was best for me, I should take you. If I took what nineteen young fellows in twenty would be glad to take, and would take at any price, I should take you. Yes, I should,' cried Mr. Tapley, shaking his head expressively enough, and looking (in a momentary state of forgetfulness) rather hard at the hostess's ripe lips. 'And no man wouldn't wonder if I did!'

Mrs. Lupin said he amazed her. She was astonished how he could say such things. She had never thought it of him.

'Why, I never thought it of myself till now!' said Mark, raising his eyebrows with a look of the merriest possible surprise. 'I always expected we should part, and never have no explanation: I meant to do it when I come in here just now; but there's something about you, as makes a man sensible. Then let us have a word or two together: letting it be understood beforehand,' he added this in a grave tone, to prevent the possibility of any mistake, 'that I'm not a-going to make no love, you know.'

There was for just one second a shade, though not by any means a dark one, on the landlady's open brow. But it passed off instantly, in a laugh that came from her very heart.

'Oh, very good!' she said; 'if there is to be no love-making, you had better take your arm away.'

'Lord, why should I!' cried Mark. 'It's quite innocent.'

'Of course it's innocent,' returned the hostess, 'or I shouldn't allow it.'

'Very well!' said Mark. 'Then let it be.'

There was so much reason in this that the landlady laughed again, suffered it to remain, and bade him say what he had to say, and be quick about it. But he was an impudent fellow, she added.

'Ha ha! I almost think I am!' cried Mark, 'though I never thought so before. Why, I can say anything to-night!'

'Say what you're going to say if you please, and be quick,' returned the landlady, 'for I want to get to bed.'

'Why, then, my dear good soul,' said Mark, 'and a kinder woman than you are never drawed breath—let me see the man as says she did!—what would be the likely consequence of us two being—'

'Oh nonsense!' cried Mrs. Lupin. 'Don't talk about that any more.'

'No, no, but it an't nonsense,' said Mark; 'and I wish you'd attend. What would be the likely consequence of us two being married? If I can't be content and comfortable in this here lively Dragon now, is it to be looked for as I should be then? By no means. Very good. Then you, even with your good humour, would be always on the fret and worrit, always uncomfortable in your own mind, always a-thinking as you was getting too old for my taste, always a-picturing me to yourself as being chained up to the Dragon door, and wanting to break away. I don't know that it would be so,' said Mark, 'but I don't know that it mightn't be. I *am* a roving sort of chap, I know. I'm fond of change. I'm always a-thinking that with my good health and spirits it would be more creditable in me to be jolly where there's things a-going on to make one dismal. It may be a mistake of mine, you see, but nothing short of trying how it acts will set it right. Then an't it best that I should go: particular when your free way has helped me out to say all this, and we can part as good friends as we have ever been since first I entered this here noble Dragon, which,' said Mr. Tapley in conclusion, 'has my good word and my good wish to the day of my death!'

The hostess sat quite silent for a little time, but she very soon put both her hands in Mark's and shook them heartily.

Mark begins to be Jolly under Creditable Circumstances

'For you are a good man,' she said; looking into his face with a smile, which was rather serious for her. 'And I do believe have been a better friend to me to-night than ever I have had in all my life.'

'Oh! as to that, you know,' said Mark, 'that's nonsense. But love my heart alive!' he added, looking at her in a sort of rapture, 'if you *are* that way disposed, what a lot of suitable husbands there is as you may drive distracted!'

She laughed again at this compliment; and, once more shaking him by both hands, and bidding him, if he should ever want a friend, to remember her, turned gaily from the little bar and up the Dragon staircase.

'Humming a tune as she goes,' said Mark, listening, 'in case I should think she's at all put out, and should be made down-hearted. Come, here's some credit in being jolly, at last!'

With that piece of comfort, very ruefully uttered, he went, in anything but a jolly manner, to bed.

He rose early next morning, and was a-foot soon after sun-rise. But it was of no use; the whole place was up to see Mark Tapley off: the boys, the dogs, the children, the old men, the busy people and the idlers: there they were, all calling out 'Good-by'e, Mark,' after their own manner, and all sorry he was going. Somehow he had a kind of sense that his old mistress was peeping from her chamber-window, but he couldn't make up his mind to look back.

'Good-by'e one, good-by'e all!' cried Mark, waving his hat on the top of his walking-stick, as he strode at a quick pace up the little street. 'Hearty chaps them wheelwrights—hurrah! Here's the butcher's dog a-coming out of the garden—down, old fellow! And Mr. Pinch a-going to his organ—good-by'e, sir! And the terrier-bitch from over the way—hie, then, lass! And children enough to hand down human natur to the latest posterity—good-by'e, boys and girls! There's some credit in it now. I'm a-coming out strong at last. These are the circum-stances that would try a ordinary mind; but I'm uncommon jolly. Not quite as jolly as I could wish to be, but very near. Good-by'e! good-by'e!'

CHAPTER VIII

Accompanies Mr. Pecksniff and his charming daughters to the City of London; and relates what fell out upon their way thither

WHEN Mr. Pecksniff and the two young ladies got into the heavy coach at the end of the lane, they found it empty, which was a great comfort; particularly as the outside was quite full and the passengers looked very frosty. For as Mr. Pecksniff justly observed—when he and his daughters had burrowed their feet deep in the straw, wrapped themselves to the chin, and pulled up both windows—it is always satisfactory to feel, in keen weather, that many other people are not as warm as you are. And this, he said, was quite natural, and a very beautiful arrangement; not confined to coaches, but extending itself into many social ramifications. 'For' (he observed), 'if every one were warm and well-fed, we should lose the satisfaction of admiring the fortitude with which certain conditions of men bear cold and hunger. And if we were no better off than anybody else, what would become of our sense of gratitude; which,' said Mr. Pecksniff with tears in his eyes, as he shook his fist at a beggar who wanted to get up behind, 'is one of the holiest feelings of our common nature.'

His children heard with becoming reverence these moral precepts from the lips of their father, and signified their acquiescence in the same, by smiles. That he might the better feed and cherish that sacred flame of gratitude in his breast, Mr. Pecksniff remarked that he would trouble his eldest daughter, even in this early stage of their journey, for the brandy-bottle. And from the narrow neck of that stone vessel he imbibed a copious refreshment.

'What are we?' said Mr. Pecksniff, 'but coaches? Some of us are slow coaches'—

'Goodness, Pa!' cried Charity.

'Some of us, I say,' resumed her parent with increased emphasis, 'are slow coaches; some of us are fast coaches. Our passions are the horses; and rampant animals too!'—

'Really, Pa!' cried both the daughters at once. 'How very unpleasant.'

'And rampant animals too!' repeated Mr. Pecksniff with so much determination, that he may be said to have exhibited, at the moment, a sort of moral rampancy himself: 'and Virtue is the drag. We start from The Mother's Arms, and we run to The Dust Shovel.'

When he had said this, Mr. Pecksniff, being exhausted, took some further refreshment. When he had done that, he corked the bottle tight, with the air of a man who had effectually corked the subject also; and went to sleep for three stages.

The tendency of mankind when it falls asleep in coaches, is to wake up cross; to find its legs in its way; and its corns an aggravation. Mr. Pecksniff not being exempt from the common lot of humanity, found himself, at the end of his nap, so decidedly the victim of these infirmities, that he had an irresistible inclination to visit them upon his daughters; which he had already begun to do in the shape of divers random kicks, and other unexpected motions of his shoes, when the coach stopped, and after a short delay the door was opened.

'Now mind,' said a thin sharp voice in the dark. 'I and my son go inside, because the roof is full, but you agree only to charge us outside prices. It's quite understood that we won't pay more. Is it?'

'All right, sir,' replied the guard.

'Is there anybody inside now?' inquired the voice.

'Three passengers,' returned the guard.

'Then I ask the three passengers to witness this bargain, if they will be so good,' said the voice. 'My boy, I think we may safely get in.'

In pursuance of which opinion, two people took their seats in the vehicle, which was solemnly licensed by Act of Parliament to carry any six persons who could be got in at the door.

'That was lucky!' whispered the old man, when they moved on again. 'And a great stroke of policy in you to observe it. He, he, he! We couldn't have gone outside. I should have died of the rheumatism!'

Whether it occurred to the dutiful son that he had in some degree over-reached himself by contributing to the prolongation of his father's days; or whether the cold had affected his temper; is doubtful. But he gave his father such a nudge in reply, that that good old gentleman was taken with a cough which lasted for full five minutes without intermission, and goaded Mr. Pecksniff to that pitch of irritation, that he said at last: and very suddenly:

'There is no room! There is really no room in this coach for any gentleman with a cold in his head!'

'Mine,' said the old man, after a moment's pause, 'is upon my chest, Pecksniff.'

The voice and manner, together, now that he spoke out; the composure of the speaker; the presence of his son; and his knowledge of Mr. Pecksniff; afforded a clue to his identity which it was impossible to mistake.

'Hem! I thought,' said Mr. Pecksniff, returning to his usual mildness, 'that I addressed a stranger. I find that I address a relative. Mr. Anthony Chuzzlewit and his son Mr. Jonas— for they, my dear children, are our travelling companions— will excuse me for an apparently harsh remark. It is not *my* desire to wound the feelings of any person with whom I am connected in family bonds. I may be a Hypocrite,' said Mr. Pecksniff, cuttingly, 'but I am not a Brute.'

'Pooh, pooh!' said the old man. 'What signifies that word, Pecksniff? Hypocrite! why, we are all hypocrites. We were all hypocrites t'other day. I am sure I felt that to be agreed upon among us, or I shouldn't have called you one. We should not have been there at all, if we had not been hypocrites. The only difference between you and the rest was—shall I tell you the difference between you and the rest now, Pecksniff?'

'If you please, my good sir; if you please.'

'Why, the annoying quality in *you*, is,' said the old man, 'that you never have a confederate or partner in *your* juggling; you would deceive everybody, even those who practise the same art; and have a way with you, as if you—he, he, he!— as if you really believed yourself. I'd lay a handsome wager now,' said the old man, 'if I laid wagers, which I don't and never did, that you keep up appearances by a tacit understanding, even before your own daughters here. Now I, when I have a business scheme in hand, tell Jonas what it is, and we discuss it openly. You're not offended, Pecksniff?'

'Offended, my good sir!' cried that gentleman, as if he had received the highest compliments that language could convey.

'Are you travelling to London, Mr. Pecksniff?' asked the son.

'Yes, Mr. Jonas, we are travelling to London. We shall have the pleasure of your company all the way, I trust?'

'Oh! ecod, you had better ask father that,' said Jonas. 'I am not a-going to commit myself.'

Mr. Pecksniff was, as a matter of course, greatly entertained by this retort. His mirth having subsided, Mr. Jonas gave him to understand that himself and parent were in fact travelling to their home in the metropolis: and that, since the memorable day of the great family gathering, they had been tarrying in that part of the country, watching the sale of certain eligible investments, which they had had in their copartnership eye when they came down; for it was their custom, Mr. Jonas said, whenever such a thing was practicable, to kill two birds with one stone, and never to throw away sprats, but as bait for whales. When he had communicated to Mr. Pecksniff these pithy scraps of intelligence, he said, 'That if it was all the same to him, he would turn him over to father, and have a chat with the gals;' and in furtherance of this polite scheme, he vacated his seat adjoining that gentleman, and established himself in the opposite corner, next to the fair Miss Mercy.

The education of Mr. Jonas had been conducted from his cradle on the strictest principles of the main chance. The very first word he learnt to spell was 'gain,' and the second (when he got into two syllables), 'money.' But for two results, which were not clearly foreseen perhaps by his watchful parent in the beginning, his training may be said to have been unexceptionable. One of these flaws was, that having been long taught by his father to over-reach everybody, he had imperceptibly acquired a love of over-reaching that venerable monitor himself. The other, that from his early habits of considering everything as a question of property, he had gradually come to look, with impatience, on his parent as a certain amount of personal estate, which had no right whatever to be going at large, but ought to be secured in that particular description of iron safe which is commonly called a coffin, and banked in the grave.

'Well, cousin!' said Mr. Jonas: 'Because we *are* cousins, you know, a few times removed: so you're going to London?'

Miss Mercy replied in the affirmative, pinching her sister's arm at the same time, and giggling excessively.

'Lots of beaux in London, cousin!' said Mr. Jonas, slightly advancing his elbow.

'Indeed, sir!' cried the young lady. 'They won't hurt us, sir, I dare say.' And having given him this answer with great demureness, she was so overcome by her own humour, that she was fain to stifle her merriment in her sister's shawl.

'Merry,' cried that more prudent damsel, 'really I am ashamed of you. How can you go on so? You wild thing!' At which Miss Merry only laughed the more, of course.

'I saw a wildness in her eye, t'other day,' said Mr. Jonas, addressing Charity. 'But you're the one to sit solemn! I say! You were regularly prim, cousin!'

'Oh! The old-fashioned fright!' cried Merry, in a whisper. 'Cherry, my dear, upon my word you must sit next him. I shall die outright if he talks to me any more; I shall, positively!' To prevent which fatal consequence, the buoyant creature skipped out of her seat as she spoke, and squeezed her sister into the place from which she had risen.

'Don't mind crowding me,' cried Mr. Jonas. 'I like to be crowded by gals. Come a little closer, cousin.'

'No, thank you, sir,' said Charity.

'There's that other one a-laughing again,' said Mr. Jonas; 'she's a-laughing at my father, I shouldn't wonder. If he puts on that old flannel nightcap of his, I don't know what she'll do! Is that my father a-snoring, Pecksniff?'

'Yes, Mr. Jonas.'

'Tread upon his foot, will you be so good?' said the young gentleman. 'The foot next you's the gouty one.'

Mr. Pecksniff hesitating to perform this friendly office, Mr. Jonas did it himself; at the same time crying:

'Come, wake up, father, or you'll be having the nightmare, and screeching out, *I* know.—Do you ever have the nightmare, cousin?' he asked his neighbour, with characteristic gallantry, as he dropped his voice again.

'Sometimes,' answered Charity. 'Not often.'

'The other one,' said Mr. Jonas, after a pause. 'Does *she* ever have the nightmare?'

'I don't know,' replied Charity. 'You had better ask her.'

'She laughs so;' said Jonas; 'there's no talking to her. Only hark how she's a-going on now! You're the sensible one, cousin!'

'Tut, tut!' cried Charity.

'Oh! But you are! You know you are!'

'Mercy is a little giddy,' said Miss Charity. 'But she'll sober down in time.'

'It'll be a very long time, then, if she does at all,' rejoined her cousin. 'Take a little more room.'

'I am afraid of crowding you,' said Charity. But she took it notwithstanding; and after one or two remarks on the extreme heaviness of the coach, and the number of places it stopped at, they fell into a silence which remained unbroken by any member of the party until supper-time.

Although Mr. Jonas conducted Charity to the hotel and sat himself beside her at the board, it was pretty clear that he had an eye to 'the other one' also, for he often glanced across at Mercy, and seemed to draw comparisons between the personal appearance of the two, which were not unfavourable to the superior plumpness of the younger sister. He allowed himself no great leisure for this kind of observation, however, being busily engaged with the supper, which, as he whispered in his fair companion's ear, was a contract business, and therefore the more she ate, the better the bargain was. His father and Mr. Pecksniff, probably acting on the same wise principle, demolished everything that came within their reach, and by that means acquired a greasy expression of countenance, indicating contentment, if not repletion, which it was very pleasant to contemplate.

When they could eat no more, Mr. Pecksniff and Mr. Jonas subscribed for two sixpenny-worths of hot brandy-and-water, which the latter gentleman considered a more politic order than one shilling's-worth; there being a chance of their getting more spirit out of the innkeeper under this arrangement than if it were all in one glass. Having swallowed his share of the enlivening fluid, Mr. Pecksniff, under pretence of going to see if the coach were ready, went secretly to the bar, and had his own little bottle filled, in order that he might refresh himself at leisure in the dark coach without being observed.

These arrangements concluded, and the coach being ready, they got into their old places and jogged on again. But before he composed himself for a nap, Mr. Pecksniff delivered a kind of grace after meat, in these words:

'The process of digestion, as I have been informed by anatomical friends, is one of the most wonderful works of nature. I do not know how it may be with others, but it is a great satisfaction to me to know, when regaling on my humble fare, that I am putting in motion the most beautiful machinery with which we have any acquaintance. I really feel at such times as if I was doing a public service. When I have wound myself up, if I may employ such a term,' said Mr. Pecksniff with exquisite tenderness, 'and know that I am Going, I feel

F

that in the lesson afforded by the works within me, I am a
Benefactor to my Kind!'

As nothing could be added to this, nothing was said; and
Mr. Pecksniff, exulting, it may be presumed, in his moral
utility, went to sleep again.

The rest of the night wore away in the usual manner. Mr.
Pecksniff and Old Anthony kept tumbling against each other
and waking up much terrified, or crushed their heads in
opposite corners of the coach and strangely tattooed the surface
of their faces—Heaven knows how—in their sleep. The coach
stopped and went on, and went on and stopped, times out of
number. Passengers got up and passengers got down, and
fresh horses came and went and came again, with scarcely any
interval between each team as it seemed to those who were
dozing, and with a gap of a whole night between every one as
it seemed to those who were broad awake. At length they began
to jolt and rumble over horribly uneven stones, and Mr. Pecksniff looking out of window said it was to-morrow morning,
and they were there.

Very soon afterwards the coach stopped at the office in the
city; and the street in which it was situated was already in
a bustle, that fully bore out Mr. Pecksniff's words about its
being morning, though for any signs of day yet appearing in
the sky it might have been midnight. There was a dense fog
too: as if it were a city in the clouds, which they had been
travelling to all night up a magic beanstalk; and there was a
thick crust upon the pavement like oil-cake: which, one of the
outsides (mad, no doubt) said to another (his keeper, of course),
was Snow.

Taking a confused leave of Anthony and his son, and leaving
the luggage of himself and daughters at the office to be called
for afterwards, Mr. Pecksniff, with one of the young ladies
under each arm, dived across the street, and then across other
streets, and so up the queerest courts, and down the strangest
alleys and under the blindest archways, in a kind of frenzy:
now skipping over a kennel, now running for his life from a
coach and horses; now thinking he had lost his way, now
thinking he had found it; now in a state of the highest confidence, now despondent to the last degree, but always in a
great perspiration and flurry; until at length they stopped in
a kind of paved yard near the Monument. That is to say, Mr.
Pecksniff told them so; for as to anything they could see of the

Monument, or anything else but the buildings close at hand, they might as well have been playing blindman's buff at Salisbury.

Mr. Pecksniff looked about him for a moment, and then knocked at the door of a very dingy edifice, even among the choice collection of dingy edifices at hand; on the front of which was a little oval board like a tea-tray, with this inscription: 'Commercial Boarding-House. M. Todgers.'

It seemed that M. Todgers was not up yet, for Mr. Pecksniff knocked twice and rang thrice, without making any impression on anything but a dog over the way. At last a chain and some bolts were withdrawn with a rusty noise, as if the weather had made the very fastenings hoarse, and a small boy with a large red head, and no nose to speak of, and a very dirty Wellington boot on his left arm, appeared; who (being surprised) rubbed the nose just mentioned with the back of a shoe-brush, and said nothing.

'Still a-bed, my man?' asked Mr. Pecksniff.

'Still a-bed!' replied the boy. 'I wish they wos still a-bed. They're very noisy a-bed; all calling for their boots at once. I thought you was the Paper, and wondered why you didn't shove yourself through the grating as usual. What do you want?'

Considering his years, which were tender, the youth may be said to have preferred this question sternly, and in something of a defiant manner. But Mr. Pecksniff, without taking umbrage at his bearing, put a card in his hand, and bade him take that up-stairs, and show them in the meanwhile into a room where there was a fire.

'Or if there's one in the eating parlour,' said Mr. Pecksniff, 'I can find it myself.' So he led his daughters, without waiting for any further introduction, into a room on the ground-floor, where a table-cloth (rather a tight and scanty fit in reference to the table it covered) was already spread for breakfast: displaying a mighty dish of pink boiled beef; an instance of that particular style of loaf which is known to housekeepers as a slack-baked, crummy quartern; a liberal provision of cups and saucers; and the usual appendages.

Inside the fender were some half-dozen pairs of shoes and boots, of various sizes, just cleaned and turned with the soles upwards to dry; and a pair of short black gaiters, on one of which was chalked—in sport, it would appear, by some gentleman who had slipped down for the purpose, pending his toilet, and gone up again—'Jinkins's Particular,' while the other exhibited a sketch in profile, claiming to be the portrait of Jinkins himself.

M. Todgers's Commercial Boarding-House was a house of that sort which is likely to be dark at any time; but that morning it was especially dark. There was an odd smell in the passage, as if the concentrated essence of all the dinners that had been cooked in the kitchen since the house was built, lingered at the top of the kitchen stairs to that hour, and, like the Black Friar in Don Juan, 'wouldn't be driven away.' In particular, there was a sensation of cabbage; as if all the greens that had ever been boiled there, were evergreens, and flourished in immortal strength. The parlour was wainscoted, and communicated to strangers a magnetic and instinctive consciousness of rats and mice. The staircase was very gloomy and very broad, with balustrades so thick and heavy that they would have served for a bridge. In a sombre corner on the first landing, stood a gruff old giant of a clock, with a preposterous coronet of three brass balls on his head; whom few had ever seen—none ever looked in the face—and who seemed to continue his heavy tick for no other reason than to warn heedless people from running into him accidentally. It had not been papered or painted, hadn't Todgers's, within the memory of man. It was very black, begrimed, and mouldy. And, at the top of the staircase, was an old, disjointed, rickety, ill-favoured skylight, patched and mended in all kinds of ways, which looked distrustfully down at everything that passed below, and covered Todgers's up as if it were a sort of human cucumber-frame, and only people of a peculiar growth were reared there.

Mr. Pecksniff and his fair daughters had not stood warming themselves at the fire ten minutes, when the sound of feet was heard upon the stairs, and the presiding deity of the establishment came hurrying in.

M. Todgers was a lady, rather a bony and hard-featured lady, with a row of curls in front of her head, shaped like little barrels of beer; and on the top of it something made of net—you couldn't call it a cap exactly—which looked like a black cobweb. She had a little basket on her arm, and in it a bunch of keys that jingled as she came. In her other hand she bore a flaming tallow candle, which, after surveying Mr. Pecksniff

for one instant by its light, she put down upon the table, to the
end that she might receive him with the greater cordiality.

'Mr. Pecksniff!' cried Mrs. Todgers. 'Welcome to London!
Who would have thought of such a visit as this, after so—dear,
dear!—so many years! How do you *do*, Mr. Pecksniff?'

'As well as ever; and as glad to see you, as ever;' Mr. Pecksniff
made response. 'Why, you are younger than you used to be!'

'*You* are, I am sure!' said Mrs. Todgers. 'You're not a bit
changed.'

'What do you say to this?' cried Mr. Pecksniff, stretching out
his hand towards the young ladies. 'Does this make me no older?'

'Not your daughters!' exclaimed the lady, raising her hands
and clasping them. 'Oh, no, Mr. Pecksniff! Your second, and
her bridesmaid!'

Mr. Pecksniff smiled complacently; shook his head; and
said, 'My daughters, Mrs. Todgers. Merely my daughters.'

'Ah!' sighed the good lady, 'I must believe you, for now I
look at 'em I think I should have known 'em anywhere. My
dear Miss Pecksniffs, how happy your Pa has made me!'

She hugged them both; and being by this time over-
powered by her feelings or the inclemency of the morning,
jerked a little pocket handkerchief out of the little basket, and
applied the same to her face.

'Now, my good madam,' said Mr. Pecksniff, 'I know the
rules of your establishment, and that you only receive gentlemen boarders. But it occurred to me, when I left home, that
perhaps you would give my daughters house-room, and make
an exception in their favour.'

'Perhaps?' cried Mrs. Todgers ecstatically. 'Perhaps?'

'I may say then, that I was sure you would,' said Mr. Pecksniff. 'I know that you have a little room of your own, and that
they can be comfortable there, without appearing at the
general table.'

'Dear girls!' said Mrs. Todgers. 'I must take that liberty
once more.'

Mrs. Todgers meant by this that she must embrace them
once more, which she accordingly did with great ardour. But
the truth was that, the house being full with the exception of
one bed, which would now be occupied by Mr. Pecksniff, she
wanted time for consideration; and so much time too (for it
was a knotty point how to dispose of them), that even when
this second embrace was over, she stood for some moments

gazing at the sisters, with affection beaming in one eye, and calculation shining out of the other.

'I think I know how to arrange it,' said Mrs. Todgers, at length. 'A sofa bedstead in the little third room which opens from my own parlour—Oh, you dear girls!'

Thereupon she embraced them once more, observing that she could not decide which was most like their poor mother (which was highly probable: seeing that she had never beheld that lady), but that she rather thought the youngest was; and then she said that as the gentlemen would be down directly, and the ladies were fatigued with travelling, would they step into her room at once?

It was on the same floor; being, in fact, the back parlour; and had, as Mrs. Todgers said, the great advantage (in London) of not being overlooked; as they would see when the fog cleared off. Nor was this a vain-glorious boast, for it commanded at a perspective of two feet, a brown wall with a black cistern on the top. The sleeping apartment designed for the young ladies was approached from this chamber by a mightily convenient little door, which would only open when fallen against by a strong person. It commanded from a similar point of sight another angle of the wall, and another side of the cistern. 'Not the damp side,' said Mrs. Todgers, '*That* is Mr. Jinkins's.'

In the first of these sanctuaries a fire was speedily kindled by the youthful porter, who, whistling at his work in the absence of Mrs. Todgers (not to mention his sketching figures on his corduroys with burnt firewood), and being afterwards taken by that lady in the fact, was dismissed with a box on his ears. Having prepared breakfast for the young ladies with her own hands, she withdrew to preside in the other room; where the joke at Mr. Jinkins's expense seemed to be proceeding rather noisily.

'I won't ask you yet, my dears,' said Mr. Pecksniff, looking in at the door, 'how you like London. Shall I?'

'We haven't seen much of it, Pa!' cried Merry.

'Nothing, I hope,' said Cherry. (Both very miserably.)

'Indeed,' said Mr. Pecksniff, 'that's true. We have our pleasure, and our business too, before us. All in good time. All in good time!'

Whether Mr. Pecksniff's business in London was as strictly professional as he had given his new pupil to understand, we shall see, to adopt that worthy man's phraseology, 'all in good time.'

CHAPTER IX

Town and Todgers's

SURELY there never was, in any other borough, city, or hamlet in the world, such a singular sort of a place as Todgers's. And surely London, to judge from that part of it which hemmed Todgers's round, and hustled it, and crushed it, and stuck its brick-and-mortar elbows into it, and kept the air from it, and stood perpetually between it and the light, was worthy of Todgers's, and qualified to be on terms of close relationship and alliance with hundreds and thousands of the odd family to which Todgers's belonged.

You couldn't walk about in Todgers's neighbourhood, as you could in any other neighbourhood. You groped your way for an hour through lanes and bye-ways, and court-yards, and passages; and you never once emerged upon anything that might be reasonably called a street. A kind of resigned distraction came over the stranger as he trod those devious mazes, and, giving himself up for lost, went in and out and round about and quietly turned back again when he came to a dead wall or was stopped by an iron railing, and felt that the means of escape might possibly present themselves in their own good time, but that to anticipate them was hopeless. Instances were known of people who, being asked to dine at Todgers's, had travelled round and round for a weary time, with its very chimney-pots in view; and finding it, at last, impossible of attainment, had gone home again with a gentle melancholy on their spirits, tranquil and uncomplaining. Nobody had ever found Todgers's on a verbal direction, though given within a minute's walk of it. Cautious emigrants from Scotland or the North of England had been known to reach it safely, by impressing a charity-boy, town-bred, and bringing him along with them; or by clinging tenaciously to the postman; but these were rare exceptions, and only went to prove the rule that Todgers's was in a labyrinth, whereof the mystery was known but to a chosen few.

Several fruit-brokers had their marts near Todgers's; and one of the first impressions wrought upon the stranger's senses was of oranges—of damaged oranges, with blue and green bruises on them, festering in boxes, or mouldering away in cellars. All day long, a stream of porters from the wharves beside the river, each bearing on his back a bursting chest of oranges, poured slowly through the narrow passages; while underneath the archway by the public-house, the knots of those who rested and regaled within, were piled from morning until night. Strange solitary pumps were found near Todgers's hiding themselves for the most part in blind alleys, and keeping company with fire-ladders. There were churches also by dozens, with many a ghostly little churchyard, all overgrown with such straggling vegetation as springs up spontaneously from damp, and graves, and rubbish. In some of these dingy resting-places, which bore much the same analogy to green churchyards, as the pots of earth for mignonette and wall-flower in the windows overlooking them did to rustic gardens, there were trees; tall trees; still putting forth their leaves in each succeeding year, with such a languishing remembrance of their kind (so one might fancy, looking on their sickly boughs) as birds in cages have of theirs. Here, paralysed old watchmen guarded the bodies of the dead at night, year after year, until at last they joined that solemn brotherhood; and, saving that they slept below the ground a sounder sleep than even they had ever known above it, and were shut up in another kind of box, their condition can hardly be said to have undergone any material change when they in turn were watched themselves.

Among the narrow thoroughfares at hand, there lingered, here and there, an ancient doorway of carved oak, from which, of old, the sounds of revelry and feasting often came; but now these mansions, only used for storehouses, were dark and dull, and, being filled with wool, and cotton, and the like—such heavy merchandise as stifles sound and stops the throat of echo —had an air of palpable deadness about them which, added to their silence and desertion, made them very grim. In like manner, there were gloomy court-yards in these parts, into which few but belated wayfarers ever strayed, and where vast bags and packs of goods, upward or downward bound, were for ever dangling between heaven and earth from lofty cranes. There were more trucks near Todgers's than you would suppose a whole city could ever need; not active trucks, but a vagabond race, for ever lounging in the narrow lanes before their masters' doors and stopping up the pass; so that when a stray hackney-coach or lumbering waggon came that way, they were the cause of such an uproar as enlivened the whole neighbourhood, and made the bells in the next church-tower vibrate again. In the throats and maws of dark no-thorough-fares near Todgers's, individual wine-merchants and wholesale dealers in grocery-ware had perfect little towns of their own; and, deep among the foundations of these buildings, the ground was undermined and burrowed out into stables, where cart-horses, troubled by rats, might be heard on a quiet Sunday rattling their halters, as disturbed spirits in tales of haunted houses are said to clank their chains.

To tell of half the queer old taverns that had a drowsy and secret existence near Todgers's, would fill a goodly book; while a second volume no less capacious might be devoted to an account of the quaint old guests who frequented their dimly-lighted parlours. These were, in general, ancient inhabitants of that region; born, and bred there from boyhood; who had long since become wheezy and asthmatical, and short of breath, except in the article of story-telling: in which respect they were still marvellously long-winded. These gentry were much opposed to steam and all new-fangled ways, and held ballooning to be sinful, and deplored the degeneracy of the times; which that particular member of each little club who kept the keys of the nearest church professionally, always attributed to the prevalence of dissent and irreligion: though the major part of the company inclined to the belief that virtue went out with hair-powder, and that Old England's greatness had decayed amain with barbers.

As to Todgers's itself—speaking of it only as a house in that neighbourhood, and making no reference to its merits as a commercial boarding establishment—it was worthy to stand where it did. There was one staircase-window in it: at the side of the house, on the ground-floor: which tradition said had not been opened for a hundred years at least, and which, abutting on an always dirty lane, was so begrimed and coated with a century's mud, that no one pane of glass could possibly fall out, though all were cracked and broken twenty times. But the grand mystery of Todgers's was the cellarage, approachable only by a little back door and a rusty grating: which cellarage within the memory of man had had no connexion with the house, but had always been the freehold property of somebody else, and was reported to be full of wealth: though in what shape—whether in silver, brass, or gold, or butts of wine, or casks of gunpowder—was matter of profound uncertainty and supreme indifference to Todgers's, and all its inmates.

The top of the house was worthy of notice. There was a sort of terrace on the roof, with posts and fragments of rotten lines, once intended to dry clothes upon; and there were two or three tea-chests out there, full of earth, with forgotten plants in them, like old walking-sticks. Whoever climbed to this observatory, was stunned at first from having knocked his head against the little door in coming out; and after that, was for the moment choked from having looked, perforce, straight down the kitchen chimney; but these two stages over, there were things to gaze at from the top of Todgers's, well worth your seeing too. For first and foremost, if the day were bright, you observed upon the housetops, stretching far away, a long dark path: the shadow of the Monument: and turning round, the tall original was close beside you, with every hair erect upon his golden head, as if the doings of the city frightened him. Then there were steeples, towers, belfries, shining vanes, and masts of ships: a very forest. Gables, housetops, garret-windows, wilderness upon wilderness. Smoke and noise enough for all the world at once.

After the first glance, there were slight features in the midst of this crowd of objects, which sprung out from the mass without any reason, as it were, and took hold of the attention whether the spectator would or no. Thus, the revolving chimney-pots on one great stack of buildings seemed to be turning gravely to each other every now and then, and whispering the result of their separate observation of what was going on below. Others, of a crook-backed shape, appeared to be maliciously holding themselves askew, that they might shut the prospect out and baffle Todgers's. The man who was mending a pen at an upper window over the way, became of paramount importance in the scene, and made a blank in it, ridiculously disproportionate in its extent, when he retired. The gambols of a piece of cloth upon the dyer's pole had far more interest for the moment than all the changing motion of the crowd. Yet even while the looker-on felt angry with himself for this, and wondered how it was, the tumult swelled into a roar; the hosts of objects seemed to thicken and expand a hundredfold; and after gazing round him, quite scared, he turned into Todgers's again, much more rapidly than he came out; and ten to one he told M. Todgers afterwards that if he hadn't done so, he would certainly have come into the street by the shortest cut; that is to say, head-foremost.

So said the two Miss Pecksniffs, when they retired with Mrs. Todgers from this place of espial, leaving the youthful porter to close the door and follow them down-stairs: who being of a playful temperament, and contemplating with a delight peculiar to his sex and time of life, any chance of dashing himself into small fragments, lingered behind to walk upon the parapet.

It being the second day of their stay in London, the Miss Pecksniffs and Mrs. Todgers were by this time highly confidential, insomuch that the last-named lady had already communicated the particulars of three early disappointments of a tender nature; and had furthermore possessed her young friends with a general summary of the life, conduct, and character of Mr. Todgers. Who, it seemed, had cut his matrimonial career rather short, by unlawfully running away from his happiness, and establishing himself in foreign countries as a bachelor.

'Your pa was once a little particular in his attentions, my dears,' said Mrs. Todgers: 'but to be your ma was too much happiness denied me. You'd hardly know who this was done for, perhaps?'

She called their attention to an oval miniature, like a little blister, which was tacked up over the kettle-holder, and in which there was a dreamy shadowing forth of her own visage.

'It's a speaking likeness!' cried the two Miss Pecksniffs.

'It was considered so once,' said Mrs. Todgers, warming herself in a gentlemanly manner at the fire: 'but I hardly thought you would have known it, my loves.'

They would have known it anywhere. If they could have met with it in the street, or seen it in a shop window, they would have cried: 'Good gracious! Mrs. Todgers!'

'Presiding over an establishment like this, makes sad havoc with the features, my dear Miss Pecksniffs,' said Mrs. Todgers. 'The gravy alone, is enough to add twenty years to one's age, I do assure you.'

'Lor!' cried the two Miss Pecksniffs.

'The anxiety of that one item, my dears,' said Mrs. Todgers, 'keeps the mind continually upon the stretch. There is no such passion in human nature, as the passion for gravy among commercial gentlemen. It's nothing to say a joint won't yield—

a whole animal wouldn't yield—the amount of gravy they expect each day at dinner. And what I have undergone in consequence,' cried Mrs. Todgers, raising her eyes and shaking her head, 'no one would believe!'

'Just like Mr. Pinch, Merry!' said Charity. 'We have always noticed it in him, you remember?'

'Yes, my dear,' giggled Merry, 'but we have never given it him, you know.'

'You, my dears, having to deal with your pa's pupils who can't help themselves, are able to take your own way,' said Mrs. Todgers, 'but in a commercial establishment, where any gentleman may say, any Saturday evening, "Mrs. Todgers, this day week we part, in consequence of the cheese," it is not so easy to preserve a pleasant understanding. Your pa was kind enough,' added the good lady, 'to invite me to take a ride with you to-day; and I think he mentioned that you were going to call upon Miss Pinch. Any relation to the gentleman you were speaking of just now, Miss Pecksniff?'

'For goodness sake; Mrs. Todgers,' interposed the lively Merry, 'don't call him a gentleman. My dear Cherry, Pinch a gentleman! The idea!'

'What a wicked girl you are!' cried Mrs. Todgers, embracing her with great affection. 'You are quite a quiz, I do declare! My dear Miss Pecksniff, what a happiness your sister's spirits must be to your pa and self!'

'He's the most hideous, goggle-eyed creature, Mrs. Todgers, in existence,' resumed Merry: 'quite an ogre. The ugliest, awkwardest, frightfullest being, you can imagine. This is his sister, so I leave you to suppose what *she* is. I shall be obliged to laugh outright, I know I shall!' cried the charming girl, 'I never shall be able to keep my countenance. The notion of a Miss Pinch presuming to exist at all is sufficient to kill one, but to see her—oh my stars!'

Mrs. Todgers laughed immensely at the dear love's humour, and declared she was quite afraid of her, that she was. She was so very severe.

'Who is severe?' cried a voice at the door. 'There is no such thing as severity in our family, I hope!' And then Mr. Pecksniff peeped smilingly into the room, and said, 'May I come in, Mrs. Todgers?'

Mrs. Todgers almost screamed, for the little door of communication between that room and the inner one being wide open, there was a full disclosure of the sofa bedstead in all its monstrous impropriety. But she had the presence of mind to close this portal in the twinkling of an eye; and having done so, said, though not without confusion, 'Oh yes, Mr. Pecksniff, you can come in, if you please.'

'How are we to-day,' said Mr. Pecksniff, jocosely; 'and what are our plans? Are we ready to go and see Tom Pinch's sister? Ha, ha, ha! Poor Thomas Pinch!'

'Are we ready,' returned Mrs. Todgers, nodding her head with mysterious intelligence, 'to send a favourable reply to Mr. Jinkins's round-robin? That's the first question, Mr. Pecksniff.'

'Why Mr. Jinkins's robin, my dear madam?' asked Mr. Pecksniff, putting one arm round Mercy, and the other round Mrs. Todgers: whom he seemed, in the abstraction of the moment, to mistake for Charity. 'Why Mr. Jinkins's?'

'Because he began to get it up, and indeed always takes the lead in the house,' said Mrs. Todgers, playfully. 'That's why, sir.'

'Jinkins is a man of superior talents,' observed Mr. Pecksniff. 'I have conceived a great regard for Jinkins. I take Jinkins's desire to pay polite attention to my daughters, as an additional proof of the friendly feeling of Jinkins, Mrs. Todgers.'

'Well now,' returned that lady, 'having said so much, you must say the rest, Mr. Pecksniff: so tell the dear young ladies all about it.'

With these words, she gently eluded Mr. Pecksniff's grasp, and took Miss Charity into her own embrace; though whether she was impelled to this proceeding solely by the irrepressible affection she had conceived for that young lady, or whether it had any reference to a lowering, not to say distinctly spiteful expression which had been visible in her face for some moments, has never been exactly ascertained. Be this as it may, Mr. Pecksniff went on to inform his daughters of the purport and history of the round-robin aforesaid, which was in brief, that the commercial gentlemen who helped to make up the sum and substance of that noun of multitude or signifying many, called Todgers's, desired the honour of their presence at the general table, so long as they remained in the house, and besought that they would grace the board at dinner-time next day, the same being Sunday. He further said, that Mrs. Todgers being a consenting party to this invitation, he was willing, for his part, to accept it; and so left them that he might write his gracious answer, the while they armed themselves with their best bonnets for the utter defeat and overthrow of Miss Pinch.

Tom Pinch's sister was governess in a family, a lofty family; perhaps the wealthiest brass and copper founders' family known to mankind. They lived at Camberwell; in a house so big and fierce, that its mere outside, like the outside of a giant's castle, struck terror into vulgar minds and made bold persons quail. There was a great front gate; with a great bell, whose handle was in itself a note of admiration; and a great lodge; which being close to the house, rather spoilt the look-out certainly, but made the look-in tremendous. At this entry, a great porter kept constant watch and ward; and when he gave the visitor high leave to pass, he rang a second great bell, responsive to whose note a great footman appeared in due time at the great hall-door, with such great tags upon his liveried shoulder that he was perpetually entangling and hooking himself among the chairs and tables, and led a life of torment which could scarcely have been surpassed, if he had been a blue-bottle in a world of cobwebs.

To this mansion Mr. Pecksniff, accompanied by his daughters and Mrs. Todgers, drove gallantly in a one-horse fly. The foregoing ceremonies having been all performed, they were ushered into the house; and so, by degrees, they got at last into a small room with books in it, where Mr. Pinch's sister was at that moment instructing her eldest pupil: to wit, a premature little woman of thirteen years old, who had already arrived at such a pitch of whalebone and education that she had nothing girlish about her: which was a source of great rejoicing to all her relations and friends.

'Visitors for Miss Pinch!' said the footman. He must have been an ingenious young man, for he said it very cleverly: with a nice discrimination between the cold respect with which he would have announced visitors to the family, and the warm personal interest with which he would have announced visitors to the cook.

'Visitors for Miss Pinch!'

Miss Pinch rose hastily; with such tokens of agitation as plainly declared that her list of callers was not numerous. At the same time, the little pupil became alarmingly upright, and prepared herself to take mental notes of all that might be said

Mrs. Todgers and the Pecksniffs call upon Miss Pinch
(*p. 136*)

and done. For the lady of the establishment was curious in the natural history and habits of the animal called Governess, and encouraged her daughters to report thereon whenever occasion served; which was, in reference to all parties concerned, very laudable, improving, and pleasant.

It is a melancholy fact; but it must be related, that Mr. Pinch's sister was not at all ugly. On the contrary, she had a good face; a very mild and prepossessing face; and a pretty little figure—slight and short, but remarkable for its neatness. There was something of her brother, much of him indeed, in a certain gentleness of manner, and in her look of timid trust-fulness; but she was so far from being a fright, or a dowdy, or a horror, or anything else, predicted by the two Miss Peck-sniffs, that those young ladies naturally regarded her with great indignation, feeling that this was by no means what they had come to see.

Miss Mercy, as having the larger share of gaiety, bore up the best against this disappointment, and carried it off, in outward show at least, with a titter; but her sister, not caring to hide her disdain, expressed it pretty openly in her looks. As to Mrs. Todgers, she leaned on Mr. Pecksniff's arm and preserved a kind of genteel grimness, suitable to any state of mind, and involving any shade of opinion.

'Don't be alarmed, Miss Pinch,' said Mr. Pecksniff, taking her hand condescendingly in one of his, and patting it with the other. 'I have called to see you, in pursuance of a promise given to your brother, Thomas Pinch. My name—compose yourself, Miss Pinch—is Pecksniff.'

The good man emphasised these words as though he would have said, 'You see in me, young person, the benefactor of your race; the patron of your house; the preserver of your brother, who is fed with manna daily from my table; and in right of whom there is a considerable balance in my favour at present standing in the books beyond the sky. But I have no pride, for I can afford to do without it!'

The poor girl felt it all as if it had been Gospel Truth. Her brother writing in the fulness of his simple heart, had often told her so, and how much more! As Mr. Pecksniff ceased to speak, she hung her head, and dropped a tear upon his hand.

'Oh very well, Miss Pinch!' thought the sharp pupil, 'crying before strangers, as if you didn't like the situation!'

'Thomas is well,' said Mr. Pecksniff; 'and sends his love and this letter. I cannot say, poor fellow, that he will ever be distinguished in our profession; but he has the will to do well, which is the next thing to having the power; and, therefore, we must bear with him. Eh?'

'I know he has the will, sir,' said Tom Pinch's sister, 'and I know how kindly and considerately you cherish it, for which neither he nor I can ever be grateful enough, as we very often say in writing to each other. The young ladies too,' she added, glancing gratefully at his two daughters, 'I know how much we owe to them.'

'My dears,' said Mr. Pecksniff, turning to them with a smile; 'Thomas's sister is saying something you will be glad to hear, I think.'

'We can't take any merit to ourselves, papa!' cried Cherry, as they both apprised Tom Pinch's sister, with a curtsey, that they would feel obliged if she would keep her distance. 'Mr. Pinch's being so well provided for is owing to you alone, and we can only say how glad we are to hear that he is as grateful as he ought to be.'

'Oh very well, Miss Pinch!' thought the pupil again. 'Got a grateful brother, living on other people's kindness!'

'It was very kind of you,' said Tom Pinch's sister, with Tom's own simplicity and Tom's own smile, 'to come here: very kind indeed: though how great a kindness you have done me in gratifying my wish to see you, and to thank you with my own lips, you, who make so light of benefits conferred, can scarcely think.'

'Very grateful; very pleasant; very proper,' murmured Mr. Pecksniff.

'It makes me happy too,' said Ruth Pinch, who now that her first surprise was over, had a chatty, cheerful way with her, and a single-hearted desire to look upon the best side of everything, which was the very moral and image of Tom; 'very happy to think that you will be able to tell him how more than comfortably I am situated here, and how unnecessary it is that he should ever waste a regret on my being cast upon my own resources. Dear me! So long as I heard that he was happy, and he heard that I was,' said Tom's sister, 'we could both bear, without one impatient or complaining thought, a great deal more than ever we have had to endure, I am very certain.' And if ever the plain truth were spoken on this occasionally false earth, Tom's sister spoke it when she said that.

'Ah!' cried Mr. Pecksniff, whose eyes had in the meantime wandered to the pupil; 'certainly. And how do *you* do, my very interesting child?'

'Quite well, I thank you, sir,' replied that frosty innocent.

'A sweet face this, my dears,' said Mr. Pecksniff, turning to his daughters. 'A charming manner!'

Both young ladies had been in ecstasies with the scion of a wealthy house (through whom the nearest road and shortest cut to her parents might be supposed to lie) from the first. Mrs. Todgers vowed that anything one quarter so angelic she had never seen. 'She wanted but a pair of wings, a dear,' said that good woman, 'to be a young syrup:' meaning, possibly, young sylph, or seraph.

'If you will give that to your distinguished parents, my amiable little friend,' said Mr. Pecksniff, producing one of his professional cards, 'and will say that I and my daughters—'

'And Mrs. Todgers, pa,' said Merry.

'And Mrs. Todgers, of London,' added Mr. Pecksniff; 'that I, and my daughters, and Mrs. Todgers, of London, did not intrude upon them, as our object simply was to take some notice of Miss Pinch, whose brother is a young man in my employment; but that I could not leave this very chaste mansion, without adding my humble tribute, as an Architect, to the correctness and elegance of the owner's taste, and to his just appreciation of that beautiful art to the cultivation of which I have devoted a life, and to the promotion of whose glory and advancement I have sacrificed a—a fortune—I shall be very much obliged to you.'

'Missis's compliments to Miss Pinch,' said the footman, suddenly appearing, and speaking in exactly the same key as before, 'and begs to know wot my young lady is a-learning of just now.'

'Oh!' said Mr. Pecksniff, 'Here is the young man. *He* will take the card. With my compliments, if you please, young man. My dears, we are interrupting the studies. Let us go.'

Some confusion was occasioned for an instant by Mrs. Todgers's unstrapping her little flat hand-basket, and hurriedly entrusting the 'young man' with one of her own cards, which, in addition to certain detailed information relative to the terms of the commercial establishment, bore a foot-note to the effect that M. T. took that opportunity of thanking those gentlemen who had honoured her with their favours, and begged they would have the goodness, if satisfied with the table, to recommend her to their friends. But Mr. Pecksniff, with admirable presence of mind, recovered this document, and buttoned it up in his own pocket.

Then he said to Miss Pinch: with more condescension and kindness than ever, for it was desirable the footman should expressly understand that they were not friends of hers, but patrons:

'Good morning. Good-bye. God bless you! You may depend upon my continued protection of your brother Thomas. Keep your mind quite at ease, Miss Pinch!'

'Thank you,' said Tom's sister heartily: 'a thousand times.'

'Not at all,' he retorted, patting her gently on the head. 'Don't mention it. You will make me angry if you do. My sweet child,' to the pupil, 'farewell! That fairy creature,' said Mr. Pecksniff, looking in his pensive mood hard at the footman, as if he meant him, 'has shed a vision on my path, refulgent in its nature, and not easily to be obliterated. My dears, are you ready?'

They were not quite ready yet, for they were still caressing the pupil. But they tore themselves away at length; and sweeping past Miss Pinch with each a haughty inclination of the head and a curtsey strangled in its birth, flounced into the passage.

The young man had rather a long job in showing them out; for Mr. Pecksniff's delight in the tastefulness of the house was such that he could not help often stopping (particularly when they were near the parlour door) and giving it expression, in a loud voice and very learned terms. Indeed, he delivered, between the study and the hall, a familiar exposition of the whole science of architecture as applied to dwelling-houses, and was yet in the freshness of his eloquence when they reached the garden.

'If you look,' said Mr. Pecksniff, backing from the steps, with his head on one side and his eyes half-shut that he might the better take in the proportions of the exterior: 'If you look, my dears, at the cornice which supports the roof, and observe the airiness of its construction, especially where it sweeps the southern angle of the building, you will feel with me—How do you do, sir? I hope you're well?'

Interrupting himself with these words, he very politely bowed to a middle-aged gentleman at an upper window, to whom he spoke: not because the gentleman could hear him (for he certainly could not), but as an appropriate accompaniment to his salutation.

'I have no doubt, my dears,' said Mr. Pecksniff, feigning to point out other beauties with his hand, 'that this is the proprietor. I should be glad to know him. It might lead to something. Is he looking this way, Charity?'

'He is opening the window, pa!'

'Ha, ha!' cried Mr. Pecksniff softly. 'All right! He has found I'm professional. He heard me inside just now, I have no doubt. Don't look! With regard to the fluted pillars in the portico, my dears—'

'Hallo!' cried the gentleman.

'Sir, your servant!' said Mr. Pecksniff, taking off his hat. 'I am proud to make your acquaintance.'

'Come off the grass, will you!' roared the gentleman.

'I beg your pardon, sir,' said Mr. Pecksniff, doubtful of his having heard aright. 'Did you—?'

'Come off the grass!' repeated the gentleman, warmly.

'We are unwilling to intrude, sir,' Mr. Pecksniff smilingly began.

'But you *are* intruding,' returned the other, 'unwarrantably intruding. Trespassing. You see a gravel walk, don't you? What do you think it's meant for? Open the gate there! Show that party out!'

With that he clapped down the window again, and disappeared.

Mr. Pecksniff put on his hat, and walked with great deliberation and in profound silence to the fly, gazing at the clouds as he went, with great interest. After helping his daughters and Mrs. Todgers into that conveyance, he stood looking at it for some moments, as if he were not quite certain whether it was a carriage or a temple; but, having settled this point in his mind, he got into his place, spread his hands out on his knees, and smiled upon the three beholders.

But his daughters, less tranquil-minded, burst into a torrent of indignation. This came, they said, of cherishing such creatures as the Pinches. This came of lowering themselves to their level. This came of putting themselves in the humiliating position of seeming to know such bold, audacious, cunning, dreadful girls as that. They had expected this. They had predicted it to Mrs. Todgers, as she (Todgers) could depone, that very morning. To this, they added, that the owner of the house, supposing them to be Miss Pinch's friends, had acted, in their opinion, quite correctly, and had done no more than, under such circumstances, might reasonably have been expected. To that they added (with a trifling inconsistency), that he was a brute and a bear; and then they merged into a flood of tears, which swept away all wandering epithets before it.

Perhaps Miss Pinch was scarcely so much to blame in the matter as the Seraph, who, immediately on the withdrawal of the visitors, had hastened to report them at head-quarters, with a full account of their having presumptuously charged her with the delivery of a message afterwards consigned to the footman; which outrage, taken in conjunction with Mr. Pecksniff's unobtrusive remarks on the establishment, might possibly have had some share in their dismissal. Poor Miss Pinch, however, had to bear the brunt of it with both parties: being so severely taken to task by the Seraph's mother for having such vulgar acquaintances, that she was fain to retire to her own room in tears, which her natural cheerfulness and submission, and the delight of having seen Mr. Pecksniff, and having received a letter from her brother, were at first insufficient to repress.

As to Mr. Pecksniff, he told them in the fly, that a good action was its own reward; and rather gave them to understand, that if he could have been kicked in such a cause, he would have liked it all the better. But this was no comfort to the young ladies, who scolded violently the whole way back, and even exhibited, more than once, a keen desire to attack the devoted Mrs. Todgers: on whose personal appearance, but particularly on whose offending card and hand-basket, they were secretly inclined to lay the blame of half their failure.

Todgers's was in a great bustle that evening, partly owing to some additional domestic preparations for the morrow, and partly to the excitement always inseparable in that house from Saturday night, when every gentleman's linen arrived at a different hour in its own little bundle, with his private account pinned on the outside. There was always a great clinking of pattens down-stairs, too, until midnight or so, on Saturdays; together with a frequent gleaming of mysterious lights in the area; much working at the pump; and a constant jangling of the iron handle of the pail. Shrill altercations from time to time arose between Mrs. Todgers and unknown females in remote back kitchens; and sounds were occasionally heard, indicative of small articles of ironmongery and hardware being thrown at the boy. It was the custom of that youth on Saturdays, to roll up his shirt sleeves to his shoulders, and pervade all parts of the house in an apron of coarse green baize; moreover, he was more strongly tempted on Saturdays than on other days (it being a busy time), to make excursive bolts into the neighbouring alleys when he answered the door, and there to play at leap-frog and other sports with vagrant lads, until pursued and brought back by the hair of his head or the lobe of his ear; thus he was quite a conspicuous feature among the peculiar incidents of the last day in the week at Todgers's.

He was especially so on this particular Saturday evening, and honoured the Miss Pecksniffs with a deal of notice; seldom passing the door of Mrs. Todgers's private room, where they sat alone before the fire, working by the light of a solitary candle, without putting in his head and greeting them with some such compliments as, 'There you are agin!' 'An't it nice?' and similar humorous attentions.

'I say,' he whispered, stopping in one of his journeys to and fro, 'young ladies, there's soup to-morrow. She's a-making it now. An't she a-putting in the water? Oh! not at all neither!'

In the course of answering another knock, he thrust in his head again.

'I say! There's fowls to-morrow. Not skinny ones. Oh no!'

Presently he called through the key-hole:

'There's a fish to-morrow. Just come. Don't eat none of him!' And, with this special warning, vanished again.

By-and-bye, he returned to lay the cloth for supper: it having been arranged between Mrs. Todgers and the young ladies, that they should partake of an exclusive veal-cutlet together in the privacy of that apartment. He entertained them on this occasion by thrusting the lighted candle into his mouth, and exhibiting his face in a state of transparency; after the performance of which feat, he went on with his professional duties; brightening every knife as he laid it on the table, by breathing on the blade and afterwards polishing the same on the apron already mentioned. When he had completed his preparations, he grinned at the sisters, and expressed his belief that the approaching collation would be of 'rather a spicy sort.'

'Will it be long before it's ready, Bailey?' asked Mercy.

'No,' said Bailey, 'it *is* cooked. When I come up, she was

dodging among the tender pieces with a fork, and eating of 'em.'

But he had scarcely achieved the utterance of these words, when he received a manual compliment on the head, which sent him staggering against the wall; and Mrs. Todgers, dish in hand, stood indignantly before him.

'Oh you little villain!' said that lady. 'Oh you bad, false boy!'

'No worse than yerself,' retorted Bailey, guarding his head, on a principle invented by Mr. Thomas Cribb. 'Ah! Come now! Do that agin, will yer?'

'He's the most dreadful child,' said Mrs. Todgers, setting down the dish, 'I ever had to deal with. The gentlemen spoil him to that extent, and teach him such things, that I'm afraid nothing but hanging will ever do him any good.'

'Won't it!' cried Bailey. 'Oh! Yes! Wot do you go a-lowerin the table-beer for then, and destroying my constitooshun?'

'Go down-stairs, you vicious boy,' said Mrs. Todgers, holding the door open. 'Do you hear me? Go along!'

After two or three dexterous feints, he went, and was seen no more that night, save once, when he brought up some tumblers and hot water, and much disturbed the two Miss Pecksniffs by squinting hideously behind the back of the unconscious Mrs. Todgers. Having done this justice to his wounded feelings, he retired underground: where, in company with a swarm of black beetles and a kitchen candle, he employed his faculties in cleaning boots and brushing clothes until the night was far advanced.

Benjamin was supposed to be the real name of this young retainer, but he was known by a great variety of names. Benjamin, for instance, had been converted into Uncle Ben, and that again had been corrupted into Uncle; which, by an easy transition, had again passed into Barnwell, in memory of the celebrated relative in that degree who was shot by his nephew George, while meditating in his garden at Camberwell. The gentlemen at Todgers's had a merry habit, too, of bestowing upon him, for the time being, the name of any notorious malefactor or minister; and sometimes when current events were flat, they even sought the pages of history for these distinctions; as Mr. Pitt, Young Brownrigg, and the like. At the period of which we write, he was generally known among the gentlemen as Bailey junior; a name bestowed upon him in contradistinction, perhaps, to Old Bailey; and possibly as involving the recollection of an unfortunate lady of the same name, who perished by her own hand early in life, and has been immortalised in a ballad.

The usual Sunday dinner-hour at Todgers's was two o'clock; a suitable time, it was considered, for all parties; convenient to Mrs. Todgers, on account of the baker's; and convenient to the gentlemen, with reference to their afternoon engagements. But on the Sunday which was to introduce the two Miss Pecksniffs to a full knowledge of Todgers's and its society, the dinner was postponed until five, in order that everything might be as genteel as the occasion demanded.

When the hour drew nigh, Bailey junior, testifying great excitement, appeared in a complete suit of cast-off clothes several sizes too large for him, and in particular, mounted a clean shirt of such extraordinary magnitude, that one of the gentlemen (remarkable for his ready wit) called him 'collars' on the spot. At about a quarter before five, a deputation, consisting of Mr. Jinkins, and another gentleman whose name was Gander, knocked at the door of Mrs. Todgers's room, and, being formally introduced to the two Miss Pecksniffs by their parent who was in waiting, besought the honour of conducting them up-stairs.

The drawing-room at Todgers's was out of the common style; so much so indeed, that you would hardly have taken it to be a drawing-room, unless you were told so by somebody who was in the secret. It was floor-clothed all over; and the ceiling, including a great beam in the middle, was papered. Besides the three little windows, with seats in them commanding the opposite archway, there was another window looking point blank, without any compromise at all about it, into Jinkins's bedroom; and high up, all along one side of the wall, was a strip of panes of glass, two-deep, giving light to the staircase. There were the oddest closets possible, with little casements in them like eight-day clocks, lurking in the wainscot and taking the shape of the stairs: and the very door itself (which was painted black) had two great glass eyes in its forehead, with an inquisitive green pupil in the middle of each.

Here the gentlemen were all assembled. There was a general cry of 'Hear, hear!' and 'Bravo Jink!' when Mr. Jinkins appeared with Charity on his arm: which became quite rapturous as Mr. Gander followed, escorting Mercy, and Mr. Pecksniff brought up the rear with Mrs. Todgers.

Then the presentations took place. They included a gentleman of a sporting turn, who propounded questions on jockey subjects to the editors of Sunday papers, which were regarded by his friends as rather stiff things to answer; and they included a gentleman of a theatrical turn, who had once entertained serious thoughts of 'coming out,' but had been kept in by the wickedness of human nature; and they included a gentleman of a debating turn, who was strong at speech-making; and a gentleman of a literary turn, who wrote squibs upon the rest, and knew the weak side of everybody's character but his own. There was a gentleman of a vocal turn, and a gentleman of a smoking turn, and a gentleman of a convivial turn; some of the gentlemen had a turn for whist, and a large proportion of the gentlemen had a strong turn for billiards and betting. They had all, it may be presumed, a turn for business; being all commercially employed in one way or other; and had, every one in his own way, a decided turn for pleasure to boot. Mr. Jinkins was of a fashionable turn; being a regular frequenter of the Parks on Sundays, and knowing a great many carriages by sight. He spoke mysteriously, too, of splendid women, and was suspected of having once committed himself with a Countess. Mr. Gander was of a witty turn, being indeed the gentleman who had originated the sally about 'collars;' which sparkling pleasantry was now retailed from mouth to mouth, under the title of Gander's Last, and was received in all parts of the room with great applause. Mr. Jinkins, it may be added, was much the oldest of the party: being a fish-salesman's book-keeper, aged forty. He was the oldest boarder also; and in right of his double seniority, took the lead in the house, as Mrs. Todgers had already said.

There was considerable delay in the production of dinner, and poor Mrs. Todgers, being reproached in confidence by Jinkins, slipped in and out, at least twenty times to see about it; always coming back as though she had no such thing upon her mind, and hadn't been out at all. But there was no hitch in the conversation, nevertheless; for one gentleman, who travelled in the perfumery line, exhibited an interesting nicknack, in the way of a remarkable cake of shaving soap which he had lately met with in Germany; and the gentleman of a literary turn repeated (by desire) some sarcastic stanzas he had recently produced on the freezing of the tank at the back of the house. These amusements, with the miscellaneous conversation arising out of them, passed the time splendidly, until dinner was announced by Bailey junior in these terms:

'The wittles is up!'

On which notice they immediately descended to the banquet-hall; some of the more facetious spirits in the rear taking down gentlemen as if they were ladies, in imitation of the fortunate possessors of the two Miss Pecksniffs.

Mr. Pecksniff said grace: a short and pious grace, invoking a blessing on the appetites of those present, and committing all persons who had nothing to eat, to the care of Providence; whose business (so said the grace, in effect) it clearly was, to look after them. This done, they fell to with less ceremony than appetite; the table groaning beneath the weight, not only of the delicacies whereof the Miss Pecksniffs had been previously forewarned, but of boiled beef, roast veal, bacon, pies, and abundance of such heavy vegetables as are favourably known to housekeepers for their satisfying qualities. Besides which, there were bottles of stout, bottles of wine, bottles of ale, and divers other strong drinks, native and foreign.

All this was highly agreeable to the two Miss Pecksniffs, who were in immense request; sitting one on either hand of Mr. Jinkins at the bottom of the table; and who were called upon to take wine with some new admirer every minute. They had hardly ever felt so pleasant, and so full of conversation, in their lives; Mercy, in particular, was uncommonly brilliant, and said so many good things in the way of lively repartee that she was looked upon as a prodigy. 'In short,' as that young lady observed, 'they felt now, indeed, that they were in London, and for the first time too.'

Their young friend Bailey sympathised in these feelings to the fullest extent, and, abating nothing of his patronage, gave them every encouragement in his power: favouring them, when the general attention was diverted from his proceedings, with many nods and winks and other tokens of recognition, and occasionally touching his nose with a corkscrew, as if to express the Bacchanalian character of the meeting. In truth, perhaps even the spirits of the two Miss Pecksniffs, and the hungry watchfulness of Mrs. Todgers, were less worthy of note than the proceedings of this remarkable boy, whom nothing disconcerted or put out of his way. If any piece of crockery, a dish or otherwise, chanced to slip through his hands (which happened once or twice), he let it go with perfect good breeding, and never added to the painful emotions of the company by exhibiting the least regret. Nor did he, by hurrying to and fro, disturb the repose of the assembly, as many well-trained servants do; on the contrary, feeling the hopelessness of waiting upon so large a party, he left the gentlemen to help themselves to what they wanted, and seldom stirred from behind Mr. Jinkins's chair: where, with his hands in his pockets, and his legs planted pretty wide apart, he led the laughter, and enjoyed the conversation.

The dessert was splendid. No waiting either. The pudding-plates had been washed in a little tub outside the door while cheese was on, and though they were moist and warm with friction, still there they were again, up to the mark, and true to time. Quarts of almonds; dozens of oranges; pounds of raisins; stacks of biffins; soup-plates full of nuts. Oh, Todgers's could do it when it chose! Mind that.

Then more wine came on; red wines and white wines; and a large china bowl of punch, brewed by the gentleman of a convivial turn, who adjured the Miss Pecksniffs not to be despondent on account of its dimensions, as there were materials in the house for the decoction of half a dozen more of the same size. Good gracious, how they laughed! How they coughed when they sipped it, because it was so strong; and how they laughed again when somebody vowed that but for its colour it might have been mistaken, in regard of its innocuous qualities, for new milk! What a shout of 'No!' burst from the gentlemen when they pathetically implored Mr. Jinkins to suffer them to qualify it with hot water; and how blushingly, by little and little, did each of them drink her whole glassful, down to its very dregs!

Now comes the trying time. The sun, as Mr. Jinkins says (gentlemanly creature, Jinkins—never at a loss!), is about to leave the firmament. 'Miss Pecksniff!' says Mrs. Todgers, softly, 'will you—?' 'Oh dear, no more, Mrs. Todgers.' Mrs. Todgers rises; the two Miss Pecksniffs rise; all rise. Miss Mercy Pecksniff looks downward for her scarf. Where is it? Dear me, where *can* it be? Sweet girl, she has it on; not on her fair neck, but loose upon her flowing figure. A dozen hands assist her. She is all confusion. The youngest gentleman in company thirsts to murder Jinkins. She skips and joins her sister at the door. Her sister has her arm about the waist of Mrs. Todgers. She winds her arm around her sister. Diana, what a picture! The last things visible are a shape and a skip. 'Gentlemen, let us drink the ladies!'

The enthusiasm is tremendous. The gentleman of a debating turn rises in the midst, and suddenly lets loose a tide of eloquence which bears down everything before it. He is reminded of a toast: a toast to which they will respond. There is an individual present; he has him in his eye; to whom they owe a debt of gratitude. He repeats it, a debt of gratitude. Their rugged natures have been softened and ameliorated that day, by the society of lovely woman. There is a gentleman in company whom two accomplished and delightful females regard with veneration, as the fountain of their existence. Yes, when yet the two Miss Pecksniffs lisped in language scarce intelligible, they called that individual 'Father!' There is great applause. He gives them 'Mr. Pecksniff, and God bless him!' They all shake hands with Mr. Pecksniff, as they drink the toast. The youngest gentleman in company does so with a thrill; for he feels that a mysterious influence pervades the man who claims that being in the pink scarf for his daughter.

What saith Mr. Pecksniff in reply? Or rather let the question be, What leaves he unsaid? Nothing. More punch is called for, and produced, and drunk. Enthusiasm mounts still higher. Every man comes out freely in his own character. The gentleman of a theatrical turn recites. The vocal gentleman regales them with a song. Gander leaves the Gander of all former feasts whole leagues behind. *He* rises to propose a toast. It is, The Father of Todgers's. It is their common friend Jink. It is Old Jink, if he may call him by that familiar and endearing appellation. The youngest gentleman in company utters a frantic negative. He won't have it, he can't bear it, it mustn't be. But his depth of feeling is misunderstood. He is supposed to be a little elevated; and nobody heeds him.

Mr. Jinkins thanks them from his heart. It is, by many degrees, the proudest day in his humble career. When he looks around him on the present occasion, he feels that he wants words in which to express his gratitude. One thing he will say. He hopes it has been shown that Todgers's can be true to itself; and that, an opportunity arising, it can come out quite as strong as its neighbours—perhaps stronger. He reminds them, amidst thunders of encouragement, that they have

heard of a somewhat similar establishment in Cannon Street;
and that they have heard it praised. He wishes to draw no
invidious comparisons; he would be the last man to do it; but
when that Cannon Street establishment shall be able to produce such a combination of wit and beauty as has graced that
board that day, and shall be able to serve up (all things considered) such a dinner as that of which they have just partaken,
he will be happy to talk to it. Until then, gentlemen, he will
stick to Todgers's.

More punch, more enthusiasm, more speeches. Everybody's
health is drunk, saving the youngest gentleman's in company.
He sits apart, with his elbow on the back of a vacant chair, and
glares disdainfully at Jinkins. Gander, in a convulsing speech,
gives them the health of Bailey junior; hiccups are heard; and
a glass is broken. Mr. Jinkins feels that it is time to join the
ladies. He proposes, as a final sentiment, Mrs. Todgers. She is
worthy to be remembered separately. Hear, hear. So she is: no
doubt of it. They all find fault with her at other times; but
every man feels, now, that he could die in her defence.

They go up-stairs, where they are not expected so soon; for
Mrs. Todgers is asleep, Miss Charity is adjusting her hair, and
Mercy, who has made a sofa of one of the window-seats, is in
a gracefully recumbent attitude. She is rising hastily, when
Mr. Jinkins implores her, for all their sakes, not to stir; she
looks too graceful and too lovely, he remarks, to be disturbed.
She laughs, and yields, and fans herself, and drops her fan, and
there is a rush to pick it up. Being now installed, by one consent, as the beauty of the party, she is cruel and capricious,
and sends gentlemen on messages to other gentlemen, and
forgets all about them before they can return with the answer,
and invents a thousand tortures, rending their hearts to pieces.
Bailey brings up the tea and coffee. There is a small cluster of
admirers round Charity; but they are only those who cannot
get near her sister. The youngest gentleman in company is
pale, but collected, and still sits apart; for his spirit loves to
hold communion with itself, and his soul recoils from noisy
revellers. She has a consciousness of his presence and adoration. He sees it flashing sometimes in the corner of her eye.
Have a care, Jinkins, ere you provoke a desperate man to
frenzy!

Mr. Pecksniff had followed his younger friends up-stairs, and
taken a chair at the side of Mrs. Todgers. He had also spilt

a cup of coffee over his legs without appearing to be aware of the circumstance; nor did he seem to know that there was muffin on his knee.

'And how have they used you down-stairs, sir?' asked the hostess.

'Their conduct has been such, my dear madam,' said Mr. Pecksniff, 'as I can never think of without emotion, or remember without a tear. Oh, Mrs. Todgers!'

'My goodness!' exclaimed that lady. 'How low you are in your spirits, sir!'

'I am a man, my dear madam,' said Mr. Pecksniff, shedding tears, and speaking with an imperfect articulation, 'but I am also a father. I am also a widower. My feelings, Mrs. Todgers, will not consent to be entirely smothered, like the young children in the Tower. They are grown up, and the more I press the bolster on them, the more they look round the corner of it.'

He suddenly became conscious of the bit of muffin, and stared at it intently: shaking his head the while, in a forlorn and imbecile manner, as if he regarded it as his evil genius, and mildly reproached it.

'She was beautiful, Mrs. Todgers,' he said, turning his glazed eye again upon her, without the least preliminary notice. 'She had a small property.'

'So I have heard,' cried Mrs. Todgers with great sympathy.

'Those are her daughters,' said Mr. Pecksniff, pointing out the young ladies, with increased emotion.

Mrs. Todgers had no doubt of it.

'Mercy and Charity,' said Mr. Pecksniff, 'Charity and Mercy. Not unholy names, I hope?'

'Mr. Pecksniff!' cried Mrs. Todgers. 'What a ghastly smile! Are you ill, sir?'

He pressed his hand upon her arm, and answered in a solemn manner, and a faint voice, 'Chronic.'

'Cholic?' cried the frightened Mrs. Todgers.

'Chron-ic,' he repeated with some difficulty. 'Chron-ic. A chronic disorder. I have been its victim from childhood. It is carrying me to my grave.'

'Heaven forbid!' cried Mrs. Todgers.

'Yes, it is,' said Mr. Pecksniff, reckless with despair. 'I am rather glad of it, upon the whole. You are like her, Mrs. Todgers.'

'Don't squeeze me so tight, pray, Mr. Pecksniff. If any of the gentlemen should notice us.'

'For her sake,' said Mr. Pecksniff. 'Permit me. In honour of her memory. For the sake of a voice from the tomb. You are *very* like her, Mrs. Todgers! What a world this is!'

'Ah! Indeed you may say that!' cried Mrs. Todgers.

'I'm afraid it is a vain and thoughtless world,' said Mr. Pecksniff, overflowing with despondency. 'These young people about us. Oh! what sense have they of their responsibilities? None. Give me your other hand, Mrs. Todgers.'

That lady hesitated, and said 'she didn't like.'.

'Has a voice from the grave no influence?' said Mr. Pecksniff, with dismal tenderness. 'This is irreligious! My dear creature.'

'Hush!' urged Mrs. Todgers. 'Really you mustn't.'

'It's not me,' said Mr. Pecksniff. 'Don't suppose it's me: it's the voice; it's her voice.'

Mrs. Pecksniff deceased, must have had an unusually thick and husky voice for a lady, and rather a stuttering voice, and to say the truth somewhat of a drunken voice, if it had ever borne much resemblance to that in which Mr. Pecksniff spoke just then. But perhaps this was delusion on his part.

'It has been a day of enjoyment, Mrs. Todgers, but still it has been a day of torture. It has reminded me of my loneliness. What am I in the world?'

'An excellent gentleman, Mr. Pecksniff,' said Mrs. Todgers.

'There is consolation in that too,' cried Mr. Pecksniff. 'Am I?'

'There is no better man living,' said Mrs. Todgers, 'I am sure.'

Mr. Pecksniff smiled through his tears, and slightly shook his head. 'You are very good,' he said, 'thank you. It is a great happiness to me, Mrs. Todgers, to make young people happy. The happiness of my pupils is my chief object. I dote upon 'em. They dote upon me too. Sometimes.'

'Always,' said Mrs. Todgers.

'When they say they haven't improved, ma'am,' whispered Mr. Pecksniff, looking at her with profound mystery, and motioning to her to advance her ear a little closer to his mouth. 'When they say they haven't improved, ma'am, and the premium was too high, they lie! I shouldn't wish it to be mentioned; you will understand me; but I say to you as to an old friend, they lie.'

'Base wretches they must be!' said Mrs. Todgers.

'Madam,' said Mr. Pecksniff, 'you are right. I respect you for that observation. A word in your ear. To Parents and Guardians. This is in confidence, Mrs. Todgers?'

'The strictest, of course!' cried that lady.

'To Parents and Guardians,' repeated Mr. Pecksniff. 'An eligible opportunity now offers, which unites the advantages of the best practical architectural education with the comforts of a home, and the constant association with some, who, however humble their sphere and limited their capacity—observe! —are not unmindful of their moral responsibilities.'

Mrs. Todgers looked a little puzzled to know what this might mean, as well she might; for it was, as the reader may perchance remember, Mr. Pecksniff's usual form of advertisement when he wanted a pupil; and seemed to have no particular reference, at present, to anything. But Mr. Pecksniff held up his finger as a caution to her not to interrupt him.

'Do you know any parent or guardian, Mrs. Todgers,' said Mr. Pecksniff, 'who desires to avail himself of such an opportunity for a young gentleman? An orphan would be preferred. Do you know of any orphan with three or four hundred pound?'

Mrs. Todgers reflected, and shook her head.

'When you hear of an orphan with three or four hundred pound,' said Mr. Pecksniff, 'let that dear orphan's friends apply, by letter post-paid, to S. P., Post Office, Salisbury. I don't know who he is, exactly. Don't be alarmed, Mrs. Todgers,' said Mr. Pecksniff, falling heavily against her: 'Chronic—chronic! Let's have a little drop of something to drink.'

'Bless my life, Miss Pecksniffs!' cried Mrs. Todgers, aloud, 'your dear pa's took very poorly!'

Mr. Pecksniff straightened himself by a surprising effort, as every one turned hastily towards him; and standing on his feet, regarded the assembly with a look of ineffable wisdom. Gradually it gave place to a smile; a feeble, helpless, melancholy smile; bland, almost to sickliness. 'Do not repine, my friends,' said Mr. Pecksniff, tenderly. 'Do not weep for me. It is chronic.' And with these words, after making a futile attempt to pull off his shoes, he fell into the fire-place.

G

The youngest gentleman in company had him out in a second. Yes, before a hair upon his head was singed, he had him on the hearth-rug.—Her father!

She was almost beside herself. So was her sister. Jinkins consoled them both. They all consoled them. Everybody had something to say, except the youngest gentleman in company, who with a noble self-devotion did the heavy work, and held up Mr. Pecksniff's head without being taken notice of by anybody. At last they gathered round, and agreed to carry him up-stairs to bed. The youngest gentleman in company was rebuked by Jinkins for tearing Mr. Pecksniff's coat! Ha, ha! But no matter.

They carried him up-stairs, and crushed the youngest gentleman at every step. His bedroom was at the top of the house, and it was a long way; but they got him there in course of time. He asked them frequently on the road for a little drop of something to drink. It seemed an idiosyncrasy. The youngest gentleman in company proposed a draught of water. Mr. Pecksniff called him opprobrious names for the suggestion.

Jinkins and Gander took the rest upon themselves, and made him as comfortable as they could, on the outside of his bed; and when he seemed disposed to sleep, they left him. But before they had all gained the bottom of the staircase, a vision of Mr. Pecksniff, strangely attired, was seen to flutter on the top landing. He desired to collect their sentiments, it seemed, upon the nature of human life.

'My friends,' cried Mr. Pecksniff, looking over the banisters, 'let us improve our minds by mutual inquiry and discussion. Let us be moral. Let us contemplate existence. Where is Jinkins?'

'Here,' cried that gentleman. 'Go to bed again!'

'To bed!' said Mr. Pecksniff. 'Bed! 'Tis the voice of the sluggard, I hear him complain, you have woke me too soon, I must slumber again. If any young orphan will repeat the remainder of that simple piece from Doctor Watts's collection an eligible opportunity now offers.'

Nobody volunteered.

'This is very soothing,' said Mr. Pecksniff, after a pause. 'Extremely so. Cool and refreshing; particularly to the legs! The legs of the human subject, my friends, are a beautiful production. Compare them with wooden legs, and observe the difference between the anatomy of nature and the anatomy of art. Do you know,' said Mr. Pecksniff, leaning over the banisters, with an odd recollection of his familiar manner among new pupils at home, 'that I should very much like to see Mrs. Todgers's notion of a wooden leg, if perfectly agreeable to herself!'

As it appeared impossible to entertain any reasonable hopes of him after this speech, Mr. Jinkins and Mr. Gander went up-stairs again, and once more got him into bed. But they had not descended to the second floor before he was out again; nor, when they had repeated the process, had they descended the first flight, before he was out again. In a word, as often as he was shut up in his own room, he darted out afresh, charged with some new moral sentiment, which he continually repeated over the banisters, with extraordinary relish, and an irrepressible desire for the improvement of his fellow creatures that nothing could subdue.

Under these circumstances, when they had got him into bed for the thirtieth time or so, Mr. Jinkins held him, while his companion went down-stairs in search of Bailey junior, with whom he presently returned. That youth, having been apprised of the service required of him, was in great spirits, and brought up a stool, a candle, and his supper; to the end that he might keep watch outside the bedroom door with tolerable comfort.

When he had completed his arrangements, they locked Mr. Pecksniff in, and left the key on the outside; charging the young page to listen attentively for symptoms of an apoplectic nature, with which the patient might be troubled, and, in case of any such presenting themselves, to summon them without delay. To which Mr. Bailey modestly replied that 'he hoped he knowed wot o'clock it wos in gineral, and didn't date his letters to his friends, from Todgers's, for nothing.'

CHAPTER X

Containing strange matter; on which many events in this history may, for their good or evil influence, chiefly depend

BUT Mr. Pecksniff came to town on business. Had he forgotten that? Was he always taking his pleasure with Todgers's jovial brood, unmindful of the serious demands, whatever they might be, upon his calm consideration? No.

Time and tide will wait for no man, saith the adage. But all men have to wait for time and tide. That tide which, taken at the flood, would lead Seth Pecksniff on to fortune, was marked down in the table, and about to flow. No idle Pecksniff lingered far inland, unmindful of the changes of the stream; but there, upon the water's edge, over his shoes already, stood the worthy creature, prepared to wallow in the very mud, so that it slid towards the quarter of his hope.

The trustfulness of his two fair daughters was beautiful indeed. They had that firm reliance on their parent's nature, which taught them to feel certain that in all he did he had his purpose straight and full before him. And that its noble end and object was himself, which almost of necessity included them, they knew. The devotion of these maids was perfect.

Their filial confidence was rendered the more touching, by their having no knowledge of their parent's real designs, in the present instance. All that they knew of his proceedings was, that every morning, after the early breakfast, he repaired to the post office and inquired for letters. That task performed, his business for the day was over; and he again relaxed, until the rising of another sun proclaimed the advent of another post.

This went on for four or five days. At length, one morning, Mr. Pecksniff returned with a breathless rapidity, strange to observe in him, at other times so calm; and, seeking immediate speech with his daughters, shut himself up with them in private conference for two whole hours. Of all that passed in this period, only the following words of Mr. Pecksniff's utterance are known.

'How he has come to change so very much (if it should turn out as I expect, that he has), we needn't stop to inquire. My dears, I have my thoughts upon the subject, but I will not impart them. It is enough that we will not be proud, resentful,

Truth prevails, and Virtue is triumphant
(p. 159)

or unforgiving. If he wants our friendship he shall have it. We know our duty, I hope!'

That same day at noon, an old gentleman alighted from a hackney-coach at the post office, and, giving his name, inquired for a letter addressed to himself, and directed to be left till called for. It had been lying there some days. The superscription was in Mr. Pecksniff's hand, and it was sealed with Mr. Pecksniff's seal.

It was very short, containing indeed nothing more than an address 'with Mr. Pecksniff's respectful, and (notwithstanding what has passed) sincerely affectionate regards.' The old gentleman tore off the direction—scattering the rest in fragments to the winds—and giving it to the coachman, bade him drive as near that place as he could. In pursuance of these instructions he was driven to the Monument; where he again alighted, and dismissed the vehicle, and walked towards Todgers's.

Though the face, and form, and gait of this old man, and even his grip of the stout stick on which he leaned, were all expressive of a resolution not easily shaken, and a purpose (it matters little whether right or wrong, just now) such as in other days might have survived the rack, and had its strongest life in weakest death; still there were grains of hesitation in his mind, which made him now avoid the house he sought, and loiter to and fro in a gleam of sunlight, that brightened the little churchyard hard by. There may have been, in the presence of those idle heaps of dust among the busiest stir of life, something to increase his wavering; but there he walked, awakening the echoes as he paced up and down, until the church clock, striking the quarters for the second time since he had been there, roused him from his meditation. Shaking off his incertitude as the air parted with the sound of the bells, he walked rapidly to the house, and knocked at the door.

Mr. Pecksniff was seated in the landlady's little room, and his visitor found him reading—by an accident: he apologised for it—an excellent theological work. There were cake and wine upon a little table—by another accident, for which he also apologised. Indeed he said, he had given his visitor up, and was about to partake of that simple refreshment with his children, when he knocked at the door.

'Your daughters are well?' said old Martin, laying down his hat and stick.

Mr. Pecksniff endeavoured to conceal his agitation as a father, when he answered, Yes, they were. They were good girls, he said, very good. He would not venture to recommend Mr. Chuzzlewit to take the easy-chair, or to keep out of the draught from the door. If he made any such suggestion, he would expose himself, he feared, to most unjust suspicion. He would, therefore, content himself with remarking that there was an easy-chair in the room; and that the door was far from being air-tight. This latter imperfection, he might perhaps venture to add, was not uncommonly to be met with in old houses.

The old man sat down in the easy-chair, and after a few moments' silence, said:

'In the first place, let me thank you for coming to London so promptly, at my almost unexplained request: I need scarcely add, at my cost.'

'At *your* cost, my good sir!' cried Mr. Pecksniff, in a tone of great surprise.

'It is not,' said Martin, waving his hand impatiently, 'my habit to put my—well! my relatives—to any personal expense to gratify my caprices.'

'Caprices, my good sir!' cried Mr. Pecksniff.

'That is scarcely the proper word either, in this instance,' said the old man. 'No. You are right.'

Mr. Pecksniff was inwardly very much relieved to hear it, though he didn't at all know why.

'You are right,' repeated Martin. 'It is not a caprice. It is built up on reason, proof, and cool comparison. Caprices never are. Moreover, I am not a capricious man. I never was.'

'Most assuredly not,' said Mr. Pecksniff.

'How do you know?' returned the other quickly. 'You are to begin to know it now. You are to test and prove it, in time to come. You and yours are to find that I can be constant, and am not to be diverted from my end. Do you hear?'

'Perfectly,' said Mr. Pecksniff.

'I very much regret,' Martin resumed, looking steadily at him, and speaking in a slow and measured tone: 'I very much regret that you and I held such a conversation together, as that which passed between us at our last meeting. I very much regret that I laid open to you what were then my thoughts of you, so freely as I did. The intentions that I bear towards you now are of another kind; deserted by all in whom I have ever trusted; hoodwinked and beset by all who should help and sustain me; I fly to you for refuge. I confide in you to be my ally; to attach yourself to me by ties of Interest and Expectation;' he laid great stress upon these words, though Mr. Pecksniff particularly begged him not to mention it; 'and to help me to visit the consequences of the very worst species of meanness, dissimulation, and subtlety, on the right heads.'

'My noble sir!' cried Mr. Pecksniff, catching at his outstretched hand. 'And *you* regret the having harboured unjust thoughts of me! *you* with those grey hairs!'

'Regrets,' said Martin, 'are the natural property of grey hairs; and I enjoy, in common with all other men, at least my share of such inheritance. And so enough of that. I regret having been severed from you so long. If I had known you sooner, and sooner used you as you well deserve, I might have been a happier man.'

Mr. Pecksniff looked up to the ceiling, and clasped his hands in rapture.

'Your daughters,' said Martin, after a short silence. 'I don't know them. Are they like you?'

'In the nose of my eldest and the chin of my youngest, Mr. Chuzzlewit,' returned the widower, 'their sainted parent (not myself, their mother) lives again.'

'I don't mean in person,' said the old man. 'Morally, morally.'

'"Tis not for me to say,' retorted Mr. Pecksniff with a gentle smile. 'I have done my best, sir.'

'I could wish to see them,' said Martin; 'are they near at hand?'

They were, very near; for they had in fact been listening at the door, from the beginning of this conversation until now, when they precipitately retired. Having wiped the signs of weakness from his eyes, and so given them time to get up-stairs, Mr. Pecksniff opened the door, and mildly cried in the passage,

'My own darlings, where are you?'

'Here, my dear pa!' replied the distant voice of Charity.

'Come down into the back parlour, if you please, my love,' said Mr. Pecksniff, 'and bring your sister with you.'

'Yes, my dear pa,' cried Merry; and down they came directly (being all obedience), singing as they came.

Nothing could exceed the astonishment of the two Miss Pecksniffs when they found a stranger with their dear papa.

Nothing could surpass their mute amazement when he said, 'My children, Mr. Chuzzlewit!' But when he told them that Mr. Chuzzlewit and he were friends, and that Mr. Chuzzlewit had said such kind and tender words as pierced his very heart, the two Miss Pecksniffs cried with one accord, 'Thank Heaven for this!' and fell upon the old man's neck. And when they had embraced him with such fervour of affection that no words can describe it, they grouped themselves about his chair, and hung over him: as figuring to themselves no earthly joy like that of ministering to his wants, and crowding into the remainder of his life, the love they would have diffused over their whole existence, from infancy, if he—dear obdurate!—had but consented to receive the precious offering.

The old man looked attentively from one to the other, and then at Mr. Pecksniff, several times.

'What,' he asked of Mr. Pecksniff, happening to catch his eye in its descent; for until now it had been piously upraised, with something of that expression which the poetry of ages has attributed to a domestic bird, when breathing its last amid the ravages of an electric storm: 'What are their names?'

Mr. Pecksniff told him, and added, rather hastily; his calumniators would have said, with a view to any testamentary thoughts that might be flitting through old Martin's mind; 'Perhaps, my dears, you had better write them down. Your humble autographs are of no value in themselves, but affection may prize them.'

'Affection,' said the old man, 'will expend itself on the living originals. Do not trouble yourselves, my girls, I shall not so easily forget you, Charity and Mercy, as to need such tokens of remembrance. Cousin!'

'Sir!' said Mr. Pecksniff, with alacrity.

'Do you never sit down?'

'Why, yes: occasionally, sir,' said Mr. Pecksniff, who had been standing all this time.

'Will you do so now?'

'Can you ask me,' returned Mr. Pecksniff, slipping into a chair immediately, 'whether I will do anything that you desire?'

'You talk confidently,' said Martin, 'and you mean well; but I fear you don't know what an old man's humours are. You don't know what it is to be required to court his likings and dislikings; to adapt yourself to his prejudices; to do his bidding, be it what it may; to bear with his distrusts and jealousies; and always still be zealous in his service. When I remember how numerous these failings are in me, and judge of their occasional enormity by the injurious thoughts I lately entertained of you, I hardly dare to claim you for my friend.'

'My worthy sir,' returned his relative, 'how *can* you talk in such a painful strain! What was more natural than that you should make one slight mistake, when in all other respects you were so very correct, and have had such reason, such very sad and undeniable reason, to judge of every one about you in the worst light!'

'True,' replied the other. 'You are very lenient with me.'

'We always said, my girls and I,' cried Mr. Pecksniff with increasing obsequiousness, 'that while we mourned the heaviness of our misfortune in being confounded with the base and mercenary, still we could not wonder at it. My dears, you remember?'

Oh vividly! A thousand times!

'We uttered no complaint,' said Mr. Pecksniff. 'Occasionally we had the presumption to console ourselves with the remark that Truth would in the end prevail, and Virtue be triumphant; but not often. My loves, you recollect?'

Recollect! Could he doubt it? Dearest pa, what strange unnecessary questions!

'And when I saw you,' resumed Mr. Pecksniff, with still greater deference, 'in the little, unassuming village where we take the liberty of dwelling, I said you were mistaken in me, my dear sir: that was all, I think?'

'No, not all,' said Martin, who had been sitting with his hand upon his brow for some time past, and now looked up again: 'you said much more, which, added to other circumstances that have come to my knowledge, opened my eyes. You spoke to me, disinterestedly, on behalf of—I needn't name him. You know whom I mean.'

Trouble was expressed in Mr. Pecksniff's visage, as he pressed his hot hands together, and replied, with humility, 'Quite disinterestedly, sir, I assure you.'

'I know it,' said old Martin, in his quiet way. 'I am sure of it. I said so. It was disinterested too, in you, to draw that herd of harpies off from me, and be their victim yourself; most other men would have suffered them to display themselves in all their rapacity, and would have striven to rise, by contrast, in my estimation. You felt for me, and drew them off, for which I owe you many thanks. Although I left the place, I know what passed behind my back, you see!'

'You amaze me, sir!' cried Mr. Pecksniff; which was true enough.

'My knowledge of your proceedings,' said the old man, 'does not stop at this. You have a new inmate in your house.'

'Yes, sir,' rejoined the architect, 'I have.'

'He must quit it,' said Martin.

'For—for yours?' asked Mr. Pecksniff, with a quavering mildness.

'For any shelter he can find,' the old man answered. 'He has deceived you.'

'I hope not,' said Mr. Pecksniff, eagerly. 'I trust not. I have been extremely well disposed towards that young man. I hope it cannot be shown that he has forfeited all claim to my protection. Deceit, deceit, my dear Mr. Chuzzlewit, would be final. I should hold myself bound, on proof of deceit, to renounce him instantly.'

The old man glanced at both his fair supporters, but especially at Miss Mercy, whom, indeed, he looked full in the face, with a greater demonstration of interest than had yet appeared in his features. His gaze again encountered Mr. Pecksniff, as he said, composedly:

'Of course you know that he has made his matrimonial choice?'

'Oh dear!' cried Mr. Pecksniff, rubbing his hair up very stiff upon his head, and staring wildly at his daughters. 'This is becoming tremendous!'

'You know the fact?' repeated Martin.

'Surely not without his grandfather's consent and approbation, my dear sir!' cried Mr. Pecksniff. 'Don't tell me that. For the honour of human nature, say you're not about to tell me that!'

'I thought he had suppressed it,' said the old man.

The indignation felt by Mr. Pecksniff at this terrible disclosure, was only to be equalled by the kindling anger of his daughters. What! Had they taken to their hearth and home a secretly contracted serpent; a crocodile, who had made a furtive offer of his hand; an imposition on society; a bankrupt bachelor with no effects, trading with the spinster world on false pretences! And oh, to think that he should have disobeyed and practised on that sweet, that venerable gentleman, whose name he bore; that kind and tender guardian; his more than father (to say nothing at all of mother), horrible, horrible! To turn him out with ignominy would be treatment much too good. Was there nothing else that could be done to him? Had he incurred no legal pains and penalties? Could it be that the statutes of the land were so remiss as to have affixed no punishment to such delinquency? Monster; how basely had they been deceived!

'I am glad to find you second me so warmly,' said the old man, holding up his hand to stay the torrent of their wrath. 'I will not deny that it is a pleasure to me to find you so full of zeal. We will consider that topic as disposed of.'

'No, my dear sir,' cried Mr. Pecksniff, 'not as disposed of, until I have purged my house of this pollution.'

'That will follow,' said the old man, 'in its own time. I look upon that as done.'

'You are very good, sir,' answered Mr. Pecksniff, shaking his hand. 'You do me honour. You *may* look upon it as done, I assure you.'

'There is another topic,' said Martin, 'on which I hope you will assist me. You remember Mary, cousin?'

'The young lady that I mentioned to you, my dears, as having interested me so very much,' remarked Mr. Pecksniff. 'Excuse my interrupting you, sir.'

'I told you her history;' said the old man.

'Which I also mentioned, you will recollect, my dears,' cried Mr. Pecksniff. 'Silly girls, Mr. Chuzzlewit. Quite moved by it, they were!'

'Why, look now!' said Martin, evidently pleased: 'I feared I should have had to urge her case upon you, and ask you to regard her favourably for my sake. But I find you have no jealousies! Well! You have no cause for any, to be sure. She has nothing to gain from me, my dears, and she knows it.'

The two Miss Pecksniffs murmured their approval of this wise arrangement, and their cordial sympathy with its interesting object.

'If I could have anticipated what has come to pass between us four,' said the old man, thoughtfully: 'but it is too late to think of that. You would receive her courteously, young ladies, and be kind to her, if need were?'

Where was the orphan whom the two Miss Pecksniffs would

not have cherished in their sisterly bosom! But when that orphan was commended to their care by one on whom the dammed-up love of years was gushing forth, what exhaustless stores of pure affection yearned to expend themselves upon her!

An interval ensued, during which Mr. Chuzzlewit, in an absent frame of mind, sat gazing at the ground, without uttering a word; and as it was plain that he had no desire to be interrupted in his meditations, Mr. Pecksniff and his daughters were profoundly silent also. During the whole of the foregoing dialogue, he had borne his part with a cold, passionless promptitude, as though he had learned and painfully rehearsed it all a hundred times. Even when his expressions were warmest and his language most encouraging, he had retained the same manner, without the least abatement. But now there was a keener brightness in his eye, and more expression in his voice, as he said, awakening from his thoughtful mood:

'You know what will be said of this? Have you reflected?'

'Said of what, my dear sir?' Mr. Pecksniff asked.

'Of this new understanding between us.'

Mr. Pecksniff looked benevolently sagacious, and at the same time far above all earthly misconstruction, as he shook his head, and observed that a great many things would be said of it, no doubt.

'A great many,' rejoined the old man. 'Some will say that I dote in my old age; that illness has shaken me; that I have lost all strength of mind; and have grown childish. You can bear that?'

Mr. Pecksniff answered that it would be dreadfully hard to bear, but he thought he could, if he made a great effort.

'Others will say—I speak of disappointed, angry people only—that you have lied, and fawned, and wormed yourself through dirty ways into my favour; by such concessions and such crooked deeds, such meannesses and vile endurances, as nothing could repay: no, not the legacy of half the world we live in. You can bear that?'

Mr. Pecksniff made reply that this would be also very hard to bear, as reflecting, in some degree, on the discernment of Mr. Chuzzlewit. Still he had a modest confidence that he could sustain the calumny, with the help of a good conscience, and that gentleman's friendship.

'With the great mass of slanderers,' said old Martin, leaning back in his chair, 'the tale, as I clearly foresee, will run thus:

That to mark my contempt for the rabble whom I despised, I chose from among them the very worst, and made him do my will, and pampered and enriched him at the cost of all the rest. That, after casting about for the means of a punishment which should rankle in the bosoms of these kites the most, and strike into their gall, I devised this scheme at a time when the last link in the chain of grateful love and duty, that held me to my race, was roughly snapped asunder; roughly, for I loved him well; roughly, for I had ever put my trust in his affection; roughly, for that he broke it when I loved him most, God help me! and he without a pang could throw me off, while I clung about his heart! Now,' said the old man, dismissing this passionate outburst as suddenly as he had yielded to it, 'is your mind made up to bear this likewise? Lay your account with having it to bear, and put no trust in being set right by me.'

'My dear Mr. Chuzzlewit,' cried Pecksniff in an ecstasy, 'for such a man as you have shown yourself to be this day; for a man so injured, yet so very humane; for a man so—I am at a loss what precise term to use—yet at the same time so remarkably—I don't know how to express my meaning: for such a man as I have described, I hope it is no presumption to say that I, and I am sure I may add my children also (my dears, we perfectly agree in this, I think?), would bear anything whatever!'

'Enough,' said Martin. 'You can charge no consequences on me. When do you return home?'

'Whenever you please, my dear sir. To-night if you desire it.'

'I desire nothing,' returned the old man, 'that is unreasonable. Such a request would be. Will you be ready to return at the end of this week?'

The very time of all others that Mr. Pecksniff would have suggested if it had been left to him to make his own choice. As to his daughters, the words, 'Let us be at home on Saturday, dear pa,' were actually upon their lips.

'Your expenses, cousin,' said Martin, taking a folded slip of paper from his pocket-book, 'may possibly exceed that amount. If so, let me know the balance that I owe you, when we next meet. It would be useless if I told you where I live just now: indeed, I have no fixed abode. When I have, you shall know it. You and your daughters may expect to see me before long: in the meantime I need not tell you that we keep our own confidence. What you will do when you get home is understood between us. Give me no account of it at any time; and never refer to it in any way. I ask that as a favour. I am commonly a man of few words, cousin; and all that need be said just now is said, I think.'

'One glass of wine, one morsel of this homely cake?' cried Mr. Pecksniff, venturing to detain him. 'My dears!'

The sisters flew to wait upon him.

'Poor girls!' said Mr. Pecksniff. 'You will excuse their agitation, my dear sir. They are made up of feeling. A bad commodity to go through the world with, Mr. Chuzzlewit! My youngest daughter is almost as much of a woman as my eldest, is she not, sir?'

'Which *is* the youngest?' asked the old man.

'Mercy, by five years,' said Mr. Pecksniff. 'We sometimes venture to consider her rather a fine figure, sir. Speaking as an artist, I may perhaps be permitted to suggest that its outline is graceful and correct. I am naturally,' said Mr. Pecksniff, drying his hands upon his handkerchief, and looking anxiously in his cousin's face at almost every word, 'proud, if I may use the expression, to have a daughter who is constructed on the best models.'

'She seems to have a lively disposition,' observed Martin.

'Dear me!' said Mr. Pecksniff. 'That is quite remarkable. You have defined her character, my dear sir, as correctly as if you had known her from her birth. She *has* a lively disposition. I assure you, my dear sir, that in our unpretending home her gaiety is delightful.'

'No doubt,' returned the old man.

'Charity, upon the other hand,' said Mr. Pecksniff, 'is remarkable for strong sense, and for rather a deep tone of sentiment, if the partiality of a father may be excused in saying so. A wonderful affection between them, my dear sir! Allow me to drink your health. Bless you!'

'I little thought,' retorted Martin, 'but a month ago, that I should be breaking bread and pouring wine with you. I drink to you.'

Not at all abashed by the extraordinary abruptness with which these latter words were spoken, Mr. Pecksniff thanked him devoutly.

'Now let me go,' said Martin, putting down the wine when he had merely touched it with his lips. 'My dears, good morning!'

But this distant form of farewell was by no means tender enough for the yearnings of the young ladies, who again embraced him with all their hearts—with all their arms at any rate—to which parting caresses their new-found friend submitted with a better grace than might have been expected from one who, not a moment before, had pledged their parent in such a very uncomfortable manner. These endearments terminated, he took a hasty leave of Mr. Pecksniff and withdrew, followed to the door by both father and daughters, who stood there kissing their hands and beaming with affection until he disappeared: though, by the way, he never once looked back, after he had crossed the threshold.

When they returned into the house, and were again alone in Mrs. Todgers's room, the two young ladies exhibited an unusual amount of gaiety; insomuch that they clapped their hands, and laughed, and looked with roguish aspects and a bantering air upon their dear papa. This conduct was so very unaccountable, that Mr. Pecksniff (being singularly grave himself) could scarcely choose but ask them what it meant; and took them to task, in his gentle manner, for yielding to such light emotions.

'If it was possible to divine any cause for this merriment, even the most remote,' he said, 'I should not reprove you. But when you can have none whatever—oh, really, really!'

This admonition had so little effect on Mercy, that she was obliged to hold her handkerchief before her rosy lips, and to throw herself back in her chair, with every demonstration of extreme amusement; which want of duty so offended Mr. Pecksniff that he reproved her in set terms, and gave her his parental advice to correct herself in solitude and contemplation. But at that juncture they were disturbed by the sound of voices in dispute; and as it proceeded from the next room, the subject matter of the altercation quickly reached their ears.

'I don't care that! Mrs. Todgers,' said the young gentleman who had been the youngest gentleman in company on the day of the festival; 'I don't care *that*, ma'am,' said he, snapping his fingers, 'for Jinkins. Don't suppose I do.'

'I am quite certain you don't, sir,' replied Mrs. Todgers. 'You have too independent a spirit, I know, to yield to anybody. And quite right. There is no reason why you should give way to any gentleman. Everybody must be well aware of that.'

'I should think no more of admitting daylight into the fellow,' said the youngest gentleman, in a desperate voice, 'than if he was a bull-dog.'

Mrs. Todgers did not stop to inquire whether, as a matter of principle, there was any particular reason for admitting daylight even into a bull-dog, otherwise than by the natural channel of his eyes: but she seemed to wring her hands, and she moaned.

'Let him be careful,' said the youngest gentleman. 'I give him warning. No man shall step between me and the current of my vengeance. I know a Cove—' he used that familiar epithet in his agitation, but corrected himself by adding, a gentleman of property, I mean—who practises with a pair of pistols (fellows too,) of his own. If I am driven to borrow 'em, and to send a friend to Jinkins, a tragedy will get into the papers. That's all.'

Again Mrs. Todgers moaned.

'I have borne this long enough,' said the youngest gentleman, 'but now my soul rebels against it, and I won't stand it any longer. I left home originally, because I had that within me which wouldn't be domineered over by a sister; and do you think I'm going to be put down by *him?* No.'

'It is very wrong in Mr. Jinkins: I know it is perfectly inexcusable in Mr. Jinkins, if he intends it,' observed Mrs. Todgers.

'If he intends it!' cried the youngest gentleman. 'Don't he interrupt and contradict me on every occasion? Does he ever fail to interpose himself between me and anything or anybody that he sees I have set my mind upon? Does he make a point of always pretending to forget me, when he's pouring out the beer? Does he make bragging remarks about his razors, and insulting allusions to people who have no necessity to shave more than once a week? But let him look out! He'll find himself shaved, pretty close, before long, and so I tell him.'

The young gentleman was mistaken in this closing sentence, inasmuch as he never told it to Jinkins, but always to Mrs. Todgers.

'However,' he said, 'these are not proper subjects for ladies' ears. All I've got to say to you, Mrs. Todgers, is, a week's notice from next Saturday. The same house can't contain that miscreant and me any longer. If we get over the intermediate time without bloodshed, you may think yourself pretty fortunate. I don't myself expect we shall.'

'Dear, dear!' cried Mrs. Todgers, 'what would I have given

to have prevented this? To lose you, sir, would be like losing the house's right-hand. So popular as you are among the gentlemen; so generally looked up to; and so much liked! I do hope you'll think better of it; if on nobody else's account, on mine.'

'There's Jinkins,' said the youngest gentleman, moodily. 'Your favourite. He'll console you, and the gentlemen too, for the loss of twenty such as me. I'm not understood in this house. I never have been.'

'Don't run away with that opinion, sir!' cried Mrs. Todgers, with a show of honest indignation. 'Don't make such a charge as that against the establishment, I must beg of you. It is not so bad as that comes to, sir. Make any remark you please against the gentlemen, or against me; but don't say you're not understood in this house.'

'I'm not treated as if I was,' said the youngest gentleman.

'There you make a great mistake, sir,' returned Mrs. Todgers, in the same strain. 'As many of the gentlemen and I have often said, you are too sensitive. That's where it is. You are of too susceptible a nature; it's in your spirit.'

The young gentleman coughed.

'And as,' said Mrs. Todgers, 'as to Mr. Jinkins, I must beg of you, if we *are* to part, to understand that I don't abet Mr. Jinkins by any means. Far from it. I could wish that Mr. Jinkins would take a lower tone in this establishment, and would not be the means of raising differences between me and gentlemen that I can much less bear to part with than I could with Mr. Jinkins. Mr. Jinkins is not such a boarder, sir,' added Mrs. Todgers, 'that all considerations of private feeling and respect give way before him. Quite the contrary, I assure you.'

The young gentleman was so much mollified by these and similar speeches on the part of Mrs. Todgers, that he and that lady gradually changed positions; so that she became the injured party, and he was understood to be the injurer; but in a complimentary, not in an offensive sense; his cruel conduct being attributable to his exalted nature, and to that alone. So, in the end, the young gentleman withdrew his notice, and assured Mrs. Todgers of his unalterable regard: and having done so, went back to business.

'Goodness me, Miss Pecksniffs!' cried that lady, as she came into the back room, and sat wearily down, with her basket on her knees, and her hands folded upon it, 'what a trial of temper it is to keep a house like this! You must have heard most of what has just passed. Now did you ever hear the like?'

'Never!' said the two Miss Pecksniffs.

'Of all the ridiculous young fellows that ever I had to deal with,' resumed Mrs. Todgers, 'that is the most ridiculous and unreasonable. Mr. Jinkins is hard upon him sometimes, but not half as hard as he deserves. To mention such a gentleman as Mr. Jinkins in the same breath with *him*. You know it's too much! And yet he's as jealous of him, bless you, as if he was his equal.'

The young ladies were greatly entertained by Mrs. Todgers's account, no less than with certain anecdotes illustrative of the youngest gentleman's character, which she went on to tell them. But Mr. Pecksniff looked quite stern and angry: and when she had concluded, said in a solemn voice:

'Pray, Mrs. Todgers, if I may inquire, what does that young gentleman contribute towards the support of these premises?'

'Why, sir, for what *he* has, he pays about eighteen shillings a week!' said Mrs. Todgers.

'Eighteen shillings a week!' repeated Mr. Pecksniff.

'Taking one week with another; as near that as possible,' said Mrs. Todgers.

Mr. Pecksniff rose from his chair, folded his arms, looked at her, and shook his head.

'And do you mean to say, ma'am, is it possible, Mrs. Todgers, that for such a miserable consideration as eighteen shillings a week, a female of your understanding can so far demean herself as to wear a double face, even for an instant?'

'I am forced to keep things on the square if I can, sir,' faltered Mrs. Todgers. 'I must preserve peace among them, and keep my connexion together, if possible, Mr. Pecksniff. The profit is very small.'

'The profit!' cried that gentleman, laying great stress upon the word. 'The profit, Mrs. Todgers! You amaze me!'

He was so severe, that Mrs. Todgers shed tears.

'The profit!' repeated Mr. Pecksniff. 'The profit of dissimulation! To worship the golden calf of Baal, for eighteen shillings a week!'

'Don't in your own goodness be too hard upon me, Mr. Pecksniff,' cried Mrs. Todgers, taking out her handkerchief.

'Oh Calf, Calf!' cried Mr. Pecksniff mournfully. 'Oh, Baal, Baal! Oh my friend, Mrs. Todgers! To barter away that

precious jewel, self-esteem, and cringe to any mortal creature
—for eighteen shillings a week!'

He was so subdued and overcome by the reflection, that he
immediately took down his hat from its peg in the passage, and
went out for a walk, to compose his feelings. Anybody passing
him in the street might have known him for a good man at
first sight; for his whole figure teemed with a consciousness of
the moral homily he had read to Mrs. Todgers.

Eighteen shillings a week! Just, most just, thy censure,
upright Pecksniff! Had it been for the sake of a ribbon, star,
or garter; sleeves of lawn, a great man's smile, a seat in parliament, a tap upon the shoulder from a courtly sword; a place,
a party, or a thriving lie, or eighteen thousand pounds, or
even eighteen hundred;—but to worship the golden calf for
eighteen shillings a week! Oh pitiful, pitiful!

CHAPTER XI

Wherein a certain gentleman becomes particular in his attentions to a certain lady; and more coming events than one, cast their shadows before

THE family were within two or three days of their departure from Mrs. Todgers's, and the commercial gentlemen were to a man despondent and not to be comforted, because of the approaching separation, when Bailey junior, at the jocund time of noon, presented himself before Miss Charity Pecksniff, then sitting with her sister in the banquet chamber, hemming six new pocket-handkerchiefs for Mr. Jinkins; and having expressed a hope, preliminary and pious, that he might be blest, gave her in his pleasant way to understand that a visitor attended to pay his respects to her, and was at that moment waiting in the drawing-room. Perhaps this last announcement showed in a more striking point of view than many lengthened speeches could have done, the trustfulness and faith of Bailey's nature; since he had, in fact, last seen the visitor on the door-mat, where, after signifying to him that he would do well to go up-stairs, he had left him to the guidance of his own sagacity. Hence it was at least an even chance that the visitor was then wandering on the roof of the house, or vainly seeking to extricate himself from a maze of bedrooms; Todgers's being precisely that kind of establishment in which an unpiloted stranger is pretty sure to find himself in some place where he least expects and least desires to be.

'A gentleman for me!' cried Charity, pausing in her work; 'my gracious, Bailey!'

'Ah!' said Bailey. 'It *is* my gracious, an't it? Wouldn't I be gracious neither, not if I wos him!'

The remark was rendered somewhat obscure in itself, by reason (as the reader may have observed) of a redundancy of negatives; but accompanied by action expressive of a faithful couple walking arm-in-arm towards a parochial church, mutually exchanging looks of love, it clearly signified this youth's conviction that the caller's purpose was of an amorous tendency. Miss Charity affected to reprove so great a liberty; but she could not help smiling. He was a strange boy, to be sure. There was always some ground of probability and likelihood mingled with his absurd behaviour. That was the best of it!

'But I don't know any gentleman, Bailey,' said Miss Pecksniff. 'I think you must have made a mistake.'

Mr. Bailey smiled at the extreme wildness of such a supposition, and regarded the young ladies with unimpaired affability.

'My dear Merry,' said Charity, 'who *can* it be? Isn't it odd? I have a great mind not to go to him really. So very strange, you know!'

The younger sister plainly considered that this appeal had its origin in the pride of being called upon and asked for; and that it was intended as an assertion of superiority, and a retaliation upon her for having captured the commercial gentlemen. Therefore, she replied, with great affection and politeness, that it was, no doubt, very strange indeed; and that she was totally at a loss to conceive what the ridiculous person unknown could mean by it.

'Quite impossible to divine!' said Charity, with some sharpness, 'though still, at the same time, you needn't be angry, my dear.'

'Thank you,' retorted Merry, singing at her needle. 'I am quite aware of that, my love.'

'I am afraid your head is turned, you silly thing,' said Cherry.

'Do you know, my dear,' said Merry, with engaging candour, 'that I have been afraid of that, myself, all along! So much incense and nonsense, and all the rest of it, is enough to turn a stronger head than mine. What a relief it must be to you, my dear, to be so very comfortable in that respect, and not to be worried by those odious men! How *do* you do it, Cherry?'

This artless inquiry might have led to turbulent results, but for the strong emotions of delight evinced by Bailey junior, whose relish in the turn the conversation had lately taken was so acute, that it impelled and forced him to the instantaneous performance of a dancing step, extremely difficult in its nature, and only to be achieved in a moment of ecstasy, which is commonly called The Frog's Hornpipe. A manifestation so lively, brought to their immediate recollection the great virtuous precept, 'Keep up appearances whatever you do,' in which they had been educated. They forbore at once, and jointly signified to Mr. Bailey that if he should presume to practise that figure any more in their presence, they would instantly acquaint Mrs. Todgers with the fact, and would demand his condign punishment at the hands of that lady. The young gentleman having expressed the bitterness of his contrition by affecting to wipe away scalding tears with his apron, and afterwards feigning to wring a vast amount of water from that garment, held the door open while Miss Charity passed out: and so that damsel went in state up-stairs to receive her mysterious adorer.

By some strange occurrence of favourable circumstances he had found out the drawing-room, and was sitting there alone.

'Ah, cousin!' he said. 'Here I am, you see. You thought I was lost, I'll be bound. Well! how do you find yourself by this time?'

Miss Charity replied that she was quite well, and gave Mr. Jonas Chuzzlewit her hand.

'That's right,' said Mr. Jonas, 'and you've got over the fatigues of the journey, have you? I say. How's the other one?'

'My sister is very well, I believe,' returned the young lady. 'I have not heard her complain of any indisposition, sir. Perhaps you would like to see her, and ask her yourself?'

'No, no, cousin!' said Mr. Jonas, sitting down beside her on the window-seat. 'Don't be in a hurry. There's no occasion for that, you know. What a cruel girl you are!'

'It's impossible for *you* to know,' said Cherry, 'whether I am or not.'

'Well, perhaps it is,' said Mr. Jonas. 'I say! Did you think I was lost? You haven't told me that.'

'I didn't think at all about it,' answered Cherry.

'Didn't you though?' said Jonas, pondering upon this strange reply. '—Did the other one?'

'I am sure it's impossible for me to say what my sister may, or may not have thought on such a subject,' cried Cherry. 'She never said anything to me about it, one way or other.'

'Didn't she laugh about it? inquired Jonas.

'No. She didn't even laugh about it,' answered Charity.

'She's a terrible one to laugh, an't she?' said Jonas, lowering his voice.

'She is very lively,' said Cherry.

'Liveliness is a pleasant thing—when it don't lead to spending money. An't it?' asked Mr. Jonas.

'Very much so, indeed,' said Cherry, with a demureness

of manner that gave a very disinterested character to her assent.

'Such liveliness as yours I mean, you know,' observed Mr. Jonas, as he nudged her with his elbow. 'I should have come to see you before, but I didn't know where you was. How quick you hurried off, that morning!'

'I was amenable to my papa's directions,' said Miss Charity.

'I wish he had given me his direction,' returned her cousin, 'and then I should have found you out before. Why, I shouldn't have found you even now, if I hadn't met him in the street this morning. What a sleek, sly chap he is! Just like a tom-cat, an't he?'

'I must trouble you to have the goodness to speak more respectfully of my papa, Mr. Jonas,' said Charity. 'I can't allow such a tone as that, even in jest.'

'Ecod, you may say what you like of *my* father, then, and so I give you leave,' said Jonas. 'I think it's liquid aggravation that circulates through his veins, and not regular blood. How old should you think my father was, cousin?'

'Old, no doubt,' replied Miss Charity; 'but a fine old gentleman.'

'A fine old gentleman!' repeated Jonas, giving the crown of his hat an angry knock. 'Ah! It's time he was thinking of being drawn out a little finer too. Why, he's eighty!'

'Is he, indeed?' said the young lady.

'And ecod,' cried Jonas, 'now he's gone so far without giving in, I don't see much to prevent his being ninety; no, nor even a hundred. Why, a man with any feeling ought to be ashamed of being eighty, let alone more. Where's his religion, I should like to know, when he goes flying in the face of the Bible like that? Three-score-and-ten's the mark; and no man with a conscience, and a proper sense of what's expected of him, has any business to live longer.'

Is any one surprised at Mr. Jonas making such a reference to such a book for such a purpose? Does any one doubt the old saw, that the Devil (being a layman) quotes Scripture for his own ends? If he will take the trouble to look about him, he may find a greater number of confirmations of the fact in the occurrences of any single day, than the steam-gun can discharge balls in a minute.

'But there's enough of my father,' said Jonas, 'it's of no use to go putting one's-self out of the way by talking about *him*.

I called to ask you to come and take a walk, cousin, and see some of the sights; and to come to our house afterwards, and have a bit of something. Pecksniff will most likely look in in the evening, he says, and bring you home. See, here's his writing; I made him put it down this morning, when he told me he shouldn't be back before I came here; in case you wouldn't believe me. There's nothing like proof, is there? Ha, ha! I say—you'll bring the other one, you know!'

Miss Charity cast her eyes upon her father's autograph, which merely said: 'Go, my children, with your cousin. Let there be union among us when it is possible;' and after enough of hesitation to impart a proper value to her consent, withdrew to prepare her sister and herself for the excursion. She soon returned, accompanied by Miss Mercy, who was by no means pleased to leave the brilliant triumphs of Todgers's for the society of Mr. Jonas and his respected father.

'Aha!' cried Jonas. 'There you are, are you?'

'Yes, fright,' said Mercy, 'here I am; and I would much rather be anywhere else, I assure you.'

'You don't mean that,' cried Mr. Jonas. 'You can't, you know. It isn't possible.'

'You can have what opinion you like, fright,' retorted Mercy. 'I am content to keep mine; and mine is that you are a very unpleasant, odious, disagreeable person.' Here she laughed heartily, and seemed to enjoy herself very much.

'Oh, you're a sharp gal!' said Mr. Jonas. 'She's a regular teazer, an't she, cousin?'

Miss Charity replied in effect, that she was unable to say what the habits and propensities of a regular teazer might be; and that even if she possessed such information, it would ill become her to admit the existence of any creature with such an unceremonious name in her family; far less in the person of a beloved sister; 'whatever,' added Cherry with an angry glance, 'whatever her real nature may be.'

'Well, my dear,' said Merry, 'the only observation I have to make is, that if we don't go out at once, I shall certainly take my bonnet off again, and stay at home.'

This threat had the desired effect of preventing any farther altercation, for Mr. Jonas immediately proposed an adjournment, and the same being carried unanimously, they departed from the house straightway. On the door-step, Mr. Jonas gave an arm to each cousin; which act of gallantry being observed by Bailey junior, from the garret window, was by him saluted with a loud and violent fit of coughing, to which paroxysm he was still the victim when they turned the corner.

Mr. Jonas inquired in the first instance if they were good walkers, and being answered, 'Yes,' submitted their pedestrian powers to a pretty severe test; for he showed them as many sights, in the way of bridges, churches, streets, outsides of theatres, and other free spectacles, in that one forenoon, as most people see in a twelvemonth. It was observable in this gentleman, that he had an insurmountable distaste to the insides of buildings; and that he was perfectly acquainted with the merits of all shows, in respect of which there was any charge for admission, which it seemed were every one detestable, and of the very lowest grade of merit. He was so thoroughly possessed with this opinion, that when Miss Charity happened to mention the circumstance of their having been twice or thrice to the theatre with Mr. Jinkins and party, he inquired, as a matter of course, 'where the orders came from?' and being told that Mr. Jinkins and party paid, was beyond description entertained, observing that 'they must be nice flats, certainly;' and often in the course of the walk, bursting out again into a perfect convulsion of laughter at the surpassing silliness of those gentlemen, and (doubtless) at his own superior wisdom.

When they had been out for some hours and were thoroughly fatigued, it being by that time twilight, Mr. Jonas intimated that he would show them one of the best pieces of fun with which he was acquainted. This joke was of a practical kind, and its humour lay in taking a hackney-coach to the extreme limits of possibility for a shilling. Happily it brought them to the place where Mr. Jonas dwelt, or the young ladies might have rather missed the point and cream of the jest.

The old-established firm of Anthony Chuzzlewit and Son, Manchester Warehousemen, and so forth, had its place of business in a very narrow street somewhere behind the Post Office; where every house was in the brightest summer morning very gloomy; and where light porters watered the pavement, each before his own employer's premises, in fantastic patterns, in the dog-days; and where spruce gentlemen with their hands in the pockets of symmetrical trousers, were always to be seen in warm weather, contemplating their undeniable boots in dusty warehouse doorways; which appeared to be the hardest work they did, except now and then carrying pens behind their ears. A dim, dirty, smoky, tumble-down, rotten old house it was, as anybody would desire to see; but there the firm of Anthony Chuzzlewit and Son transacted all their business and their pleasure too, such as it was; for neither the young man nor the old had any other residence, or any care or thought beyond its narrow limits.

Business, as may be readily supposed, was the main thing in this establishment; insomuch indeed that it shouldered comfort out of doors, and jostled the domestic arrangements at every turn. Thus in the miserable bedrooms there were files of moth-eaten letters hanging up against the walls; and linen rollers, and fragments of old patterns, and odds and ends of spoiled goods, strewed upon the ground; while the meagre bedsteads, washing-stands, and scraps of carpet, were huddled away into corners as objects of secondary consideration, not to be thought of but as disagreeable necessities, furnishing no profit, and intruding on the one affair of life. The single sitting-room was on the same principle, a chaos of boxes and old papers, and had more counting-house stools in it than chairs: not to mention a great monster of a desk straddling over the middle of the floor, and an iron safe sunk into the wall above the fire-place. The solitary little table for purposes of refection and social enjoyment, bore as fair a proportion to the desk and other business furniture, as the graces and harmless relaxations of life had ever done, in the persons of the old man and his son, to their pursuit of wealth. It was meanly laid out now for dinner; and in a chair before the fire sat Anthony himself, who rose to greet his son and his fair cousins as they entered.

An ancient proverb warns us that we should not expect to find old heads upon young shoulders; to which it may be added that we seldom meet with that unnatural combination, but we feel a strong desire to knock them off; merely from an inherent love we have of seeing things in their right places. It is not improbable that many men, in no wise choleric by nature, felt this impulse rising up within them, when they first made the acquaintance of Mr. Jonas; but if they had known him more intimately in his own house, and had sat with him at his own board, it would assuredly have been paramount to all other considerations.

'Well, ghost!' said Mr. Jonas, dutifully addressing his parent by that title. 'Is dinner nearly ready?'

'I should think it was,' rejoined the old man.

'What's the good of that?' rejoined the son. '*I* should think it was. I want to know.'

'Ah! I don't know for certain,' said Anthony.

'You don't know for certain,' rejoined his son in a lower tone. 'No. You don't know anything for certain, *you* don't. Give me your candle here. I want it for the gals.'

Anthony handed him a battered old office candlestick, with which Mr. Jonas preceded the young ladies to the nearest bedroom, where he left them to take off their shawls and bonnets; and returning, occupied himself in opening a bottle of wine, sharpening the carving-knife, and muttering compliments to his father, until they and the dinner appeared together. The repast consisted of a hot leg of mutton with greens and potatoes; and the dishes having been set upon the table by a slipshod old woman, they were left to enjoy it after their own manner.

'Bachelor's Hall, you know, cousin,' said Mr. Jonas to Charity. 'I say—the other one will be having a laugh at this when she gets home, won't she? Here; you sit on the right side of me, and I'll have her upon the left. Other one, will you come here?'

'You're such a fright,' replied Mercy, 'that I know I shall have no appetite if I sit near you: but I suppose I must.'

'An't she lively?' whispered Mr. Jonas to the elder sister, with his favourite elbow emphasis.

'Oh I really don't know!' replied Miss Pecksniff, tartly. 'I am tired of being asked such ridiculous questions.'

'What's that precious old father of mine about now?' said Mr. Jonas, seeing that his parent was travelling up and down the room, instead of taking his seat at table. 'What are you looking for?'

'I've lost my glasses, Jonas,' said old Anthony.

'Sit down without your glasses, can't you?' returned his son. 'You don't eat or drink out of 'em, I think; and where's that sleepy-headed old Chuffey got to! Now, stupid. Oh! you know your name, do you?'

It would seem that he didn't, for he didn't come until the father called. As he spoke, the door of a small glass office, which was partitioned off from the rest of the room, was slowly opened, and a little blear-eyed, weazen-faced, ancient man came creeping out. He was of a remote fashion, and dusty, like the rest of the furniture; he was dressed in a decayed suit of black; with breeches garnished at the knees with rusty wisps of ribbon, the very paupers of shoe-strings; on the lower portion of his spindle legs were dingy worsted stockings of the same colour. He looked as if he had been put away and forgotten half a century before, and somebody had just found him in a lumber-closet.

Such as he was, he came slowly creeping on towards the table, until at last he crept into the vacant chair, from which, as his dim faculties became conscious of the presence of strangers, and those strangers ladies, he rose again, apparently intending to make a bow. But he sat down once more without having made it, and breathing on his shrivelled hands to warm them, remained with his poor blue nose immovable about his plate, looking at nothing, with eyes that saw nothing, and a face that meant nothing. Take him in that state, and he was an embodiment of nothing. Nothing else.

'Our clerk,' said Mr. Jonas, as host and master of the cere-monies: 'Old Chuffey.'

'Is he deaf?' inquired one of the young ladies.

'No, I don't know that he is. He an't deaf, is he, father?'

'I never heard him say he was,' replied the old man.

'Blind?' inquired the young ladies.

'N—no. I never understood that he was at all blind,' said Jonas, carelessly. 'You don't consider him so, do you, father?'

'Certainly not,' replied Anthony.

'What is he, then?'

'Why, I'll tell you what he is,' said Mr. Jonas, apart to the young ladies, 'he's precious old, for one thing; and I an't best pleased with him for that, for I think my father must have caught it of him. He's a strange old chap, for another,' he added in a louder voice, 'and don't understand any one hardly, but *him!*' He pointed to his honoured parent with the carving-fork, in order that they might know whom he meant.

'How very strange!' cried the sisters.

'Why, you see,' said Mr. Jonas, 'he's been addling his old brains with figures and book-keeping all his life; and twenty years ago or so he went and took a fever. All the time he was out of his head (which was three weeks) he never left off casting up; and he got to so many million at last that I don't believe he's ever been quite right since. We don't do much business now though, and he an't a bad clerk.'

'A very good one,' said Anthony.

'Well! He an't a dear one at all events,' observed Jonas; 'and he earns his salt, which is enough for our look-out. I was telling you that he hardly understands any one except my father; he always understands him, though, and wakes up quite wonderful. He's been used to his ways so long, you see! Why, I've seen him play whist, with my father for a partner; and a good rubber too; when he had no more notion what sort of people he was playing against, than you have.'

'Has he no appetite?' asked Merry.

'Oh, yes,' said Jonas, plying his own knife and fork very fast. 'He eats—when he's helped. But he don't care whether he waits a minute or an hour, as long as father's here; so when I'm at all sharp set, as I am to-day, I come to him after I've taken the edge off my own hunger, you know. Now, Chuffey, stupid, are you ready?'

Chuffey remained immovable.

'Always a perverse old file, he was,' said Mr. Jonas, coolly helping himself to another slice. 'Ask him, father.'

'Are you ready for your dinner, Chuffey?' asked the old man.

'Yes, yes,' said Chuffey, lighting up into a sentient human creature at the first sound of the voice, so that it was at once a curious and quite a moving sight to see him. 'Yes, yes. Quite ready, Mr. Chuzzlewit. Quite ready, sir. All ready, all ready, all ready.' With that he stopped, smilingly, and listened for some further address; but being spoken to no more, the light forsook his face by little and little, until he was nothing again.

'He'll be very disagreeable, mind,' said Jonas, addressing his cousins as he handed the old man's portion to his father. 'He always chokes himself when it an't broth. Look at him, now! Did you ever see a horse with such a wall-eyed expression as he's got? If it hadn't been for the joke of it I wouldn't have let him come in to-day; but I thought he'd amuse you.'

The poor old subject of this humane speech was, happily for himself, as unconscious of its purport as of most other remarks that were made in his presence. But the mutton being tough, and his gums weak, he quickly verified the statement relative to his choking propensities, and underwent so much in his attempts to dine, that Mr. Jonas was infinitely amused: protesting that he had seldom seen him better company in all his life, and that he was enough to make a man split his sides with laughing. Indeed, he went so far as to assure the sisters, that in this point of view he considered Chuffey superior to his own father; which, as he significantly added, was saying a great deal.

It was strange enough that Anthony Chuzzlewit, himself so old a man, should take a pleasure in these gibings of his estimable son, at the expense of the poor shadow at their table. But he did, unquestionably: though not so much—to do him justice—with reference to their ancient clerk, as in exultation at the sharpness of Jonas. For the same reason that young man's coarse allusions, even to himself, filled him with a stealthy glee: causing him to rub his hands and chuckle covertly, as if he said in his sleeve, '*I* taught him. *I* trained him. This is the heir of my bringing-up. Sly, cunning, and covetous, he'll not squander my money. I worked for this; I hoped for this; it has been the great end and aim of my life.'

What a noble end and aim it was to contemplate in the attainment, truly! But there be some who manufacture idols after the fashion of themselves, and fail to worship them when they are made; charging their deformity on outraged nature. Anthony was better than these at any rate.

Chuffey boggled over his plate so long, that Mr. Jonas, losing patience, took it from him at last with his own hands, and requested his father to signify to that venerable person that he had better 'peg away at his bread:' which Anthony did.

'Aye, aye!' cried the old man, brightening up as before, when this was communicated to him in the same voice; 'quite right, quite right. He's your own son, Mr. Chuzzlewit! Bless him for a sharp lad! Bless him, bless him!'

Mr. Jonas considered this so particularly childish (perhaps with some reason), that he only laughed the more, and told his cousins that he was afraid one of these fine days, Chuffey would be the death of him. The cloth was then removed, and the bottle of wine set upon the table, from which Mr. Jonas filled the young ladies' glasses, calling on them not to spare it, as they might be certain there was plenty more where that came from. But he added with some haste after this sally that it was only his joke, and they wouldn't suppose him to be in earnest, he was sure.

'I shall drink,' said Anthony, 'to Pecksniff. Your father, my dears. A clever man, Pecksniff. A wary man! A hypocrite, though, eh? A hypocrite, girls, eh? Ha, ha, ha! Well, so he is. Now, among friends, he is. I don't think the worse of him for that, unless it is that he overdoes it. You may overdo anything, my darlings. You may overdo even hypocrisy. Ask Jonas!'

'You can't overdo taking care of yourself,' observed that hopeful gentleman with his mouth full.

'Do you hear that, my dears?' cried Anthony, quite enraptured. 'Wisdom, wisdom! A good exception, Jonas. No. It's not easy to overdo that.'

'Except,' whispered Mr. Jonas to his favourite cousin, 'except when one lives too long. Ha, ha! Tell the other one that. I say!'

'Good gracious me!' said Cherry, in a petulant manner. 'You can tell her yourself, if you wish, can't you?'

'She seems to make such game of one,' replied Mr. Jonas.

'Then why need you trouble yourself about her?' said Charity. 'I am sure she doesn't trouble herself much about you.'

'Don't she though?' asked Jonas.

'Good gracious me, need I tell you that she don't?' returned the young lady.

Mr. Jonas made no verbal rejoinder, but he glanced at Mercy with an odd expression in his face; and said *that* wouldn't break his heart, she might depend upon it. Then he looked on Charity with even greater favour than before, and besought her, as his polite manner was, to 'come a little closer.'

'There's another thing that's not easily overdone, father,' remarked Jonas, after a short silence.

'What's that?' asked the father; grinning already in anticipation.

'A bargain,' said the son. 'Here's the rule for bargains. "Do other men, for they would do you." That's the true business precept. All others are counterfeits.'

The delighted father applauded this sentiment to the echo; and was so much tickled by it, that he was at the pains of imparting the same to his ancient clerk, who rubbed his hands, nodded his palsied head, winked his watery eyes, and cried in his whistling tones, 'Good! good! Your own son, Mr. Chuzzlewit!' with every feeble demonstration of delight that he was capable of making. But this old man's enthusiasm had the redeeming quality of being felt in sympathy with the only creature to whom he was linked by ties of long association, and by his present helplessness. And if there had been anybody there, who cared to think about it, some dregs of a better nature unawakened, might perhaps have been descried through

H

that very medium, melancholy though it was, yet lingering at the bottom of the worn-out cask called Chuffey.

As matters stood, nobody thought or said anything upon the subject; so Chuffey fell back into a dark corner on one side of the fire-place, where he always spent his evenings, and was neither seen nor heard again that night; save once, when a cup of tea was given him, in which he was seen to soak his bread mechanically. There was no reason to suppose that he went to sleep at these seasons, or that he heard, or saw, or felt, or thought. He remained, as it were, frozen up—if any term expressive of such a vigorous process can be applied to him—until he was again thawed for the moment by a word or touch from Anthony.

Miss Charity made tea by desire of Mr. Jonas, and felt and looked so like the lady of the house that she was in the prettiest confusion imaginable; the more so from Mr. Jonas sitting close beside her, and whispering a variety of admiring expressions in her ear. Miss Mercy, for her part, felt the entertainment of the evening to be so distinctly and exclusively theirs, that she silently deplored the commercial gentleman—at that moment, no doubt, wearying for her return—and yawned over yesterday's newspaper. As to Anthony, he went to sleep outright, so Jonas and Cherry had a clear stage to themselves as long as they chose to keep possession of it.

When the tea-tray was taken away, as it was at last, Mr. Jonas produced a dirty pack of cards, and entertained the sisters with divers small feats of dexterity: whereof the main purpose of every one was, that you were to decoy somebody into laying a wager with you that you couldn't do it; and were then immediately to win and pocket his money. Mr. Jonas informed them that these accomplishments were in high vogue in the most intellectual circles, and that large amounts were constantly changing hands on such hazards. And it may be remarked that he fully believed this; for there is a simplicity of cunning no less than a simplicity of innocence; and in all matters where a lively faith in knavery and meanness was required as the ground-work of belief, Mr. Jonas was one of the most credulous of men. His ignorance, which was stupendous, may be taken into account, if the reader pleases, separately.

This fine young man had all the inclination to be a profligate of the first water, and only lacked the one good trait in the common catalogue of debauched vices—open-handedness—to be a notable vagabond. But there his griping and penurious habits stepped in; and as one poison will sometimes neutralise another, when wholesome remedies would not avail, so he was restrained by a bad passion from quaffing his full measure of evil, when virtue might have sought to hold him back in vain.

By the time he had unfolded all the peddling schemes he knew upon the cards, it was growing late in the evening; and Mr. Pecksniff not making his appearance, the young ladies expressed a wish to return home. But this, Mr. Jonas, in his gallantry, would by no means allow, until they had partaken of some bread and cheese and porter; and even then he was excessively unwilling to allow them to depart; often beseeching Miss Charity to come a little closer, or to stop a little longer, and preferring many other complimentary petitions of that nature in his own hospitable and earnest way. When all his efforts to detain them were fruitless, he put on his hat and great-coat preparatory to escorting them to Todgers's; remarking that he knew they would rather walk thither than ride; and that for his part he was quite of their opinion.

'Good night,' said Anthony. 'Good night; remember me to—ha, ha, ha!—to Pecksniff. Take care of your cousin, my dears; beware of Jonas; he's a dangerous fellow. Don't quarrel for him, in any case!'

'Oh, the creature!' cried Mercy. 'The idea of quarrelling for *him!* You may take him, Cherry, my love, all to yourself. I make you a present of my share.'

'What! I'm a sour grape, am I, cousin?' said Jonas.

Miss Charity was more entertained by this repartee than one would have supposed likely, considering its advanced age and simple character. But in her sisterly affection she took Mr. Jonas to task for leaning so very hard upon a broken reed, and said that he must not be so cruel to poor Merry any more, or she (Charity) would positively be obliged to hate him. Mercy, who really had her share of good humour, only retorted with a laugh; and they walked home in consequence without any angry passages of words upon the way. Mr. Jonas being in the middle, and having a cousin on each arm, sometimes squeezed the wrong one; so tightly too, as to cause her not a little inconvenience; but as he talked to Charity in whispers the whole time, and paid her great attention, no doubt this was an accidental circumstance. When they arrived at Todgers's, and the door was opened, Mercy broke hastily from them, and ran up-stairs; but Charity and Jonas lingered on the steps talking together for more than five minutes; so, as Mrs. Todgers observed next morning, to a third party, 'It was pretty clear what was going on *there*, and she was glad of it, for it really was high time Miss Pecksniff thought of settling.'

And now the day was coming on, when that bright vision which had burst on Todgers's so suddenly, and made a sun-shine in the shady breast of Jinkins, was to be seen no more; when it was to be packed, like a brown paper parcel, or a fish-basket, or an oyster-barrel, or a fat gentleman, or any other dull reality of life, in a stage-coach, and carried down into the country.

'Never, my dear Miss Pecksniffs,' said Mrs. Todgers, when they retired to rest on the last night of their stay; 'never have I seen an establishment so perfectly broken-hearted as mine is at this present moment of time. I don't believe the gentlemen will be the gentlemen they were, or anything like it—no, not for weeks to come. You have a great deal to answer for; both of you.'

They modestly disclaimed any wilful agency in this disas-trous state of things, and regretted it very much.

'Your pious pa, too,' said Mrs. Todgers. 'There's a loss! My dear Miss Pecksniffs, your pa is a perfect missionary of peace and love.'

Entertaining an uncertainty as to the particular kind of love supposed to be comprised in Mr. Pecksniff's mission, the young ladies received the compliment rather coldly.

'If I dared,' said Mrs. Todgers, perceiving this, 'to violate a confidence which has been reposed in me, and to tell you why I must beg of you to leave the little door between your room and mine open to-night, I think you would be interested. But I mustn't do it, for I promised Mr. Jinkins faithfully, that I would be as silent as the tomb.'

'Dear Mrs. Todgers! What can you mean?'

'Why then, my sweet Miss Pecksniffs,' said the lady of the house; 'my own loves, if you will allow me the privilege of taking that freedom on the eve of our separation, Mr. Jinkins and the gentlemen have made up a little musical party among themselves, and *do* intend, in the dead of this night, to perform a serenade upon the stairs outside the door. I could have wished, I own,' said Mrs. Todgers, with her usual foresight, 'that it had been fixed to take place an hour or two earlier;

because when gentlemen sit up late they drink, and when they drink they're not so musical, perhaps, as when they don't. But this is the arrangement; and I know you will be gratified, my dear Miss Pecksniffs, by such a mark of their attention.'

The young ladies were at first so much excited by the news, that they vowed they couldn't think of going to bed, until the serenade was over. But half an hour of cool waiting so altered their opinion that they not only went to bed, but fell asleep; and were, moreover, not ecstatically charmed to be awakened some time afterwards by certain dulcet strains breaking in upon the silent watches of the night.

It was very affecting, very. Nothing more dismal could have been desired by the most fastidious taste. The gentleman of a vocal turn was head mute, or chief mourner; Jinkins took the bass; and the rest took anything they could get. The youngest gentleman blew his melancholy into a flute. He didn't blow much out of it, but that was all the better. If the two Miss Pecksniffs and Mrs. Todgers had perished by spontaneous combustion, and the serenade had been in honour of their ashes, it would have been impossible to surpass the unutterable despair expressed in that one chorus, 'Go where glory waits thee!' It was a requiem, a dirge, a moan, a howl, a wail, a lament, an abstract of everything that is sorrowful and hideous in sound. The flute of the youngest gentleman was wild and fitful. It came and went in gusts, like the wind. For a long time together he seemed to have left off, and when it was quite settled by Mrs. Todgers and the young ladies that, overcome by his feelings, he had retired in tears, he unexpectedly turned up again at the very top of the tune, gasping for breath. He was a tremendous performer. There was no knowing where to have him; and exactly when you thought he was doing nothing at all, then was he doing the very thing that ought to astonish you most.

There were several of these concerted pieces; perhaps two or three too many, though that, as Mrs. Todgers said, was a fault on the right side. But even then, even at that solemn moment, when the thrilling sounds may be presumed to have penetrated into the very depths of his nature, if he had any depths, Jinkins couldn't leave the youngest gentleman alone. He asked him distinctly, before the second song began—as a personal favour too, mark the villain in that—not to play. Yes; he said so; not to play. The breathing of the youngest gentleman was heard through the key-hole of the door. He *didn't* play. What vent was a flute for the passions swelling up within his breast? A trombone would have been a world too mild.

The serenade approached its close. Its crowning interest was at hand. The gentleman of a literary turn had written a song on the departure of the ladies, and adapted it to an old tune. They all joined, except the youngest gentleman in company, who, for the reasons aforesaid, maintained a fearful silence. The song (which was of a classical nature) invoked the oracle of Apollo, and demanded to know what would become of Todgers's when CHARITY and MERCY were banished from its walls. The oracle delivered no opinion particularly worth remembering, according to the not infrequent practice of oracles from the earliest ages down to the present time. In the absence of enlightenment on that subject, the strain deserted it, and went on to show that the Miss Pecksniffs were nearly related to Rule Britannia, and that if Great Britain hadn't been an island, there could have been no Miss Pecksniffs. And being now on a nautical tack, it closed with this verse:

'All hail to the vessel of Pecksniff the sire!
    And favouring breezes to fan;
While Tritons flock round it, and proudly admire
    The architect, artist, and man!'

As they presented this beautiful picture to the imagination, the gentlemen gradually withdrew to bed to give the music the effect of distance; and so it died away, and Todgers's was left to its repose.

Mr. Bailey reserved his vocal offering until the morning, when he put his head into the room as the young ladies were kneeling before their trunks, packing up, and treated them to an imitation of the voice of a young dog in trying circumstances: when that animal is supposed by persons of a lively fancy, to relieve his feelings by calling for pen and ink.

'Well, young ladies,' said the youth, 'so you're a-going home, are you, worse luck?'

'Yes, Bailey, we're going home,' returned Mercy.

'An't you a-going to leave none of 'em a lock of your hair?' inquired the youth. 'It's real, an't it?'

They laughed at this, and told him of course it was.

'Oh is it of course though?' said Bailey. 'I know better than that. Hers an't. Why, I see it hanging up once, on that nail by the winder. Besides I have gone behind her at dinner-time and

pulled it; and she never know'd. I say, young ladies, I'm
a-going to leave. I an't a-going to stand being called names by
her no longer.'

Miss Mercy inquired what his plans for the future might be;
in reply to whom, Mr. Bailey intimated that he thought of
going, either into top-boots, or into the army.

'Into the army!' cried the young ladies, with a laugh.

'Ah!' said Bailey, 'why not? There's a many drummers in
the Tower. I'm acquainted with 'em. Don't their country set
a valley on 'em, mind you! Not at all!'

'You'll be shot, I see,' observed Mercy.

'Well!' cried Mr. Bailey, 'wot if I am? There's something
gamey in it, young ladies, an't there? I'd sooner be hit with a
cannon-ball than a rolling-pin, and she's always a-catching
up something of that sort, and throwing it at me, wen the
gentlemans' appetites is good. Wot,' said Mr. Bailey, stung by
the recollection of his wrongs, 'wot, if they *do* consume the per-
vishuns. It an't *my* fault, is it?'

'Surely no one says it is,' said Mercy.

'Don't they though?' retorted the youth. 'No. Yes. Ah! Oh!
No one mayn't say it is! but some one knows it is. But I an't
a-going to have every rise in prices wisited on me. I an't a-going
to be killed because the markets is dear. I won't stop. And
therefore,' added Mr. Bailey, relenting into a smile, 'wotever
you mean to give me, you'd better give me all at once, becos
if ever you come back agin, I shan't be here; and as to the
other boy, *he* won't deserve nothing, *I* know.'

The young ladies, on behalf of Mr. Pecksniff and themselves,
acted on this thoughtful advice; and in consideration of their
private friendship, presented Mr. Bailey with a gratuity so
liberal that he could hardly do enough to show his gratitude;
which found but an imperfect vent, during the remainder of
the day, in divers secret slaps upon his pocket, and other such
facetious pantomime. Nor was it confined to these ebullitions;
for besides crushing a bandbox, with a bonnet in it, he seriously
damaged Mr. Pecksniff's luggage, by ardently hauling it down
from the top of the house; and in short evinced, by every means
in his power, a lively sense of the favours he had received from
that gentleman and his family.

Mr. Pecksniff and Mr. Jinkins came home to dinner arm-
in-arm; for the latter gentleman had made half-holiday on
purpose; thus gaining an immense advantage over the youngest

gentleman and the rest, whose time, as it perversely chanced, was all bespoke, until the evening. The bottle of wine was Mr. Pecksniff's treat, and they were very sociable indeed; though full of lamentations on the necessity of parting. While they were in the midst of their enjoyment, old Anthony and his son were announced; much to the surprise of Mr. Pecksniff, and greatly to the discomfiture of Jinkins.

'Come to say good-bye, you see,' said Anthony, in a low voice, to Mr. Pecksniff, as they took their seats apart at the table, while the rest conversed among themselves. 'Where's the use of a division between you and me? We are the two halves of a pair of scissors, when apart, Pecksniff; but together we are something. Eh?'

'Unanimity, my good sir,' rejoined Mr. Pecksniff, 'is always delightful.'

'I don't know about that,' said the old man, 'for there are some people I would rather differ from than agree with. But you know my opinion of you.'

Mr. Pecksniff, still having 'Hypocrite' in his mind, only replied by a motion of his head, which was something between an affirmative bow, and a negative shake.

'Complimentary,' said Anthony. 'Complimentary, upon my word. It was an involuntary tribute to your abilities, even at the time; and it was not a time to suggest compliments either. But we agreed in the coach, you know, that we quite understood each other.'

'Oh, quite!' assented Mr. Pecksniff, in a manner which implied that he himself was misunderstood most cruelly, but would not complain.

Anthony glanced at his son as he sat beside Miss Charity, and then at Mr. Pecksniff, and then at his son again, very many times. It happened that Mr. Pecksniff's glances took a similar direction; but when he became aware of it, he first cast down his eyes, and then closed them; as if he were determined that the old man should read nothing there.

'Jonas is a shrewd lad,' said the old man.

'He appears,' rejoined Mr. Pecksniff in his most candid manner, 'to be very shrewd.'

'And careful,' said the old man.

'And careful, I have no doubt,' returned Mr. Pecksniff.

'Lookye!' said Anthony in his ear. 'I think he is sweet upon your daughter.'

'Tut, my good sir,' said Mr. Pecksniff, with his eyes still closed; 'young people, young people. A kind of cousins, too. No more sweetness than is in that, sir.'

'Why, there is very little sweetness in that, according to our experience,' returned Anthony. 'Isn't there a trifle more here?'

'Impossible to say,' rejoined Mr. Pecksniff. 'Quite impossible! You surprise me.'

'Yes, I know that,' said the old man, drily. 'It may last; I mean the sweetness, not the surprise; and it may die off. Supposing it should last, perhaps (you having feathered your nest pretty well, and I having done the same) we might have a mutual interest in the matter.'

Mr. Pecksniff, smiling gently, was about to speak, but Anthony stopped him.

'I know what you are going to say. It's quite unnecessary. You have never thought of this for a moment; and in a point so nearly affecting the happiness of your dear child, you couldn't, as a tender father, express an opinion; and so forth. Yes, quite right. And like you! But it seems to me, my dear Pecksniff,' added Anthony, laying his hand upon his sleeve, 'that if you and I kept up the joke of pretending not to see this, one of us might possibly be placed in a position of disadvantage; and as I am very unwilling to be that party myself, you will excuse my taking the liberty of putting the matter beyond a doubt thus early; and having it distinctly understood, as it is now, that we do see it, and do know it. Thank you for your attention. We are now upon an equal footing: which is agreeable to us both, I am sure.'

He rose as he spoke; and giving Mr. Pecksniff a nod of intelligence, moved away from him to where the young people were sitting: leaving that good man somewhat puzzled and discomfited by such very plain dealing, and not quite free from a sense of having been foiled in the exercise of his familiar weapons.

But the night-coach had a punctual character, and it was time to join it at the office; which was so near at hand that they had already sent their luggage and arranged to walk. Thither the whole party repaired, therefore, after no more delay than sufficed for the equipment of the Miss Pecksniffs and Mrs. Todgers. They found the coach already at its starting-place, and the horses in; there, too, were a large majority of the commercial gentlemen, including the youngest, who was visibly agitated, and in a state of deep mental dejection.

Nothing could equal the distress of Mrs. Todgers in parting from the young ladies, except the strong emotions with which she bade adieu to Mr. Pecksniff. Never surely was a pocket-handkerchief taken in and out of a flat reticule so often as Mrs. Todgers's was, as she stood upon the pavement by the coach-door, supported on either side by a commercial gentleman: and by the light of the coach-lamps caught such brief snatches and glimpses of the good man's face, as the constant interposition of Mr. Jinkins allowed. For Jinkins, to the last the youngest gentleman's rock ahead in life, stood upon the coach-step talking to the ladies. Upon the other step was Mr. Jonas, who maintained that position in right of his cousinship; where-as the youngest gentleman, who had been first upon the ground, was deep in the booking-office among the black and red placards, and the portraits of fast coaches, where he was ignominiously harassed by porters, and had to contend and strive perpetually with heavy baggage. This false position, combined with his nervous excitement, brought about the very consummation and catastrophe of his miseries; for when in the moment of parting he aimed a flower, a hot-house flower that had cost money, at the fair hand of Mercy, it reached, instead, the coachman on the box, who thanked him kindly, and stuck it in his button-hole.

They were off now; and Todgers's was alone again. The two young ladies, leaning back in their separate corners, resigned themselves to their own regretful thoughts. But Mr. Pecksniff, dismissing all ephemeral considerations of social pleasure and enjoyment, concentrated his meditations on the one great virtuous purpose before him, of casting out that ingrate and deceiver, whose presence yet troubled his domestic hearth, and was a sacrilege upon the altars of his household gods.

CHAPTER XII

Will be seen in the long run, if not in the short one, to concern Mr. Pinch and others, nearly. Mr. Pecksniff asserts the dignity of outraged virtue. Young Martin Chuzzlewit forms a desperate resolution

MR. PINCH and Martin, little dreaming of the stormy weather that impended, made themselves very comfortable in the Pecksniffian halls, and improved their friendship daily. Martin's facility, both of invention and execution, being remarkable, the grammar-school proceeded with great vigour; and Tom repeatedly declared, that if there were anything like certainty in human affairs, or impartiality in human judges, a design so new and full of merit could not fail to carry off the first prize when the time of competition arrived. Without being quite so sanguine himself, Martin had his hopeful anticipations too; and they served to make him brisk and eager at his task.

'If I should turn out a great architect, Tom,' said the new pupil one day, as he stood at a little distance from his drawing, and eyed it with much complacency, 'I'll tell you what should be one of the things I'd build.'

'Aye!' cried Tom. 'What?'

'Why, your fortune.'

'No!' said Tom Pinch, quite as much delighted as if the thing were done. 'Would you though? How kind of you to say so.'

'I'd build it up, Tom,' returned Martin, 'on such a strong foundation, that it should last your life—aye, and your children's lives too, and their children's after them. I'd be your patron, Tom. I'd take you under my protection. Let me see the man who should give the cold shoulder to anybody I chose to protect and patronise, if I were at the top of the tree, Tom!'

'Now, I don't think,' said Mr. Pinch, 'upon my word, that I was ever more gratified than by this. I really don't.'

'Oh! I mean what I say,' retorted Martin, with a manner as free and easy in its condescension to, not to say in its compassion for, the other, as if he were already First Architect in

Ordinary to all the Crowned Heads in Europe. 'I'd do it. I'd provide for you.'

'I am afraid,' said Tom, shaking his head, 'that I should be a mighty awkward person to provide for.'

'Pooh, pooh!' rejoined Martin. 'Never mind that. If I took it in my head to say, "Pinch is a clever fellow; I approve of Pinch;" I should like to know the man who would venture to put himself in opposition to me. Besides, confound it, Tom, you could be useful to me in a hundred ways.'

'If I were not useful in one or two, it shouldn't be for want of trying,' said Tom.

'For instance,' pursued Martin, after a short reflection, 'you'd be a capital fellow, now, to see that my ideas were properly carried out; and to overlook the works in their progress before they were sufficiently advanced to be very interesting to *me;* and to take all that sort of plain sailing. Then you'd be a splendid fellow to show people over my studio, and to talk about Art to 'em, when I couldn't be bored myself, and all that kind of thing. For it would be devilish creditable, Tom (I'm quite in earnest, I give you my word), to have a man of your information about one, instead of some ordinary blockhead. Oh, I'd take care of you. You'd be useful, rely upon it!'

To say that Tom had no idea of playing first fiddle in any social orchestra, but was always quite satisfied to be set down for the hundred and fiftieth violin in the band, or thereabouts, is to express his modesty in very inadequate terms. He was much delighted, therefore, by these observations.

'I should be married to her then, Tom, of course,' said Martin.

What was that which checked Tom Pinch so suddenly, in the high flow of his gladness: bringing the blood into his honest cheeks, and a remorseful feeling to his honest heart, as if he were unworthy of his friend's regard?

'I should be married to her then,' said Martin, looking with a smile towards the light: 'and we should have, I hope, children about us. They'd be very fond of you, Tom.'

But not a word said Mr. Pinch. The words he would have uttered, died upon his lips, and found a life more spiritual in self-denying thoughts.

'All the children hereabouts are fond of you, Tom, and mine would be, of course,' pursued Martin. 'Perhaps I might name one of 'em after you. Tom, eh? Well, I don't know.

Mr. Jonas Chuzzlewit entertains his Cousins
(*p. 182*)

Tom's not a bad name. Thomas Pinch Chuzzlewit. T. P. C. on his pinafores. No objection to that, I should say?'

Tom cleared his throat, and smiled.

'*She* would like you, Tom, I know,' said Martin.

'Aye!' cried Tom Pinch, faintly.

'I can tell exactly what she would think of you,' said Martin, leaning his chin upon his hand, and looking through the window-glass as if he read there what he said; 'I know her so well. She would smile, Tom, often at first when you spoke to her, or when she looked at you—merrily too—but you wouldn't mind that. A brighter smile you never saw.'

'No, no,' said Tom. 'I wouldn't mind that.'

'She would be as tender with you, Tom,' said Martin, 'as if you were a child yourself. So you are almost, in some things, an't you, Tom?'

Mr. Pinch nodded his entire assent.

'She would always be kind and good-humoured, and glad to see you,' said Martin; 'and when she found out exactly what sort of fellow you were (which she'd do very soon), she would pretend to give you little commissions to execute, and to ask little services of you, which she knew you were burning to render; so that when she really pleased you most, she would try to make you think you most pleased her. She would take to you uncommonly, Tom; and would understand you far more delicately than I ever shall; and would often say, I know, that you were a harmless, gentle, well-intentioned, good fellow.'

How silent Tom Pinch was!

'In honour of old times,' said Martin, 'and of her having heard you play the organ in this damp little church down here—for nothing too—we will have one in the house. I shall build an architectural music-room on a plan of my own, and it'll look rather knowing in a recess at one end. There you shall play away, Tom, till you tire yourself; and, as you like to do so in the dark, it shall *be* dark; and many's the summer evening she and I will sit and listen to you, Tom; be sure of that!'

It may have required a stronger effort on Tom Pinch's part to leave the seat on which he sat, and shake his friend by both hands, with nothing but serenity and grateful feeling painted on his face; it may have required a stronger effort to perform this simple act with a pure heart, than to achieve many and many a deed to which the doubtful trumpet blown by Fame has lustily resounded. Doubtful, because from its long hovering over scenes of violence, the smoke and steam of death have clogged the keys of that brave instrument; and it is not always that its notes are either true or tuneful.

'It's a proof of the kindness of human nature,' said Tom, characteristically putting himself quite out of sight in the matter, 'that everybody who comes here, as you have done, is more considerate and affectionate to me than I should have any right to hope, if I were the most sanguine creature in the world; or should have any power to express, if I were the most eloquent. It really overpowers me. But trust me,' said Tom, 'that I am not ungrateful; that I never forget; and that, if I can ever prove the truth of my words to you, I will.'

'That's all right,' observed Martin, leaning back in his chair with a hand in each pocket, and yawning drearily. 'Very fine talking, Tom; but I'm at Pecksniff's, I remember, and perhaps a mile or so out of the high-road to fortune just at this minute. So you've heard again this morning from what's his name, eh?'

'Who may that be?' asked Tom, seeming to enter a mild protest on behalf of the dignity of an absent person.

'*You* know. What is it? Northkey.'

'Westlock,' rejoined Tom, in rather a louder tone than usual.

'Ah! to be sure,' said Martin, 'Westlock. I knew it was something connected with a point of the compass and a door. Well! and what says Westlock?'

'Oh! he has come into his property,' answered Tom, nodding his head, and smiling.

'He's a lucky dog,' said Martin. 'I wish it were mine instead. Is that all the mystery you were to tell me?'

'No,' said Tom: 'not all.'

'What's the rest?' asked Martin.

'For the matter of that,' said Tom, 'it's no mystery, and you won't think much of it; but it's very pleasant to me. John always used to say when he was here, "Mark my words, Pinch. When my father's executors cash up"—he used strange expressions now and then, but that was his way.'

'Cash-up's a very good expression,' observed Martin, 'when other people don't apply it to you. Well? What a slow fellow you are, Pinch!'

'Yes, I am I know,' said Tom; 'but you'll make me nervous

if you tell me so. I'm afraid you have put me out a little now, for I forget what I was going to say.'

'When John's father's executors cashed up,' said Martin impatiently.

'Oh yes, to be sure,' cried Tom; 'yes. "Then," says John, "I'll give you a dinner, Pinch, and come down to Salisbury on purpose." Now, when John wrote the other day—the morning Pecksniff left, you know—he said his business was on the point of being immediately settled, and as he was to receive his money directly, when could I meet him at Salisbury? I wrote and said, any day this week; and I told him besides, that there was a new pupil here, and what a fine fellow you were, and what friends we had become. Upon which John writes back this letter'—Tom produced it—'fixes to-morrow; sends his compliments to you; and begs that we three may have the pleasure of dining together; not at the house where you and I were, either; but at the very first hotel in the town. Read what he says.'

'Very well,' said Martin, glancing over it with his customary coolness: 'much obliged to him. I'm agreeable.'

Tom could have wished him to be a little more astonished, a little more pleased, or in some form or other a little more interested in such a great event. But he was perfectly self-possessed: and falling into his favourite solace of whistling, took another turn at the grammar-school, as if nothing at all had happened.

Mr. Pecksniff's horse being regarded in the light of a sacred animal, only to be driven by him, the chief priest of that temple, or by some person distinctly nominated for the time being to that high office by himself, the two young men agreed to walk to Salisbury; and so, when the time came, they set off on foot; which was, after all, a better mode of travelling than in the gig, as the weather was very cold and very dry.

Better! A rare strong, hearty, healthy walk—four statute miles an hour—preferable to that rumbling, tumbling, jolting, shaking, scraping, creaking, villanous old gig? Why, the two things will not admit of comparison. It is an insult to the walk, to set them side by side. Where is an instance of a gig having ever circulated a man's blood, unless when, putting him in danger of his neck, it awakened in his veins and in his ears, and all along his spine, a tingling heat, much more peculiar than agreeable? When did a gig ever sharpen anybody's wits

and energies, unless it was when the horse bolted, and, crashing madly down a steep hill with a stone wall at the bottom,
his desperate circumstances suggested to the only gentleman
left inside, some novel and unheard-of mode of dropping out
behind? Better than the gig!

The air was cold, Tom; so it was, there was no denying it;
but would it have been more genial in the gig? The black-
smith's fire burned very bright, and leaped up high, as though
it wanted men to warm; but would it have been less tempting,
looked at from the clammy cushions of a gig? The wind blew
keenly, nipping the features of the hardy wight who fought his
way along; blinding him with his own hair if he had enough
of it, and wintry dust if he hadn't; stopping his breath as though
he had been soused in a cold bath; tearing aside his wrappings-
up, and whistling in the very marrow of his bones; but it
would have done all this a hundred times more fiercely to a
man in a gig, wouldn't it? A fig for gigs!

Better than the gig! When were travellers by wheels and
hoofs seen with such red-hot cheeks as those? when were they
so good-humouredly and merrily bloused? when did their
laughter ring upon the air, as they turned them round, what
time the stronger gusts came sweeping up; and, facing round
again as they passed by, dashed on, in such a glow of ruddy
health as nothing could keep pace with, but the high spirits it
engendered? Better than the gig! Why, here *is* a man in a gig
coming the same way now. Look at him as he passes his whip
into his left hand, chafes his numbed right fingers on his granite
leg, and beats those marble toes of his upon the foot-board.
Ha, ha, ha! Who would exchange this rapid hurry of the blood
for yonder stagnant misery, though its pace were twenty miles
for one?

Better than the gig! No man in a gig could have such interest
in the milestones. No man in a gig could see, or feel, or think,
like merry users of their legs. How, as the wind sweeps on, upon
these breezy downs, it tracks its flight in darkening ripples on
the grass, and smoothest shadows on the hills! Look round and
round upon this bare bleak plain, and see even here, upon a
winter's day, how beautiful the shadows are! Alas! it is the
nature of their kind to be so. The loveliest things in life, Tom,
are but shadows; and they come and go, and change and fade
away, as rapidly as these!

Another mile, and then begins a fall of snow, making the

crow, who skims away so close above the ground to shirk the wind, a blot of ink upon the landscape. But though it drives and drifts against them as they walk, stiffening on their skirts, and freezing in the lashes of their eyes, they wouldn't have it fall more sparingly, no, not so much as by a single flake, although they had to go a score of miles. And, lo! the towers of the Old Cathedral rise before them, even now! and by-and-bye they come into the sheltered streets, made strangely silent by their white carpet; and so to the Inn for which they are bound; where they present such flushed and burning faces to the cold waiter, and are so brimful of vigour, that he almost feels assaulted by their presence; and, having nothing to oppose to the attack (being fresh, or rather stale, from the blazing fire in the coffee-room), is quite put out of his pale countenance.

A famous Inn! the hall a very grove of dead game, and dangling joints of mutton; and in one corner an illustrious larder, with glass doors, developing cold fowls and noble joints, and tarts wherein the raspberry jam coyly withdrew itself, as such a precious creature should, behind a lattice work of pastry. And behold, on the first floor, at the court-end of the house, in a room with all the window-curtains drawn, a fire piled half-way up the chimney, plates warming before it, wax candles gleaming everywhere, and a table spread for three, with silver and glass enough for thirty—John Westlock! Not the old John of Pecksniff's, but a proper gentleman: looking another and a grander person, with the consciousness of being his own master and having money in the bank: and yet in some respects the old John too, for he seized Tom Pinch by both his hands the instant he appeared, and fairly hugged him, in his cordial welcome.

'And this,' said John, 'is Mr. Chuzzlewit. I am very glad to see him!' John had an off-hand manner of his own; so they shook hands warmly, and were friends in no time.

'Stand off a moment, Tom,' cried the old pupil, laying one hand on each of Mr. Pinch's shoulders, and holding him out at arm's length. 'Let me look at you! Just the same! Not a bit changed!'

'Why, it's not so very long ago, you know,' said Tom Pinch, 'after all.'

'It seems an age to me,' cried John; 'and so it ought to seem to you, you dog.' And then he pushed Tom down into the easiest chair, and clapped him on the back so heartily, and so like his old self in their old bedroom at old Pecksniff's that it was a toss-up with Tom Pinch whether he should laugh or cry. Laughter won it; and they all three laughed together.

'I have ordered everything for dinner, that we used to say we'd have, Tom,' observed John Westlock.

'No!' said Tom Pinch. 'Have you?'

'Everything. Don't laugh, if you can help it, before the waiters. *I* couldn't when I was ordering it. It's like a dream.'

John was wrong there, because nobody ever dreamed such soup as was put upon the table directly afterwards; or such fish; or such side-dishes; or such a top and bottom; or such a course of birds and sweets; or in short anything approaching the reality of that entertainment at ten-and-sixpence a head, exclusive of wines. As to *them*, the man who can dream such iced champagne, such claret, port, or sherry, had better go to bed and stop there.

But perhaps the finest feature of the banquet was, that nobody was half so much amazed by everything as John himself, who in his high delight was constantly bursting into fits of laughter, and then endeavouring to appear preternaturally solemn, lest the waiters should conceive he wasn't used to it. Some of the things they brought him to carve, were such outrageous practical jokes, though, that it was impossible to stand it; and when Tom Pinch insisted, in spite of the deferential advice of an attendant, not only on breaking down the outer wall of a raised pie with a tablespoon, but on trying to eat it afterwards, John lost all dignity, and sat behind the gorgeous dish-cover at the head of the table, roaring to that extent that he was audible in the kitchen. Nor had he the least objection to laugh at himself, as he demonstrated when they had all three gathered round the fire, and the dessert was on the table; at which period the head waiter inquired with respectful solicitude whether that port, being a light and tawny wine, was suited to his taste, or whether he would wish to try a fruity port with greater body. To this John gravely answered that he was well satisfied with what he had, which he esteemed, as one might say, a pretty tidy vintage: for which the waiter thanked him and withdrew. And then John told his friends, with a broad grin, that he supposed it was all right, but he didn't know; and went off into a perfect shout.

They were very merry and full of enjoyment the whole time,

but not the least pleasant part of the festival was when they all three sat about the fire, cracking nuts, drinking wine and talking cheerfully. It happened that Tom Pinch had a word to say to his friend the organist's assistant, and so deserted his warm corner for a few minutes at this season, lest it should grow too late; leaving the other two young men together.

They drank his health in his absence, of course; and John Westlock took that opportunity of saying, that he had never had even a peevish word with Tom during the whole term of their residence in Mr. Pecksniff's house. This naturally led him to dwell upon Tom's character, and to hint that Mr. Pecksniff understood it pretty well. He only hinted this, and very distantly: knowing that it pained Tom Pinch to have that gentleman disparaged, and thinking it would be as well to leave the new pupil to his own discoveries.

'Yes,' said Martin. 'It's impossible to like Pinch better than I do, or to do greater justice to his good qualities. He is the most willing fellow I ever saw.'

'He's rather too willing,' observed John, who was quick in observation. 'It's quite a fault in him.'

'So it is,' said Martin. 'Very true. There was a fellow only a week or so ago—a Mr. Tigg—who borrowed all the money he had, on a promise to repay it in a few days. It was but half a sovereign, to be sure; but it's well it was no more, for he'll never see it again.'

'Poor fellow!' said John, who had been very attentive to these few words. 'Perhaps you have not had an opportunity of observing that, in his own pecuniary transactions, Tom's proud.'

'You don't say so! No, I haven't. What do you mean? Won't he borrow?'

John Westlock shook his head.

'That's very odd,' said Martin, setting down his empty glass. 'He's a strange compound, to be sure.'

'As to receiving money as a gift,' resumed John Westlock; 'I think he'd die first.'

'He's made up of simplicity,' said Martin. 'Help yourself.'

'You, however,' pursued John, filling his own glass, and looking at his companion with some curiosity, 'who are older than the majority of Mr. Pecksniff's assistants, and have evidently had much more experience, understand him, I have no doubt, and see how liable he is to be imposed upon.'

'Certainly,' said Martin, stretching out his legs, and holding his wine between his eye and the light. 'Mr. Pecksniff knows that too. So do his daughters. Eh?'

John Westlock smiled, but made no answer.

'By-the-bye,' said Martin, 'that reminds me. What's your opinion of Pecksniff? How did he use you? What do you think of him now? Coolly, you know, when it's all over?'

'Ask Pinch,' returned the old pupil. 'He knows what my sentiments used to be upon the subject. They are not changed, I assure you.'

'No, no,' said Martin, 'I'd rather have them from you.'

'But Pinch says they are unjust,' urged John with a smile.

'Oh! well! Then I know what course they take beforehand,' said Martin; 'and, therefore, you can have no delicacy in speaking plainly. Don't mind me, I beg. I don't like him, I tell you frankly. I am with him because it happens from particular circumstances to suit my convenience. I have some ability, I believe, in that way; and the obligation, if any, will most likely be on his side and not mine. At the lowest mark, the balance will be even, and there'll be no obligation at all. So you may talk to *me*, as if I had no connexion with him.'

'If you press me to give my opinion—' returned John Westlock.

'Yes, I do,' said Martin. 'You'll oblige me.'

'—I should say,' resumed the other, 'that he is the most consummate scoundrel on the face of the earth.'

'Oh!' said Martin, as coolly as ever. 'That's rather strong.'

'Not stronger than he deserves,' said John; 'and if he called upon me to express my opinion of him to his face, I would do so in the very same terms, without the least qualification. His treatment of Pinch is in itself enough to justify them; but when I look back upon the five years I passed in that house, and remember the hypocrisy, the knavery, the meannesses, the false pretences, the lip service of that fellow, and his trading in saintly semblances for the very worst realities; when I remember how often I was the witness of all this, and how often I was made a kind of party to it, by the fact of being there, with him for my teacher; I swear to you that I almost despise myself.'

Martin drained his glass, and looked at the fire.

'I don't mean to say, that is a right feeling,' pursued John Westlock, 'because it was no fault of mine; and I can quite understand—you, for instance, fully appreciating him, and yet being simply forced by circumstances to remain there. I tell you simply what my feeling is; and even now, when, as you say, it's all over; and when I have the satisfaction of knowing that he always hated me, and we always quarrelled, and I always told him my mind; even now, I feel sorry that I didn't yield to an impulse I often had, as a boy, of running away from him and going abroad.'

'Why abroad?' asked Martin, turning his eyes upon the speaker.

'In search,' replied John Westlock, shrugging his shoulders, 'of the livelihood I couldn't have earned at home. There would have been something spirited in that. But, come! Fill your glass, and let us forget him.'

'As soon as you please,' said Martin. 'In reference to myself and my connexion with him, I have only to repeat what I said before. I have taken my own way with him so far, and shall continue to do so, even more than ever; for the fact is, to tell you the truth, that I believe he looks to me to supply his defects, and couldn't afford to lose me. I had a notion of that in first going there. Your health!'

'Thank you,' returned young Westlock. 'Yours. And may the new pupil turn out as well as you can desire!'

'What new pupil?'

'The fortunate youth, born under an auspicious star,' returned John Westlock, laughing; 'whose parents, or guardians, are destined to be hooked by the advertisement. What! Don't you know that he has advertised again?'

'No.'

'Oh, yes. I read it just before dinner in the old newspaper. I know it to be his; having some reason to remember the style. Hush! Here's Pinch. Strange, is it not, that the more he likes Pecksniff (if he can like him better than he does), the greater reason one has to like *him?* Not a word more, or we shall spoil his whole enjoyment.'

Tom entered as the words were spoken, with a radiant smile upon his face; and rubbing his hands, more from a sense of delight than because he was cold (for he had been running fast), sat down in his warm corner again, and was as happy as only Tom Pinch could be. There is no other simile that will express his state of mind.

'And so,' he said, when he had gazed at his friend for some

time in silent pleasure, 'so you really are a gentleman at last, John. Well, to be sure!'

'Trying to be, Tom; trying to be,' he rejoined good-humouredly. 'There is no saying what I may turn out, in time.'

'I suppose you wouldn't carry your own box to the mail now?' said Tom Pinch, smiling; 'although you lost it altogether by not taking it.'

'Wouldn't I?' retorted John. 'That's all you know about it, Pinch. It must be a very heavy box that I wouldn't carry to get away from Pecksniff's, Tom.'

'There!' cried Pinch, turning to Martin, 'I told you so. The great fault in his character is his injustice to Pecksniff. You mustn't mind a word he says on that subject. His prejudice is most extraordinary.'

'The absence of anything like prejudice on Tom's part, you know,' said John Westlock, laughing heartily, as he laid his hand on Mr. Pinch's shoulder, 'is perfectly wonderful. If one man ever had a profound knowledge of another, and saw him in a true light, and in his own proper colours, Tom has that knowledge of Mr. Pecksniff.'

'Why, of course I have,' cried Tom. 'That's exactly what I have so often said to you. If you knew him as well as I do—John, I'd give almost any money to bring that about—you'd admire, respect, and reverence him. You couldn't help it. Oh, how you wounded his feelings when you went away!'

'If I had known whereabout his feelings lay,' retorted young Westlock, 'I'd have done my best, Tom, with that end in view, you may depend upon it. But as I couldn't wound him in what he has not, and in what he knows nothing of, except in his ability to probe them to the quick in other people, I am afraid I can lay no claim to your compliment.'

Mr. Pinch, being unwilling to protract a discussion which might possibly corrupt Martin, forbore to say anything in reply to this speech; but John Westlock, whom nothing short of an iron gag would have silenced when Mr. Pecksniff's merits were once in question, continued notwithstanding.

'*His* feelings! Oh, he's a tender-hearted man. *His* feelings! Oh, he's a considerate, conscientious, self-examining, moral vagabond, he is! *His* feelings! Oh!—what's the matter, Tom?'

Mr. Pinch was by this time erect upon the hearth-rug, buttoning his coat with great energy.

'I can't bear it,' said Tom, shaking his head. 'No. I really cannot. You must excuse me, John. I have a great esteem and friendship for you; I love you very much; and have been perfectly charmed and overjoyed to-day, to find you just the same as ever; but I cannot listen to this.'

'Why, it's my old way, Tom; and you say yourself that you are glad to find me unchanged.'

'Not in this respect,' said Tom Pinch. 'You must excuse me, John. I cannot, really; I will not. It's very wrong; you should be more guarded in your expressions. It was bad enough when you and I used to be alone together, but under existing circumstances, I can't endure it, really. No. I cannot, indeed.'

'You are quite right!' exclaimed the other, exchanging looks with Martin; 'and I am quite wrong, Tom. I don't know how the deuce we fell on this unlucky theme. I beg your pardon with all my heart.'

'You have a free and manly temper, I know,' said Pinch; 'and therefore, your being so ungenerous in this one solitary instance, only grieves me the more. It's not my pardon you have to ask, John. You have done *me* nothing but kindnesses.'

'Well! Pecksniff's pardon, then,' said young Westlock. 'Anything, Tom, or anybody. Pecksniff's pardon. Will that do? Here! let us drink Pecksniff's health!'

'Thank you,' cried Tom, shaking hands with him eagerly, and filling a bumper. 'Thank you; I'll drink it with all my heart, John. Mr. Pecksniff's health, and prosperity to him!'

John Westlock echoed the sentiment, or nearly so; for he drank Mr. Pecksniff's health, and something to him; but what, was not quite audible. The general unanimity being then completely restored, they drew their chairs closer round the fire, and conversed in perfect harmony and enjoyment until bed-time.

No slight circumstance, perhaps, could have better illustrated the difference of character between John Westlock and Martin Chuzzlewit, than the manner in which each of the young men contemplated Tom Pinch, after the little rupture just described. There was a certain amount of jocularity in the looks of both, no doubt, but there all resemblance ceased. The old pupil could not do enough to show Tom how cordially he felt towards him, and his friendly regard seemed of a graver and more thoughtful kind than before. The new one, on the other hand, had no impulse but to laugh at the recollection of Tom's extreme absurdity; and mingled with his amusement there was something slighting and contemptuous, indicative, as it appeared, of his opinion that Mr. Pinch was much too far gone in simplicity to be admitted as the friend, on serious and equal terms, of any rational man.

John Westlock, who did nothing by halves, if he could help it, had provided beds for his two guests in the hotel; and after a very happy evening, they retired. Mr. Pinch was sitting on the side of his bed with his cravat and shoes off, ruminating on the manifold good qualities of his old friend, when he was interrupted by a knock at his chamber door, and the voice of John himself.

'You're not asleep yet, are you, Tom?'

'Bless you, no! not I. I was thinking of you,' replied Tom, opening the door. 'Come in.'

'I am not going to detain you,' said John; 'but I have for-gotten all the evening a little commission I took upon myself; and I am afraid I may forget it again, if I fail to discharge it at once. You know a Mr. Tigg, Tom, I believe?'

'Tigg!' cried Tom. 'Tigg! The gentleman who borrowed some money of me?'

'Exactly,' said John Westlock. 'He begged me to present his compliments, and to return it with many thanks. Here it is. I suppose it's a good one, but he is rather a doubtful kind of customer, Tom.'

Mr. Pinch received the little piece of gold with a face whose brightness might have shamed the metal; and said he had no fear about that. He was glad, he added, to find Mr. Tigg so prompt and honourable in his dealings; very glad.

'Why, to tell you the truth, Tom,' replied his friend, 'he is not always so. If you'll take my advice, you'll avoid him as much as you can, in the event of your encountering him again. And by no means, Tom—pray bear this in mind, for I am very serious—by no means lend him money any more.'

'Aye, aye!' said Tom, with his eyes wide open.

'He is very far from being a reputable acquaintance,' re-turned young Westlock; 'and the more you let him know you think so, the better for you, Tom.'

'I say, John,' quoth Mr. Pinch, as his countenance fell, and he shook his head in a dejected manner. 'I hope you are not getting into bad company.'

'No, no,' he replied laughing. 'Don't be uneasy on that score.'

'Oh, but I *am* uneasy,' said Tom Pinch; 'I can't help it, when I hear you talking in that way. If Mr. Tigg is what you describe him to be, you have no business to know him, John. You may laugh, but I don't consider it by any means a laughing matter, I assure you.'

'No, no,' returned his friend, composing his features. 'Quite right. It is not, certainly.'

'You know, John,' said Mr. Pinch, 'your very good nature and kindness of heart make you thoughtless; and you can't be too careful on such a point as this. Upon my word, if I thought you were falling among bad companions, I should be quite wretched, for I know how difficult you would find it to shake them off. I would much rather have lost this money, John, than I would have had it back again on such terms.'

'I tell you, my dear good old fellow,' cried his friend, shaking him to and fro with both hands, and smiling at him with a cheerful, open countenance, that would have carried conviction to a mind much more suspicious than Tom's; 'I tell you there is no danger.'

'Well!' cried Tom, 'I am glad to hear it; I am overjoyed to hear it. I am sure there is not, when you say so in that manner. You won't take it ill, John, that I said what I did just now!'

'Ill!' said the other, giving his hand a hearty squeeze; 'why what do you think I am made of? Mr. Tigg and I are not on such an intimate footing that you need be at all uneasy, I give you my solemn assurance of that, Tom. You are quite comfortable now?'

'Quite,' said Tom.

'Then once more, good night!'

'Good night!' cried Tom; 'and such pleasant dreams to you as should attend the sleep of the best fellow in the world!'

'—Except Pecksniff,' said his friend, stopping at the door for a moment, and looking gaily back.

'Except Pecksniff,' answered Tom, with great gravity; 'of course.'

And thus they parted for the night; John Westlock full of light-heartedness and good humour, and poor Tom Pinch quite satisfied; though still, as he turned over on his side in bed, he muttered to himself, 'I really do wish, for all that, though, that he wasn't acquainted with Mr. Tigg.'

They breakfasted together very early next morning, for the two young men desired to get back again in good season; and

John Westlock was to return to London by the coach that day. As he had some hours to spare, he bore them company for three or four miles on their walk, and only parted from them at last in sheer necessity. The parting was an unusually hearty one, not only as between him and Tom Pinch, but on the side of Martin also, who had found in the old pupil a very different sort of person from the milksop he had prepared himself to expect.

Young Westlock stopped upon a rising ground, when he had gone a little distance, and looked back. They were walking at a brisk pace, and Tom appeared to be talking earnestly. Martin had taken off his great-coat, the wind being now behind them, and carried it upon his arm. As he looked, he saw Tom relieve him of it, after a faint resistance, and, throwing it upon his own, encumber himself with the weight of both. This trivial incident impressed the old pupil mightily, for he stood there, gazing after them, until they were hidden from his view; when he shook his head, as if he were troubled by some uneasy reflection, and thoughtfully retraced his steps to Salisbury.

In the meantime, Martin and Tom pursued their way, until they halted, safe and sound, at Mr. Pecksniff's house, where a brief epistle from that good gentleman to Mr. Pinch announced the family's return by that night's coach. As it would pass the corner of the lane at about six o'clock in the morning, Mr. Pecksniff requested that the gig might be in waiting at the finger-post about that time, together with a cart for the luggage. And to the end that he might be received with the greater honour, the young men agreed to rise early, and be upon the spot themselves.

It was the least cheerful day they had yet passed together. Martin was out of spirits and out of humour, and took every opportunity of comparing his condition and prospects with those of young Westlock: much to his own disadvantage always. This mood of his depressed Tom: and neither that morning's parting, nor yesterday's dinner, helped to mend the matter. So the hours dragged on heavily enough; and they were glad to go to bed early.

They were not quite so glad to get up again at half-past four o'clock, in all the shivering discomfort of a dark winter's morning; but they turned out punctually, and were at the finger-post full half-an-hour before the appointed time. It was not by any means a lively morning, for the sky was black and cloudy, and it rained hard; but Martin said there was some satisfaction in seeing that brute of a horse (by this, he meant Mr. Pecksniff's Arab steed) getting very wet; and that he rejoiced, on his account, that it rained so fast. From this it may be inferred that Martin's spirits had not improved, as indeed they had not; for while he and Mr. Pinch stood waiting under a hedge, looking at the rain, the gig, the cart, and its reeking driver, he did nothing but grumble; and, but that it is indispensable to any dispute that there should be two parties to it, he would certainly have picked a quarrel with Tom.

At length the noise of wheels was faintly audible in the distance, and presently the coach came splashing through the mud and mire, with one miserable outside passenger crouching down among wet straw, under a saturated umbrella; and the coachman, guard, and horses, in a fellowship of dripping wretchedness. Immediately on its stopping, Mr. Pecksniff let down the window-glass and hailed Tom Pinch.

'Dear me, Mr. Pinch! Is it possible that you are out upon this very inclement morning?'

'Yes, sir,' cried Tom, advancing eagerly, 'Mr. Chuzzlewit and I, sir.'

'Oh!' said Mr. Pecksniff, looking not so much at Martin as at the spot on which he stood. 'Oh! Indeed! Do me the favour to see to the trunks, if you please, Mr. Pinch.'

Then Mr. Pecksniff descended, and helped his daughters to alight; but neither he nor the young ladies took the slightest notice of Martin, who had advanced to offer his assistance, but was repulsed by Mr. Pecksniff's standing immediately before his person, with his back towards him. In the same manner, and in profound silence, Mr. Pecksniff handed his daughters into the gig; and following himself and taking the reins, drove off home.

Lost in astonishment, Martin stood staring at the coach, and when the coach had driven away, at Mr. Pinch and the luggage, until the cart moved off too; when he said to Tom:

'Now will you have the goodness to tell me what *this* portends?'

'What?' asked Tom.

'This fellow's behaviour. Mr. Pecksniff's, I mean. You saw it?'

'No. Indeed I did not,' cried Tom. 'I was busy with the trunks.'

'It is no matter,' said Martin. 'Come! Let us make haste back.' And without another word started off at such a pace, that Tom had some difficulty in keeping up with him.

He had no care where he went, but walked through little heaps of mud and little pools of water with the utmost indifference; looking straight before him, and sometimes laughing in a strange manner within himself. Tom felt that anything he could say would only render him the more obstinate, and therefore trusted to Mr. Pecksniff's manner when they reached the house, to remove the mistaken impression under which he felt convinced so great a favourite as the new pupil must unquestionably be labouring. But he was not a little amazed himself, when they did reach it, and entered the parlour where Mr. Pecksniff was sitting alone before the fire, drinking some hot tea, to find that instead of taking favourable notice of his relative, and keeping him, Mr. Pinch, in the background, he did exactly the reverse, and was so lavish in his attentions to Tom, that Tom was thoroughly confounded.

'Take some tea, Mr. Pinch, take some tea,' said Pecksniff, stirring the fire. 'You must be very cold and damp. Pray take some tea, and come into a warm place, Mr. Pinch.'

Tom saw that Martin looked at Mr. Pecksniff as though he could have easily found it in his heart to give *him* an invitation to a very warm place; but he was quite silent, and standing opposite that gentleman at the table, regarded him attentively.

'Take a chair, Pinch,' said Pecksniff. 'Take a chair, if you please. How have things gone on in our absence, Mr. Pinch?'

'You—you will be very much pleased with the grammar-school, sir,' said Tom. 'It's nearly finished.'

'If you will have the goodness, Mr. Pinch,' said Pecksniff, waving his hand and smiling, 'we will not discuss anything connected with that question at present. What have *you* been doing, Thomas, humph?'

Mr. Pinch looked from master to pupil, and from pupil to master, and was so perplexed and dismayed that he wanted presence of mind to answer the question. In this awkward interval, Mr. Pecksniff (who was perfectly conscious of Martin's gaze, though he had never once glanced towards him) poked the fire very much, and when he couldn't do that any more, drank tea assiduously.

'Now, Mr. Pecksniff,' said Martin at last, in a very quiet voice, 'if you have sufficiently refreshed and recovered yourself,

I shall be glad to hear what you mean by this treatment of me.'

'And what,' said Mr. Pecksniff, turning his eyes on Tom Pinch, even more placidly and gently than before, 'what have *you* been doing, Thomas, humph?'

When he had repeated this inquiry, he looked round the walls of the room as if he were curious to see whether any nails had been left there by accident in former times.

Tom was almost at his wit's end what to say between the two, and had already made a gesture as if he would call Mr. Pecksniff's attention to the gentleman who had last addressed him, when Martin saved him further trouble by doing so himself.

'Mr. Pecksniff,' he said, softly rapping the table twice or thrice, and moving a step or two nearer, so that he could have touched him with his hand; 'you heard what I said just now. Do me the favour to reply, if you please. I ask you:' he raised his voice a little here: 'what you mean by this?'

'I will talk to you, sir,' said Mr. Pecksniff in a severe voice, as he looked at him for the first time, 'presently.'

'You are very obliging,' returned Martin; 'presently will not do. I must trouble you to talk to me at once.'

Mr. Pecksniff made a feint of being deeply interested in his pocket-book, but it shook in his hands; he trembled so.

'Now,' retorted Martin, rapping the table again. 'Now. Presently will not do. Now!'

'Do you threaten me, sir?' cried Mr. Pecksniff.

Martin looked at him, and made no answer; but a curious observer might have detected an ominous twitching at his mouth, and perhaps an involuntary attraction of his right hand in the direction of Mr. Pecksniff's cravat.

'I lament to be obliged to say, sir,' resumed Mr. Pecksniff, 'that it would be quite in keeping with your character if you did threaten me. You have deceived me. You have imposed upon a nature which you knew to be confiding and unsuspicious. You have obtained admission, sir,' said Mr. Pecksniff, rising, 'to this house, on perverted statements and on false pretences.'

'Go on,' said Martin, with a scornful smile. 'I understand you now. What more?'

'Thus much more, sir,' cried Mr. Pecksniff, trembling from head to foot, and trying to rub his hands, as though he were only cold. 'Thus much more, if you force me to publish your shame before a third party, which I was unwilling and indisposed to do. This lowly roof, sir, must not be contaminated by the presence of one who has deceived, and cruelly deceived, an honourable, beloved, venerated, and venerable gentleman; and who wisely suppressed that deceit from me when he sought my protection and favour, knowing that, humble as I am, I am an honest man, seeking to do my duty in this carnal universe, and setting my face against all vice and treachery. I weep for your depravity, sir,' said Mr. Pecksniff; 'I mourn over your corruption, I pity your voluntary withdrawal of yourself from the flowery paths of purity and peace;' here he struck himself upon his breast, or moral garden; 'but I cannot have a leper and a serpent for an inmate. Go forth,' said Mr. Pecksniff, stretching out his hand: 'go forth, young man! Like all who know you, I renounce you!'

With what intention Martin made a stride forward at these words, it is impossible to say. It is enough to know that Tom Pinch caught him in his arms, and that, at the same moment, Mr. Pecksniff stepped back so hastily, that he missed his footing, tumbled over a chair, and fell in a sitting posture on the ground; where he remained without an effort to get up again, with his head in a corner: perhaps considering it the safest place.

'Let me go, Pinch!' cried Martin, shaking him away. 'Why do you hold me? Do you think a blow could make him a more abject creature than he is? Do you think that if I spat upon him, I could degrade him to a lower level than his own? Look at him. Look at him, Pinch!'

Mr. Pinch involuntarily did so. Mr. Pecksniff sitting, as has been already mentioned, on the carpet, with his head in an acute angle of the wainscot, and all the damage and detriment of an uncomfortable journey about him, was not exactly a model of all that is prepossessing and dignified in man, certainly. Still he *was* Pecksniff; it was impossible to deprive him of that unique and paramount appeal to Tom. And he returned Tom's glance, as if he would have said, 'Aye, Mr. Pinch, look at me! Here I am! You know what the Poet says about an honest man; and an honest man is one of the few great works that can be seen for nothing! Look at me!'

'I tell you,' said Martin, 'that as he lies there, disgraced, bought, used; a cloth for dirty hands, a mat for dirty feet, a lying, fawning, servile hound, he is the very last and worst

Mr. Pecksniff renounces the Deceiver

among the vermin of the world. And mark me, Pinch! The day will come—he knows it: see it written on his face, while I speak!—when even you will find him out, and will know him as I do, and as he knows I do. *He* renounce *me!* Cast your eyes on the Renouncer, Pinch, and be the wiser for the recollection!'

He pointed at him as he spoke, with unutterable contempt, and flinging his hat upon his head, walked from the room and from the house. He went so rapidly that he was already clear of the village, when he heard Tom Pinch calling breathlessly after him in the distance.

'Well! what now?' he said, when Tom came up.

'Dear, dear!' cried Tom, 'are you going?'

'Going!' he echoed. 'Going!'

'I didn't so much mean that, as were you going now at once, in this bad weather, on foot, without your clothes, with no money?' cried Tom.

'Yes,' he answered sternly, 'I am.'

'And where?' cried Tom. 'Oh where will you go?'

'I don't know,' he said. 'Yes, I do. I'll go to America!'

'No, no,' cried Tom, in a kind of agony. 'Don't go there. Pray don't. Think better of it. Don't be so dreadfully regardless of yourself. Don't go to America!'

'My mind is made up,' he said. 'Your friend was right. I'll go to America. God bless you, Pinch!'

'Take this!' cried Tom, pressing a book upon him in great agitation. 'I must make haste back, and can't say anything I would. Heaven be with you. Look at the leaf I have turned down. Good-bye, good-bye!'

The simple fellow wrung him by the hand, with tears stealing down his cheeks; and they parted hurriedly upon their separate ways.

CHAPTER XIII

Showing what became of Martin and his desperate resolve after he left Mr. Pecksniff's house; what persons he encountered; what anxieties he suffered; and what news he heard

CARRYING Tom Pinch's book quite unconsciously under his arm, and not even buttoning his coat as a protection against the heavy rain, Martin went doggedly forward at the same quick pace, until he had passed the finger-post, and was on the high road to London. He slackened very little in his speed even then, but he began to think, and look about him, and to disengage his senses from the coil of angry passions which hitherto had held them prisoner.

It must be confessed that, at that moment, he had no very agreeable employment either for his moral or his physical perceptions. The day was dawning from a patch of watery light in the east, and sullen clouds came driving up before it, from which the rain descended in a thick, wet mist. It streamed from every twig and bramble in the hedge; made little gullies in the path; ran down a hundred channels in the road; and punched innumerable holes into the face of every pond and gutter. It fell with an oozy, slushy sound among the grass; and made a muddy kennel of every furrow in the ploughed fields. No living creature was anywhere to be seen. The prospect could hardly have been more desolate if animated nature had been dissolved in water, and poured down upon the earth again in that form.

The range of view within the solitary traveller was quite as cheerless as the scene without. Friendless and penniless; incensed to the last degree; deeply wounded in his pride and self-love; full of independent schemes, and perfectly destitute of any means of realising them; his most vindictive enemy might have been satisfied with the extent of his troubles. To add to his other miseries, he was by this time sensible of being wet to the skin, and cold at his very heart.

In this deplorable condition he remembered Mr. Pinch's book; more because it was rather troublesome to carry, than from any hope of being comforted by that parting gift. He looked at the dingy lettering on the back, and finding it to be an odd volume of the 'Bachelor of Salamanca,' in the French tongue, cursed Tom Pinch's folly twenty times. He was on the point of throwing it away, in his ill-humour and vexation, when he bethought himself that Tom had referred him to a leaf, turned down; and opening it at that place, that he might have additional cause of complaint against him for supposing that any cold scrap of the Bachelor's wisdom could cheer him in such circumstances, found—

Well, well! not much, but Tom's all. The half-sovereign. He had wrapped it hastily in a piece of paper, and pinned it to the leaf. These words were scrawled in pencil on the inside: 'I don't want it, indeed. I should not know what to do with it if I had it.'

There are some falsehoods, Tom, on which men mount, as on bright wings, towards Heaven. There are some truths, cold bitter taunting truths, wherein your worldly scholars are very apt and punctual, which bind men down to earth with leaden chains. Who would not rather have to fan him, in his dying hour, the lightest feather of a falsehood such as thine, than all the quills that have been plucked from the sharp porcupine, reproachful truth, since time began!

Martin felt keenly for himself, and he felt this good deed of Tom's keenly. After a few minutes it had the effect of raising his spirits, and reminding him that he was not altogether destitute, as he had left a fair stock of clothes behind him, and wore a gold hunting-watch in his pocket. He found a curious gratification, too, in thinking what a winning fellow he must be to have made such an impression on Tom; and in reflecting how superior he was to Tom, and how much more likely to make his way in the world. Animated by these thoughts, and strengthened in his design of endeavouring to push his fortune in another country, he resolved to get to London as a rallying-point, in the best way he could; and to lose no time about it.

He was ten good miles from the village made illustrious by being the abiding-place of Mr. Pecksniff, when he stopped to breakfast at a little road-side ale-house; and resting upon a high-backed settle before the fire, pulled off his coat, and hung it before the cheerful blaze to dry. It was a very different place from the last tavern in which he had regaled: boasting no greater extent of accommodation than the brick-floored kitchen yielded: but the mind so soon accommodates itself to the necessities of the body, that this poor waggoner's house-of-call, which he would have despised yesterday, became now quite a choice hotel; while his dish of eggs and bacon, and his mug of beer, were not by any means the coarse fare he had supposed, but fully bore out the inscription on the window-shutter, which proclaimed those viands to be 'Good entertainment for Travellers.'

He pushed away his empty plate; and with a second mug upon the hearth before him, looked thoughtfully at the fire until his eyes ached. Then he looked at the highly-coloured scripture pieces on the walls, in little black frames like common shaving-glasses, and saw how the Wise Men (with a strong family likeness among them) worshipped in a pink manger; and how the Prodigal Son came home in red rags to a purple father, and already feasted his imagination on a sea-green calf. Then he glanced through the window at the falling rain, coming down aslant upon the sign-post over against the house, and overflowing the horse-trough; and then he looked at the fire again, and seemed to descry a doubly-distant London, retreating among the fragments of the burning wood.

He had repeated this process in just the same order, many times, as if it were a matter of necessity, when the sound of wheels called his attention to the window out of its regular turn; and there he beheld a kind of light van drawn by four horses, and laden, as well as he could see (for it was covered in), with corn and straw. The driver, who was alone, stopped at the door to water his team, and presently came stamping and shaking the wet off his hat and coat, into the room where Martin sat.

He was a red-faced burly young fellow; smart in his way, and with a good-humoured countenance. As he advanced towards the fire he touched his shining forehead with the forefinger of his stiff leather glove, by way of salutation; and said (rather unnecessarily) that it was an uncommon wet day.

'Very wet,' said Martin.

'I don't know as ever I see a wetter.'

'I never felt one,' said Martin.

The driver glanced at Martin's soiled dress, and his damp shirt-sleeves, and his coat hung up to dry: and said, after a pause, as he warmed his hands:

'You have been caught in it, sir?'

'Yes,' was the short reply.

'Out riding, maybe?' said the driver.

'I should have been, if I owned a horse; but I don't,' returned Martin.

'That's bad,' said the driver.

'And may be worse,' said Martin.

Now the driver said 'That's bad,' not so much because Martin didn't own a horse, as because he said he didn't with all the reckless desperation of his mood and circumstances, and so left a great deal to be inferred. Martin put his hands in his pockets and whistled, when he had retorted on the driver: thus giving him to understand that he didn't care a pin for Fortune; that he was above pretending to be her favourite when he was not; and that he snapped his fingers at her, the driver, and everybody else.

The driver looked at him stealthily for a minute or so; and in the pauses of his warming whistled too. At length he asked, as he pointed his thumb towards the road,

'Up or down?'

'Which *is* up?' said Martin.

'London, of course,' said the driver.

'Up then,' said Martin. He tossed his head in a careless manner afterwards, as if he would have added, 'Now you know all about it;' put his hands deeper into his pockets; changed his tune, and whistled a little louder.

'*I*'m going up,' observed the driver; 'Hounslow, ten miles this side London.'

'Are you?' cried Martin, stopping short and looking at him.

The driver sprinkled the fire with his wet hat until it hissed again, and answered, 'Aye, to be sure he was.'

'Why, then,' said Martin, 'I'll be plain with you. You may suppose from my dress that I have money to spare. I have not. All I can afford for coach-hire is a crown, for I have but two. If you can take me for that, and my waist-coat, or this silk handkerchief, do. If you can't, leave it alone.'

'Short and sweet,' remarked the driver.

'You want more?' said Martin. 'Then I haven't got more, and I can't get it, so there's an end of that.' Whereupon he began to whistle again.

'I didn't say I wanted more, did I?' asked the driver, with something like indignation.

'You didn't say my offer was enough,' rejoined Martin.

'Why, how could I, when you wouldn't let me? In regard to the waistcoat, I wouldn't have a man's waistcoat, much less a gentleman's waistcoat, on my mind, for no consideration; but the silk handkerchief's another thing; and if you was satisfied when we got to Hounslow, I shouldn't object to that as a gift.'

'Is it a bargain, then?' said Martin.

'Yes, it is,' returned the other.

'Then finish this beer,' said Martin, handing him the mug, and pulling on his coat with great alacrity; 'and let us be off as soon as you like.'

In two minutes more he had paid his bill, which amounted to a shilling; was lying at full length on a truss of straw, high and dry at the top of the van, with the tilt a little open in front for the convenience of talking to his new friend; and was moving along in the right direction with a most satisfactory and encouraging briskness.

The driver's name, as he soon informed Martin, was William Simmons, better known as Bill; and his spruce appearance was sufficiently explained by his connexion with a large stage-coaching establishment at Hounslow, whither he was conveying his load from a farm belonging to the concern in Wiltshire. He was frequently up and down the road on such errands, he said, and to look after the sick and rest horses, of which animals he had much to relate that occupied a long time in the telling. He aspired to the dignity of the regular box, and expected an appointment on the first vacancy. He was musical besides, and had a little key-bugle in his pocket, on which, whenever the conversation flagged, he played the first part of a great many tunes, and regularly broke down in the second.

'Ah!' said Bill, with a sigh, as he drew the back of his hand across his lips, and put this instrument in his pocket, after screwing off the mouth-piece to drain it; 'Lummy Ned of the Light Salisbury, *he* was the one for musical talents. He *was* a guard. What you may call a Guard'an Angel, was Ned.'

'Is he dead?' asked Martin.

'Dead!' replied the other, with a contemptuous emphasis. 'Not he. You won't catch Ned a-dying easy. No, no. He knows better than that.'

'You spoke of him in the past tense,' observed Martin, 'so I supposed he was no more.'

'He's no more in England,' said Bill, 'if that's what you mean. He went to the U-nited States.'

'Did he?' asked Martin, with sudden interest. 'When?'

'Five year ago, or thenabout,' said Bill. 'He had set up in the public line here, and couldn't meet his engagements, so he cut off to Liverpool one day, without saying anything about it, and went and shipped himself for the U-nited States.'

'Well?' said Martin.

'Well! as he landed there without a penny to bless himself with, of course they was very glad to see him in the U-nited States.'

'What do you mean?' asked Martin, with some scorn.

'What do I mean?' said Bill. 'Why, *that*. All men are alike in the U-nited States, an't they? It makes no odds whether a man has a thousand pound, or nothing, there. Particular in New York, I'm told, where Ned landed.'

'New York, was it?' asked Martin, thoughtfully.

'Yes,' said Bill. 'New York. I know that, because he sent word home that it brought Old York to his mind, quite wivid, in consequence of being so exactly unlike it in every respect. I don't understand what particular business Ned turned his mind to, when he got there; but he wrote home that him and his friends was always a-singing, Ale Columbia, and blowing up the President, so I suppose it was something in the public line, or free-and-easy way again. Anyhow he made his fortune.'

'No!' cried Martin.

'Yes, he did,' said Bill. 'I know that, because he lost it all the day after, in six-and-twenty banks as broke. He settled a lot of the notes on his father, when it was ascertained that they was really stopped, and sent 'em over with a dutiful letter. I know that, because they was shown down our yard for the old gentleman's benefit, that he might treat himself with tobacco in the workus.'

'He was a foolish fellow not to take care of his money when he had it,' said Martin, indignantly.

'There you're right,' said Bill, 'especially as it was all in paper, and he might have took care of it so very easy by folding it up in a small parcel.'

Martin said nothing in reply, but soon afterwards fell asleep, and remained so for an hour or more. When he awoke, finding it had ceased to rain, he took his seat beside the driver, and asked him several questions; as how long had the fortunate guard of the Light Salisbury been in crossing the Atlantic; at what time of the year had he sailed; what was the name of the ship in which he made the voyage; how much had he paid for passage-money; did he suffer greatly from sea-sickness? and so forth. But on these points of detail his friend was possessed of little or no information; either answering obviously at random, or acknowledging that he had never heard, or had forgotten; nor, although he returned to the charge very often, could he obtain any useful intelligence on these essential particulars.

They jogged on all day, and stopped so often—now to refresh, now to change their team of horses, now to exchange or bring away a set of harness, now on one point of business, and now upon another, connected with the coaching on that line of road—that it was midnight when they reached Hounslow. A little short of the stables for which the van was bound, Martin got down, paid his crown, and forced his silk handkerchief upon his honest friend, notwithstanding the many protestations that he didn't wish to deprive him of it, with which he tried to give the lie to his longing looks. That done, they parted company; and when the van had driven into its own yard and the gates were closed, Martin stood in the dark street, with a pretty strong sense of being shut out, alone, upon the dreary world, without the key of it.

But in this moment of despondency, and often afterwards, the recollection of Mr. Pecksniff operated as a cordial to him; awakening in his breast an indignation that was very wholesome in nerving him to obstinate endurance. Under the influence of this fiery dram he started off for London without more ado. Arriving there in the middle of the night, and not knowing where to find a tavern open, he was fain to stroll about the streets and market-places until morning.

He found himself, about an hour before dawn, in the humbler regions of the Adelphi; and addressing himself to a man in a fur-cap who was taking down the shutters of an obscure public-house, informed him that he was a stranger, and inquired if he could have a bed there. It happened by good luck that he could. Though none of the gaudiest, it was tolerably clean, and Martin felt very glad and grateful when he crept into it, for warmth, rest, and forgetfulness.

It was quite late in the afternoon when he awoke; and by the time he had washed and dressed, and broken his fast, it was growing dusk again. This was all the better, for it was now a matter of absolute necessity that he should part with his watch to some obliging pawnbroker. He would have waited until after dark for this purpose, though it had been the longest day in the year, and he had begun it without a breakfast.

He passed more Golden Balls than all the jugglers in Europe have juggled with in the course of their united performances, before he could determine in favour of any particular shop where those symbols were displayed. In the end he came back to one of the first he had seen, and entering by a side-door in a court, where the three balls, with the legend 'Money Lent,' were repeated in a ghastly transparency, passed into one of a series of little closets, or private boxes, erected for the accommodation of the more bashful and uninitiated customers. He bolted himself in; pulled out his watch; and laid it on the counter.

'Upon my life and soul!' said a low voice in the next box to the shopman who was in treaty with him, 'you must make it more: you must make it a trifle more, you must indeed! You must dispense with one half-quarter of an ounce in weighing out your pound of flesh, my best of friends, and make it two-and-six.'

Martin drew back involuntarily, for he knew the voice at once.

'You're always full of your chaff,' said the shopman, rolling up the article (which looked like a shirt) quite as a matter of course, and nibbing his pen upon the counter.

'I shall never be full of my wheat,' said Mr. Tigg, 'as long as I come here. Ha, ha! Not bad! Make it two-and-six, my dear friend, positively for this occasion only. Half-a-crown is a delightful coin. Two-and-six. Going at two-and-six! For the last time at two-and-six!'

'It'll never be the last time till it's quite worn out,' rejoined the shopman. 'It's grown yellow in the service as it is.'

'Its master has grown yellow in the service, if you mean that, my friend,' said Mr. Tigg; 'in the patriotic service of an ungrateful country. You are making it two-and-six, I think?'

'I'm making it,' returned the shopman, 'what it always has been—two shillings. Same name as usual, I suppose?'

'Still the same name,' said Mr. Tigg; 'my claim to the dormant peerage not being yet established by the House of Lords.'

'The old address?'

'Not at all,' said Mr. Tigg; 'I have removed my town

establishment from thirty-eight Mayfair, to number fifteen-hundred-and-forty-two Park Lane.'

'Come, I'm not going to put down that, you know,' said the shopman with a grin.

'You may put down what you please, my friend,' quoth Mr. Tigg. 'The fact is still the same. The apartments for the under-butler and the fifth footman being of a most confounded low and vulgar kind at thirty-eight Mayfair, I have been compelled, in my regard for the feelings which do them so much honour, to take on lease for seven, fourteen, or twenty-one years, renewable at the option of the tenant, the elegant and commodious family mansion, number fifteen-hundred-and-forty-two Park Lane. Make it two-and-six, and come and see me!'

The shopman was so highly entertained by this piece of humour, that Mr. Tigg himself could not repress some little show of exultation. It vented itself, in part, in a desire to see how the occupant of the next box received his pleasantry; to ascertain which he glanced round the partition, and immediately, by the gaslight, recognised Martin.

'I wish I may die,' said Mr. Tigg, stretching out his body so far that his head was as much in Martin's little cell as Martin's own head was, 'but this is one of the most tremendous meetings in Ancient or Modern History! How are you? What is the news from the agricultural districts? How are our friends the P.'s? Ha, ha! David, pay particular attention to this gentleman immediately, as a friend of mine, I beg.'

'Here! Please to give me the most you can for this,' said Martin, handing the watch to the shopman, 'I want money sorely.'

'He wants money, sorely!' cried Mr. Tigg with excessive sympathy. 'David, will you have the goodness to do your very utmost for my friend, who wants money sorely. You will deal with my friend as if he were myself. A gold hunting-watch, David, engine-turned, capped and jewelled in four holes, escape movement, horizontal lever, and warranted to perform correctly, upon my personal reputation, who have observed it narrowly for many years, under the most trying circumstances:' here he winked at Martin, that he might understand this recommendation would have an immense effect upon the shopman: 'what do you say, David, to my friend? Be very particular to deserve my custom and recommendation, David.'

'I can lend you three pound on this, if you like,' said the shopman to Martin, confidentially. 'It's very old-fashioned. I couldn't say more.'

'And devilish handsome, too,' cried Mr. Tigg. 'Two-twelve-six for the watch, and seven-and-six for personal regard. I am gratified: it may be weakness, but I am. Three pound will do. We take it. The name of my friend is Smivey: Chicken Smivey, of Holborn, twenty-six-and-a-half B: lodger.' Here he winked at Martin again, to apprise him that all the forms and ceremonies prescribed by law were now complied with, and nothing remained but the receipt of the money.

In point of fact, this proved to be the case, for Martin, who had no resource but to take what was offered him, signified his acquiescence by a nod of his head, and presently came out with the cash in his pocket. He was joined in the entry by Mr. Tigg, who warmly congratulated him, as he took his arm and accompanied him into the street, on the successful issue of the negotiation.

'As for my part in the same,' said Mr. Tigg, 'don't mention it. Don't compliment me, for I can't bear it!'

'I have no such intention, I assure you,' retorted Martin, releasing his arm and stopping.

'You oblige me very much,' said Mr. Tigg. 'Thank you.'

'Now, sir,' observed Martin, biting his lip, 'this is a large town, and we can easily find different ways in it. If you will show me which is your way, I will take another.'

Mr. Tigg was about to speak, but Martin interposed:

'I need scarcely tell you, after what you have just seen, that I have nothing to bestow upon your friend Mr. Slyme. And it is quite as unnecessary for me to tell you that I don't desire the honour of your company.'

'Stop!' cried Mr. Tigg, holding out his hand. 'Hold! There is a most remarkably long-headed, flowing-bearded, and patriarchal proverb, which observes that it is the duty of a man to be just before he is generous. Be just now, and you can be generous presently. Do not confuse me with the man Slyme. Do not distinguish the man Slyme as a friend of mine, for he is no such thing. I have been compelled, sir, to abandon the party whom you call Slyme. I have no knowledge of the party whom you call Slyme. I am, sir,' said Mr. Tigg, striking himself upon the breast, 'a premium tulip, of a very different growth and cultivation from the cabbage Slyme, sir.'

'It matters very little to me,' said Martin coolly, 'whether you have set up as a vagabond on your own account, or are still trading on behalf of Mr. Slyme. I wish to hold no correspondence with you. In the devil's name, man,' said Martin, scarcely able, despite his vexation, to repress a smile, as Mr. Tigg stood leaning his back against the shutters of a shop window, adjusting his hair with great composure, 'will you go one way or other?'

'You will allow me to remind you, sir,' said Mr. Tigg, with sudden dignity, 'that you—not I—that you—I say emphatically, *you*—have reduced the proceedings of this evening to a cold and distant matter of business, when I was disposed to place them on a friendly footing. It being made a matter of business, sir, I beg to say that I expect a trifle (which I shall bestow in charity) as commission upon the pecuniary advance in which I have rendered you my humble services. After the terms in which you have addressed me, sir,' concluded Mr. Tigg, 'you will not insult me, if you please, by offering more than half-a-crown.'

Martin drew that piece of money from his pocket, and tossed it towards him. Mr Tigg caught it, looked at it to assure himself of its goodness, spun it in the air after the manner of a pieman, and buttoned it up. Finally, he raised his hat an inch or two from his head with a military air, and, after pausing a moment with deep gravity, as to decide in which direction he should go, and to what Earl or Marquis among his friends he should give the preference in his next call, stuck his hands in his skirt-pockets and swaggered round the corner. Martin took the directly opposite course; and so, to his great content, they parted company.

It was with a bitter sense of humiliation that he cursed, again and again, the mischance of having encountered this man in the pawnbroker's shop. The only comfort he had in the recollection was, Mr. Tigg's voluntary avowal of a separation between himself and Slyme, that would at least prevent his circumstances (so Martin argued) from being known to any member of his family, the bare possibility of which filled him with shame and wounded pride. Abstractedly there was greater reason, perhaps, for supposing any declaration of Mr. Tigg's to be false, than for attaching the least credence to it; but remembering the terms on which the intimacy between that gentleman and his bosom friend had subsisted, and the strong probability of Mr. Tigg's having established an independent business of his own on Mr. Slyme's connexion, it had a reasonable appearance of probability: at all events, Martin hoped so; and that went a long way.

His first step, now that he had a supply of ready money for his present necessities, was, to retain his bed at the public-house until further notice, and to write a formal note to Tom Pinch (for he knew Pecksniff would see it) requesting to have his clothes forwarded to London by coach, with a direction to be left at the office until called for. These measures taken, he passed the interval before the box arrived—three days—in making inquiries relative to American vessels, at the offices of various shipping-agents in the city; and in lingering about the docks and wharves, with the faint hope of stumbling upon some engagement for the voyage, as clerk or supercargo, or custodian of something or somebody, which would enable him to procure a free passage. But finding, soon, that no such means of employment were likely to present themselves, and dreading the consequences of delay, he drew up a short advertisement, stating what he wanted, and inserted it in the leading newspapers. Pending the receipt of the twenty or thirty answers which he vaguely expected, he reduced his wardrobe to the narrowest limits consistent with decent respectability, and carried the overplus at different times to the pawnbroker's shop, for conversion into money.

And it was strange, very strange, even to himself, to find how, by quick though almost imperceptible degrees, he lost his delicacy and self-respect, and gradually came to do that as a matter of course, without the least compunction, which but a few short days before had galled him to the quick. The first time he visited the pawnbroker's, he felt on his way there as if every person whom he passed suspected whither he was going; and on his way back again, as if the whole human tide he stemmed, knew well where he had come from. When did he care to think of their discernment now! In his first wanderings up and down the weary streets, he counterfeited the walk of one who had an object in his view; but soon there came upon him the sauntering, slipshod gait of listless idleness and the lounging at street-corners, and plucking and biting of stray bits of straw, and strolling up and down the same place, and looking into the same shop-windows, with a miserable indifference, fifty times a day. At first, he came out from his lodging with an uneasy sense of being observed—even by those chance passers-by, on whom he had never looked before, and hundreds to one would never see again—issuing in the morning from a public-house; but now, in his comings-out and goings-in he did not mind to lounge about the door, or to stand sunning himself in careless thought beside the wooden stem, studded from head to heel with pegs, on which the beer-pots dangled like so many boughs upon a pewter-tree. And yet it took but five weeks to reach the lowest round of this tall ladder!

Oh, moralists, who treat of happiness and self-respect, innate in every sphere of life, and shedding light on every grain of dust in God's highway, so smooth below your carriage-wheels, so rough beneath the tread of naked feet, bethink yourselves in looking on the swift descent of men who *have* lived in their own esteem, that there are scores of thousands breathing now, and breathing thick with painful toil, who in that high respect have never lived at all, nor had a chance of life! Go ye, who rest so placidly upon the sacred Bard who had been young, and when he strung his harp was old, and had never seen the righteous forsaken, or his seed begging their bread; go, Teachers of content and honest pride, into the mine, the mill, the forge, the squalid depths of deepest ignorance, and uttermost abyss of man's neglect, and say can any hopeful plant spring up in air so foul that it extinguishes the soul's bright torch as fast as it is kindled! And, oh! ye Pharisees of the nineteen hundredth year of Christian Knowledge, who soundingly appeal to human nature, see first that it be human. Take heed it has not been transformed, during your slumber and the sleep of generations, into the nature of the Beasts.

Five weeks! Of all the twenty or thirty answers, not one had come. His money, even the additional stock he had raised from the disposal of his spare clothes (and that was not much, for clothes, though dear to buy, are cheap to pawn), was fast diminishing. Yet what could he do? At times an agony came over him in which he darted forth again, though he was but newly home, and, returning to some place where he had been already twenty times, made some new attempt to gain his end, but always unsuccessfully. He was years and years too old for a cabin-boy, and years upon years too inexperienced to be accepted as a common seaman. His dress and manner, too, militated fatally against any such proposal as the latter; and yet he was reduced to making it; for even if he could have con-

*Martin meets an Acquaintance at the House of a
Mutual Relation*

(p. 220)

templated the being set down in America totally without money, he had not enough left now for a steerage passage and the poorest provisions upon the voyage.

It is an illustration of a very common tendency in the mind of man, that all this time he never once doubted, one may almost say the certainty of doing great things in the New World, if he could only get there. In proportion as he became more and more dejected by his present circumstances, and the means of gaining America receded from his grasp, the more he fretted himself with the conviction that that was the only place in which he could hope to achieve any high end, and worried his brain with the thought that men going there in the meanwhile might anticipate him in the attainment of those objects which were dearest to his heart. He often thought of John Westlock, and besides looking out for him on all occasions, actually walked about London for three days together for the express purpose of meeting with him. But although he failed in this; and although he would not have scrupled to borrow money of him; and although he believed that John would have lent it; yet still he could not bring his mind to write to Pinch and inquire where he was to be found. For although, as we have seen, he was fond of Tom after his own fashion, he could not endure the thought (feeling so superior to Tom) of making him the stepping-stone to his fortune, or being anything to him but a patron; and his pride so revolted from the idea that it restrained him even now.

It might have yielded, however; and no doubt must have yielded soon, but for a very strange and unlooked-for occurrence.

The five weeks had quite run out, and he was in a truly desperate plight, when one evening, having just returned to his lodging, and being in the act of lighting his candle at the gas jet in the bar before stalking moodily up-stairs to his own room, his landlord called him by his name. Now as he had never told it to the man, but had scrupulously kept it to himself, he was not a little startled by this; and so plainly showed his agitation that the landlord, to re-assure him, said 'it was only a letter.'

'A letter!' cried Martin.

'For Mr. Martin Chuzzlewit,' said the landlord, reading the superscription of one he held in his hand. 'Noon. Chief office. Paid.'

Martin took it from him, thanked him, and walked up-stairs. It was not sealed, but pasted close; the handwriting was quite unknown to him. He opened it and found enclosed, without any name, address, or other inscription or explanation of any kind whatever, a Bank of England note for Twenty Pounds.

To say that he was perfectly stunned with astonishment and delight; that he looked again and again at the note and the wrapper; that he hurried below stairs to make quite certain that the note was a good note; and then hurried up again to satisfy himself for the fiftieth time that he had not overlooked some scrap of writing on the wrapper; that he exhausted and bewildered himself with conjectures; and could make nothing of it but that there the note was, and he was suddenly enriched; would be only to relate so many matters of course to no purpose. The final upshot of the business at that time was, that he resolved to treat himself to a comfortable but frugal meal in his own chamber: and having ordered a fire to be kindled, went out to purchase it forthwith.

He bought some cold beef, and ham, and French bread, and butter, and came back with his pockets pretty heavily laden. It was somewhat of a damping circumstance to find the room full of smoke, which was attributable to two causes: firstly, to the flue being naturally vicious and a smoker; and secondly, to their having forgotten, in lighting the fire, an odd sack or two and some trifles, which had been put up the chimney to keep the rain out. They had already remedied this oversight, however; and propped up the window-sash with a bundle of firewood to keep it open; so that except in being rather inflammatory to the eyes and choking to the lungs, the apartment was quite comfortable.

Martin was in no vein to quarrel with it, if it had been in less tolerable order, especially when a gleaming pint of porter was set upon the table, and the servant-girl withdrew, bearing with her particular instructions relative to the production of something hot when he should ring the bell. The cold meat being wrapped in a play-bill, Martin laid the cloth by spreading that document on the little round table with the print downwards, and arranging the collation upon it. The foot of the bed, which was very close to the fire, answered for a sideboard; and when he had completed these preparations, he squeezed an old armchair into the warmest corner, and sat down to enjoy himself.

He had begun to eat with great appetite, glancing round the

room meanwhile with a triumphant anticipation of quitting it for ever on the morrow, when his attention was arrested by a stealthy footstep on the stairs, and presently by a knock at his chamber door, which, although it was a gentle knock enough, communicated such a start to the bundle of firewood, that it instantly leaped out of window, and plunged into the street.

'More coals, I suppose,' said Martin. 'Come in!'

'It an't a liberty, sir, though it seems so,' rejoined a man's voice. 'Your servant, sir. Hope you're pretty well, sir.'

Martin stared at the face that was bowing in the doorway: perfectly remembering the features and expression, but quite forgetting to whom they belonged.

'Tapley, sir,' said his visitor. 'Him as formerly lived at the Dragon, sir, and was forced to leave in consequence of a want of jollity, sir.'

'To be sure!' cried Martin. 'Why, how did you come here?'

'Right through the passage, and up the stairs, sir,' said Mark.

'How did you find me out, I mean?' asked Martin.

'Why, sir,' said Mark, 'I've passed you once or twice in the street if I'm not mistaken; and when I was a-looking in at the beef-and-ham shop just now, along with a hungry sweep, as was very much calculated to make a man jolly, sir, I see you a-buying that.'

Martin reddened as he pointed to the table, and said, somewhat hastily:

'Well! What then?'

'Why, then, sir,' said Mark, 'I made bold to foller; and as I told 'em down-stairs that you expected me, I was let up.'

'Are you charged with any message, that you told them you were expected?' inquired Martin.

'No, sir, I an't,' said Mark. 'That was what you may call a pious fraud, sir, that was.'

Martin cast an angry look at him: but there was something in the fellow's merry face, and in his manner, which with all its cheerfulness was far from being obtrusive or familiar, that quite disarmed him. He had lived a solitary life too, for many weeks, and the voice was pleasant in his ear.

'Tapley,' he said, 'I'll deal openly with you. From all I can judge, and from all I have heard of you through Pinch, you are not a likely kind of fellow to have been brought here by impertinent curiosity or any other offensive motive. Sit down. I'm glad to see you.'

'Thankee, sir,' said Mark. 'I'd as lieve stand.'

'If you don't sit down,' retorted Martin, 'I'll not talk to you.'

'Very good, sir,' observed Mark. 'Your will's a law, sir. Down it is;' and he sat down accordingly, upon the bedstead.

'Help yourself,' said Martin, handing him the only knife.

'Thankee, sir,' rejoined Mark. 'After you've done.'

'If you don't take it now, you'll not have any,' said Martin.

'Very good, sir,' rejoined Mark. 'That being your desire— now it is.' With which reply he gravely helped himself, and went on eating. Martin having done the like for a short time in silence, said abruptly:

'What are you doing in London?'

'Nothing at all, sir,' rejoined Mark.

'How's that?' asked Martin.

'I want a place,' said Mark.

'I'm sorry for you,' said Martin.

'—To attend upon a single gentleman,' resumed Mark. 'If from the country the more desirable. Makeshifts would be preferred. Wages no object.'

He said this so pointedly, that Martin stopped in his eating and said:

'If you mean me—'

'Yes, I do, sir,' interposed Mark.

'Then you may judge from my style of living here, of my means of keeping a man-servant. Besides, I am going to America immediately.'

'Well, sir,' returned Mark, quite unmoved by this intelligence, 'from all that ever I heard about it, I should say America is a very likely sort of place for me to be jolly in!'

Again Martin looked at him angrily; and again his anger melted away in spite of himself.

'Lord bless you, sir,' said Mark, 'what *is* the use of us a-going round and round, and hiding behind the corner, and dodging up and down, when we can come straight to the point in six words? I've had my eye upon you any time this fortnight. I see well enough there's a screw loose in your affairs. I know'd well enough the first time I see you down at the Dragon that it must be so, sooner or later. Now, sir, here am I, without a sitivation; without any want of wages for a year to come; for I saved up (I didn't mean to do it, but I couldn't help it) at the Dragon—here am I with a liking for what's wentersome, and a liking for you, and a wish to come out strong under circumstances as would keep other men down: and will you take me, or will you leave me?'

'How can I take you?' cried Martin.

'When I say take,' rejoined Mark, 'I mean will you let me go? and when I say will you let me go, I mean will you let me go along with you? for go I will, somehow or another. Now that you've said America, I see clear at once, that that's the place for me to be jolly in. Therefore, if I don't pay my own passage in the ship you go in, sir, I'll pay my own passage in another. And mark my words, if I go alone it shall be, to carry out the principle, in the rottenest, craziest, leakingest tub of a wessel that a place can be got in for love or money. So if I'm lost upon the way, sir, there'll be a drowned man at your door—and always a-knocking double knocks at it, too, or never trust me!'

'This is mere folly,' said Martin.

'Very good, sir,' returned Mark. 'I'm glad to hear it, because if you don't mean to let me go, you'll be more comfortable, perhaps, on account of thinking so. Therefore I contradict no gentleman. But all I say is, that if I don't emigrate to America in that case, in the beastliest old cockleshell as goes out of port, I'm——'

'You don't mean what you say, I'm sure,' said Martin.

'Yes I do,' cried Mark.

'I tell you I know better,' rejoined Martin.

'Very good, sir,' said Mark, with the same air of perfect satisfaction. 'Let it stand that way at present, sir, and wait and see how it turns out. Why, love my heart alive! the only doubt I have is, whether there's any credit in going with a gentleman like you, that's as certain to make his way there as a gimlet is to go through soft deal.'

This was touching Martin on his weak point, and having him at a great advantage. He could not help thinking, either, what a brisk fellow this Mark was, and how great a change he had wrought in the atmosphere of the dismal little room already.

'Why, certainly, Mark,' he said, 'I have hopes of doing well there, or I shouldn't go. I may have the qualifications for doing well, perhaps.'

'Of course you have, sir,' returned Mark Tapley. 'Everybody knows that.'

'You see,' said Martin, leaning his chin upon his hand, and

looking at the fire, 'ornamental architecture applied to domestic purposes, can hardly fail to be in great request in that country; for men are constantly changing their residences there, and moving further off; and it's clear they must have houses to live in.'

'I should say, sir,' observed Mark, 'that that's a state of things as opens one of the jolliest look-outs for domestic architecture that ever I heerd tell on.'

Martin glanced at him hastily, not feeling quite free from a suspicion that this remark implied a doubt of the successful issue of his plans. But Mr. Tapley was eating the boiled beef and bread with such entire good faith and singleness of purpose expressed in his visage, that he could not but be satisfied. Another doubt arose in his mind, however, as this one disappeared. He produced the blank cover in which the note had been enclosed, and fixing his eyes on Mark as he put it in his hands, said,

'Now tell me the truth. Do you know anything about that?'

Mark turned it over and over; held it near his eyes; held it away from him at arm's length; held it with the superscription upwards, and with the superscription downwards; and shook his head with such a genuine expression of astonishment at being asked the question, that Martin said, as he took it from him again:

'No, I see you don't. How should you? Though, indeed, your knowing about it would not be more extraordinary than its being here. Come, Tapley,' he added, after a moment's thought, 'I'll trust you with my history, such as it is, and then you'll see more clearly what sort of fortunes you would link yourself to, if you followed me.'

'I beg your pardon, sir,' said Mark; 'but afore you enter upon it, will you take me if I choose to go? Will you turn off me, Mark Tapley, formerly of the Blue Dragon, as can be well recommended by Mr. Pinch, and as wants a gentleman of your strength of mind to look up to? or will you, in climbing the ladder as you're certain to get to the top of, take me along with you at a respectful distance? Now, sir,' said Mark, 'it's of very little importance to you, I know; there's the difficulty; but it's of very great importance to me, and will you be so good as to consider of it?'

If this were meant as a second appeal to Martin's weak side, founded on his observation of the effect of the first, Mr. Tapley was a skilful and shrewd observer. Whether an intentional or an accidental shot, it hit the mark full; for Martin, relenting more and more, said, with a condescension which was inexpressibly delicious to him, after his recent humiliation:

'We'll see about it, Tapley. You shall tell me in what disposition you find yourself to-morrow.'

'Then, sir,' said Mark, rubbing his hands, 'the job's done. Go on, sir, if you please. I'm all attention.'

Throwing himself back in his arm-chair, and looking at the fire, with now and then a glance at Mark, who at such times nodded his head sagely, to express his profound interest and attention; Martin ran over the chief points in his history, to the same effect as he had related them, weeks before, to Mr. Pinch. But he adapted them, according to the best of his judgment, to Mr. Tapley's comprehension; and with that view made as light of his love affair as he could, and referred to it in very few words. But here he reckoned without his host; for Mark's keenest interest was keenest in this part of the business, and prompted him to ask sundry questions in relation to it; for which he apologised as one in some measure privileged to do so, from having seen (as Martin explained to him) the young lady at the Blue Dragon.

'And a young lady as any gentleman ought to feel more proud of being in love with,' said Mark, energetically, 'don't draw breath.'

'Aye! You saw her when she was not happy,' said Martin, gazing at the fire again. 'If you had seen her in the old times, indeed—'

'Why, she certainly was a little down-hearted, sir, and something paler in her colour than I could have wished,' said Mark, 'but none the worse in her looks for that. I think she seemed better, sir, after she come to London.'

Martin withdrew his eyes from the fire; stared at Mark as if he thought he had suddenly gone mad; and asked him what he meant.

'No offence intended, sir,' urged Mark. 'I don't mean to say she was any the happier without you: but I thought she was a-looking better, sir.'

'Do you mean to tell me she has been in London?' asked Martin, rising hurriedly, and pushing back his chair.

'Of course I do,' said Mark, rising too, in great amazement from the bedstead.

'Do you mean to tell me she is in London now?'

'Most likely, sir. I mean to say she was, a week ago.'

'And you know where?'

'Yes!' cried Mark. 'What! Don't you?'

'My good fellow!' exclaimed Martin, clutching him by both arms, 'I have never seen her since I left my grandfather's house.'

'Why, then!' cried Mark, giving the little table such a blow with his clenched fist that the slices of beef and ham danced upon it, while all his features seemed, with delight, to be going up into his forehead, and never coming back again any more, 'if I an't your nat'ral born servant, hired by Fate, there an't such a thing in natur' as a Blue Dragon. What! when I was a-rambling up and down a old churchyard in the City, getting myself into a jolly state, didn't I see your grandfather a-toddling to and fro for pretty nigh a mortal hour! Didn't I watch him into Todgers's commercial boarding-house, and watch him out, and watch him home to his hotel, and go and tell him as his was the service for my money, and I had said so, afore I left the Dragon! Wasn't the young lady a-sitting with him then, and didn't she fall a-laughing in a manner as was beautiful to see! Didn't your grandfather say, "Come back again next week," and didn't I go next week; and didn't he say that he couldn't make up his mind to trust nobody no more; and therefore wouldn't engage me; but at the same time stood something to drink as was handsome! Why,' cried Mr. Tapley, with a comical mixture of delight and chagrin, 'where's the credit of a man's being jolly under such circumstances! Who could help it, when things come about like this!'

For some moments Martin stood gazing at him, as if he really doubted the evidence of his senses, and could not believe that Mark stood there, in the body, before him. At length he asked him whether, if the young lady were still in London, he thought he could contrive to deliver a letter to her secretly.

'Do I think I can?' cried Mark. '*Think* I can? Here, sit down, sir. Write it out, sir!'

With that he cleared the table by the summary process of tilting everything upon it into the fire-place; snatched some writing materials from the mantel-shelf; set Martin's chair before them; forced him down into it; dipped a pen into the ink; and put it in his hand.

'Cut away, sir!' cried Mark. 'Make it strong, sir. Let it be wery pinted, sir. Do I think so? *I* should think so. Go to work, sir!'

Martin required no further adjuration, but went to work at a great rate; while Mr. Tapley, installing himself without any more formalities into the functions of his valet and general attendant, divested himself of his coat, and went on to clear the fire-place and arrange the room; talking to himself in a low voice the whole time.

'Jolly sort of lodgings,' said Mark, rubbing his nose with the knob at the end of the fire-shovel, and looking round the poor chamber: 'that's a comfort. The rain's come through the roof too. That an't bad. A lively old bedstead, I'll be bound; popilated by lots of wampires, no doubt. Come! my spirits is a-getting up again. An uncommon ragged nightcap this. A very good sign. We shall do yet! Here, Jane, my dear,' calling down the stairs, 'bring up that there hot tumbler for my master as was a-mixing when I come in. That's right, sir,' to Martin. 'Go at it as if you meant it, sir. Be very tender, sir, if you please. You can't make it too strong, sir!'

CHAPTER XIV

In which Martin bids adieu to the lady of his love; and honours an obscure individual whose fortune he intends to make, by commending her to his protection

THE letter being duly signed, sealed, and delivered, was handed to Mark Tapley for immediate conveyance if possible. And he succeeded so well in his embassy as to be enabled to return that same night, just as the house was closing, with the welcome intelligence that he had sent it up-stairs to the young lady, enclosed in a small manuscript of his own, purporting to contain his further petition to be engaged in Mr. Chuzzlewit's service; and that she had herself come down and told him, in great haste and agitation, that she would meet the gentleman at eight o'clock to-morrow morning in St. James's Park. It was then agreed between the new master and the new man, that Mark should be in waiting near the hotel in good time, to escort the young lady to the place of appointment; and when they had parted for the night with this understanding, Martin took up his pen again; and before he went to bed wrote another letter, whereof more will be seen presently.

He was up before day-break, and came upon the Park with the morning, which was clad in the least engaging of the three hundred and sixty-five dresses in the wardrobe of the year. It was raw, damp, dark, and dismal; the clouds were as muddy as the ground; and the short perspective of every street and avenue was closed up by the mist as by a filthy curtain.

'Fine weather indeed,' Martin bitterly soliloquised, 'to be wandering up and down here in, like a thief! Fine weather indeed, for a meeting of lovers in the open air, and in a public walk! I need be departing, with all speed, for another country; for I have come to a pretty pass in this!'

He might perhaps have gone on to reflect that of all mornings in the year, it was not the best calculated for a young lady's coming forth on such an errand, either. But he was stopped on the road to this reflection, if his thoughts tended that way, by her appearance at a short distance, on which he hurried forward to meet her. Her squire, Mr. Tapley, at the same time fell discreetly back, and surveyed the fog above him with an appearance of attentive interest.

'My dear Martin,' said Mary.

'My dear Mary,' said Martin; and lovers are such a singular kind of people that this is all they did say just then, though Martin took her arm, and her hand too, and they paced up and down a short walk that was least exposed to observation, half-a-dozen times.

'If you have changed at all, my love, since we parted,' said Martin at length, as he looked upon her with a proud delight, 'it is only to be more beautiful than ever!'

Had she been of the common metal of love-worn young ladies, she would have denied this in her most interesting manner: and would have told him that she knew she had become a perfect fright; or that she had wasted away with weeping and anxiety; or that she was dwindling gently into an early grave; or that her mental sufferings were unspeakable; or would, either by tears or words, or a mixture of both, have furnished him with some other information to that effect, and made him as miserable as possible. But she had been reared up in a sterner school than the minds of most young girls are formed in; she had had her nature strengthened by the hands of hard endurance and necessity; had come out from her young trials constant, self-denying, earnest, and devoted: had acquired in her maidenhood—whether happily in the end, for herself or him, is foreign to our present purpose to inquire— something of that nobler quality of gentle hearts which is developed often by the sorrows and struggles of matronly years, but often by their lessons only. Unspoiled, unpampered in her joys or griefs; with frank and full, and deep affection for the object of her early love; she saw in him one who for her sake was an outcast from his home and fortune, and she had no more idea of bestowing that love upon him in other than cheerful and sustaining words, full of high hope and grateful trust-fulness, than she had of being unworthy of it, in her lightest thought or deed, for any base temptation that the world could offer.

'What change is there in *you*, Martin,' she replied; 'for that concerns me nearest? You look more anxious and more thoughtful than you used.'

'Why, as to that, my love,' said Martin, as he drew her waist within his arm, first looking round to see that there were no observers near, and beholding Mr. Tapley more intent than ever on the fog; 'it would be strange if I did not; for my life, especially of late, has been a hard one.'

'I know it must have been,' she answered. 'When have I forgotten to think of it and you?'

'Not often, I hope,' said Martin. 'Not often, I am sure. Not often, I have some right to expect, Mary; for I have undergone a great deal of vexation and privation, and I naturally look for that return, you know.'

'A very, very poor return,' she anwered with a fainter smile. 'But you have it, and will have it always. You have paid a dear price for a poor heart, Martin; but it is at least your own, and a true one.'

'Of course I feel quite certain of that,' said Martin, 'or I shouldn't have put myself in my present position. And don't say a poor heart, Mary, for I say a rich one. Now, I am about to break a design to you, dearest, which will startle you at first, but which is undertaken for your sake. I am going,' he added slowly, looking far into the deep wonder of her bright dark eyes, 'abroad.'

'Abroad, Martin!'

'Only to America. See now. How you droop directly!'

'If I do, or, I hope I may say, if I did,' she answered, raising her head after a short silence, and looking once more into his face, 'it was for grief to think of what you are resolved to undergo for me. I would not venture to dissuade you, Martin; but it is a long, long distance; there is a wide ocean to be crossed; illness and want are sad calamities in any place, but in a foreign country dreadful to endure. Have you thought of all this?'

'Thought of it!' cried Martin, abating, in his fondness—and he *was* very fond of her—hardly an iota of his usual impetuosity. 'What am I to do? It's very well to say, Have I thought of it? my love; but you should ask me in the same breath, have I thought of starving at home; have I thought of doing porter's work for a living; have I thought of holding horses in the streets to earn my roll of bread from day to day? Come, come,' he added, in a gentler tone, 'do not hang down your head, my dear, for I need the encouragement that your sweet face alone can give me. Why, that's well! Now you are brave again.'

'I am endeavouring to be,' she answered, smiling through her tears.

'Endeavouring to be anything that's good, and being it, is, with you, all one. Don't I know that of old?' cried Martin, gaily. 'So! That's famous! Now I can tell you all my plans as cheerfully as if you were my little wife already, Mary.'

She hung more closely on his arm, and looking upwards in his face, bade him speak on.

'You see,' said Martin, playing with the little hand upon his wrist, 'that my attempts to advance myself at home have been baffled and rendered abortive. I will not say by whom, Mary, for that would give pain to us both. But so it is. Have you heard him speak of late of any relative of mine or his, called Pecksniff? Only tell me what I ask you, no more.'

'I have heard, to my surprise, that he is a better man than was supposed.'

'I thought so,' interrupted Martin.

'And that it is likely we may come to know him, if not to visit and reside with him and—I think—his daughters. He *has* daughters, has he, love?'

'A pair of them,' Martin answered. 'A precious pair! Gems of the first water!'

'Ah! You are jesting!'

'There is a sort of jesting which is very much in earnest, and includes some pretty serious disgust,' said Martin. 'I jest in reference to Mr. Pecksniff (at whose house I have been living as his assistant, and at whose hands I have received insult and injury), in that vein. Whatever betides, or however closely you may be brought into communication with his family, never forget that, Mary; and never for an instant, whatever appearances may seem to contradict me, lose sight of this assurance: Pecksniff is a scoundrel.'

'Indeed!'

'In thought, and in deed, and in everything else. A scoundrel from the topmost hair of his head, to the nethermost atom of his heel. Of his daughters I will only say that, to the best of my knowledge and belief, they are dutiful young ladies, and take after their father closely. This is a digression from the main point, and yet it brings me to what I was going to say.'

He stopped to look into her eyes again, and seeing, in a hasty glance over his shoulder, that there was no one near, and that Mark was still intent upon the fog, not only looked at her lips too, but kissed them into the bargain.

'Now I am going to America, with great prospects of doing

well, and of returning home myself very soon; it may be to take you there for a few years, but, at all events, to claim you for my wife: which, after such trials, I should do with no fear of your still thinking it a duty to cleave to him who will not suffer me to live (for this is true), if he can help it, in my own land. How long I may be absent is, of course, uncertain; but it shall not be very long. Trust me for that.'

'In the meantime, dear Martin—'

'That's the very thing I am coming to. In the meantime you shall hear, constantly, of all my goings-on. Thus.'

He paused to take from his pocket the letter he had written over-night, and then resumed:

'In this fellow's employment, and living in this fellow's house (by fellow, I mean Mr. Pecksniff, of course), there is a certain person of the name of Pinch. Don't forget; a poor, strange, simple oddity, Mary; but thoroughly honest and sincere; full of zeal; and with a cordial regard for me. Which I mean to return one of these days, by setting him up in life in some way or other.'

'Your old kind nature, Martin!'

'Oh!' said Martin, 'that's not worth speaking of, my love. He's very grateful and desirous to serve me; and I am more than repaid. Now one night I told this Pinch my history, and all about myself and you; in which he was not a little interested, I can tell you, for he knows you! Aye, you may look surprised—and the longer the better, for it becomes you—but you have heard him play the organ in the church of that village before now; and he has seen you listening to his music; and has caught his inspiration from you, too!'

'Was *he* the organist?' cried Mary. 'I thank him from my heart!'

'Yes, he was,' said Martin, 'and is, and gets nothing for it either. There never was such a simple fellow! Quite an infant! But a very good sort of creature, I assure you.'

'I am sure of that,' she said, with great earnestness. 'He must be!'

'Oh, yes, no doubt at all about it,' rejoined Martin, in his usual careless way. 'He is. Well! It has occurred to me—but stay. If I read you what I have written and intend sending to him by post to-night, it will explain itself. "My dear Tom Pinch." That's rather familiar perhaps,' said Martin, suddenly remembering that he was proud when they had last met, 'but

Mr. Tapley acts Third Party with great Discretion

I call him my dear Tom Pinch because he likes it, and it pleases him.'

'Very right, and very kind,' said Mary.

'Exactly so!' cried Martin. 'It's as well to be kind whenever one can; and, as I said before, he really is an excellent fellow. "My dear Tom Pinch. I address this under cover to Mrs. Lupin, at the Blue Dragon, and have begged her in a short note to deliver it to you without saying anything about it elsewhere; and to do the same with all future letters she may receive from me. My reason for so doing will be at once apparent to you." I don't know that it will be, by-the-bye,' said Martin, breaking off, 'for he's slow of comprehension, poor fellow; but he'll find it out in time. My reason simply is, that I don't want my letters to be read by other people; and particulary by the scoundrel whom he thinks an angel.'

'Mr. Pecksniff again?' asked Mary.

'The same,' said Martin: ' "—will be at once apparent to you. I have completed my arrangements for going to America; and you will be surprised to hear that I am to be accompanied by Mark Tapley, upon whom I have stumbled strangely in London, and who insists on putting himself under my protection:" meaning, my love,' said Martin, breaking off again, 'our friend in the rear, of course.'

She was delighted to hear this, and bestowed a kind glance upon Mark, which he brought his eyes down from the fog to encounter, and received with immense satisfaction. She said in his hearing, too, that he was a good soul and a merry creature, and would be faithful, she was certain; commendations which Mr. Tapley inwardly resolved to deserve, from such lips, if he died for it.

' "Now, my dear Pinch," ' resumed Martin, proceeding with his letter; ' "I am going to repose great trust in you, knowing that I may do so with perfect reliance on your honour and secrecy, and having nobody else just now to trust in." '

'I don't think I would say that, Martin.'

'Wouldn't you? Well! I'll take that out. It's perfectly true, though.'

'But it might seem ungracious, perhaps.'

'Oh, I don't mind Pinch,' said Martin. 'There's no occasion to stand on any ceremony with *him*. However, I'll take it out, as you wish it, and make the full stop at "secrecy." Very well! "I shall not only"—this is the letter again, you know.'

'I understand.'

' " I shall not only enclose my letters to the young lady of whom I have told you, to your charge, to be forwarded as she may request; but I most earnestly commit her, the young lady herself, to your care and regard, in the event of your meeting in my absence. I have reason to think that the probabilities of your encountering each other—perhaps very frequently—are now neither remote nor few; and although in our position you can do very little to lessen the uneasiness of hers, I trust to you implicitly to do that much, and so deserve the confidence I have reposed in you." You see, my dear Mary,' said Martin, 'it will be a great consolation to you to have anybody, no matter how simple, with whom you can speak about ME; and the very first time you talk to Pinch, you'll feel at once that there is no more occasion for any embarrassment or hesitation in talking to him, than if he were an old woman.'

'However that may be,' she returned, smiling, 'he is your friend, and that is enough.'

'Oh, yes, he's my friend,' said Martin, 'certainly. In fact, I have told him in so many words that we'll always take notice of him, and protect him: and it's a good trait in his character that he's grateful, very grateful indeed. You'll like him of all things, my love, I know. You'll observe very much that's comical and old-fashioned about Pinch, but you needn't mind laughing at him; for he'll not care about it. He'll rather like it indeed!'

'I don't think I shall put that to the test, Martin.'

'You won't if you can help it, of course,' he said, 'but I think you'll find him a little too much for your gravity. However, that's neither here nor there, and it certainly is not the letter; which ends thus: "Knowing that I need not impress the nature and extent of that confidence upon you at any greater length, as it is already sufficiently established in your mind, I will only say, in bidding you farewell and looking forward to our next meeting, that I shall charge myself from this time, through all changes for the better, with your advancement and happiness, as if they were my own. You may rely upon that. And always believe me, my dear Tom Pinch, faithfully your friend, Martin Chuzzlewit. P.S. I enclose the amount which you so kindly"— Oh,' said Martin, checking himself, and folding up the letter, 'that's nothing!'

At this crisis Mark Tapley interposed, with an apology for

remarking that the clock at the Horse Guards was strik-ing.

'Which I shouldn't have said nothing about, sir,' added Mark, 'if the young lady hadn't begged me to be particular in mentioning it.'

'I did,' said Mary. 'Thank you. You are quite right. In another minute I shall be ready to return. We have time for a very few words more, dear Martin, and although I had much to say, it must remain unsaid until the happy time of our next meeting. Heaven send it may come speedily and prosperously! But I have no fear of that.'

'Fear!' cried Martin. 'Why, who has? What are a few months? What is a whole year? When I come gaily back, with a road through life hewn out before me, then indeed, looking back upon this parting, it may seem a dismal one. But now! I swear I wouldn't have it happen under more favourable auspices, if I could: for then I should be less inclined to go, and less impressed with the necessity.'

'Yes, yes. I feel that too. When do you go?'

'To-night. We leave for Liverpool to-night. A vessel sails from that port, as I hear, in three days. In a month, or less, we shall be there. Why, what's a month! How many months have flown by, since our last parting!'

'Long to look back upon,' said Mary, echoing his cheerful tone, 'but nothing in their course!'

'Nothing at all!' cried Martin. 'I shall have change of scene and change of place; change of people, change of manners, change of cares and hopes! Time will wear wings indeed! I can bear anything, so that I have swift action, Mary.'

Was he thinking solely of her care for him, when he took so little heed of her share in the separation; of her quiet monoton-ous endurance, and her slow anxiety from day to day? Was there nothing jarring and discordant even in his tone of courage, with this one note 'self' for ever audible, however high the strain? Not in her ears. It had been better otherwise, perhaps, but so it was. She heard the same bold spirit which had flung away as dross all gain and profit for her sake, making light of peril and privation that she might be calm and happy; and she heard no more. That heart where self has found no place and raised no throne, is slow to recognise its ugly presence when it looks upon it. As one possessed of an evil spirit was held in old time to be alone conscious of the lurking demon in the breasts of other men, so kindred vices know each other in their hiding-places every day, when Virtue is incredulous and blind.

'The quarter's gone!' cried Mr. Tapley, in a voice of admonition.

'I shall be ready to return immediately,' she said. 'One thing, dear Martin, I am bound to tell you. You entreated me a few minutes since only to answer what you asked me in reference to one theme, but you should and must know (otherwise I could not be at ease), that since that separation of which I was the unhappy occasion, he has never once uttered your name; has never coupled it, or any faint allusion to it, with passion or reproach; and has never abated in his kindness to me.'

'I thank him for that last act,' said Martin, 'and for nothing else. Though on consideration I may thank him for his other forbearance also, inasmuch as I neither expect nor desire that he will mention my name again. He may once, perhaps—to couple it with reproach—in his will. Let him, if he please! By the time it reaches me, he will be in his grave: a satire on his own anger, God help him!'

'Martin! If you would but sometimes, in some quiet hour; beside the winter fire; in the summer air; when you hear gentle music, or think of Death, or Home, or Childhood; if you would at such a season resolve to think, but once a month, or even once a year, of him, or any one who ever wronged you, you would forgive him in your heart, I know!'

'If I believed that to be true, Mary,' he replied, 'I would resolve at no such time to bear him in my mind: wishing to spare myself the shame of such a weakness. I was not born to be the toy and puppet of any man, far less his; to whose pleasure and caprice, in return for any good he did me, my whole youth was sacrificed. It became between us two a fair exchange, a barter, and no more: and there is no such balance against me that I need throw in a mawkish forgiveness to poise the scale. He has forbidden all mention of me to you, I know,' he added hastily. 'Come! Has he not?'

'That was long ago,' she returned; 'immediately after your parting; before you had left the house. He has never done so since.'

'He has never done so since because he has seen no occasion,' said Martin; 'but that is of little consequence, one way or other. Let all allusion to him between you and me be interdicted from this time forth. And therefore, love:' he drew her quickly to him, for the time of parting had now come: 'in the first letter that you write to me through the Post Office, addressed to New York; and in all the others that you send through Pinch; remember he has no existence, but has become to us as one who is dead. Now, God bless you! This is a strange place for such a meeting and such a parting; but our next meeting shall be in a better, and our next and last parting in a worse.'

'One other question, Martin, I must ask. Have you provided money for this journey?'

'Have I?' cried Martin; it might have been in his pride; it might have been in his desire to set her mind at ease: 'Have I provided money? Why, there's a question for an emigrant's wife! How could I move on land or sea without it, love?'

'I mean, enough.'

'Enough! More than enough. Twenty times more than enough. A pocket-full. Mark and I, for all essential ends, are quite as rich as if we had the purse of Fortunatus in our baggage.'

'The half-hour's a-going!' cried Mr. Tapley.

'Good-bye a hundred times!' cried Mary, in a trembling voice.

But how cold the comfort in Good-bye! Mark Tapley knew it perfectly. Perhaps he knew it from his reading, perhaps from his experience, perhaps from intuition. It is impossible to say; but however he knew it, his knowledge instinctively suggested to him the wisest course of proceeding that any man could have adopted under the circumstances. He was taken with a violent fit of sneezing, and was obliged to turn his head another way. In doing which, he, in a manner, fenced and screened the lovers into a corner by themselves.

There was a short pause, but Mark had an undefined sensation that it was a satisfactory one in its way. Then Mary, with her veil lowered, passed him with a quick step, and beckoned him to follow. She stopped once more before they lost that corner; looked back; and waved her hand to Martin. He made a start towards them at the moment as if he had some other farewell words to say; but she only hurried off the faster, and Mr. Tapley followed as in duty bound.

When he rejoined Martin again in his own chamber, he found that gentleman seated moodily before the dusty grate, with his two feet on the fender, his two elbows on his knees, and his chin supported, in a not very ornamental manner, on the palms of his hands.

'Well, Mark!'

'Well, sir,' said Mark, taking a long breath, 'I see the young lady safe home, and I feel pretty comfortable after it. She sent a lot of kind words, sir, and this,' handing him a ring, 'for a parting keepsake.'

'Diamonds!' said Martin, kissing it—let us do him justice, it was for her sake; not for theirs—and putting it on his little finger. 'Splendid diamonds! My grandfather is a singular character, Mark. He must have given her this, now.'

Mark Tapley knew as well that she had bought it, to the end that that unconscious speaker might carry some article of sterling value with him in his necessity; as he knew that it was day, and not night. Though he had no more acquaintance of his own knowledge with the history of the glittering trinket on Martin's outspread finger, than Martin himself had, he was as certain that in its purchase she had expended her whole stock of hoarded money, as if he had seen it paid down coin by coin. Her lover's strange obtuseness in relation to this little incident, promptly suggested to Mark's mind its real cause and root; and from that moment he had a clear and perfect insight into the one absorbing principle of Martin's character.

'She is worthy of the sacrifices I have made,' said Martin, folding his arms, and looking at the ashes in the stove, as if in resumption of some former thoughts. 'Well worthy of them. No riches:' here he stroked his chin, and mused: 'could have compensated for the loss of such a nature. Not to mention that in gaining her affection I have followed the bent of my own wishes, and baulked the selfish schemes of others who had no right to form them. She is quite worthy, more than worthy, of the sacrifices I have made. Yes, she is. No doubt of it.'

These ruminations might or might not have reached Mark Tapley; for though they were by no means addressed to him, yet they were softly uttered. In any case, he stood there, watching Martin with an indescribable and most involved expression on his visage, until that young man roused himself and looked towards him; when he turned away, as being suddenly intent upon certain preparations for the journey, and, without giving vent to any articulate sound, smiled with surpassing ghastliness, and seemed by a twist of his features and a motion of his lips, to release himself of this word:

'Jolly!'

CHAPTER XV

The burden whereof is, Hail, Columbia!

A DARK and dreary night; people nestling in their beds or circling late about the fire; Want, colder than Charity, shivering at the street corners; church-towers humming with the faint vibration of their own tongues, but newly resting from the ghostly preachment 'One!' The earth covered with a sable pall as for the burial of yesterday; the clumps of dark trees, its giant plumes of funeral feathers, waving sadly to and fro: all hushed, all noiseless, and in deep repose, save the swift clouds that skim across the moon, and the cautious wind, as, creeping after them upon the ground, it stops to listen, and goes rustling on, and stops again, and follows, like a savage on the trail.

Whither go the clouds and wind so eagerly? If, like guilty spirits, they repair to some dread conference with powers like themselves, in what wild regions do the elements hold council, or where unbend in terrible disport?

Here! Free from that cramped prison called the earth, and out upon the waste of waters. Here, roaring, raging, shrieking, howling, all night long. Hither come the sounding voices from the caverns on the coast of that small island, sleeping, a thousand miles away, so quietly in the midst of angry waves; and hither, to meet them, rush the blasts from unknown desert places of the world. Here, in the fury of their unchecked liberty, they storm and buffet with each other, until the sea, lashed into passion like their own, leaps up, in ravings mightier than theirs, and the whole scene is madness.

On, on, on, over the countless miles of angry space roll the long heaving billows. Mountains and caves are here, and yet are not; for what is now the one, is now the other; then all is but a boiling heap of rushing water. Pursuit, and flight, and mad return of wave on wave, and savage struggle, ending in a spouting-up of foam that whitens the black night; incessant change of place, and form, and hue; constancy in nothing, but eternal strife; on, on, on, they roll, and darker grows the night, and louder howls the wind, and more clamorous and fierce become the million voices in the sea, when the wild cry goes forth upon the storm 'A ship!'

Onward she comes, in gallant combat with the elements, her tall masts trembling, and her timbers starting on the strain; onward she comes, now high upon the curling billows, now low down in the hollows of the sea, as hiding for the moment from its fury; and every storm-voice in the air and water cries more loudly yet, 'A ship!'

Still she comes striving on: and at her boldness and the spreading cry, the angry waves rise up above each other's hoary heads to look; and round about the vessel, far as the mariners on the decks can pierce into the gloom, they press upon her, forcing each other down, and starting up, and rushing forward from afar, in dreadful curiosity. High over her they break; and round her surge and roar; and giving place to others, moaningly depart, and dash themselves to fragments in their baffled anger. Still she comes onward bravely. And though the eager multitude crowd thick and fast upon her all the night, and dawn of day discovers the untiring train yet bearing down upon the ship in an eternity of troubled water, onward she comes, with dim lights burning in her hull, and people there, asleep: as if no deadly element were peering in at every seam and chink, and no drowned seaman's grave, with but a plank to cover it, were yawning in the unfathomable depths below.

Among these sleeping voyagers were Martin and Mark Tapley, who, rocked into a heavy drowsiness by the unaccustomed motion, were as insensible to the foul air in which they lay, as to the uproar without. It was broad day, when the latter awoke with a dim idea that he was dreaming of having gone to sleep in a four-post bedstead which had turned bottom upwards in the course of the night. There was more reason in this too, than in the roasting of eggs; for the first objects Mr. Tapley recognised when he opened his eyes were his own heels —looking down to him, as he afterwards observed, from a nearly perpendicular elevation.

'Well!' said Mark, getting himself into a sitting posture, after various ineffectual struggles with the rolling of the ship. 'This is the first time as ever I stood on my head all night.'

'You shouldn't go to sleep upon the ground with your head to leeward then,' growled a man in one of the berths.

'With my head to *where?*' asked Mark.

The man repeated his previous sentiment.

'No, I won't another time,' said Mark, 'when I know whereabouts on the map that country is. In the meanwhile I can give you a better piece of advice. Don't you nor any other friend of mine never go to sleep with his head in a ship any more.'

The man gave a grunt of discontented acquiescence, turned over in his berth, and drew his blanket over his head.

'—For,' said Mr. Tapley, pursuing the theme by way of soliloquy, in a low tone of voice: 'the sea is as nonsensical a thing as any going. It never knows what to do with itself. It hasn't got no employment for its mind, and is always in a state of vacancy. Like them Polar bears in the wild-beast shows as is constantly a-nodding their heads from side to side, it never *can* be quiet. Which is entirely owing to its uncommon stupidity.'

'Is that you, Mark?' asked a faint voice from another berth.

'It's as much of me as is left, sir, after a fortnight of this work,' Mr. Tapley replied. 'What with leading the life of a fly, ever since I've been aboard—for I've been perpetually holding-on to something or other, in a upside-down position—what with that, sir, and putting a very little into myself, and taking a good deal out of myself, there an't too much of me to swear by. How do *you* find yourself this morning, sir?'

'Very miserable,' said Martin, with a peevish groan. 'Ugh! This is wretched, indeed!'

'Creditable,' muttered Mark, pressing one hand upon his aching head and looking round him with a rueful grin. 'That's the great comfort. It *is* creditable to keep up one's spirits here. Virtue's its own reward. So's jollity.'

Mark was so far right, that unquestionably any man who retained his cheerfulness among the steerage accommodations of that noble and fast-sailing line-of-packet ship, 'The Screw,' was solely indebted to his own resources, and shipped his good humour, like his provisions, without any contribution or assistance from the owners. A dark, low, stifling cabin, surrounded by berths all filled to overflowing with men, women, and children, in various stages of sickness and misery, is not the liveliest place of assembly at any time; but when it is so crowded (as the steerage cabin of 'The Screw' was, every passage out), that mattresses and beds are heaped upon the floor, to the extinction of everything like comfort, cleanliness, and decency, it is liable to operate not only as a pretty strong barrier against amiability of temper, but as a positive encourager of selfish and rough humours. Mark felt this, as he sat looking about him; and his spirits rose proportionately.

There were English people, Irish people, Welsh people, and Scotch people there; all with their little store of coarse food and shabby clothes; and nearly all with their families of children. There were children of all ages; from the baby at the breast, to the slattern-girl who was as much a grown woman as her mother. Every kind of domestic suffering that is bred in poverty, illness, banishment, sorrow, and long travel in bad weather, was crammed into the little space; and yet was there infinitely less of complaint and querulousness, and infinitely more of mutual assistance and general kindness to be found in that unwholesome ark, than in many brilliant ball-rooms.

Mark looked about him wistfully, and his face brightened as he looked. Here an old grandmother was crooning over a sick child, and rocking it to and fro, in arms hardly more wasted than its own young limbs; here a poor woman with an infant in her lap, mended another little creature's clothes, and quieted another who was creeping up about her from their scanty bed upon the floor. Here were old men awkwardly engaged in little household offices, wherein they would have been ridiculous but for their good-will and kind purpose; and here were swarthy fellows—giants in their way—doing such little acts of tenderness for those about them, as might have belonged to gentlest-hearted dwarfs. The very idiot in the corner who sat mowing there, all day, had his faculty of imitation roused by what he saw about him; and snapped his fingers to amuse a crying child.

'Now, then,' said Mark, nodding to a woman who was dressing her three children at no great distance from him; and the grin upon his face had by this time spread from ear to ear: 'Hand over one of them young uns according to custom.'

'I wish you'd get breakfast, Mark, instead of worrying with people who don't belong to you,' observed Martin, petulantly.

'All right,' said Mark. '*She*'ll do that. It's a fair division of labour, sir. I wash her boys, and she makes our tea. I never *could* make tea, but any one can wash a boy.'

The woman, who was delicate and ill, felt and understood his kindness, as well she might, for she had been covered every night with his great-coat, while he had had for his own bed the bare boards and a rug. But Martin, who seldom got up or looked about him, was quite incensed by the folly of this speech, and expressed his dissatisfaction by an impatient groan.

'So it is, certainly,' said Mark, brushing the child's hair as coolly as if he had been born and bred a barber.

'What are you talking about, now?' asked Martin.

'What you said,' replied Mark; 'or what you meant, when you gave that there dismal vent to your feelings. I quite go along with it, sir. It *is* very hard upon her.'

'What is?'

'Making the voyage by herself along with these young impediments here, and going such a way at such a time of the year to join her husband. If you don't want to be driven mad with yellow soap in your eye, young man,' said Mr. Tapley to the second urchin, who was by this time under his hands at the basin, 'you'd better shut it.'

'Where does she join her husband?' asked Martin, yawning.

'Why, I'm very much afraid,' said Mr. Tapley, in a low voice, 'that she don't know. I hope she mayn't miss him. But she sent her last letter by hand, and it don't seem to have been very clearly understood between 'em without it, and if she don't see him a-waving his pocket-handkerchief on the shore, like a pictur out of a song-book, my opinion is she'll break her heart.'

'Why, how, in Folly's name, does the woman come to be on board ship on such a wild-goose venture!' cried Martin.

Mr. Tapley glanced at him for a moment as he lay prostrate in his berth, and then said, very quietly:

'Ah! How indeed! I can't think! He's been away from her for two year: she's been very poor and lonely in her own country; and has always been a-looking forward to meeting him. It's very strange she should be here. Quite amazing! A little mad perhaps! There can't be no other way of accounting for it.'

Martin was too far gone in the lassitude of sea-sickness to make any reply to these words, or even to attend to them as they were spoken. And the subject of their discourse returning at this crisis with some hot tea, effectually put a stop to any resumption of the theme by Mr. Tapley; who, when the meal was over and he had adjusted Martin's bed, went up on deck to wash the breakfast service, which consisted of two half-pint tin mugs, and a shaving-pot of the same metal.

It is due to Mark Tapley to state that he suffered at least

as much from sea-sickness as any man, woman, or child, on
board; and that he had a peculiar faculty of knocking himself
about on the smallest provocation, and losing his legs at every
lurch of the ship. But resolved, in his usual phrase, to 'come
out strong' under disadvantageous circumstances, he was the
life and soul of the steerage, and made no more of stopping
in the middle of a facetious conversation to go away and be
excessively ill by himself, and afterwards come back in the very
best and gayest of tempers to resume it, than if such a course
of proceeding had been the commonest in the world.

It cannot be said that as his illness wore off, his cheerfulness
and good nature increased, because they would hardly admit
of augmentation; but his usefulness among the weaker members
of the party was much enlarged; and at all times and seasons
there he was exerting it. If a gleam of sun shone out of the dark
sky, down Mark tumbled into the cabin, and presently up he
came again with a woman in his arms, or half-a-dozen children,
or a man, or a bed, or a saucepan, or a basket, or something
animate or inanimate, that he thought would be the better for
the air. If an hour or two of fine weather in the middle of the
day tempted those who seldom or never came on deck at other
times to crawl into the long-boat, or lie down upon the spare
spars, and try to eat, there, in the centre of the group, was Mr.
Tapley, handing about salt beef and biscuit, or dispensing
tastes of grog, or cutting up the children's provisions with his
pocket-knife, for their greater ease and comfort, or reading
aloud from a venerable newspaper, or singing some roaring old
song to a select party, or writing the beginnings of letters to
their friends at home for people who couldn't write, or cracking
jokes with the crew, or nearly getting blown over the side, or
emerging, half-drowned, from a shower of spray, or lending
a hand somewhere or other: but always doing something for the
general entertainment. At night, when the cooking-fire was
lighted on the deck, and the driving sparks that flew among the
rigging, and the cloud of sails, seemed to menace the ship with
certain annihilation by fire, in case the elements of air and
water failed to compass her destruction; there, again, was
Mr. Tapley, with his coat off and his shirt-sleeves turned up to
his elbows, doing all kinds of culinary offices; compounding the
strangest dishes; recognised by every one as an established
authority; and helping all parties to achieve something which,
left to themselves, they never could have done, and never

would have dreamed of. In short, there never was a more popular character than Mark Tapley became, on board that noble and fast-sailing line-of-packet ship, the Screw; and he attained at last to such a pitch of universal admiration, that he began to have grave doubts within himself whether a man might reasonably claim any credit for being jolly under such exciting circumstances.

'If this was going to last,' said Tapley, 'there'd be no great difference as I can perceive, between the Screw and the Dragon. I never *am* to get credit, I think. I begin to be afraid that the Fates is determined to make the world easy to me.'

'Well, Mark,' said Martin, near whose berth he had ruminated to this effect. 'When will this be over?'

'Another week, they say, sir,' returned Mark, 'will most likely bring us into port. The ship's a-going along at present, as sensible as a ship can, sir; though I don't mean to say as that's any very high praise.'

'I don't think it is, indeed,' groaned Martin.

'You'd feel all the better for it, sir, if you was to turn out,' observed Mark.

'And be seen by the ladies and gentlemen on the after-deck,' returned Martin, with a scornful emphasis upon the words, 'mingling with the beggarly crowd that are stowed away in this vile hole. I should be greatly the better for that, no doubt!'

'I'm thankful that I can't say from my own experience what the feelings of a gentleman may be,' said Mark, 'but I should have thought, sir, as a gentleman would feel a deal more uncomfortable down here than up in the fresh air, especially when the ladies and gentlemen in the after-cabin know just as much about him as he does about them, and are likely to trouble their heads about him in the same proportion. I should have thought that, certainly.'

'I tell you, then,' rejoined Martin, 'you would have thought wrong, and do think wrong.'

'Very likely, sir,' said Mark, with imperturbable good temper. 'I often do.'

'As to lying here,' cried Martin, raising himself on his elbow, and looking angrily at his follower. 'Do you suppose it's a pleasure to lie here?'

'All the madhouses in the world,' said Mr. Tapley, 'couldn't produce such a maniac as the man must be who could think that.'

'Then why are you for ever goading and urging me to get up?' asked Martin. 'I lie here because I don't wish to be recognised, in the better days to which I aspire, by any purse-proud citizen, as the man who came over with him among the steerage passengers. I lie here because I wish to conceal my circumstances and myself, and not to arrive in a new world badged and ticketed as an utterly poverty-stricken man. If I could have afforded a passage in the after-cabin, I should have held up my head with the rest. As I couldn't, I hide it. Do you understand that?'

'I am very sorry, sir,' said Mark. 'I didn't know you took it so much to heart as this comes to.'

'Of course you didn't know,' returned his master. 'How should you know, unless I told you? It's no trial to *you*, Mark, to make yourself comfortable and to bustle about. It's as natural for you to do so under the circumstances as it is for me not to do so. Why, you don't suppose there is a living creature in this ship who can by possibility have half so much to undergo on board of her as *I* have? Do you?' he asked, sitting upright in his berth and looking at Mark, with an expression of great earnestness not unmixed with wonder.

Mark twisted his face into a tight knot, and with his head very much on one side pondered upon this question as if he felt it an extremely difficult one to answer. He was relieved from his embarrassment by Martin himself, who said, as he stretched himself upon his back again and resumed the book he had been reading:

'But what is the use of my putting such a case to you, when the very essence of what I have been saying is, that you cannot by possibility understand it! Make me a little brandy-and-water, cold and very weak, and give me a biscuit, and tell your friend, who is a nearer neighbour of ours than I could wish, to try and keep her children a little quieter to-night than she did last night; that's a good fellow.'

Mr. Tapley set himself to obey these orders with great alacrity, and pending their execution, it may be presumed his flagging spirits revived: inasmuch as he several times observed, below his breath, that in respect of its power of imparting a credit to jollity, the Screw unquestionably had some decided advantages over the Dragon. He also remarked that it was a high gratification to him to reflect that he would carry its main excellence ashore with him, and have it constantly beside him wherever he went; but what he meant by these consolatory thoughts he did not explain.

And now a general excitement began to prevail on board; and various predictions relative to the precise day, and even the precise hour at which they would reach New York, were freely broached. There was infinitely more crowding on deck and looking over the ship's side than there had been before; and an epidemic broke out for packing up things every morning, which required unpacking again every night. Those who had any letters to deliver, or any friends to meet, or any settled plans of going anywhere or doing anything, discussed their prospects a hundred times a day; and as this class of passengers was very small, and the number of those who had no prospects whatever was very large, there were plenty of listeners and few talkers. Those who had been ill all along, got well now, and those who had been well, got better. An American gentleman in the after-cabin, who had been wrapped up in fur and oilskin the whole passage, unexpectedly appeared in a very shiny, tall, black hat, and constantly overhauled a very little valise of pale leather, which contained his clothes, linen, brushes, shaving apparatus, books, trinkets, and other baggage. He likewise stuck his hands deep into his pockets, and walked the deck with his nostrils dilated, as already inhaling the air of Freedom which carries death to all tyrants, and can never (under any circumstances worth mentioning) be breathed by slaves. An English gentleman who was strongly suspected of having run away from a bank, with something in his possession belonging to its strong-box besides the key, grew eloquent upon the subject of the rights of man, and hummed the Marseillaise Hymn constantly. In a word, one great sensation pervaded the whole ship, and the soil of America lay close before them: so close at last, that, upon a certain starlight night, they took a pilot on board, and within a few hours afterwards lay to until the morning, awaiting the arrival of a steamboat in which the passengers were to be conveyed ashore.

Off she came, soon after it was light next morning, and lying alongside an hour or more—during which period her very firemen were objects of hardly less interest and curiosity than if they had been so many angels, good or bad—took all her living freight aboard. Among them Mark, who still had his friend and her three children under his close protection: and Martin, who had once more dressed himself in his usual attire, but wore a soiled, old cloak above his ordinary clothes, until such time as he should separate for ever from his late companions.

The steamer—which, with its machinery on deck, looked, as it worked its long slim legs, like some enormously magnified insect or antediluvian monster—dashed at great speed up a beautiful bay; and presently they saw some heights, and islands, and a long, flat, straggling city.

'And this,' said Mr. Tapley, looking far ahead, 'is the Land of Liberty, is it? Very well. I'm agreeable. Any land will do for me, after so much water!'

CHAPTER XVI

Martin disembarks from that noble and fast-sailing line-of-packet ship, The Screw, at the port of New York, in the United States of America. He makes some acquaintances, and dines at a boarding-house. The particulars of those transactions

SOME trifling excitement prevailed upon the very brink and margin of the land of liberty; for an alderman had been elected the day before; and Party Feeling naturally running rather high on such an exciting occasion, the friends of the disappointed candidate had found it necessary to assert the great principles of Purity of Election and Freedom of Opinion by breaking a few legs and arms, and furthermore pursuing one obnoxious gentleman through the streets with the design of slitting his nose. These good-humoured little outbursts of the popular fancy were not in themselves sufficiently remarkable to create any great stir, after the lapse of a whole night; but they found fresh life and notoriety in the breath of the newsboys, who not only proclaimed them with shrill yells in all the highways and byways of the town, upon the wharves and among the shipping, but on the deck and down in the cabins of the steamboat; which, before she touched the shore, was boarded and overrun by a legion of those young citizens.

'Here's this morning's New York Sewer!' cried one. 'Here's this morning's New York Stabber! Here's the New York Family Spy! Here's the New York Private Listener! Here's the New York Peeper! Here's the New York Plunderer! Here's the New York Keyhole Reporter! Here's the New York Rowdy Journal! Here's all the New York papers! Here's full particulars of the patriotic loco-foco movement yesterday, in which the whigs was so chawed up; and the last Alabama gouging case; and the interesting Arkansas dooel with Bowie knives; and all the Political, Commercial, and Fashionable News. Here they are! Here they are! Here's the papers, here's the papers!'

'Here's the Sewer!' cried another. 'Here's the New York Sewer! Here's some of the twelfth thousand of to-day's Sewer, with the best accounts of the markets, and all the shipping news, and four whole columns of country correspondence, and a full account of the Ball at Mrs. White's last night, where all the beauty and fashion of New York was assembled; with the Sewer's own particulars of the private lives of all the ladies that was there! Here's the Sewer! Here's some of the twelfth thousand of the New York Sewer! Here's the Sewer's exposure of the Wall Street Gang, and the Sewer's exposure of the Washington Gang, and the Sewer's exclusive account of a flagrant act of dishonesty committed by the Secretary of State when he was eight years old; now communicated, at a great expense, by his own nurse. Here's the Sewer! Here's the New York Sewer, in its twelfth thousand, with a whole column of New Yorkers to be shown up, and all their names printed! Here's the Sewer's article upon the Judge that tried him, day afore yesterday, for libel, and the Sewer's tribute to the independent Jury that didn't convict him, and the Sewer's account of what they might have expected if they had! Here's the Sewer, here's the Sewer! Here's the wide-awake Sewer; always on the look-out; the leading Journal of the United States, now in its twelfth thousand, and still a-printing off. Here's the New York Sewer!'

'It is in such enlightened means,' said a voice almost in Martin's ear, 'that the bubbling passions of my country find a vent.'

Martin turned involuntarily, and saw, standing close at his side, a sallow gentleman, with sunken cheeks, black hair, small twinkling eyes, and a singular expression hovering about that region of his face, which was not a frown, nor a leer, and yet might have been mistaken at the first glance for either. Indeed it would have been difficult, on a much closer acquaintance, to describe it in any more satisfactory terms than as a mixed expression of vulgar cunning and conceit. This gentleman wore a rather broad-brimmed hat for the greater wisdom of his appearance; and had his arms folded for the greater impressiveness of his attitude. He was somewhat shabbily dressed in a blue surtout reaching nearly to his ankles, short loose trousers of the same colour, and a faded buff waistcoat, through which a discoloured shirt-frill struggled to force itself into notice, as asserting an equality of civil rights with the other portions of his dress, and maintaining a declaration of Independence on its own account. His feet, which were of unusually large proportions, were leisurely crossed before him as he half leaned against, half sat upon, the steamboat's bulwark; and his thick cane, shod with a mighty ferule at one end and armed with a great metal knob at the other, depended from a line-and-tassel on his wrist. Thus attired, and thus composed into an aspect of great profundity, the gentleman twitched up the right-hand corner of his mouth and his right eye simultaneously, and said, once more:

'It is in such enlightened means that the bubbling passions of my country find a vent.'

As he looked at Martin, and nobody else was by, Martin inclined his head, and said:

'You allude to—?'

'To the Palladium of rational Liberty at home, sir, and the dread of Foreign oppression abroad,' returned the gentleman, as he pointed with his cane to an uncommonly dirty newsboy with one eye. 'To the Envy of the world, sir, and the leaders of Human Civilization. Let me ask you, sir,' he added, bringing the ferule of his stick heavily upon the deck with the air of a man who must not be equivocated with, 'how do you like my Country?'

'I am hardly prepared to answer that question yet,' said Martin, 'seeing that I have not been ashore.'

'Well, I should expect you were not prepared, sir,' said the gentleman, 'to behold such signs of National Prosperity as those?'

He pointed to the vessels lying at the wharves; and then gave a vague flourish with his stick, as if he would include the air and water, generally, in this remark.

'Really,' said Martin, 'I don't know. Yes. I think I was.'

The gentleman glanced at him with a knowing look, and said he liked his policy. It was natural, he said, and it pleased him as a philosopher to observe the prejudices of human nature.

'You have brought, I see, sir,' he said, turning round towards Martin, and resting his chin on the top of his stick, 'the usual amount of misery and poverty and ignorance and crime, to be located in the bosom of the great Republic. Well, sir! let 'em come on in ship-loads from the old country. When vessels are about to founder, the rats are said to leave 'em. There is considerable of truth, I find, in that remark.'

'The old ship will keep afloat a year or two longer yet, perhaps,' said Martin with a smile, partly occasioned by what the gentleman said, and partly by his manner of saying it, which was odd enough, for he emphasised all the small words and syllables in his discourse, and left the others to take care of themselves: as if he thought the larger parts of speech could be trusted alone, but the little ones required to be constantly looked after.

'Hope is said by the poet, sir,' observed the gentleman, 'to be the nurse of young Desire.'

Martin signified that he had heard of the cardinal virtue in question serving occasionally in that domestic capacity.

'She will not rear her infant in the present instance, sir, you'll find,' observed the gentleman.

'Time will show,' said Martin.

The gentleman nodded his head gravely; and said, 'What is your name, sir?'

Martin told him.

'How old are you, sir?'

Martin told him.

'What is your profession, sir?'

Martin told him that also.

'What is your destination, sir?' inquired the gentleman.

'Really,' said Martin, laughing. 'I can't satisfy you in that particular, for I don't know it myself.'

'Yes?' said the gentleman.

'No,' said Martin.

The gentleman adjusted his cane under his left arm, and took a more deliberate and complete survey of Martin than he had yet had leisure to make. When he had completed his inspection, he put out his right hand, shook Martin's hand, and said:

'My name is Colonel Diver, sir. I am the Editor of the New York Rowdy Journal.'

Martin received the communication with that degree of respect which an announcement so distinguished appeared to demand.

'The New York Rowdy Journal, sir,' resumed the colonel, 'is, as I expect you know, the organ of our aristocracy in this city.'

'Oh! there *is* an aristocracy here, then?' said Martin. 'Of what is it composed?'

'Of intelligence, sir,' replied the colonel; 'of intelligence and virtue. And of their necessary consequence in this republic. Dollars, sir.'

Martin was very glad to hear this, feeling well assured that if intelligence and virtue led, as a matter of course, to the acquisition of dollars, he would speedily become a great capitalist. He was about to express the gratification such news afforded him, when he was interrupted by the captain of the ship, who came up at the moment to shake hands with the colonel; and who, seeing a well-dressed stranger on the deck (for Martin had thrown aside his cloak), shook hands with him also. This was an unspeakable relief to Martin, who, in spite of the acknowledged supremacy of intelligence and virtue in that happy country, would have been deeply mortified to appear before Colonel Diver in the poor character of a steerage passenger.

'Well, cap'en!' said the colonel.

'Well, colonel,' cried the captain. 'You're looking most uncommon bright, sir. I can hardly realise its being you, and that's a fact.'

'A good passage, cap'en?' inquired the colonel, taking him aside.

'Well now! It was a pretty spanking run, sir,' said, or rather sung, the captain, who was a genuine New Englander: 'considerin the weather.'

'Yes?' said the colonel.

'Well! It was, sir,' said the captain. 'I've just now sent a boy up to your office with the passenger-list, colonel.'

'You haven't got another boy to spare, p'raps, cap'en?' said the colonel, in a tone almost amounting to severity.

'I guess there air a dozen if you want 'em, colonel,' said the captain.

'One moderate big 'un could convey a dozen of champagne, perhaps,' observed the colonel, musing, 'to my office. You said a spanking run, I think?'

'Well, so I did,' was the reply.

'It's very nigh, you know,' observed the colonel. 'I'm glad it was a spanking run, cap'en. Don't mind about quarts if you're short of 'em. The boy can as well bring four-and-twenty pints, and travel twice as once.—A first-rate spanker, cap'en, was it? Yes?'

'A most e—tarnal spanker,' said the skipper.

'I admire at your good fortun, cap'en. You might loan me a corkscrew at the same time, and half-a-dozen glasses if you liked. However bad the elements combine against my country's noble packet-ship, the Screw, sir,' said the colonel, turning to Martin, and drawing a flourish on the surface of the deck with

his cane, 'her passage either way is almost certain to eventuate
a spanker!'

The captain, who had the Sewer below at that moment,
lunching expensively in one cabin, while the amiable Stabber
was drinking himself into a state of blind madness in another,
took a cordial leave of his friend the colonel, and hurried
away to dispatch the champagne: well knowing (as it afterwards appeared) that if he failed to conciliate the editor of the
Rowdy Journal, that potentate would denounce him and his
ship in large capitals before he was a day older; and would
probably assault the memory of his mother also, who had not
been dead more than twenty years. The colonel being again
left alone with Martin, checked him as he was moving away,
and offered, in consideration of his being an Englishman, to
show him the town and to introduce him, if such were his
desire, to a genteel boarding-house. But before they entered on
these proceedings (he said), he would beseech the honour of
his company at the office of the Rowdy Journal, to partake of
a bottle of champagne of his own importation.

All this was so extremely kind and hospitable, that Martin,
though it was quite early in the morning, readily acquiesced.
So, instructing Mark, who was deeply engaged with his friend
and her three children, that when he had done assisting them,
and had cleared the baggage, he was to wait for further orders
at the Rowdy Journal Office, Martin accompanied his new
friend on shore.

They made their way as they best could through the melancholy crowd of emigrants upon the wharf, who, grouped about
their beds and boxes, with the bare ground below them and the
bare sky above, might have fallen from another planet, for anything they knew of the country; and walked for some short distance along a busy street, bounded on one side by the quays and
shipping; and on the other by a long row of staring red-brick
storehouses and offices, ornamented with more black boards
and white letters, and more white boards and black letters, than
Martin had ever seen before, in fifty times the space. Presently
they turned up a narrow street, and presently into other narrow
streets, until at last they stopped before a house whereon was
painted in great characters, 'ROWDY JOURNAL.'

The colonel, who had walked the whole way with one hand
in his breast, his head occasionally wagging from side to side,
and his hat thrown back upon his ears, like a man who was

oppressed to inconvenience by a sense of his own greatness, led the way up a dark and dirty flight of stairs into a room of similar character, all littered and bestrewn with odds and ends of newspapers and other crumpled fragments, both in proof and manuscript. Behind a mangy old writing-table in this apartment sat a figure with a stump of a pen in its mouth and a great pair of scissors in its right hand, clipping and slicing at a file of Rowdy Journals; and it was such a laughable figure that Martin had some difficulty in preserving his gravity, though conscious of the close observation of Colonel Diver.

The individual who sat clipping and slicing as aforesaid at the Rowdy Journals, was a small young gentleman of very juvenile appearance, and unwholesomely pale in the face; partly, perhaps, from intense thought, but partly, there is no doubt, from the excessive use of tobacco, which he was at that moment chewing vigorously. He wore his shirt-collar turned down over a black ribbon; and his lank hair, a fragile crop, was not only smoothed and parted back from his brow, that none of the Poetry of his aspect might be lost, but had, here and there, been grubbed up by the roots: which accounted for his loftiest developments being somewhat pimply. He had that order of nose on which the envy of mankind has bestowed the appellation 'snub,' and it was very much turned up at the end, as with a lofty scorn. Upon the upper lip of this young gentleman were tokens of a sandy down: so very, very smooth and scant, that, though encouraged to the utmost, it looked more like a recent trace of gingerbread than the fair promise of a moustache; and this conjecture his apparently tender age went far to strengthen. He was intent upon his work. Every time he snapped the great pair of scissors, he made a corresponding motion with his jaws, which gave him a very terrible appearance.

Martin was not long in determining within himself that this must be Colonel Diver's son; the hope of the family, and future mainspring of the Rowdy Journal. Indeed he had begun to say that he presumed this was the colonel's little boy, and that it was very pleasant to see him playing at Editor in all the guilelessness of childhood, when the colonel proudly interposed and said:

'My War Correspondent, sir. Mr. Jefferson Brick!'

Martin could not help starting at this unexpected announcement, and the consciousness of the irretrievable mistake he had nearly made.

Mr. Brick seemed pleased with the sensation he produced
upon the stranger, and shook hands with him, with an air of
patronage designed to reassure him, and to let him know that
there was no occasion to be frightened, for he (Brick) wouldn't
hurt him.

'You have heard of Jefferson Brick I see, sir,' quoth the
colonel, with a smile. 'England has heard of Jefferson Brick.
Europe has heard of Jefferson Brick. Let me see. When did you
leave England, sir?'

'Five weeks ago,' said Martin.

'Five weeks ago,' repeated the colonel, thoughtfully; as he
took his seat upon the table, and swung his legs. 'Now let me
ask you, sir, which of Mr. Brick's articles had become at that
time the most obnoxious to the British Parliament and the
Court of Saint James's?'

'Upon my word,' said Martin, 'I—'

'I have reason to know, sir,' interrupted the colonel, 'that
the aristocratic circles of your country quail before the name
of Jefferson Brick. I should like to be informed, sir, from
your lips, which of his sentiments has struck the deadliest
blow—'

'At the hundred heads of the Hydra of Corruption now
grovelling in the dust beneath the lance of Reason, and spout-
ing up to the universal arch above us, its sanguinary gore,' said
Mr. Brick, putting on a little blue cloth cap with a glazed front,
and quoting his last article.

'The libation of freedom, Brick,' hinted the colonel.

'Must sometimes be quaffed in blood, colonel,' cried Brick.
And when he said 'blood,' he gave the great pair of scissors a
sharp snap, as if *they* said blood too, and were quite of his
opinion.

This done, they both looked at Martin, pausing for a
reply.

'Upon my life,' said Martin, who had by this time quite
recovered his usual coolness, 'I can't give you any satisfactory
information about it; for the truth is that I—'

'Stop!' cried the colonel, glancing sternly at his war correspondent, and giving his head one shake after every sentence.
'That you never heard of Jefferson Brick, sir. That you never
read Jefferson Brick, sir. That you never saw the Rowdy
Journal, sir. That you never knew, sir, of its mighty influence
upon the cabinets of Eu—rope. Yes?'

Mr. Jefferson Brick proposes an appropriate Sentiment

'That's what I was about to observe, certainly,' said Martin.

'Keep cool, Jefferson,' said the colonel gravely. 'Don't bust! oh you Europeans! Arter that, let's have a glass of wine!' So saying, he got down from the table, and produced, from a basket outside the door, a bottle of champagne, and three glasses.

'Mr. Jefferson Brick, sir,' said the colonel, filling Martin's glass and his own, and pushing the bottle to that gentleman, 'will give us a sentiment.'

'Well, sir!' cried the war correspondent, 'since you have concluded to call upon me, I will respond. I will give you, sir, The Rowdy Journal and its brethren; the well of Truth, whose waters are black from being composed of printers' ink, but are quite clear enough for my country to behold the shadow of her Destiny reflected in.'

'Hear, hear!' cried the colonel, with great complacency. 'There are flowery components, sir, in the language of my friend?'

'Very much so, indeed,' said Martin.

'There is to-day's Rowdy, sir,' observed the colonel, handing him a paper. 'You'll find Jefferson Brick at his usual post in the van of human civilisation and moral purity.'

The colonel was by this time seated on the table again. Mr. Brick also took up a position on that same piece of furniture; and they fell to drinking pretty hard. They often looked at Martin as he read the paper, and then at each other. When he laid it down, which was not until they had finished a second bottle, the colonel asked him what he thought of it.

'Why, it's horribly personal,' said Martin.

The colonel seemed much flattered by this remark; and said he hoped it was.

'We are independent here, sir,' said Mr. Jefferson Brick. 'We do as we like.'

'If I may judge from this specimen,' returned Martin, 'there must be a few thousands here, rather the reverse of independent, who do as they don't like.'

'Well! They yield to the mighty mind of the Popular Instructor, sir,' said the colonel. 'They rile up, sometimes; but in general we have a hold upon our citizens, both in public and in private life, which is as much one of the ennobling institutions of our happy country as—'

'As nigger slavery itself,' suggested Mr. Brick.

'En—tirely so,' remarked the colonel.

'Pray,' said Martin, after some hesitation, 'may I venture to ask, with reference to a case I observe in this paper of yours, whether the Popular Instructor often deals in—I am at a loss to express it without giving you offence—in forgery? In forged letters, for instance,' he pursued, for the colonel was perfectly calm and quite at his ease, 'solemnly purporting to have been written at recent periods by living men?'

'Well, sir!' replied the colonel. 'It does, now and then.'

'And the popular instructed; what do they do?' asked Martin.

'Buy 'em:' said the colonel.

Mr. Jefferson Brick expectorated and laughed; the former copiously, the latter approvingly.

'Buy 'em by hundreds of thousands,' resumed the colonel. 'We are a smart people here, and can appreciate smartness.'

'Is smartness American for forgery?' asked Martin.

'Well!' said the colonel, 'I expect it's American for a good many things that you call by other names. But you can't help yourselves in Europe. We can.'

'And do, sometimes,' thought Martin. 'You help yourselves with very little ceremony, too!'

'At all events, whatever name we choose to employ,' said the colonel, stooping down to roll the third empty bottle into a corner after the other two, 'I suppose the art of forgery was not invented here, sir?'

'I suppose not,' replied Martin.

'Nor any other kind of smartness, I reckon?'

'Invented! No, I presume not.'

'Well!' said the colonel; 'then we got it all from the old country, and the old country's to blame for it, and not the new 'un. There's an end of *that*. Now, if Mr. Jefferson Brick and you will be so good as clear, I'll come out last, and lock the door.'

Rightly interpreting this as the signal for their departure, Martin walked down-stairs after the war correspondent, who preceded him with great majesty. The colonel following, they left the Rowdy Journal Office and walked forth into the streets: Martin feeling doubtful whether he ought to kick the colonel for having presumed to speak to him, or whether it came within the bounds of possibility that he and his establishment could be among the boasted usages of that regenerated land.

It was clear that Colonel Diver, in the security of his strong position, and in his perfect understanding of the public sentiment, cared very little what Martin or anybody else thought about him. His high-spiced wares were made to sell, and they sold; and his thousands of readers could as rationally charge their delight in filth upon him, as a glutton can shift upon his cook the responsibility of his beastly excess. Nothing would have delighted the colonel more than to be told that no such man as he could walk in high success the streets of any other country in the world: for that would only have been a logical assurance to him of the correct adaptation of his labours to the prevailing taste, and of his being strictly and peculiarly a national feature of America.

They walked a mile or more along a handsome street which the colonel said was called Broadway, and which Mr. Jefferson Brick said 'whipped the universe.' Turning, at length, into one of the numerous streets which branched from this main thoroughfare, they stopped before a rather mean-looking house with jalousie blinds to every window; a flight of steps before the green street-door; a shining white ornament on the rails on either side like a petrified pine-apple, polished; a little oblong plate of the same material over the knocker, whereon the name of 'Pawkins' was engraved; and four accidental pigs looking down the area.

The colonel knocked at this house with the air of a man who lived there; and an Irish girl popped her head out of one of the top windows to see who it was. Pending her journey downstairs, the pigs were joined by two or three friends from the next street, in company with whom they lay down sociably in the gutter.

'Is the major in-doors?' inquired the colonel, as he entered.

'Is it the master, sir?' returned the girl, with a hesitation which seemed to imply that they were rather flush of majors in that establishment.

'The master!' said Colonel Diver, stopping short and looking round at his war correspondent.

'Oh! The depressing institutions of that British empire, colonel!' said Jefferson Brick. 'Master!'

'What's the matter with the word?' asked Martin.

'I should hope it was never heard in our country, sir: that's all,' said Jefferson Brick: 'except when it is used by some

degraded Help, as new to the blessings of our form of government, as this Help is. There are no masters here.'

'All "owners," are they?' said Martin.

Mr. Jefferson Brick followed in the Rowdy Journal's footsteps without returning any answer. Martin took the same
course, thinking as he went, that perhaps the free and independent citizens, who in their moral elevation, owned the
colonel for their master, might render better homage to the
goddess, Liberty, in nightly dreams upon the oven of a Russian
Serf.

The colonel led the way into a room at the back of the house
upon the ground-floor, light, and of fair dimensions, but exquisitely uncomfortable: having nothing in it but the four cold
white walls and ceiling, a mean carpet, a dreary waste of
dining-table reaching from end to end, and a bewildering
collection of cane-bottomed chairs. In the further region of
this banqueting-hall was a stove, garnished on either side with
a great brass spittoon, and shaped in itself like three little iron
barrels set up on end in a fender, and joined together on the
principle of the Siamese Twins. Before it, swinging himself in a
rocking-chair, lounged a large gentleman with his hat on, who
amused himself by spitting alternately into the spittoon on the
right hand of the stove, and the spittoon on the left, and then
working his way back again in the same order. A negro lad in
a soiled white jacket was busily engaged in placing on the
table two long rows of knives and forks, relieved at intervals by
jugs of water; and as he travelled down one side of this festive
board, he straightened with his dirty hands the dirtier cloth,
which was all askew, and had not been removed since breakfast. The atmosphere of this room was rendered intensely hot
and stifling by the stove; but being further flavoured by a sickly
gush of soup from the kitchen, and by such remote suggestions
of tobacco as lingered within the brazen receptacles already
mentioned, it became, to a stranger's senses, almost insupportable.

The gentleman in the rocking-chair having his back towards
them, and being much engaged in his intellectual pastime,
was not aware of their approach until the colonel walking up
to the stove, contributed his mite towards the support of the
left-hand spittoon, just as the major—for it was the major—
bore down upon it. Major Pawkins then reserved his fire, and
looking upward, said, with a peculiar air of quiet weariness,

like a man who had been up all night: an air which Martin
had already observed both in the colonel and Mr. Jefferson
Brick:

'Well, colonel!'

'Here is a gentleman from England, major,' the colonel
replied, 'who has concluded to locate himself here if the amount
of compensation suits him.'

'I am glad to see you, sir,' observed the major, shaking
hands with Martin, and not moving a muscle of his face. 'You
are pretty bright, I hope?'

'Never better,' said Martin.

'You are never likely to be,' returned the major. 'You will
see the sun shine *here*.'

'I think I remember to have seen it shine at home sometimes,' said Martin, smiling.

'I think not,' replied the major. He said so with a stoical
indifference certainly, but still in a tone of firmness which
admitted of no further dispute on that point. When he had
thus settled the question, he put his hat a little on one side for
the greater convenience of scratching his head, and saluted
Mr. Jefferson Brick with a lazy nod.

Major Pawkins (a gentleman of Pennsylvanian origin) was
distinguished by a very large skull, and a great mass of yellow
forehead; in deference to which commodities it was currently
held in bar-rooms and other such places of resort that the
major was a man of huge sagacity. He was further to be
known by a heavy eye and a dull slow manner; and for being
a man of that kind who, mentally speaking, requires a deal of
room to turn himself in. But, in trading on his stock of wisdom,
he invariably proceeded on the principle of putting all the
goods he had (and more) into his window; and that went a
great way with his constituency of admirers. It went a great
way, perhaps, with Mr. Jefferson Brick, who took occasion to
whisper in Martin's ear:

'One of the most remarkable men in our country, sir!'

It must not be supposed, however, that the perpetual exhibition in the market-place of all his stock-in-trade for sale or
hire, was the major's sole claim to a very large share of
sympathy and support. He was a great politician; and the one
article of his creed, in reference to all public obligations involving the good faith and integrity of his country, was, 'run
a moist pen slick through everything, and start fresh.' This

L

made him a patriot. In commercial affairs he was a bold speculator. In plainer words he had a most distinguished genius for swindling, and could start a bank, or negotiate a loan, or form a land-jobbing company (entailing ruin, pestilence, and death, on hundreds of families), with any gifted creature in the Union. This made him an admirable man of business. He could hang about a bar-room, discussing the affairs of the nation, for twelve hours together; and in that time could hold forth with more intolerable dulness, chew more tobacco, smoke more tobacco, drink more rum-toddy, mint-julep, gin-sling, and cock-tail, than any private gentleman of his acquaintance. This made him an orator and a man of the people. In a word, the major was a rising character, and a popular character, and was in a fair way to be sent by the popular party to the State House of New York, if not in the end to Washington itself. But as a man's private prosperity does not always keep pace with his patriotic devotion to public affairs; and as fraudulent transactions have their downs as well as ups, the major was occasionally under a cloud. Hence, just now, Mrs. Pawkins kept a boarding-house, and Major Pawkins rather 'loafed' his time away than otherwise.

'You have come to visit our country, sir, at a season of great commercial depression,' said the major.

'At an alarming crisis,' said the colonel.

'At a period of unprecedented stagnation,' said Mr. Jefferson Brick.

'I am sorry to hear that,' returned Martin. 'It's not likely to last, I hope?'

Martin knew nothing about America, or he would have known perfectly well that if its individual citizens, to a man, are to be believed, it always *is* depressed, and always *is* stagnated, and always *is* at an alarming crisis, and never was otherwise; though as a body they are ready to make oath upon the Evangelists at any hour of the day or night, that it is the most thriving and prosperous of all countries on the habitable globe.

'It's not likely to last, I hope?' said Martin.

'Well!' returned the major, 'I expect we shall get along somehow, and come right in the end.'

'We are an elastic country,' said the Rowdy Journal.

'We are a young lion,' said Mr. Jefferson Brick.

'We have revivifying and vigorous principles within ourselves,' observed the major. 'Shall we drink a bitter afore dinner, colonel?'

The colonel assenting to this proposal with great alacrity, Major Pawkins proposed an adjournment to a neighbouring bar-room, which, as he observed, was 'only in the next block.' He then referred Martin to Mrs. Pawkins for all particulars connected with the rate of board and lodging, and informed him that he would have the pleasure of seeing that lady at dinner, which would soon be ready, as the dinner hour was two o'clock, and it only wanted a quarter now. This reminded him that if the bitter were to be taken at all, there was no time to lose; so he walked off without more ado, and left them to follow if they thought proper.

When the major rose from his rocking-chair before the stove, and so disturbed the hot air and balmy whiff of soup which fanned their brows, the odour of stale tobacco became so decidedly prevalent as to leave no doubt of its proceeding mainly from that gentleman's attire. Indeed, as Martin walked behind him to the bar-room, he could not help thinking that the great square major, in his listlessness and languor, looked very much like a stale weed himself: such as might be hoed out of the public garden, with great advantage to the decent growth of that preserve, and tossed on some congenial dung-hill.

They encountered more weeds in the bar-room, some of whom (being thirsty souls as well as dirty) were pretty stale in one sense, and pretty fresh in another. Among them was a gentleman who, as Martin gathered from the conversation that took place over the bitter, started that afternoon for the Far West on a six months' business tour; and who, as his outfit and equipment for this journey, had just such another shiny hat and just such another little pale valise as had composed the luggage of the gentleman who came from England in the Screw.

They were walking back very leisurely; Martin arm-in-arm with Mr. Jefferson Brick, and the major and the colonel side-by-side before them; when, as they came within a house or two of the major's residence, they heard a bell ringing violently. The instant this sound struck upon their ears, the colonel and the major darted off, dashed up the steps and in at the street-door (which stood ajar) like lunatics; while Mr. Jefferson Brick, detaching his arm from Martin's, made a precipitate dive in the same direction, and vanished also.

'Good Heaven!' thought Martin. 'The premises are on fire!
It was an alarm bell!'

But there was no smoke to be seen, nor any flame, nor was
there any smell of fire. As Martin faltered on the pavement,
three more gentlemen, with horror and agitation depicted in
their faces, came plunging wildly round the street corner;
jostled each other on the steps; struggled for an instant; and
rushed into the house, a confused heap of arms and legs. Unable
to bear it any longer, Martin followed. Even in his rapid progress he was run down, thrust aside, and passed, by two more
gentlemen, stark mad, as it appeared, with fierce excitement.

'Where is it?' cried Martin, breathlessly, to a negro whom
he encountered in the passage.

'In a eatin room, sa. 'Kernell, sa, him kep a seat 'side himself, sa.'

'A seat!' cried Martin.

'For a dinnar, sa.'

Martin stared at him for a moment, and burst into a hearty
laugh; to which the negro, out of his natural good humour and
desire to please, so heartily responded, that his teeth shone like
a gleam of light. 'You're the pleasantest fellow I have seen yet,'
said Martin, clapping him on the back, 'and give me a better
appetite than bitters.'

With this sentiment he walked into the dining-room and
slipped into a chair next the colonel, which that gentleman (by
this time nearly through his dinner) had turned down in reserve
for him, with its back against the table.

It was a numerous company, eighteen or twenty perhaps.
Of these some five or six were ladies, who sat wedged together
in a little phalanx by themselves. All the knives and forks were
working away at a rate that was quite alarming; very few
words were spoken; and everybody seemed to eat his utmost
in self-defence, as if a famine were expected to set in before
breakfast time to-morrow morning, and it had become high
time to assert the first law of nature. The poultry, which may
perhaps be considered to have formed the staple of the entertainment—for there was a turkey at the top, a pair of ducks at
the bottom, and two fowls in the middle—disappeared as
rapidly as if every bird had had the use of its wings, and had
flown in desperation down a human throat. The oysters,
stewed and pickled, leaped from their capacious reservoirs, and
slid by scores into the mouths of the assembly. The sharpest

pickles vanished, whole cucumbers at once, like sugar-plums, and no man winked his eye. Great heaps of indigestible matter melted away as ice before the sun. It was a solemn and an awful thing to see. Dyspeptic individuals bolted their food in wedges; feeding, not themselves, but broods of nightmares, who were continually standing at livery within them. Spare men, with lank and rigid cheeks, came out unsatisfied from the destruction of heavy dishes, and glared with watchful eyes upon the pastry. What Mrs. Pawkins felt each day at dinner-time is hidden from all human knowledge. But she had one comfort. It was very soon over.

When the colonel had finished his dinner, which event took place while Martin, who had sent his plate for some turkey, was waiting to begin, he asked him what he thought of the boarders, who were from all parts of the Union, and whether he would like to know any particulars concerning them.

'Pray,' said Martin, 'who is that sickly little girl opposite, with the tight round eyes? I don't see anybody here, who looks like her mother, or who seems to have charge of her.'

'Do you mean the matron in blue, sir?' asked the colonel, with emphasis. 'That is Mrs. Jefferson Brick, sir.'

'No, no,' said Martin, 'I mean the little girl, like a doll; directly opposite.'

'Well, sir!' cried the colonel. '*That* is Mrs. Jefferson Brick.'

Martin glanced at the colonel's face, but he was quite serious.

'Bless my soul! I suppose there will be a young Brick then, one of these days?' said Martin.

'There are two young Bricks already, sir,' returned the colonel.

The matron looked so uncommonly like a child herself, that Martin could not help saying as much. 'Yes, sir,' returned the colonel, 'but some institutions develop human natur: others re—tard it.'

'Jefferson Brick,' he observed after a short silence, in commendation of his correspondent, 'is one of the most remarkable men in our country, sir!'

This had passed almost in a whisper, for the distinguished gentleman alluded to sat on Martin's other hand.

'Pray, Mr. Brick,' said Martin, turning to him, and asking a question more for conversation's sake than from any feeling of interest in its subject, 'who is that:' he was going to say 'young' but thought it prudent to eschew the word: 'that very short gentleman yonder, with the red nose?'

'That is Pro—fessor Mullit, sir,' replied Jefferson.

'May I ask what he is professor of?' asked Martin.

'Of education, sir,' said Jefferson Brick.

'A sort of schoolmaster, possibly?' Martin ventured to observe.

'He is a man of fine moral elements, sir, and not commonly endowed,' said the war correspondent. 'He felt it necessary, at the last election for President, to repudiate and denounce his father, who voted on the wrong interest. He has since written some powerful pamphlets, under the signature of 'Suturb', or Brutus reversed. He is one of the most remarkable men in our country, sir.'

'There seem to be plenty of 'em,' thought Martin; 'at any rate.'

Pursuing his inquiries, Martin found that there were no fewer than four majors present, two colonels, one general, and a captain, so that he could not help thinking how strongly officered the American militia must be; and wondering very much whether the officers commanded each other; or if they did not, where on earth the privates came from. There seemed to be no man there without a title: for those who had not attained to military honours were either doctors, professors, or reverends. Three very hard and disagreeable gentlemen were on missions from neighbouring States; one on monetary affairs, one on political, one on sectarian. Among the ladies, there were Mrs. Pawkins, who was very straight, bony, and silent; and a wiry-faced old damsel, who held strong sentiments touching the rights of women, and had diffused the same in lectures; but the rest were strangely devoid of individual traits of character, insomuch that any one of them might have changed minds with the other, and nobody would have found it out. These, by the way, were the only members of the party who did not appear to be among the most remarkable people in the country.

Several of the gentlemen got up, one by one, and walked off as they swallowed their last morsel; pausing generally by the stove for a minute or so to refresh themselves at the brass spittoons. A few sedentary characters, however, remained at table full a quarter of an hour, and did not rise until the ladies rose, when all stood up.

'Where are they going?' asked Martin, in the ear of Mr. Jefferson Brick.

'To their bedrooms, sir.'

'Is there no dessert, or other interval of conversation?' asked Martin, who was disposed to enjoy himself after his long voyage.

'We are a busy people here, sir, and have no time for that,' was the reply.

So the ladies passed out in single file; Mr. Jefferson Brick and such other married gentlemen as were left, acknowledging the departure of their other halves by a nod; and there was an end of *them*. Martin thought this an uncomfortable custom, but he kept his opinion to himself for the present, being anxious to hear, and inform himself by, the conversation of the busy gentlemen, who now lounged about the stove as if a great weight had been taken off their minds by the withdrawal of the other sex; and who made a plentiful use of the spittoons and their toothpicks.

It was rather barren of interest, to say the truth; and the greater part of it may be summed up in one word. Dollars. All their cares, hopes, joys, affections, virtues, and associations, seemed to be melted down into dollars. Whatever the chance contributions that fell into the slow cauldron of their talk, they made the gruel thick and slab with dollars. Men were weighed by their dollars, measures gauged by their dollars; life was auctioneered, appraised, put up, and knocked down for its dollars. The next respectable thing to dollars was any venture having their attainment for its end. The more of that worthless ballast, honour and fair-dealing, which any man cast overboard from the ship of his Good Name and Good Intent, the more ample stowage-room he had for dollars. Make commerce one huge lie and mighty theft. Deface the banner of the nation for an idle rag; pollute it star by star; and cut out stripe by stripe as from the arm of a degraded soldier. Do anything for dollars! What is a flag to *them!*

One who rides at all hazards of limb and life in the chase of a fox, will prefer to ride recklessly at most times. So it was with these gentlemen. He was the greatest patriot, in their eyes, who brawled the loudest, and who cared the least for decency. He was their champion who, in the brutal fury of his own pursuit, could cast no stigma upon them for the hot knavery of theirs. Thus Martin learned in the five minutes' straggling talk about the stove, that to carry pistols into legislative assemblies, and swords in sticks, and other such peaceful toys; to seize opponents by the throat, as dogs or rats might do; to bluster, bully, and overbear by personal assailment; were glowing deeds. Not thrusts and stabs at Freedom, striking far deeper into her House of Life than any sultan's scimitar could reach; but rare incense on her altars, having a grateful scent in patriotic nostrils, and curling upward to the seventh heaven of Fame.

Once or twice, when there was a pause, Martin asked such questions as naturally occurred to him, being a stranger, about the national poets, the theatre, literature, and the arts. But the information which these gentlemen were in a condition to give him on such topics, did not extend beyond the effusions of such master-spirits of the time as Colonel Diver, Mr. Jefferson Brick, and others; renowned, as it appeared, for excellence in the achievement of a peculiar style of broadside-essay called 'a screamer.'

'We are a busy people, sir,' said one of the captains, who was from the West, 'and have no time for reading mere notions. We don't mind 'em if they come to us in newspapers along with almighty strong stuff of another sort, but darn your books.'

Here the general, who appeared to grow quite faint at the bare thought of reading anything which was neither mercantile nor political, and was not in a newspaper, inquired 'if any gentleman would drink some?' Most of the company, considering this a very choice and seasonable idea, lounged out, one by one, to the bar-room in the next block. Thence they probably went to their stores and counting-houses; thence to the bar-room again, to talk once more of dollars, and enlarge their minds with the perusal and discussion of screamers; and thence each man to snore in the bosom of his own family.

'Which would seem,' said Martin, pursuing the current of his own thoughts, 'to be the principal recreation they enjoy in common.' With that, he fell a-musing again on dollars, demagogues, and bar-rooms; debating within himself whether busy people of this class were really as busy as they claimed to be, or only had an inaptitude for social and domestic pleasure.

It was a difficult question to solve; and the mere fact of its being strongly presented to his mind by all that he had seen and heard, was not encouraging. He sat down at the deserted board, and becoming more and more despondent, as he thought

of all the uncertainties and difficulties of his precarious situation, sighed heavily.

Now, there had been at the dinner-table a middle-aged man
with a dark eye and a sunburnt face, who had attracted
Martin's attention by having something very engaging and
honest in the expression of his features; but of whom he could
learn nothing from either of his neighbours, who seemed to
consider him quite beneath their notice. He had taken no part
in the conversation round the stove, nor had he gone forth with
the rest; and now, when he heard Martin sigh for the third or
fourth time, he interposed with some casual remark, as if he
desired, without obtruding himself upon a stranger's notice, to
engage him in cheerful conversation if he could. His motive
was so obvious, and yet so delicately expressed, that Martin
felt really grateful to him, and showed him so in the manner of
his reply.

'I will not ask you,' said this gentleman with a smile, as he
rose and moved towards him, 'how you like my country, for I
can quite anticipate your feeling on that point. But, as I am
an American, and consequently bound to begin with a question, I'll ask you how you like the colonel?'

'You are so very frank,' returned Martin, 'that I have no
hesitation in saying I don't like him at all. Though I must add
that I am beholden to him for his civility in bringing me here
—and arranging for my stay, on pretty reasonable terms, by the
way,' he added: remembering that the colonel had whispered
him to that effect, before going out.

'Not much beholden,' said the stranger drily. 'The colonel
occasionally boards packet-ships, I have heard, to glean the
latest information for his journal; and he occasionally brings
strangers to board here, I believe, with a view to the little
percentage which attaches to those good offices; and which the
hostess deducts from his weekly bill. I don't offend you, I hope?'
he added, seeing that Martin reddened.

'My dear sir,' returned Martin, as they shook hands, 'how
is that possible! to tell you the truth, I—am—'

'Yes?' said the gentleman, sitting down beside him.

'I am rather at a loss, since I must speak plainly,' said
Martin, getting the better of his hesitation, 'to know how this
colonel escapes being beaten.'

'Well! He has been beaten once or twice,' remarked the
gentleman quietly. 'He is one of a class of men, in whom our

own Franklin, so long ago as ten years before the close of the last century, foresaw our danger and disgrace. Perhaps you don't know that Franklin, in very severe terms, published his opinion that those who were slandered by such fellows as this colonel, having no sufficient remedy in the administration of this country's laws or in the decent and right-minded feeling of its people, were justified in retorting on such public nuisances by means of a stout cudgel?'

'I was not aware of that,' said Martin, 'but I am very glad to know it, and I think it worthy of his memory; especially'— here he hesitated again.

'Go on,' said the other, smiling as if he knew what stuck in Martin's throat.

'Especially,' pursued Martin, 'as I can already understand that it may have required great courage, even in his time, to write freely on any question which was not a party one in this very free country.'

'Some courage, no doubt,' returned his new friend. 'Do you think it would require any to do so, now?'

'Indeed I think it would; and not a little,' said Martin.

'You are right. So very right, that I believe no satirist could breathe this air. If another Juvenal or Swift could rise up among us to-morrow, he would be hunted down. If you have any knowledge of our literature, and can give me the name of any man, American born and bred, who has anatomised our follies as a people, and not as this or that party; and who has escaped the foulest and most brutal slander, the most inveterate hatred and intolerant pursuit; it will be a strange name in my ears, believe me. In some cases I could name to you, where a native writer has ventured on the most harmless and good-humoured illustrations of our vices or defects, it has been found necessary to announce, that in a second edition the passage has been expunged, or altered, or explained away, or patched into praise.'

'And how has this been brought about?' asked Martin, in dismay.

'Think of what you have seen and heard to-day, beginning with the colonel,' said his friend, 'and ask yourself. How *they* came about, is another question. Heaven forbid that they should be samples of the intelligence and virtue of America, but they come uppermost, and in great numbers, and too often represent it. Will you walk?'

There was a cordial candour in his manner, and an engaging confidence that it would not be abused; a manly bearing on his own part, and a simple reliance on the manly faith of a stranger; which Martin had never seen before. He linked his arm readily in that of the American gentleman, and they walked out together.

It was perhaps to men like this, his new companion, that a traveller of honoured name, who trod those shores now nearly forty years ago, and woke upon that soil, as many have done since, to blots and stains upon its high pretensions, which in the brightness of his distant dreams were lost to view, appealed in these words:

> 'Oh but for such, Columbia's days were done;
> Rank without ripeness, quickened without sun,
> Crude at the surface, rotten at the core,
> Her fruits would fall before her spring were o'er!'

CHAPTER XVII

Martin enlarges his circle of acquaintance; increases his stock of wisdom; and has an excellent opportunity of comparing his own experiences with those of Lummy Ned of the Light Salisbury, as related by his friend Mr. William Simmons

IT was characteristic of Martin, that all this while he had either forgotten Mark Tapley as completely as if there had been no such person in existence, or, if for a moment the figure of that gentleman rose before his mental vision, had dismissed it as something by no means of a pressing nature, which might be attended to by-and-bye, and could wait his perfect leisure. But, being now in the streets again, it occurred to him as just coming within the bare limits of possibility that Mr. Tapley might, in course of time, grow tired of waiting on the threshold of the Rowdy Journal Office, so he intimated to his new friend, that if they could conveniently walk in that direction, he would be glad to get this piece of business off his mind.

'And speaking of business,' said Martin, 'may I ask, in order that I may not be behind-hand with questions either, whether your occupation holds you to this city, or like myself, you are a visitor here?'

'A visitor,' replied his friend. 'I was "raised" in the State of Massachusetts, and reside there still. My home is in a quiet country town. I am not often in these busy places; and my inclination to visit them does not increase with our better acquaintance, I assure you.'

'You have been abroad?' asked Martin.

'Oh yes.'

'And, like most people who travel, have become more than ever attached to your home and native country,' said Martin, eyeing him curiously.

'To my home, yes,' rejoined his friend. 'To my native country *as* my home—yes, also.'

'You imply some reservation,' said Martin.

'Well,' returned his new friend, 'if you ask me whether I came back here with a greater relish for my country's faults; with a greater fondness for those who claim (at the rate of so many dollars a day) to be her friends; with a cooler indifference to the growth of principles among us in respect of public matters and of private dealings between man and man, the advocacy of which, beyond the foul atmosphere of a criminal trial, would disgrace your own Old Bailey lawyers; why, then I answer plainly, No.'

'Oh!' said Martin; in so exactly the same key as his friend's No, that it sounded like an echo.

'If you ask me,' his companion pursued, 'whether I came back here better satisfied with a state of things which broadly divides society into two classes—whereof one, the great mass, asserts a spurious independence, most miserably dependent for its mean existence on the disregard of humanising conventionalities of manner and social custom, so that the coarser a man is, the more distinctly it shall appeal to his taste; while the other, disgusted with the low standard thus set up and made adaptable to everything, takes refuge among the graces and refinements it can bring to bear on private life, and leaves the public weal to such fortune as may betide it in the press and uproar of a general scramble—then again I answer, No.'

And again Martin said 'Oh!' in the same odd way as before, being anxious and disconcerted; not so much, to say the truth, on public grounds, as with reference to the fading prospects of domestic architecture.

'In a word,' resumed the other, 'I do not find and cannot believe, and therefore will not allow, that we are a model of wisdom, and an example to the world, and the perfection of human reason, and a great deal more to the same purpose, which you may hear any hour in the day; simply because we began our political life with two inestimable advantages.'

'What were they?' asked Martin.

'One, that our history commenced at so late a period as to escape the ages of bloodshed and cruelty through which other nations have passed; and so had all the light of their probation, and none of its darkness. The other, that we have a vast territory, and not—as yet—too many people on it. These facts considered, we have done little enough, I think.'

'Education?' suggested Martin, faintly.

'Pretty well on that head,' said the other, shrugging his shoulders, 'still no mighty matter to boast of; for old countries, and despotic countries too, have done as much, if not more, and made less noise about it. We shine out brightly in comparison with England, certainly; but hers is a very extreme case. You complimented me on my frankness, you know,' he added, laughing.

'Oh! I am not at all astonished at your speaking thus openly when my country is in question,' returned Martin. 'It is your plain-speaking in reference to your own that surprises me.'

'You will not find it a scarce quality here, I assure you, saving among the Colonel Divers, and Jefferson Bricks, and Major Pawkinses; though the best of us are something like the man in Goldsmith's comedy, who wouldn't suffer anybody but himself to abuse his master. Come!' he added. 'Let us talk of something else. You have come here on some design of improving your fortune, I dare say; and I should grieve to put you out of heart. I am some years older than you, besides; and may, on a few trivial points, advise you, perhaps.'

There was not the least curiosity or impertinence in the manner of this offer, which was open-hearted, unaffected, and good-natured. As it was next to impossible that he should not have his confidence awakened by a deportment so prepossessing and kind, Martin plainly stated what had brought him into those parts, and even made the very difficult avowal that he was poor. He did not say how poor, it must be admitted, rather throwing off the declaration with an air which might have implied that he had money enough for six months, instead of as many weeks; but poor he said he was, and grateful he said he would be, for any counsel that his friend would give him.

It would not have been very difficult for any one to see; but it was particularly easy for Martin, whose perceptions were sharpened by his circumstances, to discern; that the stranger's face grew infinitely longer as the domestic-architecture project was developed. Nor, although he made a great effort to be as encouraging as possible, could he prevent his head from shaking once involuntarily, as if it said in the vulgar tongue, upon its own account, 'No go!' But he spoke in a cheerful tone, and said, that although there was no such opening as Martin wished, in that city, he would make it matter of immediate consideration and inquiry where one was most likely to exist; and then he made Martin acquainted with his name, which was Bevan; and with his profession, which was physic, though he seldom or never practised; and with other circumstances connected with himself and family, which fully occupied the time, until they reached the Rowdy Journal Office.

Mr. Tapley appeared to be taking his ease on the landing of the first floor; for sounds as of some gentleman established in that region, whistling 'Rule Britannia' with all his might and main, greeted their ears before they reached the house. On ascending to the spot from whence this music proceeded, they found him recumbent in the midst of a fortification of luggage, apparently performing his national anthem for the gratification of a grey-haired black man, who sat on one of the outworks (a portmanteau), staring intently at Mark, while Mark, with his head reclining on his hand, returned the compliment in a thoughtful manner, and whistled all the time. He seemed to have recently dined, for his knife, a case-bottle, and certain broken meats in a handkerchief, lay near at hand. He had employed a portion of his leisure in the decoration of the Rowdy Journal door, whereon his own initials now appeared in letters nearly half a foot long, together with the day of the month in smaller type: the whole surrounded by an ornamental border, and looking very fresh and bold.

'I was a'most afraid you was lost, sir!' cried Mark, rising, and stopping the tune at that point where Britons generally are supposed to declare (when it is whistled) that they never, never, never.

'Nothing gone wrong, I hope, sir?'

'No, Mark. Where's your friend?'

'The mad woman, sir?' said Mr. Tapley. 'Oh! she's all right, sir.'

'Did she find her husband?'

'Yes, sir. Leastways she's found his remains,' said Mark, correcting himself.

'The man's not dead, I hope?'

'Not altogether dead, sir,' returned Mark; 'but he's had more fevers and agues than is quite reconcileable with being alive. When she didn't see him a-waiting for her, I thought she'd have died herself, I did!'

'Was he not here, then?'

'*He* wasn't here. There was a feeble old shadow come a-creeping down at last, as much like his substance when she know'd him, as your shadow when it's drawn out to its very finest and longest by the sun, is like you. But it was his remains, there's no doubt about that. She took on with joy, poor thing, as much as if it had been all of him!'

'Had he bought land?' asked Mr. Bevan.

'Ah! He'd bought land,' said Mark, shaking his head, 'and paid for it too. Every sort of nateral advantage was connected with it, the agents said; and there certainly was *one*, quite unlimited. No end to the water!'

'It's a thing he couldn't have done without, I suppose,' observed Martin, peevishly.

'Certainly not, sir. There it was, any way; always turned on, and no water-rate. Independent of three or four slimy old rivers close by, it varied on the farm from four to six foot deep in the dry season. He couldn't say how deep it was in the rainy time, for he never had anything long enough to sound it with.'

'Is this true?' asked Martin of his companion.

'Extremely probable,' he answered. 'Some Mississippi or Missouri lot, I dare say.'

'However,' pursued Mark, 'he came from I-don't-know-where-and-all, down to New York here, to meet his wife and children; and they started off again in a steam-boat this blessed afternoon, as happy to be along with each other, as if they were going to Heaven. I should think they was, pretty straight, if I may judge from the poor man's looks.'

'And may I ask,' said Martin, glancing, but not with any displeasure, from Mark to the negro, 'who this gentleman is? Another friend of yours?'

'Why, sir,' returned Mark, taking him aside, and speaking confidentially in his ear, 'he's a man of colour, sir!'

'Do you take me for a blind man,' asked Martin, somewhat impatiently, 'that you think it necessary to tell me that, when his face is the blackest that ever was seen?'

'No, no, when I say a man of colour,' returned Mark, 'I mean that he's been one of them as there's picters of in the shops. A man and a brother, you know, sir,' said Mr. Tapley, favouring his master with a significant indication of the figure so often represented in tracts and cheap prints.

'A slave!' cried Martin, in a whisper.

'Ah!' said Mark in the same tone. 'Nothing else. A slave. Why, when that there man was young—don't look at him while I'm a-telling it—he was shot in the leg; gashed in the arm; scored in his live limbs, like crimped fish; beaten out of shape; had his neck galled with an iron collar, and wore iron rings upon his wrists and ankles. The marks are on him to this day. When I was having my dinner just now, he stripped off his coat, and took away my appetite.'

*Mr. Tapley succeeds in finding a Jolly Subject for
Contemplation*

(p. 281)

'Is *this* true?' asked Martin of his friend, who stood beside them.

'I have no reason to doubt it,' he answered, shaking his head. 'It very often is.'

'Bless you,' said Mark, 'I know it is, from hearing his whole story. That master died; so did his second master from having his head cut open with a hatchet by another slave, who, when he'd done it, went and drowned himself: then he got a better one. In years and years he saved up a little money, and bought his freedom, which he got pretty cheap at last, on account of his strength being nearly gone, and he being ill. Then he come here. And now he's a-saving up to treat himself, afore he dies, to one small purchase; it's nothing to speak of; only his own daughter; that's all!' cried Mr. Tapley, becoming excited. 'Liberty for ever! Hurrah! Hail, Columbia!'

'Hush!' cried Martin, clapping his hand upon his mouth: 'and don't be an idiot. What is he doing here?'

'Waiting to take our luggage off upon a truck,' said Mark. 'He'd have come for it by-and-bye, but I engaged him for a very reasonable charge (out of my own pocket) to sit along with me and make me jolly; and I *am* jolly; and if I was rich enough to contract with him to wait upon me once a day, to be looked at, I'd never be anything else.'

The fact may cause a solemn impeachment of Mark's veracity, but it must be admitted nevertheless, that there was that in his face and manner at the moment, which militated strongly against this emphatic declaration of his state of mind.

'Lord love you, sir,' he added, 'they're so fond of Liberty in this part of the globe, that they buy her and sell her and carry her to market with 'em. They've such a passion for Liberty, that they can't help taking liberties with her. That's what it's owing to.'

'Very well,' said Martin, wishing to change the theme. 'Having come to that conclusion, Mark, perhaps you'll attend to me. The place to which the luggage is to go is printed on this card. Mrs. Pawkins's Boarding House.'

'Mrs. Pawkins's boarding-house,' repeated Mark. 'Now, Cicero.'

'Is that his name?' asked Martin.

'That's his name, sir,' rejoined Mark. And the negro grinning assent from under a leathern portmanteau, than which his own face was many shades deeper, hobbled downstairs with his portion of their worldly goods: Mark Tapley having already gone before with his share.

Martin and his friend followed them to the door below, and were about to pursue their walk, when the latter stopped, and asked, with some hesitation, whether that young man was to be trusted?

'Mark! Oh certainly! with anything.'

'You don't understand me. I think he had better go with us. He is an honest fellow, and speaks his mind so very plainly.'

'Why, the fact is,' said Martin, smiling, 'that being un-accustomed to a free republic, he is used to do so.'

'I think he had better go with us,' returned the other. 'He may get into some trouble otherwise. This is not a slave State; but I am ashamed to say that a spirit of Tolerance is not so common anywhere in these latitudes as the form. We are not remarkable for behaving very temperately to each other when we differ: but to strangers!—No, I really think he had better go with us.'

Martin called to him immediately to be of their party; so Cicero and the truck went one way, and they three went another.

They walked about the city for two or three hours; seeing it from the best points of view, and pausing in the principal streets, and before such public buildings as Mr. Bevan pointed out. Night then coming on apace, Martin proposed that they should adjourn to Mrs. Pawkins's establishment for coffee; but in this he was overruled by his new acquaintance, who seemed to have set his heart on carrying him, though it were only for an hour, to the house of a friend of his who lived hard by. Feeling (however disinclined he was, being weary) that it would be in bad taste, and not very gracious, to object that he was unintroduced, when this open-hearted gentleman was so ready to be his sponsor, Martin—for once in his life, at all events—sacrificed his own will and pleasure to the wishes of another, and consented with a fair grace. So travelling had done him that much good, already.

Mr. Bevan knocked at the door of a very neat house of moderate size, from the parlour windows of which, lights were shining brightly into the now dark street. It was quickly opened by a man with such a thoroughly Irish face, that it seemed as if he ought, as a matter of right and principle, to be in rags, and could have no sort of business to be looking cheerfully at anybody out of a whole suit of clothes.

Commending Mark to the care of this phenomenon, for such he may be said to have been in Martin's eyes, Mr. Bevan led the way into the room which had shed its cheerfulness upon the street, to whose occupants he introduced Mr. Chuzzlewit as a gentleman from England, whose acquaintance he had recently had the pleasure to make. They gave him welcome in all courtesy and politeness; and in less than five minutes' time he found himself sitting very much at his ease by the fireside, and becoming vastly well acquainted with the whole family.

There were two young ladies—one eighteen; the other twenty—both very slender, but very pretty; their mother, who looked, as Martin thought, much older and more faded than she ought to have looked; and their grandmother, a little sharp-eyed, quick old woman, who seemed to have got past that stage, and to have come all right again. Besides these, there were the young ladies' father, and the young ladies' brother; the first engaged in mercantile affairs; the second, a student at college; both, in a certain cordiality of manner, like his own friend, and not unlike him in face. Which was no great wonder, for it soon appeared that he was their near relation. Martin could not help tracing the family pedigree from the two young ladies, because they were foremost in his thoughts; not only from being, as aforesaid, very pretty, but by reason of their wearing miraculously small shoes, and the thinnest possible silk stockings: the which their rocking-chairs developed to a distracting extent.

There is no doubt that it was a monstrous comfortable circumstance to be sitting in a snug, well-furnished room, warmed by a cheerful fire, and full of various pleasant decorations, including four small shoes, and the like amount of silk stockings, and——yes, why not?—the feet and legs therein enshrined. And there is no doubt that Martin was monstrous well-disposed to regard his position in that light, after his recent experience of the Screw, and of Mrs. Pawkins's boarding-house. The consequence was that he made himself very agreeable indeed; and by the time the tea and coffee arrived (with sweet preserves, and cunning tea-cakes in its train), was in a highly genial state, and much esteemed by the whole family.

Another delightful circumstance turned up before the first cup of tea was drunk. The whole family had been in England.

There was a pleasant thing! But Martin was not quite so glad of this, when he found that they knew all the great dukes, lords, viscounts, marquesses, duchesses, knights, and baronets, quite affectionately, and were beyond everything interested in the least particular concerning them. However, when they asked after the wearer of this or that coronet, and said, 'Was he quite well?' Martin answered, 'Yes, oh yes. Never better;' and when they said, 'his lordship's mother, the duchess, was she much changed?' Martin said, 'Oh dear no, they would know her anywhere, if they saw her to-morrow;' and so got on pretty well. In like manner when the young ladies questioned him touching the Gold Fish in that Grecian fountain in such and such a nobleman's conservatory, and whether there were as many as there used to be, he gravely reported, after mature consideration, that there must be at least twice as many: and as to the exotics, 'Oh! well! it was of no use talking about *them;* they must be seen to be believed;' which improved state of circumstances reminded the family of the splendour of that brilliant festival (comprehending the whole British Peerage and Court Calendar) to which they were specially invited, and which indeed had been partly given in their honour: and recollections of what Mr. Norris the father had said to the marquess, and of what Mrs. Norris the mother had said to the marchioness, and of what the marquess and marchioness had both said, when they said that upon their words and honours they wished Mr. Norris the father and Mrs. Norris the mother, and the Misses Norris the daughters, and Mr. Norris Junior, the son, would only take up their permanent residence in England, and give them the pleasure of their everlasting friendship, occupied a very considerable time.

Martin thought it rather strange, and in some sort inconsistent, that during the whole of these narrations, and in the very meridian of their enjoyment thereof, both Mr. Norris the father, and Mr. Norris Junior, the son (who corresponded, every post, with four members of the English Peerage), enlarged upon the inestimable advantage of having no such arbitrary distinctions in that enlightened land, where there were no noblemen but nature's noblemen, and where all society was based on one broad level of brotherly love and natural equality. Indeed, Mr. Norris the father, gradually expanding into an oration on this swelling theme, was becoming tedious, when Mr. Bevan diverted his thoughts by happening to make some casual inquiry relative to the occupier of the next house; in reply to which, this same Mr. Norris the father observed, that 'that person entertained religious opinions of which he couldn't approve; and therefore he hadn't the honour of knowing the gentleman.' Mrs. Norris the mother added another reason of her own, the same in effect, but varying in words; to wit, that she believed the people were well enough in their way, but they were not genteel.

Another little trait came out, which impressed itself on Martin forcibly. Mr. Bevan told them about Mark and the negro, and then it appeared that all the Norrises were abolitionists. It was a great relief to hear this, and Martin was so much encouraged on finding himself in such company, that he expressed his sympathy with the oppressed and wretched blacks. Now, one of the young ladies—the prettiest and most delicate—was mightily amused at the earnestness with which he spoke; and on his craving leave to ask her why, was quite unable for a time to speak for laughing. As soon however as she could, she told him that the negroes were such a funny people, so excessively ludicrous in their manners and appearance, that it was wholly impossible for those who knew them well, to associate any serious ideas with such a very absurd part of the creation. Mr. Norris the father, and Mrs. Norris the mother, and Miss Norris the sister, and Mr. Norris Junior the brother, and even Mrs. Norris Senior the grandmother, were all of this opinion, and laid it down as an absolute matter of fact. As if there were nothing in suffering and slavery, grim enough to cast a solemn air on any human animal; though it were as ridiculous, physically, as the most grotesque of apes, or, morally, as the mildest Nimrod among tuft-hunting republicans!

'In short,' said Mr. Norris the father, settling the question comfortably, 'there is a natural antipathy between the races.'

'Extending,' said Martin's friend, in a low voice, 'to the cruellest of tortures, and the bargain and sale of unborn generations.'

Mr. Norris the son said nothing, but he made a wry face, and dusted his fingers as Hamlet might after getting rid of Yorick's skull: just as though he had that moment touched a negro, and some of the black had come off upon his hands.

In order that their talk might fall again into its former pleasant channel, Martin dropped the subject, with a shrewd

suspicion that it would be a dangerous theme to revive under
the best of circumstances: and again addressed himself to
the young ladies, who were very gorgeously attired in very
beautiful colours, and had every article of dress on the same
extensive scale as the little shoes and the thin silk stockings.
This suggested to him that they were great proficients in the
French fashions, which soon turned out to be the case, for
though their information appeared to be none of the newest, it
was very extensive: and the eldest sister in particular, who was
distinguished by a talent for metaphysics, the laws of hydraulic
pressure, and the rights of human kind, had a novel way of
combining these acquirements and bringing them to bear on
any subject from Millinery to the Millennium, both inclusive,
which was at once improving and remarkable; so much so, in
short, that it was usually observed to reduce foreigners to a
state of temporary insanity in five minutes.

Martin felt his reason going; and as a means of saving himself, besought the other sister (seeing a piano in the room) to
sing. With this request she willingly complied; and a bravura
concert, solely sustained by the Misses Norris, presently began.
They sang in all languages—except their own. German,
French, Italian, Spanish, Portuguese, Swiss; but nothing
native; nothing so low as native. For, in this respect, languages
are like many other travellers: ordinary and commonplace
enough at home, but specially genteel abroad.

There is little doubt that in course of time the Misses Norris
would have come to Hebrew, if they had not been interrupted
by an announcement from the Irishman, who flinging open
the door, cried in a loud voice:

'Jiniral Fladdock!'

'My!' cried the sisters, desisting suddenly. 'The general
come back!'

As they made the exclamation, the general, attired in full
uniform for a ball, came darting in with such precipitancy that,
hitching his boot in the carpet, and getting his sword between
his legs, he came down headlong, and presented a curious little
bald place on the crown of his head to the eyes of the astonished company. Nor was this the worst of it; for being rather
corpulent and very tight, the general, being down, could not
get up again, but lay there writhing and doing such things with
his boots, as there is no other instance of in military history.

Of course there was an immediate rush to his assistance; and the general was promptly raised. But his uniform was so fearfully and wonderfully made, that he came up stiff and without a bend in him, like a dead clown, and had no command whatever of himself until he was put quite flat upon the soles of his feet, when he became animated as by a miracle, and moving edgewise that he might go in a narrower compass and be in less danger of fraying the gold lace on his epaulettes by brushing them against anything, advanced with a smiling visage to salute the lady of the house.

To be sure, it would have been impossible for the family to testify purer delight and joy than at this unlooked-for appearance of General Fladdock! The general was as warmly received as if New York had been in a state of siege and no other general was to be got for love or money. He shook hands with the Norrises three times all round, and then reviewed them from a little distance as a brave commander might, with his ample cloak drawn forward over the right shoulder and thrown back upon the left side to reveal his manly breast.

'And do I then,' cried the general, 'once again behold the choicest spirits of my country!'

'Yes,' said Mr. Norris the father. 'Here we are, general.'

Then all the Norrises pressed round the general, inquiring how and where he had been since the date of his letter, and how he had enjoyed himself in foreign parts, and particularly and above all, to what extent he had become acquainted with the great dukes, lords, viscounts, marquesses, duchesses, knights, and baronets, in whom the people of those benighted countries had delight.

'Well then, don't ask me,' said the general, holding up his hand. 'I was among 'em all the time, and have got public journals in my trunk with my name printed:' he lowered his voice and was very impressive here: 'among the fashionable news. But, oh the conventionalities of that a-mazing Eu—rope!'

'Ah!' cried Mr. Norris the father, giving his head a melancholy shake, and looking towards Martin as though he would say, 'I can't deny it, sir. I would if I could.'

'The limited diffusion of a moral sense in that country!' exclaimed the general. 'The absence of a moral dignity in man!'

'Ah!' sighed all the Norrises, quite overwhelmed with despondency.

'I couldn't have realised it,' pursued the general, 'without being located on the spot. Norris, your imagination is the imagination of a strong man, but *you* couldn't have realised it, without being located on the spot!'

'Never,' said Mr. Norris.

'The ex-clusiveness, the pride, the form, the ceremony,' exclaimed the general, emphasising the article more vigorously at every repetition. 'The artificial barriers set up between man and man; the division of the human race into court cards and plain cards, of every denomination—into clubs, diamonds, spades, anything but hearts!'

'Ah!' cried the whole family. 'Too true, general!'

'But stay!' cried Mr. Norris the father, taking him by the arm. 'Surely you crossed in the Screw, general?'

'Well! so I did,' was the reply.

'Possible!' cried the young ladies. 'Only think!'

The general seemed at a loss to understand why his having come home in the Screw should occasion such a sensation, nor did he seem at all clearer on the subject when Mr. Norris, introducing him to Martin, said:

'A fellow-passenger of yours, I think?'

'Of mine?' exclaimed the general; 'No!'

He had never seen Martin, but Martin had seen him, and recognised him, now that they stood face to face, as the gentleman who had stuck his hands in his pockets towards the end of the voyage, and walked the deck with his nostrils dilated.

Everybody looked at Martin. There was no help for it. The truth must out.

'I came over in the same ship as the general,' said Martin, 'but not in the same cabin. It being necessary for me to observe strict economy, I took my passage in the steerage.'

If the general had been carried up bodily to a loaded cannon, and required to let it off that moment, he could not have been in a state of greater consternation than when he heard these words. He, Fladdock, Fladdock in full militia uniform, Fladdock the General, Fladdock the caressed of foreign noblemen, expected to know a fellow who had come over in the steerage of a line-of-packet ship, at the cost of four pound ten! And meeting that fellow in the very sanctuary of New York fashion, and nestling in the bosom of the New York aristocracy! He almost laid his hand upon his sword.

A death-like stillness fell upon the Norrises. If this story should get wind, their country relation had, by his imprudence, for ever disgraced them. They were the bright particular stars of an exalted New York sphere. There were other fashionable spheres above them, and other fashionable spheres below, and none of the stars in any one of these spheres had anything to say to the stars in any other of these spheres. But, through all the spheres it would go forth, that the Norrises, deceived by gentlemanly manners and appearances, had, falling from their high estate, 'received' a dollarless and unknown man. O guardian eagle of the pure Republic, had they lived for this!

'You will allow me,' said Martin, after a terrible silence, 'to take my leave. I feel that I am the cause of at least as much embarrassment here, as I have brought upon myself. But I am bound, before I go, to exonerate this gentleman, who, in introducing me to such society, was quite ignorant of my unworthiness, I assure you.'

With that he made his bow to the Norrises, and walked out like a man of snow: very cool externally, but pretty hot within.

'Come, come,' said Mr. Norris the father, looking with a pale face on the assembled circle as Martin closed the door, 'the young man has this night beheld a refinement of social manner, and an easy magnificence of social decoration, to which he is a stranger in his own country. Let us hope it may awake a moral sense within him.'

If that peculiarly transatlantic article, a moral sense,—for if native statesmen, orators, and pamphleteers, are to be believed, America quite monopolises the commodity,—if that peculiarly transatlantic article be supposed to include a benevolent love of all mankind, certainly Martin's would have borne, just then, a deal of waking. As he strode along the street, with Mark at his heels, his immoral sense was in active operation; prompting him to the utterance of some rather sanguinary remarks, which it was well for his own credit that nobody over-heard. He had so far cooled down however, that he had begun to laugh at the recollection of these incidents, when he heard another step behind him, and turning round encountered his friend Bevan, quite out of breath.

He drew his arm through Martin's, and entreating him to walk slowly, was silent for some minutes. At length he said:

'I hope you exonerate me in another sense?'

'How do you mean?' asked Martin.

'I hope you acquit me of intending or foreseeing the termina-tion of our visit. But I scarcely need ask you that.'

'Scarcely indeed,' said Martin. 'I am the more beholden to you for your kindness, when I find what kind of stuff the good citizens here are made of.'

'I reckon,' his friend returned, 'that they are made of pretty much the same stuff as other folks, if they would but own it, and not set up on false pretences.'

'In good faith, that's true,' said Martin.

'I dare say,' resumed his friend, 'you might have such a scene as that in an English comedy, and not detect any gross improbability or anomaly in the matter of it?'

'Yes, indeed!'

'Doubtless it is more ridiculous here than anywhere else,' said his companion; 'but our professions are to blame for that. So far as I myself am concerned, I may add that I was perfectly aware from the first that you came over in the steerage, for I had seen the list of passengers, and knew it did not comprise your name.'

'I feel more obliged to you than before,' said Martin.

'Norris is a very good fellow in his way,' observed Mr. Bevan.

'Is he?' said Martin drily.

'Oh yes! there are a hundred good points about him. If you or anybody else addressed him as another order of being, and sued to him *in formâ pauperis*, he would be all kindness and consideration.'

'I needn't have travelled three thousand miles from home to find such a character as *that*,' said Martin. Neither he nor his friend said anything more on the way back; each appearing to find sufficient occupation in his own thoughts.

The tea, or the supper, or whatever else they called the evening meal, was over when they reached the Major's; but the cloth, ornamented with a few additional smears and stains, was still upon the table. At one end of the board Mrs. Jefferson Brick and two other ladies were drinking tea; out of the ordinary course, evidently, for they were bonneted and shawled, and seemed to have just come home. By the light of three flaring candles of different lengths, in as many candlesticks of different patterns, the room showed to almost as little advantage as in broad day.

These ladies were all three talking together in a very loud tone when Martin and his friend entered; but seeing those gentlemen, they stopped directly, and became excessively genteel, not to say frosty. As they went on to exchange some few remarks in whispers, the very water in the tea-pot might have fallen twenty degrees in temperature beneath their chilling coldness.

'Have you been to meeting, Mrs. Brick?' asked Martin's friend, with something of a roguish twinkle in his eye.

'To lecture, sir.'

'I beg your pardon. I forgot. You don't go to meeting, I think?'

Here the lady on the right of Mrs. Brick gave a pious cough, as much as to say '*I* do!' As, indeed, she did nearly every night in the week.

'A good discourse, ma'am?' asked Mr. Bevan, addressing this lady.

The lady raised her eyes in a pious manner, and answered 'Yes.' She had been much comforted by some good, strong, peppery doctrine, which satisfactorily disposed of all her friends and acquaintances, and quite settled *their* business. Her bonnet, too, had far outshone every bonnet in the congregation: so she was tranquil on all accounts.

'What course of lectures are you attending now, ma'am?' said Martin's friend, turning again to Mrs. Brick.

'The Philosophy of the Soul, on Wednesdays.'

'On Mondays?'

'The Philosophy of Crime.'

'On Fridays?'

'The Philosophy of Vegetables.'

'You have forgotten Thursdays; the Philosophy of Government, my dear,' observed the third lady.

'No,' said Mrs. Brick. 'That's Tuesdays.'

'So it is!' cried the lady. 'The Philosophy of Matter on Thursdays, of course.'

'You see, Mr. Chuzzlewit, our ladies are fully employed,' said Bevan.

'Indeed you have reason to say so,' answered Martin. 'Between these very grave pursuits abroad, and family duties at home, their time must be pretty well engrossed.'

Martin stopped here, for he saw that the ladies regarded him with no very great favour, though what he had done to deserve the disdainful expression which appeared in their faces he was at a loss to divine. But on their going up-stairs to their bedrooms: which they very soon did: Mr. Bevan informed him that domestic drudgery was far beneath the exalted range of these Philosophers, and that the chances were a hundred to one that not one of the three could perform the easiest woman's work for herself, or make the simplest article of dress for any of her children.

'Though whether they might not be better employed with such blunt instruments as knitting-needles, than with these edge-tools,' he said, 'is another question; but I can answer for one thing: they don't often cut themselves. Devotions and lectures are our balls and concerts. They go to these places of resort, as an escape from monotony; look at each other's clothes; and come home again.'

'When you say "home," do you mean a house like this?'

'Very often. But I see you are tired to death, and will wish you good night. We will discuss your projects in the morning. You cannot but feel already that it is useless staying here, with any hope of advancing them. You will have to go farther.'

'And to fare worse?' said Martin, pursuing the old adage.

'Well, I hope not. But sufficient for the day, you know. Good night.'

They shook hands heartily and separated. As soon as Martin was left alone, the excitement of novelty and change which had sustained him through all the fatigues of the day, departed; and he felt so thoroughly dejected and worn out, that he even lacked the energy to crawl up-stairs to bed.

In twelve or fifteen hours, how great a change had fallen on his hopes and sanguine plans! New and strange as he was to the ground on which he stood, and to the air he breathed, he could not—recalling all that he had crowded into that one day—but entertain a strong misgiving that his enterprise was doomed. Rash and ill-considered as it had often looked on shipboard, but had never seemed on shore, it wore a dismal aspect, now, that frightened him. Whatever thoughts he called up to his aid, they came upon him in depressing and discouraging shapes, and gave him no relief. Even the diamonds on his finger sparkled with the brightness of tears, and had no ray of hope in all their brilliant lustre.

He continued to sit in gloomy rumination by the stove, unmindful of the boarders who dropped in one by one from their stores and counting-houses, or the neighbouring bar-rooms, and after taking long pulls from a great white water-jug upon the sideboard, and lingering with a kind of hideous fascination near the brass spittoons, lounged heavily to bed; until at length Mark Tapley came and shook him by the arm, supposing him asleep.

'Mark!' he cried, starting.

'All right, sir,' said that cheerful follower, snuffing with his fingers the candle he bore. 'It ain't a very large bed, your'n, sir; and a man as wasn't thirsty might drink, afore breakfast, all the water you've got to wash in, and arterwards eat the towel. But you'll sleep without rocking to-night, sir.'

'I feel as if the house were on the sea,' said Martin, staggering when he rose; 'and am utterly wretched.'

'I'm as jolly as a sandboy, myself, sir,' said Mark. 'But, Lord, I have reason to be! I ought to have been born here; that's my opinion. Take care how you go:' for they were now ascending the stairs. 'You recollect the gentleman aboard the Screw as had the very small trunk, sir?'

'The valise? Yes.'

'Well, sir, there's been a delivery of clean clothes from the wash to-night, and they're put outside the bedroom doors here. If you take notice as we go up, what a very few shirts there are, and what a many fronts, you'll penetrate the mystery of his packing.'

But Martin was too weary and despondent to take heed of anything, so had no interest in this discovery. Mr. Tapley, nothing dashed by his indifference, conducted him to the top of the house, and into the bed-chamber prepared for his reception: which was a very little narrow room, with half a window in it; a bedstead like a chest without a lid; two chairs; a piece of carpet, such as shoes are commonly tried upon at a ready-made establishment in England; a little looking-glass nailed against the wall; and a washing-table, with a jug and ewer that might have been mistaken for a milk-pot and slop-basin.

'I suppose they polish themselves with a dry cloth in this country,' said Mark. 'They've certainly got a touch of the 'phoby, sir.'

'I wish you would pull off my boots for me,' said Martin, dropping into one of the chairs. 'I am quite knocked up. Dead beat, Mark.'

'You won't say that to-morrow morning, sir,' returned Mr. Tapley; 'nor even to-night, sir, when you've made a trial of this.' With which he produced a very large tumbler, piled up to the brim with little blocks of clear transparent ice, through which one or two thin slices of lemon, and a golden liquid of delicious appearance, appealed from the still depths below, to the loving eye of the spectator.

'What do you call this?' said Martin.

But Mr. Tapley made no answer: merely plunging a reed into the mixture—which caused a pleasant commotion among the pieces of ice—and signifying by an expressive gesture that it was to be pumped up through that agency by the enraptured drinker.

Martin took the glass, with an astonished look; applied his lips to the reed; and cast up his eyes once in ecstasy. He paused no more until the goblet was drained to the last drop.

'There, sir!' said Mark, taking it from him with a triumphant face; 'if ever you should happen to be dead beat again, when I ain't in the way, all you've got to do is, to ask the nearest man to go and fetch a cobbler.'

'To go and fetch a cobbler?' repeated Martin.

'This wonderful invention, sir,' said Mark, tenderly patting the empty glass, 'is called a cobbler. Sherry cobbler when you name it long; cobbler, when you name it short. Now you're equal to having your boots took off, and are, in every particular worth mentioning, another man.'

Having delivered himself of this solemn preface, he brought the boot-jack.

'Mind! I am not going to relapse, Mark,' said Martin; 'but, good Heaven, if we should be left in some wild part of this country without goods or money!'

'Well, sir!' replied the imperturbable Tapley; 'from what we've seen already, I don't know whether, under those circumstances, we shouldn't do better in the wild parts than in the tame ones.'

'Oh, Tom Pinch, Tom Pinch!' said Martin, in a thoughtful tone; 'what would I give to be again beside you, and able to hear your voice, though it were even in the old bedroom at Pecksniff's!'

'Oh, Dragon, Dragon!' echoed Mark, cheerfully, 'if there warn't any water between you and me, and nothing faint-hearted-like in going back, I don't know that I mightn't say the same. But here am I, Dragon, in New York, America; and there are you in Wiltshire, Europe; and there's a fortune to make, Dragon, and a beautiful young lady to make it for; and whenever you go to see the Monument, Dragon, you mustn't give in on the door-steps, or you'll never get up to the top!'

'Wisely said, Mark,' cried Martin. 'We must look forward.'

'In all the story-books as ever I read, sir, the people as looked backward was turned into stones,' replied Mark; 'and my opinion always was, that they brought it on themselves, and it served 'em right. I wish you good night, sir, and pleasant dreams!'

'They must be of home, then, said Martin, as he lay down in bed.

'So I say, too,' whispered Mark Tapley, when he was out of hearing and in his own room; 'for if there don't come a time afore we're well out of this, when there'll be a little more credit in keeping up one's jollity, I'm a United Statesman!'

Leaving them to blend and mingle in their sleep the shadows of objects afar off, as they take fantastic shapes upon the wall in the dim light of thought without control, be it the part of this slight chronicle—a dream within a dream—as rapidly to change the scene, and cross the ocean to the English shore.

CHAPTER XVIII

Does business with the house of Anthony Chuzzlewit and son, from which one of the partners retires unexpectedly

CHANGE begets change. Nothing propagates so fast. If a man habituated to a narrow circle of cares and pleasures, out of which he seldom travels, step beyond it, though for never so brief a space, his departure from the monotonous scene on which he has been an actor of importance, would seem to be the signal for instant confusion. As if, in the gap he had left, the wedge of change were driven to the head, rending what was a solid mass to fragments, things cemented and held together by the usages of years, burst asunder in as many weeks. The mine which Time has slowly dug beneath familiar objects is sprung in an instant; and what was rock before becomes but sand and dust.

Most men, at one time or other, have proved this in some degree. The extent to which the natural laws of change asserted their supremacy in that limited sphere of action which Martin had deserted, shall be faithfully set down in these pages.

'What a cold spring it is!' whimpered old Anthony, drawing near the evening fire. 'It was a warmer season, sure, when I was young!'

'You needn't go scorching your clothes into holes, whether it was or not,' observed the amiable Jonas, raising his eyes from yesterday's newspaper. 'Broadcloth ain't so cheap as that comes to.'

'A good lad!' cried the father, breathing on his cold hands, and feebly chafing them against each other. 'A prudent lad! He never delivered himself up to the vanities of dress. No, no!'

'I don't know but I would though, mind you, if I could do it for nothing,' said his son, as he resumed the paper.

'Ah!' chuckled the old man. '*If*, indeed! But it's very cold.'

'Let the fire be!' cried Mr. Jonas, stopping his honoured parent's hand in the use of the poker. 'Do you mean to come to want in your old age, that you take to wasting now?'

'There's not time for that, Jonas,' said the old man.

'Not time for what?' bawled his heir.

'For me to come to want. I wish there was!'

'You always were as selfish an old blade as need be,' said

The Dissolution of Partnership
(*p. 307*)

Jonas, in a voice too low for him to hear, and looking at him with an angry frown. 'You act up to your character. You wouldn't mind coming to want, wouldn't you! I dare say you wouldn't. And your own flesh and blood might come to want too, might they, for anything you cared? Oh you precious old flint!'

After this dutiful address he took his tea-cup in his hand: for that meal was in progress, and the father and son and Chuffey were partakers of it. Then, looking steadfastly at his father, and stopping now and then to carry a spoonful of tea to his lips, he proceeded in the same tone, thus:

'Want, indeed! You're a nice old man to be talking of want at this time of day. Beginning to talk of want, are you? Well, I declare! There isn't time? No, I should hope not. But you'd live to be a couple of hundred if you could; and after all be discontented. *I* know you!'

The old man sighed, and still sat cowering before the fire. Mr. Jonas shook his Britannia-metal teaspoon at him, and taking a loftier position went on to argue the point on high moral grounds.

'If you're in such a state of mind as that,' he grumbled, but in the same subdued key, 'why don't you make over your property? Buy an annuity cheap, and make your life interesting to yourself and everybody else that watches the speculation. But no, that wouldn't suit *you*. That would be natural conduct to your own son, and you like to be unnatural, and to keep him out of his rights. Why, I should be ashamed of myself if I was you, and glad to hide my head in the what-you-may-call-it.'

Possibly this general phrase supplied the place of grave, or tomb, or sepulchre, or cemetery, or mausoleum, or other such word which the filial tenderness of Mr. Jonas made him delicate of pronouncing. He pursued the theme no further; for Chuffey, somehow discovering, from his old corner by the fireside, that Anthony was in the attitude of a listener, and that Jonas appeared to be speaking, suddenly cried out, like one inspired:

'He is your own son, Mr. Chuzzlewit. Your own son, sir!'

Old Chuffey little suspected what depth of application these words had, or that, in the bitter satire which they bore, they might have sunk into the old man's very soul, could he have known what words were hanging on his own son's lips, or what was passing in his thoughts. But the voice diverted the current of Anthony's reflections, and roused him.

'Yes, yes, Chuffey, Jonas is a chip of the old block. It's a very old block, now, Chuffey,' said the old man, with a strange look of discomposure.

'Precious old,' assented Jonas.

'No, no, no,' said Chuffey. 'No, Mr. Chuzzlewit. Not old at all, sir.'

'Oh! He's worse than ever, you know!' cried Jonas, quite disgusted. 'Upon my soul, father, he's getting too bad. Hold your tongue, will you?'

'He says you're wrong!' cried Anthony to the old clerk.

'Tut, tut!' was Chuffey's answer. 'I know better. I say *he's* wrong. I say *he's* wrong. He's a boy. That's what he is. So are you, Mr. Chuzzlewit—a kind of boy. Ha! ha! ha! You're quite a boy to many I have known; you're a boy to me; you're a boy to hundreds of us. Don't mind him!'

With which extraordinary speech—for in the case of Chuffey this was a burst of eloquence without a parallel—the poor old shadow drew through his palsied arm his master's hand, and held it there, with his own folded upon it, as if he would defend him.

'I grow deafer every day, Chuff,' said Anthony, with as much softness of manner, or, to describe it more correctly, with as little hardness as he was capable of expressing.

'No, no,' cried Chuffey. 'No, you don't. What if you did? I've been deaf this twenty year.'

'I grow blinder, too,' said the old man, shaking his head.

'That's a good sign!' cried Chuffey. 'Ha! ha! The best sign in the world! You saw too well before.'

He patted Anthony upon the hand as one might comfort a child, and drawing the old man's arm still further through his own, shook his trembling fingers towards the spot where Jonas sat, as though he would wave him off. But, Anthony remaining quite still and silent, he relaxed his hold by slow degrees and lapsed into his usual niche in the corner: merely putting forth his hand at intervals and touching his old employer gently on the coat, as with the design of assuring himself that he was yet beside him.

Mr. Jonas was so very much amazed by these proceedings that he could do nothing but stare at the two old men, until Chuffey had fallen into his usual state, and Anthony had sunk into a doze; when he gave some vent to his emotions by going close up to the former personage, and making as though he would, in vulgar parlance, 'punch his head.'

'They've been carrying on this game,' thought Jonas in a brown study, 'for the last two or three weeks. I never saw my father take so much notice of him as he has in that time. What! You're legacy hunting, are you, Mister Chuff? Eh?'

But Chuffey was as little conscious of the thought as of the bodily advance of Mr. Jonas's clenched fist, which hovered fondly about his ear. When he had scowled at him to his heart's content, Jonas took the candle from the table, and walking into the glass office, produced a bunch of keys from his pocket. With one of these he opened a secret drawer in the desk: peeping stealthily out, as he did so, to be certain that the two old men were still before the fire.

'All as right as ever,' said Jonas, propping the lid of the desk open with his forehead, and unfolding a paper. 'Here's the will, Mister Chuff. Thirty pound a year for your maintenance, old boy, and all the rest to his only son, Jonas. You needn't trouble yourself to be too affectionate. You won't get anything by it. What's that?'

It *was* startling, certainly. A face on the other side of the glass partition looking curiously in: and not at him but at the paper in his hand. For the eyes were attentively cast down upon the writing, and were swiftly raised when he cried out. Then they met his own, and were as the eyes of Mr. Pecksniff.

Suffering the lid of the desk to fall with a loud noise, but not forgetting even then to lock it, Jonas, pale and breathless, gazed upon this phantom. It moved, opened the door, and walked in.

'What's the matter?' cried Jonas, falling back. 'Who is it? Where do you come from? What do you want?'

'Matter!' cried the voice of Mr. Pecksniff, as Pecksniff in the flesh smiled amiably upon him. 'The matter, Mr. Jonas!'

'What are you prying and peering about here for?' said Jonas, angrily. 'What do you mean by coming up to town in this way, and taking one unawares? It's precious odd a man can't read the—the newspaper—in his own office without being startled out of his wits by people coming in without notice. Why didn't you knock at the door?'

'So I did, Mr. Jonas,' answered Pecksniff, 'but no one heard me. I was curious,' he added in his gentle way as he laid his hand upon the young man's shoulder, 'to find out what part of the newspaper interested you so much; but the glass was too dim and dirty.'

Jonas glanced in haste at the partition. Well. It wasn't very clean. So far he spoke the truth.

'Was it poetry now?' said Mr. Pecksniff, shaking the fore-finger of his right hand with an air of cheerful banter. 'Or was it politics? Or was it the price of stock? The main chance, Mr. Jonas, the main chance, I suspect.'

'You ain't far from the truth,' answered Jonas, recovering himself and snuffing the candle: 'but how the deuce do you come to be in London again? Ecod! it's enough to make a man stare, to see a fellow looking at him all of a sudden, who he thought was sixty or seventy mile away.'

'So it is,' said Mr. Pecksniff. 'No doubt of it, my dear Mr. Jonas. For while the human mind is constituted as it is—'

'Oh, bother the human mind,' interrupted Jonas with impatience, 'what have you come up for?'

'A little matter of business,' said Mr. Pecksniff, 'which has arisen quite unexpectedly.'

'Oh!' cried Jonas, 'is that all? Well. Here's father in the next room. Hallo father, here's Pecksniff! He gets more addlepated every day he lives, I do believe,' muttered Jonas, shaking his honoured parent roundly. 'Don't I tell you Pecksniff's here, stupid head?'

The combined effects of the shaking and this loving remon-strance soon awoke the old man, who gave Mr. Pecksniff a chuckling welcome, which was attributable in part to his being glad to see that gentleman, and in part to his unfading delight in the recollection of having called him a hypocrite. As Mr. Pecksniff had not yet taken tea (indeed he had, but an hour before, arrived in London) the remains of the late collation, with a rasher of bacon, were served up for his entertainment; and as Mr. Jonas had a business appointment in the next street, he stepped out to keep it: promising to return before Mr. Peck-sniff could finish his repast.

'And now, my good sir,' said Mr. Pecksniff to Anthony: 'now that we are alone, pray tell me what I can do for you. I say alone, because I believe that our dear friend Mr. Chuffey is, metaphysically speaking, a—shall I say a dummy?' asked Mr. Pecksniff with his sweetest smile, and his head very much on one side.

'He neither hears us,' replied Anthony, 'nor sees us.'

'Why, then,' said Mr. Pecksniff, 'I will be bold to say, with the utmost sympathy for his afflictions, and the greatest admiration of those excellent qualities which do equal honour to his head and to his heart, that he *is* what is playfully termed a dummy. You were going to observe, my dear sir—?'

'I was not going to make any observation that I know of,' replied the old man.

'*I* was,' said Mr. Pecksniff, mildly.

'Oh! *you* were? What was it?'

'That I never,' said Mr. Pecksniff, previously rising to see that the door was shut, and arranging his chair when he came back, so that it could not be opened in the least without his immediately becoming aware of the circumstance; 'that I never in my life was so astonished as by the receipt of your letter yesterday. That you should do me the honour to wish to take counsel with me on any matter, amazed me; but that you should desire to do so, to the exclusion even of Mr. Jonas, showed an amount of confidence in one to whom you had done a verbal injury, merely a verbal injury you were anxious to repair, which gratified, which moved, which overcame me.'

He was always a glib speaker, but he delivered this short address very glibly; having been at some pains to compose it outside the coach.

Although he paused for a reply, and truly said that he was there at Anthony's request, the old man sat gazing at him in profound silence and with a perfectly blank face. Nor did he seem to have the least desire or impulse to pursue the conversation, though Mr. Pecksniff looked towards the door, and pulled out his watch, and gave him many other hints that their time was short, and Jonas, if he kept his word, would soon return. But the strangest incident in all this strange behaviour was, that of a sudden, in a moment, so swiftly that it was impossible to trace how, or to observe any process of change, his features fell into their old expression, and he cried, striking his hand passionately upon the table as if no interval at all had taken place:

'Will you hold your tongue, sir, and let me speak?'

Mr. Pecksniff deferred to him with a submissive bow; and said within himself, 'I knew his hand was changed, and that his writing staggered. I said so yesterday. Ahem! Dear me!'

'Jonas is sweet upon your daughter, Pecksniff,' said the old man, in his usual tone.

'We spoke of that, if you remember, sir, at Mrs. Todgers's,' replied the courteous architect.

'You needn't speak so loud,' retorted Anthony. 'I'm not so deaf as that.'

Mr. Pecksniff had certainly raised his voice pretty high: not so much because he thought Anthony was deaf, as because he felt convinced that his perceptive faculties were waxing dim: but this quick resentment of his considerate behaviour greatly disconcerted him, and, not knowing what tack to shape his course upon, he made another inclination of the head, yet more submissive than the last.

'I have said,' repeated the old man, 'that Jonas is sweet upon your daughter.'

'A charming girl, sir,' murmured Mr. Pecksniff, seeing that he waited for an answer. 'A dear girl, Mr. Chuzzlewit, though I say it who should not.'

'You know better,' cried the old man, advancing his weazen face at least a yard, and starting forward in his chair to do it. 'You lie! What, you *will* be a hypocrite, will you?'

'My good sir,' Mr. Pecksniff began.

'Don't call me a good sir,' retorted Anthony, 'and don't claim to be one yourself. If your daughter was what you would have me believe, she wouldn't do for Jonas. Being what she is, I think she will. He might be deceived in a wife. She might run riot, contract debts, and waste his substance. Now when I am dead—'

His face altered so horribly as he said the word, that Mr. Pecksniff really was fain to look another way.

'—It will be worse for me to know of such doings than if I was alive: for to be tormented for getting that together, which even while I suffer for its acquisition is flung into the very kennels of the streets, would be insupportable torture. No,' said the old man, hoarsely, 'let that be saved at least; let there be something gained, and kept fast hold of, when so much is lost.'

'My dear Mr. Chuzzlewit,' said Pecksniff, 'these are unwholesome fancies; quite unnecessary, sir, quite uncalled for, I am sure. The truth is, my dear sir, that you are not well!'

'Not dying though!' cried Anthony, with something like the snarl of a wild animal. 'Not yet! There are years of life in me. Why, look at him,' pointing to his feeble clerk. 'Death has no right to leave him standing, and to mow me down!'

Mr. Pecksniff was so much afraid of the old man, and so completely taken aback by the state in which he found him, that he had not even presence of mind enough to call up a scrap of morality from the great storehouse within his own breast. Therefore he stammered out that no doubt it was, in fairness and decency, Mr. Chuffey's turn to expire; and that from all he had heard of Mr. Chuffey, and the little he had the pleasure of knowing of that gentleman, personally, he felt convinced in his own mind that he would see the propriety of expiring with as little delay as possible.

'Come here!' said the old man, beckoning him to draw nearer. 'Jonas will be my heir, Jonas will be rich, and a great catch for you. You know that. Jonas is sweet upon your daughter.'

'I know that too,' thought Mr. Pecksniff, 'for you have said it often enough.'

'He might get more money than with her,' said the old man, 'but she will help him to take care of what they have. She is not too young or heedless, and comes of a good hard griping stock. But don't you play too fine a game. She only holds him by a thread; and if you draw it too tight (I know his temper) it'll snap. Bind him when he's in the mood, Pecksniff; bind him. You're too deep. In your way of leading him on, you'll leave him miles behind. Bah, you man of oil, have I no eyes to see how you have angled with him from the first?'

'Now I wonder,' thought Mr. Pecksniff, looking at him with a wistful face, 'whether this is all he has to say!'

Old Anthony rubbed his hands and muttered to himself; complained again that he was cold; drew his chair before the fire; and, sitting with his back to Mr. Pecksniff, and his chin sunk down upon his breast, was, in another minute, quite regardless or forgetful of his presence.

Uncouth and unsatisfactory as this short interview had been, it had furnished Mr. Pecksniff with a hint which, supposing nothing further were imparted to him, repaid the journey up and home again. For the good gentleman had never (for want of an opportunity) dived into the depths of Mr. Jonas's nature; and any recipe for catching such a son-in-law (much more one written on a leaf out of his own father's book) was worth the having. In order that he might lose no chance of improving so fair an opportunity by allowing Anthony to fall asleep before he had finished all he had to say, Mr. Pecksniff, in the disposal of the refreshments on the table, a work to which he now applied himself in earnest, resorted to many ingenious contrivances for attracting his attention: such as coughing, sneezing, clattering the tea-cups, sharpening the knives, dropping the loaf, and so forth. But all in vain, for Mr. Jonas returned, and Anthony had said no more.

'What! My father asleep again?' he cried, as he hung up his hat, and cast a look at him. 'Ah! and snoring. Only hear!'

'He snores very deep,' said Mr. Pecksniff.

'Snores deep?' repeated Jonas. 'Yes; let him alone for that. He'll snore for six, at any time.'

'Do you know, Mr. Jonas,' said Pecksniff, 'that I think your father is—don't let me alarm you—breaking?'

'Oh, is he though?' replied Jonas, with a shake of the head which expressed the closeness of his dutiful observation. 'Ecod, you don't know how tough he is. He ain't upon the move yet.'

'It struck me that he was changed, both in his appearance and manner,' said Mr. Pecksniff.

'That's all you know about it,' returned Jonas, seating himself with a melancholy air. 'He never was better than he is now. How are they all at home? How's Charity?'

'Blooming, Mr. Jonas, blooming.'

'And the other one; how's she?'

'Volatile trifler!' said Mr. Pecksniff, fondly musing. 'She is well, she is well. Roving from parlour to bedroom, Mr. Jonas, like the bee; skimming from post to pillar, like the butterfly; dipping her young beak into our currant wine, like the humming-bird! Ah! were she a little less giddy than she is; and had she but the sterling qualities of Cherry, my young friend!'

'Is she so very giddy, then?' asked Jonas.

'Well, well!' said Mr. Pecksniff, with great feeling; 'let me not be hard upon my child. Beside her sister Cherry she appears so. A strange noise that, Mr. Jonas!'

'Something wrong in the clock, I suppose,' said Jonas, glancing towards it. 'So the other one ain't your favourite, ain't she?'

The fond father was about to reply, and had already summoned into his face a look of most intense sensibility, when the sound he had already noticed was repeated.

'Upon my word, Mr. Jonas, that is a very extraordinary clock,' said Pecksniff.

It would have been, if it had made the noise which startled them: but another kind of time-piece was fast running down, and from that the sound proceeded. A scream from Chuffey, rendered a hundred times more loud and formidable by his silent habits, made the house ring from roof to cellar; and, looking round, they saw Anthony Chuzzlewit extended on the floor, with the old clerk upon his knees beside him.

He had fallen from his chair in a fit, and lay there, battling for each gasp of breath, with every shrivelled vein and sinew starting in its place, as if it were bent on bearing witness to his age, and sternly pleading with Nature against his recovery. It was frightful to see how the principle of life, shut up within his withered frame, fought like a strong devil, mad to be released, and rent its ancient prison-house. A young man in the fulness of his vigour, struggling with so much strength of desperation, would have been a dismal sight; but an old, old, shrunken body, endowed with preternatural might, and giving the lie in every motion of its every limb and joint to its enfeebled aspect, was a hideous spectacle indeed.

They raised him up, and fetched a surgeon with all haste, who bled the patient and applied some remedies; but the fits held him so long, that it was past midnight when they got him, quiet now, but quite unconscious and exhausted, into bed.

'Don't go,' said Jonas, putting his ashy lips to Mr. Pecksniff's ear, and whispering across the bed. 'It was a mercy you were present when he was taken ill. Some one might have said it was my doing.'

'*Your* doing!' cried Mr. Pecksniff.

'I don't know but they might,' he replied, wiping the moisture from his white face. 'People say such things. How does he look now?'

Mr. Pecksniff shook his head.

'I used to joke, you know,' said Jonas: 'but I—I never wished him dead. Do you think he's very bad?'

'The doctor said he was. You heard,' was Mr. Pecksniff's answer.

'Ah! but he might say that to charge us more, in case of his getting well,' said Jonas. 'You mustn't go away, Pecksniff. Now it's come to this, I wouldn't be without a witness for a thousand pound.'

Chuffey said not a word, and heard not a word. He had sat himself down in a chair at the bedside, and there he remained, motionless; except that he sometimes bent his head over the pillow, and seemed to listen. He never changed in this. Though once in the dreary night Mr. Pecksniff, having dozed, awoke with a confused impression that he had heard him praying, and strangely mingling figures: not of speech, but arithmetic: with his broken prayers.

Jonas sat there, too, all night: not where his father could have seen him, had his consciousness returned, but hiding, as it were, behind him, and only reading how he looked, in Mr. Pecksniff's eyes. *He*, the coarse upstart, who had ruled the house so long? That craven cur, who was afraid to move, and shook so, that his very shadow fluttered on the wall!

It was broad, bright, stirring day when, leaving the old clerk to watch him, they went down to breakfast. People hurried up and down the street; windows and doors were opened; thieves and beggars took their usual posts; workmen bestirred themselves; tradesmen set forth their shops; bailiffs and constables were on the watch; all kinds of human creatures strove, in their several ways, as hard to live, as the one sick old man who combated for every grain of sand in his fast-emptying glass, as eagerly as if it were an empire.

'If anything happens, Pecksniff,' said Jonas, 'you must promise me to stop here till it's all over. You shall see that I do what's right.'

'I know that you will do what's right, Mr. Jonas,' said Pecksniff.

'Yes, yes, but I won't be doubted. No one shall have it in his power to say a syllable against me,' he returned. 'I know how people will talk. Just as if he wasn't old, or I had the secret of keeping him alive!'

Mr. Pecksniff promised that he would remain, if circumstances should render it, in his esteemed friend's opinion, desirable; they were finishing their meal in silence, when suddenly an apparition stood before them, so ghastly to the view that Jonas shrieked aloud, and both recoiled in horror.

Old Anthony, dressed in his usual clothes, was in the room—beside the table. He leaned upon the shoulder of his solitary friend; and on his livid face, and on his horny hands, and in his glassy eyes, and traced by an eternal finger in the very drops of sweat upon his brow, was one word—Death.

He spoke to them in something of his own voice too, but sharpened and made hollow, like a dead man's face. What he would have said, God knows. He seemed to utter words, but they were such as man had never heard. And this was the most fearful circumstance of all, to see him standing there, gabbling in an unearthly tongue.

'He's better now,' said Chuffey. 'Better now. Let him sit in his old chair, and he'll be well again. I told him not to mind. I said so, yesterday.'

They put him in his easy-chair, and wheeled it near the window; then, setting open the door, exposed him to the free current of morning air. But not all the air that is, nor all the winds that ever blew 'twixt Heaven and Earth, could have brought new life to him.

Plunge him to the throat in golden pieces now, and his heavy fingers shall not close on one!

CHAPTER XIX

The reader is brought into communication with some professional persons, and sheds a tear over the filial piety of good Mr. Jonas

MR. PECKSNIFF was in a hackney cabriolet, for Jonas Chuzzlewit had said 'Spare no expense.' Mankind is evil in its thoughts and in its base constructions, and Jonas was resolved it should not have an inch to stretch into an ell against him. It never should be charged upon his father's son that he had grudged the money for his father's funeral. Hence, until the obsequies should be concluded, Jonas had taken for his motto 'Spend, and spare not!'

Mr. Pecksniff had been to the undertaker, and was now upon his way to another officer in the train of mourning: a female functionary, a nurse, and watcher, and performer of nameless offices about the persons of the dead: whom he had recommended. Her name, as Mr. Pecksniff gathered from a scrap of writing in his hand, was Gamp; her residence in Kingsgate Street, High Holborn. So Mr. Pecksniff, in a hackney cab, was rattling over Holborn stones, in quest of Mrs. Gamp.

This lady lodged at a bird-fancier's, next door but one to the celebrated mutton-pie shop, and directly opposite to the original cat's-meat warehouse; the renown of which establishments was duly heralded on their respective fronts. It was a little house, and this was the more convenient; for Mrs. Gamp being, in her highest walk of art, a monthly nurse, or, as her sign-board boldly had it, 'Midwife,' and lodging in the first-floor front, was easily assailable at night by pebbles, walking-sticks, and fragments of tobacco-pipe: all much more efficacious than the street-door knocker, which was so constructed as to wake the street with ease, and even spread alarms of fire in Holborn, without making the smallest impression on the premises to which it was addressed.

It chanced on this particular occasion, that Mrs. Gamp had been up all the previous night, in attendance upon a ceremony to which the usage of gossips has given that name which expresses, in two syllables, the curse pronounced on Adam. It chanced that Mrs. Gamp had not been regularly engaged, but had been called in at a crisis, in consequence of her great

Mr. Pecksniff on his Mission
(p. 311)

repute, to assist another professional lady with her advice; and thus it happened that, all points of interest in the case being over, Mrs. Gamp had come home again to the bird-fancier's, and gone to bed. So when Mr. Pecksniff drove up in the hackney cab, Mrs. Gamp's curtains were drawn close, and Mrs. Gamp was fast asleep behind them.

If the bird-fancier had been at home, as he ought to have been, there would have been no great harm in this; but he was out, and his shop was closed. The shutters were down certainly; and in every pane of glass there was at least one tiny bird in a tiny bird-cage, twittering and hopping his little ballet of despair, and knocking his head against the roof: while one unhappy goldfinch who lived outside a red villa with his name on the door, drew the water for his own drinking, and mutely appealed to some good man to drop a farthing's-worth of poison in it. Still, the door was shut. Mr. Pecksniff tried the latch, and shook it, causing a cracked bell inside to ring most mournfully; but no one came. The bird-fancier was an easy shaver also, and a fashionable hairdresser also; and perhaps he had been sent for, express, from the court end of the town, to trim a lord, or cut and curl a lady; but however that might be, there, upon his own ground, he was not; nor was there any more distinct trace of him to assist the imagination of an inquirer, than a professional print or emblem of his calling (much favoured in the trade), representing a hair-dresser of easy manners curling a lady of distinguished fashion, in the presence of a patent upright grand pianoforte.

Noting these circumstances, Mr. Pecksniff, in the innocence of his heart, applied himself to the knocker; but at the first double knock every window in the street became alive with female heads; and before he could repeat the performance whole troops of married ladies (some about to trouble Mrs. Gamp themselves very shortly) came flocking round the steps, all crying out with one accord, and with uncommon interest, 'Knock at the winder, sir, knock at the winder. Lord bless you, don't lose no more time than you can help; knock at the winder!'

Acting upon this suggestion, and borrowing the driver's whip for the purpose, Mr. Pecksniff soon made a commotion among the first-floor flower-pots, and roused Mrs. Gamp, whose voice—to the great satisfaction of the matrons—was heard to say, 'I'm coming.'

'He's as pale as a muffin,' said one lady, in allusion to Mr. Pecksniff.

'So he ought to be, if he's the feelings of a man,' observed another.

A third lady (with her arms folded) said she wished he had chosen any other time for fetching Mrs. Gamp, but it always happened so with *her*.

It gave Mr. Pecksniff much uneasiness to find, from these remarks, that he was supposed to have come to Mrs. Gamp upon an errand touching—not the close of life, but the other end. Mrs. Gamp herself was under the same impression, for, throwing open the window, she cried behind the curtains, as she hastily attired herself:

'Is it Mrs. Perkins?'

'No!' returned Mr. Pecksniff, sharply. 'Nothing of the sort.'

'What, Mr. Whilks!' cried Mrs. Gamp. 'Don't say it's you, Mr. Whilks, and that poor creetur Mrs. Whilks with not even a pincushion ready. Don't say it's you, Mr. Whilks!'

'It isn't Mr. Whilks,' said Pecksniff. 'I don't know the man. Nothing of the kind. A gentleman is dead; and some person being wanted in the house, you have been recommended by Mr. Mould the undertaker.'

As she was by this time in a condition to appear, Mrs. Gamp, who had a face for all occasions, looked out of the window with her mourning countenance, and said she would be down directly. But the matrons took it very ill that Mr. Pecksniff's mission was of so unimportant a kind; and the lady with her arms folded rated him in good round terms, signifying that she would be glad to know what he meant by terrifying delicate females 'with his corpses;' and giving it as her opinion that he was quite ugly enough to know better. The other ladies were not at all behind-hand in expressing similar sentiments; and the children, of whom some scores had now collected, hooted and defied Mr. Pecksniff quite savagely. So when Mrs. Gamp appeared, the unoffending gentleman was glad to hustle her with very little ceremony into the cabriolet, and drive off, overwhelmed with popular execration.

Mrs. Gamp had a large bundle with her, a pair of pattens, and a species of gig umbrella; the latter article in colour like a faded leaf, except where a circular patch of a lively blue had been dexterously let in at the top. She was much flurried by the haste she had made, and laboured under the most erroneous views of cabriolets, which she appeared to confound with mail-coaches or stage-waggons, inasmuch as she was constantly endeavouring for the first half mile to force her luggage through the little front window, and clamouring to the driver to 'put it in the boot.' When she was disabused of this idea, her whole being resolved itself into an absorbing anxiety about her pattens, with which she played innumerable games at quoits on Mr. Pecksniff's legs. It was not until they were close upon the house of mourning that she had enough composure to observe:

'And so the gentleman's dead, sir! Ah! The more's the pity.' She didn't even know his name. 'But it's what we must all come to. It's as certain as being born, except that we can't make our calculations as exact. Ah! Poor dear!'

She was a fat old woman, this Mrs. Gamp, with a husky voice and a moist eye, which she had a remarkable power of turning up, and only showing the white of it. Having very little neck, it cost her some trouble to look over herself, if one may say so, at those to whom she talked. She wore a very rusty black gown, rather the worse for snuff, and a shawl and bonnet to correspond. In these dilapidated articles of dress she had, on principle, arrayed herself, time out of mind, on such occasions as the present; for this at once expressed a decent amount of veneration for the deceased, and invited the next of kin to present her with a fresher suit of weeds: an appeal so frequently successful, that the very fetch and ghost of Mrs. Gamp, bonnet and all, might be seen hanging up, any hour in the day, in at least a dozen of the second-hand clothes shops about Holborn. The face of Mrs. Gamp—the nose in particular—was somewhat red and swollen, and it was difficult to enjoy her society without becoming conscious of a smell of spirits. Like most persons who have attained to great eminence in their profession, she took to hers very kindly; insomuch that, setting aside her natural predilections as a woman, she went to a lying-in or a laying-out with equal zest and relish.

'Ah!' repeated Mrs. Gamp; for it was always a safe sentiment in cases of mourning. 'Ah dear! When Gamp was summoned to his long home, and I see him a-lying in Guy's Hospital with a penny-piece on each eye, and his wooden leg under his left arm, I thought I should have fainted away. But I bore up.'

If certain whispers current in the Kingsgate Street circles

had any truth in them, she had indeed borne up surprisingly; and had exerted such uncommon fortitude as to dispose of Mr. Gamp's remains for the benefit of science. But it should be added, in fairness, that this had happened twenty years before; and that Mr. and Mrs. Gamp had long been separated on the ground of incompatibility of temper in their drink.

'You have become indifferent since then, I suppose?' said Mr. Pecksniff. 'Use is second nature, Mrs. Gamp.'

'You may well say second natur, sir,' returned that lady. 'One's first ways is to find sich things a trial to the feelings, and so is one's lasting custom. If it wasn't for the nerve a little sip of liquor gives me (I never was able to do more than taste it), I never could go through with what I sometimes has to do. "Mrs. Harris," I says, at the very last case as ever I acted in, which it was but a young person, "Mrs. Harris," I says, "leave the bottle on the chimley-piece, and don't ask me to take none, but let me put my lips to it when I am so dispoged, and then I will do what I'm engaged to do, according to the best of my ability." "Mrs. Gamp," she says, in answer, "if ever there was a sober creetur to be got at eighteen pence a day for working people, and three and six for gentlefolks—night watching,"' said Mrs. Gamp, with emphasis, ' "being a extra charge—you are that inwallable person." "Mrs. Harris," I says to her, "don't name the charge, for if I could afford to lay all my feller creeturs out for nothink, I would gladly do it, sich is the love I bears 'em. But what I always says to them as has the management of matters, Mrs. Harris:"' here she kept her eye on Mr. Pecksniff: ' "be they gents or be they ladies, is, don't ask me whether I won't take none, or whether I will, but leave the bottle on the chimley-piece, and let me put my lips to it when I am so dispoged."'

The conclusion of this affecting narrative brought them to the house. In the passage they encountered Mr. Mould the undertaker: a little elderly gentleman, bald, and in a suit of black; with a note-book in his hand, a massive gold watch-chain dangling from his fob, and a face in which a queer attempt at melancholy was at odds with a smirk of satisfaction; so that he looked as a man might, who, in the very act of smacking his lips over choice old wine, tried to make believe it was physic.

'Well, Mrs. Gamp, and how are *you*, Mrs. Gamp?' said this gentleman, in a voice as soft as his step.

'Pretty well, I thank you, sir,' dropping a curtsey.

'You'll be very particular here, Mrs. Gamp. This is not a common case, Mrs. Gamp. Let everything be very nice and comfortable, Mrs. Gamp, if you please,' said the undertaker, shaking his head with a solemn air.

'It shall be, sir,' she replied, curtseying again. 'You knows me of old, sir, I hope.'

'I hope so, too, Mrs. Gamp,' said the undertaker; 'and I think so, also.' Mrs. Gamp curtseyed again. 'This is one of the most impressive cases, sir,' he continued, addressing Mr. Pecksniff, 'that I have seen in the whole course of my professional experience.'

'Indeed, Mr. Mould!' cried that gentleman.

'Such affectionate regret, sir, I never saw. There is no limitation, there is positively NO limitation:' opening his eyes wide, and standing on tiptoe: 'in point of expense! I have orders, sir, to put on my whole establishment of mutes; and mutes come very dear, Mr. Pecksniff; not to mention their drink. To provide silver-plated handles of the very best description, ornamented with angels' heads from the most expensive dies. To be perfectly profuse in feathers. In short, sir, to turn out something absolutely gorgeous.'

'My friend Mr. Jonas is an excellent man,' said Mr. Pecksniff.

'I have seen a good deal of what is filial in my time, sir,' retorted Mould, 'and what is unfilial too. It is our lot. We come into the knowledge of those secrets. But anything so filial as this; anything so honourable to human nature; so calculated to reconcile all of us to the world we live in; never yet came under my observation. It only proves, sir, what was so forcibly observed by the lamented theatrical poet—buried at Stratford—that there is good in everything.'

'It is very pleasant to hear you say so, Mr. Mould,' observed Pecksniff.

'You are very kind, sir. And what a man Mr. Chuzzlewit was, sir! Ah! what a man he was. You may talk of your lord mayors,' said Mould, waving his hand at the public in general, 'your sheriffs, your common councilmen, your trumpery; but show me a man in this city who is worthy to walk in the shoes of the departed Mr. Chuzzlewit. No, no,' cried Mould, with bitter sarcasm. 'Hang 'em up, hang 'em up; sole 'em and heel 'em, and have 'em ready for his son against he's old enough to wear 'em; but don't try 'em on yourselves, for they won't fit you. We knew him,' said Mould, in the same biting vein, as he pocketed his note-book; 'we knew him, and are not to be caught with chaff. Mr. Pecksniff, sir, good morning.'

Mr. Pecksniff returned the compliment; and Mould, sensible of having distinguished himself, was going away with a brisk smile, when he fortunately remembered the occasion. Quickly becoming depressed again, he sighed; looked into the crown of his hat, as if for comfort; put it on without finding any; and slowly departed.

Mrs. Gamp and Mr. Pecksniff then ascended the staircase; and the former, having been shown to the chamber in which all that remained of Anthony Chuzzlewit lay covered up, with but one loving heart, and that a halting one, to mourn it, left the latter free to enter the darkened room below, and rejoin Mr. Jonas, from whom he had now been absent nearly two hours.

He found that example to bereaved sons, and pattern in the eyes of all performers of funerals, musing over a fragment of writing-paper on the desk, and scratching figures on it with a pen. The old man's chair, and hat, and walking-stick, were removed from their accustomed places, and put out of sight; the window-blinds, as yellow as November fogs, were drawn down close; Jonas himself was so subdued, that he could scarcely be heard to speak, and only seen to walk across the room.

'Pecksniff,' he said, in a whisper, 'you shall have the regulation of it all, mind! You shall be able to tell anybody who talks about it that everything was correctly and freely done. There isn't any one you'd like to ask to the funeral, is there?'

'No, Mr. Jonas, I think not.'

'Because if there is, you know,' said Jonas, 'ask him. We don't want to make a secret of it.'

'No,' repeated Mr. Pecksniff, after a little reflection. 'I am not the less obliged to you on that account, Mr. Jonas, for your liberal hospitality; but there really is no one.'

'Very well,' said Jonas; 'then you, and I, and Chuffey, and the doctor, will be just a coachful. We'll have the doctor, Pecksniff, because he knows what was the matter with him, and that it couldn't be helped.'

'Where *is* our dear friend, Mr. Chuffey?' asked Pecksniff, looking round the chamber, and winking both his eyes at once. For he was overcome by his feelings.

But here he was interrupted by Mrs. Gamp, who, divested of her bonnet and shawl, came sidling and bridling into the room; and with some sharpness demanded a conference outside the door with Mr. Pecksniff.

'You may say whatever you wish to say here, Mrs. Gamp,' said that gentleman, shaking his head with a melancholy expression.

'It is not much as I have to say when people is a-mourning for the dead and gone,' said Mrs. Gamp; 'but what I have to say is *to* the pint and purpose, and no offence intended, must be so considered. I have been at a many places in my time, gentlemen, and I hope I knows what my duties is, and how the same should be performed: in course, if I did not, it would be very strange, and very wrong in sich a gentleman as Mr. Mould, which has undertook the highest families in this land, and given every satisfaction, so to recommend me as he does. I have seen a deal of trouble my own self,' said Mrs. Gamp, laying greater and greater stress upon her words, 'and I can feel for them as has their feelings tried, but I am not a Rooshan or a Prooshan, and consequently cannot suffer spies to be set over me.'

Before it was possible that an answer could be returned, Mrs. Gamp, growing redder in the face, went on to say:

'It is not a easy matter, gentlemen, to live when you are left a widder woman; particular when your feelings works upon you to that extent that you often find yourself a-going out on terms which is a certain loss, and never can repay. But in whatever way you earns your bread, you may have rules and regulations of your own which cannot be broke through. Some people,' said Mrs. Gamp, again entrenching herself behind her strong point, as if it were not assailable by human ingenuity, 'may be Rooshans, and others may be Prooshans; they are born so, and will please themselves. Them which is of other naturs thinks different.'

'If I understand this good lady,' said Mr. Pecksniff, turning to Jonas, 'Mr. Chuffey is troublesome to her. Shall I fetch him down?'

'Do,' said Jonas. 'I was going to tell you he was up there, when she came in. I'd go myself and bring him down, only— only I'd rather you went, if you don't mind.'

Mr. Pecksniff promptly departed, followed by Mrs. Gamp, who, seeing that he took a bottle and glass from the cupboard, and carried it in his hand, was much softened.

'I am sure,' she said, 'that if it wasn't for his own happiness, I should no more mind his being there, poor dear, than if he was a fly. But them as isn't used to these things, thinks so much of 'em afterwards, that it's a kindness to 'em not to let 'em have their wish. And even,' said Mrs. Gamp, probably in reference to some flowers of speech she had already strewn on Mr. Chuffey, 'even if one calls 'em names, it's only done to rouse 'em.'

Whatever epithets she had bestowed on the old clerk, they had not roused *him*. He sat beside the bed, in the chair he had occupied all the previous night, with his hands folded before him, and his head bowed down; and neither looked up, on their entrance, nor gave any sign of consciousness, until Mr. Pecksniff took him by the arm, when he meekly rose.

'Three score and ten,' said Chuffey, 'ought and carry seven. Some men are so strong that they live to four score—four times ought's an ought, four times two's an eight—eighty. Oh! why —why—why—didn't he live to four times ought's an ought, and four times two's an eight, eighty?'

'Ah! what a wale of grief!' cried Mrs. Gamp, possessing herself of the bottle and glass.

'Why did he die before his poor old crazy servant?' said Chuffey, clasping his hands and looking up in anguish. 'Take him from me, and what remains?'

'Mr. Jonas,' returned Pecksniff, 'Mr. Jonas, my good friend.'

'I loved him,' cried the old man, weeping. 'He was good to me. We learnt Tare and Tret together, at school. I took him down once, six boys in the arithmetic class. God forgive me! Had I the heart to take him down!'

'Come, Mr. Chuffey,' said Pecksniff. 'Come with me. Summon up your fortitude, Mr. Chuffey.'

'Yes, I will,' returned the old clerk. 'Yes. I'll sum up my forty—How many times forty—Oh, Chuzzlewit and Son— Your own son, Mr. Chuzzlewit; your own son, sir!'

He yielded to the hand that guided him, as he lapsed into this familiar expression, and submitted to be led away. Mrs. Gamp, with the bottle on one knee, and the glass in the other, sat upon a stool, shaking her head for a long time, until, in a moment of abstraction, she poured out a dram of spirits, and raised it to her lips. It was succeeded by a second, and by a third, and then her eyes—either in the sadness of her reflections upon life and death, or in her admiration of the liquor —were so turned up, as to be quite invisible. But she shook her head still.

Poor Chuffey was conducted to his accustomed corner, and there he remained, silent and quiet, save at long intervals, when he would rise, and walk about the room, and wring his hands, or raise some strange and sudden cry. For a whole week they all three sat about the hearth and never stirred abroad. Mr. Pecksniff would have walked out in the evening time, but Mr. Jonas was so averse to his being absent for a minute, that he abandoned the idea, and so, from morning until night, they brooded together in the dark room, without relief or occupation.

The weight of that which was stretched out, stiff and stark, in the awful chamber above-stairs, so crushed and bore down Jonas, that he bent beneath the load. During the whole long seven days and nights, he was always oppressed and haunted by a dreadful sense of its presence in the house. Did the door move, he looked towards it with a livid face and starting eye, as if he fully believed that ghostly fingers clutched the handle. Did the fire flicker in a draught of air, he glanced over his shoulder, as almost dreading to behold some shrouded figure fanning and flapping at it with its fearful dress. The lightest noise disturbed him; and once, in the night, at the sound of a footstep overhead, he cried out that the dead man was walking, tramp, tramp, tramp, about his coffin.

He lay at night upon a mattress on the floor of the sitting-room; his own chamber having been assigned to Mrs. Gamp; and Mr. Pecksniff was similarly accommodated. The howling of a dog before the house, filled him with a terror he could not disguise. He avoided the reflection in the opposite windows of the light that burned above, as though it had been an angry eye. He often, in every night, rose up from his fitful sleep, and looked and longed for dawn; all directions and arrangements, even to the ordering of their daily meals, he abandoned to Mr. Pecksniff. That excellent gentleman, deeming that the mourner wanted comfort, and that high feeding was likely to do him infinite service, availed himself of these opportunities to such good purpose, that they kept quite a dainty table during this melancholy season; with sweetbreads, stewed kidneys, oysters, and other such light viands for supper every night; over which, and sundry jorums of hot punch, Mr. Pecksniff delivered such moral reflections and spiritual consolation as might have converted a Heathen—especially if he had had but an imperfect acquaintance with the English tongue.

Nor did Mr. Pecksniff alone indulge in the creature comforts during this sad time. Mrs. Gamp proved to be very choice in her eating, and repudiated hashed mutton with scorn. In her drinking too, she was very punctual and particular, requiring a pint of mild porter at lunch, a pint at dinner, half-a-pint as a species of stay or holdfast between dinner and tea, and a pint of the celebrated staggering ale, or Real Old Brighton Tipper, at supper; besides the bottle on the chimney-piece, and such casual invitations to refresh herself with wine as the good breeding of her employers might prompt them to offer. In like manner, Mr. Mould's men found it necessary to drown their grief, like a young kitten in the morning of its existence; for which reason they generally fuddled themselves before they began to do anything, lest it should make head and get the better of them. In short, the whole of that strange week was a round of dismal joviality and grim enjoyment; and every one, except poor Chuffey, who came within the shadow of Anthony Chuzzlewit's grave, feasted like a Ghoul.

At length the day of the funeral, pious and truthful ceremony that it was, arrived. Mr. Mould, with a glass of generous port between his eye and the light, leaned against the desk in the little glass office with his gold watch in his unoccupied hand, and conversed with Mrs. Gamp; two mutes were at the house-door, looking as mournful as could be reasonably expected of men with such a thriving job in hand; the whole of Mr. Mould's establishment were on duty within the house or without; feathers waved, horses snorted, silk and velvets fluttered; in a word, as Mr. Mould emphatically said, 'everything that money could do was done.'

'And what can do more, Mrs. Gamp?' exclaimed the undertaker, as he emptied his glass and smacked his lips.

'Nothing in the world, sir.'

'Nothing in the world,' repeated Mr. Mould. 'You are right, Mrs. Gamp. Why do people spend more money:' here he filled his glass again: 'upon a death, Mrs. Gamp, than upon a birth? Come, that's in your way; you ought to know. How do you account for that now?'

'Perhaps it is because an undertaker's charges comes dearer than a nurse's charges, sir,' said Mrs. Gamp, tittering, and smoothing down her new black dress with her hands.

'Ha, ha!' laughed Mr. Mould. 'You have been breakfasting at somebody's expense this morning, Mrs. Gamp.' But seeing, by the aid of a little shaving-glass which hung opposite, that he looked merry, he composed his features and became sorrowful.

'Many's the time that I've not breakfasted at my own expense along of your kind recommending, sir; and many's the time I hope to do the same in time to come,' said Mrs. Gamp, with an apologetic curtsey.

'So be it,' replied Mr. Mould, 'please Providence. No, Mrs. Gamp; I'll tell you why it is. It's because the laying out of money with a well-conducted establishment, where the thing is performed upon the very best scale, binds the broken heart, and sheds balm upon the wounded spirit. Hearts want binding, and spirits want balming when people die: not when people are born. Look at this gentleman to-day; look at him.'

'An open-handed gentleman?' cried Mrs. Gamp, with enthusiasm.

'No, no,' said the undertaker; 'not an open-handed gentleman in general, by any means. There you mistake him: but an afflicted gentleman, an affectionate gentleman, who knows what it is in the power of money to do, in giving him relief, and in testifying his love and veneration for the departed. It can give him,' said Mr. Mould, waving his watch-chain slowly round and round, so that he described one circle after every item; 'it can give him four horses to each vehicle; it can give him velvet trappings; it can give him drivers in cloth cloaks and top-boots; it can give him the plumage of the ostrich, dyed black; it can give him any number of walking attendants, dressed in the first style of funeral fashion, and carrying batons tipped with brass; it can give him a handsome tomb; it can give him a place in Westminster Abbey itself, if he choose to invest it in such a purchase. Oh! do not let us say that gold is dross, when it can buy such things as these, Mrs. Gamp.'

'But what a blessing, sir,' said Mrs. Gamp, 'that there are such as you, to sell or let 'em out on hire!'

'Aye, Mrs. Gamp, you are right,' rejoined the undertaker. 'We should be an honoured calling. We do good by stealth, and blush to have it mentioned in our little bills. How much consolation may I, even I,' cried Mr. Mould, 'have diffused among my fellow-creatures by means of my four long-tailed prancers, never harnessed under ten pund ten!'

Mrs. Gamp had begun to make a suitable reply, when she was interrupted by the appearance of one of Mr. Mould's assistants—his chief mourner in fact—an obese person, with his waistcoat in closer connexion with his legs than is quite reconcilable with the established ideas of grace; with that cast of feature which is figuratively called a bottle-nose; and with a face covered all over with pimples. He had been a tender plant once upon a time, but from constant blowing in the fat atmosphere of funerals, had run to seed.

'Well, Tacker,' said Mr. Mould, 'is all ready below?'

'A beautiful show, sir,' rejoined Tacker. 'The horses are prouder and fresher than ever I see 'em; and toss their heads, they do, as if they knowed how much their plumes cost. One, two, three, four,' said Mr. Tacker, heaping that number of black cloaks upon his left arm.

'Is Tom there, with the cake and wine?' asked Mr. Mould.

'Ready to come in at a moment's notice, sir,' said Tacker.

'Then,' rejoined Mr. Mould, putting up his watch, and glancing at himself in the little shaving-glass, that he might be sure his face had the right expression on it: 'then I think we may proceed to business. Give me the paper of gloves, Tacker. Ah, what a man he was! Ah, Tacker, Tacker, what a man he was!'

Mr. Tacker, who from his great experience in the performance of funerals, would have made an excellent pantomime actor, winked at Mrs. Gamp without at all disturbing the gravity of his countenance, and followed his master into the next room.

It was a great point with Mr. Mould, and a part of his professional tact, not to seem to know the doctor; though in reality they were near neighbours, and very often, as in the present instance, worked together. So he advanced to fit on his black kid gloves as if he had never seen him in all his life; while the doctor, on his part, looked as distant and unconscious as if he had heard and read of undertakers, and had passed their shops, but had never before been brought into communication with one.

'Gloves, eh?' said the doctor. 'Mr. Pecksniff, after you.'

'I couldn't think of it,' returned Mr. Pecksniff.

'You are very good,' said the doctor, taking a pair. 'Well, sir, as I was saying, I was called up to attend that case at about half-past one o'clock. Cake and wine, eh? Which is port? Thank you.'

Mr. Pecksniff took some also.

'At about half-past one o'clock in the morning, sir,' resumed the doctor, 'I was called up to attend that case. At the first pull of the night-bell I turned out, threw up the window, and put out my head. Cloak, eh? Don't tie it too tight. That'll do.'

Mr. Pecksniff having been likewise inducted into a similar garment, the doctor resumed.

'And put out my head. Hat, eh? My good friend, that is not mine. Mr. Pecksniff, I beg your pardon, but I think we have unintentionally made an exchange. Thank you. Well, sir, I was going to tell you—'

'We are quite ready,' interrupted Mould in a low voice.

'Ready, eh?' said the doctor. 'Very good. Mr. Pecksniff, I'll take an opportunity of relating the rest in the coach. It's rather curious. Ready, eh? No rain, I hope?'

'Quite fair, sir,' returned Mould.

'I was afraid the ground would have been wet,' said the doctor, 'for my glass fell yesterday. We may congratulate ourselves upon our good fortune.' But seeing by this time that Mr. Jonas and Chuffey were going out at the door, he put a white pocket-handkerchief to his face as if a violent burst of grief had suddenly come upon him, and walked down side by side with Mr. Pecksniff.

Mr. Mould and his men had not exaggerated the grandeur of the arrangements. They were splendid. The four hearse-horses, especially, reared and pranced, and showed their highest action, as if they knew a man was dead, and triumphed in it. 'They break us, drive us, ride us; ill-treat, abuse, and maim us for their pleasure—But they die; Hurrah, they die!'

So through the narrow streets and winding city ways, went Anthony Chuzzlewit's funeral: Mr. Jonas glancing stealthily out of the coach-window now and then, to observe its effect upon the crowd; Mr. Mould as he walked along, listening with a sober pride to the exclamations of the bystanders; the doctor whispering his story to Mr. Pecksniff, without appearing to come any nearer the end of it; and poor old Chuffey sobbing unregarded in a corner. But he had greatly scandalised Mr. Mould at an early stage of the ceremony by carrying his handkerchief in his hat in a perfectly informal manner, and wiping his eyes with his knuckles. And as Mr. Mould himself had said already, his behaviour was indecent, and quite unworthy of such an occasion; and he never ought to have been there.

There he was, however; and in the churchyard there he was, also, conducting himself in a no less unbecoming manner, and leaning for support on Tacker, who plainly told him that he was fit for nothing better than a walking funeral. But Chuffey, Heaven help him! heard no sound but the echoes, lingering in his own heart, of a voice for ever silent.

'I loved him,' cried the old man, sinking down upon the grave when all was done. 'He was very good to me. Oh, my dear old friend and master!'

'Come, come, Mr. Chuffey,' said the doctor, 'this won't do; it's a clayey soil, Mr. Chuffey. You mustn't, really.'

'If it had been the commonest thing we do, and Mr. Chuffey had been a Bearer, gentlemen,' said Mould, casting an imploring glance upon them, as he helped to raise him, 'he couldn't have gone on worse than this.'

'Be a man, Mr. Chuffey,' said Pecksniff.

'Be a gentleman, Mr. Chuffey,' said Mould.

'Upon my word, my good friend,' murmured the doctor, in a tone of stately reproof, as he stepped up to the old man's side, 'this is worse than weakness. This is bad, selfish, very wrong, Mr. Chuffey. You should take example from others, my good sir. You forget that you were not connected by ties of blood with our deceased friend; and that he had a very near and very dear relation, Mr. Chuffey.'

'Aye, his own son!' cried the old man, clasping his hands with remarkable passion. 'His own, own, only son!'

'He's not right in his head, you know,' said Jonas, turning pale. 'You're not to mind anything he says. I shouldn't wonder if he was to talk some precious nonsense. But don't you mind him, any of you. I don't. My father left him to my charge; and whatever he says or does, that's enough. *I'*ll take care of him.'

A hum of admiration rose from the mourners (including Mr. Mould and his merry men) at this new instance of magnanimity and kind feeling on the part of Jonas. But Chuffey put it to the test no farther. He said not a word more, and being left to himself for a little while, crept back again to the coach.

It has been said that Mr. Jonas turned pale when the behaviour of the old clerk attracted general attention; his discomposure, however, was but momentary, and he soon recovered. But these were not the only changes he had exhibited that day. The curious eyes of Mr. Pecksniff had observed that as soon as they left the house upon their mournful errand, he began to mend; that as the ceremonies proceeded he gradually, by little and little, recovered his old condition, his old looks, his old bearing, his old agreeable characteristics of speech and manner, and became, in all respects, his old pleasant self. And now that they were seated in the coach on their return home; and more when they got there, and found the windows open, the light and air admitted, and all traces of the late event removed; he felt so well convinced that Jonas was again the Jonas he had known a week ago, and not the Jonas of the intervening time, that he voluntarily gave up his recently-acquired power without one faint attempt to exercise it, and at once fell back into his former position of mild and deferential guest.

Mrs. Gamp went home to the bird-fancier's, and was knocked up again that very night for a birth of twins; Mr. Mould dined gaily in the bosom of his family, and passed the evening facetiously at his club; the hearse, after standing for a long time at the door of a roistering public-house, repaired to its stables with the feathers inside and twelve red-nosed undertakers on the roof, each holding on by a dingy peg, to which, in times of state, a waving plume was fitted; the various trappings of sorrow were carefully laid by in presses for the next hirer; the fiery steeds were quenched and quiet in their stalls; the doctor got merry with wine at a wedding-dinner, and forgot the middle of the story which had no end to it; the pageant of a few short hours ago was written nowhere half so legibly as in the undertaker's books.

Not in the churchyard? Not even there. The gates were closed; the night was dark and wet; the rain fell silently, among the stagnant weeds and nettles. One new mound was there which had not been there last night. Time, burrowing like a mole below the ground, had marked his track by throwing up another heap of earth. And that was all.

'PECKSNIFF,' said Jonas, taking off his hat, to see that the black crape band was all right; and finding that it was, putting it on again, complacently; 'what do you mean to give your daughters when they marry?'

'My dear Mr. Jonas,' cried the affectionate parent, with an ingenuous smile, 'what a very singular inquiry!'

'Now, don't you mind whether it's a singular inquiry or a plural one,' retorted Jonas, eyeing Mr. Pecksniff with no great favour, 'but answer it, or let it alone. One or the other.'

'Hum! The question, my dear friend,' said Mr. Pecksniff, laying his hand tenderly upon his kinsman's knee, 'is involved with many considerations. What would I give them? Eh?'

'Ah! what would you give 'em?' repeated Jonas.

'Why, that,' said Mr. Pecksniff, 'would naturally depend in a great measure upon the kind of husbands they might choose, my dear young friend.'

Mr. Jonas was evidently disconcerted, and at a loss how to proceed. It was a good answer. It seemed a deep one, but such is the wisdom of simplicity!

'My standard for the merits I would require in a son-in-law,' said Mr. Pecksniff, after a short silence, 'is a high one. Forgive me, my dear Mr. Jonas,' he added, greatly moved, 'if I say that you have spoiled me, and made it a fanciful one; an imaginative one; a prismatically tinged one, if I may be permitted to call it so.'

'What do you mean by that?' growled Jonas, looking at him with increased disfavour.

'Indeed, my dear friend,' said Mr. Pecksniff, 'you may well inquire. The heart is not always a royal mint, with patent machinery to work its metal into current coin. Sometimes it throws it out in strange forms, not easily recognised as coin at all. But it is sterling gold. It has at least that merit. It is sterling gold.'

'Is it?' grumbled Jonas, with a doubtful shake of the head.

'Aye!' said Mr. Pecksniff, warming with his subject, 'it is. To be plain with you, Mr. Jonas, if I could find two such sons-in-law as you will one day make to some deserving man, capable of appreciating a nature such as yours, I would—forgetful of myself—bestow upon my daughters portions reaching to the very utmost limit of my means.'

This was strong language, and it was earnestly delivered. But who can wonder that such a man as Mr. Pecksniff, after all he had seen and heard of Mr. Jonas, should be strong and earnest upon such a theme; a theme that touched even the worldly lips of undertakers with the honey of eloquence!

Mr. Jonas was silent, and looked thoughtfully at the landscape. For they were seated on the outside of the coach, at the back, and were travelling down into the country. He accompanied Mr. Pecksniff home for a few days' change of air and scene after his recent trials.

'Well,' he said, at last, with captivating bluntness, 'suppose you got one such son-in-law as me, what then?'

Mr. Pecksniff regarded him at first with inexpressible surprise; then gradually breaking into a sort of dejected vivacity, said:

'Then well I know whose husband he would be!'

'Whose?' asked Jonas, drily.

'My eldest girl's, Mr. Jonas,' replied Pecksniff, with moistening eyes. 'My dear Cherry's: my staff, my scrip, my treasure, Mr. Jonas. A hard struggle, but it is in the nature of things! I must one day part with her to a husband. I know it, my dear friend. I am prepared for it.'

'Ecod! you've been prepared for that a pretty long time, I should think,' said Jonas.

'Many have sought to bear her from me,' said Mr. Pecksniff. 'All have failed. "I never will give my hand, papa:" those were her words: "unless my heart is won." She has not been quite so happy as she used to be, of late. I don't know why.'

Again Mr. Jonas looked at the landscape; then at the coachman; then at the luggage on the roof; finally at Mr. Pecksniff.

'I suppose you'll have to part with the other one, some of these days?' he observed, as he caught that gentleman's eye.

'Probably,' said the parent. 'Years will tame down the wildness of my foolish bird, and then it will be caged. But Cherry, Mr. Jonas, Cherry.'

'Oh, ah!' interrupted Jonas. 'Years have made her all right enough. Nobody doubts that. But you haven't answered what I asked you. Of course, you're not obliged to do it, you know, if you don't like. You're the best judge.'

There was a warning sulkiness in the manner of this speech, which admonished Mr. Pecksniff that his dear friend was not to be trifled with or fenced off, and that he must either return a straightforward reply to his question, or plainly give him to understand that he declined to enlighten him upon the subject to which it referred. Mindful in this dilemma of the caution Old Anthony had given him almost with his latest breath, he resolved to speak to the point, and so told Mr. Jonas (enlarging upon the communication as a proof of his great attachment and confidence), that in the case he had put; to wit, in the event of such a man as he proposing for his daughter's hand; he would endow her with a fortune of four thousand pounds.

'I should sadly pinch and cramp myself to do so,' was his fatherly remark; 'but that would be my duty, and my conscience would reward me. For myself, my conscience is my bank. I have a trifle invested there, a mere trifle, Mr. Jonas; but I prize it as a store of value, I assure you.'

The good man's enemies would have divided upon this question into two parties. One would have asserted without scruple that if Mr. Pecksniff's conscience were his bank, and he kept a running account there, he must have overdrawn it beyond all mortal means of computation. The other would have contended that it was a mere fictitious form; a perfectly blank book; or one in which entries were only made with a peculiar kind of invisible ink to become legible at some indefinite time; and that he never troubled it at all.

'It would sadly pinch and cramp me, my dear friend,' repeated Mr. Pecksniff, 'but Providence, perhaps I may be permitted to say a special Providence, has blessed my endeavours, and I could guarantee to make the sacrifice.'

A question of philosophy arises here, whether Mr. Pecksniff had or had not good reason to say, that he was specially patronised and encouraged in his undertakings. All his life long he had been walking up and down the narrow ways and by-places, with a hook in one hand and a crook in the other, scraping all sorts of valuable odds and ends into his pouch. Now, there being a special Providence in the fall of a sparrow, it follows (so Mr. Pecksniff would have reasoned), that there must also be a special Providence in the alighting of the stone, or stick, or other substance which is aimed at the sparrow. And Mr. Pecksniff's hook, or crook, having invariably knocked the sparrow on the head and brought him down, that gentleman may have been led to consider himself as specially licensed to bag sparrows, and as being specially seised and possessed of all the birds he had got together. That many undertakings, national as well as individual—but especially the former—are held to be specially brought to a glorious and successful issue, which never could be so regarded on any other process of reasoning, must be clear to all men. Therefore the precedents would seem to show that Mr. Pecksniff had good argument for what he said, and might be permitted to say it, and did not say it presumptuously, vainly, or arrogantly, but in a spirit of high faith and great wisdom meriting all praise.[1]

Mr. Jonas, not being much accustomed to perplex his mind with theories of this nature, expressed no opinion on the subject. Nor did he receive his companion's announcement with one solitary syllable, good, bad, or indifferent. He preserved this taciturnity for a quarter of an hour at least, and during the whole of that time appeared to be steadily engaged in subjecting some given amount to the operation of every known rule in figures; adding to it, taking from it, multiplying it, reducing it by long and short division; working it by the rule-of-three direct and inversed; exchange or barter; practice; simple interest; compound interest; and other means of arithmetical calculation. The result of these labours appeared to be satisfactory, for when he did break silence, it was as one who had arrived at some specific result, and freed himself from a state of distressing uncertainty.

'Come, old Pecksniff!' Such was his jocose address, as he slapped that gentleman on the back, at the end of the stage; 'let's have something!'

'With all my heart,' said Mr. Pecksniff.

'Let's treat the driver,' cried Jonas.

'If you think it won't hurt the man, or render him discontented with his station; certainly,' faltered Mr. Pecksniff.

Jonas only laughed at this, and getting down from the coach-top with great alacrity, cut a cumbersome kind of caper in the road. After which, he went into the public-house, and there ordered spirituous drink to such an extent, that Mr. Pecksniff had some doubts of his perfect sanity, until Jonas set them quite at rest by saying, when the coach could wait no longer:

[1] The most credulous reader will scarcely believe that Mr. Pecksniff's reasoning was once set upon as the Author's!!

'I've been standing treat for a whole week and more, and letting you have all the delicacies of the season. *You* shall pay for this, Pecksniff.' It was not a joke either, as Mr. Pecksniff at first supposed; for he went off to the coach without further ceremony, and left his respected victim to settle the bill.

But Mr. Pecksniff was a man of meek endurance, and Mr. Jonas was his friend. Moreover, his regard for that gentleman was founded, as we know, on pure esteem, and a knowledge of the excellence of his character. He came out from the tavern with a smiling face, and even went so far as to repeat the performance, on a less expensive scale, at the next ale-house. There was a certain wildness in the spirits of Mr. Jonas (not usually a part of his character) which was far from being subdued by these means, and, for the rest of the journey, he was so very buoyant—it may be said, boisterous—that Mr. Pecksniff had some difficulty in keeping pace with him.

They were not expected. Oh dear, no! Mr. Pecksniff had proposed in London to give the girls a surprise, and had said he wouldn't write a word to prepare them on any account, in order that he and Mr. Jonas might take them unawares, and just see what they were doing, when they thought their dear papa was miles and miles away. As a consequence of this playful device, there was nobody to meet them at the finger-post, but that was of small consequence, for they had come down by the day coach, and Mr. Pecksniff had only a carpet-bag, while Mr. Jonas had only a portmanteau. They took the portmanteau between them, put the bag upon it, and walked off up the lane without delay: Mr. Pecksniff already going on tiptoe as if, without this precaution, his fond children, being then at a distance of a couple of miles or so, would have some filial sense of his approach.

It was a lovely evening in the spring-time of the year; and in the soft stillness of the twilight, all nature was very calm and beautiful. The day had been fine and warm; but at the coming on of night, the air grew cool, and in the mellowing distance smoke was rising gently from the cottage chimneys. There were a thousand pleasant scents diffused around, from young leaves and fresh buds; the cuckoo had been singing all day long, and was but just now hushed; the smell of earth newly-upturned, first breath of hope to the first labourer after his garden withered, was fragrant in the evening breeze. It was a time when most men cherish good resolves, and sorrow for the wasted past; when most men, looking on the shadows as they gather, think of that evening which must close on all, and that to-morrow which has none beyond.

'Precious dull,' said Mr. Jonas, looking about. 'It's enough to make a man go melancholy mad.'

'We shall have lights and a fire soon,' observed Mr. Pecksniff.

'We shall need 'em by the time we get there,' said Jonas. 'Why the devil don't you talk? What are you thinking of?'

'To tell you the truth, Mr. Jonas,' said Pecksniff with great solemnity, 'my mind was running at that moment on our late dear friend, your departed father.'

Mr. Jonas immediately let his burden fall, and said, threatening him with his hand:

'Drop that, Pecksniff!'

Mr. Pecksniff not exactly knowing whether allusion was made to the subject or the portmanteau, stared at his friend in unaffected surprise.

'Drop it, I say!' cried Jonas, fiercely. 'Do you hear? Drop it, now and for ever. You had better, I give you notice!'

'It was quite a mistake,' urged Mr. Pecksniff, very much dismayed; 'though I admit it was foolish. I might have known it was a tender string.'

'Don't talk to me about tender strings,' said Jonas, wiping his forehead with the cuff of his coat. 'I'm not going to be crowed over by you, because I don't like dead company.'

Mr. Pecksniff had got out the words 'Crowed over, Mr. Jonas!' when that young man, with a dark expression in his countenance, cut him short once more:

'Mind!' he said. 'I won't have it. I advise you not to revive the subject, neither to me nor anybody else. You can take a hint, if you choose, as well as another man. There's enough said about it. Come along!'

Taking up his part of the load again, when he had said these words, he hurried on so fast that Mr. Pecksniff, at the other end of the portmanteau, found himself dragged forward, in a very inconvenient and ungraceful manner, to the great detriment of what is called by fancy gentlemen 'the bark' upon his shins, which were most unmercifully bumped against the hard leather and the iron buckles. In the course of a few minutes, however, Mr. Jonas relaxed his speed, and suffered his companion to come up with him, and to bring the port-manteau into a tolerably straight position.

It was pretty clear that he regretted his late outbreak, and
that he mistrusted its effect on Mr. Pecksniff; for as often as
that gentleman glanced towards Mr. Jonas, he found Mr.
Jonas glancing at him, which was a new source of embarrassment. It was but a short-lived one, though, for Mr. Jonas soon
began to whistle, whereupon Mr. Pecksniff, taking his cue from
his friend, began to hum a tune melodiously.

'Pretty nearly there, ain't we?' said Jonas, when this had
lasted some time.

'Close, my dear friend,' said Mr. Pecksniff.

'What'll they be doing, do you suppose?' asked Jonas.

'Impossible to say,' cried Mr. Pecksniff. 'Giddy truants!
They may be away from home, perhaps. I was going to—he!
he! he!—I was going to propose,' said Mr. Pecksniff, 'that we
should enter by the back way, and come upon them like a clap
of thunder, Mr. Jonas.'

It might not have been easy to decide in respect of which of
their manifold properties, Jonas, Mr. Pecksniff, the carpet-bag,
and the portmanteau, could be likened to a clap of thunder.
But Mr. Jonas giving his assent to this proposal, they stole
round into the back yard, and softly advanced towards the
kitchen window, through which the mingled light of fire and
candle shone upon the darkening night.

Truly Mr. Pecksniff is blessed in his children. In one of
them, at any rate. The prudent Cherry—staff and scrip, and
treasure of her doting father—there she sits, at a little table
white as driven snow, before the kitchen fire, making up
accounts! See the neat maiden, as with pen in hand, and calculating look addressed towards the ceiling, and bunch of keys
within a little basket at her side, she checks the housekeeping
expenditure! From flat-iron, dish-cover, and warming-pan;
from pot and kettle, face of brass footman, and black-leaded
stove; bright glances of approbation wink and glow upon her.
The very onions dangling from the beam, mantle and shine
like cherubs' cheeks. Something of the influence of those
vegetables sinks into Mr. Pecksniff's nature. He weeps.

It is but for a moment, and he hides it from the observation
of his friend—very carefully—by a somewhat elaborate use of
his pocket-handkerchief, in fact: for he would not have his
weakness known.

'Pleasant,' he murmured, 'pleasant to a father's feelings!
My dear girl! Shall we let her know we are here, Mr. Jonas?'

'Why, I suppose you don't mean to spend the evening in the stable or the coach-house,' he returned.

'That, indeed, is not such hospitality as I would show to *you*, my friend,' cried Mr. Pecksniff, pressing his hand. And then he took a long breath, and tapping at the window, shouted with stentorian blandness:

'Boh!'

Cherry dropped her pen and screamed. But innocence is ever bold, or should be. As they opened the door, the valiant girl exclaimed in a firm voice, and with a presence of mind which even in that trying moment did not desert her, 'Who are you? What do you want? Speak! Or I will call my Pa.'

Mr. Pecksniff held out his arms. She knew him instantly, and rushed into his fond embrace.

'It was thoughtless of us, Mr. Jonas, it was very thoughtless,' said Pecksniff, smoothing his daughter's hair. 'My darling, do you see that I am not alone!'

Not she. She had seen nothing but her father until now. She saw Mr. Jonas now, though; and blushed, and hung her head down, as she gave him welcome.

But where was Merry? Mr. Pecksniff didn't ask the question in reproach, but in a vein of mildness touched with a gentle sorrow. She was up-stairs, reading on the parlour couch. Ah! Domestic details had no charms for *her*. 'But call her down,' said Mr. Pecksniff, with a placid resignation. 'Call her down, my love.'

She was called and came, all flushed and tumbled from reposing on the sofa; but none the worse for that. No, not at all. Rather the better, if anything.

'Oh my goodness me!' cried the arch girl, turning to her cousin when she had kissed her father on both cheeks, and in her frolicsome nature had bestowed a supernumerary salute upon the tip of his nose, '*you* here, fright! Well, I'm very thankful that you won't trouble *me* much!'

'What! you're as lively as ever, are you?' said Jonas. 'Oh! You're a wicked one!'

'There, go along!' retorted Merry, pushing him away. 'I'm sure I don't know what I shall ever do, if I have to see much of you. Go along, for gracious' sake!'

Mr. Pecksniff striking in here, with a request that Mr. Jonas would immediately walk up-stairs, he so far complied with the young lady's adjuration as to go at once. But though he had the fair Cherry on his arm, he could not help looking back at her sister, and exchanging some further dialogue of the same bantering description, as they all four ascended to the parlour; where—for the young ladies happened, by good fortune, to be a little later than usual that night—the tea-board was at that moment being set out.

Mr. Pinch was not at home, so they had it all to themselves, and were very snug and talkative, Jonas sitting between the two sisters, and displaying his gallantry in that engaging manner which was peculiar to him. It was a hard thing, Mr. Pecksniff said, when tea was done, and cleared away, to leave so pleasant a little party, but having some important papers to examine in his own apartment, he must beg them to excuse him for half an hour. With this apology he withdrew, singing a careless strain as he went. He had not been gone five minutes, when Merry, who had been sitting in the window, apart from Jonas and her sister, burst into a half-smothered laugh, and skipped towards the door.

'Hallo!' cried Jonas. 'Don't go.'

'Oh, I dare say!' rejoined Merry, looking back. 'You're very anxious I should stay, fright, ain't you?'

'Yes, I am,' said Jonas. 'Upon my word I am. I want to speak to you.' But as she left the room notwithstanding, he ran out after her, and brought her back, after a short struggle in the passage which scandalised Miss Cherry very much.

'Upon my word, Merry,' urged that young lady, 'I wonder at you! There are bounds even to absurdity, my dear.'

'Thank you, my sweet,' said Merry, pursing up her rosy lips. 'Much obliged to it for its advice. Oh! do leave me alone, you monster, do!' This entreaty was wrung from her by a new proceeding on the part of Mr. Jonas, who pulled her down, all breathless as she was, into a seat beside him on the sofa, having at the same time Miss Cherry upon the other side.

'Now,' said Jonas, clasping the waist of each: 'I have got both arms full, haven't I?'

'One of them will be black and blue to-morrow, if you don't let me go,' cried the playful Merry.

'Ah! I don't mind *your* pinching,' grinned Jonas, 'a bit.'

'Pinch him for me, Cherry, pray,' said Mercy. 'I never did hate anybody so much as I hate this creature, I declare!'

'No, no, don't say that,' urged Jonas, 'and don't pinch either, because I want to be serious. I say! Cousin Charity!'

'Well! what?' she answered sharply.

'I want to have some sober talk,' said Jonas: 'I want to prevent any mistakes, you know, and to put everything upon a pleasant understanding. That's desirable and proper, ain't it?'

Neither of the sisters spoke a word. Mr. Jonas paused and cleared his throat, which was very dry.

'She'll not believe what I am going to say, will she, cousin?' said Jonas, timidly squeezing Miss Charity.

'Really, Mr. Jonas, I don't know, until I hear what it is. It's quite impossible!'

'Why, you see,' said Jonas, 'her way always being to make game of people, I know she'll laugh, or pretend to; I know that, beforehand. But you can tell her I'm in earnest, cousin; can't you? You'll confess you know, won't you? You'll be honourable, I'm sure,' he added persuasively.

No answer. His throat seemed to grow hotter and hotter, and to be more and more difficult of control.

'You see, Cousin Charity,' said Jonas, 'nobody but you can tell her what pains I took to get into her company when you were both at the boarding-house in the city, because nobody's so well aware of it, you know. Nobody else can tell her how hard I tried to get to know you better, in order that I might get to know her without seeming to wish it; can they? I always asked you about her, and said where had she gone, and when would she come, and how lively she was, and all that; didn't I, cousin? I know you'll tell her so, if you haven't told her so already, and—and—I dare say you have, because I'm sure you're honourable, ain't you?'

Still not a word. The right arm of Mr. Jonas—the elder sister sat upon his right—may have been sensible of some tumultuous throbbing which was not within itself; but nothing else apprised him that his words had had the least effect.

'Even if you kept it to yourself, and haven't told her,' resumed Jonas, 'it don't much matter, because you'll bear honest witness now; won't you? We've been very good friends from the first; haven't we? And of course we shall be quite friends in future, and so I don't mind speaking before you a bit. Cousin Mercy, you've heard what I've been saying. She'll confirm it, every word; she must. Will you have me for your husband? Eh?'

As he released his hold of Charity, to put this question with better effect, she started up and hurried away to her own room, marking her progress as she went by such a train of passionate and incoherent sound, as nothing but a slighted woman in her anger could produce.

'Let me go away. Let me go after her,' said Merry, pushing him off, and giving him—to tell the truth—more than one sounding slap upon his outstretched face.

'Not till you say Yes. You haven't told me. Will you have me for your husband?'

'No, I won't. I can't bear the sight of you. I have told you so a hundred times. You are a fright. Besides, I always thought you liked my sister best. We all thought so.'

'But that wasn't my fault,' said Jonas.

'Yes, it was; you know it was.'

'Any trick is fair in love,' said Jonas. 'She may have thought I liked her best, but you didn't.'

'I did!'

'No, you didn't. You never could have thought I liked her best, when you were by.'

'There's no accounting for tastes,' said Merry; 'at least I didn't mean to say that. I don't know what I mean. Let me go to her.'

'Say "Yes," and then I will.'

'If I ever brought myself to say so, it should only be that I might hate and tease you all my life.'

'That's as good,' cried Jonas, 'as saying it right out. It's a bargain, cousin. We're a pair, if ever there was one.'

This gallant speech was succeeded by a confused noise of kissing and slapping; and then the fair but much dishevelled Merry broke away, and followed in the footsteps of her sister.

Now whether Mr. Pecksniff had been listening—which in one of his character appears impossible: or divined almost by inspiration what the matter was—which, in a man of his sagacity is far more probable: or happened by sheer good fortune to find himself in exactly the right place, at precisely the right time—which, under the special guardianship in which he lived might very reasonably happen: it is quite certain that at the moment when the sisters came together in their own room, he appeared at the chamber door. And a marvellous contrast it was. They so heated, noisy, and vehement; he so calm, so self-possessed, so cool and full of peace, that not a hair upon his head was stirred.

'Children!' said Mr. Pecksniff, spreading out his hands in

wonder, but not before he had shut the door, and set his back against it. 'Girls! Daughters! What is this?'

'The wretch; the apostate; the false, mean, odious villain; has before my very face proposed to Mercy!' was his eldest daughter's answer.

'Who has proposed to Mercy?' asked Mr. Pecksniff.

'*He* has. That thing, Jonas, down-stairs.'

'Jonas proposed to Mercy?' said Mr. Pecksniff. 'Aye, aye! Indeed!'

'Have you nothing else to say?' cried Charity. 'Am I to be driven mad, papa? He has proposed to Mercy, not to me.'

'Oh, fie! For shame!' said Mr. Pecksniff, gravely. 'Oh, for shame! Can the triumph of a sister move you to this terrible display, my child? Oh, really this is very sad! I am sorry; I am surprised and hurt to see you so. Mercy, my girl, bless you! See to her. Ah, envy, envy, what a passion you are!'

Uttering this apostrophe in a tone full of grief and lamentation, Mr. Pecksniff left the room (taking care to shut the door behind him), and walked down-stairs into the parlour. There he found his intended son-in-law, whom he seized by both hands.

'Jonas!' cried Mr. Pecksniff. 'Jonas! the dearest wish of my heart is now fulfilled!'

'Very well; I'm glad to hear it,' said Jonas. 'That'll do. I say! As it ain't the one you're so fond of, you must come down with another thousand, Pecksniff. You must make it up five. It's worth that, to keep your treasure to yourself, you know. You get off very cheap that way, and haven't a sacrifice to make.'

The grin with which he accompanied this, set off his other attractions to such unspeakable advantage, that even Mr. Pecksniff lost his presence of mind for a moment, and looked at the young man as if he were quite stupefied with wonder and admiration. But he quickly regained his composure, and was in the very act of changing the subject, when a hasty step was heard without, and Tom Pinch, in a state of great excitement, came darting into the room.

On seeing a stranger there, apparently engaged with Mr. Pecksniff in private conversation, Tom was very much abashed, though he still looked as if he had something of great importance to communicate, which would be a sufficient apology for his intrusion.

'Mr. Pinch,' said Pecksniff, 'this is hardly decent. You will excuse my saying that I think your conduct scarcely decent, Mr. Pinch.'

'I beg your pardon, sir,' replied Tom, 'for not knocking at the door.'

'Rather beg this gentleman's pardon, Mr. Pinch,' said Pecksniff. '*I* know you; he does not. My young man, Mr. Jonas.'

The son-in-law that was to be gave him a slight nod: not actively disdainful or contemptuous, only passively; for he was in a good humour.

'Could I speak a word with you, sir, if you please?' said Tom. 'It's rather pressing.'

'It should be very pressing to justify this strange behaviour, Mr. Pinch,' returned his master. 'Excuse me for one moment, my dear friend. Now, sir, what is the reason of this rough intrusion?'

'I am very sorry, sir, I am sure,' said Tom, standing, cap in hand, before his patron in the passage; 'and I know it must have a very rude appearance—'

'It *has* a very rude appearance, Mr. Pinch.'

'Yes, I feel that, sir; but the truth is, I was so surprised to see them, and knew you would be too, that I ran home very fast indeed, and really hadn't enough command over myself to know what I was doing very well. I was in the church just now, sir, touching the organ for my own amusement, when I happened to look round, and saw a gentleman and lady standing in the aisle listening. They seemed to be strangers, sir, as well as I could make out in the dusk: and I thought I didn't know them: so presently I left off, and said, would they walk up into the organ-loft, or take a seat? No, they said, they wouldn't do that; but they thanked me for the music they had heard. In fact,' observed Tom, blushing, 'they said, "Delicious music!" at least, *she* did; and I am sure that was a greater pleasure and honour to me than any compliment I could have had. I—I—beg your pardon, sir;' he was all in a tremble, and dropped his hat for the second time; 'but I—I'm rather flurried, and I fear I've wandered from the point.'

'If you will come back to it, Thomas,' said Mr. Pecksniff, with an icy look, 'I shall feel obliged.'

'Yes, sir,' returned Tom, 'certainly. They had a posting carriage at the porch, sir, and had stopped to hear the organ, they said. And then they said—*she* said, I mean, "I believe you live with Mr. Pecksniff, sir?" I said I had that honour, and I took the liberty, sir,' added Tom, raising his eyes to his benefactor's face, 'of saying, as I always will and must, with your permission, that I was under great obligations to you, and never could express my sense of them sufficiently.'

'That,' said Mr. Pecksniff, 'was very, very wrong. Take your time, Mr. Pinch.'

'Thank you, sir,' cried Tom. 'On that they asked me—she asked, I mean—"Wasn't there a bridle road to Mr. Pecksniff's house—?"'

Mr. Pecksniff suddenly became full of interest.

' "Without going by the Dragon?" When I said there was, and said how happy I should be to show it 'em, they sent the carriage on by the road, and came with me across the meadows. I left 'em at the turnstile to run forward and tell you they were coming, and they'll be here, sir, in—in less than a minute's time, I should say,' added Tom, fetching his breath with difficulty.

'Now, who,' said Mr. Pecksniff, pondering, 'who may these people be?'

'Bless my soul, sir!' cried Tom, 'I meant to mention that at first, I thought I had. I knew them—her, I mean—directly. The gentleman who was ill at the Dragon, sir, last winter; and the young lady who attended him.'

Tom's teeth chattered in his head, and he positively staggered with amazement, at witnessing the extraordinary effect produced on Mr. Pecksniff by these simple words. The dread of losing the old man's favour almost as soon as they were reconciled, through the mere fact of having Jonas in the house; the impossibility of dismissing Jonas, or shutting him up, or tying him hand and foot and putting him in the coal-cellar, without offending him beyond recall; the horrible discordance prevailing in the establishment, and the impossibility of reducing it to decent harmony, with Charity in loud hysterics, Mercy in the utmost disorder, Jonas in the parlour, and Martin Chuzzlewit and his young charge upon the very door-steps; the total hopelessness of being able to disguise or feasibly explain this state of rampant confusion; the sudden accumulation over his devoted head of every complicated perplexity and entanglement for his extrication from which he had trusted to time, good fortune, chance, and his own plotting, so filled the entrapped architect with dismay, that if Tom could have been a Gorgon staring at Mr. Pecksniff, and Mr. Pecksniff could have been a Gorgon staring at Tom, they could not have horrified each other half so much as in their own bewildered persons.

'Dear, dear!' cried Tom, 'what have I done? I hoped it would be a pleasant surprise, sir. I thought you would like to know.'

But at that moment a loud knocking was heard at the hall door.

CHAPTER XXI

More American experiences. Martin takes a partner, and makes a purchase. Some account of Eden, as it appeared on paper. Also of the British Lion. Also of the kind of sympathy professed and entertained by the Watertoast Association of United Sympathisers

THE knocking at Mr. Pecksniff's door, though loud enough, bore no resemblance whatever to the noise of an American railway train at full speed. It may be well to begin the present chapter with this frank admission, lest the reader should imagine that the sounds now deafening this history's ears have any connexion with the knocker on Mr. Pecksniff's door, or with the great amount of agitation pretty equally divided between that worthy man and Mr. Pinch, of which its strong performance was the cause.

Mr. Pecksniff's house is more than a thousand leagues away; and again this happy chronicle has Liberty and Moral Sensibility for its high companions. Again it breathes the blessed air of Independence; again it contemplates with pious awe that moral sense which renders unto Cæsar nothing that is his; again inhales that sacred atmosphere which was the life of him —oh noble patriot, with many followers!—who dreamed of Freedom in a slave's embrace, and waking sold her offspring and his own in public markets.

How the wheels clank and rattle, and the tram-road shakes, as the train rushes on! And now the engine yells, as it were lashed and tortured like a living labourer, and writhed in agony. A poor fancy; for steel and iron are of infinitely greater account, in this commonwealth, than flesh and blood. If the cunning work of man be urged beyond its power of endurance, it has within it the elements of its own revenge; whereas the wretched mechanism of the Divine Hand is dangerous with no such property, but may be tampered with, and crushed, and broken, at the driver's pleasure. Look at that engine! It shall cost a man more dollars in the way of penalty and fine, and satisfaction of the outraged law, to deface in wantonness that senseless mass of metal, than to take the lives of twenty human creatures! Thus the stars wink upon the bloody stripes; and Liberty pulls down her cap upon her eyes, and owns Oppression in its vilest aspect, for her sister.

The engine-driver of the train whose noise awoke us to the present chapter, was certainly troubled with no such reflections as these; nor is it very probable that his mind was disturbed by any reflections at all. He leaned with folded arms and crossed legs against the side of the carriage, smoking: and, except when he expressed, by a grunt as short as his pipe, his approval of some particularly dexterous aim on the part of his colleague, the fireman, who beguiled his leisure by throwing logs of wood from the tender at the numerous stray cattle on the line, he preserved a composure so immovable, and an indifference so complete, that if the locomotive had been a sucking-pig, he could not have been more perfectly indifferent to its doings. Notwithstanding the tranquil state of this officer, and his unbroken peace of mind, the train was proceeding with tolerable rapidity; and the rails being but poorly laid, the jolts and bumps it met with in its progress were neither slight nor few.

There were three great caravans or cars attached. The ladies' car, the gentlemen's car, and the car for negroes: the latter painted black, as an appropriate compliment to its company. Martin and Mark Tapley were in the first, as it was the most comfortable; and, being far from full, received other gentlemen who, like them, were unblessed by the society of ladies of their own. They were seated side by side, and were engaged in earnest conversation.

'And so, Mark,' said Martin, looking at him with an anxious expression, 'and so you are glad we have left New York far behind us, are you?'

'Yes, sir,' said Mark. 'I am. Precious glad.'

'Were you not "jolly" there?' asked Martin.

'On the contrairy, sir,' returned Mark. 'The jolliest week as ever I spent in my life, was that there week at Pawkins's.'

'What do you think of our prospects?' inquired Martin, with an air that plainly said he had avoided the question for some time.

'Uncommon bright, sir,' returned Mark. 'Impossible for a place to have a better name, sir, than the Walley of Eden. No man couldn't think of settling in a better place than the Walley of Eden. And I'm told,' added Mark, after a pause, 'as there's lots of serpents there, so we shall come out quite complete and reg'lar.'

So far from dwelling upon this agreeable piece of information with the least dismay, Mark's face grew radiant as he called it to mind: so very radiant, that a stranger might have supposed he had all his life been yearning for the society of serpents, and now hailed with delight the approaching consummation of his fondest wishes.

'Who told you that?' asked Martin, sternly.

'A military officer,' said Mark.

'Confound you for a ridiculous fellow!' cried Martin, laughing heartily in spite of himself. 'What military officer? You know they spring up in every field.'

'As thick as scarecrows in England, sir,' interposed Mark, 'which is a sort of militia themselves, being entirely coat and wescoat, with a stick inside. Ha, ha! Don't mind me, sir; it's my way sometimes. I can't help being jolly. Why it was one of them inwading conquerors at Pawkins's, as told me. "Am I rightly informed," he says: not exactly through his nose, but as if he'd got a stoppage in it, very high up: "that you're a-going to the Walley of Eden?" "I heard some talk on it," I told him. "Oh!" says he, "if you should ever happen to go to bed there—you *may*, you know," he says, "in course of time as civilisation progresses—don't forget to take a axe with you." I looks at him tolerable hard. "Fleas?" says I. "And more," says he. "Wampires?" says I. "And more," says he. "Musquitoes, perhaps?" says I. "And more," says he. "What more?" says I. "Snakes more," says he; "rattlesnakes. You're right to a certain extent, stranger. There air some catawampous chawers in the small way too, as graze upon a human pretty strong; but don't mind *them*, they're company. It's snakes," he says, "as you'll object to: and whenever you wake and see one in a upright poster on your bed," he says, "like a cork-screw with the handle off a-sittin' on its bottom ring, cut him down, for he means wenom."'

'Why didn't you tell me this before!' cried Martin, with an expression of face which set off the cheerfulness of Mark's visage to great advantage.

'I never thought on it, sir,' said Mark. 'It come in at one ear, and went out at the other. But Lord love us, he was one of another Company I dare say, and only made up the story that we might go to his Eden, and not the opposition one.'

'There's some probability in that,' observed Martin. 'I can honestly say that I hope so, with all my heart.'

'I've not a doubt about it, sir,' returned Mark, who, full of the inspiriting influence of the anecdote upon himself, had for the moment forgotten its probable effect upon his master; 'anyhow, we must live, you know, sir.'

'Live!' cried Martin. 'Yes, it's easy to say live; but if we should happen not to wake when rattlesnakes are making corkscrews of themselves upon our beds, it may be not so easy to do it.'

'And that's a fact,' said a voice so close in his ear that it tickled him. 'That's dreadful true.'

Martin looked round, and found that a gentleman, on the seat behind, had thrust his head between himself and Mark, and sat with his chin resting on the back rail of their little bench, entertaining himself with their conversation. He was as languid and listless in his looks, as most of the gentlemen they had seen; his cheeks were so hollow that he seemed to be always sucking them in; and the sun had burnt him, not a wholesome red or brown, but dirty yellow. He had bright dark eyes, which he kept half closed; only peeping out of the corners, and even then with a glance that seemed to say, 'Now you won't overreach me: you want to, but you won't.' His arms rested carelessly on his knees as he leant forward; in the palm of his left hand, as English rustics have their slice of cheese, he had a cake of tobacco; in his right a penknife. He struck into the dialogue with as little reserve as if he had been specially called in, days before, to hear the arguments on both sides, and favour them with his opinion; and he no more contemplated or cared for the possibility of their not desiring the honour of his acquaintance or interference in their private affairs, than if he had been a bear or a buffalo.

'That,' he repeated, nodding condescendingly to Martin, as to an outer barbarian and foreigner, 'is dreadful true. Darn all manner of vermin.'

Martin could not help frowning for a moment, as if he were disposed to insinuate that the gentleman had unconsciously 'darned' himself. But remembering the wisdom of doing at Rome as Romans do, he smiled with the pleasantest expression he could assume upon so short a notice.

Their new friend said no more just then, being busily employed in cutting a quid or plug from his cake of tobacco, and whistling softly to himself the while. When he had shaped it to his liking, he took out his old plug, and deposited the same on the back of the seat between Mark and Martin, while he thrust the new one into the hollow of his cheek, where it looked like a large walnut, or tolerable pippin. Finding it quite satisfactory, he struck the point of his knife into the old plug, and holding it out for their inspection, remarked with the air of a man who had not lived in vain, that it was 'used up considerable.' Then he tossed it away; put his knife into one pocket and his tobacco into another; rested his chin upon the rail as before; and approving of the pattern on Martin's waistcoat, reached out his hand to feel the texture of that garment.

'What do you call this now?' he asked.

'Upon my word,' said Martin, 'I don't know what it's called.'

'It'll cost a dollar or more a yard, I reckon?'

'I really don't know.'

'In my country,' said the gentleman, 'we know the cost of our own prŏdūce.'

Martin not discussing the question, there was a pause.

'Well!' resumed their new friend, after staring at them intently during the whole interval of silence: 'how's the unnat'ral old parent by this time?'

Mr. Tapley regarding this inquiry as only another version of the impertinent English question, 'How's your mother?' would have resented it instantly, but for Martin's prompt interposition.

'You mean the old country?' he said.

'Ah!' was the reply. 'How's she? Progressing back'ards, I expect, as usual? Well! How's Queen Victoria?'

'In good health, I believe,' said Martin.

'Queen Victoria won't shake in her royal shoes at all, when she hears to-morrow named,' observed the stranger. 'No.'

'Not that I am aware of. Why should she?'

'She won't be taken with a cold chill, when she realiscs what is being done in these diggings,' said the stranger. 'No.'

'No,' said Martin. 'I think I could take my oath of that.'

The strange gentleman looked at him as if in pity for his ignorance or prejudice, and said:

'Well, sir, I tell you this—there ain't a ĕn-gīne with its biler bust, in God A'mighty's free U-nited States, so fixed, and nipped, and frizzled to a most e-tarnal smash, as that young critter, in her luxurious location in the Tower of London, will be, when she reads the next double-extra Watertoast Gazette.'

Several other gentlemen had left their seats and gathered round during the foregoing dialogue. They were highly delighted with this speech. One very lank gentleman, in a loose limp white cravat, long white waistcoat, and a black greatcoat, who seemed to be in authority among them, felt called upon to acknowledge it.

'Hem! Mr. La Fayette Kettle,' he said, taking off his hat.

There was a grave murmur of 'Hush!'

'Mr. La Fayette Kettle! Sir!'

Mr. Kettle bowed.

'In the name of this company, sir, and in the name of our common country, and in the name of that righteous cause of holy sympathy in which we are engaged, I thank you. I thank you, sir, in the name of the Watertoast Sympathisers; and I thank you, sir, in the name of the Watertoast Gazette; and I thank you, sir, in the name of the star-spangled banner of the Great United States, for your eloquent and categorical exposition. And if, sir,' said the speaker, poking Martin with the handle of his umbrella to bespeak his attention, for he was listening to a whisper from Mark; 'if, sir, in such a place, and at such a time, I might venture to con-clude with a sentiment, glancing—however slantin'dicularly—at the subject in hand, I would say, sir, may the British Lion have his talons eradicated by the noble bill of the American Eagle, and be taught to play upon the Irish Harp and the Scotch Fiddle that music which is breathed in every empty shell that lies upon the shores of green Co-lumbia!'

Here the lank gentleman sat down again, amidst a great sensation; and every one looked very grave.

'General Choke,' said Mr. La Fayette Kettle, 'you warm my heart; sir, you warm my heart. But the British Lion is not unrepresented here, sir; and I should be glad to hear his answer to those remarks.'

'Upon my word,' cried Martin, laughing, 'since you do me the honour to consider me his representative, I have only to say that I never heard of Queen Victoria reading the What's-his-name Gazette, and that I should scarcely think it probable.'

General Choke smiled upon the rest, and said, in patient and benignant explanation:

'It is sent to her, sir. It is sent to her. Per mail.'

'But if it is addressed to the Tower of London, it would

hardly come to hand, I fear,' returned Martin: 'for she don't live there.'

'The Queen of England, gentlemen,' observed Mr. Tapley, affecting the greatest politeness, and regarding them with an immovable face, 'usually lives in the Mint to take care of the money. She *has* lodgings, in virtue of her office, with the Lord Mayor at the Mansion-House; but don't often occupy them, in consequence of the parlour chimney smoking.'

'Mark,' said Martin, 'I shall be very much obliged to you if you'll have the goodness not to interfere with preposterous statements, however jocose they may appear to you. I was merely remarking, gentlemen—though it's a point of very little import—that the Queen of England does not happen to live in the Tower of London.'

'General!' cried Mr. La Fayette Kettle. 'You hear?'

'General!' echoed several others. 'General!'

'Hush! Pray, silence!' said General Choke, holding up his hand, and speaking with a patient and complacent benevolence that was quite touching. 'I have always remarked it as a very extraordinary circumstance, which I impute to the natur' of British Institutions and their tendency to suppress that popular inquiry and information which air so widely diffused even in the trackless forests of this vast Continent of the Western Ocean; that the knowledge of Britishers themselves on such points is not to be compared with that possessed by our intelligent and locomotive citizens. This is interesting, and confirms my observation. When you say, sir,' he continued, addressing Martin, 'that your Queen does not reside in the Tower of London, you fall into an error, not uncommon to your countrymen, even when their abilities and moral elements air such as to command respect. But, sir, you air wrong. She *does* live there—'

'When she is at the Court of Saint James's;' interposed Kettle.

'When she is at the Court of Saint James's, of course,' returned the General, in the same benignant way: 'for if her location was in Windsor Pavilion it couldn't be in London at the same time. Your Tower of London, sir,' pursued the General, smiling with a mild consciousness of his knowledge, 'is nat'rally your royal residence. Being located in the immediate neighbourhood of your Parks, your Drives, your Triumphant Arches, your Opera, and your Royal Almacks, it nat'rally suggests itself as the place for holding a luxurious and thoughtless court. And, consequently,' said the General, 'consequently, the court is held there.'

'Have you been in England?' asked Martin.

'In print I have, sir,' said the General, 'not otherwise. We air a reading people here, sir. You will meet with much information among us that will surprise you, sir.'

'I have not the least doubt of it,' returned Martin. But here he was interrupted by Mr. La Fayette Kettle, who whispered in his ear:

'You know General Choke?'

'No,' returned Martin, in the same tone.

'You know what he is considered?'

'One of the most remarkable men in the country?' said Martin, at a venture.

'That's a fact,' rejoined Kettle. 'I was sure you must have heard of him!'

'I think,' said Martin, addressing himself to the General again, 'that I have the pleasure of being the bearer of a letter of introduction to you, sir. From Mr. Bevan, of Massachusetts,' he added, giving it to him.

The General took it and read it attentively; now and then stopping to glance at the two strangers. When he had finished the note, he came over to Martin, sat down by him, and shook hands.

'Well!' he said, 'and you think of settling in Eden?'

'Subject to your opinion, and the agent's advice,' replied Martin. 'I am told there is nothing to be done in the old towns.'

'I can introduce you to the agent, sir,' said the General. 'I know him. In fact, I am a member of the Eden Land Corporation myself.'

This was serious news to Martin, for his friend had laid great stress upon the General's having no connexion, as he thought, with any land company, and therefore being likely to give him disinterested advice. The General explained that he had joined the Corporation only a few weeks ago, and that no communication had passed between himself and Mr. Bevan since.

'We have very little to venture,' said Martin anxiously: 'only a few pounds; but it is our all. Now, do you think that for one of my profession, this would be a speculation with any hope or chance in it?'

'Well,' observed the General, gravely, 'if there wasn't any

hope or chance in the speculation, it wouldn't have engaged my dollars, I opinionate.'

'I don't mean for the sellers,' said Martin. 'For the buyers, for the buyers!'

'For the buyers, sir?' observed the General, in a most impressive manner. 'Well! you come from an old country: from a country, sir, that has piled up golden calves as high as Babel, and worshipped 'em for ages. We are a new country, sir; man is in a more primeval state here, sir; we have not the excuse of having lapsed in the slow course of time into degenerate practices; we have no false gods; man, sir, here, is man in all his dignity. We fought for that or nothing. Here am I, sir,' said the General, setting up his umbrella to represent himself; and a villanous-looking umbrella it was; a very bad counter to stand for the sterling coin of his benevolence; 'here am I with grey hairs, sir, and a moral sense. Would I, with my principles, invest capital in this speculation if I didn't think it full of hopes and chances for my brother man?'

Martin tried to look convinced, but he thought of New York, and found it difficult.

'What are the Great United States for, sir,' pursued the General, 'if not for the regeneration of man? But it is nat'ral in you to make such an enquerry, for you come from England, and you do not know my country.'

'Then you think,' said Martin, 'that allowing for the hardships we are prepared to undergo, there is a reasonable—Heaven knows we don't expect much—a reasonable opening in this place?'

'A reasonable opening in Eden, sir! But see the agent, see the agent; see the maps and plans, sir; and conclude to go or stay, according to the natur' of the settlement. Eden hadn't need to go a-begging yet, sir,' remarked the General.

'It is an awful lovely place, sure-ly. And frightful wholesome, likewise!' said Mr. Kettle, who had made himself a party to this conversation as a matter of course.

Martin felt that to dispute such testimony, for no better reason than because he had his secret misgivings on the subject, would be ungentlemanly and indecent. So he thanked the General for his promise to put him in personal communication with the agent; and 'concluded' to see that officer next morning. He then begged the General to inform him who the Watertoast Sympathisers were, of whom he had spoken in addressing Mr. La Fayette Kettle, and on what grievances they bestowed their Sympathy. To which the General, looking very serious, made answer, that he might fully enlighten himself on those points to-morrow by attending a Great Meeting of the Body, which would then be held at the town to which they were travelling: 'over which, sir,' said the General, 'my fellow-citizens have called on me to preside.'

They came to their journey's end late in the evening. Close to the railway was an immense white edifice, like an ugly hospital, on which was painted 'NATIONAL HOTEL.' There was a wooden gallery or verandah in front, in which it was rather startling, when the train stopped, to behold a great many pairs of boots and shoes, and the smoke of a great many cigars, but no other evidences of human habitation. By slow degrees, however, some heads and shoulders appeared, and connecting themselves with the boots and shoes, led to the discovery that certain gentlemen boarders, who had a fancy for putting their heels where the gentlemen boarders in other countries usually put their heads, were enjoying themselves after their own manner in the cool of the evening.

There was a great bar-room in this hotel, and a great public room in which the general table was being set out for supper. There were interminable whitewashed staircases, long whitewashed galleries up-stairs and down-stairs, scores of little whitewashed bedrooms, and a four-sided verandah to every story in the house, which formed a large brick square with an uncomfortable court-yard in the centre, where some clothes were drying. Here and there, some yawning gentlemen lounged up and down with their hands in their pockets; but within the house and without, wherever half a dozen people were collected together, there, in their looks, dress, morals, manners, habits, intellect, and conversation, were Mr. Jefferson Brick, Colonel Diver, Major Pawkins, General Choke, and Mr. La Fayette Kettle, over, and over, and over again. They did the same things; said the same things; judged all subjects by, and reduced all subjects to, the same standard. Observing how they lived, and how they were always in the enchanting company of each other, Martin even began to comprehend their being the social, cheerful, winning, airy men they were.

At the sounding of a dismal gong, this pleasant company went trooping down from all parts of the house to the public room; while from the neighbouring stores other guests came flocking in, in shoals; for half the town, married folks as well as single, resided at the National Hotel. Tea, coffee, dried meats, tongue, ham, pickles, cake, toast, preserves, and bread and butter, were swallowed with the usual ravaging speed; and then, as before, the company dropped off by degrees, and lounged away to the desk, the counter, or the bar-room. The ladies had a smaller ordinary of their own, to which their husbands and brothers were admitted if they chose; and in all other respects they enjoyed themselves as at Pawkins's.

'Now, Mark, my good fellow,' said Martin, closing the door of his little chamber, 'we must hold a solemn council, for our fate is decided to-morrow morning. You are determined to invest these savings of yours in the common stock, are you?'

'If I hadn't been determined to make that wentur, sir,' answered Mr. Tapley, 'I shouldn't have come.'

'How much is there here, did you say?' asked Martin, holding up a little bag.

'Thirty-seven pound ten and sixpence. The Savings' Bank said so, at least. I never counted it. But *they* know, bless you!' said Mark, with a shake of the head expressive of his unbounded confidence in the wisdom and arithmetic of those Institutions.

'The money we brought with us,' said Martin, 'is reduced to a few shillings less than eight pounds.'

Mr. Tapley smiled, and looked all manner of ways, that he might not be supposed to attach any importance to this fact.

'Upon the ring—*her* ring, Mark,' said Martin, looking ruefully at his empty finger—

'Ah!' sighed Mr. Tapley. 'Beg your pardon, sir.'

'—We raised, in English money, fourteen pounds. So, even with that, your share of the stock is still very much the larger of the two, you see. Now, Mark,' said Martin, in his old way, just as he might have spoken to Tom Pinch, 'I have thought of a means of making this up to you, more than making it up to you, I hope, and very materially elevating your prospects in life.'

'Oh! don't talk of that, you know, sir,' returned Mark. 'I don't want no elevating, sir. I'm all right enough, sir, *I* am.'

'No, but hear me,' said Martin, 'because this is very important to you, and a great satisfaction to me. Mark, you shall be a partner in the business: an equal partner with myself. I will put in, as my additional capital, my professional knowledge and ability; and half the annual profits, as long as it is carried on, shall be yours.'

Poor Martin! For ever building castles in the air. For ever, in his very selfishness, forgetful of all but his own teeming hopes and sanguine plans. Swelling, at that instant, with the consciousness of patronising and most munificently rewarding Mark!

'I don't know, sir,' Mark rejoined, much more sadly than his custom was, though from a very different cause than Martin supposed, 'what I can say to this, in the way of thanking you. I'll stand by you, sir, to the best of my ability, and to the last. That's all.'

'We quite understand each other, my good fellow,' said Martin, rising in self-approval and condescension. 'We are no longer master and servant, but friends and partners; and are mutually gratified. If we determine on Eden, the business shall be commenced as soon as we get there. Under the name,' said Martin, who never hammered upon an idea that wasn't red hot, 'under the name of Chuzzlewit and Tapley.'

'Lord love you, sir,' cried Mark, 'don't have my name in it. I ain't acquainted with the business, sir. I must be Co., I must. I've often thought,' he added, in a low voice, 'as I should like to know a Co.; but I little thought as ever I should live to be one.'

'You shall have your own way, Mark.'

'Thank'ee, sir. If any country gentleman thereabouts, in the public way, or otherwise, wanted such a thing as a skittle-ground made, I could take that part of the bis'ness, sir.'

'Against any architect in the States,' said Martin. 'Get a couple of sherry-cobblers, Mark, and we'll drink success to the firm.'

Either he forgot already (and often afterwards), that they were no longer master and servant, or considered this kind of duty to be among the legitimate functions of the Co. But Mark obeyed with his usual alacrity; and before they parted for the night, it was agreed between them that they should go together to the agent's in the morning, but that Martin should decide the Eden question, on his own sound judgment. And Mark made no merit, even to himself in his jollity, of this concession; perfectly well knowing that the matter would come to that in the end, any way.

The General was one of the party at the public table next

day, and after breakfast suggested that they should wait upon
the agent without loss of time. They, desiring nothing more,
agreed; so off they all four started for the office of the Eden
Settlement, which was almost within rifle-shot of the National
Hotel.

It was a small place: something like a turnpike. But a great
deal of land may be got into a dice-box, and why may not
a whole territory be bargained for in a shed? It was but
a temporary office too; for the Edeners were 'going' to build a
superb establishment for the transaction of their business, and
had already got so far as to mark out the site. Which is a great
way in America. The office-door was wide open, and in the
doorway was the agent: no doubt a tremendous fellow to get
through his work, for he seemed to have no arrears, but was
swinging backwards and forwards in a rocking-chair, with one
of his legs planted high up against the door-post, and the other
doubled up under him, as if he were hatching his foot.

He was a gaunt man in a huge straw hat, and a coat of green
stuff. The weather being hot, he had no cravat, and wore his
shirt collar wide open; so that every time he spoke something
was seen to twitch and jerk up in his throat, like the little
hammers in a harpsichord when the notes are struck. Perhaps
it was the Truth feebly endeavouring to leap to his lips. If so,
it never reached them.

Two grey eyes lurked deep within this agent's head, but one
of them had no sight in it, and stood stock still. With that side
of his face he seemed to listen to what the other side was doing.
Thus each profile had a distinct expression; and when the
movable side was most in action, the rigid one was in its coldest
state of watchfulness. It was like turning the man inside out,
to pass to that view of his features in his liveliest mood, and see
how calculating and intent they were.

Each long black hair upon his head hung down as straight as
any plummet line; but rumpled tufts were on the arches of his
eyes, as if the crow whose foot was deeply printed in the corners
had pecked and torn them in a savage recognition of his
kindred nature as a bird of prey.

Such was the man whom they now approached, and whom
the General saluted by the name of Scadder.

'Well, Gen'ral,' he returned, 'and how are you?'

'Ac-tive and spry, sir, in my country's service and the
sympathetic cause. Two gentlemen on business, Mr. Scadder.'

He shook hands with each of them (nothing is done in America without shaking hands), then went on rocking.

'I think I know what bis'ness you have brought these strangers here upon, then, Gen'ral?'

'Well, sir. I expect you may.'

'You air a tongue-y person, Gen'ral. For you talk too much, and that's a fact,' said Scadder. 'You speak a-larming well in public, but you didn't ought to go ahead so fast in private. Now!'

'If I can realise your meaning, ride me on a rail!' returned the General, after pausing for consideration.

'You know we didn't wish to sell the lots off right away to any loafer as might bid,' said Scadder; 'but had con-cluded to reserve 'em for Aristocrats of Natur'. Yes!'

'And they are here, sir!' cried the General with warmth. 'They are here, sir!'

'If they air here,' returned the agent, in reproachful accents, 'that's enough. But you didn't ought to have your dander ris with *me*, Gen'ral.'

The General whispered Martin that Scadder was the honest-est fellow in the world, and that he wouldn't have given him offence designedly, for ten thousand dollars.

'I do my duty; and I raise the dander of my feller critters, as I wish to serve,' said Scadder in a low voice, looking down the road and rocking still. 'They rile up rough, along of my objecting to their selling Eden off too cheap. That's human natur'! Well!

'Mr. Scadder,' said the General, assuming his oratorical deportment. 'Sir! Here is my hand, and here my heart. I esteem you, sir, and ask your pardon. These gentlemen air friends of mine, or I would not have brought 'em here, sir, being well aware, sir, that the lots at present go entirely too cheap. But these air friends, sir; these air partick'ler friends.'

Mr. Scadder was so satisfied by this explanation, that he shook the General warmly by the hand, and got out of the rocking-chair to do it. He then invited the General's particular friends to accompany him into the office. As to the General, he observed, with his usual benevolence, that being one of the company, he wouldn't interfere in the transaction on any account; so he appropriated the rocking-chair to himself, and looked at the prospect, like a good Samaritan waiting for a traveller.

'Heyday!' cried Martin, as his eye rested on a great plan which occupied one whole side of the office. Indeed, the office had little else in it, but some geological and botanical specimens, one or two rusty ledgers, a homely desk, and a stool. 'Heyday! what's that?'

'That's Eden,' said Scadder, picking his teeth with a sort of young bayonet that flew out of his knife when he touched a spring.

'Why, I had no idea it was a city.'

'Hadn't you? Oh, it's a city.'

A flourishing city, too! An architectural city! There were banks, churches, cathedrals, market-places, factories, hotels, stores, mansions, wharves; an exchange, a theatre; public buildings of all kinds, down to the office of the Eden Stinger, a daily journal; all faithfully depicted in the view before them.

'Dear me! It's really a most important place!' cried Martin, turning round.

'Oh! it's very important,' observed the agent.

'But, I am afraid,' said Martin, glancing again at the Public Buildings, 'that there's nothing left for me to do.'

'Well! it ain't all built,' replied the agent. 'Not quite.'

This was a great relief.

'The market-place, now,' said Martin. 'Is that built?'

'That?' said the agent, sticking his toothpick into the weathercock on the top. 'Let me see. No: that ain't built.'

'Rather a good job to begin with. Eh, Mark?' whispered Martin, nudging him with his elbow.

Mark, who with a very stolid countenance had been eyeing the plan and the agent by turns, merely rejoined 'Uncommon!'

A dead silence ensued, Mr. Scadder in some short recesses or vacations of his toothpick, whistled a few bars of Yankee Doodle, and blew the dust off the roof of the Theatre.

'I suppose,' said Martin, feigning to look more narrowly at the plan, but showing by his tremulous voice how much depended, in his mind, upon the answer; 'I suppose there are—several architects there?'

'There ain't a single one,' said Scadder.

'Mark,' whispered Martin, pulling him by the sleeve, 'do you hear that? But whose work is all this before us, then?' he asked aloud.

'The soil being very fruitful, public buildings grows spontaneous, perhaps,' said Mark.

He was on the agent's dark side as he said it; but Scadder instantly changed his place, and brought his active eye to bear upon him.

'Feel of my hands, young man,' he said.

'What for?' asked Mark, declining.

'Air they dirty, or air they clean, sir?' said Scadder, holding them out.

In a physical point of view they were decidedly dirty. But it being obvious that Mr. Scadder offered them for examination in a figurative sense, as emblems of his moral character, Martin hastened to pronounce them pure as the driven snow.

'I entreat, Mark,' he said, with some irritation, 'that you will not obtrude remarks of that nature, which, however harmless and well-intentioned, are quite out of place, and cannot be expected to be very agreeable to strangers. I am quite surprised.'

'The Co.'s a-putting his foot in it already,' thought Mark. 'He must be a sleeping partner: fast asleep and snoring, Co. must: I see.'

Mr. Scadder said nothing, but he set his back against the plan, and thrust his toothpick into the desk some twenty times: looking at Mark all the while as if he were stabbing him in effigy.

'You haven't said whose work it is,' Martin ventured to observe, at length, in a tone of mild propitiation.

'Well, never mind whose work it is, or isn't,' said the agent sulkily. 'No matter how it did eventuate. P'raps he cleared off, handsome, with a heap of dollars; p'raps he wasn't worth a cent. P'raps he was a loafin' rowdy; p'raps a ring-tailed roarer. Now!'

'All your doing, Mark!' said Martin.

'P'raps,' pursued the agent, 'them an't plants of Eden's raising. No! P'raps that desk and stool ain't made from Eden lumber. No! P'raps no end of squatters ain't gone out there. No! P'raps there ain't no such location in the territoary of the Great U-nited States. Oh, no!'

'I hope you're satisfied with the success of your joke, Mark,' said Martin.

But here, at a most opportune and happy time, the General interposed, and called out to Scadder from the doorway to give his friends the particulars of that little lot of fifty acres with the house upon it; which, having belonged to the company formerly, had lately lapsed again into their hands.

The thriving City of Eden as it appeared on Paper

'You air a deal too open-handed, Gen'ral,' was the answer. 'It is a lot as should be rose in price. It is.'

He grumblingly opened his books notwithstanding, and always keeping his bright side towards Mark, no matter at what amount of inconvenience to himself, displayed a certain leaf for their perusal. Martin read it greedily, and then inquired:

'Now where upon the plan may this place be?'

'Upon the plan?' said Scadder.

'Yes.'

He turned towards it, and reflected for a short time, as if, having been put upon his mettle, he was resolved to be particular to the very minutest hair's breadth of a shade. At length, after wheeling his toothpick slowly round and round in the air, as if it were a carrier pigeon just thrown up, he suddenly made a dart at the drawing, and pierced the very centre of the main wharf, through and through.

'There!' he said, leaving his knife quivering in the wall; 'that's where it is!'

Martin glanced with sparkling eyes upon his Co., and his Co. saw that the thing was done.

The bargain was not concluded as easily as might have been expected though, for Scadder was caustic and ill-humoured, and cast much unnecessary opposition in the way; at one time requesting them to think of it, and call again in a week or a fortnight; at another, predicting that they wouldn't like it; at another, offering to retract and let them off, and muttering strong imprecations upon the folly of the General. But the whole of the astoundingly small sum-total of purchase-money —it was only one hundred and fifty dollars, or something more than thirty pounds of the capital brought by Co. into the architectural concern—was ultimately paid down; and Martin's head was two inches nearer the roof of the little wooden office, with the consciousness of being a landed proprietor in the thriving city of Eden.

'If it shouldn't happen to fit,' said Scadder, as he gave Martin the necessary credentials on receipt of his money, 'don't blame me.'

'No, no,' he replied merrily. 'We'll not blame you. General, are you going?'

'I am at your service, sir; and I wish you,' said the General, giving him his hand with grave cordiality, 'joy of your po-ssession. You air now, sir, a denizen of the most powerful and highly-civilised do-minion that has ever graced the world; a do-minion, sir, where man is bound to man in one vast bond of equal love and truth. May you, sir, be worthy of your a-dopted country!'

Martin thanked him, and took leave of Mr. Scadder; who had resumed his post in the rocking-chair, immediately on the General's rising from it, and was once more swinging away as if he had never been disturbed. Mark looked back several times as they went down the road towards the National Hotel, but now his blighted profile was towards them, and nothing but attentive thoughtfulness was written on it. Strangely different to the other side! He was not a man much given to laughing, and never laughed outright; but every line in the print of the crow's foot, and every little wiry vein in that division of his head, was wrinkled up into a grin! The compound figure of Death and the Lady at the top of the old ballad was not divided with a greater nicety, and hadn't halves more monstrously unlike each other, than the two profiles of Zephaniah Scadder.

The General posted along at a great rate, for the clock was on the stroke of twelve; and at that hour precisely, the Great Meeting of the Watertoast Sympathisers was to be holden in the public room of the National Hotel. Being very curious to witness the demonstration, and know what it was all about, Martin kept close to the General: and, keeping closer than ever when they entered the Hall, got by that means upon a little platform of tables at the upper end: where an arm-chair was set for the General, and Mr. La Fayette Kettle, as secretary, was making a great display of some foolscap documents. Screamers, no doubt.

'Well, sir!' he said, as he shook hands with Martin, 'here is a spectacle calc'lated to make the British Lion put his tail between his legs, and howl with anguish, I expect!'

Martin certainly thought it possible that the British Lion might have been rather out of his element in that Ark: but he kept the idea to himself. The General was then voted to the chair, on the motion of a pallid lad of the Jefferson Brick school: who forthwith set in for a high-spiced speech, with a good deal about hearths and homes in it, and unriveting the chains of Tyranny.

Oh but it was a clincher for the British Lion, it was! The

indignation of the glowing young Columbian knew no bounds.
If he could only have been one of his own forefathers, he said,
wouldn't he have peppered that same Lion, and been to him
as another Brute Tamer with a wire whip, teaching him lessons
not easily forgotten. 'Lion! (cried that young Columbian)
where is he? Who is he? What is he? Show him to me. Let
me have him here. Here!' said the young Columbian, in a
wrestling attitude, 'upon this sacred altar. Here!' cried the
young Columbian, idealising the dining-table, 'upon ancestral
ashes, cemented with the glorious blood poured out like water
on our native plains of Chickabiddy Lick! Bring forth that
Lion!' said the young Columbian. 'Alone, I dare him! I taunt
that Lion. I tell that Lion, that Freedom's hand once twisted
in his mane, he rolls a corse before me, and the Eagles of the
Great Republic laugh ha, ha!'

When it was found that the Lion didn't come, but kept out
of the way; that the young Columbian stood there, with folded
arms, alone in his glory; and consequently that the Eagles
were no doubt laughing wildly on the mountain tops; such
cheers arose as might have shaken the hands upon the Horse-
Guards' clock, and changed the very mean time of the day in
England's capital.

'Who is this?' Martin telegraphed to La Fayette.

The Secretary wrote something, very gravely, on a piece of
paper, twisted it up, and had it passed to him from hand to
hand. It was an improvement on the old sentiment: 'Perhaps
as remarkable a man as any in our country.'

This young Columbian was succeeded by another, to the full
as eloquent as he, who drew down storms of cheers. But both
remarkable youths, in their great excitement (for your true
poetry can never stoop to details), forgot to say with whom or
what the Watertoasters sympathised, and likewise why or
wherefore they were sympathetic. Thus Martin remained for
a long time as completely in the dark as ever; until at length
a ray of light broke in upon him through the medium of the
Secretary, who, by reading the minutes of their past proceedings, made the matter somewhat clearer. He then learned that
the Watertoast Association sympathised with a certain Public
Man in Ireland, who held a contest upon certain points with
England: and that they did so, because they didn't love England at all—not by any means because they loved Ireland
much; being indeed horribly jealous and distrustful of its

people always, and only tolerating them because of their working hard, which made them very useful; labour being held in greater indignity in the simple republic than in any other country upon earth. This rendered Martin curious to see what grounds of sympathy the Watertoast Association put forth; nor was he long in suspense, for the General rose to read a letter to the Public Man, which with his own hands he had written.

'Thus,' said the General, 'thus, my friends and fellow-citizens, it runs:

' "SIR,

' "I address you on behalf of the Watertoast Association of United Sympathisers. It is founded, sir, in the great republic of America! and now holds its breath, and swells the blue veins in its forehead nigh to bursting, as it watches, sir, with feverish intensity and sympathetic ardour, your noble efforts in the cause of Freedom." '

At the name of Freedom, and at every repetition of that name, all the Sympathisers roared aloud; cheering with nine times nine, and nine times over.

' "In Freedom's name, sir—holy Freedom—I address you. In Freedom's name, I send herewith a contribution to the funds of your society. In Freedom's name, sir, I advert with indignation and disgust to that accursed animal, with gore-stained whiskers, whose rampant cruelty and fiery lust have ever been a scourge, a torment to the world. The naked visitors to Crusoe's Island, sir; the flying wives of Peter Wilkins; the fruit-smeared children of the tangled bush; nay, even the men of large stature, anciently bred in the mining districts of Corn-wall; alike bear witness to its savage nature. Where, sir, are the Cormorans, the Blunderbores, the Great Feefofums, named in History? All, all, exterminated by its destroying hand.

' "I allude, sir, to the British Lion.

' "Devoted, mind and body, heart and soul, to Freedom, sir·—to Freedom, blessed solace to the snail upon the cellar-door, the oyster in his pearly bed, the still mite in his home of cheese, the very winkle of your country in his shelly lair—in her unsullied name, we offer you our sympathy. Oh, sir, in this our cherished and our happy land, her fires burn bright and clear and smokeless: once lighted up in yours, the lion shall be roasted whole.

' "I am sir, in Freedom's name,
 ' "Your affectionate friend and faithful Sympathiser,
  ' "Cyrus Choke, General, U.S.M." '

It happened that just as the General began to read this letter, the railroad train arrived, bringing a new mail from England; and a packet had been handed in to the Secretary, which during its perusal and the frequent cheerings in homage to freedom, he had opened. Now, its contents disturbed him very much, and the moment the General sat down, he hurried to his side, and placed in his hand a letter and several printed extracts from English newspapers; to which, in a state of infinite excitement, he called his immediate attention.

The General, being greatly heated by his own composition, was in a fit state to receive any inflammable influence; but he had no sooner possessed himself of the contents of these documents, than a change came over his face, involving such a huge amount of choler and passion, that the noisy concourse were silent in a moment, in very wonder at the sight of him.

'My friends!' cried the General, rising; 'my friends and fellow-citizens, we have been mistaken in this man.'

'In what man?' was the cry.

'In this,' panted the General, holding up the letter he had read aloud a few minutes before. 'I find that he has been, and is, the advocate—consistent in it always too—of Nigger emancipation!'

If anything beneath the sky be real, those Sons of Freedom would have pistolled, stabbed—in some way slain—that man by coward hands and murderous violence, if he had stood among them at that time. The most confiding of their own countrymen would not have wagered then; no, nor would they ever peril one dung-hill straw, upon the life of any man in such a strait. They tore the letter, cast the fragments in the air, trod down the pieces as they fell; and yelled, and groaned, and hissed, till they could cry no longer.

'I shall move,' said the General, when he could make himself heard, 'that the Watertoast Association of United Sympathisers be immediately dissolved!'

Down with it! Away with it! Don't hear of it! Burn its records! Pull the room down! Blot it out of human memory!

'But, my fellow-countrymen!' said the General, 'the contributions. We have funds. What is to be done with the funds?'

It was hastily resolved that a piece of plate should be presented to a certain constitutional Judge, who had laid down from the Bench the noble principle that it was lawful for any white mob to murder any black man: and that another piece of plate, of similar value, should be presented to a certain Patriot, who had declared from his high place in the Legislature, that he and his friends would hang, without trial, any Abolitionist who might pay them a visit. For the surplus, it was agreed that it should be devoted to aiding the enforcement of those free and equal laws, which render it incalculably more criminal and dangerous to teach a negro to read and write than to roast him alive in a public city. These points adjusted, the meeting broke up in great disorder, and there was an end of the Watertoast Sympathy.

As Martin ascended to his bedroom, his eye was attracted by the Republican banner, which had been hoisted from the house-top in honour of the occasion, and was fluttering before a window which he passed.

'Tut!' said Martin. 'You're a gay flag in the distance. But let a man be near enough to get the light upon the other side and see through you; and you are but sorry fustian!'

CHAPTER XXII

From which it will be seen that Martin became a lion on his own account. Together with the reason why

AS soon as it was generally known in the National Hotel, that the young Englishman, Mr. Chuzzlewit, had purchased a 'lo-cation' in the Valley of Eden, and intended to betake himself to that earthly Paradise by the next steamboat, he became a popular character. Why this should be, or how it had come to pass, Martin no more knew than Mrs. Gamp, of Kingsgate Street, High Holborn, did; but that he was for the time being the lion, by popular election, of the Watertoast community, and that his society was in rather inconvenient request, there could be no kind of doubt.

The first notification he received of this change in his position, was the following epistle, written in a thin running hand,—with here and there a fat letter or two, to make the general effect more striking,—on a sheet of paper, ruled with blue lines.

'*National Hotel, Monday Morning.*

'Dear Sir,

'When I had the privillidge of being your fellow-traveller in the cars, the day before yesterday, you offered some remarks upon the subject of the Tower of London, which (in common with my fellow-citizens generally) I could wish to hear repeated to a public audience.

'As secretary to the Young Men's Watertoast Association of this town, I am requested to inform you that the Society will be proud to hear you deliver a lecture upon the Tower of London, at their Hall to-morrow evening, at seven o'clock; and as a large issue of quarter-dollar tickets may be expected, your answer and consent by bearer will be considered obliging.

'Dear Sir, yours truly,

'La Fayette Kettle.

'The Honourable Mr. Chuzzlewit.

'P.S.—The Society would not be particular in limiting you to the Tower of London. Permit me to suggest that any remarks upon the Elements of Geology, or (if more convenient) upon the Writings of your talented and witty countryman, the honourable Mr. Miller, would be well received.'

Very much aghast at this invitation, Martin wrote back, civilly declining it; and had scarcely done so, when he received another letter.

'(Private).
'*No.* 47, *Bunker Hill Street, Monday Morning.*
'Sir,
'I was raised in those interminable solitudes where our mighty Mississippi (or Father of Waters) rolls his turbid flood.

'I am young, and ardent. For there is a poetry in wildness, and every alligator basking in the slime is in himself an Epic, self-contained. I aspire for fame. It is my yearning and my thirst.

'Are you, sir, aware of any member of Congress in England, who would undertake to pay my expenses to that country, and for six months after my arrival?

'There is something within me which gives me the assurance that this enlightened patronage would not be thrown away. In literature or art; the bar, the pulpit, or the stage; in one or other, if not all, I feel that I am certain to succeed.

'If too much engaged to write to any such yourself, please let me have a list of three or four of those most likely to respond, and I will address them through the Post Office. May I also ask you to favour me with any critical observations that have ever presented themselves to your reflective faculties, on "Cain: a Mystery," by the Right Honourable Lord Byron?
'I am, Sir,
'Yours (forgive me if I add, soaringly),
'PUTNAM SMIF.
'P.S.—Address your answer to America Junior, Messrs. Hancock & Floby, Dry Goods Store, as above.'

Both of which letters, together with Martin's reply to each, were, according to a laudable custom, much tending to the promotion of gentlemanly feeling and social confidence, published in the next number of the Watertoast Gazette.

He had scarcely got through this correspondence when Captain Kedgick, the landlord, kindly came up-stairs to see how he was getting on. The Captain sat down upon the bed before he spoke; and finding it rather hard, moved to the pillow.

'Well, sir!' said the Captain, putting his hat a little more on one side, for it was rather tight in the crown: 'You're quite a public man I calc'late.'

'So it seems,' retorted Martin, who was very tired.

'Our citizens, sir,' pursued the Captain, 'intend to pay their respects to you. You will have to hold a sort of lĕ—vĕe, sir, while you're here.'

'Powers above!' cried Martin, 'I couldn't do that, my good fellow!'

'I reckon you *must* then,' said the Captain.

'Must is not a pleasant word, Captain,' urged Martin.

'Well! I didn't fix the mother language, and I can't unfix it,' said the Captain, coolly: 'else I'd make it pleasant. You must re-ceive. That's all.'

'But why should I receive people who care as much for me as I care for them?' asked Martin.

'Well! because I have had a muniment put up in the bar,' returned the Captain.

'A what?' cried Martin.

'A muniment,' rejoined the Captain.

Martin looked despairingly at Mark, who informed him that the Captain meant a written notice that Mr. Chuzzlewit would receive the Watertoasters that day, at and after two o'clock: which was in effect then hanging in the bar, as Mark, from ocular inspection of the same, could testify.

'You wouldn't be unpop'lar, *I* know,' said the Captain, paring his nails. 'Our citizens an't long of riling up, I tell you; and our Gazette could flay you like a wild cat.'

Martin was going to be very wroth, but he thought better of it, and said:

'In Heaven's name let them come, then.'

'Oh, *they*'ll come,' returned the Captain. 'I have seen the big room fixed a'purpose, with my eyes.'

'But will you,' said Martin, seeing that the Captain was about to go; 'will you at least tell me this? What do they want to see me for? what have I done? and how do they happen to have such a sudden interest in me?'

Captain Kedgick put a thumb and three fingers to each side of the brim of his hat; lifted it a little way off his head; put it on again carefully; passed one hand all down his face, beginning at the forehead and ending at the chin; looked at Martin; then at Mark; then at Martin again; winked; and walked out.

'Upon my life, now!' said Martin, bringing his hand heavily upon the table; 'such a perfectly unaccountable fellow as that, I never saw. Mark, what do you say to this?'

'Why, sir,' returned his partner, 'my opinion is that we must have got to the MOST remarkable man in the country at last. So I hope there's an end to the breed, sir.'

Although this made Martin laugh, it couldn't keep off two o'clock. Punctually, as the hour struck, Captain Kedgick returned to hand him to the room of state; and he had no sooner got him safe there, than he bawled down the staircase to his fellow-citizens below, that Mr. Chuzzlewit was 'receiving.'

Up they came with a rush. Up they came until the room was full, and, through the open door, a dismal perspective of more to come, was shown upon the stairs. One after another, one after another, dozen after dozen, score after score, more, more, more, up they came: all shaking hands with Martin. Such varieties of hands, the thick, the thin, the short, the long, the fat, the lean, the coarse, the fine; such differences of temperature, the hot, the cold, the dry, the moist, the flabby; such diversities of grasp, the tight, the loose, the short-lived, and the lingering! Still up, up, up, more, more, more: and ever and anon the Captain's voice was heard above the crowd: 'There's more below! there's more below. Now, gentlemen, you that have been introduced to Mr. Chuzzlewit, will you clear, gentlemen? Will you clear? Will you be so good as clear, gentlemen, and make a little room for more?'

Regardless of the Captain's cries, they didn't clear at all, but stood there, bolt upright and staring. Two gentlemen connected with the Watertoast Gazette had come express to get the matter for an article on Martin. They had agreed to divide the labour. One of them took him below the waistcoat; one above. Each stood directly in front of his subject with his head a little on one side, intent on his department. If Martin put one boot before the other, the lower gentleman was down upon him; he rubbed a pimple on his nose, and the upper gentleman booked it. He opened his mouth to speak, and the same gentleman was on one knee before him, looking in at his teeth, with the nice scrutiny of a dentist. Amateurs in the physiognomical and phrenological sciences roved about him with watchful eyes and itching fingers, and sometimes one, more daring than the rest, made a mad grasp at the back of his head, and vanished in the crowd. They had him in all points of view: in front, in profile, three-quarter face, and behind. Those who were not professional or scientific, audibly exchanged opinions on his looks. New lights shone in upon him, in respect of his nose. Contradictory rumours were abroad on the subject of his hair. And still the Captain's voice was heard —so stifled by the concourse, that he seemed to speak from underneath a feather-bed, exclaiming, 'Gentlemen, you that have been introduced to Mr. Chuzzlewit, *will* you clear?'

Even when they began to clear it was no better; for then a stream of gentlemen, every one with a lady on each arm (exactly like the chorus to the National Anthem when Royalty goes in state to the play), came gliding in: every new group fresher than the last, and bent on staying to the latest moment. If they spoke to him, which was not often, they invariably asked the same questions, in the same tone: with no more remorse, or delicacy, or consideration, than if he had been a figure of stone, purchased, and paid for, and set up there for their delight. Even when, in the slow course of time, these died off, it was as bad as ever, if not worse; for then the boys grew bold, and came in as a class of themselves, and did everything that the grown-up people had done. Uncouth stragglers, too, appeared; men of a ghostly kind, who being in, didn't know how to get out again: insomuch that one silent gentleman with glazed and fishy eyes, and only one button on his waistcoat (which was a very large metal one, and shone prodigiously), got behind the door, and stood there, like a clock, long after everybody else was gone.

Martin felt, from pure fatigue, and heat, and worry, as if he could have fallen on the ground and willingly remained there, if they would but have had the mercy to leave him alone. But as letters and messages, threatening his public denouncement if he didn't see the senders, poured in like hail; and as more visitors came while he took his coffee by himself; and as Mark, with all his vigilance, was unable to keep them from the door; he resolved to go to bed. Not that he felt at all sure of bed being any protection, but that he might not leave a forlorn hope untried.

He had communicated this design to Mark, and was on the eve of escaping, when the door was thrown open in a great hurry, and an elderly gentleman entered: bringing with him a lady who certainly could not be considered young—that was matter of fact; and probably could not be considered handsome—but that was matter of opinion. She was very straight, very tall, and not at all flexible in face or figure. On her head she wore a great straw bonnet, with trimmings of the same, in which she looked as if she had been thatched by an unskilful labourer; and in her hand she held a most enormous fan.

'Mr. Chuzzlewit, I believe?' said the gentleman.

'That is my name.'

'Sir,' said the gentleman, 'I am pressed for time.'

'Thank God!' thought Martin.

'I go back Toe my home, sir,' pursued the gentleman, 'by the return train, which starts immediate. Start is not a word you use in your country, sir.'

'Oh yes, it is,' said Martin.

'You air mistaken, sir,' returned the gentleman, with great decision: 'but we will not pursue the subject, lest it should awake your prĕjŭ-dīce. Sir, Mrs. Hominy.'

Martin bowed.

'Mrs. Hominy, sir, is the lady of Major Hominy, one of our chicest spirits; and belongs Toe one of our most aristocratic families. You air, p'raps, acquainted, sir, with Mrs. Hominy's writings.'

Martin couldn't say he was.

'You have much Toe learn, and Toe enjoy, sir,' said the gentleman. 'Mrs. Hominy is going Toe stay until the end of the Fall, sir, with her married daughter at the settlement of New Thermopylæ, three days this side of Eden. Any attention, sir, that you can show Toe Mrs. Hominy upon the journey, will be very grateful Toe the Major and our fellow-citizens. Mrs. Hominy, I wish you good night, ma'am, and a pleasant progress on your rout!'

Martin could scarcely believe it; but he had gone, and Mrs. Hominy was drinking the milk.

'A'most used-up I am, I do declare!' she observed. 'The jolting in the cars is pretty nigh as bad as if the rail was full of snags and sawyers.'

'Snags and sawyers, ma'am?' said Martin.

'Well, then, I do suppose you'll hardly realise my meaning, sir,' said Mrs. Hominy. 'My! Only think! *Do* tell!'

It did not appear that these expressions, although they seemed to conclude with an urgent entreaty, stood in need of any answer; for Mrs. Hominy, untying her bonnet-strings, observed that she would withdraw to lay that article of dress aside, and would return immediately.

'Mark!' said Martin. 'Touch me, will you. Am I awake?'

'Hominy is, sir,' returned his partner: 'Broad awake! Just the sort of woman, sir, as would be discovered with her eyes wide open, and her mind a-working for her country's good, at any hour of the day or night.'

They had no opportunity of saying more, for Mrs. Hominy stalked in again; very erect, in proof of her aristocratic blood; and holding in her clasped hands a red cotton pocket-handkerchief, perhaps a parting gift from that choice spirit, the Major. She had laid aside her bonnet, and now appeared in a highly aristocratic and classical cap, meeting beneath her chin: a style of head-dress so admirably adapted to her countenance, that if the late Mr. Grimaldi had appeared in the lappets of Mrs. Siddons, a more complete effect could not have been produced.

Martin handed her to a chair. Her first words arrested him before he could get back to his own seat.

'Pray, sir!' said Mrs. Hominy, 'where do you hail from?'

'I am afraid I am dull of comprehension,' answered Martin, 'being extremely tired; but upon my word I don't understand you.'

Mrs. Hominy shook her head with a melancholy smile that said, not inexpressively, 'They corrupt even the language in that old country!' and added then, as coming down a step or two to meet his low capacity, 'Where was you rose?'

'Oh!' said Martin, 'I was born in Kent.'

'And how do you like our country, sir?' asked Mrs. Hominy.

'Very much indeed,' said Martin, half asleep. 'At least— that is—pretty well, ma'am.'

'Most strangers—and partick'larly Britishers—are much surprised by what they see in the U-nited States,' remarked Mrs. Hominy.

'They have excellent reason to be so, ma'am,' said Martin. 'I never was so much surprised in all my life.'

'Our institutions make our people smart much, sir,' Mrs. Hominy remarked.

'The most short-sighted man could see that at a glance, with his naked eye,' said Martin.

Mrs. Hominy was a philosopher and an authoress, and consequently had a pretty strong digestion; but this coarse, this indecorous phrase, was almost too much for her. For a gentleman sitting alone with a lady—although the door *was* open— to talk about a naked eye!

A long interval elapsed before even she, woman of masculine

and towering intellect though she was, could call up fortitude enough to resume the conversation. But Mrs. Hominy was a traveller. Mrs. Hominy was a writer of reviews and analytical disquisitions. Mrs. Hominy had had her letters from abroad, beginning 'My ever dearest blank,' and signed 'The Mother of the Modern Gracchi' (meaning the married Miss Hominy), regularly printed in a public journal, with all the indignation in capitals, and all the sarcasm in italics. Mrs. Hominy had looked on foreign countries with the eye of a perfect republican hot from the model oven; and Mrs. Hominy could talk (or write) about them by the hour together. So Mrs. Hominy at last came down on Martin heavily, and as he was fast asleep, she had it all her own way, and bruised him to her heart's content.

It is no great matter what Mrs. Hominy said, save that she had learnt it from the cant of a class, and a large class, of her fellow-countrymen, who, in their every word, avow themselves to be as senseless to the high principles on which America sprang, a nation, into life, as any Orson in her legislative halls. Who are no more capable of feeling, or of caring if they did feel, that by reducing their own country to the ebb of honest men's contempt, they put in hazard the rights of nations yet unborn, and very progress of the human race, than are the swine who wallow in their streets. Who think that crying out to other nations, old in their iniquity, 'We are no worse than you!' (No worse!) is high defence and 'vantage-ground enough for that Republic, but yesterday let loose upon her noble course, and but to-day so maimed and lame, so full of sores and ulcers, foul to the eye and almost hopeless to the sense, that her best friends turn from the loathsome creature with disgust. Who, having by their ancestors declared and won their Independence, because they would not bend the knee to certain Public vices and corruptions, and would not abrogate the truth, run riot in the Bad, and turn their backs upon the Good; and lying down contented with the wretched boast that other Temples also are of glass, and stones which batter theirs may be flung back; show themselves, in that alone, as immeasurably behind the import of the trust they hold, and as unworthy to possess it as if the sordid hucksterings of all their little governments—each one a kingdom in its small depravity—were brought into a heap for evidence against them.

Martin by degrees became so far awake, that he had a sense

of a terrible oppression on his mind; an imperfect dream that he had murdered a particular friend, and couldn't get rid of the body. When his eyes opened it was staring him full in the face. There was the horrible Hominy talking deep truths in a melodious snuffle, and pouring forth her mental endowments to such an extent that the Major's bitterest enemy, hearing her, would have forgiven him from the bottom of his heart. Martin might have done something desperate if the gong had not sounded for supper; but sound it did most opportunely; and having stationed Mrs. Hominy at the upper end of the table, he took refuge at the lower end himself; whence, after a hasty meal, he stole away, while the lady was yet busied with dried beef and a saucer-full of pickled fixings.

It would be difficult to give an adequate idea of Mrs. Hominy's freshness next day, or of the avidity with which she went headlong into moral philosophy at breakfast. Some little additional degree of asperity, perhaps, was visible in her features, but not more than the pickles would have naturally produced. All that day she clung to Martin. She sat beside him while he received his friends (for there was another Reception, yet more numerous than the former), propounded theories, and answered imaginary objections, so that Martin really began to think he must be dreaming, and speaking for two; she quoted interminable passages from certain essays on government, written by herself; used the Major's pocket-handkerchief as if the snuffle were a temporary malady, of which she was determined to rid herself by some means or other; and, in short, was such a remarkable companion, that Martin quite settled it between himself and his conscience, that in any new settlement it would be absolutely necessary to have such a person knocked on the head for the general peace of society.

In the meantime Mark was busy, from early in the morning until late at night, in getting on board the steamboat such provisions, tools, and other necessaries, as they had been forewarned it would be wise to take. The purchase of these things, and the settlement of their bill at the National, reduced their finances to so low an ebb, that if the captain had delayed his departure any longer, they would have been in almost as bad a plight as the unfortunate poorer emigrants, who (seduced on board by solemn advertisement) had been living on the lower deck a whole week, and exhausting their miserable stock of provisions before the voyage commenced. There they were, all huddled together with the engine and the fires. Farmers who had never seen a plough; woodmen who had never used an axe; builders who couldn't make a box; cast out of their own land, with not a hand to aid them: newly come into an unknown world, children in helplessness, but men in wants, with younger children at their backs, to live or die as it might happen!

The morning came, and they would start at noon. Noon came, and they would start at night. But nothing is eternal in this world: not even the procrastination of an American skipper: and at night all was ready.

Dispirited and weary to the last degree, but a greater lion than ever (he had done nothing all the afternoon but answer letters from strangers: half of them about nothing: half about borrowing money: and all requiring an instantaneous reply), Martin walked down to the wharf, through a concourse of people, with Mrs. Hominy upon his arm; and went on board. But Mark was bent on solving the riddle of this lionship, if he could; and so, not without the risk of being left behind, ran back to the hotel.

Captain Kedgick was sitting in the colonnade, with a julep on his knee, and a cigar in his mouth. He caught Mark's eye, and said:

'Why, what the 'Tarnal brings you here?'

'I'll tell you plainly what it is, Captain,' said Mark. 'I want to ask you a question.'

'A man may *ask* a question, so he may,' returned Kedgick: strongly implying that another man might not answer a question, so he mightn't.

'What have they been making so much of him for, now?' said Mark, slyly, 'Come!'

'Our people like ex-citement,' answered Kedgick, sucking his cigar.

'But how has he excited 'em?' asked Mark.

The Captain looked at him as if he were half inclined to unburden his mind of a capital joke.

'You air a-going?' he said.

'Going!' cried Mark. 'Ain't every moment precious?'

'Our people like ex-citement,' said the Captain, whispering. 'He ain't like emigrants in gin'ral; and he excited 'em along of this;' he winked and burst into a smothered laugh; 'along of this. Scadder is a smart man, and—and—nobody as goes to Eden ever comes back a-live!'

The wharf was close at hand, and at that instant Mark could hear them shouting out his name; could even hear Martin calling to him to make haste, or they would be separated. It was too late to mend the matter, or put any face upon it but the best. He gave the Captain a parting benediction, and ran off like a race-horse.

'Mark! Mark!' cried Martin.

'Here am I, sir!' shouted Mark, suddenly replying from the edge of the quay, and leaping at a bound on board. 'Never was half so jolly, sir. All right. Haul in! Go ahead!'

The sparks from the wood fire streamed upward from the two chimneys, as if the vessel were a great firework just lighted; and they roared away upon the dark water.

CHAPTER XXIII

Martin and his partner take possession of their estate. The joyful occasion involves some further account of Eden

THERE happened to be on board the steamboat several gentlemen passengers, of the same stamp as Martin's New York friend Mr. Bevan; and in their society he was cheerful and happy. They released him as well as they could from the intellectual entanglements of Mrs. Hominy; and exhibited, in all they said and did, so much good sense and high feeling, that he could not like them too well. 'If this were a republic of Intellect and Worth,' he said, 'instead of vapouring and jobbing, they would not want the levers to keep it in motion.'

'Having good tools, and using bad ones,' returned Mr. Tapley, 'would look as if they was rather a poor sort of carpenters, sir, wouldn't it?'

Martin nodded. 'As if their work were infinitely above their powers and purpose, Mark; and they botched it in consequence.'

'The best on it is,' said Mark, 'that when they do happen to make a decent stroke; such as better workmen, with no such opportunities, make every day of their lives and think nothing of; they begin to sing out so surprising loud. Take notice of my words, sir. If ever the defaulting part of this here country pays its debts—along of finding that not paying 'em won't do in a commercial point of view, you see, and is inconvenient in its consequences—they'll take such a shine out of it, and make such bragging speeches, that a man might suppose no borrowed money had ever been paid afore, since the world was first begun. That's the way they gammon each other, sir. Bless you, *I* know 'em. Take notice of my words, now!'

'You seem to be growing profoundly sagacious!' cried Martin, laughing.

'Whether that is,' thought Mark, 'because I'm a day's journey nearer Eden, and am brightening up afore I die, I can't say. P'rhaps by the time I get there I shall have growed into a prophet.'

He gave no utterance to these sentiments; but the excessive joviality they inspired within him, and the merriment they brought upon his shining face, were quite enough for Martin.

Although he might sometimes profess to make light of his partner's inexhaustible cheerfulness, and might sometimes, as in the case of Zephaniah Scadder, find him too jocose a commentator, he was always sensible of the effect of his example in rousing him to hopefulness and courage. Whether he were in the humour to profit by it, mattered not a jot. It was contagious, and he could not choose but be affected.

At first they parted with some of their passengers once or twice a day, and took in others to replace them. But by degrees, the towns upon their route became more thinly scattered; and for many hours together they would see no other habitations than the huts of the wood-cutters, where the vessel stopped for fuel. Sky, wood, and water all the livelong day; and heat that blistered everything it touched.

On they toiled through great solitudes, where the trees upon the banks grew thick and close; and floated in the stream; and held up shrivelled arms from out the river's depths; and slid down from the margin of the land, half growing, half decaying, in the miry water. On through the weary day and melancholy night: beneath the burning sun, and in the mist and vapour of the evening: on, until return appeared impossible, and restoration to their home a miserable dream.

They had now but few people on board, and these few were as flat, as dull, and stagnant, as the vegetation that oppressed their eyes. No sound of cheerfulness or hope was heard; no pleasant talk beguiled the tardy time; no little group made common cause against the dull depression of the scene. But that, at certain periods, they swallowed food together from a common trough, it might have been old Charon's boat, conveying melancholy shades to judgment.

At length they drew near New Thermopylæ; where, that same evening, Mrs. Hominy would disembark. A gleam of comfort sunk into Martin's bosom when she told him this. Mark needed none; but he was not displeased.

It was almost night when they came alongside the landing-place. A steep bank with an hotel like a barn on the top of it; a wooden store or two; and a few scattered sheds.

'You sleep here to-night, and go on in the morning, I suppose, ma'am?' said Martin.

'Where should I go on to?' cried the mother of the modern Gracchi.

'To New Thermopylæ.'

'My! ain't I there?' said Mrs. Hominy.

Martin looked for it all round the darkening panorama, but he couldn't see it, and was obliged to say so.

'Why that's it!' cried Mrs. Hominy, pointing to the sheds just mentioned.

'*That!*' exclaimed Martin.

'Ah! that; and work it which way you will, it whips Eden,' said Mrs. Hominy, nodding her head with great expression.

The married Miss Hominy, who had come on board with her husband, gave to this statement her most unqualified support, as did that gentleman also. Martin gratefully declined their invitation to regale himself at their house during the half hour of the vessel's stay; and having escorted Mrs. Hominy and the red pocket-handkerchief (which was still on active service) safely across the gangway, returned in a thoughtful mood to watch the emigrants as they removed their goods ashore.

Mark, as he stood beside him, glanced in his face from time to time; anxious to discover what effect this dialogue had had upon him, and not unwilling that his hopes should be dashed before they reached their destination, so that the blow he feared might be broken in its fall. But saving that he sometimes looked up quickly at the poor erections on the hill, he gave him no clue to what was passing in his mind, until they were again upon their way.

'Mark,' he said then, 'are there really none but ourselves on board this boat who are bound for Eden?'

'None at all, sir. Most of 'em, as you know, have stopped short; and the few that are left are going further on. What matters that! More room there for us, sir.'

'Oh, to be sure!' said Martin. 'But I was thinking'—and there he paused.

'Yes, sir?' observed Mark.

'How odd it was that the people should have arranged to try their fortune at a wretched hole like that, for instance, when there is such a much better, and such a very different kind of place, near at hand, as one may say.'

He spoke in a tone so very different from his usual confidence, and with such an obvious dread of Mark's reply, that the good-natured fellow was full of pity.

'Why, you know, sir,' said Mark, as gently as he could by any means insinuate the observation, 'we must guard against being too sanguine. There's no occasion for it, either, because we're determined to make the best of everything, after we know the worst of it. Ain't we, sir?'

Martin looked at him, but answered not a word.

'Even Eden, you know, ain't all built,' said Mark.

'In the name of Heaven, man,' cried Martin angrily, 'don't talk of Eden in the same breath with that place. Are you mad? There—God forgive me!—don't think harshly of me for my temper!'

After that, he turned away, and walked to and fro upon the deck full two hours. Nor did he speak again, except to say 'Good night,' until next day; nor even then upon this subject, but on other topics quite foreign to the purpose.

As they proceeded further on their track, and came more and more towards their journey's end, the monotonous desolation of the scene increased to that degree, that for any redeeming feature it presented to their eyes, they might have entered, in the body, on the grim domains of Giant Despair. A flat morass, bestrewn with fallen timber; a marsh on which the good growth of the earth seemed to have been wrecked and cast away, that from its decomposing ashes vile and ugly things might rise; where the very trees took the aspect of huge weeds, begotten of the slime from which they sprung, by the hot sun that burnt them up; where fatal maladies, seeking whom they might infect, came forth at night in misty shapes, and creeping out upon the water, hunted them like spectres until day; where even the blessed sun, shining down on festering elements of corruption and disease, became a horror; this was the realm of Hope through which they moved.

At last they stopped. At Eden too. The waters of the Deluge might have left it but a week before: so choked with slime and matted growth was the hideous swamp which bore that name.

There being no depth of water close in shore, they landed from the vessel's boat, with all their goods beside them. There were a few log-houses visible among the dark trees: the best, a cow-shed or a rude stable. But for the wharves, the market-place, the public buildings!

'Here comes an Edener,' said Mark. 'He'll get us help to carry these things up. Keep a good heart, sir. Hallo there!'

The man advanced toward them through the thickening gloom, very slowly: leaning on a stick. As he drew nearer, they observed that he was pale and worn, and that his anxious eyes were deeply sunken in his head. His dress of homespun blue hung about him in rags; his feet and head were bare. He sat down on a stump half-way, and beckoned them to come to him. When they complied, he put his hand upon his side as if in pain, and while he fetched his breath stared at them, wondering.

'Strangers!' he exclaimed, as soon as he could speak.

'The very same,' said Mark. 'How are you, sir?'

'I've had the fever very bad,' he answered faintly. 'I haven't stood upright these many weeks. Those are your notions I see,' pointing to their property.

'Yes, sir,' said Mark, 'they are. You couldn't recommend us some one as would lend a hand to help carry 'em up to the—to the town, could you, sir?'

'My eldest son would do it if he could,' replied the man; 'but to-day he has his chill upon him, and is lying wrapped up in the blankets. My youngest died last week.'

'I'm sorry for it, governor, with all my heart,' said Mark, shaking him by the hand. 'Don't mind us. Come along with me, and I'll give you an arm back. The goods is safe enough, sir:' to Martin: 'there ain't many people about, to make away with 'em. What a comfort that is!'

'No,' cried the man. 'You must look for such folk here,' knocking his stick upon the ground, 'or yonder in the bush, towards the north. We've buried most of 'em. The rest have gone away. Them that we have here, don't come out at night.'

'The night air ain't quite wholesome, I suppose?' said Mark.

'It's deadly poison,' was the settler's answer.

Mark showed no more uneasiness than if it had been commended to him as ambrosia; but he gave the man his arm, and as they went along explained to him the nature of their purchase, and inquired where it lay. Close to his own log-house, he said: so close that he had used their dwelling as a store-house for some corn: they must excuse it that night, but he would endeavour to get it taken out upon the morrow. He then gave them to understand, as an additional scrap of local chit-chat, that he had buried the last proprietor with his own hands; a piece of information which Mark also received without the least abatement of his equanimity.

In a word, he conducted them to a miserable cabin, rudely constructed of the trunks of trees; the door of which had either fallen down or been carried away long ago; and which was consequently open to the wild landscape and the dark night. Saving for the little store he had mentioned, it was perfectly bare of all furniture; but they had left a chest upon the landing-place, and he gave them a rude torch in lieu of candle. This latter acquisition Mark planted in the earth, and then declaring that the mansion 'looked quite comfortable,' hurried Martin off again to help bring up the chest. And all the way to the landing-place and back, Mark talked incessantly: as if he would infuse into his partner's breast some faint belief that they had arrived under the most auspicious and cheerful of all imaginable circumstances.

But many a man who would have stood within a home dismantled, strong in his passion and design of vengeance, has had the firmness of his nature conquered by the razing of an air-built castle. When the log-hut received them for the second time, Martin lay down upon the ground, and wept aloud.

'Lord love you, sir!' cried Mr. Tapley, in great terror; 'Don't do that! Don't do that, sir! Anything but that! It never helped man, woman, or child, over the lowest fence yet, sir, and it never will. Besides its being of no use to you, it's worse than of no use to me, for the least sound of it will knock me flat down. I can't stand up agin it, sir. Anything but that!'

There is no doubt he spoke the truth, for the extraordinary alarm with which he looked at Martin as he paused upon his knees before the chest, in the act of unlocking it, to say these words, sufficiently confirmed him.

'I ask your forgiveness a thousand times, my dear fellow,' said Martin. 'I couldn't have helped it, if death had been the penalty.'

'Ask my forgiveness!' said Mark, with his accustomed cheerfulness, as he proceeded to unpack the chest. 'The head partner a-asking forgiveness of Co., eh? There must be something wrong in the firm when that happens. I must have the books inspected, and the accounts gone over immediate. Here we are. Everything in its proper place. Here's the salt pork. Here's the biscuit. Here's the whiskey. Uncommon good it smells too. Here's the tin pot. This tin pot's a small fortun' in itself! Here's the blankets. Here's the axe. Who says we ain't got a first-rate fit out? I feel as if I was a cadet gone out to Indy, and my noble father was chairman of the Board of Directors. Now, when I've got some water from the stream afore the door and mixed the grog,' cried Mark, running out

to suit the action to the word, 'there's a supper ready, comprising every delicacy of the season. Here we are, sir, all complete. For what we are going to receive, et cetrer. Lord bless
you, sir, it's very like a gipsy party!'

It was impossible not to take heart, in the company of such
a man as this. Martin sat upon the ground beside the box; took
out his knife; and ate and drank sturdily.

'Now you see,' said Mark, when they had made a hearty
meal; 'with your knife and mine, I sticks this blanket right
afore the door, or where, in a state of high civilisation, the
door would be. And very neat it looks. Then I stops the aper-
ture below, by putting the chest agin it. And very neat *that*
looks. Then there's your blanket, sir. Then here's mine. And
what's to hinder our passing a good night?'

For all his light-hearted speaking, it was long before he slept
himself. He wrapped his blanket round him, put the axe ready
to his hand, and lay across the threshold of the door: too
anxious and too watchful to close his eyes. The novelty of their
dreary situation, the dread of some rapacious animal or human
enemy, the terrible uncertainty of their means of subsistence,
the apprehension of death, the immense distance and the hosts
of obstacles between themselves and England, were fruitful
sources of disquiet in the deep silence of the night. Though
Martin would have had him think otherwise, Mark felt that
he was waking also, and a prey to the same reflections. This
was almost worse than all, for if he began to brood over their
miseries instead of trying to make head against them, there
could be little doubt that such a state of mind would power-
fully assist the influence of the pestilent climate. Never had the
light of day been half so welcome to his eyes, as when awaking
from a fitful doze, Mark saw it shining through the blanket in
the doorway.

He stole out gently, for his companion was sleeping now;
and having refreshed himself by washing in the river, where it
flowed before the door, took a rough survey of the settlement.
There were not above a score of cabins in the whole; half of
these appeared untenanted; all were rotten and decayed. The
most tottering, abject, and forlorn among them was called,
with great propriety, the Bank, and National Credit Office.
It had some feeble props about it, but was settling deep down
in the mud, past all recovery.

Here and there an effort had been made to clear the land,

The thriving City of Eden as it appeared in Fact
(*p. 382*)

and something like a field had been marked out, where, among the stumps and ashes of burnt trees, a scanty crop of Indian corn was growing. In some quarters, a snake or zigzag fence had been begun, but in no instance had it been completed; and the fallen logs, half hidden in the soil, lay mouldering away. Three or four meagre dogs, wasted and vexed with hunger; some long-legged pigs, wandering away into the woods in search of food; some children, nearly naked, gazing at him from the huts; were all the living things he saw. A fetid vapour, hot and sickening as the breath of an oven, rose up from the earth, and hung on everything around; and as his foot-prints sunk into the marshy ground, a black ooze started forth to blot them out.

Their own land was mere forest. The trees had grown so thick and close that they shouldered one another out of their places, and the weakest, forced into shapes of strange distortion, languished like cripples. The best were stunted, from the pressure and the want of room; and high about the stems of all grew long rank grass, dank weeds, and frowsy underwood: not divisible into their separate kinds, but tangled all together in a heap; a jungle deep and dark, with neither earth nor water at its roots, but putrid matter, formed of the pulpy offal of the two, and of their own corruption.

He went down to the landing-place where they had left their goods last night; and there he found some half-dozen men —wan and forlorn to look at, but ready enough to assist—who helped him to carry them to the log-house. They shook their heads in speaking of the settlement, and had no comfort to give him. Those who had the means of going away had all deserted it. They who were left had lost their wives, their children, friends, or brothers there, and suffered much themselves. Most of them were ill then; none were the men they had been once. They frankly offered their assistance and advice, and, leaving him for that time, went sadly off upon their several tasks.

Martin was by this time stirring; but he had greatly changed, even in one night. He was very pale and languid; he spoke of pains and weakness in his limbs, and complained that his sight was dim, and his voice feeble. Increasing in his own briskness as the prospect grew more and more dismal, Mark brought away a door from one of the deserted houses, and fitted it to their own habitation; then went back again for a rude bench he had observed, with which he presently returned in triumph; and having put this piece of furniture outside the house, arranged the notable tin pot and other such movables upon it, that it might represent a dresser or a sideboard. Greatly satisfied with this arrangement, he next rolled their cask of flour into the house, and set it up on end in one corner, where it served for a side-table. No better dining-table could be required than the chest, which he solemnly devoted to that useful service thenceforth. Their blankets, clothes, and the like, he hung on pegs and nails. And lastly, he brought forth a great placard (which Martin in the exultation of his heart had prepared with his own hands at the National Hotel), bearing the inscription, CHUZZLEWIT & CO., ARCHITECTS AND SURVEYORS, which he displayed upon the most conspicuous part of the premises, with as much gravity as if the thriving city of Eden had a real existence, and they expected to be overwhelmed with business.

'These here tools,' said Mark, bringing forward Martin's case of instruments and sticking the compasses upright in a stump before the door, 'shall be set out in the open air to show that we come provided. And now, if any gentleman wants a house built, he'd better give his orders, afore we're other ways bespoke.'

Considering the intense heat of the weather, this was not a bad morning's work; but without pausing for a moment, though he was streaming at every pore, Mark vanished into the house again, and presently reappeared with a hatchet: intent on performing some impossibilities with that implement.

'Here's a ugly old tree in the way, sir,' he observed, 'which'll be all the better down. We can build the oven in the afternoon. There never was such a handy spot for clay as Eden is. That's convenient, anyhow.'

But Martin gave him no answer. He had sat the whole time with his head upon his hands, gazing at the current as it rolled swiftly by; thinking, perhaps, how fast it moved towards the open sea, the high road to the home he never would behold again.

Not even the vigorous strokes which Mark dealt at the tree awoke him from his mournful meditation. Finding all his endeavours to rouse him of no use, Mark stopped in his work and came towards him.

'Don't give in, sir,' said Mr. Tapley.

'Oh, Mark,' returned his friend, 'what have I done in all my life that has deserved this heavy fate?'

'Why, sir,' returned Mark, 'for the matter of that, ev'rybody as is here might say the same thing; many of 'em with better reason p'raps than you or me. Hold up, sir. Do something. Couldn't you ease your mind, now, don't you think, by making some personal obserwations in a letter to Scadder?'

'No,' said Martin, shaking his head sorrowfully: 'I am past that.'

'But if you're past that already,' returned Mark, 'you must be ill, and ought to be attended to.'

'Don't mind me,' said Martin. 'Do the best you can for yourself. You'll soon have only yourself to consider. And then God speed you home, and forgive me for bringing you here! I am destined to die in this place. I felt it the instant I set foot upon the shore. Sleeping or waking, Mark, I dreamed it all last night.'

'I said you must be ill,' returned Mark, tenderly, 'and now I'm sure of it. A touch of fever and ague caught on these rivers, I dare say; but bless you, *that*'s nothing. It's only a seasoning; and we must all be seasoned, one way or another. That's religion, that is, you know,' said Mark.

He only sighed and shook his head.

'Wait half a minute,' said Mark cheerily, 'till I run up to one of our neighbours and ask what's best to be took, and borrow a little of it to give you; and to-morrow you'll find yourself as strong as ever again. I won't be gone a minute. Don't give in while I'm away, whatever you do!'

Throwing down his hatchet, he sped away immediately, but stopped when he had got a little distance, and looked back: then hurried on again.

'Now, Mr. Tapley,' said Mark, giving himself a tremendous blow in the chest by way of reviver, 'just you attend to what I've got to say. Things is looking about as bad as they *can* look, young man. You'll not have such another opportunity for showing your jolly disposition, my fine fellow, as long as you live. And therefore, Tapley, Now's your time to come out strong; or Never!'

CHAPTER XXIV

Reports progress in certain homely matters of Love, Hatred, Jealousy, and Revenge

'HALLO, Pecksniff!' cried Mr. Jonas from the parlour. 'Isn't somebody a-going to open that precious old door of yours?'

'Immediately, Mr. Jonas. Immediately.'

'Ecod,' muttered the orphan, 'not before it's time neither. Whoever it is, has knocked three times, and each one loud enough to wake the—' he had such a repugnance to the idea of waking the Dead, that he stopped even then with the words upon his tongue, and said, instead, 'the Seven Sleepers.'

'Immediately, Mr. Jonas; immediately,' repeated Pecksniff. 'Thomas Pinch:' he couldn't make up his mind, in his great agitation, whether to call Tom his dear friend or a villain, so he shook his fist at him *pro tem.*: 'go up to my daughters' room, and tell them who is here. Say, Silence. Silence! Do you hear me, sir?'

'Directly, sir!' cried Tom, departing, in a state of much amazement, on his errand.

'You'll—ha, ha, ha!—you'll excuse me, Mr. Jonas, if I close this door a moment, will you?' said Pecksniff. 'This may be a professional call. Indeed I am pretty sure it is. Thank you.' Then Mr. Pecksniff, gently warbling a rustic stave, put on his garden hat, seized a spade, and opened the street door: calmly appearing on the threshold, as if he thought he had, from his vineyard, heard a modest rap, but was not quite certain.

Seeing a gentleman and lady before him, he started back in as much confusion as a good man with a crystal conscience might betray in mere surprise. Recognition came upon him the next moment, and he cried:

'Mr. Chuzzlewit! Can I believe my eyes! My dear sir; my good sir! A joyful hour, a happy hour indeed. Pray, my dear sir, walk in. You find me in my garden-dress. You will excuse it, I know. It is an ancient pursuit, gardening. Primitive, my dear sir; or, if I am not mistaken, Adam was the first of our calling. *My* Eve, I grieve to say, is no more, sir; but:' here he pointed to his spade, and shook his head, as if he were not cheerful without an effort: 'but I do a little bit of Adam still.'

He had by this time got them into the best parlour, where the portrait by Spiller, and the bust by Spoker, were.

'My daughters,' said Mr. Pecksniff, 'will be overjoyed. If I could feel weary upon such a theme, I should have been worn out long ago, my dear sir, by their constant anticipation of this happiness, and their repeated allusions to our meeting at Mrs. Todgers's. Their fair young friend, too,' said Mr. Pecksniff, 'whom they so desire to know and love—indeed to know her, *is* to love—I hope I see her well. I hope in saying, "Welcome to my humble roof!" I find some echo in her own sentiments. If features are an index to the heart, I have no fears of that. An extremely engaging expression of countenance, Mr. Chuzzlewit, my dear sir; very much so!'

'Mary,' said the old man, 'Mr. Pecksniff flatters you. But flattery from him is worth the having. He is not a dealer in it, and it comes from his heart. We thought Mr.——'

'Pinch,' said Mary.

'Mr. Pinch would have arrived before us, Pecksniff.'

'He did arrive before you, my dear sir,' retorted Pecksniff, raising his voice for the edification of Tom upon the stairs, 'and was about, I dare say, to tell me of your coming, when I begged him first to knock at my daughters' chamber, and inquire after Charity, my dear child, who is not so well as I could wish. No,' said Mr. Pecksniff, answering their looks, 'I am sorry to say, she is not. It is merely an hysterical affection; nothing more. I am not uneasy. Mr. Pinch! Thomas!' exclaimed Pecksniff, in his kindest accents. 'Pray come in. I shall make no stranger of you. Thomas is a friend of mine, of rather long-standing, Mr. Chuzzlewit, you must know.'

'Thank you, sir,' said Tom. 'You introduce me very kindly, and speak of me in terms of which I am very proud.'

'Old Thomas!' cried his master, pleasantly. 'God bless you!'

Tom reported that the young ladies would appear directly, and that the best refreshments which the house afforded were even then in preparation, under their joint superintendence. While he was speaking, the old man looked at him intently, though with less harshness than was common to him; nor did the mutual embarrassment of Tom and the young lady, to whatever cause he attributed it, seem to escape his observation.

'Pecksniff,' he said after a pause, rising and taking him aside towards the window, 'I was much shocked on hearing of my

P

brother's death. We had been strangers for many years. My only comfort is, that he must have lived the happier and better man for having associated no hopes or schemes with me. Peace to his memory! We were playfellows once; and it would have been better for us both if we had died then.'

Finding him in this gentle mood, Mr. Pecksniff began to see another way out of his difficulties, besides the casting overboard of Jonas.

'That any man, my dear sir, could possibly be the happier for not knowing you,' he returned, 'you will excuse my doubting. But that Mr. Anthony, in the evening of his life, was happier in the affection of his excellent son—a pattern, my dear sir, a pattern to all sons—and in the care of a distant relation who, however lowly in his means of serving him, had no bounds to his inclination; *I* can inform you.'

'How's this?' said the old man. 'You are not a legatee?'

'You don't,' said Mr. Pecksniff, with a melancholy pressure of his hand, 'quite understand my nature yet, I find. No, sir, I am not a legatee. I am proud to say I am not a legatee. I am proud to say that neither of my children is a legatee. And yet, sir, I was with him at his own request. *He* understood me somewhat better, sir. He wrote and said, "I am sick. I am sinking. Come to me!" I went to him. I sat beside his bed, sir, and I stood beside his grave. Yes, at the risk of offending even *you*, I did it, sir. Though the avowal should lead to our instant separation, and to the severing of those tender ties between us which have recently been formed, I make it. But I am not a legatee,' said Mr. Pecksniff, smiling dispassionately; 'and I never expected to be a legatee. I knew better!'

'His son a pattern!' cried old Martin. 'How can you tell me that? My brother had in his wealth the usual doom of wealth, and root of misery. He carried his corrupting influence with him, go where he would; and shed it round him, even on his hearth. It made of his own child a greedy expectant, who measured every day and hour the lessening distance between his father and the grave, and cursed his tardy progress on that dismal road.'

'No!' cried Mr. Pecksniff, boldly. 'Not at all, sir!'

'But I saw that shadow in his house,' said Martin Chuzzlewit, 'the last time we met, and warned him of its presence. I know it when I see it, do I not? I, who have lived within it all these years!'

'I deny it,' Mr. Pecksniff answered, warmly. 'I deny it altogether. That bereaved young man is now in this house, sir, seeking in change of scene the peace of mind he has lost. Shall I be backward in doing justice to that young man, when even undertakers and coffin-makers have been moved by the conduct he has exhibited; when even mutes have spoken in his praise, and the medical man hasn't known what to do with himself in the excitement of his feelings! There is a person of the name of Gamp, sir—Mrs. Gamp—ask her. She saw Mr. Jonas in a trying time. Ask *her*, sir. She is respectable, but not sentimental, and will state the fact. A line addressed to Mrs. Gamp, at the Bird-shop, Kingsgate Street, High Holborn, London, will meet with every attention, I have no doubt. Let her be examined, my good sir. Strike, but hear! Leap, Mr. Chuzzlewit, but look! Forgive me, my dear sir,' said Mr. Pecksniff, taking both his hands, 'if I am warm; but I am honest, and must state the truth.'

In proof of the character he gave himself, Mr. Pecksniff suffered tears of honesty to ooze out of his eyes.

The old man gazed at him for a moment with a look of wonder, repeating to himself, 'Here now! In this house!' But he mastered his surprise, and said, after a pause:

'Let me see him.'

'In a friendly spirit, I hope?' said Mr. Pecksniff. 'Forgive me, sir, but he is in the receipt of my humble hospitality.'

'I said,' replied the old man, 'let me see him. If I were disposed to regard him in any other than a friendly spirit, I should have said, keep us apart.'

'Certainly, my dear sir. So you would. You are frankness itself, I know. I will break this happiness to him,' said Mr. Pecksniff, as he left the room, 'if you will excuse me for a minute, gently.'

He paved the way to the disclosure so very gently, that a quarter of an hour elapsed before he returned with Mr. Jonas. In the meantime the young ladies had made their appearance, and the table had been set out for the refreshment of the travellers.

Now, however well Mr. Pecksniff, in his morality, had taught Jonas the lesson of dutiful behaviour to his uncle, and however perfectly Jonas, in the cunning of his nature, had learnt it, that young man's bearing, when presented to his father's brother, was anything but manly or engaging.

Perhaps, indeed, so singular a mixture of defiance and obse-quiousness, of fear and hardihôod, of dogged sullenness and an attempt at cringing and propitiation, never was expressed in any one human figure as in that of Jonas, when, having raised his downcast eyes to Martin's face, he let them fall again, and uneasily closing and unclosing his hands without a moment's intermission, stood swinging himself from side to side, waiting to be addressed.

'Nephew,' said the old man. 'You have been a dutiful son, I hear.'

'As dutiful as sons in general, I suppose,' returned Jonas, looking up and down once more. 'I don't brag to have been any better than other sons; but I haven't been any worse, I dare say.'

'A pattern to all sons, I am told,' said the old man, glancing towards Mr. Pecksniff.

'Ecod!' said Jonas, looking up again for a moment, and shaking his head, 'I've been as good a son as ever you were a brother. It's the pot and the kettle, if you come to that.'

'You speak bitterly, in the violence of your regret,' said Martin, after a pause. 'Give me your hand.'

Jonas did so, and was almost at his ease. 'Pecksniff,' he whispered, as they drew their chairs about the table; 'I gave him as good as he brought, eh? He had better look at home, before he looks out of window, I think?'

Mr. Pecksniff only answered by a nudge of the elbow, which might either be construed into an indignant remonstrance or a cordial assent; but which, in any case, was an emphatic admonition to his chosen son-in-law to be silent. He then pro-ceeded to do the honours of the house with his accustomed ease and amiability.

But not even Mr. Pecksniff's guileless merriment could set such a party at their ease, or reconcile materials so utterly discordant and conflicting as those with which he had to deal. The unspeakable jealousy and hatred which that night's explanation had sown in Charity's breast, was not to be so easily kept down; and more than once it showed itself in such intensity, as seemed to render a full disclosure of all the cir-cumstances then and there, impossible to be avoided. The beauteous Merry, too, with all the glory of her conquest fresh upon her, so probed and lanced the rankling disappointment of her sister by her capricious airs and thousand little trials of

Mr. Jonas's obedience, that she almost goaded her into a fit of madness, and obliged her to retire from table in a burst of passion, hardly less vehement than that to which she had abandoned herself in the first tumult of her wrath. The constraint imposed upon the family by the presence among them for the first time of Mary Graham (for by that name old Martin Chuzzlewit had introduced her) did not at all improve this state of things: gentle and quiet though her manner was. Mr. Pecksniff's situation was peculiarly trying: for, what with having constantly to keep the peace between his daughters; to maintain a reasonable show of affection and unity in his household; to curb the growing ease and gaiety of Jonas, which vented itself in sundry insolences towards Mr. Pinch, and an indefinable coarseness of manner in reference to Mary (they being the two dependants); to make no mention at all of his having perpetually to conciliate his rich old relative, and to smooth down, or explain away, some of the ten thousand bad appearances and combinations of bad appearances, by which they were surrounded on that unlucky evening—what with having to do this, and it would be difficult to sum up how much more, without the least relief or assistance from anybody, it may be easily imagined that Mr. Pecksniff had in his enjoyment something more than that usual portion of alloy which is mixed up with the best of men's delights. Perhaps he had never in his life felt such relief as when old Martin, looking at his watch, announced that it was time to go.

'We have rooms,' he said, 'at the Dragon, for the present. I have a fancy for the evening walk. The nights are dark just now: perhaps Mr. Pinch would not object to light us home?'

'My dear sir!' cried Pecksniff, '*I* shall be delighted. Merry, my child, the lantern.'

'The lantern, if you please, my dear,' said Martin; 'but I couldn't think of taking your father out of doors to-night; and, to be brief, I won't.'

Mr. Pecksniff already had his hat in his hand, but it was so emphatically said that he paused.

'I take Mr. Pinch, or go alone,' said Martin. 'Which shall it be?'

'It shall be Thomas, sir,' cried Pecksniff, 'since you are so resolute upon it. Thomas, my friend, be very careful, if you please.'

Tom was in some need of this injunction, for he felt so

nervous, and trembled to such a degree, that he found it difficult to hold the lantern. How much more difficult when, at the old man's bidding, she drew her hand through his, Tom Pinch's, arm!

'And so, Mr. Pinch,' said Martin, on the way, 'you are very comfortably situated here; are you?'

Tom answered, with even more than his usual enthusiasm, that he was under obligations to Mr. Pecksniff which the devotion of a lifetime would but imperfectly repay.

'How long have you known my nephew?' asked Martin.

'Your nephew, sir?' faltered Tom.

'Mr. Jonas Chuzzlewit,' said Mary.

'Oh dear, yes,' cried Tom, greatly relieved, for his mind was running upon Martin. 'Certainly. I never spoke to him before to-night, sir!'

'Perhaps half a lifetime will suffice for the acknowledgment of *his* kindness,' observed the old man.

Tom felt that this was a rebuff for him, and could not but understand it as a left-handed hit at his employer. So he was silent. Mary felt that Mr. Pinch was not remarkable for presence of mind, and that she could not say too little under existing circumstances. So *she* was silent. The old man, disgusted by what in his suspicious nature he considered a shameless and fulsome puff of Mr. Pecksniff, which was a part of Tom's hired service and in which he was determined to persevere, set him down at once for a deceitful, servile, miserable fawner. So *he* was silent. And though they were all sufficiently uncomfortable, it is fair to say that Martin was perhaps the most so; for he had felt kindly towards Tom at first, and had been interested by his seeming simplicity.

'You're like the rest,' he thought, glancing at the face of the unconscious Tom. 'You had nearly imposed upon me, but you have lost your labour. You are too zealous a toad-eater, and betray yourself, Mr. Pinch.'

During the whole remainder of the walk, not another word was spoken. First among the meetings to which Tom had long looked forward with a beating heart, it was memorable for nothing but embarrassment and confusion. They parted at the Dragon door; and sighing as he extinguished the candle in the lantern, Tom turned back again over the gloomy fields.

As he approached the first stile, which was in a lonely part, made very dark by a plantation of young firs, a man slipped past him and went on before. Coming to the stile he stopped, and took his seat upon it. Tom was rather startled, and for a moment stood still; but he stepped forward again immediately, and went close up to him.

It was Jonas; swinging his legs to and fro, sucking the head of a stick, and looking with a sneer at Tom.

'Good gracious me!' cried Tom, 'who would have thought of its being you! You followed us, then?'

'What's that to you?' said Jonas. 'Go to the devil!'

'You are not very civil, I think,' remarked Tom.

'Civil enough for *you*,' retorted Jonas. 'Who are you?'

'One who has as good a right to common consideration as another,' said Tom, mildly.

'You're a liar,' said Jonas. 'You haven't a right to any consideration. You haven't a right to anything. You're a pretty sort of fellow to talk about your rights, upon my soul! Ha, ha! Rights, too!'

'If you proceed in this way,' returned Tom, reddening, 'you will oblige me to talk about my wrongs. But I hope your joke is over.'

'It's the way with you curs,' said Mr. Jonas, 'that when you know a man's in real earnest, you pretend to think he's joking, so that you may turn it off. But that won't do with me. It's too stale. Now just attend to me for a bit, Mr. Pitch, or Witch, or Stitch, or whatever your name is.'

'My name is Pinch,' observed Tom. 'Have the goodness to call me by it.'

'What! You mustn't even be called out of your name, mustn't you!' cried Jonas. 'Pauper 'prentices are looking up, I think. Ecod, we manage 'em a little better in the city!'

'Never mind what you do in the city,' said Tom. 'What have you got to say to me?'

'Just this, Mister Pinch,' retorted Jonas, thrusting his face so close to Tom's that Tom was obliged to retreat a step, 'I advise you to keep your own counsel, and to avoid tittle-tattle, and not to cut in where you're not wanted. I've heard something of you, my friend, and your meek ways; and I recommend you to forget 'em till I am married to one of Pecksniff's gals, and not to curry favour among my relations, but to leave the course clear. You know, when curs won't leave the course clear, they're whipped off; so this is kind advice. Do you understand? Eh? Damme, who are you,' cried Jonas, with increased contempt, 'that you should walk home with *them*, unless it was behind 'em, like any other servant out of livery?'

'Come!' cried Tom, 'I see that you had better get off the stile, and let me pursue my way home. Make room for me, if you please.'

'Don't think it!' said Jonas, spreading out his legs. 'Not till I choose. And I don't choose now. What! You're afraid of my making you split upon some of your babbling just now, are you, Sneak?'

'I am not afraid of many things, I hope,' said Tom; 'and certainly not of anything that you will do. I am not a tale-bearer, and I despise all meanness. You quite mistake me. Ah!' cried Tom, indignantly. 'Is this manly from one in your position to one in mine? Please to make room for me to pass. The less I say, the better.'

'The less you say!' retorted Jonas, dangling his legs the more, and taking no heed of this request. 'You say very little, don't you? Ecod, I should like to know what goes on between you and a vagabond member of my family. There's very little in that too, I dare say!'

'I know no vagabond member of your family,' cried Tom, stoutly.

'You do!' said Jonas.

'I don't,' said Tom. 'Your uncle's namesake, if you mean him, is no vagabond. Any comparison between you and him:' Tom snapped his fingers at him, for he was rising fast in wrath: 'is immeasurably to your disadvantage.'

'Oh indeed!' sneered Jonas. 'And what do you think of his deary, his beggarly leavings, eh, Mister Pinch?'

'I don't mean to say another word, or stay here another instant,' replied Tom.

'As I told you before, you're a liar,' said Jonas, coolly. 'You'll stay here till I give you leave to go. Now, keep where you are, will you?'

He flourished his stick over Tom's head; but in a moment it was spinning harmlessly in the air, and Jonas himself lay sprawling in the ditch. In the momentary struggle for the stick, Tom had brought it into violent contact with his opponent's forehead; and the blood welled out profusely from a deep cut on the temple. Tom was first apprised of this by seeing that he pressed his handkerchief to the wounded part, and staggered as he rose: being stunned.

Balm for the Wounded Orphan

'Are you hurt?' said Tom. 'I am very sorry. Lean on me for a moment. You can do that without forgiving me, if you still bear me malice. But I don't know why; for I never offended you before we met on this spot.'

He made him no answer: not appearing at first to understand him, or even to know that he was hurt, though he several times took his handkerchief from the cut to look vacantly at the blood upon it. After one of these examinations, he looked at Tom, and then there was an expression in his features, which showed that he understood what had taken place, and would remember it.

Nothing more passed between them as they went home. Jonas kept a little in advance, and Tom Pinch sadly followed, thinking of the grief which the knowledge of this quarrel must occasion his excellent benefactor. When Jonas knocked at the door, Tom's heart beat high; higher when Miss Mercy answered it, and seeing her wounded lover, shrieked aloud; higher, when he followed them into the family parlour; higher than at any other time, when Jonas spoke.

'Don't make a noise about it,' he said. 'It's nothing worth mentioning. I didn't know the road; the night's very dark; and just as I came up with Mr. Pinch:' he turned his face towards Tom, but not his eyes: 'I ran against a tree. It's only skin deep.'

'Cold water, Merry, my child!' cried Mr. Pecksniff. 'Brown paper! Scissors! A piece of old linen! Charity, my dear, make a bandage. Bless me, Mr. Jonas!'

'Oh, bother *your* nonsense,' returned the gracious son-in-law elect. 'Be of some use if you can. If you can't, get out!'

Miss Charity, though called upon to lend her aid, sat upright in one corner, with a smile upon her face, and didn't move a finger. Though Mercy laved the wound herself; and Mr. Pecksniff held the patient's head between his two hands, as if without that assistance it must inevitably come in half; and Tom Pinch, in his guilty agitation, shook a bottle of Dutch Drops until they were nothing but English Froth, and in his other hand sustained a formidable carving-knife, really intended to reduce the swelling, but apparently designed for the ruthless infliction of another wound as soon as that was dressed; Charity rendered not the least assistance, nor uttered a word. But when Mr. Jonas's head was bound up, and he had gone to bed, and everybody else had retired, and the house was quiet, Mr. Pinch, as he sat mournfully on his bedstead, ruminating, heard a gentle tap at his door; and opening it, saw her, to his great astonishment, standing before him with her finger on her lip.

'Mr. Pinch,' she whispered. 'Dear Mr. Pinch! Tell me the truth! You did that? There was some quarrel between you, and you struck him? I am sure of it!'

It was the first time she had ever spoken kindly to Tom, in all the many years they had passed together. He was stupefied with amazement.

'Was it so, or not?' she eagerly demanded.

'I was very much provoked,' said Tom.

'Then it was?' cried Charity, with sparkling eyes.

'Ye-yes. We had a struggle for the path,' said Tom. 'But I didn't mean to hurt him so much.'

'Not so much!' she repeated, clenching her hand and stamping her foot, to Tom's great wonder. 'Don't say that. It was brave of you. I honour you for it. If you should ever quarrel again, don't spare him for the world, but beat him down and set your shoe upon him. Not a word of this to anybody. Dear Mr. Pinch, I am your friend from to-night. I am always your friend from this time.'

She turned her flushed face upon Tom to confirm her words by its kindling expression; and seizing his right hand, pressed it to her breast, and kissed it. And there was nothing personal in this to render it at all embarrassing, for even Tom, whose power of observation was by no means remarkable, knew from the energy with which she did it that she would have fondled any hand, no matter how bedaubed or dyed, that had broken the head of Jonas Chuzzlewit.

Tom went into his room, and went to bed, full of uncomfortable thoughts. That there should be any such tremendous division in the family as he knew must have taken place to convert Charity Pecksniff into his friend, for any reason, but, above all, for that which was clearly the real one; that Jonas, who had assailed him with such exceeding coarseness, should have been sufficiently magnanimous to keep the secret of their quarrel; and that any train of circumstances should have led to the commission of an assault and battery by Thomas Pinch upon any man calling himself the friend of Seth Pecksniff; were matters of such deep and painful cogitation that he could not close his eyes. His own violence, in particular, so preyed upon the generous mind of Tom, that coupling it with the many former occasions on which he had given Mr. Pecksniff pain and anxiety (occasions of which that gentleman often reminded him), he really began to regard himself as destined by a mysterious fate to be the evil genius and bad angel of his patron. But he fell asleep at last, and dreamed—new source of waking uneasiness—that he had betrayed his trust, and run away with Mary Graham.

It must be acknowledged that, asleep or awake, Tom's position in reference to this young lady was full of uneasiness. The more he saw of her, the more he admired her beauty, her intelligence, the amiable qualities that even won on the divided house of Pecksniff, and in a few days restored at all events the semblance of harmony and kindness between the angry sisters. When she spoke, Tom held his breath, so eagerly he listened; when she sang, he sat like one entranced. She touched his organ, and from that bright epoch, even it, the old companion of his happiest hours, incapable as he had thought of elevation, began a new and deified existence.

God's love upon thy patience, Tom! Who, that had beheld thee, for three summer weeks, poring through half the deadlong night over the jingling anatomy of that inscrutable old harpsichord in the back parlour, could have missed the entrance to thy secret heart: albeit it was dimly known to thee? Who that had seen the glow upon thy cheek when leaning down to listen, after hours of labour, for the sound of one incorrigible note, thou foundest that it had a voice at last, and wheezed out a flat something, distantly akin to what it ought to be, would not have known that it was destined for no common touch, but one that smote, though gently as an angel's hand, upon the deepest chord within thee! And if a friendly glance—aye, even though it were as guileless as thine own, dear Tom—could but have pierced the twilight of that evening, when, in a voice well tempered to the time, sad, sweet, and low, yet hopeful, she first sang to the altered instrument, and wondered at the change; and thou, sitting apart at the open window, kept a glad silence and a swelling heart; must not that glance have read perforce the dawning of a story, Tom, that it were well for thee had never been begun!

Tom Pinch's situation was not made the less dangerous or difficult, by the fact of no one word passing between them in reference to Martin. Honourably mindful of his promise, Tom gave her opportunities of all kinds. Early and late he was in the church; in her favourite walks; in the village, in the garden, in the meadows; and in any or all of these places he might have spoken freely. But no: at all such times she carefully avoided him, or never came in his way unaccompanied. It could not be that she disliked or distrusted him, for by a thousand little delicate means, too slight for any notice but his own, she singled him out when others were present, and showed herself the very soul of kindness. Could it be that she had broken with Martin, or had never returned his affection, save in his own bold and heightened fancy? Tom's cheek grew red with self-reproach as he dismissed the thought.

All this time old Martin came and went in his own strange manner, or sat among the rest absorbed within himself, and holding little intercourse with any one. Although he was unsocial, he was not wilful in other things, or troublesome, or morose: being never better pleased than when they left him quite unnoticed at his book, and pursued their own amusements in his presence, unreserved. It was impossible to discern in whom he took an interest, or whether he had an interest in any of them. Unless they spoke to him directly, he never showed that he had ears or eyes for anything that passed.

One day the lively Merry, sitting with downcast eyes under a shady tree in the churchyard, whither she had retired after fatiguing herself by the imposition of sundry trials on the temper of Mr. Jonas, felt that a new shadow came between her and the sun. Raising her eyes in the expectation of seeing her betrothed, she was not a little surprised to see old Martin instead. Her surprise was not diminished when he took his seat upon the turf beside her, and opened a conversation thus:

'When are you to be married?'

'Oh! dear Mr. Chuzzlewit, my goodness me! I'm sure I don't know. Not yet awhile, I hope.'

'You hope?' said the old man.

It was very gravely said, but she took it for banter, and giggled excessively.

'Come!' said the old man, with unusual kindness, 'you are young, good-looking, and I think good-natured! Frivolous you are, and love to be, undoubtedly; but you must have some heart.'

'I have not given it all away, I can tell you,' said Merry, nodding her head shrewdly, and plucking up the grass.

'Have you parted with any of it?'

She threw the grass about, and looked another way, but said nothing.

Martin repeated his question.

'Lor, my dear Mr. Chuzzlewit! really you must excuse me! How very odd you are.'

'If it be odd in me to desire to know whether you love the young man whom I understand you are to marry, I *am* very odd,' said Martin. 'For that is certainly my wish.'

'He's such a monster, you know,' said Merry, pouting.

'Then you don't love him?' returned the old man. 'Is that your meaning?'

'Why, my dear Mr. Chuzzlewit, I'm sure I tell him a hundred times a day that I hate him. You must have heard me tell him that.'

'Often,' said Martin.

'And so I do,' cried Merry. 'I do positively.'

'Being at the same time engaged to marry him,' observed the old man.

'Oh yes,' said Merry. 'But I told the wretch—my dear Mr. Chuzzlewit, I told him when he asked me—that if I ever did marry him, it should only be that I might hate and teaze him all my life.'

She had a suspicion that the old man regarded Jonas with anything but favour, and intended these remarks to be extremely captivating. He did not appear, however, to regard them in that light by any means; for when he spoke again, it was in a tone of severity.

'Look about you,' he said, pointing to the graves; 'and remember that from your bridal hour to the day which sees you brought as low as these, and laid in such a bed, there will be no appeal against him. Think, and speak, and act, for once, like an accountable creature. Is any control put upon your inclinations? Are you forced into this match? Are you insidiously advised or tempted to contract it, by any one? I will not ask by whom. By any one?'

'No,' said Merry, shrugging her shoulders. 'I don't know that I am.'

'Don't know that you are! Are you?'

'No,' replied Merry. 'Nobody ever said anything to me about it. If any one had tried to make me have him, I wouldn't have had him at all.'

'I am told that he was at first supposed to be your sister's admirer,' said Martin.

'Oh, good gracious! My dear Mr. Chuzzlewit, it would be very hard to make him, though he *is* a monster, accountable for other people's vanity,' said Merry. 'And poor dear Cherry is the vainest darling!'

'It was her mistake, then?'

'I hope it was,' cried Merry; 'but, all along, the dear child has been so dreadfully jealous, and *so* cross, that, upon my word and honour, it's impossible to please her, and it's of no use trying.'

'Not forced, persuaded, or controlled,' said Martin, thoughtfully. 'And that's true, I see. There is one chance yet. You may have lapsed into this engagement in very giddiness. It may have been the wanton act of a light head. Is that so?'

'My dear Mr. Chuzzlewit,' simpered Merry, 'as to light-headedness, there never was such a feather of a head as mine. It's a perfect balloon, I declare! You never *did*, you know!'

He waited quietly till she had finished, and then said, steadily and slowly, and in a softened voice, as if he would still invite her confidence:

'Have you any wish: or is there anything within your breast that whispers you may form the wish, if you have time to think: to be released from this engagement?'

Again Miss Merry pouted, and looked down, and plucked the grass, and shrugged her shoulders. No. She didn't know that she had. She was pretty sure she hadn't. Quite sure, she might say. She 'didn't mind it.'

'Has it ever occurred to you,' said Martin, 'that your married life may perhaps be miserable, full of bitterness, and most unhappy?'

Merry looked down again; and now she tore the grass up by the roots.

'My dear Mr. Chuzzlewit, what shocking words! Of course, I shall quarrel with him. I should quarrel with any husband. Married people always quarrel, I believe. But as to being miserable, and bitter, and all those dreadful things, you know, why I couldn't be absolutely that, unless he always had the best of it; and I mean to have the best of it myself. I always do now,' cried Merry, nodding her head and giggling very much; 'for I make a perfect slave of the creature.'

'Let it go on,' said Martin, rising. 'Let it go on! I sought to know your mind, my dear, and you have shown it me. I wish you joy. Joy!' he repeated, looking full upon her, and pointing to the wicket-gate where Jonas entered at the moment. And then, without waiting for his nephew, he passed out at another gate, and went away.

'Oh you terrible old man!' cried the facetious Merry to herself. 'What a perfectly hideous monster to be wandering about churchyards in the broad daylight, frightening people out of their wits! Don't come here, Griffin, or I'll go away directly.'

Mr. Jonas was the Griffin. He sat down upon the grass at her side, in spite of this warning, and sulkily inquired:

'What's my uncle been a-talking about?'

'About you,' rejoined Merry. 'He says you're not half good enough for me.'

'Oh yes, I dare say! We all know that. He means to give you some present worth having, I hope. Did he say anything that looked like it?'

'*That* he didn't!' cried Merry, most decisively.

'A stingy old dog he is,' said Jonas. 'Well?'

'Griffin!' cried Miss Mercy, in counterfeit amazement; 'what are you doing, Griffin?'

'Only giving you a squeeze,' said the discomfited Jonas. 'There's no harm in that, I suppose?'

'But there is a great deal of harm in it, if I don't consider it agreeable,' returned his cousin. 'Do go along, will you? You make me so hot!'

Mr. Jonas withdrew his arm; and for a moment looked at her more like a murderer than a lover. But he cleared his brow by degrees, and broke silence with:

'I say, Mel!'

'What do you say, you vulgar thing, you low savage?' cried his fair betrothed.

'When is it to be? I can't afford to go on dawdling about here half my life, I needn't tell you, and Pecksniff says that father's being so lately dead makes very little odds: for we can be married as quiet as we please down here, and my being lonely is a good reason to the neighbours for taking a wife home so soon, especially one that he knew. As to cross-bones (my uncle, I mean), he's sure not to put a spoke in the wheel, whatever we settle on, for he told Pecksniff only this morning, that if *you* liked it he'd nothing at all to say. So, Mel,' said Jonas, venturing on another squeeze; 'when shall it be?'

'Upon my word!' cried Merry.

'Upon my soul, if you like,' said Jonas. 'What do you say to next week, now?'

'To next week! If you had said next quarter, I should have wondered at your impudence.'

'But I didn't say next quarter,' retorted Jonas. 'I said next week.'

'Then, Griffin,' cried Miss Merry, pushing him off, and rising. 'I say no! not next week. It shan't be till I choose, and I may not choose it to be for months. There!'

He glanced up at her from the ground, almost as darkly as he had looked at Tom Pinch; but held his peace.

'No fright of a Griffin with a patch over his eye, shall dictate to me, or have a voice in the matter,' said Merry. 'There!'

Still Mr. Jonas held his peace.

'If it's next month, that shall be the very earliest; but I won't say when it shall be till to-morrow; and if you don't like that, it shall never be at all,' said Merry; 'and if you follow me about and won't leave me alone, it shall never be at all. There! And if you don't do everything I order you to do, it shall never be at all. So don't follow me. There, Griffin!'

And with that, she skipped away, among the trees.

'Ecod, my lady!' said Jonas, looking after her, and biting a piece of straw, almost to powder; 'you'll catch it for this, when you *are* married! It's all very well now—it keeps one on, somehow, and you know it—but I'll pay you off scot and lot by-and-bye. This is a plaguy dull sort of a place for a man to be sitting by himself in. I never could abide a mouldy old churchyard.'

As he turned into the avenue himself, Miss Merry, who was far ahead, happened to look back.

'Ah!' said Jonas, with a sullen smile, and a nod that was not addressed to her. 'Make the most of it while it lasts. Get in your hay while the sun shines. Take your own way as long as it's in your power, my lady!'

CHAPTER XXV

Is in part professional; and furnishes the reader with some valuable hints in relation to the management of a sick chamber

MR. MOULD was surrounded by his household gods. He was enjoying the sweets of domestic repose, and gazing on them with a calm delight. The day being sultry, and the window open, the legs of Mr. Mould were on the window-seat, and his back reclined against the shutter. Over his shining head a handkerchief was drawn, to guard his baldness from the flies. The room was fragrant with the smell of punch, a tumbler of which grateful compound stood upon a small round table, convenient to the hand of Mr. Mould; so deftly mixed, that as his eye looked down into the cool transparent drink, another eye, peering brightly from behind the crisp lemon-peel, looked up at him, and twinkled like a star.

Deep in the City, and within the ward of Cheap, stood Mr. Mould's establishment. His Harem, or, in other words, the common sitting-room of Mrs. Mould and family, was at the back, over the little counting-house behind the shop; abutting on a churchyard small and shady. In this domestic chamber Mr. Mould now sat; gazing, a placid man, upon his punch and home. If, for a moment at a time, he sought a wider prospect, whence he might return with freshened zest to these enjoyments, his moist glance wandered like a sunbeam through a rural screen of scarlet runners, trained on strings before the window; and he looked down, with an artist's eye, upon the graves.

The partner of his life, and daughters twain, were Mr. Mould's companions. Plump as any partridge was each Miss Mould, and Mrs. M. was plumper than the two together. So round and chubby were their fair proportions, that they might have been the bodies once belonging to the angels' faces in the shop below, grown up, with other heads attached to make them mortal. Even their peachy cheeks were puffed out and distended, as though they ought of right to be performing on celestial trumpets. The bodiless cherubs in the shop, who were depicted as constantly blowing those instruments for ever and ever without any lungs, played, it is to be presumed, entirely by ear.

Mr. Mould looked lovingly at Mrs. Mould, who sat hard by, and was a helpmate to him in his punch as in all other things. Each seraph daughter, too, enjoyed her share of his regards, and smiled upon him in return. So bountiful were Mr. Mould's possessions, and so large his stock in trade, that even there, within his household sanctuary, stood a cumbrous press, whose mahogany maw was filled with shrouds, and winding-sheets, and other furniture of funerals. But, though the Misses Mould had been brought up, as one may say, beneath his eye, it had cast no shadow on their timid infancy or blooming youth. Sporting behind the scenes of death and burial from cradle-hood, the Misses Mould knew better. Hatbands, to them, were but so many yards of silk or crape; the final robe but such a quantity of linen. The Misses Mould could idealise a player's habit, or a court-lady's petticoat, or even an act of parliament. But they were not to be taken in by palls. They made them sometimes.

The premises of Mr. Mould were hard of hearing to the boisterous noises in the great main streets, and nestled in a quiet corner, where the City strife became a drowsy hum, that sometimes rose and sometimes fell and sometimes altogether ceased: suggesting to a thoughtful mind a stoppage in Cheap-side. The light came sparkling in among the scarlet runners, as if the churchyard winked at Mr. Mould, and said, 'We understand each other;' and from the distant shop a pleasant sound arose of coffin-making with a low melodious hammer, rat, tat, tat, tat, alike promoting slumber and digestion.

'Quite the buzz of insects,' said Mr. Mould, closing his eyes in a perfect luxury. 'It puts one in mind of the sound of animated nature in the agricultural districts. It's exactly like the woodpecker tapping.'

'The woodpecker tapping the hollow *elm* tree,' observed Mrs. Mould, adapting the words of the popular melody to the description of wood commonly used in the trade.

'Ha, ha!' laughed Mr. Mould. 'Not at all bad, my dear. We shall be glad to hear from you again, Mrs. M. Hollow elm tree, eh! Ha, ha! Very good indeed. I've seen worse than that in the Sunday papers, my love.'

Mrs. Mould, thus encouraged, took a little more of the punch, and handed it to her daughters, who dutifully followed the example of their mother.

'Hollow *elm* tree, eh?' said Mr. Mould, making a slight

motion with his legs in his enjoyment of the joke. It's beech in the song. Elm, eh? Yes, to be sure. Ha, ha, ha! Upon my soul, that's one of the best things I know!' He was so excessively tickled by the jest that he couldn't forget it, but repeated twenty times, 'Elm, eh? Yes, to be sure. Elm, of course. Ha, ha, ha! Upon my life, you know, that ought to be sent to somebody who could make use of it. It's one of the smartest things that ever was said. Hollow *elm* tree, eh? Of course. Very hollow. Ha, ha, ha!'

Here a knock was heard at the room door.

'That's Tacker, *I* know,' said Mrs. Mould, 'by the wheezing he makes. Who that hears him now, would suppose he'd ever had wind enough to carry the feathers on his head! Come in, Tacker.'

'Beg your pardon, ma'am,' said Tacker, looking in a little way. 'I thought our Governor was here.'

'Well! so he is,' cried Mould.

'Oh! I didn't see you, I'm sure,' said Tacker, looking in a little farther. 'You wouldn't be inclined to take a walking one of two, with the plain wood and a tin plate, I suppose?'

'Certainly not,' replied Mr. Mould, 'much too common. Nothing to say to it.'

'I told 'em it was precious low,' observed Mr. Tacker.

'Tell 'em to go somewhere else. We don't do that style of business here,' said Mr. Mould. 'Like their impudence to propose it. Who is it?'

'Why,' returned Tacker, pausing, 'that's where it is, you see. It's the beadle's son-in-law.'

'The beadle's son-in-law, eh?' said Mould. 'Well! I'll do it if the beadle follows in his cocked hat; not else. We carry it off that way, by looking official, but it'll be low enough then. His cocked hat, mind!'

'I'll take care, sir,' rejoined Tacker. 'Oh! Mrs. Gamp's below, and wants to speak to you.'

'Tell Mrs. Gamp to come up-stairs,' said Mould. 'Now, Mrs. Gamp, what's *your* news?'

The lady in question was by this time in the doorway, curtseying to Mrs. Mould. At the same moment a peculiar fragrance was borne upon the breeze, as if a passing fairy had hiccoughed, and had previously been to a wine-vaults.

Mrs. Gamp made no response to Mr. Mould, but curtseyed to Mrs. Mould again, and held up her hands and eyes, as in a devout thanksgiving that she looked so well. She was neatly, but not gaudily attired, in the weeds she had worn when Mr. Pecksniff had the pleasure of making her acquaintance; and was perhaps the turning of a scale more snuffy.

'There are some happy creeturs,' Mrs. Gamp observed, 'as time runs back'ards with, and you are one, Mrs. Mould; not that he need do nothing except use you in his most owldacious way for years to come, I'm sure; for young you are and will be. I says to Mrs. Harris,' Mrs. Gamp continued, 'only t'other day; the last Monday evening fortnight as ever dawned upon this Piljian's Projiss of a mortal wale; I says to Mrs. Harris when she says to me, "Years and our trials, Mrs. Gamp, sets marks upon us all."—"Say not the words, Mrs. Harris, if you and me is to be continual friends, for sech is not the case. Mrs. Mould," I says, making so free, I will confess, as use the name,' (she curtseyed here,) ' " is one of them that goes agen the obserwation straight; and never, Mrs. Harris, whilst I've a drop of breath to draw, will I set by, and not stand up, don't think it."—"I ast your pardon, ma'am," says Mrs. Harris, "and I humbly grant your grace; for if ever a woman lived as would see her feller creeturs into fits to serve her friends, well do I know that woman's name is Sairey Gamp."'

At this point she was fain to stop for breath; and advantage may be taken of the circumstance, to state that a fearful mystery surrounded this lady of the name of Harris, whom no one in the circle of Mrs. Gamp's acquaintance had ever seen; neither did any human being know her place of residence, though Mrs. Gamp appeared on her own showing to be in constant communication with her. There were conflicting rumours on the subject; but the prevalent opinion was that she was a phantom of Mrs. Gamp's brain—as Messrs. Doe and Roe are fictions of the law—created for the express purpose of holding visionary dialogues with her on all manner of subjects, and invariably winding up with a compliment to the excellence of her nature.

'And likeways what a pleasure,' said Mrs. Gamp, turning with a tearful smile towards the daughters, 'to see them two young ladies as I know'd afore a tooth in their pretty heads was cut, and have many a day seen—ah, the sweet creeturs!— playing at berryins down in the shop, and follerin' the order-book to its long home in the iron safe! But that's all past and over, Mr. Mould;' as she thus got in a carefully regulated routine to that gentleman, she shook her head waggishly; 'That's all past and over now, sir, an't it?'

'Changes, Mrs. Gamp, changes!' returned the under-taker.

'More changes too, to come, afore we've done with changes, sir,' said Mrs. Gamp, nodding yet more waggishly than before. 'Young ladies with such faces thinks of something else besides berryins, don't they, sir?'

'I am sure I don't know, Mrs. Gamp,' said Mould, with a chuckle—'Not bad in Mrs. Gamp, my dear?'

'Oh yes, you do know, sir!' said Mrs. Gamp, 'and so does Mrs. Mould, your ansome pardner too, sir; and so do I, although the blessing of a daughter was deniged me; which, if we had had one, Gamp would certainly have drunk its little shoes right off its feet, as with our precious boy he did, and arterwards send the child a errand to sell his wooden leg for any money it would fetch as matches in the rough, and bring it home in liquor: which was truly done beyond his years, for ev'ry individgle penny that child lost at toss or buy for kidney ones; and come home arterwards quite bold, to break the news, and offering to drown himself if that would be a satisfac-tion to his parents.—Oh yes, you do know, sir,' said Mrs. Gamp, wiping her eye with her shawl, and resuming the thread of her discourse. 'There's something besides births and berryins in the newspapers, an't there, Mr. Mould?'

Mr. Mould winked at Mrs. Mould, whom he had by this time taken on his knee, and said: 'No doubt. A good deal more, Mrs. Gamp. Upon my life, Mrs. Gamp is very far from bad, my dear!'

'There's marryings, an't there, sir?' said Mrs. Gamp, while both the daughters blushed and tittered. 'Bless their precious hearts, and well they knows it! Well you know'd it too, and well did Mrs. Mould, when you was at their time of life! But my opinion is, you're all of one age now. For as to you and Mrs. Mould, sir, ever having grandchildren—'

'Oh! Fie, fie! Nonsense, Mrs. Gamp,' replied the under-taker. 'Devilish smart, though. Ca-pi-tal!' This was in a whisper. 'My dear'—aloud again—'Mrs. Gamp can drink a glass of rum, I dare say. Sit down, Mrs. Gamp, sit down.'

Mrs. Gamp took the chair that was nearest the door, and casting up her eyes towards the ceiling, feigned to be wholly insensible to the fact of a glass of rum being in preparation, until it was placed in her hand by one of the young ladies, when she exhibited the greatest surprise.

'A thing,' she said, 'as hardly ever, Mrs. Mould, occurs with me unless it is when I am indisposged, and find my half a pint of porter settling heavy on the chest. Mrs. Harris often and often says to me, "Sairey Gamp," she says, "you raly do amaze me!" "Mrs. Harris," I says to her, "why so? Give it a name, I beg." "Telling the truth then, ma'am," says Mrs. Harris, "and shaming him as shall be nameless betwixt you and me, never did I think till I know'd you, as any woman could sick-nurse and monthly likeways, on the little that you takes to drink." "Mrs. Harris," I says to her, "none on us knows what we can do till we tries; and wunst, when me and Gamp kept ouse, I thought so too. But now," I says, "my half a pint of porter fully satisfies; perwisin', Mrs. Harris, that it is brought reg'lar, and draw'd mild. Whether I sicks or monthlies, ma'am, I hope I does my duty, but I am but a poor woman, and I earns my living hard; therefore I *do* require it, which I makes confession, to be brought reg'lar and draw'd mild."'

The precise connexion between these observations and the glass of rum, did not appear; for Mrs. Gamp proposing as a toast 'The best of lucks to all!' took off the dram in quite a scientific manner, without any further remarks.

'And what's your news, Mrs. Gamp?' asked Mould again, as that lady wiped her lips upon her shawl, and nibbled a corner off a soft biscuit, which she appeared to carry in her pocket as a provision against contingent drams. 'How's Mr. Chuffey?'

'Mr. Chuffey, sir,' she replied, 'is jest as usual; he an't no better and he an't no worse. I take it very kind in the gentle-man to have wrote up to you and said, "let Mrs. Gamp take care of him till I come home;" but ev'ry think he does is kind. There an't a many like him. If there was, we shouldn't want no churches.'

'What do you want to speak to me about, Mrs. Gamp?' said Mould, coming to the point.

'Jest this, sir,' Mrs. Gamp returned, 'with thanks to you for asking. There *is* a gent, sir, at the Bull in Holborn, as has been took ill there, and is bad abed. They have a day nurse as was recommended from Bartholomew's; and well I knows her, Mr. Mould, her name bein' Mrs. Prig, the best of creeturs. But she is otherways engaged at night, and they are in wants of night-watching; consequent she says to them, having reposed the greatest friendliness in me for twenty year, "The soberest person going, and the best of blessings in a sick room, is Mrs. Gamp. Send a boy to Kingsgate Street," she says, "and snap her up at any price, for Mrs. Gamp is worth her weight and more in goldian guineas." My landlord brings the message down to me, and says, "bein' in a light place where you are, and this job promising so well, why not unite the two?" "No, sir," I says, "not unbeknown to Mr. Mould, and therefore do not think it. But I will go to Mr. Mould," I says, "and ast him, if you like."' Here she looked sideways at the undertaker, and came to a stop.

'Night-watching, eh?' said Mould, rubbing his chin.

'From eight o'clock till eight, sir. I will not deceive you,' Mrs. Gamp rejoined.

'And then go back, eh?' said Mould.

'Quite free then, sir, to attend to Mr. Chuffey. His ways bein' quiet, and his hours early, he'd be abed, sir, nearly all the time. I will not deny,' said Mrs. Gamp with meekness, 'that I am but a poor woman, and that the money is a object; but do not let that act upon you, Mr. Mould. Rich folks may ride on camels, but it ain't so easy for 'em to see out of a needle's eye. That is my comfort, and I hope I knows it.'

'Well, Mrs. Gamp,' observed Mould, 'I don't see any particular objection to your earning an honest penny under such circumstances. I should keep it quiet, I think, Mrs. Gamp. I wouldn't mention it to Mr. Chuzzlewit on his return, for instance, unless it were necessary, or he asked you point-blank.'

'The very words was on my lips, sir,' Mrs. Gamp rejoined. 'Suppoging that the gent should die, I hope I might take the liberty of saying as I know'd some one in the undertaking line, and yet give no offence to you, sir?'

'Certainly, Mrs. Gamp,' said Mould, with much condescension. 'You may casually remark, in such a case, that we do the thing pleasantly and in a great variety of styles, and are generally considered to make it as agreeable as possible to the feelings of the survivors. But don't obtrude it, don't obtrude it. Easy, easy! My dear, you may as well give Mrs. Gamp a card or two, if you please.'

Mrs. Gamp received them, and scenting no more rum in the wind (for the bottle was locked up again) rose to take her departure.

'Wishing ev'ry happiness to this happy family,' said Mrs. Gamp, 'with all my heart. Good arternoon, Mrs. Mould! If I was Mr. Mould, I should be jealous of you, ma'am; and I'm sure, if I was you, I should be jealous of Mr. Mould.'

'Tut, tut! Bah, bah! Go along, Mrs. Gamp!' cried the delighted undertaker.

'As to the young ladies,' said Mrs. Gamp, dropping a curtsey, 'bless their sweet looks—how they can ever reconsize it with their duties to be so grown up with such young parents, it an't for sech as me to give a guess at.'

'Nonsense, nonsense. Be off, Mrs. Gamp!' cried Mould. But in the height of his gratification he actually pinched Mrs. Mould as he said it.

'I'll tell you what, my dear,' he observed, when Mrs. Gamp had at last withdrawn and shut the door, 'that's a ve-ry shrewd woman. That's a woman whose intellect is immensely superior to her station in life. That's a woman who observes and reflects in an uncommon manner. She's the sort of woman now,' said Mould, drawing his silk handkerchief over his head again, and composing himself for a nap, 'one would almost feel disposed to bury for nothing: and do it neatly, too!'

Mrs. Mould and her daughters fully concurred in these remarks; the subject of which had by this time reached the street, where she experienced so much inconvenience from the air, that she was obliged to stand under an archway for a short time, to recover herself. Even after this precaution, she walked so unsteadily as to attract the compassionate regards of divers kind-hearted boys, who took the liveliest interest in her disorder; and in their simple language, bade her be of good cheer, for she was 'only a little screwed.'

Whatever she was, or whatever name the vocabulary of medical science would have bestowed upon her malady, Mrs. Gamp was perfectly acquainted with the way home again; and arriving at the house of Anthony Chuzzlewit & Son, lay down to rest. Remaining there until seven o'clock in the evening, and then persuading poor old Chuffey to betake himself to bed, she sallied forth upon her new engagement. First, she went to her private lodgings in Kingsgate Street, for a bundle of robes and wrappings comfortable in the night season; and then repaired to the Bull in Holborn, which she reached as the clocks were striking eight.

As she turned into the yard, she stopped; for the landlord,

landlady, and head chambermaid, were all on the threshold together, talking earnestly with a young gentleman who seemed to have just come or to be just going away. The first words that struck upon Mrs. Gamp's ear obviously bore reference to the patient; and it being expedient that all good attendants should know as much as possible about the case on which their skill is brought to bear, Mrs. Gamp listened as a matter of duty.

'No better, then?' observed the gentleman.

'Worse!' said the landlord.

'Much worse,' added the landlady.

'Oh! a deal badder,' cried the chambermaid from the background, opening her eyes very wide, and shaking her head.

'Poor fellow!' said the gentleman, 'I am sorry to hear it. The worst of it is, that I have no idea what friends or relations he has, or where they live, except that it certainly is not in London.'

The landlord looked at the landlady; the landlady looked at the landlord; and the chambermaid remarked, hysterically, 'that of all the many wague directions she had ever seen or heerd of (and they wasn't few in an hotel), *that* was the waguest.'

'The fact is, you see,' pursued the gentleman, 'as I told you yesterday when you sent to me, I really know very little about him. We were school-fellows together; but since that time I have only met him twice. On both occasions I was in London for a boy's holiday (having come up for a week or so from Wiltshire), and lost sight of him again directly. The letter bearing my name and address which you found upon his table, and which led to your applying to me, is in answer, you will observe, to one he wrote from this house the very day he was taken ill, making an appointment with him at his own request. Here is his letter, if you wish to see it.'

The landlord read it: the landlady looked over him. The chambermaid, in the background, made out as much of it as she could, and invented the rest; believing it all from that time forth as a positive piece of evidence.

'He has very little luggage, you say?' observed the gentleman, who was no other than our old friend, John Westlock.

'Nothing but a portmanteau,' said the landlord; 'and very little in it.'

'A few pounds in his purse, though?'

'Yes. It's sealed up, and in the cash-box. I made a memorandum of the amount, which you're welcome to see.'

'Well!' said John, 'as the medical gentleman says the fever must take its course, and nothing can be done just now beyond giving him his drinks regularly and having him carefully attended to, nothing more can be said that I know of, until he is in a condition to give us some information. Can you suggest anything else?'

'N-no,' replied the landlord, 'except—'

'Except, who's to pay, I suppose?' said John.

'Why,' hesitated the landlord, 'it would be as well.'

'Quite as well,' said the landlady.

'Not forgetting to remember the servants,' said the chambermaid in a bland whisper.

'It is but reasonable, I fully admit,' said John Westlock. 'At all events, you have the stock in hand to go upon for the present; and I will readily undertake to pay the doctor and the nurses.'

'Ah!' cried Mrs. Gamp. 'A rayal gentleman!'

She groaned her admiration so audibly, that they all turned round. Mrs. Gamp felt the necessity of advancing, bundle in hand, and introducing herself.

'The night-nurse,' she observed, 'from Kingsgate Street, well beknown to Mrs. Prig the day-nurse, and the best of creeturs. How is the poor dear gentleman, to-night? If he an't no better yet, still that is what must be expected and prepared for. It an't the fust time by a many score, ma'am,' dropping a curtsey to the landlady, 'that Mrs. Prig and me has nussed together, turn and turn about, one off, one on. We knows each other's ways, and often gives relief when others failed. Our charges is but low, sir:' Mrs. Gamp addressed herself to John on this head: 'considerin' the nater of our painful dooty. If they wos made accordin' to our wishes, they would be easy paid.'

Regarding herself as having now delivered her inauguration address, Mrs. Gamp curtseyed all round, and signified her wish to be conducted to the scene of her official duties. The chambermaid led her, through a variety of intricate passages, to the top of the house; and pointing at length to a solitary door at the end of a gallery, informed her that yonder was the chamber where the patient lay. That done, she hurried off with all the speed she could make.

Mrs. Gamp traversed the gallery in a great heat from having

carried her large bundle up so many stairs, and tapped at the door, which was immediately opened by Mrs. Prig, bonneted and shawled and all impatience to be gone. Mrs. Prig was of the Gamp build, but not so fat; and her voice was deeper and more like a man's. She had also a beard.

'I began to think you warn't a-coming!' Mrs. Prig observed, in some displeasure.

'It shall be made good to-morrow night,' said Mrs. Gamp, '*h*onorable. I had to go and fetch my things.' She had begun to make signs of inquiry in reference to the position of the patient and his overhearing them—for there was a screen before the door—when Mrs. Prig settled that point easily.

'Oh!' she said aloud, 'he's quiet, but his wits is gone. It an't no matter wot you say.'

'Anythin' to tell afore you goes, my dear?' asked Mrs. Gamp, setting her bundle down inside the door, and looking affectionately at her partner.

'The pickled salmon,' Mrs. Prig replied, 'is quite delicious. I can partick'ler recommend it. Don't have nothink to say to the cold meat, for it tastes of the stable. The drinks is all good.'

Mrs. Gamp expressed herself much gratified.

'The physic and them things is on the drawers and mankle-shelf,' said Mrs. Prig, cursorily. 'He took his last slime draught at seven. The easy-chair an't soft enough. You'll want his piller.'

Mrs. Gamp thanked her for these hints, and giving her a friendly good night, held the door open until she had disappeared at the other end of the gallery. Having thus performed the hospitable duty of seeing her safely off, she shut it, locked it on the inside, took up her bundle, walked round the screen, and entered on her occupation of the sick chamber.

'A little dull, but not so bad as might be,' Mrs. Gamp remarked. 'I'm glad to see a parapidge, in case of fire, and lots of roofs and chimley-pots to walk upon.'

It will be seen from these remarks that Mrs. Gamp was looking out of window. When she had exhausted the prospect, she tried the easy-chair, which she indignantly declared was 'harder than a brickbadge.' Next she pursued her researches among the physic-bottles, glasses, jugs, and tea-cups; and when she had entirely satisfied her curiosity on all these subjects of investigation, she untied her bonnet-strings and strolled up to the bedside to take a look at the patient.

'A young man—dark and not ill-looking—with long black hair, that seemed the blacker for the whiteness of the bed-clothes. His eyes were partly open, and he never ceased to roll his head from side to side upon the pillow, keeping his body almost quiet. He did not utter words; but every now and then gave vent to an expression of impatience or fatigue, sometimes of surprise; and still his restless head—oh, weary, weary hour! —went to and fro without a moment's intermission.

Mrs. Gamp solaced herself with a pinch of snuff, and stood looking at him with her head inclined a little sideways, as a connoisseur might gaze upon a doubtful work of art. By degrees, a horrible remembrance of one branch of her calling took possession of the woman; and stooping down, she pinned his wandering arms against his sides, to see how he would look if laid out as a dead man. Hideous as it may appear, her fingers itched to compose his limbs in that last marble attitude.

'Ah!' said Mrs. Gamp, walking away from the bed, 'he'd make a lovely corpse.'

She now proceeded to unpack her bundle; lighted a candle with the aid of a fire-box on the drawers; filled a small kettle, as a preliminary to refreshing herself with a cup of tea in the course of the night; laid what she called 'a little bit of fire,' for the same philanthropic purpose; and also set forth a small tea-board, that nothing might be wanting for her comfortable enjoyment. These preparations occupied so long, that when they were brought to a conclusion it was high time to think about supper; so she rang the bell and ordered it.

'I think, young woman,' said Mrs. Gamp to the assistant chambermaid, in a tone expressive of weakness, 'that I could pick a little bit of pickled salmon, with a nice little sprig of fennel, and a sprinkling of white pepper. I takes new bread, my dear, with jest a little pat of fresh butter, and a mossel of cheese. In case there should be such a thing as a cowcumber in the 'ouse, will you be so kind as bring it, for I'm rather partial to 'em, and they does a world of good in a sick room. If they draws the Brighton Old Tipper here, I takes *that* ale at night, my love; it bein' considered wakeful by the doctors. And whatever you do, young woman, don't bring more than a shilling's-worth of gin and water-warm when I rings the bell a second time; for that is always my allowance, and I never takes a drop beyond!'

Having preferred these moderate requests, Mrs. Gamp

observed that she would stand at the door until the order was executed, to the end that the patient might not be disturbed by her opening it a second time; and therefore she would thank the young woman to 'look sharp.'

A tray was brought with everything upon it, even to the cucumber; and Mrs. Gamp accordingly sat down to eat and drink in high good humour. The extent to which she availed herself of the vinegar, and supped up that refreshing fluid with the blade of her knife, can scarcely be expressed in narrative.

'Ah!' sighed Mrs. Gamp, as she meditated over the warm shilling's-worth, 'what a blessed thing it is—living in a wale— to be contented! What a blessed thing it is to make sick people happy in their beds, and never mind one's self as long as one can do a service! I don't believe a finer cowcumber was ever grow'd. I'm sure I never see one!'

She moralised in the same vein until her glass was empty, and then administered the patient's medicine, by the simple process of clutching his windpipe to make him gasp, and immediately pouring it down his throat.

'I a'most forgot the piller, I declare!' said Mrs. Gamp, drawing it away. 'There! Now he's comfortable as he can be, *I*'m sure! I must try to make myself as much so as I can.'

With this view, she went about the construction of an extemporaneous bed in the easy-chair, with the addition of the next easy one for her feet. Having formed the best couch that the circumstances admitted of, she took out of her bundle a yellow night-cap, of prodigious size, in shape resembling a cabbage; which article of dress she fixed and tied on with the utmost care, previously divesting herself of a row of bald old curls that could scarcely be called false, they were so very innocent of anything approaching to deception. From the same repository she brought forth a night-jacket, in which she also attired herself. Finally, she produced a watchman's coat, which she tied round her neck by the sleeves, so that she became two people; and looked, behind, as if she were in the act of being embraced by one of the old patrol.

All these arrangements made, she lighted the rushlight, coiled herself up on her couch, and went to sleep. Ghostly and dark the room became, and full of lowering shadows. The distant noises in the streets were gradually hushed; the house was quiet as a sepulchre; the dead of night was coffined in the silent city.

Oh, weary, weary hour! Oh, haggard mind, groping darkly through the past; incapable of detaching itself from the miserable present; dragging its heavy chain of care through imaginary feasts and revels, and scenes of awful pomp; seeking but a moment's rest among the long-forgotten haunts of childhood, and the resorts of yesterday; and dimly finding fear and horror everywhere! Oh, weary, weary hour! What were the wanderings of Cain, to these!

Still, without a moment's interval, the burning head tossed to and fro. Still, from time to time, fatigue, impatience, suffering, and surprise, found utterance upon that rack, and plainly too, though never once in words. At length, in the solemn hour of midnight, he began to talk; waiting awfully for answers sometimes; as though invisible companions were about his bed; and so replying to their speech and questioning again.

Mrs. Gamp awoke, and sat up in her bed: presenting on the wall the shadow of a gigantic night constable, struggling with a prisoner.

'Come! Hold your tongue!' she cried, in sharp reproof. 'Don't make none of that noise here.'

There was no alteration in the face, or in the incessant motion of the head, but he talked on wildly.

'Ah!' said Mrs. Gamp, coming out of the chair with an impatient shiver; 'I thought I was a-sleepin' too pleasant to last! The devil's in the night, I think, it's turned so chilly!'

'Don't drink so much!' cried the sick man. 'You'll ruin us all. Don't you see how the fountain sinks? Look at the mark where the sparkling water was just now!'

'Sparkling water, indeed!' said Mrs. Gamp. 'I'll have a sparkling cup o' tea, I think. I wish you'd hold your noise!'

He burst into a laugh, which, being prolonged, fell off into a dismal wail. Checking himself, with fierce inconstancy he began to count, fast.

'One—two—three—four—five—six.'

' "One, two, buckle my shoe,"' said Mrs. Gamp, who was now on her knees, lighting the fire, ' "three, four, shut the door,"—I wish you'd shut your mouth, young man—"five, six, picking up sticks." If I'd got a few handy, I should have the kettle biling all the sooner.'

Awaiting this desirable consummation, she sat down so close to the fender (which was a high one) that her nose rested upon it; and for some time she drowsily amused herself by sliding that feature backwards and forwards along the brass top, as far as she could, without changing her position to do it. She maintained, all the while, a running commentary upon the wanderings of the man in bed.

'That makes five hundred and twenty-one men, all dressed alike, and with the same distortion on their faces, that have passed in at the window, and out at the door,' he cried, anxiously. 'Look there! Five hundred and twenty-two—twenty-three—twenty-four. Do you see them?'

'Ah! *I* see 'em,' said Mrs. Gamp; 'all the whole kit of 'em numbered like hackney-coaches, ain't they?'

'Touch me! Let me be sure of this. Touch me!'

'You'll take your next draught when I've made the kettle bile,' retorted Mrs. Gamp, composedly, 'and you'll be touched then. You'll be touched up, too, if you don't take it quiet.'

'Five hundred and twenty-eight, five hundred and twenty-nine, five hundred and thirty,—look here!'

'What's the matter now?' said Mrs. Gamp.

'They're coming four abreast, each man with his arm entwined in the next man's, and his hand upon his shoulder. What's that upon the arm of every man, and on the flag?'

'Spiders, p'raps,' said Mrs. Gamp.

'Crape! Black crape! Good God! why do they wear it outside?'

'Would you have 'em carry black crape in their insides?' Mrs. Gamp retorted. 'Hold your noise, hold your noise.'

The fire beginning by this time to impart a grateful warmth, Mrs. Gamp became silent; gradually rubbed her nose more and more slowly along the top of the fender; and fell into a heavy doze. She was awakened by the room ringing (as she fancied) with a name she knew:

'Chuzzlewit!'

The sound was so distinct and real, and so full of agonised entreaty, that Mrs. Gamp jumped up in terror, and ran to the door. She expected to find the passage filled with people, come to tell her that the house in the City had taken fire. But the place was empty: not a soul was there. She opened the window, and looked out. Dark, dull, dingy, and desolate house-tops. As she passed to her seat again, she glanced at the patient. Just the same; but silent. Mrs. Gamp was so warm now, that she threw off the watchman's coat, and fanned herself.

Q

'It seemed to make the wery bottles ring,' she said. 'What could I have been a-dreaming of? That dratted Chuffey, I'll be bound.'

The supposition was probable enough. At any rate, a pinch of snuff, and the song of the steaming kettle, quite restored the tone of Mrs. Gamp's nerves, which were none of the weakest. She brewed her tea; made some buttered toast; and sat down at the tea-board, with her face to the fire.

When once again, in a tone more terrible than that which had vibrated in her slumbering ear, these words were shrieked out:

'Chuzzlewit! Jonas! No!'

Mrs. Gamp dropped the cup she was in the act of raising to her lips, and turned round with a start that made the little tea-board leap. The cry had come from the bed.

It was bright morning the next time Mrs. Gamp looked out of the window, and the sun was rising cheerfully. Lighter and lighter grew the sky, and noisier the streets; and high into the summer air uprose the smoke of newly kindled fires, until the busy day was broad awake.

Mrs. Prig relieved punctually, having passed a good night at her other patient's. Mr. Westlock came at the same time, but he was not admitted, the disorder being infectious. The doctor came too. The doctor shook his head. It was all he could do, under the circumstances, and he did it well.

'What sort of a night, nurse?'

'Restless, sir,' said Mrs. Gamp.

'Talk much?'

'Middling, sir,' said Mrs. Gamp.

'Nothing to the purpose, I suppose?'

'Oh bless you, no, sir. Only jargon.'

'Well!' said the doctor, 'we must keep him quiet; keep the room cool: give him his draughts regularly; and see that he's carefully looked to. That's all!'

'And as long as Mrs. Prig and me waits upon him, sir, no fear of that,' said Mrs. Gamp.

'I suppose,' observed Mrs. Prig, when they had curtseyed the doctor out: 'there's nothin' new?'

'Nothin' at all, my dear,' said Mrs. Gamp. 'He's rather wearin' in his talk from making up a lot of names; elseways you needn't mind him.'

'Oh, I sha'n't mind him,' Mrs. Prig returned. 'I have somethin' else to think of.'

'I pays my debts to-night, you know, my dear, and comes afore my time,' said Mrs. Gamp. 'But, Betsey Prig:' speaking with great feeling, and laying her hand upon her arm: 'try the cowcumbers, God bless you!'

CHAPTER XXVI

An unexpected meeting, and a promising prospect

THE laws of sympathy between beards and birds, and the secret source of that attraction which frequently impels a shaver of the one to be a dealer in the other, are questions for the subtle reasoning of scientific bodies: not the less so, because their investigation would seem calculated to lead to no particular result. It is enough to know that the artist who had the honour of entertaining Mrs. Gamp as his first-floor lodger, united the two pursuits of barbering and bird-fancying; and that it was not an original idea of his, but one in which he had, dispersed about the by-streets and suburbs of the town, a host of rivals.

The name of the householder was Paul Sweedlepipe. But he was commonly called Poll Sweedlepipe: and was not uncommonly believed to have been so christened, among his friends and neighbours.

With the exception of the staircase, and his lodger's private apartment, Poll Sweedlepipe's house was one great bird's nest. Game-cocks resided in the kitchen; pheasants wasted the brightness of their golden plumage on the garret; bantams roosted in the cellar; owls had possession of the bedroom; and specimens of all the smaller fry of birds chirruped and twittered in the shop. The staircase was sacred to rabbits. There in hutches of all shapes and kinds, made from old packing-cases, boxes, drawers, and tea-chests, they increased in a prodigious degree, and contributed their share towards that complicated whiff which, quite impartially, and without distinction of persons, saluted every nose that was put into Sweedlepipe's easy shaving-shop.

Many noses found their way there, for all that, especially on Sunday morning, before church-time. Even archbishops shave, or must be shaved, on a Sunday, and beards *will* grow after twelve o'clock on Saturday night, though it be upon the chins of base mechanics: who, not being able to engage their valets by the quarter, hire them by the job, and pay them—oh, the wickedness of copper coin!—in dirty pence. Poll Sweedlepipe, the sinner, shaved all comers at a penny each, and cut the hair of any customer for twopence; and being a lone unmarried man, and having some connexion in the bird line, Poll got on tolerably well.

He was a little elderly man, with a clammy cold right hand, from which even rabbits and birds could not remove the smell of shaving-soap. Poll had something of the bird in his nature; not of the hawk or eagle, but of the sparrow, that builds in chimney-stacks and inclines to human company. He was not quarrelsome, though, like the sparrow; but peaceful, like the dove. In his walk he strutted; and, in this respect, he bore a faint resemblance to the pigeon, as well as in a certain prosiness of speech, which might, in its monotony, be likened to the cooing of that bird. He was very inquisitive; and when he stood at his shop-door in the evening-tide, watching the neighbours, with his head on one side, and his eye cocked knowingly, there was a dash of the raven in him. Yet there was no more wickedness in Poll than in a robin. Happily, too, when any of his ornithological properties were on the verge of going too far, they were quenched, dissolved, melted down, and neutralised in the barber; just as his bald head—otherwise, as the head of a shaved magpie—lost itself in a wig of curly black ringlets, parted on one side, and cut away almost to the crown, to indicate immense capacity of intellect.

Poll had a very small, shrill, treble voice, which might have led the wags of Kingsgate Street to insist the more upon his feminine designation. He had a tender heart, too; for, when he had a good commission to provide three or four score sparrows for a shooting-match, he would observe, in a compassionate tone, how singular it was that sparrows should have been made expressly for such purposes. The question, whether men were made to shoot them, never entered into Poll's philosophy.

Poll wore in his sporting character, a velveteen coat, a great deal of blue stocking, ankle boots, a neckerchief of some bright colour, and a very tall hat. Pursuing his more quiet occupation of barber, he generally subsided into an apron not over-clean, a flannel jacket, and corduroy knee-shorts. It was in this latter costume, but with his apron girded round his waist, as a token of his having shut up shop for the night, that he closed the door one evening, some weeks after the occurrences detailed in the last chapter, and stood upon the steps in Kingsgate Street, listening until the little cracked bell within should leave off ringing. For until it did—this was Mr. Sweedlepipe's reflection—the place never seemed quiet enough to be left to itself.

'It's the greediest little bell to ring,' said Poll, 'that ever was. But it's quiet at last.'

He rolled his apron up a little tighter as he said these words, and hastened down the street. Just as he was turning into Holborn, he ran against a young gentleman in a livery. This youth was bold, though small, and with several lively expressions of displeasure, turned upon him instantly.

'Now, STOO-PID!' cried the young gentleman. 'Can't you look where you're a-going to—eh? Can't you mind where you're a-coming to—eh? What do you think your eyes was made for—eh? Ah! Yes. Oh! Now then!'

The young gentleman pronounced the two last words in a very loud tone and with frightful emphasis, as though they contained within themselves the essence of the direst aggravation. But he had scarcely done so, when his anger yielded to surprise, and he cried, in a milder tone:

'What! Polly!'

'Why, it ain't you, sure!' cried Poll. 'It can't be you!'

'No. It ain't me,' returned the youth. 'It's my son, my oldest one. He's a credit to his father, ain't he, Polly?' With this delicate little piece of banter, he halted on the pavement, and went round and round in circles, for the better exhibition of his figure: rather to the inconvenience of the passengers generally, who were not in an equal state of spirits with himself.

'I wouldn't have believed it,' said Poll. 'What! You've left your old place, then? Have you?'

'Have I!' returned his young friend, who had by this time stuck his hands into the pockets of his white cord breeches, and was swaggering along at the barber's side. 'D'ye know a pair of top-boots when you see 'em, Polly? Look here!'

'Beau-ti-ful!' cried Mr. Sweedlepipe.

'D'ye know a slap-up sort of button, when you see it?' said the youth. 'Don't look at mine, if you ain't a judge, because these lions' heads was made for men of taste: not snobs.'

'Beau-ti-ful!' cried the barber again. 'A grass-green frock-coat, too, bound with gold! And a cockade in your hat!'

'I should hope so,' replied the youth. 'Blow the cockade, though; for, except that it don't turn round, it's like the wentilator that used to be in the kitchen winder at Todgers's.

You ain't seen the old lady's name in the Gazette, have you?'

'No,' returned the barber. 'Is she a bankrupt?'

'If she ain't, she will be,' retorted Bailey. 'That bis'ness never can be carried on without *me*. Well! How are you?'

'Oh! I'm pretty well,' said Poll. 'Are you living at this end of the town, or were you coming to see me? Was that the bis'ness that brought you to Holborn?'

'I haven't got no bis'ness in Holborn,' returned Bailey, with some displeasure. 'All my bis'ness lays at the West-end. I've got the right sort of governor now. You can't see his face for his whiskers, and can't see his whiskers for the dye upon 'em. That's a gentleman, ain't it? You wouldn't like a ride in a cab, would you? Why, it wouldn't be safe to offer it. You'd faint away, only to see me a-comin' at a mild trot round the corner.'

To convey a slight idea of the effect of this approach, Mr. Bailey counterfeited in his own person the action of a high-trotting horse, and threw up his head so high, in backing against a pump, that he shook his hat off.

'Why, he's own uncle to Capricorn,' said Bailey, 'and brother to Cauliflower. He's been through the winders of two chaney shops since we've had him, and wos sold for killin' his missis. That's a horse, I hope?'

'Ah! you'll never want to buy any more red-polls, now,' observed Poll, looking on his young friend with an air of melancholy. 'You'll never want to buy any more red-polls now, to hang up over the sink, will you?'

'I should think not,' replied Bailey. 'Reether so. I wouldn't have nothin' to say to any bird below a Peacock; and *he*'d be wulgar. Well, how are you?'

'Oh! I'm pretty well,' said Poll. He answered the question again because Mr. Bailey asked it again; Mr. Bailey asked it again, because—accompanied with a straddling action of the white cords, a bend of the knees, and a striking forth of the top-boots—it was an easy, horse-fleshy, turfy sort of thing to do.

'Wot are you up to, old feller?' added Mr. Bailey, with the same graceful rakishness. He was quite the man-about-town of the conversation, while the easy-shaver was the child.

'Why, I am going to fetch my lodger home,' said Paul.

'A woman!' cried Mr. Bailey, 'for a twenty-pun' note!'

The little barber hastened to explain that she was neither a young woman, nor a handsome woman, but a nurse, who had been acting as a kind of house-keeper to a gentleman for some weeks past, and left her place that night, in consequence of being superseded by another and a more legitimate house-keeper: to wit, the gentleman's bride.

'He's newly married, and he brings his young wife home to-night,' said the barber. 'So I'm going to fetch my lodger away—Mr. Chuzzlewit's, close behind the Post Office—and carry her box for her.'

'Jonas Chuzzlewit's?' said Bailey.

'Ah!' returned Paul: 'that's the name sure enough. Do you know him?'

'Oh, no!' cried Mr. Bailey; 'not at all. And I don't know her! Not neither! Why, they first kept company through me, a'most.'

'Ah?' said Paul.

'Ah!' said Mr. Bailey, with a wink; 'and she ain't bad-looking, mind you. But her sister was the best. *She* was the merry one. I often used to have a bit of fun with her, in the hold times!'

Mr. Bailey spoke as if he already had a leg and three-quarters in the grave, and this had happened twenty or thirty years ago. Paul Sweedlepipe, the meek, was so perfectly confounded by his precocious self-possession, and his patronising manner, as well as by his boots, cockade, and livery, that a mist swam before his eyes, and he saw—not the Bailey of acknowledged juvenility, from Todgers's Commercial Boarding House, who had made his acquaintance within a twelve-month, by purchasing, at sundry times, small birds at two-pence each —but a highly-condensed embodiment of all the sporting grooms in London; an abstract of all the stable-knowledge of the time; a something at a high-pressure that must have had existence many years, and was fraught with terrible experiences. And truly, though in the cloudy atmosphere of Todgers's, Mr. Bailey's genius had ever shone out brightly in this particular respect, it now eclipsed both time and space, cheated beholders of their senses, and worked on their belief in defiance of all natural laws. He walked along the tangible and real stones of Holborn Hill, an under-sized boy; and yet he winked the winks, and thought the thoughts, and did the deeds, and said the sayings of an ancient man. There was an old principle within him, and a young surface without. He became an inexplicable creature: a breeched and booted

Sphinx. There was no course open to the barber but to go distracted himself, or to take Bailey for granted: and he wisely chose the latter.

Mr. Bailey was good enough to continue to bear him company, and to entertain him, as they went, with easy conversation on various sporting topics; especially on the comparative merits, as a general principle, of horses with white stockings and horses without. In regard to the style of tail to be preferred, Mr. Bailey had opinions of his own, which he explained, but begged they might by no means influence his friend's, as here he knew he had the misfortune to differ from some excellent authorities. He treated Mr. Sweedlepipe to a dram, compounded agreeably to his own directions, which he informed him had been invented by a member of the Jockey Club; and, as they were by this time near the barber's destination, he observed that, as he had an hour to spare, and knew the parties, he would, if quite agreeable, be introduced to Mrs. Gamp.

Paul knocked at Jonas Chuzzlewit's: and, on the door being opened by that lady, made the two distinguished persons known to one another. It was a happy feature in Mrs. Gamp's twofold profession, that it gave her an interest in everything that was young as well as in everything that was old. She received Mr. Bailey with much kindness.

'It's very good, I'm sure, of you to come,' she said to her landlord, 'as well as bring so nice a friend. But I'm afraid that I must trouble you so far as to step in, for the young couple has not yet made appearance.'

'They're late, ain't they?' inquired her landlord, when she had conducted them down-stairs into the kitchen.

'Well, sir, considerin' the Wings of Love, they are,' said Mrs. Gamp.

Mr. Bailey inquired whether the Wings of Love had ever won a plate, or could be backed to do anything remarkable; and being informed that it was not a horse, but merely a poetical or figurative expression, evinced considerable disgust. Mrs. Gamp was so very much astonished by his affable manners and great ease, that she was about to propound to her landlord in a whisper the staggering inquiry, whether he was a man or a boy, when Mr. Sweedlepipe, anticipating her design, made a timely diversion.

'He knows Mrs. Chuzzlewit,' said Paul aloud.

'There's nothin' he don't know; that's my opinion,' observed Mrs. Gamp. 'All the wickedness of the world is Print to him.'

Mr. Bailey received this as a compliment, and said, adjusting his cravat, 'reether so.'

'As you knows Mrs. Chuzzlewit, you knows, p'raps, what her chris'n name is?' Mrs. Gamp observed.

'Charity,' said Bailey.

'That it ain't!' cried Mrs. Gamp.

'Cherry, then,' said Bailey. 'Cherry's short for it. It's all the same.'

'It don't begin with a C at all,' retorted Mrs. Gamp, shaking her head. 'It begins with a M.'

'Whew!' cried Mr. Bailey, slapping a little cloud of pipeclay out of his left leg, 'then he's been and married the merry one!'

As these words were mysterious, Mrs. Gamp called upon him to explain, which Mr. Bailey proceeded to do: that lady listening greedily to everything he said. He was yet in the fulness of his narrative when the sound of wheels, and a double knock at the street door, announced the arrival of the newly-married couple. Begging him to reserve what more he had to say, for her hearing on the way home, Mrs. Gamp took up the candle, and hurried away to receive and welcome the young mistress of the house.

'Wishing you appiness and joy with all my art,' said Mrs. Gamp, dropping a curtsey as they entered the hall; 'and you, too, sir. Your lady looks a little tired with the journey, Mr. Chuzzlewit, a pretty dear!'

'She has bothered enough about it,' grumbled Mr. Jonas. 'Now, show a light, will you?'

'This way, ma'am, if you please,' said Mrs. Gamp, going up-stairs before them. 'Things has been made as comfortable as they could be; but there's many things you'll have to alter your own self when you gets time to look about you! Ah! sweet thing! But you don't,' added Mrs. Gamp, internally, 'you don't look much like a merry one, I must say!'

It was true: she did not. The death that had gone before the bridal seemed to have left its shade upon the house. The air was heavy and oppressive; the rooms were dark; a deep gloom filled up every chink and corner. Upon the hearthstone, like a creature of ill omen, sat the aged clerk, with his eyes fixed on some withered branches in the stove. He rose and looked at her.

Mrs. Gamp has her Eye on the Future

'So there you are, Mr. Chuff,' said Jonas carelessly, as he dusted his boots; 'still in the land of the living, eh?'

'Still in the land of the living, sir,' retorted Mrs. Gamp. 'And Mr. Chuffey may thank you for it, as many and many a time I've told him.'

Mr. Jonas was not in the best of humours, for he merely said, as he looked round, 'We don't want you any more, you know, Mrs. Gamp.'

'I'm a-going immediate, sir,' returned the nurse; 'unless there's nothink I can do for you, ma'am. Ain't there,' said Mrs. Gamp, with a look of great sweetness, and rummaging all the time in her pocket; 'ain't there nothink I can do for you, my little bird?'

'No,' said Merry, almost crying. 'You had better go away, please!'

With a leer of mingled sweetness and slyness; with one eye on the future, one on the bride, and an arch expression in her face, partly spiritual, partly spirituous, and wholly professional and peculiar to her art; Mrs. Gamp rummaged in her pocket again, and took from it a printed card, whereon was an inscription copied from her sign-board.

'Would you be so good, my darling dovey of a dear young married lady,' Mrs. Gamp observed, in a low voice, 'as put that somewheres where you can keep it in your mind? I'm well beknown to many ladies, and it's my card. Gamp is my name, and Gamp my nater. Livin' quite handy, I will make so bold as call in now and then, and make inquiry how your health and spirits is, my precious chick!'

And with innumerable leers, winks, coughs, nods, smiles, and curtseys, all leading to the establishment of a mysterious and confidential understanding between herself and the bride, Mrs. Gamp, invoking a blessing upon the house, leered, winked, coughed, nodded, smiled, and curtseyed herself out of the room.

'But I will say, and I would if I was led a Martha to the Stakes for it,' Mrs. Gamp remarked below stairs, in a whisper, 'that she don't look much like a merry one at this present moment of time.'

'Ah! wait till you hear her laugh!' said Bailey.

'Hem!' cried Mrs. Gamp, in a kind of groan. 'I will, child.'

They said no more in the house, for Mrs. Gamp put on her bonnet, Mr. Sweedlepipe took up her box, and Mr. Bailey accompanied them towards Kingsgate Street; recounting to Mrs. Gamp as they went along, the origin and progress of his acquaintance with Mrs. Chuzzlewit and her sister. It was a pleasant instance of this youth's precocity, that he fancied Mrs. Gamp had conceived a tenderness for him, and was much tickled by her misplaced attachment.

As the door closed heavily behind them, Mrs. Jonas sat down in a chair, and felt a strange chill creep upon her, whilst she looked about the room. It was pretty much as she had known it, but appeared more dreary. She had thought to see it brightened to receive her.

'It ain't good enough for you, I suppose?' said Jonas, watching her looks.

'Why, it *is* dull,' said Merry, trying to be more herself.

'It'll be duller before you're done with it,' retorted Jonas, 'if you give me any of your airs. You're a nice article, to turn sulky on first coming home! Ecod, you used to have life enough, when you could plague me with it. The gal's down-stairs. Ring the bell for supper, while I take my boots off!'

She roused herself from looking after him as he left the room, to do what he had desired: when the old man Chuffey laid his hand softly on her arm.

'You are not married?' he said eagerly. 'Not married?'

'Yes. A month ago. Good Heaven, what is the matter?'

He answered nothing was the matter; and turned from her. But in her fear and wonder, turning also, she saw him raise his trembling hands above his head, and heard him say:

'Oh! woe, woe, woe, upon this wicked house!'

It was her welcome,—HOME.

CHAPTER XXVII

Showing that old friends may not only appear with new faces, but in false colours. That people are prone to bite; and that biters may sometimes be bitten

MR. BAILEY, Junior—for the sporting character, whilom of general utility at Todgers's, had now regularly set up in life under that name, without troubling himself to obtain from the legislature a direct licence in the form of a Private Bill, which of all kinds and classes of bills is without exception the most unreasonable in its charges—Mr. Bailey, Junior, just tall enough to be seen by an inquiring eye, gazing indolently at society from beneath the apron of his master's cab, drove slowly up and down Pall Mall about the hour of noon, in waiting for his 'Governor.' The horse of distinguished family, who had Capricorn for his nephew, and Cauliflower for his brother, showed himself worthy of his high relations by champing at the bit until his chest was white with foam, and rearing like a horse in heraldry; the plated harness and the patent leather glittered in the sun; pedestrians admired; Mr. Bailey was complacent, but unmoved. He seemed to say, 'A barrow, good people, a mere barrow; nothing to what we could do, if we chose!' and on he went, squaring his short green arms outside the apron, as if he were hooked on to it by his armpits.

Mr. Bailey had a great opinion of brother to Cauliflower, and estimated his powers highly. But he never told him so. On the contrary, it was his practice, in driving that animal, to assail him with disrespectful, if not injurious, expressions, as, 'Ah! would you!' 'Did you think it, then?' 'Where are you going to now?' 'No, you won't, my lad!' and similar fragmentary remarks. These being usually accompanied by a jerk of the rein, or a crack of the whip, led to many trials of strength between them, and to many contentions for the upper hand, terminating, now and then, in china shops, and other unusual goals, as Mr. Bailey had already hinted to his friend Poll Sweedlepipe.

On the present occasion Mr. Bailey, being in spirits, was more than commonly hard upon his charge; in consequence of which that fiery animal confined himself almost entirely to his hind legs in displaying his paces, and constantly got himself

into positions with reference to the cabriolet that very much
amazed the passengers in the street. But Mr. Bailey, not at all
disturbed, had still a shower of pleasantries to bestow on any
one who crossed his path: as, calling to a full-grown coal-
heaver in a wagon, who for a moment blocked the way, 'Now,
young 'un, who trusted you with a cart?' inquiring of elderly
ladies who wanted to cross, and ran back again, 'Why they
didn't go to the workhouse and get an order to be buried?'
tempting boys, with friendly words, to get up behind, and immediately afterwards cutting them down; and the like flashes
of a cheerful humour, which he would occasionally relieve by
going round St. James's Square at a hand gallop, and coming
slowly into Pall Mall by another entry, as if, in the interval,
his pace had been a perfect crawl.

It was not until these amusements had been very often repeated, and the apple-stall at the corner had sustained so many
miraculous escapes as to appear impregnable, that Mr. Bailey
was summoned to the door of a certain house in Pall Mall, and
turning short, obeyed the call and jumped out. It was not until
he had held the bridle for some minutes longer—every jerk of
Cauliflower's brother's head, and every twitch of Cauliflower's
brother's nostril, taking him off his legs in the meanwhile—
that two persons entered the vehicle, one of whom took the
reins and drove rapidly off. Nor was it until Mr. Bailey had
run after it some hundreds of yards in vain, that he managed
to lift his short leg into the iron step, and finally to get his boots
upon the little footboard behind. Then, indeed, he became a
sight to see: and—standing now on one foot and now upon the
other, now trying to look round the cab on this side, now on
that, and now endeavouring to peep over the top of it, as it
went dashing in among the carts and coaches—was from head
to heel Newmarket.

The appearance of Mr. Bailey's governor as he drove along
fully justified that enthusiastic youth's description of him to
the wondering Poll. He had a world of jet-black shining hair
upon his head, upon his cheeks, upon his chin, upon his upper
lip. His clothes, symmetrically made, were of the newest fashion
and the costliest kind. Flowers of gold and blue, and green and
blushing red, were on his waistcoat; precious chains and jewels
sparkled on his breast; his fingers, clogged with brilliant rings,
were as unwieldy as summer flies but newly rescued from a
honey-pot. The daylight mantled in his gleaming hat and boots

as in a polished glass. And yet, though changed his name, and changed his outward surface, it was Tigg. Though turned and twisted upside down, and inside out, as great men have been sometimes known to be; though no longer Montague Tigg, but Tigg Montague; still it was Tigg; the same Satanic, gallant, military Tigg. The brass was burnished, lacquered, newly-stamped; yet it was the true Tigg metal notwithstanding.

Beside him sat a smiling gentleman, of less pretensions and of business looks, whom he addressed as David. Surely not the David of the—how shall it be phrased?—the triumvirate of golden balls? Not David, tapster at the Lombards' Arms? Yes. The very man.

'The secretary's salary, David,' said Mr. Montague, 'the office being now established, is eight hundred pounds per annum, with his house-rent, coals, and candles free. His five-and-twenty shares he holds, of course. Is that enough?'

David smiled and nodded, and coughed behind a little locked portfolio which he carried; with an air that proclaimed him to be the secretary in question.

'If that's enough,' said Montague, 'I will propose it at the Board to-day, in my capacity as chairman.'

The secretary smiled again; laughed, indeed, this time; and said, rubbing his nose slily with one end of the portfolio:

'It was a capital thought, wasn't it?'

'What was a capital thought, David?' Mr. Montague inquired.

'The Anglo-Bengalee,' tittered the secretary.

'The Anglo-Bengalee Disinterested Loan and Life Assurance Company is rather a capital concern, I hope, David,' said Montague.

'Capital indeed!' cried the secretary, with another laugh —'in one sense.'

'In the only important one,' observed the chairman; 'which is number one, David.'

'What,' asked the secretary, bursting into another laugh, 'what will be the paid-up capital, according to the next prospectus?'

'A figure of two, and as many oughts after it as the printer can get into the same line,' replied his friend. 'Ha, ha!'

At this they both laughed; the secretary so vehemently, that in kicking up his feet, he kicked the apron open, and nearly started Cauliflower's brother into an oyster-shop; not to

mention Mr. Bailey's receiving such a sudden swing, that he
held on for a moment, quite a young Fame, by one strap and
no legs.

'What a chap you are!' exclaimed David admiringly, when
this little alarm had subsided.

'Say, genius, David, genius.'

'Well, upon my soul, you *are* a genius then,' said David. 'I
always knew you had the gift of the gab, of course; but I never
believed you were half the man you are. How could I?'

'I rise with circumstances, David. That's a point of genius
in itself,' said Tigg. 'If you were to lose a hundred pound wager
to me at this minute, David, and were to pay it (which is most
confoundedly improbable), I should rise, in a mental point of
view, directly.'

It is due to Mr. Tigg to say that he had really risen with his
opportunities; peculating on a grander scale, he had become
a grander man altogether.

'Ha, ha,' cried the secretary, laying his hand, with growing
familiarity, upon the chairman's arm. 'When I look at you,
and think of your property in Bengal being—ha, ha, ha!—'

The half-expressed idea seemed no less ludicrous to Mr.
Tigg than to his friend, for he laughed, too, heartily.

'—Being,' resumed David, 'being amenable—your property
in Bengal being amenable—to all claims upon the company;
when I look at you and think of that, you might tickle me into
fits by waving the feather of a pen at me. Upon my soul you
might!'

'It's a devilish fine property,' said Tigg Montague, 'to be
amenable to any claims. The preserve of tigers alone is worth
a mint of money, David.'

David could only reply in the intervals of his laughter, 'Oh,
what a chap you are!' and so continued to laugh, and hold
his sides, and wipe his eyes, for some time, without offering
any other observation.

'A capital idea?' said Tigg, returning after a time to his
companion's first remark: 'no doubt it was a capital idea. It
was my idea.'

'No, no. It was my idea,' said David. 'Hang it, let a man
have some credit. Didn't I say to you that I'd saved a few
pounds?—'

'You said! Didn't I say to you,' interposed Tigg, 'that *I* had
come into a few pounds?'

'Certainly you did,' returned David, warmly, 'but that's not the idea. Who said, that if we put the money together we could furnish an office, and make a show?'

'And who said,' retorted Mr. Tigg, 'that, provided we did it on a sufficiently large scale, we could furnish an office and make a show, without any money at all? Be rational, and just, and calm, and tell me whose idea was that.'

'Why, there,' David was obliged to confess, 'you had the advantage of me, I admit. But I don't put myself on a level with you. I only want a little credit in the business.'

'All the credit you deserve to have,' said Tigg. 'The plain work of the company, David—figures, books, circulars, advertisements, pen, ink and paper, sealing-wax and wafers—is admirably done by you. You are a first-rate groveller. I don't dispute it. But the ornamental department, David; the inventive and poetical department—'

'Is entirely yours,' said his friend. 'No question of it. But with such a swell turn-out as this, and all the handsome things you've got about you, and the life you lead, I mean to say it's a precious comfortable department too.'

'Does it gain the purpose? Is it Anglo-Bengalee?' asked Tigg.

'Yes,' said David.

'Could you undertake it yourself?' demanded Tigg.

'No,' said David.

'Ha, ha!' laughed Tigg. 'Then be contented with your station and your profits, David, my fine fellow, and bless the day that made us acquainted across the counter of our common uncle, for it was a golden day to you.'

It will have been already gathered from the conversation of these worthies, that they were embarked in an enterprise of some magnitude, in which they addressed the public in general from the strong position of having everything to gain and nothing at all to lose; and which, based upon this great principle, was thriving pretty comfortably.

The Anglo-Bengalee Disinterested Loan and Life Assurance Company started into existence one morning, not an Infant Institution, but a Grown-up Company running alone at a great pace, and doing business right and left: with a 'branch' in a first floor over a tailor's at the West-end of the town, and main offices in a new street in the City, comprising the upper part of a spacious house resplendent in stucco and plate-glass, with wire blinds in all the windows, and 'Anglo-Bengalee' worked into the pattern of every one of them. On the door-post was painted again in large letters, 'Offices of the Anglo-Bengalee Disinterested Loan and Life Assurance Company,' and on the door was a large brass plate with the same inscription: always kept very bright, as courting inquiry; staring the City out of countenance after office hours on working days, and all day long on Sundays; and looking bolder than the Bank. Within, the offices were newly plastered, newly painted, newly papered, newly countered, newly floor-clothed, newly tabled, newly chaired, newly fitted up in every way, with goods that were substantial and expensive, and designed (like the company) to last. Business! Look at the green ledgers with red backs, like strong cricket-balls beaten flat; the court-guides, directories, day-books, almanacks, letter-boxes, weighing-machines for letters, rows of fire-buckets for dashing out a conflagration in its first spark, and saving the immense wealth in notes and bonds belonging to the company; look at the iron safes, the clock, the office seal—in its capacious self, security for anything. Solidity! Look at the massive blocks of marble in the chimney-pieces, and the gorgeous parapet on the top of the house! Publicity! Why, Anglo-Bengalee Disinterested Loan and Life Assurance Company is painted on the very coal-scuttles. It is repeated at every turn until the eyes are dazzled with it, and the head is giddy. It is engraved upon the top of all the letter paper, and it makes a scroll-work round the seal, and it shines out of the porter's buttons, and it is repeated twenty times in every circular and public notice wherein one David Crimple, Esquire, Secretary and resident Director, takes the liberty of inviting your attention to the accompanying statement of the advantages offered by the Anglo-Bengalee Disinterested Loan and Life Assurance Company: and fully proves to you that any connexion on your part with that establishment must result in a perpetual Christmas Box and constantly increasing Bonus to yourself, and that nobody can run any risk by the transaction except the office, which, in its great liberality, is pretty sure to lose. And this, David Crimple, Esquire, submits to you (and the odds are heavy you believe him), is the best guarantee that can reasonably be suggested by the Board of Management for its permanence and stability.

This gentleman's name, by the way, had been originally Crimp; but as the word was susceptible of an awkward construction and might be misrepresented, he had altered it to Crimple.

Lest with all these proofs and confirmations, any man should be suspicious of the Anglo-Bengalee Disinterested Loan and Life Assurance Company; should doubt in tiger, cab, or person, Tigg Montague, Esquire, (of Pall Mall and Bengal), or any other name in the imaginative List of Directors; there was a porter on the premises—a wonderful creature, in a vast red waistcoat and a short-tailed pepper-and-salt coat—who carried more conviction to the minds of sceptics than the whole establishment without him. No confidences existed between him and the Directorship; nobody knew where he had served last; no character or explanation had been given or required. No questions had been asked on either side. This mysterious being, relying solely on his figure, had applied for the situation, and had been instantly engaged on his own terms. They were high; but he knew, doubtless, that no man could carry such an extent of waistcoat as himself, and felt the full value of his capacity to such an institution. When he sat upon a seat erected for him in a corner of the office, with his glazed hat hanging on a peg over his head, it was impossible to doubt the respectability of the concern. It went on doubling itself with every square inch of his red waistcoat until, like the problem of the nails in the horse's shoes, the total became enormous. People had been known to apply to effect an insurance on their lives for a thousand pounds, and looking at him, to beg, before the form of proposal was filled up, that it might be made two. And yet he was not a giant. His coat was rather small than otherwise. The whole charm was in his waistcoat. Respectability, competence, property in Bengal or anywhere else, responsibility to any amount on the part of the company that employed him, were all expressed in that one garment.

Rival offices had endeavoured to lure him away; Lombard Street itself had beckoned to him; rich companies had whispered 'Be a Beadle!' but he still continued faithful to the Anglo-Bengalee. Whether he was a deep rogue, or a stately simpleton, it was impossible to make out, but he appeared to believe in the Anglo-Bengalee. He was grave with imaginary cares of office; and having nothing whatever to do, and something less to take care of, would look as if the pressure of his numerous duties, and a sense of the treasure in the company's strong-room, made him a solemn and a thoughtful man.

As the cabriolet drove up to the door, this officer appeared bareheaded on the pavement, crying aloud 'Room for the chairman, room for the chairman, if you please!' much to the admiration of the bystanders, who, it is needless to say, had their attention directed to the Anglo-Bengalee Company thenceforth, by that means. Mr. Tigg leaped gracefully out, followed by the Managing Director (who was by this time very distant and respectful), and ascended the stairs, still preceded by the porter: who cried as he went, 'By your leave there! by your leave! The Chairman of the Board, Gentle—MEN!' In like manner, but in a still more stentorian voice, he ushered the chairman through the public office, where some humble clients were transacting business, into an awful chamber, labelled Board-room: the door of which sanctuary immediately closed, and screened the great capitalist from vulgar eyes.

The board-room had a Turkey carpet in it, a sideboard, a portrait of Tigg Montague, Esquire, as chairman; a very imposing chair of office, garnished with an ivory hammer and a little hand-bell; and a long-table, set out at intervals with sheets of blotting-paper, foolscap, clean pens, and ink-stands. The chairman having taken his seat with great solemnity, the secretary supported him on his right hand, and the porter stood bolt upright behind them, forming a warm background of waistcoat. This was the board; everything else being a light-hearted little fiction.

'Bullamy!' said Mr. Tigg.

'Sir!' replied the Porter.

'Let the Medical Officer know, with my compliments, that I wish to see him.'

Bullamy cleared his throat, and bustled out into the office, crying 'The Chairman of the Board wishes to see the Medical Officer. By your leave there! By your leave!' He soon returned with the gentleman in question; and at both openings of the board-room door—at his coming in and at his going out—simple clients were seen to stretch their necks and stand upon their toes, thirsting to catch the slightest glimpse of that mysterious chamber.

'Jobling, my dear friend!' said Mr. Tigg, 'how are you? Bullamy, wait outside. Crimple, don't leave us. Jobling, my good fellow, I am glad to see you.'

'And how are *you*, Mr. Montague, eh?' said the Medical Officer, throwing himself luxuriously into an easy-chair (they were all easy-chairs in the board-room), and taking a handsome gold snuff-box from the pocket of his black satin waistcoat. 'How are you? A little worn with business, eh? If so, rest. A little feverish from wine, humph? If so, water. Nothing at all the matter, and quite comfortable? Then take some lunch. A very wholesome thing at this time of day to strengthen the gastric juices with lunch, Mr. Montague.'

The Medical Officer (he was the same medical officer who had followed poor old Anthony Chuzzlewit to the grave, and who had attended Mrs. Gamp's patient at the Bull) smiled in saying these words; and casually added, as he brushed some grains of snuff from his shirt-frill, 'I always take it myself about this time of day, do you know!'

'Bullamy!' said the Chairman, ringing the little bell.

'Sir!'

'Lunch.'

'Not on my account, I hope?' said the doctor. 'You are very good. Thank you. I'm quite ashamed. Ha, ha! if I had been a sharp practitioner, Mr. Montague, I shouldn't have mentioned it without a fee; for you may depend upon it, my dear sir, that if you don't make a point of taking lunch, you'll very soon come under my hands. Allow me to illustrate this. In Mr. Crimple's leg—'

The resident Director gave an involuntary start, for the doctor, in the heat of his demonstration, caught it up and laid it across his own, as if he were going to take it off, then and there.

'In Mr. Crimple's leg, you'll observe,' pursued the doctor, turning back his cuffs and spanning the limb with both hands, 'where Mr. Crimple's knee fits into the socket, here, there is— that is to say, between the bone and the socket—a certain quantity of animal oil.'

'What do you pick *my* leg out for?' said Mr. Crimple, looking with something of an anxious expression at his limb. 'It's the same with other legs, ain't it?'

'Never you mind, my good sir,' returned the doctor, shaking his head, 'whether it is the same with other legs, or not the same.'

'But I do mind,' said David.

'I take a particular case, Mr. Montague,' returned the doctor, 'as illustrating my remark, you observe. In this portion of Mr. Crimple's leg, sir, there is a certain amount of animal

oil. In every one of Mr. Crimple's joints, sir, there is more or
less of the same deposit. Very good. If Mr. Crimple neglects
his meals, or fails to take his proper quantity of rest, that oil
wanes, and becomes exhausted. What is the consequence?
Mr. Crimple's bones sink down into their sockets, sir, and Mr.
Crimple becomes a weazen, puny, stunted, miserable man!'

The doctor let Mr. Crimple's leg fall suddenly, as if he were
already in that agreeable condition: turned down his wrist-
bands again, and looked triumphantly at the chairman.

'We know a few secrets of nature in our profession, sir,' said
the doctor. 'Of course we do. We study for that; we pass the
Hall and the College for that; and we take our station in
society *by* that. It's extraordinary how little is known on these
subjects generally. Where do you suppose, now:' the doctor
closed one eye, as he leaned back smilingly in his chair, and
formed a triangle with his hands, of which his two thumbs
composed the base: 'where do you suppose Mr. Crimple's
stomach is?'

Mr. Crimple, more agitated than before, clapped his hand
immediately below his waistcoat.

'Not at all,' cried the doctor; 'not at all. Quite a popular
mistake! My good sir, you're altogether deceived.'

'I feel it there, when it's out of order; that's all I know,'
said Crimple.

'You think you do,' replied the doctor; 'but science knows
better. There was a patient of mine once:' touching one of the
many mourning rings upon his fingers, and slightly bowing his
head: 'a gentleman who did me the honour to make a very
handsome mention of me in his will—"in testimony," as he
was pleased to say, "of the unremitting zeal, talent, and attention of my friend and medical attendant, John Jobling,
Esquire, M.R.C.S.,"—who was so overcome by the idea of
having all his life laboured under an erroneous view of the
locality of this important organ, that when I assured him, on
my professional reputation, he was mistaken, he burst into
tears, put out his hand, and said, "Jobling, God bless you!"
Immediately afterwards he became speechless, and was ultimately buried at Brixton.'

'By your leave there!' cried Bullamy, without. 'By your
leave! Refreshment for the Board-room!'

'Ha!' said the doctor, jocularly, as he rubbed his hands, and
drew his chair nearer to the table. 'The true Life Assurance,

Mr. Montague. The best Policy in the world, my dear sir. We should be provident, and eat and drink whenever we can. Eh, Mr. Crimple?'

The resident Director acquiesced rather sulkily, as if the gratification of replenishing his stomach had been impaired by the unsettlement of his preconceived opinions in reference to its situation. But the appearance of the porter and under porter with a tray covered with a snow-white cloth, which, being thrown back, displayed a pair of cold roast fowls, flanked by some potted meats and a cool salad, quickly restored his good humour. It was enhanced still further by the arrival of a bottle of excellent madeira, and another of champagne; and he soon attacked the repast with an appetite scarcely inferior to that of the medical officer.

The lunch was handsomely served, with a profusion of rich glass, plate, and china; which seemed to denote that eating and drinking on a showy scale formed no unimportant item in the business of the Anglo-Bengalee Directorship. As it proceeded, the Medical Officer grew more and more joyous and red-faced, insomuch that every mouthful he ate, and every drop of wine he swallowed, seemed to impart new lustre to his eyes, and to light up new sparks in his nose and forehead.

In certain quarters of the City and its neighbourhood, Mr. Jobling was, as we have already seen in some measure, a very popular character. He had a portentously sagacious chin, and a pompous voice, with a rich huskiness in some of its tones that went directly to the heart, like a ray of light shining through the ruddy medium of choice old burgundy. His neckerchief and shirt-frill were ever of the whitest, his clothes of the blackest and sleekest, his gold watch-chain of the heaviest, and his seals of the largest. His boots, which were always of the brightest, creaked as he walked. Perhaps he could shake his head, rub his hands, or warm himself before a fire, better than any man alive; and he had a peculiar way of smacking his lips and saying, 'Ah!' at intervals while patients detailed their symptoms, which inspired great confidence. It seemed to express, 'I know what you're going to say better than you do; but go on, go on.' As he talked on all occasions whether he had anything to say or not, it was unanimously observed of him that he was 'full of anecdote;' and his experience and profit from it were considered, for the same reason, to be something much too extensive for description. His female patients could never praise him too highly; and the coldest of his male admirers would always say this for him to their friends, 'that whatever Jobling's professional skill might be (and it could not be denied that he had a very high reputation), he was one of the most comfortable fellows you ever saw in your life!'

Jobling was for many reasons, and not last in the list because his connexion lay principally among tradesmen and their families, exactly the sort of person whom the Anglo-Bengalee Company wanted for a medical officer. But Jobling was far too knowing to connect himself with the company in any closer ties than as a paid (and well-paid) functionary, or to allow his connexion to be misunderstood abroad, if he could help it. Hence he always stated the case to an inquiring patient, after this manner:

'Why, my dear sir, with regard to the Anglo-Bengalee, my information, you see, is limited: very limited. I am the medical officer, in consideration of a certain monthly payment. The labourer is worthy of his hire; *Bis dat qui citò dat*'—('Classical scholar, Jobling!' thinks the patient, 'well-read man!')—'and I receive it regularly. Therefore I am bound, so far as my own knowledge goes, to speak well of the establishment.' ('Nothing can be fairer than Jobling's conduct,' thinks the patient, who has just paid Jobling's bill himself.) 'If you put any question to me, my dear friend,' says the doctor, 'touching the responsibility or capital of the company, there I am at fault; for I have no head for figures, and not being a shareholder, am delicate of showing any curiosity whatever on the subject. Delicacy—your amiable lady will agree with me I am sure—should be one of the first characteristics of a medical man.' ('Nothing can be finer or more gentlemanly than Jobling's feeling,' thinks the patient.) 'Very good, my dear sir, so the matter stands. You don't know Mr. Montague? I'm sorry for it. A remarkably handsome man, and quite the gentleman in every respect. Property, I am told, in India. House and everything belonging to him, beautiful. Costly furniture on the most elegant and lavish scale. And pictures, which, even in an anatomical point of view, are per—fection. In case you should ever think of doing anything with the company, I'll pass you, you may depend upon it. I can conscientiously report you a healthy subject. If I understand any man's constitution, it is yours; and this little indisposition has done him more good, ma'am,' says the doctor, turning to the patient's wife, 'than if he had swallowed the contents of half the nonsensical bottles in my surgery. For they *are* nonsense—to tell the honest truth, one half of them *are* nonsense—compared with such a constitution as his!' ('Jobling is the most friendly creature I ever met with in my life,' thinks the patient; 'and upon my word and honour, I'll consider of it!')

'Commission to you, doctor, on four new policies, and a loan this morning, eh?' said Crimple, looking, when they had finished lunch, over some papers brought in by the porter. 'Well done!'

'Jobling, my dear friend,' said Tigg, 'long life to you.'

'No, no. Nonsense. Upon my word I've no right to draw the commission,' said the doctor, 'I haven't really. It's picking your pocket. I don't recommend anybody here. I only say what I know. My patients ask me what I know, and I tell 'em what I know. Nothing else. Caution is my weak side, that's the truth; and always was from a boy. That is,' said the doctor, filling his glass, 'caution in behalf of other people. Whether I would repose confidence in this company myself, if I had not been paying money elsewhere for many years—that's quite another question.'

He tried to look as if there were no doubt about it; but feeling that he did it but indifferently, changed the theme, and praised the wine.

'Talking of wine,' said the doctor, 'reminds me of one of the finest glasses of light old port I ever drank in my life; and that was at a funeral. You have not seen anything of—of *that* party, Mr. Montague, have you?' handing him a card.

'He is not buried, I hope?' said Tigg, as he took it. 'The honour of his company is not requested if he is.'

'Ha, ha!' laughed the doctor. 'No; not quite. He was honourably connected with that very occasion though.'

'Oh!' said Tigg, smoothing his moustache, as he cast his eyes upon the name. 'I recollect. No. He has not been here.'

The words were on his lips, when Bullamy entered, and presented a card to the Medical Officer.

'Talk of the what's his name,' observed the doctor rising.

'And he's sure to appear, eh?' said Tigg.

'Why, no, Mr. Montague, no,' returned the doctor. 'We will not say that in the present case, for this gentleman is very far from it.'

'So much the better,' retorted Tigg. 'So much the more

adaptable to the Anglo-Bengalee. Bullamy, clear the table and take the things out by the other door. Mr. Crimple, business.'

'Shall I introduce him?' asked Jobling.

'I shall be eternally delighted,' answered Tigg, kissing his hand and smiling sweetly.

The doctor disappeared into the outer office, and immediately returned with Jonas Chuzzlewit.

'Mr. Montague,' said Jobling. 'Allow me. My friend Mr. Chuzzlewit. My dear friend—our chairman. Now do you know,' he added, checking himself with infinite policy, and looking round with a smile: 'that's a very singular instance of the force of example. It really is a very remarkable instance of the force of example. I say *our* chairman. Why do I say our chairman? Because he is not *my* chairman, you know. I have no connexion with the company, farther than giving them, for a certain fee and reward, my poor opinion as a medical man, precisely as I may give it any day to Jack Noakes or Tom Styles. Then why do I say our chairman? Simply because I hear the phrase constantly repeated about me. Such is the involuntary operation of the mental faculty in the imitative biped man. Mr. Crimple, I believe you never take snuff? Injudicious. You should.'

Pending these remarks on the part of the doctor, and the lengthened and sonorous pinch with which he followed them up, Jonas took a seat at the board: as ungainly a man as ever he has been within the reader's knowledge. It is too common with all of us, but it is especially in the nature of a mean mind, to be overawed by fine clothes and fine furniture. They had a very decided influence on Jonas.

'Now you two gentlemen have business to discuss, I know,' said the doctor, 'and your time is precious. So is mine; for several lives are waiting for me in the next room, and I have a round of visits to make after—after I have taken 'em. Having had the happiness to introduce you to each other, I may go about my business. Good-bye. But allow me, Mr. Montague, before I go, to say this of my friend who sits beside you: That gentleman has done more, sir,' rapping his snuff-box solemnly, 'to reconcile me to human nature, than any man alive or dead. Good-bye!'

With these words Jobling bolted abruptly out of the room, and proceeded in his own official department, to impress the lives in waiting with a sense of his keen conscientiousness in

The Board
(*p. 436*)

the discharge of his duty, and the great difficulty of getting into the Anglo-Bengalee; by feeling their pulses, looking at their tongues, listening at their ribs, poking them in the chest, and so forth; though, if he didn't well know beforehand that whatever kind of lives they were, the Anglo-Bengalee would accept them readily, he was far from being the Jobling that his friend considered him; and was not the original Jobling, but a spurious imitation.

Mr. Crimple also departed on the business of the morning; and Jonas Chuzzlewit and Tigg were left alone.

'I learn from our friend,' said Tigg, drawing his chair towards Jonas with a winning ease of manner, 'that you have been thinking—'

'Oh! Ecod then he'd no right to say so,' cried Jonas, interrupting. 'I didn't tell *him* my thoughts. If he took it into his head that I was coming here for such or such a purpose, why, that's his look-out. I don't stand committed by that.'

Jonas said this offensively enough; for over and above the habitual distrust of his character, it was in his nature to seek to revenge himself on the fine clothes and the fine furniture, in exact proportion as he had been unable to withstand their influence.

'If I come here to ask a question or two, and get a document or two to consider of, I don't bind myself to anything. Let's understand that, you know,' said Jonas.

'My dear fellow!' cried Tigg, clapping him on the shoulder, 'I applaud your frankness. If men like you and I speak openly at first, all possible misunderstanding is avoided. Why should I disguise what you know so well, but what the crowd never dream of? We companies are all birds of prey: mere birds of prey. The only question is, whether, in serving our own turn, we can serve yours too: whether in double-lining our own nest, we can put a single lining into yours. Oh, you're in our secret. You're behind the scenes. We'll make a merit of dealing plainly with you, when we know we can't help it.'

It was remarked, on the first introduction of Mr. Jonas into these pages, that there is a simplicity of cunning no less than a simplicity of innocence, and that in all matters involving a faith in knavery, he was the most credulous of men. If Mr. Tigg had preferred any claim to high and honourable dealing, Jonas would have suspected him though he had been a very model of probity; but when he gave utterance to Jonas's own thoughts of everything and everybody, Jonas began to feel that he was a pleasant fellow, and one to be talked to freely.

He changed his position in the chair; not for a less awkward, but for a more boastful attitude; and smiling in his miserable conceit, rejoined:

'You an't a bad man of business, Mr. Montague. You know how to set about it, I *will* say.'

'Tut, tut,' said Tigg, nodding confidentially, and showing his white teeth: 'we are not children, Mr. Chuzzlewit; we are grown men, I hope.'

Jonas assented, and said after a short silence, first spreading out his legs, and sticking one arm akimbo to show how perfectly at home he was,

'The truth is—'

'Don't say, the truth,' interposed Tigg, with another grin. 'It's so like humbug.'

Greatly charmed by this, Jonas began again.

'The long and the short of it is—'

'Better,' muttered Tigg. 'Much better!'

'—That I didn't consider myself very well used by one or two of the old companies in some negotiations I have had with 'em. Once had, I mean. They started objections they had no right to start, and put questions they had no right to put, and carried things much too high for my taste.'

As he made these observations he cast down his eyes, and looked curiously at the carpet. Mr. Tigg looked curiously at him.

He made so long a pause, that Tigg came to the rescue, and said, in his pleasantest manner:

'Take a glass of wine.'

'No, no,' returned Jonas, with a cunning shake of the head; 'none of that, thankee. No wine over business. All very well for you, but it wouldn't do for me.'

'What an old hand you are, Mr. Chuzzlewit!' said Tigg, leaning back in his chair, and leering at him through his half-shut eyes.

Jonas shook his head again, as much as to say, 'You're right there;' and then resumed, jocosely:

'Not such an old hand, either, but that I've been and got married. That's rather green, you'll say. Perhaps it is, especially as she's young. But one never knows what may happen to these women, so I'm thinking of insuring her life. It is but fair, you know, that a man should secure some consolation in case of meeting with such a loss.'

'If anything *can* console him under such heart-breaking circumstances,' murmured Tigg, with his eyes shut up as before.

'Exactly,' returned Jonas; 'if anything can. Now, supposing I did it here, I should do it cheap, I know, and easy, without bothering her about it; which I'd much rather not do, for it's just in a woman's way to take it into her head, if you talk to her about such things, that she's going to die directly.'

'So it is,' cried Tigg, kissing his hand in honour of the sex. 'You're quite right. Sweet, silly, fluttering little simpletons!'

'Well,' said Jonas, 'on that account, you know, and because offence has been given me in other quarters, I wouldn't mind patronising this Company. But I want to know what sort of security there is for the Company's going on. That's the—'

'Not the truth?' cried Tigg, holding up his jewelled hand. 'Don't use that Sunday School expression, please!'

'The long and the short of it,' said Jonas. 'The long and the short of it is, what's the security?'

'The paid-up capital, my dear sir,' said Tigg, referring to some papers on the table, 'is, at this present moment—'

'Oh! I understand all about paid-up capitals, you know,' said Jonas.

'You do?' cried Tigg, stopping short.

'I should hope so.'

He turned the papers down again, and moving nearer to him, said in his ear:

'I know you do. I know you do. Look at me!'

It was not much in Jonas's way to look straight at anybody; but thus requested, he made shift to take a tolerable survey of the chairman's features. The chairman fell back a little, to give him the better opportunity.

'You know me?' he inquired, elevating his eyebrows. 'You recollect? You've seen me before?'

'Why, I thought I remembered your face when I first came in,' said Jonas, gazing at it: 'but I couldn't call to mind where I had seen it. No. I don't remember, even now. Was it in the street?'

'Was it in Pecksniff's parlour?' said Tigg.

'In Pecksniff's parlour!' echoed Jonas, fetching a long breath. 'You don't mean when—'

R

'Yes,' cried Tigg, 'when there was a very charming and delightful little family party, at which yourself and your respected father assisted.'

'Well, never mind *him*,' said Jonas. 'He's dead, and there's no help for it.'

'Dead, is he!' cried Tigg. 'Venerable old gentleman, is he dead! You're very like him.'

Jonas received this compliment with anything but a good grace; perhaps because of his own private sentiments in reference to the personal appearance of his deceased parent; perhaps because he was not best pleased to find that Montague and Tigg were one. That gentleman perceived it, and tapping him familiarly on the sleeve, beckoned him to the window. From this moment, Mr. Montague's jocularity and flow of spirits were remarkable.

'Do you find me at all changed since that time?' he asked. 'Speak plainly.'

Jonas looked hard at his waistcoat and jewels; and said, 'Rather, ecod!'

'Was I at all seedy in those days?' asked Montague.

'Precious seedy,' said Jonas.

Mr. Montague pointed down into the street, where Bailey and the cab were in attendance.

'Neat: perhaps dashing. Do you know whose it is?'

'No.'

'Mine. Do you like this room?'

'It must have cost a lot of money,' said Jonas.

'You're right. Mine too. Why don't you'—he whispered this, and nudged him in the side with his elbow—'why don't you take premiums, instead of paying 'em? That's what a man like you should do. Join us!'

Jonas stared at him in amazement.

'Is that a crowded street?' asked Montague, calling his attention to the multitude without.

'Very,' said Jonas, only glancing at it, and immediately afterwards looking at him again.

'There are printed calculations,' said his companion, 'which will tell you pretty nearly how many people will pass up and down that thoroughfare in the course of a day. *I* can tell you how many of 'em will come in here, merely because they find this office here; knowing no more about it than they do of the Pyramids. Ha, ha! Join us. You shall come in cheap.'

Jonas looked at him harder and harder.

'I can tell you,' said Tigg in his ear, 'how many of 'em will buy annuities, effect insurances, bring us their money in a hundred shapes and ways, force it upon us, trust us as if we were the Mint; yet know no more about us than you do of that crossing-sweeper at the corner. Not so much. Ha, ha!'

Jonas gradually broke into a smile.

'Yah!' said Montague, giving him a pleasant thrust in the breast; 'you're too deep for us, you dog, or I wouldn't have told you. Dine with me to-morrow, in Pall Mall!'

'I will,' said Jonas.

'Done!' cried Montague. 'Wait a bit. Take these papers with you, and look 'em over. See,' he said, snatching some printed forms from the table. 'B is a little tradesman, clerk, parson, artist, author, any common thing you like.'

'Yes,' said Jonas, looking greedily over his shoulder. 'Well!'

'B wants a loan. Say fifty or a hundred pound; perhaps more; no matter. B proposes self and two securities. B is accepted. Two securities give a bond. B assures his own life for double the amount, and brings two friends' lives also—just to patronise the office. Ha, ha, ha! Is that a good notion?'

'Ecod, that's a capital notion!' cried Jonas. 'But does he really do it?'

'Do it!' repeated the chairman. 'B's hard-up, my good fellow, and will do anything. Don't you see? It's my idea.'

'It does you honour. I'm blest if it don't,' said Jonas.

'I think it does,' replied the chairman, 'and I'm proud to hear you say so. B pays the highest lawful interest—'

'That an't much,' interrupted Jonas.

'Right! quite right!' retorted Tigg. 'And hard it is upon the part of the law that it should be so confoundedly down upon us unfortunate victims; when it takes such amazing good interest for itself from all its clients. But charity begins at home, and justice begins next door. Well! The law being hard upon us, we're not exactly soft upon B; for besides charging B the regular interest, we get B's premium, and B's friends' premiums, and we charge B for the bond, and, whether we accept him or not, we charge B for "inquiries" (we keep a man, at a pound a week, to make 'em), and we charge B a trifle for the secretary; and in short, my good fellow, we stick it into B, up hill and down dale, and make a devilish comfortable little property out of him. Ha, ha, ha! I drive B, in point of fact,' said Tigg, pointing to the cabriolet, 'and a thorough-bred horse he is. Ha, ha, ha!'

Jonas enjoyed this joke very much indeed. It was quite in his peculiar vein of humour.

'Then,' said Tigg Montague, 'we grant annuities on the very lowest and most advantageous terms known in the money market; and the old ladies and gentlemen down in the country buy 'em. Ha, ha, ha! And we pay 'em too—perhaps. Ha, ha, ha!'

'But there's responsibility in that,' said Jonas, looking doubtful.

'I take it all myself,' said Tigg Montague. 'Here I am responsible for everything. The only responsible person in the establishment! Ha, ha, ha! Then there are the Life Assurances without loans: the common policies. Very profitable, very comfortable. Money down, you know; repeated every year; capital fun!'

'But when they begin to fall in,' observed Jonas. 'It's all very well, while the office is young, but when the policies begin to die; that's what I am thinking of.'

'At the first start, my dear fellow,' said Montague, 'to show you how correct your judgment is, we had a couple of unlucky deaths that brought us down to a grand piano.'

'Brought you down where?' cried Jonas.

'I give you my sacred word of honour,' said Tigg Montague, 'that I raised money on every other individual piece of property, and was left alone in the world with a grand piano. And it was an upright-grand too, so that I couldn't even sit upon it. But, my dear fellow, we got over it. We granted a great many new policies that week (liberal allowance to solicitors, by-the-bye), and got over it in no time. Whenever they should chance to fall in heavily, as you very justly observe they may, one of these days; then—' he finished the sentence in so low a whisper, that only one disconnected word was audible, and that imperfectly. But it sounded like 'Bolt.'

'Why, you're as bold as brass!' said Jonas, in the utmost admiration.

'A man can well afford to be as bold as brass, my good fellow, when he gets gold in exchange!' cried the chairman, with a laugh that shook him from head to foot. 'You'll dine with me to-morrow?'

'At what time?' asked Jonas.

'Seven. Here's my card. Take the documents. I see you'll join us!'

'I don't know about that,' said Jonas. 'There's a good deal to be looked into first.'

'You shall look,' said Montague, slapping him on the back, 'into anything and everything you please. But you'll join us, I am convinced. You were made for it. Bullamy!'

Obedient to the summons and the little bell, the waistcoat appeared. Being charged to show Jonas out, it went before; and the voice within it cried, as usual, 'By your leave there, by your leave! Gentleman from the board-room, by your leave!'

Mr. Montague being left alone, pondered for some moments, and then said, raising his voice,

'Is Nadgett in the office there?'

'Here he is, sir.' And he promptly entered: shutting the board-room door after him, as carefully as if he were about to plot a murder.

He was the man at a pound a week who made the inquiries. It was no virtue or merit in Nadgett that he transacted all his Anglo-Bengalee business secretly and in the closest confidence; for he was born to be a secret. He was a short, dried-up, withered old man, who seemed to have secreted his very blood; for nobody would have given him credit for the possession of six ounces of it in his whole body. How he lived was a secret; where he lived was a secret; and even what he was, was a secret. In his musty old pocket-book he carried contradictory cards, in some of which he called himself a coal-merchant, in others a wine-merchant, in others a commission-agent, in others a collector, in others an accountant: as if he really didn't know the secret himself. He was always keeping appointments in the City, and the other man never seemed to come. He would sit on 'Change for hours, looking at everybody who walked in and out, and would do the like at Garraway's, and in other business coffee-houses, in some of which he would be occasionally seen drying a very damp pocket-handkerchief before the fire, and still looking over his shoulder for the man who never appeared. He was mildewed, threadbare, shabby; always had flue upon his legs and back; and kept his linen so secret by buttoning up and wrapping over, that he might have had none—perhaps he hadn't. He carried one stained beaver glove, which he dangled before him by the forefinger as he walked or sat; but even its fellow was a secret. Some people said he had been a bankrupt, others that he had gone an infant into an ancient Chancery suit which was still depending, but it was all a secret. He carried bits of sealing-wax and a hieroglyphical old copper seal in his pocket, and often secretly indited letters in corner boxes of the trysting-places before mentioned; but they never appeared to go to anybody, for he would put them into a secret place in his coat, and deliver them to himself weeks afterwards, very much to his own surprise, quite yellow. He was that sort of man that if he had died worth a million of money, or had died worth twopence halfpenny, everybody would have been perfectly satisfied, and would have said it was just as they expected. And yet he belonged to a class; a race peculiar to the City; who are secrets as profound to one another, as they are to the rest of mankind.

'Mr. Nadgett,' said Montague, copying Jonas Chuzzlewit's address upon a piece of paper, from the card which was still lying on the table, 'any information about this name, I shall be glad to have myself. Don't you mind what it is. Any you can scrape together, bring me. Bring it *to me*, Mr. Nadgett.'

Nadgett put on his spectacles, and read the name attentively; then looked at the chairman over his glasses, and bowed; then took them off, and put them in their case; and then put the case in his pocket. When he had done so, he looked, without his spectacles, at the paper as it lay before him, and at the same time produced his pocket-book from somewhere about the middle of his spine. Large as it was, it was very full of documents, but he found a place for this one; and having clasped it carefully, passed it by a kind of solemn legerdemain into the same region as before.

He withdrew with another bow and without a word; opening the door no wider than was sufficient for his passage out; and shutting it as carefully as before. The chairman of the board employed the rest of the morning in affixing his signmanual of gracious acceptance to various new proposals of annuity-purchase and assurance. The Company was looking up, for they flowed in gaily.

CHAPTER XXVIII

Mr. Montague at home. And Mr. Jonas Chuzzlewit at home

THERE were many powerful reasons for Jonas Chuzzlewit being strongly prepossessed in favour of the scheme which its great originator had so boldly laid open to him; but three among them stood prominently forward. Firstly, there was money to be made by it. Secondly, the money had the peculiar charm of being sagaciously obtained at other people's cost. Thirdly, it involved much outward show of homage and distinction: a board being an awful institution in its own sphere, and a director a mighty man. 'To make a swingeing profit, have a lot of chaps to order about, and get into regular good society by one and the same means, and them so easy to one's hand, ain't such a bad look-out,' thought Jonas. The latter considerations were only second to his avarice; for, conscious that there was nothing in his person, conduct, character, or accomplishments, to command respect, he was greedy of power, and was, in his heart, as much a tyrant as any laurelled conqueror on record.

But he determined to proceed with cunning and caution, and to be very keen in his observation of the gentility of Mr. Montague's private establishment. For it no more occurred to this shallow knave that Montague wanted him to be so, or he wouldn't have invited him while his decision was yet in abeyance, than the possibility of that genius being able to over-reach him in any way, pierced through his self-conceit by the inlet of a needle's point. He had said, in the outset, that Jonas was too sharp for him; and Jonas, who would have been sharp enough to believe him in nothing else, though he had solemnly sworn it, believed him in that, instantly.

It was with a faltering hand, and yet with an imbecile attempt at a swagger, that he knocked at his new friend's door in Pall Mall when the appointed hour arrived. Mr. Bailey quickly answered to the summons. He was not proud, and was kindly disposed to take notice of Jonas; but Jonas had forgotten him.

'Mr. Montague at home?'

'I should hope he wos at home, and waiting dinner, too,'

said Bailey, with the ease of an old acquaintance. 'Will you take your hat up along with you, or leave it here?'

Mr. Jonas preferred leaving it there.

'The hold name, I suppose?' said Bailey, with a grin.

Mr. Jonas stared at him in mute indignation.

'What, don't you remember hold mother Todgers's?' said Mr. Bailey, with his favourite action of the knees and boots. 'Don't you remember my taking your name up to the young ladies, when you come a-courting there? A reg'lar scaly old shop, warn't it? Times is changed, ain't they. I say, how you've growed!'

Without pausing for any acknowledgement of this compliment, he ushered the visitor up-stairs; and having announced him, retired with a private wink.

The lower story of the house was occupied by a wealthy tradesman, but Mr. Montague had all the upper portion, and splendid lodging it was. The room in which he received Jonas was a spacious and elegant apartment, furnished with extreme magnificence: decorated with pictures, copies from the antique in alabaster and marble, china vases, lofty mirrors, crimson hangings of the richest silk, gilded carvings, luxurious couches, glistening cabinets inlaid with precious woods: costly toys of every sort in negligent abundance. The only guests besides Jonas were the doctor, the resident Director, and two other gentlemen, whom Montague presented in due form.

'My dear friend, I am delighted to see you. Jobling you know, I believe?'

'I think so,' said the doctor pleasantly, as he stepped out of the circle to shake hands. 'I trust I have that honour. I hope so. My dear sir, I see you well. Quite well? *That*'s well!'

'Mr. Wolf,' said Montague, as soon as the doctor would allow him to introduce the two others, 'Mr. Chuzzlewit. Mr. Pip, Mr. Chuzzlewit.'

Both gentlemen were exceedingly happy to have the honour of making Mr. Chuzzlewit's acquaintance. The doctor drew Jonas a little apart, and whispered behind his hand:

'Men of the world, my dear sir—men of the world. Hem! Mr. Wolf—literary character—you needn't mention it—remarkably clever weekly paper—oh, remarkably clever! Mr. Pip—theatrical man—capital man to know—oh, capital man!'

'Well!' said Wolf, folding his arms and resuming a conversation which the arrival of Jonas had interrupted. 'And what did Lord Nobley say to that?'

'Why,' returned Pip, with an oath. 'He didn't know what to say. Damme, sir, if he wasn't as mute as a poker. But you know what a good fellow Nobley is!'

'The best fellow in the world!' cried Wolf. 'It was only last week that Nobley said to me, "By Gad, Wolf, I've got a living to bestow, and if you had but been brought up at the University, strike me blind if I wouldn't have made a parson of you!"'

'Just like him,' said Pip with another oath. 'And he'd have done it!'

'Not a doubt of it,' said Wolf. 'But you were going to tell us?—'

'Oh, yes!' cried Pip. 'To be sure. So I was. At first he was dumb—sewn up, dead, sir—but after a minute he said to the Duke, "Here's Pip. Ask Pip. Pip's our mutual friend. Ask Pip. He knows." "Damme!" said the Duke, "I appeal to Pip then. Come, Pip. Bandy or not bandy? Speak out!" "Bandy, your Grace, by the Lord Harry!" said I. "Ha, ha!" laughed the Duke. "To be sure she is. Bravo, Pip. Well said, Pip. I wish I may die if you're not a trump, Pip. Pop me down among your fashionable visitors whenever I'm in town, Pip." And so I do, to this day.'

The conclusion of this story gave immense satisfaction, which was in no degree lessened by the announcement of dinner. Jonas repaired to the dining-room, along with his distinguished host, and took his seat at the board between that individual and his friend the doctor. The rest fell into their places like men who were well accustomed to the house; and dinner was done full justice to, by all parties.

It was as good a one as money (or credit, no matter which) could produce. The dishes, wines, and fruits were of the choicest kind. Everything was elegantly served. The plate was gorgeous. Mr. Jonas was in the midst of a calculation of the value of this item alone, when his host disturbed him.

'A glass of wine?'

'Oh!' said Jonas, who had had several glasses already. 'As much of that, as you like! It's too good to refuse.'

'Well said, Mr. Chuzzlewit!' cried Wolf.

'Tom Gag, upon my soul!' said Pip.

'Positively, you know, that's—ha, ha, ha!' observed the doctor, laying down his knife and fork for one instant, and then going to work again, pell-mell—'that's epigrammatic; quite!'

'You're tolerably comfortable, I hope?' said Tigg, apart to Jonas.

'Oh! You needn't trouble your head about *me*,' he replied. 'Famous!'

'I thought it best not to have a party,' said Tigg. 'You feel that?'

'Why, what do you call this?' retorted Jonas. 'You don't mean to say you do this every day, do you?'

'My dear fellow,' said Montague, shrugging his shoulders, 'every day of my life, when I dine at home. This is my common style. It was of no use having anything uncommon for you. You'd have seen through it. "You'll have a party?" said Crimple. "No, I won't," I said; "he shall take us in the rough!"'

'And pretty smooth, too, ecod!' said Jonas, glancing round the table. 'This don't cost a trifle.'

'Why, to be candid with you, it does not,' returned the other. 'But I like this sort of thing. It's the way I spend my money.'

Jonas thrust his tongue into his cheek, and said, 'Was it?'

'When you join us, you won't get rid of your share of the profits in the same way?' said Tigg.

'Quite different,' retorted Jonas.

'Well, and you're right,' said Tigg, with friendly candour. 'You needn't. It's not necessary. One of a Company must do it to hold the connexion together; but, as I take a pleasure in it, that's my department. You don't mind dining expensively at another man's expense, I hope?'

'Not a bit,' said Jonas.

'Then I hope you'll often dine with me?'

'Ah!' said Jonas, 'I don't mind. On the contrary.'

'And I'll never attempt to talk business to you over wine, I take my oath,' said Tigg. 'Oh deep, deep, deep of you this morning! I must tell 'em that. They're the very men to enjoy it. Pip, my good fellow, I've a splendid little trait to tell you of my friend Chuzzlewit, who is the deepest dog I know. I give you my sacred word of honour he is the deepest dog I know, Pip!'

Pip swore a frightful oath that he was sure of it already; and the anecdote, being told, was received with loud applause, as an incontestable proof of Mr. Jonas's greatness. Pip, in a natural spirit of emulation, then related some instances of his own depth; and Wolf, not to be left behindhand, recited the leading points of one or two vastly humorous articles he was then preparing. These lucubrations, being of what he called 'a warm complexion,' were highly approved; and all the company agreed that they were full of point.

'Men of the world, my dear sir,' Jobling whispered to Jonas; 'thorough men of the world! To a professional person like myself it's quite refreshing to come into this kind of society. It's not only agreeable—and nothing *can* be more agreeable—but it's philosophically improving. It's character, my dear sir; character!'

It is so pleasant to find real merit appreciated, whatever its particular walk in life may be, that the general harmony of the company was doubtless much promoted by their knowing that the two men of the world were held in great esteem by the upper classes of society, and by the gallant defenders of their country in the army and navy, but particularly the former. The least of their stories had a colonel in it; lords were as plentiful as oaths; and even the Blood Royal ran in the muddy channel of their personal recollections.

'Mr. Chuzzlewit didn't know him, I'm afraid,' said Wolf, in reference to a certain personage of illustrious descent, who had previously figured in a reminiscence.

'No,' said Tigg. 'But we must bring him into contact with this sort of fellows.'

'He was very fond of literature,' observed Wolf.

'Was he?' said Tigg.

'Oh, yes; he took my paper regularly for many years. Do you know he said some good things now and then? He asked a certain Viscount, who's a friend of mine—Pip knows him— "What's the editor's name, what's the editor's name?" "Wolf." "Wolf, eh? Sharp biter, Wolf. We must keep the Wolf from the door, as the proverb says." It was very well. And being complimentary, I printed it.'

'But the Viscount's the boy!' cried Pip, who invented a new oath for the introduction of everything he said. 'The Viscount's the boy! He came into our place one night to take Her home; rather slued, but not much; and said, "Where's Pip? I want to see/ Pip. Produce Pip!"—"What's the row, my lord?"— "Shakspeare's an infernal humbug, Pip! What's the good of

Shakspeare, Pip? I never read him. What the devil is it all about, Pip? There's a lot of feet in Shakspeare's verse, but there ain't any legs worth mentioning in Shakspeare's plays, are there, Pip? Juliet, Desdemona, Lady Macbeth, and all the rest of 'em, whatever their names are, might as well have no legs at all, for anything the audience know about it, Pip. Why, in that respect they're all Miss Biffins to the audience, Pip. I'll tell you what it is. What the people call dramatic poetry is a collection of sermons. Do I go to the theatre to be lectured? No, Pip. If I wanted that, I'd go to church. What's the legitimate object of the drama, Pip? Human nature. What are legs? Human nature. Then let us have plenty of leg pieces, Pip, and I'll stand by you, my buck!" And I am proud to say,' added Pip, 'that he *did* stand by me, handsomely.'

The conversation now becoming general, Mr. Jonas's opinion was requested on this subject; and as it was in full accordance with the sentiments of Mr. Pip, that gentleman was extremely gratified. Indeed, both himself and Wolf had so much in common with Jonas, that they became very amicable; and between their increasing friendship and the fumes of wine, Jonas grew talkative.

It does not follow in the case of such a person that the more talkative he becomes, the more agreeable he is; on the contrary, his merits show to most advantage, perhaps, in silence. Having no means, as he thought, of putting himself on an equality with the rest, but by the assertion of that depth and sharpness on which he had been complimented, Jonas exhibited that faculty to the utmost; and was so deep and sharp that he lost himself in his own profundity, and cut his fingers with his own edge-tools.

It was especially in his way and character to exhibit his quality at his entertainer's expense; and while he drank of his sparkling wines, and partook of his monstrous profusion, to ridicule the extravagance which had set such costly fare before him. Even at such a wanton board, and in such more than doubtful company, this might have proved a disagreeable experiment, but that Tigg and Crimple, studying to understand their man thoroughly, gave him what license he chose: knowing that the more he took, the better for their purpose. And thus while the blundering cheat—gull that he was, for all his cunning—thought himself rolled up hedgehog fashion, with his sharpest points towards them, he was, in fact, betraying all his vulnerable parts to their unwinking watchfulness.

Whether the two gentlemen who contributed so much to the doctor's philosophical knowledge (by the way, the doctor slipped off quietly, after swallowing his usual amount of wine) had had their cue distinctly from the host, or took it from what they saw and heard, they acted their parts very well. They solicited the honour of Jonas's better acquaintance; trusted that they would have the pleasure of introducing him into that elevated society in which he was so well qualified to shine; and informed him, in the most friendly manner, that the advantages of their respective establishments were entirely at his control. In a word, they said 'Be one of us!' And Jonas said he was infinitely obliged to them, and he would be: adding within himself, that so long as they 'stood treat,' there was nothing he would like better.

After coffee, which was served in the drawing-room, there was a short interval (mainly sustained by Pip and Wolf) of conversation; rather highly spiced and strongly seasoned. When it flagged, Jonas took it up and showed considerable humour in appraising the furniture; inquiring whether such an article was paid for; what it had originally cost; and the like. In all of this, he was, as he considered, desperately hard on Montague, and very demonstrative of his own brilliant parts.

Some Champagne Punch gave a new though temporary fillip to the entertainments of the evening. For after leading to some noisy proceedings, which were not intelligible, it ended in the unsteady departure of the two gentlemen of the world, and the slumber of Mr. Jonas upon one of the sofas.

As he could not be made to understand where he was, Mr. Bailey received orders to call a hackney-coach, and take him home: which that young gentleman roused himself from an uneasy sleep in the hall, to do. It being now almost three o'clock in the morning.

'Is he hooked, do you think?' whispered Crimple, as himself and partner stood in a distant part of the room observing him as he lay.

'Aye!' said Tigg, in the same tone. 'With a strong iron, perhaps. Has Nadgett been here to-night?'

'Yes. I went out to him. Hearing you had company, he went away.'

'Why did he do that?'

'He said he would come back early in the morning, before you were out of bed.'

'Tell them to be sure and send him up to my bedside. Hush! Here's the boy! Now Mr. Bailey, take this gentleman home, and see him safely in. Hallo here! Why Chuzzlewit, halloa!'

They got him upright with some difficulty, and assisted him down-stairs, where they put his hat upon his head, and tumbled him into the coach. Mr. Bailey, having shut him in, mounted the box beside the coachman, and smoked his cigar with an air of particular satisfaction; the undertaking in which he was engaged having a free and sporting character about it, which was quite congenial to his taste.

Arriving in due time at the house in the City, Mr. Bailey jumped down, and expressed the lively nature of his feelings in a knock: the like of which had probably not been heard in that quarter since the great fire of London. Going out into the road to observe the effect of this feat, he saw that a dim light, previously visible at an upper window, had been already removed and was travelling down-stairs. To obtain a fore-knowledge of the bearer of this taper, Mr. Bailey skipped back to the door again, and put his eye to the keyhole.

It was the merry one herself. But sadly, strangely altered! So careworn and dejected, so faltering and full of fear; so fallen, humbled, broken; that to have seen her quiet in her coffin would have been a less surprise.

She set the light upon a bracket in the hall, and laid her hand upon her heart; upon her eyes; upon her burning head. Then she came on towards the door with such a wild and hurried step that Mr. Bailey lost his self-possession, and still had his eye where the keyhole had been, when she opened it.

'Aha!' said Mr. Bailey, with an effort. 'There you are, are you? What's the matter? Ain't you well, though?'

In the midst of her astonishment as she recognised him in his altered dress, so much of her old smile came back to her face that Bailey was glad. But next moment he was sorry again, for he saw tears standing in her poor dim eyes.

'Don't be frightened,' said Bailey. 'There ain't nothing the matter. I've brought home Mr. Chuzzlewit. He ain't ill. He's only a little swipey, you know.' Mr. Bailey reeled in his boots, to express intoxication.

'Have you come from Mrs. Todgers's?' asked Merry, trembling.

'Todgers's, bless you! No!' cried Mr. Bailey. 'I haven't got nothing to do with Todgers's. I cut that connexion long ago. He's been a-dining with my governor at the West-end. Didn't you know he was a-coming to see us?'

'No,' she said, faintly.

'Oh yes! We're heavy swells too, and so I tell you. Don't you come out, a-catching cold in your head. *I*'ll wake him!' Mr. Bailey expressing in his demeanour a perfect confidence that he could carry him in with ease, if necessary, opened the coach door, let down the steps, and giving Jonas a shake, cried 'We've got home, my flower! Tumble up, then!'

He was so far recovered as to be able to respond to this appeal, and to come stumbling out of the coach in a heap, to the great hazard of Mr. Bailey's person. When he got upon the pavement, Mr. Bailey first butted at him in front, and then dexterously propped him up behind; and having steadied him by these means, he assisted him into the house.

'You go up first with the light,' said Bailey to Mrs. Jonas, 'and we'll foller. Don't tremble so. He won't hurt you. When *I*'ve had a drop too much, I'm full of good natur myself.'

She went on before; and her husband and Bailey, by dint of tumbling over each other, and knocking themselves about, got at last into the sitting-room abovestairs, where Jonas staggered into a seat.

'There!' said Mr. Bailey. 'He's all right now. You ain't got nothing to cry for, bless you! He's righter than a trivet!'

The ill-favoured brute, with dress awry, and sodden face, and rumpled hair, sat blinking and drooping, and rolling his idiotic eyes about, until, becoming conscious by degrees, he recognised his wife, and shook his fist at her.

'Ah!' cried Mr. Bailey, squaring his arms with a sudden emotion. 'What, you're wicious, are you? Would you though! You'd better not!'

'Pray, go away!' said Merry. 'Bailey, my good boy, go home. Jonas!' she said; timidly laying her hand upon his shoulder, and bending her head down over him; 'Jonas!'

'Look at her!' cried Jonas, pushing her off with his extended arm. 'Look here! Look at her! Here's a bargain for a man!'

'Dear Jonas!'

'Dear Devil!' he replied, with a fierce gesture. 'You're a pretty clog to be tied to a man for life, you mewling, white-faced cat! Get out of my sight!'

'I know you don't mean it, Jonas. You wouldn't say it if you were sober.'

With affected gaiety she gave Bailey a piece of money, and again implored him to be gone. Her entreaty was so earnest, that the boy had not the heart to stay there. But he stopped at the bottom of the stairs, and listened.

'I wouldn't say it if I was sober!' retorted Jonas. 'You know better. Have I never said it when I was sober?'

'Often, indeed!' she answered through her tears.

'Hark ye!' cried Jonas, stamping his foot upon the ground. 'You made me bear your pretty humours once, and ecod I'll make you bear mine now. I always promised myself I would. I married you that I might. I'll know who's master, and who's slave!'

'Heaven knows I am obedient!' said the sobbing girl. 'Much more so than I ever thought to be!'

Jonas laughed in his drunken exultation. 'What! you're finding it out, are you! Patience, and you will in time! Griffins have claws, my girl. There's not a pretty slight you ever put upon me, nor a pretty trick you ever played me, nor a pretty insolence you ever showed me, that I won't pay back a hundred-fold. What else did I marry you for? *You*, too!' he said, with coarse contempt.

It might have softened him to hear her turn a little fragment of a song he used to say he liked; trying, with a heart so full, to win him back.

'Oho!' he said, 'you're deaf, are you? You don't hear me, eh? So much the better for you. I hate you. I hate myself, for having been fool enough to strap a pack upon my back for the pleasure of treading on it whenever I choose. Why, things have opened to me, now, so that I might marry almost where I liked. But I wouldn't; I'd keep single. I ought to be single, among the friends *I* know. Instead of that, here I am, tied like a log to you. Pah! Why do you show your pale face when I come home? Am I never to forget you?'

'How late it is!' she said cheerfully: opening the shutter after an interval of silence. 'Broad day, Jonas!'

'Broad day or black night, what do *I* care!' was the kind rejoinder.

'The night passed quickly, too. I don't mind sitting up, at all.'

'Sit up for me again, if you dare!' growled Jonas.

'I was reading,' she proceeded, 'all night long. I began when you went out, and read till you came home again. The strangest story, Jonas! And true, the book says. I'll tell it you tomorrow.'

'True, was it?' said Jonas, doggedly.

'So the book says.'

'Was there anything in it, about a man's being determined to conquer his wife, break her spirit, bend her temper, crush all her humours like so many nut-shells—kill her, for aught I know?' said Jonas.

'No. Not a word,' she answered quickly.

'Ah!' he returned. 'That'll be a true story though, before long; for all the book says nothing about it. It's a lying book, I see. A fit book for a lying reader. But you're deaf. I forgot that.'

There was another interval of silence; and the boy was stealing away, when he heard her footstep on the floor, and stopped. She went up to him, as it seemed, and spoke lovingly: saying that she would defer to him in everything, and would consult his wishes and obey them, and they might be very happy if he would be gentle with her. He answered with an imprecation, and—

Not with a blow? Yes. Stern truth against the base-souled villain: with a blow.

No angry cries; no loud reproaches. Even her weeping and her sobs were stifled by her clinging round him. She only said, repeating it in agony of heart, How could he, could he, could he! And lost utterance in tears.

Oh woman, God beloved in old Jerusalem! The best among us need deal lightly with thy faults, if only for the punishment thy nature will endure, in bearing heavy evidence against us on the Day of Judgment!

CHAPTER XXIX

In which some people are precocious, others professional, and others mysterious: all in their several ways

IT may have been the restless remembrance of what he had seen and heard overnight, or it may have been no deeper mental operation than the discovery that he had nothing to do, which caused Mr. Bailey, on the following afternoon, to feel particularly disposed for agreeable society, and prompted him to pay a visit to his friend Poll Sweedlepipe.

On the little bell giving clamorous notice of a visitor's approach (for Mr. Bailey came in at the door with a lunge, to get as much sound out of the bell as possible), Poll Sweedlepipe desisted from the contemplation of a favourite owl, and gave his young friend hearty welcome.

'Why, you look smarter by day,' said Poll, 'than you do by candle-light. I never see such a tight young dasher.'

'Reether so, Polly. How's our fair friend Sairah?'

'Oh, she's pretty well,' said Poll. 'She's at home.'

'There's the remains of a fine woman about Sairah, Poll,' observed Mr. Bailey, with genteel indifference.

'Oh!' thought Poll, 'he's old. He must be very old!'

'Too much crumb, you know,' said Mr. Bailey; 'too fat, Poll. But there's many worse at her time of life.'

'The very owl's a-opening his eyes!' thought Poll. 'I don't wonder at it, in a bird of his opinions.'

He happened to have been sharpening his razors, which were lying open in a row, while a huge strop dangled from the wall. Glancing at these preparations, Mr. Bailey stroked his chin, and a thought appeared to occur to him.

'Poll,' he said, 'I ain't as neat as I could wish about the gills. Being here, I may as well have a shave, and get trimmed close.'

The barber stood aghast; but Mr. Bailey divested himself of his neck-cloth, and sat down in the easy shaving chair with all the dignity and confidence in life. There was no resisting his manner. The evidence of sight and touch became as nothing. His chin was as smooth as a new-laid egg or a scraped Dutch cheese; but Poll Sweedlepipe wouldn't have ventured to deny, on affidavit, that he had the beard of a Jewish rabbi.

'Go *with* the grain, Poll, all round, please,' said Mr. Bailey, screwing up his face for the reception of the lather. 'You may do wot you like with the bits of whisker. I don't care for 'em.'

The meek little barber stood gazing at him with the brush and soap-dish in his hand, stirring them round and round in a ludicrous uncertainty, as if he were disabled by some fascination from beginning. At last he made a dash at Mr. Bailey's cheek. Then he stopped again, as if the ghost of a beard had suddenly receded from his touch; but receiving mild encouragement from Mr. Bailey, in the form of an adjuration to 'Go in and win,' he lathered him bountifully. Mr. Bailey smiled through the suds in his satisfaction.

'Gently over the stones, Poll. Go a tip-toe over the pimples!'

Poll Sweedlepipe obeyed, and scraped the lather off again with particular care. Mr. Bailey squinted at every successive dab, as it was deposited on a cloth on his left shoulder, and seemed, with a microscopic eye, to detect some bristles in it; for he murmured more than once, 'Reether redder than I could wish, Poll.' The operation being concluded, Poll fell back and stared at him again, while Mr. Bailey, wiping his face on the jack-towel, remarked, 'that arter late hours nothing freshened up a man so much as a easy shave.'

He was in the act of tying his cravat at the glass, without his coat, and Poll had wiped his razor, ready for the next customer, when Mrs. Gamp, coming down-stairs, looked in at the shop-door to give the barber neighbourly good day. Feeling for her unfortunate situation, in having conceived a regard for himself which it was not in the nature of things that he could return, Mr. Bailey hastened to soothe her with words of kindness.

'Hallo!' he said, 'Sairah! I needn't ask you how you've been this long time, for you're in full bloom. All a-blowin and a-growin; ain't she, Polly?'

'Why, drat the Bragian boldness of that boy!' cried Mrs. Gamp, though not displeased. 'What a imperent young sparrow it is! I wouldn't be that creetur's mother not for fifty pound!'

Mr. Bailey regarded this as a delicate confession of her attachment, and a hint that no pecuniary gain could recompense her for its being rendered hopeless. He felt flattered. Disinterested affection is always flattering.

'Ah, dear!' moaned Mrs. Gamp, sinking into the shaving chair, 'that there blessed Bull, Mr. Sweedlepipe, has done his wery best to conker me. Of all the trying inwalieges in this walley of the shadder, that one beats 'em black and blue.'

It was the practice of Mrs. Gamp and her friends in the profession, to say this of all the easy customers; as having at once the effect of discouraging competitors for office, and accounting for the necessity of high living on the part of the nurses.

'Talk of constitooshun!' Mrs. Gamp observed. 'A person's constitooshun need be made of bricks to stand it. Mrs. Harris jestly says to me, but t'other day, "Oh! Sairey Gamp," she says, "how is it done?" "Mrs. Harris, ma'am," I says to her, "we gives no trust ourselves, and puts a deal o' trust elsevere; these is our religious feelins, and we finds 'em answer." "Sairey," says Mrs. Harris, "sech is life. Vich likeways is the hend of all things!"'

The barber gave a soft murmur, as much as to say that Mrs. Harris's remark, though perhaps not quite so intelligible as could be desired from such an authority, did equal honour to her head and to her heart.

'And here,' continued Mrs. Gamp, 'and here am I a-goin twenty mile in distant, on as wentersome a chance as ever any one as monthlied ever run, I do believe. Says Mrs. Harris, with a woman's and a mother's art a-beatin in her human breast, she says to me, "You're not a-goin, Sairey, Lord forgive you!" "Why am I not a-goin, Mrs. Harris?" I replies. "Mrs. Gill," I says, "wos never wrong with six; and is it likely, ma'am— I ast you as a mother—that she will begin to be unreg'lar now? Often and often have I heerd him say," I says to Mrs. Harris, meaning Mr. Gill, "that he would back his wife agen Moore's almanack, to name the very day and hour, for ninepence farden. Is it likely, ma'am," I says, "as she will fail this once?" Says Mrs. Harris, "No, ma'am, not in the course of nater. But," she says, the tears a-fillin in her eyes, "you knows much betterer than me, with your experienge, how little puts us out. A Punch's show," she says, "a chimbley sweep, a newfundlandog, or a drunkin man a-comin round the corner sharp, may do it." So it may, Mr. Sweedlepipes,' said Mrs. Gamp, 'there's no deniging of it; and though my books is clear for a full week, I takes a anxious art along with me, I do assure you, sir.'

'You're so full of zeal, you see!' said Poll. 'You worrit yourself so.'

'Worrit myself!' cried Mrs. Gamp, raising her hands and turning up her eyes. 'You speak truth in that, sir, if you never speaks no more 'twixt this and when two Sundays jines together. I feels the sufferins of other people more than I feels my own, though no one mayn't suppoge it. The families I've had,' said Mrs. Gamp, 'if all was knowd, and credit done where credit's doo, would take a week to chris'en at Saint Polge's fontin!'

'Where's the patient going?' asked Sweedlepipe.

'Into Har'fordshire, which is his native air. But native airs nor native graces neither,' Mrs. Gamp observed, 'won't bring *him* round.'

'So bad as that?' inquired the wistful barber. 'Indeed!'

Mrs. Gamp shook her head mysteriously, and pursed up her lips. 'There's fevers of the mind,' she said, 'as well as body. You may take your slime drafts till you flies into the air with efferwescence; but you won't cure that.'

'Ah!' said the barber, opening his eyes, and putting on his raven aspect, 'Lor!'

'No. You may make yourself as light as any gash balloon,' said Mrs. Gamp. 'But talk, when you're wrong in your head and when you're in your sleep, of certain things; and you'll be heavy in your mind.'

'Of what kind of things now?' inquired Poll, greedily biting his nails in his great interest. 'Ghosts?'

Mrs. Gamp, who perhaps had been already tempted further than she had intended to go, by the barber's stimulating curiosity, gave a sniff of uncommon significance, and said, it didn't signify.

'I'm a-goin down with my patient in the coach this arternoon,' she proceeded. 'I'm a-goin to stop with him a day or so, till he gets a country nuss (drat them country nusses, much the orkard hussies knows about their bis'ness); and then I'm a-comin back; and that's my trouble, Mr. Sweedlepipes. But I hope that everythink 'll only go on right and comfortable as long as I'm away; perwisin which, as Mrs. Harris says, Mrs. Gill is welcome to choose her own time: all times of the day and night bein' equally the same to me.'

During the progress of the foregoing remarks, which Mrs. Gamp had addressed exclusively to the barber, Mr. Bailey had been tying his cravat, getting on his coat, and making hideous faces at himself in the glass. Being now personally addressed

by Mrs. Gamp, he turned round, and mingled in the conversation.

'You ain't been in the City, I suppose, sir, since we was all
three there together,' said Mrs. Gamp, 'at Mr. Chuzzlewit's?'

'Yes, I have, Sairah. I was there last night.'

'Last night!' cried the barber.

'Yes, Poll, reether so. You can call it this morning, if you
like to be particular. He dined with us.'

'Who does that young Limb mean by "hus?"' said Mrs.
Gamp, with most impatient emphasis.

'Me and my Governor, Sairah. He dined at our house. We
wos very merry, Sairah. So much so, that I was obliged to see
him home in a hackney coach at three o'clock in the morning.'
It was on the tip of the boy's tongue to relate what had followed;
but remembering how easily it might be carried to his master's
ears, and the repeated cautions he had had from Mr. Crimple
'not to chatter,' he checked himself: adding only, 'She was
sitting up, expecting him.'

'And all things considered,' said Mrs. Gamp sharply, 'she
might have know'd better than to go a-tirin herself out, by
doin' anythink of the sort. Did they seem pretty pleasant
together, sir?'

'Oh, yes,' answered Bailey, 'pleasant enough.'

'I'm glad on it,' said Mrs. Gamp, with a second sniff of
significance.

'They haven't been married so long,' observed Poll, rubbing
his hands, 'that they need be anything but pleasant yet awhile.'

'No,' said Mrs. Gamp, with a third significant signal.

'Especially,' pursued the barber, 'when the gentleman bears
such a character as you gave him.'

'I speak as I find, Mr. Sweedlepipes,' said Mrs. Gamp.
'Forbid it should be otherways! But we never knows wot's
hidden in each other's hearts; and if we had glass winders
there, we'd need keep the shetters up, some on us, I do
assure you!'

'But you don't mean to say,' Poll Sweedlepipe began.

'No,' said Mrs. Gamp, cutting him very short, 'I don't.
Don't think I do. The torters of the Imposition shouldn't
make me own I did. All I says is,' added the good woman,
rising and folding her shawl about her, 'that the Bull's a-waitin,
and the precious moments is a-flyin fast.'

The little barber having in his eager curiosity a great desire to see Mrs. Gamp's patient, proposed to Mr. Bailey that they should accompany her to the Bull, and witness the departure of the coach. That young gentleman assenting, they all went out together.

Arriving at the tavern, Mrs. Gamp (who was full-dressed for the journey, in her latest suit of mourning) left her friends to entertain themselves in the yard, while she ascended to the sick room, where her fellow-labourer Mrs. Prig was dressing the invalid.

He was so wasted, that it seemed as if his bones would rattle when they moved him. His cheeks were sunken, and his eyes unnaturally large. He lay back in the easy-chair like one more dead than living; and rolled his languid eyes towards the door when Mrs. Gamp appeared, as painfully as if their weight alone were burdensome to move.

'And how are we by this time?' Mrs. Gamp observed. 'We looks charming.'

'We looks a deal charminger than we are, then,' returned Mrs. Prig, a little chafed in her temper. 'We got out of bed back'ards, I think, for we're as cross as two sticks. I never see sich a man. He wouldn't have been washed, if he'd had his own way.'

'She put the soap in my mouth,' said the unfortunate patient, feebly.

'Couldn't you keep it shut then?' retorted Mrs. Prig. 'Who do you think's to wash one feater, and miss another, and wear one's eyes out with all manner of fine-work of that description, for half-a-crown a day! If you wants to be tittivated, you must pay accordin.'

'Oh dear me!' cried the patient, 'oh dear, dear!'

'There!' said Mrs. Prig, 'that's the way he's been a-conductin of himself, Sarah, ever since I got him out of bed, if you'll believe it.'

'Instead of being grateful,' Mrs. Gamp observed, 'for all our little ways. Oh, fie for shame, sir, fie for shame!'

Here Mrs. Prig seized the patient by the chin, and began to rasp his unhappy head with a hair-brush.

'I suppose you don't like that, neither!' she observed, stopping to look at him.

It was just possible that he didn't, for the brush was a specimen of the hardest kind of instrument producible by modern art; and his very eye-lids were red with the friction.

Mrs. Prig was gratified to observe the correctness of her supposition, and said triumphantly, 'she know'd as much.'

When his hair was smoothed down comfortably into his eyes, Mrs. Prig and Mrs. Gamp put on his neckerchief: adjusting his shirt-collar with great nicety, so that the starched points should also invade those organs, and afflict them with an artificial ophthalmia. His waistcoat and coat were next arranged: and as every button was wrenched into a wrong button-hole, and the order of his boots was reversed, he presented on the whole rather a melancholy appearance.

'I don't think it's right,' said the poor weak invalid. 'I feel as if I was in somebody else's clothes. I'm all on one side; and you've made one of my legs shorter than the other. There's a bottle in my pocket too. What do you make me sit upon a bottle for?'

'Deuce take the man!' cried Mrs. Gamp, drawing it forth. 'If he ain't been and got my night-bottle here. I made a little cupboard of his coat when it hung behind the door, and quite forgot it, Betsey. You'll find a ingun or two, and a little tea and sugar in his t'other pocket, my dear, if you'll just be good enough to take 'em out.'

Betsey produced the property in question, together with some other articles of general chandlery; and Mrs. Gamp transferred them to her own pocket, which was a species of nankeen pannier. Refreshment then arrived in the form of chops and strong ale for the ladies, and a basin of beef-tea for the patient: which refection was barely at an end when John Westlock appeared.

'Up and dressed!' cried John, sitting down beside him. 'That's brave. How do you feel?'

'Much better. But very weak.'

'No wonder. You have had a hard bout of it. But country air, and change of scene,' said John, 'will make another man of you! Why, Mrs. Gamp,' he added, laughing, as he kindly arranged the sick man's garments, 'you have odd notions of a gentleman's dress!'

'Mr. Lewsome an't a easy gent to get into his clothes, sir,' Mrs. Gamp replied with dignity; 'as me and Betsey Prig can certify afore the Lord Mayor and Uncommon Counsellors, if needful!'

John at that moment was standing close in front of the sick man, in the act of releasing him from the torture of the collars before mentioned, when he said in a whisper:

'Mr. Westlock! I don't wish to be overheard. I have something very particular and strange to say to you; something that has been a dreadful weight on my mind, through this long illness.'

Quick in all his motions, John was turning round to desire the women to leave the room: when the sick man held him by the sleeve.

'Not now. I've not the strength. I've not the courage. May I tell it when I have? May I write it, if I find that easier and better?'

'May you!' cried John. 'Why, Lewsome, what is this!'

'Don't ask me what it is. It's unnatural and cruel. Frightful to think of. Frightful to tell. Frightful to know. Frightful to have helped in. Let me kiss your hand for all your goodness to me. Be kinder still, and don't ask me what it is!'

At first John gazed at him, in great surprise; but remembering how very much reduced he was, and how recently his brain had been on fire with fever, believed that he was labouring under some imaginary horror or despondent fancy. For farther information on this point, he took an opportunity of drawing Mrs. Gamp aside, while Betsy Prig was wrapping him in cloaks and shawls, and asked her whether he was quite collected in his mind.

'Oh bless you, no!' said Mrs. Gamp. 'He hates his nusses to this hour. They always does it, sir. It's a certain sign. If you could have heerd the poor dear soul a-findin fault with me and Betsey Prig, not half an hour ago, you would have wondered how it is we don't get fretted to the tomb.'

This almost confirmed John in his suspicion; so, not taking what had passed into any serious account, he resumed his former cheerful manner, and assisted by Mrs. Gamp and Betsey Prig, conducted Lewsome down-stairs to the coach: just then upon the point of starting.

Poll Sweedlepipe was at the door with his arms tight folded and his eyes wide open, and looked on with absorbing interest, while the sick man was slowly moved into the vehicle. His bony hands and haggard face impressed Poll wonderfully; and he informed Mr. Bailey, in confidence, that he wouldn't have missed seeing him for a pound. Mr. Bailey, who was of a different constitution, remarked that he would have stayed away for five shillings.

It was a troublesome matter to adjust Mrs. Gamp's luggage

to her satisfaction; for every package belonging to that lady had the inconvenient property of requiring to be put in a boot by itself, and to have no other luggage near it, on pain of actions at law for heavy damages against the proprietors of the coach. The umbrella with the circular patch was particularly hard to be got rid of, and several times thrust out its battered brass nozzle from improper crevices and chinks, to the great terror of the other passengers. Indeed, in her intense anxiety to find a haven of refuge for this chattel, Mrs. Gamp so often moved it, in the course of five minutes, that it seemed not one umbrella but fifty. At length it was lost, or said to be; and for the next five minutes she was face to face with the coachman, go wherever he might, protesting that it should be 'made good,' though she took the question to the House of Commons.

At last, her bundle, and her pattens, and her basket, and everything else, being disposed of, she took a friendly leave of Poll and Mr. Bailey, dropped a curtsey to John Westlock, and parted as from a cherished member of the sisterhood with Betsey Prig.

'Wishin you lots of sickness, my darlin creetur,' Mrs. Gamp observed, 'and good places. It won't be long, I hope, afore we works together, off and on, again, Betsey; and may our next meetin' be at a large family's, where they all takes it reg'lar, one from another, turn and turn about, and has it business-like.'

'I don't care how soon it is,' said Mrs. Prig; 'nor how many weeks it lasts.'

Mrs. Gamp with a reply in a congenial spirit was backing to the coach, when she came in contact with a lady and gentleman who were passing along the footway.

'Take care, take care here!' cried the gentleman. 'Halloo! My dear! Why, it's Mrs. Gamp!'

'What, Mr. Mould!' exclaimed the nurse. 'And Mrs. Mould! who would have thought as we should ever have a meetin' here, I'm sure!'

'Going out of town, Mrs. Gamp?' cried Mould. 'That's unusual, isn't it?'

'It *is* unusual, sir,' said Mrs. Gamp. 'But only for a day or two at most. The gent,' she whispered, 'as I spoke about.'

'What, in the coach!' cried Mould. 'The one you thought of recommending? Very odd. My dear, this will interest you. The gentleman that Mrs. Gamp thought likely to suit us is in the coach, my love.'

Mrs. Mould was greatly interested.

'Here, my dear. You can stand upon the door-step,' said Mould, 'and take a look at him. Ha! There he is. Where's my glass? Oh! all right. I've got it. Do you see him, my dear?'

'Quite plain,' said Mrs. Mould.

'Upon my life you know, this is a very singular circumstance,' said Mould, quite delighted. 'This is the sort of thing, my dear, I wouldn't have missed on any account. It tickles one. It's interesting. It's almost a little play, you know. Ah! There he is! To be sure. Looks poorly, Mrs. M., don't he?'

Mrs. Mould assented.

'He's coming our way, perhaps, after all,' said Mould. 'Who knows! I feel as if I ought to show him some little attention, really. He don't seem a stranger to me. I'm very much inclined to move my hat, my dear.'

'He's looking hard this way,' said Mrs. Mould.

'Then I will!' cried Mould. 'How d'ye do, sir? I wish you good day. Ha! He bows too. Very gentlemanly. Mrs. Gamp has the cards in her pocket, I have no doubt. This is very singular, my dear—and very pleasant. I am not superstitious, but it really seems as if one was destined to pay him those little melancholy civilities which belong to our peculiar line of business. There can be no kind of objection to your kissing your hand to him, my dear.'

Mrs. Mould did so.

'Ha!' said Mould. 'He's evidently gratified. Poor fellow! I'm quite glad you did it, my love. Bye bye, Mrs. Gamp!' waving his hand. 'There he goes; there he goes!'

So he did; for the coach rolled off as the words were spoken. Mr. and Mrs. Mould, in high good humour, went their merry way. Mr. Bailey retired with Poll Sweedlepipe as soon as possible; but some little time elapsed before he could remove his friend from the ground, owing to the impression wrought upon the barber's nerves by Mrs. Prig, whom he pronounced, in admiration of her beard, to be a woman of transcendent charms.

When the light cloud of bustle hanging round the coach was thus dispersed, Nadgett was seen in the darkest box of the Bull coffee-room, looking wistfully up at the clock—as if the man who never appeared were a little behind his time.

CHAPTER XXX

Proves that changes may be rung in the best-regulated families, and that Mr. Pecksniff was a special hand at a Triple-bob-major

AS the surgeon's first care after amputating a limb is to take up the arteries the cruel knife has severed, so it is the duty of this history, which in its remorseless course has cut from the Pecksniffian trunk its right arm, Mercy, to look to the parent stem, and see how in all its various ramifications it got on without her.

And first of Mr. Pecksniff it may be observed, that having provided for his youngest daughter that choicest of blessings, a tender and indulgent husband; and having gratified the dearest wish of his parental heart by establishing her in life so happily; he renewed his youth, and spreading the plumage of his own bright conscience, felt himself equal to all kinds of flights. It is customary with fathers in stage-plays, after giving their daughters to the men of their hearts, to congratulate themselves on having no other business on their hands but to die immediately: though it is rarely found that they are in a hurry to do it. Mr. Pecksniff, being a father of a more sage and practical class, appeared to think that his immediate business was to live; and having deprived himself of one comfort, to surround himself with others.

But however much inclined the good man was to be jocose and playful, and in the garden of his fancy to disport himself (if one may say so), like an architectural kitten, he had one impediment constantly opposed to him. The gentle Cherry, stung by a sense of slight and injury, which far from softening down or wearing out, rankled and festered in her heart, was in flat rebellion. She waged fierce war against her dear papa; she led her parent what is usually called, for want of a better figure of speech, the life of a dog. But never did that dog live, in kennel, stable-yard, or house, whose life was half as hard as Mr. Pecksniff's with his gentle child.

The father and daughter were sitting at their breakfast. Tom had retired, and they were alone. Mr. Pecksniff frowned at first; but having cleared his brow, looked stealthily at his child. Her nose was very red indeed, and screwed up tight, with hostile preparation.

'Cherry,' cried Mr. Pecksniff, 'what is amiss between us? My child, why are we disunited?'

Miss Pecksniff's answer was scarcely a response to this gush of affection, for it was simply, 'Bother, Pa!'

'Bother!' repeated Mr. Pecksniff, in a tone of anguish.

'Oh! 'tis too late, Pa,' said his daughter, calmly, 'to talk to me like this. I know what it means, and what its value is.'

'This is hard!' cried Mr. Pecksniff, addressing his breakfast-cup. 'This is very hard! She is my child. I carried her in my arms when she wore shapeless worsted shoes—I might say, mufflers—many years ago!'

'You needn't taunt me with that, Pa,' retorted Cherry, with a spiteful look. 'I am not so many years older than my sister, either, though she *is* married to your friend!'

'Ah, human nature, human nature! Poor human nature!' said Mr. Pecksniff, shaking his head at human nature, as if he didn't belong to it. 'To think that this discord should arise from such a cause! oh dear, oh dear!'

'From such a cause indeed!' cried Cherry. 'State the real cause, Pa, or I'll state it myself. Mind! I will!'

Perhaps the energy with which she said this was infectious. However that may be, Mr. Pecksniff changed his tone and the expression of his face for one of anger, if not downright violence, when he said:

'You will! you have. You did yesterday. You do always. You have no decency; you make no secret of your temper; you have exposed yourself to Mr. Chuzzlewit a hundred times.'

'Myself!' cried Cherry, with a bitter smile. 'Oh indeed! I don't mind that.'

'Me too, then,' said Mr. Pecksniff.

His daughter answered with a scornful laugh.

'And since we have come to an explanation, Charity,' said Mr. Pecksniff, rolling his head portentously, 'let me tell you that I won't allow it. None of your nonsense, Miss! I won't permit it to be done.'

'I shall do,' said Charity, rocking her chair backwards and forwards, and raising her voice to a high pitch, 'I shall do, Pa, what I please and what I have done. I am not going to be crushed in everything, depend upon it. I've been more shamefully used than anybody ever was in this world,' here she began to cry and sob, 'and may expect the worse treatment from you, I know. But I don't care for that. No, I don't!'

Mr. Pecksniff was made so desperate by the loud tone in which she spoke, that, after looking about him in frantic uncertainty for some means of softening it, he rose and shook her until the ornamental bow of hair upon her head nodded like a plume. She was so very much astonished by this assault, that it really had the desired effect.

'I'll do it again!' cried Mr. Pecksniff, as he resumed his seat and fetched his breath, 'if you dare to talk in that loud manner. How do you mean about being shamefully used? If Mr. Jonas chose your sister in preference to you, who could help it, I should wish to know. What have *I* to do with it?'

'Wasn't I made a convenience of? Wern't my feelings trifled with? Didn't he address himself to me first?' sobbed Cherry, clasping her hands; 'and oh, good gracious, that I should live to be shook!'

'You'll live to be shaken again,' returned her parent, 'if you drive me to that means of maintaining the decorum of this humble roof. You surprise me. I wonder you have not more spirit. If Mr. Jonas didn't care for you, how could you wish to have him?'

'*I* wish to have him!' exclaimed Cherry. '*I* wish to have him, Pa!'

'Then what are you making all this piece of work for,' retorted her father, 'if you didn't wish to have him?'

'Because I was treated with duplicity,' said Cherry; 'and because my own sister and my own father conspired against me. I am not angry with *her*,' said Cherry, looking much more angry than ever. 'I pity her. I'm sorry for her. I know the fate that's in store for her, with that Wretch.'

'Mr. Jonas will survive your calling him a wretch, my child, I dare say,' said Mr. Pecksniff, with returning resignation; 'but call him what you like and make an end of it.'

'Not an end, Pa,' said Charity. 'No, not an end. That's not the only point on which we're not agreed. I won't submit to it. It's better you should know that at once. No; I won't submit to it indeed, Pa! I am not quite a fool, and I am not blind. All I have got to say is, I won't submit to it.'

Whatever she meant, she shook Mr. Pecksniff now; for his lame attempt to seem composed was melancholy in the last degree. His anger changed to meekness, and his words were mild and fawning.

'My dear,' he said; 'if in the short excitement of an angry

moment I resorted to an unjustifiable means of suppressing a little outbreak calculated to injure you as well as myself—it's possible I may have done so; perhaps I did—I ask your pardon. A father asking pardon of his child,' said Mr. Pecksniff, 'is, I believe, a spectacle to soften the most rugged nature.'

But it didn't at all soften Miss Pecksniff: perhaps because her nature was not rugged enough. On the contrary, she persisted in saying, over and over again, that she wasn't quite a fool, and wasn't blind, and wouldn't submit to it.

'You labour under some mistake, my child!' said Mr. Pecksniff: 'but I will not ask you what it is; I don't desire to know. No, pray!' he added, holding out his hand and colouring again, 'let us avoid the subject, my dear, whatever it is!'

'It's quite right that the subject should be avoided between us, sir,' said Cherry. 'But I wish to be able to avoid it altogether, and consequently must beg you to provide me with a home.'

Mr. Pecksniff looked about the room, and said, 'A home, my child!'

'Another home, papa,' said Cherry, with increasing stateliness. 'Place me at Mrs. Todgers's or somewhere, on an independent footing; but I will not live here, if such is to be the case.'

It is possible that Miss Pecksniff saw in Mrs. Todgers's a vision of enthusiastic men, pining to fall in adoration at her feet. It is possible that Mr. Pecksniff, in his new-born juvenility, saw in the suggestion of that same establishment, an easy means of relieving himself from an irksome charge in the way of temper and watchfulness. It is undoubtedly a fact that in the attentive ears of Mr. Pecksniff, the proposition did not sound quite like the dismal knell of all his hopes.

But he was a man of great feeling and acute sensibility; and he squeezed his pocket-handkerchief against his eyes with both hands—as such men always do; especially when they are observed. 'One of my birds,' Mr. Pecksniff said, 'has left me for the stranger's breast; the other would take wing to Todgers's! Well, well, what am I? I don't know what I am, exactly. Never mind!'

Even this remark, made more pathetic perhaps by his breaking down in the middle of it, had no effect upon Charity. She was grim, rigid, and inflexible.

'But I have ever,' said Mr. Pecksniff, 'sacrificed my children's happiness to my own—I mean my own happiness to my children's—and I will not begin to regulate my life by other rules of conduct now. If you can be happier at Mrs. Todgers's than in your father's house, my dear, go to Mrs. Todgers's! Do not think of me, my girl!' said Mr. Pecksniff with emotion: 'I shall get on pretty well, no doubt.'

Miss Charity, who knew he had a secret pleasure in the contemplation of the proposed change, suppressed her own, and went on to negotiate the terms. His views upon this subject were at first so very limited that another difference, involving possibly another shaking, threatened to ensue; but by degrees they came to something like an understanding, and the storm blew over. Indeed, Miss Charity's idea was so agreeable to both, that it would have been strange if they had not come to an amicable agreement. It was soon arranged between them that the project should be tried, and that immediately; and that Cherry's not being well, and needing change of scene, and wishing to be near her sister, should form the excuse for her departure to Mr. Chuzzlewit and Mary, to both of whom she had pleaded indisposition for some time past. These premises agreed on, Mr. Pecksniff gave her his blessing, with all the dignity of a self-denying man who had made a hard sacrifice, but comforted himself with the reflection that virtue is its own reward. Thus they were reconciled for the first time since that not easily forgiven night, when Mr. Jonas, repudiating the elder, had confessed his passion for the younger sister, and Mr. Pecksniff had abetted him on moral grounds.

But how happened it—in the name of an unexpected addition to that small family, the Seven Wonders of the World, whatever and wherever they may be, how happened it—that Mr. Pecksniff and his daughter were about to part? How happened it that their mutual relations were so greatly altered? Why was Miss Pecksniff so clamorous to have it understood that she was neither blind nor foolish, and she wouldn't bear it? It is not possible that Mr. Pecksniff had any thoughts of marrying again; or that his daughter, with the sharp eye of a single woman, fathomed his design!

Let us inquire into this.

Mr. Pecksniff, as a man without reproach, from whom the breath of slander passed like common breath from any other polished surface, could afford to do what common men could not. He knew the purity of his own motives; and when he had a motive worked at it as only a very good man (or a very bad one) can. Did he set before himself any strong and palpable motives for taking a second wife? Yes: and not one or two of them, but a combination of very many.

Old Martin Chuzzlewit had gradually undergone an important change. Even upon the night when he made such an ill-timed arrival at Mr. Pecksniff's house, he was comparatively subdued and easy to deal with. This Mr. Pecksniff attributed, at the time, to the effect his brother's death had had upon him. But from that hour his character seemed to have modified by regular degrees, and to have softened down into a dull indifference for almost every one but Mr. Pecksniff. His looks were much the same as ever, but his mind was singularly altered. It was not that this or that passion stood out in brighter or in dimmer hues; but that the colour of the whole man was faded. As one trait disappeared, no other trait sprung up to take its place. His senses dwindled too. He was less keen of sight; was deaf sometimes; took little notice of what passed before him; and would be profoundly taciturn for days together. The process of this alteration was so easy, that almost as soon as it began to be observed it was complete. But Mr. Pecksniff saw it first, and having Anthony Chuzzlewit fresh in his recollection, saw in his brother Martin the same process of decay.

To a gentleman of Mr. Pecksniff's tenderness, this was a very mournful sight. He could not but foresee the probability of his respected relative being made the victim of designing persons, and of his riches falling into worthless hands. It gave him so much pain that he resolved to secure the property to himself; to keep bad testamentary suitors at a distance: to wall up the old gentleman, as it were, for his own use. By little and little, therefore, he began to try whether Mr. Chuzzlewit gave any promise of becoming an instrument in his hands, and finding that he did, and indeed that he was very supple in his plastic fingers, he made it the business of his life, kind soul! to establish an ascendancy over him: and every little test he durst apply meeting with a success beyond his hopes, he began to think he heard old Martin's cash already chinking in his own unworldly pockets.

But when Mr. Pecksniff pondered on this subject (as, in his zealous way, he often did), and thought with an uplifted heart of the train of circumstances which had delivered the old gentleman into his hands for the confusion of evil-doers and the triumph of a righteous nature, he always felt that Mary

S

Graham was his stumbling-block. Let the old man say what he would, Mr. Pecksniff knew he had a strong affection for her. He knew that he showed it in a thousand little ways; that he liked to have her near him, and was never quite at ease when she was absent long. That he had ever really sworn to leave her nothing in his will, Mr. Pecksniff greatly doubted. That even if he had, there were many ways by which he could evade the oath and satisfy his conscience, Mr. Pecksniff knew. That her unprotected state was no light burden on the old man's mind, he also knew, for Mr. Chuzzlewit had plainly told him so. 'Then,' said Mr. Pecksniff, 'what if I married her! What,' repeated Mr. Pecksniff, sticking up his hair and glancing at his bust by Spoker: 'what if, making sure of his approval first— he is nearly imbecile, poor gentleman—I married her!'

Mr. Pecksniff had a lively sense of the Beautiful: especially in women. His manner towards the sex was remarkable for its insinuating character. It is recorded of him in another part of these pages, that he embraced Mrs. Todgers on the smallest provocation: and it was a way he had: it was a part of the gentle placidity of his disposition. Before any thought of matrimony was in his mind, he had bestowed on Mary many little tokens of his spiritual admiration. They had been in-dignantly received, but that was nothing. True, as the idea expanded within him, these had become too ardent to escape the piercing eye of Cherry, who read his scheme at once; but he had always felt the power of Mary's charms. So Interest and Inclination made a pair, and drew the curricle of Mr. Pecksniff's plan.

As to any thought of revenging himself on young Martin for his insolent expressions when they parted, and of shutting him out still more effectually from any hope of reconciliation with his grandfather, Mr. Pecksniff was much too meek and for-giving to be suspected of harbouring it. As to being refused by Mary, Mr. Pecksniff was quite satisfied that in her position she could never hold out if he and Mr. Chuzzlewit were both against her. As to consulting the wishes of her heart in such a case, it formed no part of Mr. Pecksniff's moral code; for he knew what a good man he was, and what a blessing he must be to anybody. His daughter having broken the ice, and the murder being out between them, Mr. Pecksniff had now only to pursue his design as cleverly as he could, and by the craftiest approaches.

'Well, my good sir,' said Mr. Pecksniff, meeting old Martin in the garden, for it was his habit to walk in and out by that way, as the fancy took him: 'and how is my dear friend this delicious morning?'

'Do you mean me?' asked the old man.

'Ah!' said Mr. Pecksniff, 'one of his deaf days, I see. Could I mean any one else, my dear sir?'

'You might have meant Mary,' said the old man.

'Indeed I might. Quite true. I might speak of her as a dear, dear friend, I hope?' observed Mr. Pecksniff.

'I hope so,' returned old Martin. 'I think she deserves it.'

'Think!' cried Pecksniff, 'think, Mr. Chuzzlewit!'

'You are speaking, I know,' returned Martin, 'but I don't catch what you say. Speak up!'

'He's getting deafer than a flint,' said Pecksniff. 'I was saying, my dear sir, that I am afraid I must make up my mind to part with Cherry.'

'What has *she* been doing?' asked the old man.

'He puts the most ridiculous questions I ever heard!' muttered Mr. Pecksniff. 'He's a child to-day.' After which he added, in a mild roar: 'She hasn't been doing anything, my dear friend.

'What are you going to part with her for?' demanded Martin.

'She hasn't her health by any means,' said Mr. Pecksniff. 'She misses her sister, my dear sir; they doted on each other from the cradle. And I think of giving her a run in London for a change. A good long run, sir, if I find she likes it.'

'Quite right,' cried Martin. 'It's judicious.'

'I am glad to hear you say so. I hope you mean to bear me company in this dull part, while she's away?' said Mr. Pecksniff.

'I have no intention of removing from it,' was Martin's answer.

'Then why,' said Mr. Pecksniff, taking the old man's arm in his, and walking slowly on: 'Why, my good sir, can't you come and stay with me? I am sure I could surround you with more comforts, lowly as is my cot, than you can obtain at a village house of entertainment. And pardon me, Mr. Chuzzlewit, pardon me if I say that such a place as the Dragon, however well-conducted (and, as far as I know, Mrs. Lupin is one of the worthiest creatures in this county), is hardly a home for Miss Graham.'

Martin mused a moment: and then said, as he shook him by the hand,

'No. You're quite right; it is not.'

'The very sight of skittles,' Mr. Pecksniff eloquently pursued, 'is far from being congenial to a delicate mind.'

'It's an amusement of the vulgar,' said old Martin, 'certainly.'

'Of the very vulgar,' Mr. Pecksniff answered. 'Then why not bring Miss Graham here, sir? Here is the house. Here am I alone in it, for Thomas Pinch I do not count as any one. Our lovely friend shall occupy my daughter's chamber! you shall choose your own; we shall not quarrel, I hope!'

'We are not likely to do that,' said Martin.

Mr. Pecksniff pressed his hand. 'We understand each other, my dear sir, I see!—I can wind him,' he thought, with exultation, 'round my little finger!'

'You leave the recompense to me?' said the old man, after a minute's silence.

'Oh! do not speak of recompense!' cried Pecksniff.

'I say,' repeated Martin, with a glimmer of his old obstinacy, 'you leave the recompense to me. Do you?'

'Since you desire it, my good sir.'

'I always desire it,' said the old man. 'You know I always desire it. I wish to pay as I go, even when I buy of you. Not that I do not leave a balance to be settled one day, Pecksniff.'

The architect was too much overcome to speak. He tried to drop a tear upon his patron's hand, but couldn't find one in his dry distillery.

'May that day be very distant!' was his pious exclamation. 'Ah, sir! If I could say how deep an interest I have in you and yours! I allude to our beautiful young friend.'

'True,' he answered. 'True. She need have some one interested in her. I did her wrong to train her as I did. Orphan though she was, she would have found some one to protect her whom she might have loved again. When she was a child, I pleased myself with the thought that in gratifying my whim of placing her between me and false-hearted knaves, I had done her a kindness. Now she is a woman, I have no such comfort. She has no protector but herself. I have put her at such odds with the world, that any dog may bark or fawn upon her at his pleasure. Indeed she stands in need of delicate consideration. Yes; indeed she does!'

'If her position could be altered and defined, sir?' Mr. Pecksniff hinted.

'How can that be done? Should I make a seamstress of her, or a governess?'

'Heaven forbid!' said Mr. Pecksniff. 'My dear sir, there are other ways. There are indeed. But I am much excited and embarrassed at present, and would rather not pursue the subject. I scarcely know what I mean. Permit me to resume it at another time.'

'You are not unwell?' asked Martin anxiously.

'No, no!' cried Pecksniff. 'No. Permit me to resume it at another time. I'll walk a little. Bless you!'

Old Martin blessed him in return, and squeezed his hand. As he turned away, and slowly walked towards the house, Mr. Pecksniff stood gazing after him: being pretty well recovered from his late emotion, which, in any other man, one might have thought had been assumed as a machinery for feeling Martin's pulse. The change in the old man found such a slight expression in his figure, that Mr. Pecksniff, looking after him, could not help saying to himself:

'And I can wind him round my little finger! Only think!'

Old Martin happening to turn his head, saluted him affectionately. Mr. Pecksniff returned the gesture.

'Why, the time was,' said Mr. Pecksniff; 'and not long ago, when he wouldn't look at me! How soothing is this change. Such is the delicate texture of the human heart; so complicated is the process of its being softened! Externally he looks the same, and I can wind him round my little finger. Only think!'

In sober truth, there did appear to be nothing on which Mr. Pecksniff might not have ventured with Martin Chuzzlewit; for whatever Mr. Pecksniff said or did was right, and whatever he advised was done. Martin had escaped so many snares from needy fortune-hunters, and had withered in the shell of his suspicion and distrust for so many years, but to become the good man's tool and plaything. With the happiness of this conviction painted on his face, the architect went forth upon his morning walk.

The summer weather in his bosom was reflected in the breast of Nature. Through deep green vistas where the boughs arched over-head, and showed the sunlight flashing in the beautiful perspective; through dewy fern from which the startled hares leaped up, and fled at his approach; by mantled pools, and fallen trees, and down in hollow places, rustling among last year's leaves whose scent woke memory of the past; the placid Pecksniff strolled. By meadow gates and hedges fragrant with wild roses; and by thatched-roof cottages whose inmates humbly bowed before him as a man both good and wise; the worthy Pecksniff walked in tranquil meditation. The bee passed onward, humming of the work he had to do; the idle gnats for ever going round and round in one contract-ing and expanding ring, yet always going on as fast as he, danced merrily before him; the colour of the long grass came and went, as if the light clouds made it timid as they floated through the distant air. The birds, so many Pecksniff con-sciences, sang gaily upon every branch; and Mr. Pecksniff paid *his* homage to the day by ruminating on his projects as he walked along.

Chancing to trip, in his abstraction, over the spreading root of an old tree, he raised his pious eyes to take a survey of the ground before him. It startled him to see the embodied image of his thoughts not far ahead. Mary herself. And alone.

At first Mr. Pecksniff stopped as if with the intention of avoiding her; but his next impulse was to advance, which he did at a brisk pace; carolling as he went so sweetly and with so much innocence that he only wanted feathers and wings to be a bird.

Hearing notes behind her, not belonging to the songsters of the grove, she looked round. Mr. Pecksniff kissed his hand, and was at her side immediately.

'Communing with nature?' said Mr. Pecksniff. 'So am I.'

She said the morning was so beautiful that she had walked further than she intended, and would return. Mr. Pecksniff said it was exactly his case, and he would return with her.

'Take my arm, sweet girl,' said Mr. Pecksniff.

Mary declined it, and walked so very fast that he remon-strated. 'You were loitering when I came upon you,' Mr. Peck-sniff said. 'Why be so cruel as to hurry now? You would not shun me, would you?'

'Yes, I would,' she answered, turning her glowing cheek indignantly upon him, 'you know I would. Release me, Mr. Pecksniff. Your touch is disagreeable to me.'

His touch! What? That chaste patriarchal touch which Mrs. Todgers—surely a discreet lady—had endured, not only without complaint, but with apparent satisfaction! This was positively wrong. Mr. Pecksniff was sorry to hear her say it.

'If you have not observed,' said Mary, 'that it is so, pray take assurance from my lips, and not, as you are a gentleman, continue to offend me.'

'Well, well!' said Mr. Pecksniff, mildly, 'I feel that I might consider this becoming in a daughter of my own, and why should I object to it in one so beautiful! It's harsh. It cuts me to the soul,' said Mr. Pecksniff: 'but I cannot quarrel with you, Mary.'

She tried to say she was sorry to hear it, but burst into tears. Mr. Pecksniff now repeated the Todgers performance on a comfortable scale, as if he intended it to last some time; and in his disengaged hand, catching hers, employed himself in separating the fingers with his own, and sometimes kissing them, as he pursued the conversation thus:

'I am glad we met. I am very glad we met. I am able now to ease my bosom of a heavy load, and speak to you in confidence. Mary,' said Mr. Pecksniff in his tenderest tones: indeed, they were so very tender that he almost squeaked: 'My soul! I love you!'

A fantastic thing, that maiden affectation! She made believe to shudder.

'I love you,' said Mr. Pecksniff, 'my gentle life, with a devotion which is quite surprising, even to myself. I did suppose that the sensation was buried in the silent tomb of a lady, only second to you in qualities of the mind and form: but I find I am mistaken.'

She tried to disengage her hand, but might as well have tried to free herself from the embrace of an affectionate boa-constrictor: if anything so wily may be brought into comparison with Pecksniff.

'Although I am a widower,' said Mr. Pecksniff, examining the rings upon her fingers, and tracing the course of one delicate blue vein with his fat thumb, 'a widower with two daughters, still I am not encumbered, my love. One of them, as you know, is married. The other, by her own desire, but with a view, I will confess—why not?—to my altering my condition, is about to leave her father's house. I have a character, I hope. People are pleased to speak well of me, I think. My person and manner are not absolutely those of a monster, I trust. Ah, naughty Hand!' said Mr. Pecksniff, apostrophising the reluctant prize, 'why did you take me prisoner! Go, go!'

He slapped the hand to punish it; but relenting, folded it in his waistcoat to comfort it again.

'Blessed in each other, and in the society of our venerable friend, my darling,' said Mr. Pecksniff, 'we shall be happy. When he is wafted to a haven of rest, we will console each other. My pretty primrose, what do you say?'

'It is possible,' Mary answered, in a hurried manner, 'that I ought to feel grateful for this mark of your confidence. I cannot say that I do, but I am willing to suppose you may deserve my thanks. Take them; and pray leave me, Mr. Pecksniff.'

The good man smiled a greasy smile; and drew her closer to him.

'Pray, pray release me, Mr. Pecksniff. I cannot listen to your proposal. I cannot receive it. There are many to whom it may be acceptable, but it is not so to me. As an act of kindness and an act of pity, leave me!'

Mr. Pecksniff walked on with his arm round her waist, and her hand in his, as contentedly as if they had been all in all to each other, and were joined in the bonds of truest love.

'If you force me by your superior strength,' said Mary, who finding that good words had not the least effect upon him, made no further effort to suppress her indignation: 'if you force me by your superior strength to accompany you back, and to be the subject of your insolence upon the way, you cannot constrain the expression of my thoughts. I hold you in the deepest abhorrence. I know your real nature and despise it.'

'No, no,' said Mr. Pecksniff, sweetly. 'No, no, no!'

'By what arts or unhappy chances you have gained your influence over Mr. Chuzzlewit, I do not know,' said Mary: 'it may be strong enough to soften even this, but he shall know of this, trust me, sir.'

Mr. Pecksniff raised his heavy eyelids languidly, and let them fall again. It was saying with perfect coolness, 'Aye, aye! Indeed!'

'Is it not enough,' said Mary, 'that you warp and change his nature, adapt his every prejudice to your bad ends, and harden a heart naturally kind by shutting out the truth and allowing none but false and distorted views to reach it; is it not enough that you have the power of doing this, and that you

Easy Shaving
(*p. 461*)

exercise it, but must you also be so coarse, so cruel, and so cowardly to me?'

Still Mr. Pecksniff led her calmly on, and looked as mild as any lamb that ever pastured in the fields.

'Will nothing move you, sir?' cried Mary.

'My dear,' observed Mr. Pecksniff, with a placid leer, 'a habit of self-examination, and the practice of—shall I say of virtue?'

'Of hypocrisy,' said Mary.

'No, no,' resumed Mr. Pecksniff, chafing the captive hand reproachfully, 'of virtue—have enabled me to set such guards upon myself, that it is really difficult to ruffle me. It is a curious fact, but it is difficult, do you know, for any one to ruffle me. And did she think,' said Mr. Pecksniff, with a playful tightening of his grasp, 'that *she* could! How little did she know his heart!'

Little, indeed! Her mind was so strangely constituted that she would have preferred the caresses of a toad, an adder, or a serpent: nay, the hug of a bear: to the endearments of Mr. Pecksniff.

'Come, come,' said that good gentleman, 'a word or two will set this matter right, and establish a pleasant understanding between us. I am not angry, my love.'

'*You* angry!'

'No,' said Mr. Pecksniff, 'I am not. I say so. Neither are you.'

There was a beating heart beneath his hand that told another story though.

'I am sure you are not,' said Mr. Pecksniff: 'and I will tell you why. There are two Martin Chuzzlewits, my dear; and your carrying your anger to one might have a serious effect—who knows!—upon the other. You wouldn't wish to hurt him, would you?'

She trembled violently, and looked at him with such a proud disdain that he turned his eyes away. No doubt lest he should be offended with her in spite of his better self.

'A passive quarrel, my love,' said Mr. Pecksniff, 'may be changed into an active one, remember. It would be sad to blight even a disinherited young man in his already blighted prospects: but how easy to do it. Ah, how easy! *Have* I influence with our venerable friend, do you think? Well, perhaps I have. Perhaps I have.'

He raised his eyes to hers; and nodded with an air of banter that was charming.

'No,' he continued, thoughtfully. 'Upon the whole, my sweet, if I were you I'd keep my secret to myself. I am not at all sure: very far from it: that it would surprise our friend in any way, for he and I have had some conversation together only this morning, and he is anxious, very anxious, to establish you in some more settled manner. But whether he was surprised or not surprised, the consequence of your imparting it might be the same. Martin junior might suffer severely. I'd have compassion on Martin junior, do you know?' said Mr. Pecksniff, with a persuasive smile. 'Yes. He don't deserve it, but I would.'

She wept so bitterly now, and was so much distressed, that he thought it prudent to unclasp her waist, and hold her only by the hand.

'As to our own share in the precious little mystery,' said Mr. Pecksniff, 'we will keep it to ourselves, and talk of it between ourselves, and you shall think it over. You will consent, my love; you will consent, I know. Whatever you may think; you will. I seem to remember to have heard: I really don't know where, or how:' he added, with bewitching frankness, 'that you and Martin junior, when you were children, had a sort of childish fondness for each other. When we are married, you shall have the satisfaction of thinking that it didn't last to ruin him, but passed away to do him good; for we'll see then what we can do to put some trifling help in Martin junior's way. *Have* I any influence with our venerable friend? Well! Perhaps I have. Perhaps I have.'

The outlet from the wood in which these tender passages occurred, was close to Mr. Pecksniff's house. They were now so near it that he stopped, and holding up her little finger, said in playful accents, as a parting fancy:

'Shall I bite it?'

Receiving no reply he kissed it instead; and then stooping down, inclined his flabby face to hers (he had a flabby face, although he *was* a good man), and with a blessing, which from such a source was quite enough to set her up in life, and prosper her from that time forth, permitted her to leave him.

Gallantry in its true sense is supposed to ennoble and dignify a man; and love has shed refinements on innumerable Cymons. But Mr. Pecksniff: perhaps because to one of his exalted nature these were mere grossnesses: certainly did not appear to any unusual advantage, now that he was left alone. On the contrary, he seemed to be shrunk and reduced; to be trying to hide himself within himself; and to be wretched at not having the power to do it. His shoes looked too large; his sleeve looked too long; his hair looked too limp; his features looked too mean; his exposed throat looked as if a halter would have done it good. For a minute or two, in fact, he was hot, and pale, and mean, and shy, and slinking, and consequently not at all Pecksniffian. But after that, he recovered himself, and went home with as beneficent an air as if he had been the High Priest of the summer weather.

'I have arranged to go, Papa,' said Charity, 'to-morrow.'

'So soon, my child!'

'I can't go too soon,' said Charity, 'under the circumstances. I have written to Mrs. Todgers to propose an arrangement, and have requested her to meet me at the coach, at all events. You'll be quite your own master now, Mr. Pinch!'

Mr. Pecksniff had just gone out of the room, and Tom had just come into it.

'My own master!' repeated Tom.

'Yes, you'll have nobody to interfere with you,' said Charity. 'At least I hope you won't. Hem! It's a changing world.'

'What! are *you* going to be married, Miss Pecksniff?' asked Tom in great surprise.

'Not exactly,' faltered Cherry. 'I haven't made up my mind to be. I believe I could be, if I chose, Mr. Pinch.'

'Of course you could!' said Tom. And he said it in perfect good faith. He believed it from the bottom of his heart.

'No,' said Cherry, '*I* am not going to be married. Nobody is, that I know of. Hem! But I am not going to live with Papa. I have my reasons, but it's all a secret. I shall always feel very kindly towards you, I assure you, for the boldness you showed that night. As to you and me, Mr. Pinch, *we* part the best friends possible!'

Tom thanked her for her confidence, and for her friendship, but there was a mystery in the former which perfectly bewildered him. In his extravagant devotion to the family, he had felt the loss of Merry more than any one but those who knew that for all the slights he underwent he thought his own demerits were to blame, could possibly have understood. He had scarcely reconciled himself to that when here was Charity about to leave them. She had grown up, as it were, under Tom's eye. The sisters were a part of Pecksniff, and a part of Tom; items in Pecksniff's goodness, and in Tom's service. He couldn't bear it: not two hours' sleep had Tom that night, through dwelling in his bed upon these dreadful changes.

When morning dawned he thought he must have dreamed this piece of ambiguity; but no, on going down-stairs he found them packing trunks and cording boxes, and making other preparations for Miss Charity's departure, which lasted all day long. In good time for the evening coach, Miss Charity deposited her housekeeping keys with much ceremony upon the parlour table: took a gracious leave of all the house; and quitted her paternal roof—a blessing, for which the Pecksniffian servant was observed by some profane persons to be particularly active in the thanksgiving at church next Sunday.

CHAPTER XXXI

*Mr. Pinch is discharged of a duty which he never owed to anybody;
and Mr. Pecksniff discharges a duty which he owes to society*

THE closing words of the last chapter lead naturally to the
commencement of this, its successor; for it has to do with a
church. With the church, so often mentioned heretofore, in
which Tom Pinch played the organ for nothing.

One sultry afternoon, about a week after Miss Charity's
departure for London, Mr. Pecksniff being out walking by
himself, took it into his head to stray into the churchyard. As
he was lingering among the tombstones, endeavouring to
extract an available sentiment or two from the epitaphs—for
he never lost an opportunity of making up a few moral crackers,
to be let off as occasion served—Tom Pinch began to practise.
Tom could run down to the church and do so whenever he had
time to spare; for it was a simple little organ, provided with
wind by the action of the musician's feet; and he was independent, even of a bellows-blower. Though if Tom had wanted
one at any time, there was not a man or boy in all the village,
and away to the turnpike (tollman included), but would have
blown away for him till he was black in the face.

Mr. Pecksniff had no objection to music; not the least. He
was tolerant of everything; he often said so. He considered it
a vagabond kind of trifling, in general, just suited to Tom's
capacity. But in regard to Tom's performance upon this same
organ, he was remarkably lenient, singularly amiable; for
when Tom played it on Sundays, Mr. Pecksniff in his unbounded sympathy felt as if he played it himself, and were a
benefactor to the congregation. So whenever it was impossible
to devise any other means of taking the value of Tom's wages
out of him, Mr. Pecksniff gave him leave to cultivate this
instrument. For which mark of his consideration Tom was
very grateful.

The afternoon was remarkably warm, and Mr. Pecksniff
had been strolling a long way. He had not what may be called
a fine ear for music, but he knew when it had a tranquillising
influence on his soul; and that was the case now, for it sounded
to him like a melodious snore. He approached the church, and

looking through the diamond lattice of a window near the porch, saw Tom, with the curtains in the loft drawn back, playing away with great expression and tenderness.

The church had an inviting air of coolness. The old oak roof supported by cross-beams, the hoary walls, the marble tablets, and the cracked stone pavement, were refreshing to look at. There were leaves of ivy tapping gently at the opposite windows; and the sun poured in through only one: leaving the body of the church in tempting shade. But the most tempting spot of all, was one red-curtained and soft-cushioned pew, wherein the official dignitaries of the place (of whom Mr. Pecksniff was the head and chief) enshrined themselves on Sundays. Mr. Pecksniff's seat was in the corner: a remarkably comfortable corner; where his very large Prayer-Book was at that minute making the most of its quarto self upon the desk. He determined to go in and rest.

He entered very softly; in part because it was a church; in part because his tread was always soft; in part because Tom played a solemn tune; in part because he thought he would surprise him when he stopped. Unbolting the door of the high pew of state, he glided in and shut it after him; then sitting in his usual place, and stretching out his legs upon the hassocks, he composed himself to listen to the music.

It is an unaccountable circumstance that he should have felt drowsy there, where the force of association might surely have been enough to keep him wide awake; but he did. He had not been in the snug little corner five minutes before he began to nod. He had not recovered himself one minute before he began to nod again. In the very act of opening his eyes indolently, he nodded again. In the very act of shutting them, he nodded again. So he fell out of one nod into another until at last he ceased to nod at all, and was as fast as the church itself.

He had a consciousness of the organ, long after he fell asleep, though as to its being an organ he had no more idea of that than he had of its being a Bull. After a while he began to have at intervals the same dreamy impressions of voices; and awakening to an indolent curiosity upon the subject, opened his eyes.

He was so indolent, that after glancing at the hassocks and the pew, he was already half-way off to sleep again, when it occurred to him that there really were voices in the church:

low voices, talking earnestly hard by: while the echoes seemed to mutter responses. He roused himself, and listened.

Before he had listened half a dozen seconds, he became as broad awake as ever he had been in all his life. With eyes, and ears, and mouth, wide open, he moved himself a very little with the utmost caution, and gathering the curtain in his hand, peeped out.

Tom Pinch and Mary. Of course. He had recognised their voices, and already knew the topic they discussed. Looking like the small end of a guillotined man, with his chin on a level with the top of the pew, so that he might duck down immediately in case of either of them turning round, he listened. Listened with such concentrated eagerness, that his very hair and shirt-collar stood bristling up to help him.

'No,' cried Tom. 'No letters have ever reached me, except that one from New York. But don't be uneasy on that account, for it's very likely they have gone away to some far-off place, where the posts are neither regular nor frequent. He said in that very letter that it might be so, even in that city to which they thought of travelling—Eden, you know.'

'It is a great weight upon my mind,' said Mary.

'Oh, but you mustn't let it be,' said Tom. 'There's a true saying that nothing travels so fast as ill news; and if the slightest harm had happened to Martin, you may be sure you would have heard of it long ago. I have often wished to say this to you,' Tom continued with an embarrassment that became him very well, 'but you have never given me an opportunity.'

'I have sometimes been almost afraid,' said Mary, 'that you might suppose I hesitated to confide in you, Mr. Pinch.'

'No,' Tom stammered, 'I—I am not aware that I ever supposed that. I am sure that if I have, I have checked the thought directly, as an injustice to you. I feel the delicacy of your situation in having to confide in me at all,' said Tom, 'but I would risk my life to save you from one day's uneasiness: indeed I would!'

Poor Tom!

'I have dreaded sometimes,' Tom continued, 'that I might have displeased you by—by having the boldness to try and anticipate your wishes now and then. At other times I have fancied that your kindness prompted you to keep aloof from me.'

'Indeed!'

'It was very foolish: very presumptuous and ridiculous: to think so,' Tom pursued: 'but I feared you might suppose it possible that I—I—should admire you too much for my own peace; and so denied yourself the slight assistance you would otherwise have accepted from me. If such an idea has ever presented itself to you,' faltered Tom, 'pray dismiss it. I am easily made happy: and I shall live contented here long after you and Martin have forgotten me. I am a poor, shy, awkward creature: not at all a man of the world: and you should think no more of me, bless you, than if I were an old friar!'

If friars bear such hearts as thine, Tom, let friars multiply; though they have no such rule in all their stern arithmetic.

'Dear Mr. Pinch!' said Mary, giving him her hand; 'I cannot tell you how your kindness moves me. I have never wronged you by the lightest doubt, and have never for an instant ceased to feel that you were all—much more than all —that Martin found you. Without the silent care and friend-ship I have experienced from you, my life here would have been unhappy. But you have been a good angel to me; filling me with gratitude of heart, hope, and courage.'

'I am as little like an angel, I am afraid,' replied Tom, shaking his head, 'as any stone cherubim among the grave-stones; and I don't think there are many real angels of *that* pattern. But I should like to know (if you will tell me) why you have been so very silent about Martin.'

'Because I have been afraid,' said Mary, 'of injuring you.'

'Of injuring me!' cried Tom.

'Of doing you an injury with your employer.'

The gentleman in question dived.

'With Pecksniff!' rejoined Tom, with cheerful confidence. 'Oh dear, he'd never think of us! He's the best of men. The more at ease you were, the happier he would be. Oh dear, you needn't be afraid of Pecksniff. He is not a spy.'

Many a man in Mr. Pecksniff's place, if he could have dived through the floor of the pew of state and come out at Calcutta or any inhabited region on the other side of the earth, would have done it instantly. Mr. Pecksniff sat down upon a hassock, and listening more attentively than ever, smiled.

Mary seemed to have expressed some dissent in the mean-while, for Tom went on to say, with honest energy:

'Well, I don't know how it is, but it always happens, when-ever I express myself in this way to anybody almost, that I find they won't do justice to Pecksniff. It is one of the most extra-ordinary circumstances that ever came within my knowledge, but it is so. There's John Westlock, who used to be a pupil here, one of the best-hearted young men in the world, in all other matters: I really believe John would have Pecksniff flogged at the cart's tail if he could. And John is not a solitary case, for every pupil we have had in my time has gone away with the same inveterate hatred of him. There was Mark Tapley, too, quite in another station of life,' said Tom: 'the mockery he used to make of Pecksniff when he was at the Dragon was shocking. Martin too: Martin was worse than any of 'em. But I forgot. He prepared you to dislike Pecksniff, of course. So you came with a prejudice, you know, Miss Graham, and are not a fair witness.'

Tom triumphed very much in this discovery, and rubbed his hands with great satisfaction.

'Mr. Pinch,' said Mary, 'you mistake him.'

'No, no!' cried Tom. '*You* mistake him. But,' he added, with a rapid change in his tone, 'what is the matter? Miss Graham, what is the matter?'

Mr. Pecksniff brought up to the top of the pew, by slow degrees, his hair, his forehead, his eyebrow, his eye. She was sitting on a bench beside the door with her hands before her face; and Tom was bending over her.

'What is the matter?' cried Tom. 'Have I said anything to hurt you? Has any one said anything to hurt you? Don't cry. Pray tell me what it is. I cannot bear to see you so distressed. Mercy on us, I never was so surprised and grieved in all my life!'

Mr. Pecksniff kept his eye in the same place. He could have moved it now for nothing short of a gimlet or a red-hot wire.

'I wouldn't have told you, Mr. Pinch,' said Mary, 'if I could have helped it; but your delusion is so absorbing, and it is so necessary that we should be upon our guard; that you should not be compromised; and to that end that you should know by whom I am beset; that no alternative is left me. I came here purposely to tell you, but I think I should have wanted courage if you had not chanced to lead me so directly to the object of my coming.'

Tom gazed at her steadfastly, and seemed to say, 'What else?' But he said not a word.

'That person whom you think the best of men,' said Mary, looking up, and speaking with a quivering lip and flashing eye:

'Lord bless me!' muttered Tom, staggering back. 'Wait a moment. That person whom I think the best of men! You mean Pecksniff, of course. Yes, I see you mean Pecksniff. Good gracious me, don't speak without authority. What has he done? If he is not the best of men, what is he?'

'The worst. The falsest, craftiest, meanest, cruellest, most sordid, most shameless,' said the trembling girl—trembling with her indignation.

Tom sat down on a seat, and clasped his hands.

'What is he,' said Mary, 'who receiving me in his house as his guest; his unwilling guest: knowing my history, and how defenceless and alone I am, presumes before his daughters to affront me so, that if I had a brother but a child, who saw it, he would instinctively have helped me?'

'He is a scoundrel!' exclaimed Tom. 'Whoever he may be, he is a scoundrel.'

Mr. Pecksniff dived again.

'What is he,' said Mary, 'who, when my only friend: a dear and kind one, too: was in full health of mind, humbled himself before him, but was spurned away (for he knew him then) like a dog. Who, in his forgiving spirit, now that that friend is sunk into a failing state, can crawl about him again, and use the influence he basely gains for every base and wicked purpose, and not for one—not one—that's true or good?'

'I say he is a scoundrel!' answered Tom.

'But what is he: oh Mr. Pinch, what *is* he: who, thinking he could compass these designs the better if I were his wife, assails me with the coward's argument that if I marry him, Martin, on whom I have brought so much misfortune, shall be restored to something of his former hopes; and if I do not, shall be plunged in deeper ruin? What is he who makes my very constancy to one I love with all my heart a torture to myself and wrong to him; who makes me, do what I will, the instrument to hurt a head I would heap blessings on! What is he who, winding all these cruel snares about me, explains their purpose to me, with a smooth tongue and a smiling face, in the broad light of day: dragging me on, the while, in his embrace, and holding to his lips a hand,' pursued the agitated girl, extending it, 'which I would have struck off, if with it I could lose the shame and degradation of his touch?'

'I say,' cried Tom, in great excitement, 'he is a scoundrel and a villain! I don't care who he is, I say he is a double-dyed and most intolerable villain!'

Covering her face with her hands again, as if the passion which had sustained her through these disclosures lost itself in an overwhelming sense of shame and grief, she abandoned herself to tears.

Any sight of distress was sure to move the tenderness of Tom, but this especially. Tears and sobs from her were arrows in his heart. He tried to comfort her; sat down beside her; expended all his store of homely eloquence; and spoke in words of praise and hope of Martin. Aye, though he loved her from his soul with such a self-denying love as woman seldom wins: he spoke from first to last of Martin. Not the wealth of the rich Indies would have tempted Tom to shirk one mention of her lover's name.

When she was more composed, she impressed upon Tom that this man she had described, was Pecksniff in his real colours; and word by word and phrase by phrase, as well as she remembered it, related what had passed between them in the wood: which was no doubt a source of high gratification to that gentleman himself, who in his desire to see and his dread of being seen, was constantly diving down into the state pew, and coming up again like the intelligent householder in Punch's Show, who avoids being knocked on the head with a cudgel. When she had concluded her account, and had besought Tom to be very distant and unconscious in his manner towards her after this explanation, and had thanked him very much, they parted on the alarm of footsteps in the burial-ground; and Tom was left alone in the church again.

And now the full agitation and misery of the disclosure came rushing upon Tom indeed. The star of his whole life from boyhood had become, in a moment, putrid vapour. It was not that Pecksniff, Tom's Pecksniff, had ceased to exist, but that he never had existed. In his death Tom would have had the comfort of remembering what he used to be, but in this discovery, he had the anguish of recollecting what he never was. For as Tom's blindness in this matter had been total and not partial, so was his restored sight. *His* Pecksniff could never have worked the wickedness of which he had just now heard, but any other Pecksniff could; and the Pecksniff who could do that could do anything, and no doubt had been doing anything and everything except the right thing all through his career.

From the lofty height on which poor Tom had placed his idol it was tumbled down headlong, and

> Not all the king's horses, nor all the king's men,
> Could have set Mr. Pecksniff up again.

Legions of Titans couldn't have got him out of the mud; and serve him right! But it was not he who suffered; it was Tom. His compass was broken, his chart destroyed, his chronometer had stopped, his masts were gone by the board; his anchor was adrift, ten thousand leagues away.

Mr. Pecksniff watched him with a lively interest, for he divined the purpose of Tom's ruminations, and was curious to see how he conducted himself. For some time, Tom wandered up and down the aisle like a man demented, stopping occasionally to lean against a pew and think it over; then he stood staring at a blank old monument bordered tastefully with skulls and cross-bones, as if it were the finest work of Art he had ever seen, although at other times he held it in unspeakable contempt; then he sat down; then walked to and fro again; then went wandering up into the organ-loft, and touched the keys. But their minstrelsy was changed, their music gone; and sounding one long melancholy chord, Tom drooped his head upon his hands and gave it up as hopeless.

'I wouldn't have cared,' said Tom Pinch, rising from his stool, and looking down into the church as if he had been the Clergyman, 'I wouldn't have cared for anything he might have done to Me, for I have tried his patience often, and have lived upon his sufferance, and have never been the help to him that others could have been. I wouldn't have minded, Pecksniff,' Tom continued, little thinking who heard him, 'if you had done Me any wrong; I could have found plenty of excuses for that; and though you might have hurt me, could have still gone on respecting you. But why did you ever fall so low as this in my esteem! Oh Pecksniff, Pecksniff, there is nothing I would not have given, to have had you deserve my old opinion of you; nothing!'

Mr. Pecksniff sat upon the hassock pulling up his shirt-collar, while Tom, touched to the quick, delivered this apostrophe. After a pause he heard Tom coming down the stairs, jingling the church keys; and bringing his eye to the top of the pew again, saw him go slowly out and lock the door.

Mr. Pecksniff durst not issue from his place of concealment;

for through the windows of the church he saw Tom passing on among the graves, and sometimes stopping at a stone, and leaning there as if he were a mourner who had lost a friend. Even when he had left the churchyard, Mr. Pecksniff still remained shut up: not being at all secure but that in his restless state of mind Tom might come wandering back. At length he issued forth, and walked with a pleasant countenance into the vestry; where he knew there was a window near the ground, by which he could release himself by merely stepping out.

He was in a curious frame of mind, Mr. Pecksniff: being in no hurry to go, but rather inclining to a dilatory trifling with the time, which prompted him to open the vestry cupboard, and look at himself in the parson's little glass that hung within the door. Seeing that his hair was rumpled, he took the liberty of borrowing the canonical brush and arranging it. He also took the liberty of opening another cupboard; but he shut it up again quickly, being rather startled by the sight of a black and a white surplice dangling against the wall; which had very much the appearance of two curates who had committed suicide by hanging themselves. Remembering that he had seen in the first cupboard a port-wine bottle and some biscuits, he peeped into it again, and helped himself with much deliberation: cogitating all the time though, in a very deep and weighty manner, as if his thoughts were otherwise employed.

He soon made up his mind, if it had ever been in doubt; and putting back the bottle and biscuits, opened the casement. He got out into the churchyard without any difficulty; shut the window after him; and walked straight home.

'Is Mr. Pinch in-doors?' asked Mr. Pecksniff of his serving-maid.

'Just come in, sir.'

'Just come in, eh?' repeated Mr. Pecksniff, cheerfully. 'And gone up-stairs, I suppose?'

'Yes, sir. Gone up-stairs. Shall I call him, sir?'

'No,' said Mr. Pecksniff, 'no. You needn't call him, Jane. Thank you, Jane. How are your relations, Jane?'

'Pretty well, I thank you, sir.'

'I am glad to hear it. Let them know I asked about them, Jane. Is Mr. Chuzzlewit in the way, Jane?'

'Yes, sir. He's in the parlour, reading.'

'He's in the parlour, reading, is he, Jane?' said Mr. Pecksniff. 'Very well. Then I think I'll go and see him, Jane.'

Never had Mr. Pecksniff been beheld in a more pleasant humour!

But when he walked into the parlour where the old man was engaged as Jane had said; with pen and ink and paper on a table close at hand (for Mr. Pecksniff was always very particular to have him well supplied with writing materials); he became less cheerful. He was not angry, he was not vindictive, he was not cross, he was not moody, but he was grieved: he was sorely grieved. As he sat down by the old man's side, two tears: not tears like those with which recording angels blot their entries out, but drops so precious that they use them for their ink: stole down his meritorious cheeks.

'What is the matter?' asked old Martin. 'Pecksniff, what ails you, man?'

'I am sorry to interrupt you, my dear sir, and I am still more sorry for the cause. My good, my worthy friend, I am deceived.'

'You are deceived!'

'Ah!' cried Mr. Pecksniff, in an agony, 'deceived in the tenderest point. Cruelly deceived in that quarter, sir, in which I placed the most unbounded confidence. Deceived, Mr. Chuzzlewit, by Thomas Pinch.'

'Oh! bad, bad, bad!' said Martin, laying down his book. 'Very bad! I hope not. Are you certain?'

'Certain, my good sir! My eyes and ears are witnesses. I wouldn't have believed it otherwise. I wouldn't have believed it, Mr. Chuzzlewit, if a Fiery Serpent had proclaimed it from the top of Salisbury Cathedral. I would have said,' cried Mr. Pecksniff, 'that the Serpent lied. Such was my faith in Thomas Pinch, that I would have cast the falsehood back into the Serpent's teeth, and would have taken Thomas to my heart. But I am not a Serpent, sir, myself, I grieve to say, and no excuse or hope is left me.'

Martin was greatly disturbed to see him so much agitated, and to hear such unexpected news. He begged him to compose himself, and asked upon what subject Mr. Pinch's treachery had been developed.

'That is almost the worst of all, sir,' Mr. Pecksniff answered. 'On a subject nearly concerning *you*. Oh! is it not enough,' said Mr. Pecksniff, looking upward, 'that these blows must fall on me, but must they also hit my friends!'

'You alarm me,' cried the old man, changing colour. 'I am not so strong as I was. You terrify me, Pecksniff!'

'Cheer up, my noble sir,' said Mr. Pecksniff, taking courage, 'and we will do what is required of us. You shall know all, sir, and shall be righted. But first excuse me, sir, ex-cuse me. I have a duty to discharge, which I owe to society.'

He rang the bell, and Jane appeared. 'Send Mr. Pinch here, if you please, Jane.'

Tom came. Constrained and altered in his manner, downcast and dejected, visibly confused; not liking to look Pecksniff in the face.

The honest man bestowed a glance on Mr. Chuzzlewit, as who should say 'You see!' and addressed himself to Tom in these terms:

'Mr. Pinch, I have left the vestry-window unfastened. Will you do me the favour to go and secure it; then bring the keys of the sacred edifice to me!'

'The vestry-window, sir?' cried Tom.

'You understand me, Mr. Pinch, I think,' returned his patron. 'Yes, Mr. Pinch, the vestry-window. I grieve to say that sleeping in the church after a fatiguing ramble, I overheard just now some fragments,' he emphasised that word, 'of a dialogue between two parties; and one of them locking the church when he went out, I was obliged to leave it myself by the vestry-window. Do me the favour to secure that vestry-window, Mr. Pinch, and then come back to me.'

No physiognomist that ever dwelt on earth could have construed Tom's face when he heard these words. Wonder was in it, and a mild look of reproach, but certainly no fear or guilt, although a host of strong emotions struggled to display themselves. He bowed, and without saying one word, good or bad, withdrew.

'Pecksniff,' cried Martin, in a tremble, 'what does all this mean? You are not going to do anything in haste, you may regret!'

'No, my good sir,' said Mr. Pecksniff, firmly, 'No. But I have a duty to discharge which I owe to society; and it shall be discharged, my friend, at any cost!'

Oh late-remembered, much-forgotten, mouthing, braggart duty, always owed, and seldom paid in any other coin than punishment and wrath, when will mankind begin to know thee! When will men acknowledge thee in thy neglected cradle, and thy stunted youth, and not begin their recognition in thy sinful manhood and thy desolate old age! Oh ermined

Judge whose duty to society is, now, to doom the ragged criminal to punishment and death, hadst thou never, Man, a duty to discharge in barring up the hundred open gates that wooed him to the felon's dock, and throwing but ajar the portals to a decent life! Oh prelate, prelate, whose duty to society it is to mourn in melancholy phrase the sad degeneracy of these bad times in which thy lot of honours has been cast, did nothing go before thy elevation to the lofty seat, from which thou dealest out thy homilies to other tarriers for dead men's shoes, whose duty to society has not begun! Oh magistrate, so rare a country gentleman and brave a squire, had you no duty to society, before the ricks were blazing and the mob were mad; or did it spring up, armed and booted from the earth, a corps of yeomanry, full-grown!

Mr. Pecksniff's duty to society could not be paid till Tom came back. The interval which preceded the return of that young man, he occupied in a close conference with his friend; so that when Tom did arrive, he found the two quite ready to receive him. Mary was in her own room above, whither Mr. Pecksniff, always considerate, had besought old Martin to entreat her to remain some half-hour longer, that her feelings might be spared.

When Tom came back, he found old Martin sitting by the window, and Mr. Pecksniff in an imposing attitude at the table. On one side of him was his pocket-handkerchief; and on the other a little heap (a very little heap) of gold and silver, and odd pence. Tom saw, at a glance, that it was his own salary for the current quarter.

'Have you fastened the vestry-window, Mr. Pinch?' said Pecksniff.

'Yes, sir.'

'Thank you. Put down the keys if you please, Mr. Pinch.'

Tom placed them on the table. He held the bunch by the key of the organ-loft (though it was one of the smallest), and looked hard at it as he laid it down. It had been an old, old friend of Tom's; a kind companion to him, many and many a day.

'Mr. Pinch,' said Pecksniff, shaking his head: 'Oh Mr. Pinch! I wonder you can look me in the face!'

Tom did it though; and notwithstanding that he has been described as stooping generally, he stood as upright then as man could stand.

'Mr. Pinch,' said Pecksniff, taking up his handkerchief, as if he felt that he should want it soon, 'I will not dwell upon the past. I will spare you, and I will spare myself, that pain at least.'

Tom's was not a very bright eye, but it was a very expressive one when he looked at Mr. Pecksniff, and said:

'Thank you, sir. I am very glad you will not refer to the past.'

'The present is enough,' said Mr. Pecksniff, dropping a penny, 'and the sooner *that* is past, the better. Mr. Pinch, I will not dismiss you without a word of explanation. Even such a course would be quite justifiable under the circumstances; but it might wear an appearance of hurry, and I will not do it; for I am,' said Mr. Pecksniff, knocking down another penny, 'perfectly self-possessed. Therefore I will say to you, what I have already said to Mr. Chuzzlewit.'

Tom glanced at the old gentleman, who nodded now and then as approving of Mr. Pecksniff's sentences and sentiments, but interposed between them in no other way.

'From fragments of a conversation which I overheard in the church, just now, Mr. Pinch,' said Pecksniff, 'between yourself and Miss Graham—I say fragments, because I was slumbering at a considerable distance from you, when I was roused by your voices—and from what I saw, I ascertained (I would have given a great deal not to have ascertained, Mr. Pinch) that you, forgetful of all ties of duty and of honour, sir; regardless of the sacred laws of hospitality, to which you were pledged as an inmate of this house; have presumed to address Miss Graham with un-returned professions of attachment and proposals of love.'

Tom looked at him steadily.

'Do you deny it, sir?' asked Mr. Pecksniff, dropping one pound two and fourpence, and making a great business of picking it up again.

'No, sir,' replied Tom. 'I do not.'

'You do not,' said Mr. Pecksniff, glancing at the old gentleman. 'Oblige me by counting this money, Mr. Pinch, and putting your name to this receipt. You do not?'

No, Tom did not. He scorned to deny it. He saw that Mr. Pecksniff having overheard his own disgrace, cared not a jot for sinking lower yet in his contempt. He saw that he had devised this fiction as the readiest means of getting rid of him

at once, but that it must end in that any way. He saw that
Mr. Pecksniff reckoned on his not denying it, because his doing
so and explaining would incense the old man more than ever
against Martin and against Mary: while Pecksniff himself
would only have been mistaken in his 'fragments.' Deny it!
No.

'You find the amount correct, do you, Mr. Pinch?' said
Pecksniff.

'Quite correct, sir,' answered Tom.

'A person is waiting in the kitchen,' said Mr. Pecksniff, 'to
carry your luggage wherever you please. We part, Mr. Pinch,
at once, and are strangers from this time.'

Something without a name; compassion, sorrow, old
tenderness, mistaken gratitude, habit: none of these, and yet
all of them; smote upon Tom's gentle heart at parting. There
was no such soul as Pecksniff's in that carcase; and yet, though
his speaking out had not involved the compromise of one he
loved, he couldn't have denounced the very shape and figure
cf the man. Not even then.

'I will not say,' cried Mr. Pecksniff, shedding tears, 'what
a blow this is. I will not say how much it tries me; how it works
upon my nature; how it grates upon my feelings. I do not care
for that. I can endure as well as another man. But what I have
to hope, and what you have to hope, Mr. Pinch (otherwise
a great responsibility rests upon you), is, that this deception
may not alter my ideas of humanity; that it may not impair
my freshness, or contract, if I may use the expression, my
Pinions. I hope it will not; I don't think it will. It may be a
comfort to you, if not now, at some future time, to know that I
shall endeavour not to think the worse of my fellow-creatures
in general, for what has passed between us. Farewell!'

Tom had meant to spare him one little puncturation with
a lancet, which he had it in his power to administer, but he
changed his mind on hearing this, and said:

'I think you left something in the church, sir.'

'Thank you, Mr. Pinch,' said Pecksniff. 'I am not aware
that I did.'

'This is your double eye-glass, I believe?' said Tom.

'Oh!' cried Pecksniff, with some degree of confusion. 'I am
obliged to you. Put it down, if you please.'

'I found it,' said Tom, slowly, 'when I went to bolt the
vestry-window, in the pew.'

So he had. Mr. Pecksniff had taken it off when he was bobbing up and down, lest it should strike against the panelling: and had forgotten it. Going back to the church with his mind full of having been watched, and wondering very much from what part, Tom's attention was caught by the door of the state pew standing open. Looking into it he found the glass. And thus he knew, and by returning it gave Mr. Pecksniff the information that he knew, where the listener had been; and that instead of overhearing fragments of the conversation, he must have rejoiced in every word of it.

'I am glad he's gone,' said Martin, drawing a long breath when Tom had left the room.

'It *is* a relief,' assented Mr. Pecksniff. 'It is a great relief. But having discharged—I hope with tolerable firmness—the duty which I owed to society, I will now, my dear sir, if you will give me leave, retire to shed a few tears in the back garden, as an humble individual.'

Tom went up-stairs: cleared his shelf of books: packed them up with his music and an old fiddle in his trunk; got out his clothes (they were not so many that they made his head ache); put them on the top of his books; and went into the workroom for his case of instruments. There was a ragged stool there, with the horsehair all sticking out of the top like a wig: a very Beast of a stool in itself: on which he had taken up his daily seat, year after year, during the whole period of his service. They had grown older and shabbier in company. Pupils had served their time; seasons had come and gone; Tom and the worn-out stool had held together through it all. That part of the room was traditionally called 'Tom's Corner.' It had been assigned to him at first because of its being situated in a strong draught, and a great way from the fire; and he had occupied it ever since. There were portraits of him on the walls, with all his weak points monstrously portrayed. Diabolical sentiments, foreign to his character, were represented as issuing from his mouth in fat balloons. Every pupil had added something, even unto fancy portraits of his father with one eye, and of his mother with a disproportionate nose, and especially of his sister; who always being presented as extremely beautiful, made full amends to Tom for any other joke. Under less uncommon circumstances, it would have cut Tom to the heart to leave these things, and think that he saw them for the last time; but it didn't now. There was no Pecksniff; there never had been a Pecksniff; and all his other griefs were swallowed up in that.

So when he returned into the bedroom, and, having fastened his box and a carpet-bag, put on his walking gaiters, and his great-coat, and his hat, and taken his stick in his hand, looked round it for the last time. Early on summer mornings, and by the light of private candle-ends on winter nights, he had read himself half blind in this same room. He had tried in this same room to learn the fiddle under the bedclothes, but yielding to objections from the other pupils, had reluctantly abandoned the design. At any other time he would have parted from it with a pang, thinking of all he had learned there, of the many hours he had passed there; for the love of his very dreams. But there was no Pecksniff; there never had been a Pecksniff, and the unreality of Pecksniff extended itself to the chamber, in which, sitting on one particular bed, the thing supposed to be that Great Abstraction had often preached morality with such effect that Tom had felt a moisture in his eyes, while hanging breathless on the words.

The man engaged to bear his box—Tom knew him well; a Dragon man—came stamping up the stairs, and made a roughish bow to Tom (to whom in common times he would have nodded with a grin), as though he were aware of what had happened, and wished him to perceive it made no differ-ence to *him*. It was clumsily done; he was a mere waterer of horses; but Tom liked the man for it, and felt it more than going away.

Tom would have helped him with the box, but he made no more of it, though it was a heavy one, than an elephant would have made of a castle: just swinging it on his back and bowling down-stairs as if, being naturally a heavy sort of fellow, he could carry a box infinitely better than he could go alone. Tom took the carpet-bag, and went down-stairs along with him. At the outer door stood Jane, crying with all her might: and on the steps was Mrs. Lupin, sobbing bitterly, and putting out her hand for Tom to shake.

'You're coming to the Dragon, Mr. Pinch?'

'No,' said Tom, 'no. I shall walk to Salisbury to-night. I couldn't stay here. For goodness' sake, don't make me so un-happy, Mrs. Lupin.'

'But you'll come to the Dragon, Mr. Pinch. If it's only for to-night. To see me, you know: not as a traveller.'

Mr. Pecksniff discharges a Duty which he owes to Society

'God bless my soul!' said Tom, wiping his eyes. 'The kindness of people is enough to break one's heart! I mean to go to Salisbury to-night, my dear good creature. If you'll take care of my box for me till I write for it, I shall consider it the greatest kindness you can do me.'

'I wish,' cried Mrs. Lupin, 'there were twenty boxes, Mr. Pinch, that I might have 'em all.'

'Thank'ee,' said Tom. 'It's like you. Good-bye. Good-bye.'

There were several people, young and old, standing about the door, some of whom cried with Mrs. Lupin; while others tried to keep up a stout heart, as Tom did; and others were absorbed in admiration of Mr. Pecksniff—a man who could build a church, as one may say, by squinting at a sheet of paper; and others were divided between that feeling and sympathy with Tom. Mr. Pecksniff had appeared on the top of the steps, simultaneously with his old pupil, and while Tom was talking with Mrs. Lupin kept his hand stretched out, as though he said 'Go forth!' When Tom went forth, and had turned the corner, Mr. Pecksniff shook his head, shut his eyes, and heaving a deep sigh, shut the door. On which, the best of Tom's supporters said he must have done some dreadful deed, or such a man as Mr. Pecksniff never could have felt like that. If it had been a common quarrel (they observed) he would have said something, but when he didn't, Mr. Pinch must have shocked him dreadfully.

Tom was out of hearing of their shrewd opinions, and plodded on as steadily as he could go, until he came within sight of the turnpike where the tollman's family had cried out 'Mr. Pinch!' that frosty morning when he went to meet young Martin. He had got through the village, and this toll-bar was his last trial; but when the infant toll-takers came screeching out, he had half a mind to run for it, and make a bolt across the country.

'Why deary Mr. Pinch! oh deary sir!' cried the tollman's wife. 'What an unlikely time for you to be a-going this way with a bag!'

'I am going to Salisbury,' said Tom.

'Why, goodness, where's the gig then?' cried the tollman's wife, looking down the road, as if she thought Tom might have been upset without observing it.

'I haven't got it,' said Tom. 'I—' he couldn't evade it; he

T

felt she would have him in the next question, if he got over this one. 'I have left Mr. Pecksniff.'

The tollman—a crusty customer, always smoking solitary pipes in a Windsor chair, inside, set artfully between two little windows that looked up and down the road, so that when he saw anything coming up, he might hug himself on having toll to take, and when he saw it going down, might hug himself on having taken it—the tollman was out in an instant.

'Left Mr. Pecksniff!' cried the tollman.

'Yes,' said Tom, 'left him.'

The tollman looked at his wife, uncertain whether to ask her if she had anything to suggest, or to order her to mind the children. Astonishment making him surly, he preferred the latter, and sent her into the toll-house with a flea in her ear.

'You left Mr. Pecksniff!' cried the tollman, folding his arms, and spreading his legs. 'I should as soon have thought of his head leaving him.'

'Aye!' said Tom, 'so should I, yesterday. Good night!'

If a heavy drove of oxen hadn't come by immediately, the tollman would have gone down to the village straight, to inquire into it. As things turned out, he smoked another pipe, and took his wife into his confidence. But their united sagacity could make nothing of it, and they went to bed—meta-phorically—in the dark. But several times that night, when a waggon or other vehicle came through, and the driver asked the tollkeeper 'What news?' he looked at the man by the light of his lantern, to assure himself that he had an interest in the subject, and then said, wrapping his watch-coat round his legs:

'You've heerd of Mr. Pecksniff down yonder?'

'Ah! sure-ly!'

'And of his young man Mr. Pinch, p'raps?'

'Ah!'

'They've parted.'

After every one of these disclosures, the tollman plunged into his house again, and was seen no more, while the other side went on in great amazement.

But this was long after Tom was abed, and Tom was now with his face towards Salisbury, doing his best to get there. The evening was beautiful at first, but it became cloudy and dull at sunset, and the rain fell heavily soon afterwards. For ten long miles he plodded on, wet through, until at last the lights appeared, and he came into the welcome precincts of the city.

He went to the inn where he had waited for Martin, and briefly answering their inquiries after Mr. Pecksniff, ordered a bed. He had no heart for tea or supper, meat or drink of any kind, but sat by himself before an empty table in the public room while the bed was getting ready, revolving in his mind all that had happened that eventful day, and wondering what he could or should do for the future. It was a great relief when the chambermaid came in, and said the bed was ready.

It was a low four-poster shelving downward in the centre like a trough, and the room was crowded with impracticable tables and exploded chests of drawers, full of damp linen. A graphic representation in oil of a remarkably fat ox hung over the fireplace, and the portrait of some former landlord (who might have been the ox's brother, he was so like him) stared roundly in, at the foot of the bed. A variety of queer smells were partially quenched in the prevailing scent of very old lavender; and the window had not been opened for such a long space of time that it pleaded immemorial usage, and wouldn't come open now.

These were trifles in themselves, but they added to the strangeness of the place, and did not induce Tom to forget his new position. Pecksniff had gone out of the world—had never been in it—and it was as much as Tom could do to say his prayers without him. But he felt happier afterwards, and went to sleep, and dreamed about him as he Never Was.

CHAPTER XXXII

Treats of Todgers's again; and of another blighted plant besides the plants upon the leads

EARLY on the day next after that on which she bade adieu to the halls of her youth and the scenes of her childhood, Miss Pecksniff, arriving safely at the coach-office in London, was there received, and conducted to her peaceful home beneath the shadow of the Monument, by Mrs. Todgers. M. Todgers looked a little worn by cares of gravy and other such solicitudes arising out of her establishment, but displayed her usual earnestness and warmth of manner.

'And how, my sweet Miss Pecksniff,' said she, 'how is your princely pa?'

Miss Pecksniff signified (in confidence) that he contemplated the introduction of a princely ma; and repeated the sentiment that she wasn't blind, and wasn't quite a fool, and wouldn't bear it.

Mrs. Todgers was more shocked by the intelligence than any one could have expected. She was quite bitter. She said there was no truth in man, and that the warmer he expressed himself, as a general principle, the falser and more treacherous he was. She foresaw with astonishing clearness that the object of Mr. Pecksniff's attachment was designing, worthless, and wicked; and receiving from Charity the fullest confirmation of these views, protested with tears in her eyes that she loved Miss Pecksniff like a sister, and felt her injuries as if they were her own.

'Your real darling sister, I have not seen her more than once since her marriage,' said Mrs. Todgers, 'and then I thought her looking poorly. My sweet Miss Pecksniff, I always thought that you was to be the lady?'

'Oh dear no!' cried Cherry, shaking her head. 'Oh no, Mrs. Todgers. Thank you. No! not for any consideration he could offer.'

'I dare say you are right,' said Mrs. Todgers with a sigh. 'I feared it all along. But the misery we have had from that match, here among ourselves, in this house, my dear Miss Pecksniff, nobody would believe.'

'Lor, Mrs. Todgers!'

'Awful, awful!' repeated Mrs. Todgers, with strong emphasis. 'You recollect our youngest gentleman, my dear?'

'Of course I do,' said Cherry.

'You might have observed,' said Mrs. Todgers, 'how he used to watch your sister; and that a kind of stony dumbness came over him whenever she was in company?'

'I am sure I never saw anything of the sort,' said Cherry. in a peevish manner. 'What nonsense, Mrs. Todgers!'

'My dear,' returned that lady in a hollow voice, 'I have seen him, again and again, sitting over his pie at dinner, with his spoon a perfect fixture in his mouth, looking at your sister. I have seen him standing in a corner of our drawing-room, gazing at her, in such a lonely, melancholy state, that he was more like a Pump than a man, and might have drawed tears.'

'I never saw it!' cried Cherry; 'that's all I can say.'

'But when the marriage took place,' said Mrs. Todgers, proceeding with her subject, 'when it was in the paper, and was read out here at breakfast, I thought he had taken leave of his senses, I did indeed. The violence of that young man, my dear Miss Pecksniff; the frightful opinions he expressed upon the subject of self-destruction; the extraordinary actions he performed with his tea; the clenching way in which he bit his bread and butter; the manner in which he taunted Mr. Jinkins; all combined to form a picture never to be forgotten.'

'It's a pity he didn't destroy himself, I think,' observed Miss Pecksniff.

'Himself!' said Mrs. Todgers, 'it took another turn at night. He was for destroying other people then. There was a little chaffing going on—I hope you don't consider that a low expression, Miss Pecksniff; it is always in our gentlemen's mouths—a little chaffing going on, my dear, among 'em, all in good nature, when suddenly he rose up, foaming with his fury, and but for being held by three, would have had Mr. Jinkins's life with a boot-jack.'

Miss Pecksniff's face expressed supreme indifference.

'And now,' said Mrs. Todgers, 'now he is the meekest of men. You can almost bring the tears into his eyes by looking at him. He sits with me the whole day long on Sundays, talking in such a dismal way that I find it next to impossible to keep my spirits up equal to the accommodation of the boarders. His only comfort is in female society. He takes me half-price to the play, to an extent which I sometimes fear is beyond his means; and I see the tears a-standing in his eyes during the whole performance—particularly if it is anything of a comic nature. The turn I experienced only yesterday,' said Mrs. Todgers, putting her hand to her side, 'when the housemaid threw his bedside carpet out of the window of his room, while I was sitting here, no one can imagine. I thought it was him, and that he had done it at last!'

The contempt with which Miss Charity received this pathetic account of the state to which the youngest gentleman in company was reduced, did not say much for her power of sympathising with that unfortunate character. She treated it with great levity, and went on to inform herself, then and afterwards, whether any other changes had occurred in the commercial boarding-house.

Mr. Bailey was gone, and had been succeeded (such is the decay of human greatness!) by an old woman whose name was reported to be Tamaroo—which seemed an impossibility. Indeed it appeared in the fulness of time that the jocular boarders had appropriated the word from an English ballad, in which it is supposed to express the bold and fiery nature of a certain hackney coachman; and that it was bestowed upon Mr. Bailey's successor by reason of her having nothing fiery about her, except an occasional attack of that fire which is called St. Anthony's. This ancient female had been engaged, in fulfilment of a vow, registered by Mrs. Todgers, that no more boys should darken the commercial doors; and she was chiefly remarkable for a total absence of all comprehension upon every subject whatever. She was a perfect Tomb for messages and small parcels; and when dispatched to the Post Office with letters, had been frequently seen endeavouring to insinuate them into casual chinks in private doors, under the delusion that any door with a hole in it would answer the purpose. She was a very little old woman, and always wore a very coarse apron with a bib before and a loop behind, together with bandages on her wrists, which appeared to be afflicted with an everlasting sprain. She was on all occasions chary of opening the street-door, and ardent to shut it again; and she waited at table in a bonnet.

This was the only great change over and above the change which had fallen on the youngest gentleman. As for him, he more than corroborated the account of Mrs. Todgers: possessing greater sensibility than even she had given him credit for.

He entertained some terrible notions of Destiny, among other matters, and talked much about people's 'Missions:' upon which he seemed to have some private information not generally attainable, as he knew it had been poor Merry's mission to crush him in the bud. He was very frail and tearful; for being aware that a shepherd's mission was to pipe to his flocks, and that a boatswain's mission was to pipe all hands, and that one man's mission was to be a paid piper, and another man's mission was to pay the piper, so he had got it into his head that his own peculiar mission was to pipe his eye. Which he did perpetually.

He often informed Mrs. Todgers that the sun had set upon him; that the billows had rolled over him; that the Car of Juggernaut had crushed him; and also that the deadly Upas tree of Java had blighted him. His name was Moddle.

Towards this most unhappy Moddle, Miss Pecksniff conducted herself at first with distant haughtiness, being in no humour to be entertained with dirges in honour of her married sister. The poor young gentleman was additionally crushed by this, and remonstrated with Mrs. Todgers on the subject.

'Even she turns from me, Mrs. Todgers,' said Moddle.

'Then why don't you try and be a little bit more cheerful, sir?' retorted Mrs. Todgers.

'Cheerful, Mrs. Todgers! cheerful!' cried the youngest gentleman: 'when she reminds me of days for ever fled, Mrs. Todgers!'

'Then you had better avoid her for a short time, if she does,' said Mrs. Todgers, 'and come to know her again, by degrees. That's my advice.'

'But I can't avoid her,' replied Moddle. 'I haven't strength of mind to do it. Oh, Mrs. Todgers, if you knew what a comfort her nose is to me!'

'Her nose, sir!' Mrs. Todgers cried.

'Her profile, in general,' said the youngest gentleman, 'but particularly her nose. It's so like;' here he yielded to a burst of grief; 'it's so like hers who is Another's, Mrs. Todgers!'

The observant matron did not fail to report this conversation to Charity, who laughed at the time, but treated Mr. Moddle that very evening with increased consideration, and presented her side-face to him as much as possible. Mr. Moddle was not less sentimental than usual; was rather more so, if anything; but he sat and stared at her with glistening eyes, and seemed grateful.

'Well, sir!' said the lady of the Boarding-House next day. 'You held up your head last night. You're coming round, I think.'

'Only because she's so like her who is Another's, Mrs. Todgers,' rejoined the youth. 'When she talks, and when she smiles, I think I'm looking on HER brow again, Mrs. Todgers.'

This was likewise carried to Charity, who talked and smiled next evening in her most engaging manner, and rallying Mr. Moddle on the lowness of his spirits, challenged him to play a rubber at cribbage. Mr. Moddle taking up the gauntlet, they played several rubbers for sixpences, and Charity won them all. This may have been partially attributable to the gallantry of the youngest gentleman, but it was certainly referable to the state of his feelings also: for his eyes being frequently dimmed by tears, he thought that aces were tens, and knaves queens, which at times occasioned some confusion in his play.

On the seventh night of cribbage, when Mrs. Todgers, sitting by, proposed that instead of gambling they should play for 'love,' Mr. Moddle was seen to change colour. On the fourteenth night, he kissed Miss Pecksniff's snuffers, in the passage, when she went up-stairs to bed: meaning to have kissed her hand, but missing it.

In short, Mr. Moddle began to be impressed with the idea that Miss Pecksniff's mission was to comfort him; and Miss Pecksniff began to speculate on the probability of its being her mission to become ultimately Mrs. Moddle. He was a young gentleman (Miss Pecksniff was not a very young lady) with rising prospects, and 'almost' enough to live on. Really it looked very well.

Besides, besides, he had been regarded as devoted to Merry. Merry had joked about him, and had once spoken of it to her sister as a conquest. He was better looking, better shaped, better spoken, better tempered, better mannered than Jonas. He was easy to manage, could be made to consult the humours of his Betrothed, and could be shown off like a lamb when Jonas was a bear. There was the rub!

In the meantime the cribbage went on, and Mrs. Todgers went off; for the youngest gentleman, dropping her society, began to take Miss Pecksniff to the play. He also began, as Mrs. Todgers said, to slip home 'in his dinner-times,' and to get away from 'the office' at unholy seasons; and twice, as he informed Mrs. Todgers himself, he received anonymous letters,

*Mr. Moddle is both particular and peculiar in his
Attentions*

(p. 511)

enclosing cards from Furniture Warehouses—clearly the act of that ungentlemanly ruffian Jinkins: only he hadn't evidence enough to call him out upon. All of which, so Mrs. Todgers told Miss Pecksniff, spoke as plain English as the shining sun.

'My dear Miss Pecksniff, you may depend upon it,' said Mrs. Todgers, 'that he is burning to propose.'

'My goodness me, why don't he then?' cried Cherry.

'Men are so much more timid than we think 'em, my dear,' returned Mrs. Todgers. 'They baulk themselves continually. I saw the words on Todgers's lips for months and months and months, before he said 'em.'

Miss Pecksniff submitted that Todgers might not have been a fair specimen.

'Oh yes, he was. Oh bless you, yes, my dear. I was very particular in those days, I assure you,' said Mrs. Todgers, bridling. 'No, no. You give Mr. Moddle a little encouragement, Miss Pecksniff, if you wish him to speak; and he'll speak fast enough, depend upon it.'

'I am sure I don't know what encouragement he would have, Mrs. Todgers,' returned Charity. 'He walks with me, and plays cards with me, and he comes and sits alone with me.'

'Quite right,' said Mrs. Todgers. 'That's indispensable, my dear.'

'And he sits very close to me.'

'Also quite correct,' said Mrs. Todgers.

'And he looks at me.'

'To be sure he does,' said Mrs. Todgers.

'And he has his arm upon the back of the chair or sofa, or whatever it is—behind me, you know.'

'*I* should think so,' said Mrs. Todgers.

'And then he begins to cry!'

Mrs. Todgers admitted that he might do better than that; and might undoubtedly profit by the recollection of the great Lord Nelson's signal at the battle of Trafalgar. Still, she said, he would come round, or, not to mince the matter, would be brought round, if Miss Pecksniff took up a decided position, and plainly showed him that it must be done.

Determining to regulate her conduct by this opinion, the young lady received Mr. Moddle, on the earliest subsequent occasion, with an air of constraint: and gradually leading him to inquire, in a dejected manner, why she was so changed, confessed to him that she felt it necessary for their mutual peace and happiness to take a decided step. They had been much together lately, she observed, much together, and had tasted the sweets of a genuine reciprocity of sentiment. She never could forget him, nor could she ever cease to think of him with feelings of the liveliest friendship; but people had begun to talk, the thing had been observed, and it was necessary that they should be nothing more to each other, than any gentleman and lady in society usually are. She was glad she had had the resolution to say thus much before her feelings had been tried too far; they had been greatly tried, she would admit; but though she was weak and silly, she would soon get the better of it, she hoped.

Moddle, who had by this time become in the last degree maudlin, and wept abundantly, inferred from the foregoing avowal, that it was his mission to communicate to others the blight which had fallen on himself; and that, being a kind of unintentional Vampire, he had had Miss Pecksniff assigned to him by the Fates, as Victim Number One. Miss Pecksniff controverting this opinion as sinful, Moddle was goaded on to ask whether she could be contented with a blighted heart; and it appearing on further examination that she could be, plighted his dismal troth, which was accepted and returned.

He bore his good fortune with the utmost moderation. Instead of being triumphant, he shed more tears than he had ever been known to shed before: and, sobbing, said:

'Oh! what a day this has been! I can't go back to the office this afternoon. Oh, what a trying day this has been, Good Gracious!'

*Mr. Tapley is recognised by some Fellow-Citizens
of Eden*
(p. 514)

CHAPTER XXXIII

Further proceedings in Eden, and a proceeding out of it.
Martin makes a discovery of some importance

FROM Mr. Moddle to Eden is an easy and natural transition. Mr. Moddle, living in the atmosphere of Miss
Pecksniff's love, dwelt (if he had but known it) in a terrestrial Paradise. The thriving city of Eden was also a terrestrial
Paradise, upon the showing of its proprietors. The beautiful
Miss Pecksniff might have been poetically described as a something too good for man in his fallen and degraded state. That
was exactly the character of the thriving city of Eden, as
poetically heightened by Zephaniah Scadder, General Choke,
and other worthies: part and parcel of the talons of that great
American Eagle, which is always airing itself sky-high in
purest æther, and never, no never, never, tumbles down with
draggled wings into the mud.

When Mark Tapley, leaving Martin in the architectural
and surveying offices, had effectually strengthened and encouraged his own spirits by the contemplation of their joint
misfortunes, he proceeded, with new cheerfulness, in search
of help: congratulating himself, as he went along, on the
enviable position to which he had at last attained.

'I used to think, sometimes,' said Mr. Tapley, 'as a desolate
island would suit me, but I should only have had myself to
provide for there, and being naterally a easy man to manage,
there wouldn't have been much credit in *that*. Now here I've
got my partner to take care on, and he's something like the
sort of man for the purpose. I want a man as is always a-sliding
off his legs when he ought to be on 'em. I want a man as is so
low down in the school of life that he's always a-making figures
of one in his copy-book, and can't get no further. I want a man
as is his own great-coat and cloak, and is always a-wrapping
himself up in himself. And I have got him too,' said Mr.
Tapley, after a moment's silence. 'What a happiness!'

He paused to look round, uncertain to which of the log-
houses he should repair.

'I don't know which to take,' he observed; 'that's the truth.
They're equally prepossessing outside, and equally commodious, no doubt, within; being fitted up with every convenience

that a Alligator, in a state of natur', could possibly require. Let me see! The citizen as turned out last night, lives under water, in the right-handed dog-kennel at the corner. I don't want to trouble him if I can help it, poor man, for he is a melancholy object; a reg'lar Settler in every respect. There's a house with a winder, but I am afraid of their being proud. I don't know whether a door ain't too aristocratic; but here goes for the first one!'

He went up to the nearest cabin, and knocked with his hand. Being desired to enter, he complied.

'Neighbour,' said Mark: 'for I *am* a neighbour, though you don't know me; I've come a-begging. Hallo! hal—lo!——Am I a-bed, and dreaming!'

He made this exclamation on hearing his own name pronounced, and finding himself clasped about the skirts by two little boys, whose faces he had often washed, and whose suppers he had often cooked, on board of that noble and fast-sailing line-of-packet ship, the Screw.

'My eyes is wrong!' said Mark. 'I don't believe 'em. That ain't my fellow-passenger yonder, a-nursing her little girl, who, I am sorry to see, is so delicate; and that ain't her husband as come to New York to fetch her. Nor these,' he added, looking down upon the boys, 'ain't them two young shavers as was so familiar to me; though they are uncommon like 'em. That I must confess.'

The woman shed tears in very joy to see him; the man shook both his hands and would not let them go; the two boys hugged his legs; the sick child in the mother's arms stretched out her burning little fingers, and muttered, in her hoarse, dry throat, his well-remembered name.

It was the same family, sure enough. Altered by the salubrious air of Eden. But the same.

'This is a new sort of a morning call,' said Mark, drawing a long breath. 'It strikes one all of a heap. Wait a little bit! I'm a-coming round fast. That'll do! These gentlemen ain't my friends. Are they on the visiting list of the house?'

The inquiry referred to certain gaunt pigs, who had walked in after him, and were much interested in the heels of the family. As they did not belong to the mansion, they were expelled by the two little boys.

'I ain't superstitious about toads,' said Mark, looking round the room, 'but if you could prevail upon the two or three I see in company, to step out at the same time, my young friends, I think they'd find the open air refreshing. Not that I at all object to 'em. A very handsome animal is a toad,' said Mr. Tapley, sitting down upon a stool: 'very spotted; very like a partickler style of old gentleman about the throat; very bright-eyed, very cool, and very slippy. But one sees 'em to the best advantage out of doors perhaps.'

While pretending, with such talk as this, to be perfectly at his ease, and to be the most indifferent and careless of men, Mark Tapley had an eye on all around him. The wan and meagre aspect of the family, the changed looks of the poor mother, the fevered child she held in her lap, the air of great despondency and little hope on everything, were plain to him, and made a deep impression on his mind. He saw it all as clearly and as quickly as with his bodily eyes he saw the rough shelves supported by pegs driven between the logs, of which the house was made; the flour-cask in the corner, serving also for a table; the blankets, spades, and other articles against the walls; the damp that blotched the ground; or the crop of vegetable rottenness in every crevice of the hut.

'How is it that you have come here?' asked the man, when their first expressions of surprise were over.

'Why, we come by the steamer last night,' replied Mark. 'Our intention is to make our fortuns with punctuality and dispatch; and to retire upon our property as soon as ever it's realised. But how are you all? You're looking noble!'

'We are but sickly now,' said the poor woman, bending over her child. 'But we shall do better when we are seasoned to the place.'

'There are some here,' thought Mark, 'whose seasoning will last for ever.'

But he said cheerfully, 'Do better! To be sure you will. We shall all do better. What we've got to do is, to keep up our spirits, and be neighbourly. We shall come all right in the end, never fear. That reminds me, by-the-bye, that my partner's all wrong just at present; and that I looked in to beg for him. I wish you'd come and give me your opinion of him, master.'

That must have been a very unreasonable request on the part of Mark Tapley, with which, in their gratitude for his kind offices on board the ship, they would not have complied instantly. The man rose to accompany him without a moment's delay. Before they went, Mark took the sick child in his arms, and tried to comfort the mother; but the hand of death was on it then, he saw.

They found Martin in the house, lying wrapped up in his blanket on the ground. He was, to all appearance, very ill indeed, and shook and shivered horribly: not as people do from cold, but in a frightful kind of spasm or convulsion, that racked his whole body. Mark's friend pronounced his disease an aggravated kind of fever, accompanied with ague; which was very common in those parts, and which he predicted would be worse to-morrow, and for many more to-morrows. He had had it himself off and on, he said, for a couple of years or so; but he was thankful that, while so many he had known had died about him, he had escaped with life.

'And with not too much of that,' thought Mark, surveying his emaciated form. 'Eden for ever!'

They had some medicine in their chest; and this man of sad experience showed Mark how and when to administer it, and how he could best alleviate the sufferings of Martin. His attentions did not stop there; for he was backwards and forwards constantly, and rendered Mark good service in all his brisk attempts to make their situation more endurable. Hope or comfort for the future he could not bestow. The season was a sickly one; the settlement a grave. His child died that night; and Mark, keeping the secret from Martin, helped to bury it, beneath a tree, next day.

With all his various duties of attendance upon Martin (who became the more exacting in his claims, the worse he grew), Mark worked out of doors, early and late; and with the assistance of his friend and others, laboured to do something with their land. Not that he had the least strength of heart or hope, or steady purpose in so doing, beyond the habitual cheerfulness of his disposition, and his amazing power of self-sustainment; for within himself, he looked on their condition as beyond all hope, and, in his own words, 'came out strong' in consequence.

'As to coming out as strong as I could wish, sir,' he confided to Martin in a leisure moment; that is to say, one evening, while he was washing the linen of the establishment, after a hard day's work, 'that I give up. It's a piece of good fortune as never is to happen to me, I see!'

'Would you wish for circumstances stronger than these?' Martin retorted with a groan, from underneath his blanket.

'Why, only see how easy they might have been stronger, sir,' said Mark, 'if it wasn't for the envy of that uncommon fortun of mine, which is always after me, and tripping me up. The night we landed here, I thought things did look pretty jolly. I won't deny it. I thought they did look pretty jolly.'

'How do they look now?' groaned Martin.

'Ah!' said Mark, 'Ah, to be sure. That's the question. How do they look now? On the very first morning of my going out, what do I do? Stumble on a family I know, who are constantly assisting of us in all sorts of ways, from that time to this! That won't do, you know: that ain't what I'd a right to expect. If I had stumbled on a serpent, and got bit; or stumbled on a first-rate patriot, and got bowie-knifed; or stumbled on a lot of Sympathisers with inverted shirt-collars, and got made a lion of; I might have distinguished myself, and earned some credit. As it is, the great object of my voyage is knocked on the head. So it would be, wherever I went. How do you feel to-night, sir?'

'Worse than ever,' said poor Martin.

'That's something,' returned Mark, 'but not enough. Nothing but being very bad myself, and jolly to the last, will ever do me justice.'

'In Heaven's name, don't talk of that,' said Martin, with a thrill of terror. 'What should I do, Mark, if you were taken ill!'

Mr. Tapley's spirits appeared to be stimulated by this remark, although it was not a very flattering one. He proceeded with his washing in a brighter mood; and observed 'that his glass was a-rising.'

'There's one good thing in this place, sir,' said Mr. Tapley, scrubbing away at the linen, 'as disposes me to be jolly; and that is, that it's a reg'lar little United States in itself. There's two or three American settlers left; and they coolly comes over one, even here, sir, as if it was the wholesomest and loveliest spot in the world. But they're like the cock that went and hid himself to save his life, and was found out by the noise he made. They can't help crowing. They was born to do it, and do it they must, whatever comes of it.'

Glancing from his work out at the door as he said these words, Mark's eyes encountered a lean person in a blue frock and a straw hat, with a short black pipe in his mouth, and a great hickory stick, studded all over with knots, in his hand;

who smoking and chewing as he came along, and spitting frequently, recorded his progress by a train of decomposed tobacco on the ground.

'Here's one on 'em,' cried Mark, 'Hannibal Chollop.'

'Don't let him in,' said Martin, feebly.

'He won't want any letting in,' replied Mark. 'He'll come in, sir.' Which turned out to be quite true, for he did. His face was almost as hard and knobby as his stick; and so were his hands. His head was like an old black hearth-broom. He sat down on the chest with his hat on; and crossing his legs and looking up at Mark, said without removing his pipe:

'Well, Mr. Co! and how do you git along, sir?'

It may be necessary to observe that Mr. Tapley had gravely introduced himself to all strangers, by that name.

'Pretty well, sir; pretty well,' said Mark.

'If this ain't Mr. Chuzzlewit, ain't it!' exclaimed the visitor. 'How do *you* git along, sir?'

Martin shook his head, and drew the blanket over it involuntarily; for he felt that Hannibal was going to spit; and his eye, as the song says, was upon him.

'You need not regard me, sir,' observed Mr. Chollop, complacently. 'I am fever-proof, and likewise agur.'

'Mine was a more selfish motive,' said Martin, looking out again. 'I was afraid you were going to——'

'I can calc'late my distance, sir,' returned Mr. Chollop, 'to an inch.'

With a proof of which happy faculty he immediately favoured him.

'I re-quire, sir,' said Hannibal, 'two foot clear in a circ'lar di-rection, and can engage my-self toe keep within it. I *have* gone ten foot, in a circ'lar di-rection, but that was for a wager.'

'I hope you won it, sir,' said Mark.

'Well, sir, I realised the stakes,' said Chollop. 'Yes, sir.'

He was silent for a time, during which he was actively engaged in the formation of a magic circle round the chest on which he sat. When it was completed, he began to talk again.

'How do you like our country, sir?' he inquired, looking at Martin.

'Not at all,' was the invalid's reply.

Chollop continued to smoke without the least appearance of emotion, until he felt disposed to speak again. That time at length arriving, he took his pipe from his mouth, and said:

'I am not surprised to hear you say so. It re-quires An elevation, and A preparation of the intellect. The mind of man must be prepared for Freedom, Mr. Co.'

He addressed himself to Mark: because he saw that Martin, who wished him to go, being already half-mad with feverish irritation, which the droning voice of this new horror rendered almost insupportable, had closed his eyes, and turned on his uneasy bed.

'A little bodily preparation wouldn't be amiss, either, would it, sir,' said Mark, 'in the case of a blessed old swamp like this?'

'Do you con-sider this a swamp, sir?' inquired Chollop gravely.

'Why yes, sir,' returned Mark. 'I haven't a doubt about it myself.'

'The sentiment is quite Europian,' said the major, 'and does not surprise me: what would your English millions say to such a swamp in England, sir?'

'They'd said it was an uncommon nasty one, I should think,' said Mark; 'and that they would rather be inoculated for fever in some other way.'

'Europian!' remarked Chollop, with sardonic pity. 'Quite Europian!'

And there he sat. Silent and cool, as if the house were his; smoking away like a factory chimney.

Mr. Chollop was, of course, one of the most remarkable men in the country; but he really was a notorious person besides. He was usually described by his friends, in the South and West, as 'a splendid sample of our na-tive raw material, sir,' and was much esteemed for his devotion to rational Liberty; for the better propagation whereof he usually carried a brace of re-volving-pistols in his coat pocket, with seven barrels a-piece. He also carried, amongst other trinkets, a sword-stick, which he called his 'Tickler;' and a great knife, which (for he was a man of a pleasant turn of humour) he called 'Ripper', in allusion to its usefulness as a means of ventilating the stomach of any adversary in a close contest. He had used these weapons with distinguished effect in several instances, all duly chronicled in the newspapers; and was greatly beloved for the gallant manner in which he had 'jobbed out' the eye of one gentleman, as he was in the act of knocking at his own street-door.

Mr. Chollop was a man of a roving disposition; and, in any

less advanced community, might have been mistaken for a
violent vagabond. But his fine qualities being perfectly understood and appreciated in those regions where his lot was cast,
and where he had many kindred spirits to consort with, he
may be regarded as having been born under a fortunate star,
which is not always the case with a man so much before the
age in which he lives. Preferring, with a view to the gratification of his tickling and ripping fancies, to dwell upon the outskirts of society, and in the more remote towns and cities, he
was in the habit of emigrating from place to place, and
establishing in each some business—usually a newspaper—
which he presently sold: for the most part closing the bargain
by challenging, stabbing, pistolling, or gouging the new editor, before he had quite taken possession of the property.

He had come to Eden on a speculation of this kind, but had
abandoned it, and was about to leave. He always introduced
himself to strangers as a worshipper of Freedom; was the
consistent advocate of Lynch law, and slavery; and invariably
recommended, both in print and speech, the 'tarring and
feathering' of any unpopular person who differed from himself.
He called this 'planting the standard of civilisation in the
wilder gardens of My country.'

There is little doubt that Chollop would have planted this
standard in Eden at Mark's expense, in return for his plainness
of speech (for the genuine Freedom is dumb, save when she
vaunts herself), but for the utter desolation and decay prevailing in the settlement, and his own approaching departure
from it. As it was, he contented himself with showing Mark
one of the revolving-pistols, and asking him what he thought
of that weapon.

'It ain't long since I shot a man down with that, sir, in the
State of Illinoy,' observed Chollop.

'Did you, indeed!' said Mark, without the smallest agitation. 'Very free of you. And very independent!'

'I shot him down, sir,' pursued Chollop, 'for asserting in
the Spartan Portico, a tri-weekly journal, that the ancient
Athenians went a-head of the present Locofoco Ticket.'

'And what's that?' asked Mark.

'Europian not to know,' said Chollop, smoking placidly.
'Europian quite!'

After a short devotion to the interests of the magic circle, he
resumed the conversation by observing:

'You won't half feel yourself at home in Eden, now?'

'No,' said Mark, 'I don't.'

'You miss the imposts of your country. You miss the house dues?' observed Chollop.

'And the houses—rather,' said Mark.

'No window dues here, sir,' observed Chollop.

'And no windows to put 'em on,' said Mark.

'No stakes, no dungeons, no blocks, no racks, no scaffolds, no thumbscrews, no pikes, no pillories,' said Chollop.

'Nothing but rewolwers and bowie-knives,' returned Mark. 'And what are they? Not worth mentioning!'

The man who had met them on the night of their arrival came crawling up at this juncture, and looked in at the door.

'Well, sir,' said Chollop. 'How do *you* git along?'

He had considerable difficulty in getting along at all, and said as much in reply.

'Mr. Co. And me, sir,' observed Chollop, 'are disputating a piece. He ought to be slicked up pretty smart to dispute between the Old World and the New, I do expect?'

'Well!' returned the miserable shadow. 'So he had.'

'I was merely observing, sir,' said Mark, addressing this new visitor, 'that I looked upon the city in which we have the honour to live, as being swampy. What's your sentiments?'

'I opinionate it's moist perhaps, at certain times,' returned the man.

'But not as moist as England, sir?' cried Chollop, with a fierce expression in his face.

'Oh! Not as moist as England; let alone its Institutions,' said the man.

'I should hope there ain't a swamp in all Americay, as don't whip *that* small island into mush and molasses,' observed Chollop, decisively. 'You bought slick, straight, and right away, of Scadder, sir?' to Mark.

He answered in the affirmative. Mr. Chollop winked at the other citizen.

'Scadder is a smart man, sir? He is a rising man? He is a man as will come up'ards, right side up, sir?' Mr. Chollop winked again at the other citizen.

'He should have his right side very high up, if I had my way,' said Mark. 'As high up as the top of a good tall gallows, perhaps.'

Mr. Chollop was so delighted at the smartness of his excellent countryman having been too much for the Britisher, and at the Britisher's resenting it, that he could contain himself no longer, and broke forth in a shout of delight. But the strangest exposition of this ruling passion was in the other: the pestilence-stricken, broken, miserable shadow of a man: who derived so much entertainment from the circumstance that he seemed to forget his own ruin in thinking of it, and laughed outright when he said 'that Scadder was a smart man, and had draw'd a lot of British capital that way, as sure as sun-up.'

After a full enjoyment of this joke, Mr. Hannibal Chollop sat smoking and improving the circle, without making any attempts either to converse or to take leave; apparently labouring under the not uncommon delusion that for a free and enlightened citizen of the United States to convert another man's house into a spittoon for two or three hours together, was a delicate attention, full of interest and politeness, of which nobody could ever tire. At last he rose.

'I am a-going easy,' he observed.

Mark entreated him to take particular care of himself.

'Afore I go,' he said sternly, 'I have got a leetle word to say to you. You are darnnation 'cute, you are.'

Mark thanked him for the compliment.

'But you are much too 'cute to last. I can't con-ceive of any spotted Painter in the bush, as ever was so riddled through and through as you will be, I bet.'

'What for?' asked Mark.

'We must be cracked-up, sir,' retorted Chollop, in a tone of menace. 'You are not now in A despotic land. We are a model to the airth, and must be jist cracked-up, I tell you.'

'What! I speak too free, do I?' cried Mark.

'I have draw'd upon A man, and fired upon A man for less,' said Chollop, frowning. 'I have know'd strong men obleeged to make themselves uncommon skase for less. I have know'd men Lynched for less, and beaten into punkin'-sarse for less, by an enlightened people. We are the intellect and virtue of the airth, the cream Of human natur', and the flower Of moral force. Our backs is easy ris. We must be cracked-up, or they rises, and we snarls. We shows our teeth, I tell you, fierce. You'd better crack us up, you had!'

After the delivery of this caution, Mr. Chollop departed; with Ripper, Tickler, and the revolvers, all ready for action on the shortest notice.

'Come out from under the blanket, sir,' said Mark, 'he's gone. What's this!' he added softly: kneeling down to look into his partner's face, and taking his hot hand. 'What's come of all that chattering and swaggering? He's wandering in his mind to-night, and don't know me!'

Martin indeed was dangerously ill; very near his death. He lay in that state many days, during which time Mark's poor friends, regardless of themselves, attended him. Mark, fatigued in mind and body; working all the day and sitting up at night; worn with hard living and the unaccustomed toil of his new life; surrounded by dismal and discouraging circumstances of every kind; never complained or yielded in the least degree. If ever he had thought Martin selfish or inconsiderate, or had deemed him energetic only by fits and starts, and then too passive for their desperate fortunes, he now forgot it all. He remembered nothing but the better qualities of his fellow-wanderer, and was devoted to him, heart and hand.

Many weeks elapsed before Martin was strong enough to move about with the help of a stick and Mark's arm; and even then his recovery, for want of wholesome air and proper nourishment, was very slow. He was yet in a feeble and weak condition, when the misfortune he had so much dreaded fell upon them. Mark was taken ill.

Mark fought against it; but the malady fought harder, and his efforts were in vain.

'Floored for the present, sir,' he said one morning, sinking back upon his bed: 'but jolly!'

Floored indeed, and by a heavy blow! As any one but Martin might have known beforehand.

If Mark's friends had been kind to Martin (and they had been very), they were twenty times kinder to Mark. And now it was Martin's turn to work, and sit beside the bed and watch, and listen through the long, long nights, to every sound in the gloomy wilderness; and hear poor Mr. Tapley, in his wandering fancy, playing at skittles in the Dragon, making love-remonstrances to Mrs. Lupin, getting his sea-legs on board the Screw, travelling with old Tom Pinch on English roads, and burning stumps of trees in Eden, all at once.

But whenever Martin gave him drink or medicine, or tended him in any way, or came into the house returning from some drudgery without, the patient Mr. Tapley brightened up and cried: 'I'm jolly, sir: I'm jolly!'

Now, when Martin began to think of this, and to look at Mark as he lay there; never reproaching him by so much as an expression of regret; never murmuring; always striving to be manful and staunch; he began to think, how was it that this man who had had so few advantages, was so much better than he who had had so many? And attendance upon a sick bed, but especially the sick bed of one whom we have been accustomed to see in full activity and vigour, being a great breeder of reflection, he began to ask himself in what they differed.

He was assisted in coming to a conclusion on this head by the frequent presence of Mark's friend, their fellow-passenger across the ocean: which suggested to him that in regard to having aided her, for example, they had differed very much. Somehow he coupled Tom Pinch with this train of reflection; and thinking that Tom would be very likely to have struck up the same sort of acquaintance under similar circumstances, began to think in what respects two people so extremely different were like each other, and were unlike him. At first sight there was nothing very distressing in these meditations, but they did undoubtedly distress him for all that.

Martin's nature was a frank and generous one; but he had been bred up in his grandfather's house; and it will usually be found that the meaner domestic vices propagate themselves to be their own antagonists. Selfishness does this especially; so do suspicion, cunning, stealth, and covetous propensities. Martin had unconsciously reasoned as a child, 'My guardian takes so much thought of himself, that unless I do the like by *myself*, I shall be forgotten.' So he had grown selfish.

But he had never known it. If any one had taxed him with the vice, he would have indignantly repelled the accusation, and conceived himself unworthily aspersed. He never would have known it, but that being newly risen from a bed of dangerous sickness, to watch by such another couch, he felt how nearly Self had dropped into the grave, and what a poor dependent, miserable thing it was.

It was natural for him to reflect—he had months to do it in —upon his own escape, and Mark's extremity. This led him to consider which of them could be the better spared, and why? Then the curtain slowly rose a very little way; and Self, Self, Self, was shown below.

He asked himself, besides, when dreading Mark's decease

(as all men do and must, at such a time), whether he had done his duty by him, and had deserved and made a good response to his fidelity and zeal. No. Short as their companionship had been, he felt in many, many instances, that there was blame against himself; and still inquiring why, the curtain slowly rose a little more, and Self, Self, Self, dilated on the scene.

It was long before he fixed the knowledge of himself so firmly in his mind that he could thoroughly discern the truth; but in the hideous solitude of that most hideous place, with Hope so far removed, Ambition quenched, and Death beside him rattling at the very door, reflection came, as in a plague-beleaguered town; and so he felt and knew the failing of his life, and saw distinctly what an ugly spot it was.

Eden was a hard school to learn so hard a lesson in; but there were teachers in the swamp and thicket, and the pestilential air, who had a searching method of their own.

He made a solemn resolution that when his strength returned he would not dispute the point or resist the conviction, but would look upon it as an established fact, that selfishness was in his breast, and must be rooted out. He was so doubtful (and with justice) of his own character, that he determined not to say one word of vain regret or good resolve to Mark, but steadily to keep his purpose before his own eyes solely: and there was not a jot of pride in this; nothing but humility and steadfastness: the best armour he could wear. So low had Eden brought him down. So high had Eden raised him up.

After a long and lingering illness (in certain forlorn stages of which, when too far gone to speak, he had feebly written 'jolly!' on a slate), Mark showed some symptoms of returning health. They came and went, and flickered for a time; but he began to mend at last decidedly; and after that continued to improve from day to day.

As soon as he was well enough to talk without fatigue, Martin consulted him upon a project he had in his mind, and which a few months back he would have carried into execution without troubling anybody's head but his own.

'Ours is a desperate case,' said Martin. 'Plainly. The place is deserted; its failure must have become known; and selling what we have bought to any one, for anything, is hopeless, even if it were honest. We left home on a mad enterprise, and have failed. The only hope left us: the only one end for which we have now to try, is to quit this settlement for ever, and get back to England. Anyhow! by any means! Only to get back there, Mark.'

'That's all, sir,' returned Mr. Tapley, with a significant stress upon the words: 'only that!'

'Now, upon this side of the water,' said Martin, 'we have but one friend who can help us, and that is Mr. Bevan.'

'I thought of him when you was ill,' said Mark.

'But for the time that would be lost, I would even write to my grandfather,' Martin went on to say, 'and implore him for money to free us from this trap into which we were so cruelly decoyed. Shall I try Mr. Bevan first?'

'He's a very pleasant sort of a gentleman,' said Mark. 'I think so.'

'The few goods we brought here, and in which we spent our money, would produce something if sold,' resumed Martin; 'and whatever they realise shall be paid him instantly. But they can't be sold here.'

'There's nobody but corpses to buy 'em,' said Mr. Tapley, shaking his head with a rueful air, 'and pigs.'

'Shall I tell him so, and only ask him for money enough to enable us by the cheapest means to reach New York, or any port from which we may hope to get a passage home, by serving in any capacity? Explaining to him at the same time how I am connected, and that I will endeavour to repay him, even through my grandfather, immediately on our arrival in England?'

'Why to be sure,' said Mark: 'he can only say no, and he may say yes. If you don't mind trying him, sir—'

'Mind!' exclaimed Martin. 'I am to blame for coming here, and I would do anything to get away. I grieve to think of the past. If I had taken your opinion sooner, Mark, we never should have been here, I am certain.'

Mr. Tapley was very much surprised at this admission, but protested, with great vehemence, that they would have been there all the same; and that he had set his heart upon coming to Eden, from the first word he had ever heard of it.

Martin then read him a letter to Mr. Bevan, which he had already prepared. It was frankly and ingenuously written, and described their situation without the least concealment; plainly stated the miseries they had undergone; and preferred their request in modest but straightforward terms. Mark highly commended it; and they determined to dispatch it by the next steamboat going the right way, that might call to take in wood at Eden,—where there was plenty of wood to spare. Not knowing how to address Mr. Bevan at his own place of abode, Martin superscribed it to the care of the memorable Mr. Norris of New York, and wrote upon the cover an entreaty that it might be forwarded without delay.

More than a week elapsed before a boat appeared; but at length they were awakened very early one morning by the high-pressure snorting of the 'Esau Slodge;' named after one of the most remarkable men in the country, who had been very eminent somewhere. Hurrying down to the landing-place, they got it safe on board; and waiting anxiously to see the boat depart, stopped up the gangway: an instance of neglect which caused the 'Capting' of the Esau Slodge to 'wish he might be sifted fine as flour, and whittled small as chips; that if they didn't come off that there fixing right smart too, he'd spill 'em in the drink:' whereby the Capting metaphorically said he'd throw them in the river.

They were not likely to receive an answer for eight or ten weeks at the earliest. In the meantime they devoted such strength as they had to the attempted improvement of their land; to clearing some of it, and preparing it for useful purposes. Monstrously defective as their farming was, still it was better than their neighbours'; for Mark had some practical knowledge of such matters, and Martin learned of him; whereas the other settlers who remained upon the putrid swamp (a mere handful, and those withered by disease), appeared to have wandered there with the idea that husbandry was the natural gift of all mankind. They helped each other after their own manner in these struggles, and in all others; but they worked as hopelessly and sadly as a gang of convicts in a penal settlement.

Often at night when Mark and Martin were alone, and lying down to sleep, they spoke of home, familiar places, houses, roads, and people whom they knew; sometimes in the lively hope of seeing them again, and sometimes with a sorrowful tranquillity, as if that hope were dead. It was a source of great amazement to Mark Tapley to find, pervading all these conversations, a singular alteration in Martin.

'I don't know what to make of him,' he thought one night, 'he ain't what I supposed. He don't think of himself half as much. I'll try him again. Asleep, sir?'

'No, Mark.'

'Thinking of home, sir?'

'Yes, Mark.'

'So was I, sir. I was wondering how Mr. Pinch and Mr. Pecksniff gets on now.'

'Poor Tom!' said Martin, thoughtfully.

'Weak-minded man, sir,' observed Mr. Tapley. 'Plays the organ for nothing, sir. Takes no care of himself?'

'I wish he took a little more, indeed,' said Martin. 'Though I don't know why I should. We shouldn't like him half as well, perhaps.'

'He gets put upon, sir,' hinted Mark.

'Yes,' said Martin, after a short silence. '*I* know that, Mark.'

He spoke so regretfully that his partner abandoned the theme, and was silent for a short time, until he had thought of another.

'Ah, sir!' said Mark, with a sigh. 'Dear. me! You've ventured a good deal for a young lady's love!'

'I tell you what. I'm not so sure of that, Mark,' was the reply; so hastily and energetically spoken, that Martin sat up in his bed to give it. 'I begin to be far from clear upon it. You may depend upon it she is very unhappy. She has sacrificed her peace of mind; she has endangered her interests very much; she can't run away from those who are jealous of her, and opposed to her, as I have done. She has to endure, Mark: to endure without the possibility of action, poor girl! I begin to think that she has more to bear than ever I have had. Upon my soul I do!'

Mr. Tapley opened his eyes wide in the dark; but did not interrupt.

'And I'll tell you a secret, Mark,' said Martin, 'since we *are* upon this subject. That ring—'

'Which ring, sir?' Mark inquired, opening his eyes still wider.

'That ring she gave me when we parted, Mark. She bought it; bought it; knowing I was poor and proud (Heaven help me! Proud!) and wanted money.'

'Who says so, sir?' asked Mark.

'I say so. I know it. I thought of it, my good fellow, hundreds of times, while you were lying ill. And like a beast, I took it from her hand, and wore it on my own, and never dreamed of this even at the moment when I parted with it, when some faint glimmering of the truth might surely have possessed me! But it's late,' said Martin, checking himself, 'and you are weak and tired, I know. You only talk to cheer me up. Good night! God bless you, Mark!'

'God bless you, sir! But I'm reg'larly defrauded,' thought Mr. Tapley, turning round with a happy face. 'It's a swindle. I never entered for this sort of service. There'll be no credit in being jolly with *him!*'

The time wore on, and other steamboats coming from the point on which their hopes were fixed, arrived to take in wood; but still no answer to the letter. Rain, heat, foul slime, and noxious vapour, with all the ills and filthy things they bred, prevailed. The earth, the air, the vegetation, and the water that they drank, all teemed with deadly properties. Their fellow-passenger had lost two children long before; and buried now her last. Such things are much too common to be widely known or cared for. Smart citizens grow rich, and friendless victims smart and die, and are forgotten. That is all.

At last a boat came panting up the ugly river, and stopped at Eden. Mark was waiting at the wood hut when it came, and had a letter handed to him from on board. He bore it off to Martin. They looked at one another, trembling.

'It feels heavy,' faltered Martin. And opening it a little roll of dollar-notes fell out upon the ground.

What either of them said, or did, or felt, at first, neither of them knew. All Mark could ever tell was, that he was at the river's bank again out of breath, before the boat had gone, inquiring when it would retrace its track, and put in there.

The answer was, in ten or twelve days: notwithstanding which they began to get their goods together and to tie them up that very night. When this stage of excitement was passed, each of them believed (they found this out, in talking of it afterwards) that he would surely die before the boat returned.

They lived, however, and it came, after the lapse of three long crawling weeks. At sunrise, on an autumn day, they stood upon her deck.

'Courage! We shall meet again!' cried Martin, waving his hand to two thin figures on the bank. 'In the Old World!'

'Or in the next one,' added Mark below his breath. 'To see them standing side by side, so quiet, is a'most the worst of all!'

They looked at one another as the vessel moved away, and then looked backward at the spot from which it hurried fast.

The log-house, with the open door, and drooping trees about it; the stagnant morning mist, and red sun, dimly seen beyond; the vapour rising up from land and river; the quick stream making the loathsome banks it washed more flat and dull: how often they returned in dreams! How often it was happiness to wake and find them Shadows that had vanished!

CHAPTER XXXIV

In which the travellers move homeward, and encounter some distinguished characters upon the way

AMONG the passengers on board the steamboat, there was a faint gentleman sitting on a low camp-stool, with his legs on a high barrel of flour, as if he were looking at the prospect with his ankles; who attracted their attention speedily.

He had straight black hair, parted up the middle of his head and hanging down upon his coat; a little fringe of hair upon his chin; wore no neckcloth; a white hat; a suit of black, long in the sleeves and short in the legs; soiled brown stockings and laced shoes. His complexion, naturally muddy, was rendered muddier by too strict an economy of soap and water; and the same observation will apply to the washable part of his attire, which he might have changed with comfort to himself and gratification to his friends. He was about five and thirty; was crushed and jammed up in a heap, under the shade of a large green cotton umbrella; and ruminated over his tobacco-plug like a cow.

He was not singular, to be sure, in these respects; for every gentleman on board appeared to have had a difference with his laundress, and to have left off washing himself in early youth. Every gentleman, too, was perfectly stopped up with tight plugging, and was dislocated in the greater part of his joints. But about this gentleman there was a peculiar air of sagacity and wisdom, which convinced Martin that he was no common character; and this turned out to be the case.

'How do you do, sir?' said a voice in Martin's ear.

'How do you do, sir?' said Martin.

It was a tall thin gentleman who spoke to him, with a carpet-cap on, and a long loose coat of green baize, ornamented about the pockets with black velvet.

'You air from Europe, sir?'

'I am,' said Martin.

'You air fortunate, sir.'

Martin thought so too; but he soon discovered that the gentleman and he attached different meanings to this remark.

'You air fortunate, sir, in having an opportunity of behold-ing our Elijah Pogram, sir.'

'Your Elijahpogram!' said Martin, thinking it was all one word, and a building of some sort.

'Yes, sir.'

Martin tried to look as if he understood him, but he couldn't make it out.

'Yes, sir,' repeated the gentleman. 'Our Elijah Pogram, sir, is, at this minute, identically settin' by the en-gine biler.'

The gentleman under the umbrella put his right forefinger to his eyebrow, as if he were revolving schemes of state.

'That is Elijah Pogram, is it?' said Martin.

'Yes, sir,' replied the other. 'That is Elijah Pogram.'

'Dear me!' said Martin. 'I am astonished.' But he had not the least idea who this Elijah Pogram was; having never heard the name in all his life.

'If the biler of this vessel was Toe bust, sir,' said his new acquaintance, 'and Toe bust now, this would be a festival day in the calendar of despotism; pretty nigh equallin', sir, in its effects upon the human race, our Fourth of glorious July. Yes, sir, that is the Honourable Elijah Pogram, Member of Con-gress; one of the master-minds of our country, sir. There is a brow, sir, there!'

'Quite remarkable,' said Martin.

'Yes, sir. Our own immortal Chiggle, sir, is said to have observed, when he made the celebrated Pogram statter in marble, which rose so much con-test and preju-dice in Europe, that the brow was more than mortal. This was before the Pogram Defiance, and was, therefore, a pre-diction, cruel smart.'

'What is the Pogram Defiance?' asked Martin, thinking, perhaps, it was the sign of a public-house.

'An o-ration, sir,' returned his friend.

'Oh! to be sure,' cried Martin. 'What am I thinking of! It defied—'

'It defied the world, sir,' said the other, gravely. 'Defied the world in general to com-pete with our country upon any hook; and devellop'd our internal resources for making war upon the universal airth. You would like to know Elijah Pogram, sir?'

'If you please,' said Martin.

'Mr. Pogram,' said the stranger—Mr. Pogram having over-heard every word of the dialogue—'this is a gentleman from

Europe, sir: from England, sir. But gen'rous ene-mies may meet upon the neutral sile of private life, I think.'

The languid Mr. Pogram shook hands with Martin, like a clock-work figure that was just running down. But he made amends by chewing like one that was just wound up.

'Mr. Pogram,' said the introducer, 'is a public servant, sir. When Congress is recessed, he makes himself acquainted with those free United States, of which he is the gifted son.'

It occurred to Martin that if the Honourable Elijah Pogram had stayed at home, and sent his shoes upon a tour, they would have answered the same purpose; for they were the only part of him in a situation to see anything.

In course of time, however, Mr. Pogram rose; and having ejected certain plugging consequences which would have impeded his articulation, took up a position where there was something to lean against, and began to talk to Martin: shading himself with the green umbrella all the time.

As he began with the words, 'How do you like—?' Martin took him up and said:

'The country, I presume?'

'Yes, sir,' said Elijah Pogram. A knot of passengers gathered round to hear what followed: and Martin heard his friend say, as he whispered to another friend, and rubbed his hands, 'Pogram will smash him into sky-blue fits, I know!'

'Why,' said Martin, after a moment's hesitation, 'I have learned by experience, that you take an unfair advantage of a stranger, when you ask that question. You don't mean it to be answered, except in one way. Now, I don't choose to answer it in that way, for I cannot honestly answer it in that way. And therefore, I would rather not answer it at all.'

But Mr. Pogram was going to make a great speech in the next session about foreign relations, and was going to write strong articles on the subject; and as he greatly favoured the free and independent custom (a very harmless and agreeable one) of procuring information of any sort in any kind of confidence, and afterwards perverting it publicly in any manner that happened to suit him, he had determined to get at Martin's opinions somehow or other. For if he could have got nothing out of him, he would have had to invent it for him, and that would have been laborious. He made a mental note of his answer, and went in again.

'You are from Eden, sir? How did you like Eden?'

Martin said what he thought of that part of the country, in pretty strong terms.

'It is strange,' said Pogram, looking round upon the group, 'this hatred of our country, and her Institutions! This national antipathy is deeply rooted in the British mind!'

'Good Heaven, sir,' cried Martin. 'Is the Eden Land Corporation, with Mr. Scadder at its head, and all the misery it has worked, at its door, an Institution of America? A part of any form of government that ever was known or heard of?'

'I con-sider the cause of this to be,' said Pogram, looking round again and taking himself up where Martin had interrupted him, 'partly jealousy and pre-judice, and partly the nat'ral unfitness of the British people to appreciate the ex-alted Institutions of our native land. I expect, sir,' turning to Martin again, 'that a gentleman named Chollop happened in upon you during your lo-cation in the town of Eden?'

'Yes,' answered Martin; 'but my friend can answer this better than I can, for I was very ill at the time. Mark! The gentleman is speaking of Mr. Chollop.'

'Oh. Yes, sir. Yes. *I* see him,' observed Mark.

'A splendid example of our na-tive raw material, sir?' said Pogram, interrogatively.

'Indeed, sir!' cried Mark.

The Honourable Elijah Pogram glanced at his friends as though he would have said, 'Observe this! See what follows!' and they rendered tribute to the Pogram genius by a gentle murmur.

'Our fellow-countryman is a model of a man, quite fresh from Natur's mould!' said Pogram, with enthusiasm. 'He is true-born child of this free hemisphere! Verdant as the mountains of our country; bright and flowing as our mineral Licks; unspiled by withering conventionalities as air our broad and boundless Perearers! Rough he may be. So air our Barrs. Wild he may be. So air our Buffalers. But he is a child of Natur', and a child of Freedom; and his boastful answer to the Despot and the Tyrant is, that his bright home is in the Settin Sun.'

Part of this referred to Chollop, and part to a Western postmaster, who, being a public defaulter not very long before (a character not at all uncommon in America), had been removed from office; and on whose behalf Mr. Pogram (he voted for Pogram) had thundered the last sentence from his seat in Congress, at the head of an unpopular President. It told brilliantly; for the bystanders were delighted, and one of them said to Martin, 'that he guessed he had now seen something of the eloquential aspect of our country, and was chawed up pritty small.'

Mr. Pogram waited until his hearers were calm again, before he said to Mark:

'You do not seem to coincide, sir?'

'Why,' said Mark, 'I didn't like him much; and that's the truth, sir. I thought he was a bully; and I didn't admire his carryin' them murderous little persuaders, and being so ready to use 'em.'

'It's singler!' said Pogram, lifting his umbrella high enough to look all round from under it. 'It's strange! You observe the settled opposition to our Institutions which pervades the British mind!'

'What an extraordinary people you are!' cried Martin. 'Are Mr. Chollop and the class he represents, an Institution here? Are pistols with revolving barrels, sword-sticks, bowie-knives, and such things, Institutions on which you pride yourselves? Are bloody duels, brutal combats, savage assaults, shooting down and stabbing in the streets, your Institutions! Why, I shall hear next that Dishonour and Fraud are among the Institutions of the great republic!'

The moment the words passed his lips, the Honourable Elijah Pogram looked round again.

'This morbid hatred of our Institutions,' he observed, 'is quite a study for the psychological observer. He's alludin' to Repudiation now!'

'Oh! You may make anything an Institution if you like,' said Martin, laughing, 'and I confess you had me there, for you certainly have made that one. But the greater part of these things are one Institution with us, and we call it by the generic name of Old Bailey!'

The bell being rung for dinner at this moment, everybody ran away into the cabin, whither the Honourable Elijah Pogram fled with such precipitation that he forgot his umbrella was up, and fixed it so tightly in the cabin door that it could neither be let down nor got out. For a minute or so this accident created a perfect rebellion among the hungry passengers behind, who, seeing the dishes, and hearing the knives and forks at work, well knew what would happen unless they got there instantly, and were nearly mad: while several virtuous citizens at the table were in deadly peril of choking themselves in their unnatural efforts to get rid of all the meat before these others came.

They carried the umbrella by storm, however, and rushed in at the breach. The Honourable Elijah Pogram and Martin found themselves, after a severe struggle, side by side, as they might have come together in the pit of a London theatre; and for four whole minutes afterwards, Pogram was snapping up great blocks of everything he could get hold of, like a raven. When he had taken this unusually protracted dinner, he began to talk to Martin; and begged him not to have the least delicacy in speaking with perfect freedom to him, for he was a calm philosopher. Which Martin was extremely glad to hear; for he had begun to speculate on Elijah being a disciple of that other school of republican philosophy, whose noble sentiments are carved with knives upon a pupil's body, and written, not with pen and ink, but tar and feathers.

'What do you think of my countrymen who are present, sir?' inquired Elijah Pogram.

'Oh! very pleasant,' said Martin.

They were a very pleasant party. No man had spoken a word; every one had been intent, as usual, on his own private gorging; and the greater part of the company were decidedly dirty feeders.

The Honourable Elijah Pogram looked at Martin as if he thought 'You don't mean that, I know!' and he was soon confirmed in this opinion.

Sitting opposite to them was a gentleman in a high state of tobacco, who wore quite a little beard, composed of the overflowings of that weed, as they had dried about his mouth and chin: so common an ornament that it would scarcely have attracted Martin's observation, but that this good citizen, burning to assert his equality against all comers, sucked his knife for some moments, and made a cut with it at the butter, just as Martin was in the act of taking some. There was a juiciness about the deed that might have sickened a scavenger.

When Elijah Pogram (to whom this was an every-day incident) saw that Martin put the plate away, and took no butter, he was quite delighted, and said,

'Well! The morbid hatred of you British to the Institutions of our country is as-TONishing!'

'Upon my life!' cried Martin, in his turn. 'This is the most wonderful community that ever existed. A man deliberately makes a hog of himself, and *that's* an Institution!'

'We have no time to ac-quire forms, sir,' said Elijah Pogram.

'Acquire!' cried Martin. 'But it's not a question of acquiring anything. It's a question of losing the natural politeness of a savage, and that instinctive good breeding which admonishes one man not to offend and disgust another. Don't you think that man over the way, for instance, naturally knows better, but considers it a very fine and independent thing to be a brute in small matters?'

'He is a na-tive of our country, and is nat'rally bright and spry, of course,' said Mr. Pogram.

'Now, observe what this comes to, Mr. Pogram,' pursued Martin. 'The mass of your countrymen begin by stubbornly neglecting little social observances, which have nothing to do with gentility, custom, usage, government, or country, but are acts of common, decent, natural, human politeness. You abet them in this, by resenting all attacks upon their social offences as if they were a beautiful national feature. From disregarding small obligations they come in regular course to disregard great ones; and so refuse to pay their debts. What they may do, or what they may refuse to do next, I don't know; but any man may see if he will, that it will be something following in natural succession, and a part of one great growth, which is rotten at the root.'

The mind of Mr. Pogram was too philosophical to see this; so they went on deck again, where, resuming his former post, he chewed until he was in a lethargic state, amounting to insensibility.

After a weary voyage of several days, they came again to that same wharf where Mark had been so nearly left behind, on the night of starting for Eden. Captain Kedgick, the landlord, was standing there, and was greatly surprised to see them coming from the boat.

'Why, what the 'tarnal!' cried the Captain. 'Well! I do admire at this, I do!'

'We can stay at your house until to-morrow, Captain, I suppose?' said Martin.

'I reckon you can stay there for a twelvemonth if you like,' retorted Kedgick coolly. 'But our people won't best like your coming back.'

'Won't like it, Captain Kedgick!' said Martin.

'They did ex-pect you was a-going to settle,' Kedgick answered, as he shook his head. 'They've been took in, you can't deny!'

'What do you mean?' cried Martin.

'You didn't ought to have received 'em,' said the Captain. 'No, you didn't!'

'My good friend,' returned Martin, 'did I want to receive them? Was it any act of mine? Didn't you tell me they would rile up, and that I should be flayed like a wild cat—and threaten all kinds of vengeance, if I didn't receive them?'

'I don't know about that,' returned the Captain. 'But when our people's frills is out, they're starched up pretty stiff, I tell you!'

With that, he fell into the rear to walk with Mark, while Martin and Elijah Pogram went on to the National.

'We've come back alive, you see!' said Mark.

'It ain't the thing I did expect,' the Captain grumbled. 'A man ain't got no right to be a public man, unless he meets the public views. Our fashionable people wouldn't have attended his le-vee, if they had know'd it.'

Nothing mollified the Captain, who persisted in taking it very ill that they had not both died in Eden. The boarders at the National felt strongly on the subject too; but it happened by good fortune that they had not much time to think about this grievance, for it was suddenly determined to pounce upon the Honourable Elijah Pogram, and give *him* a le-vee forthwith.

As the general evening meal of the house was over before the arrival of the boat, Martin, Mark, and Pogram were taking tea and fixings at the public table by themselves, when the deputation entered to announce this honour: consisting of six gentlemen boarders and a very shrill boy.

'Sir!' said the spokesman.

'Mr. Pogram!' cried the shrill boy.

The spokesman thus reminded of the shrill boy's presence, introduced him. 'Doctor Ginery Dunkle, sir. A gentleman of great poetical elements. He has recently jined us here, sir, and is an acquisition to us, sir, I do assure you. Yes, sir. Mr. Jodd, sir. Mr. Izzard, sir. Mr. Julius Bib, sir.'

'Julius Washington Merryweather Bib,' said the gentleman himself *to* himself.

'I beg your pardon, sir. Excuse me. Mr. Julius Washington

Merryweather Bib, sir; a gentleman in the lumber line, sir, and much esteemed. Colonel Groper, sir. Pro-fessor Piper, sir. My own name, sir, is Oscar Buffum.'

Each man took one slide forward as he was named; butted at the Honourable Elijah Pogram with his head; shook hands, and slid back again. The introductions being completed, the spokesman resumed.

'Sir!'

'Mr. Pogram!' cried the shrill boy.

'Perhaps,' said the spokesman, with a hopeless look, 'you will be so good, Dr. Ginery Dunkle, as to charge yourself with the execution of our little office, sir?'

As there was nothing the shrill boy desired more, he immediately stepped forward.

'Mr. Pogram! Sir! A handful Of your fellow-citizens, sir, hearing Of your arrival at the National Hotel, and feeling the patriotic character Of your public services, wish, sir, to have the gratification Of beholding you, and mixing with you, sir; and unbending with you, sir, in those moments which—'

'Air,' suggested Buffum.

'Which air so peculiarly the lot, sir, Of our great and happy country.'

'Hear!' cried Colonel Groper, in a loud voice. 'Good! Hear him! Good!'

'And therefore, sir,' pursued the Doctor, 'they request; as A mark Of their respect; the honour of your company at a little le-Vee, sir, in the ladies' ordinary, at eight o'clock.'

Mr. Pogram bowed, and said:

'Fellow-countrymen!'

'Good!' cried the Colonel. 'Hear him! Good!'

Mr. Pogram bowed to the Colonel individually, and then resumed:

'Your approbation of My labours in the common cause goes to My heart. At all times and in all places; in the ladies' ordinary, My friends, and in the Battle Field—'

'Good, very good! Hear him! Hear him!' said the Colonel.

'The name Of Pogram will be proud to jine you. And may it, My friends, be written on My tomb, "He was a member of the Con-gress of our common country, and was ac-Tive in his trust."'

'The Com-mittee, sir,' said the shrill boy, 'will wait upon you at five minutes afore eight. I take My leave, sir!'

Mr. Pogram shook hands with him, and everybody else, once more; and when they came back again at five minutes before eight, they said, one by one, in a melancholy voice, 'How do you do, sir?' and shook hands with Mr. Pogram all over again, as if he had been abroad for a twelvemonth in the meantime, and they met, now, at a funeral.

But by this time Mr. Pogram had freshened himself up, and had composed his hair and features after the Pogram statue, so that any one with half an eye might cry out, 'There he is! as he delivered the Defiance!' The Committee were embellished also; and when they entered the ladies' ordinary in a body, there was much clapping of hands from ladies and gentlemen, accompanied by cries of 'Pogram! Pogram!' and some standing up on chairs to see him.

The object of the popular caress looked round the room as he walked up it, and smiled: at the same time observing to the shrill boy, that he knew something of the beauty of the daughters of their common country, but had never seen it in such lustre and perfection as at that moment. Which the shrill boy put in the paper next day; to Elijah Pogram's great surprise.

'We will re-quest you, sir, if you please,' said Buffum, laying hands on Mr. Pogram as if he were taking his measure for a coat, 'to stand up with your back agin the wall right in the furthest corner, that there may be more room for our fellow cit-izens. If you could set your back right slap agin that curtain-peg, sir, keeping your left leg everlastingly behind the stove, we should be fixed quite slick.'

Mr. Pogram did as he was told, and wedged himself into such a little corner that the Pogram statue wouldn't have known him.

The entertainments of the evening then began. Gentlemen brought ladies up, and brought themselves up, and brought each other up; and asked Elijah Pogram what he thought of this political question, and what he thought of that; and looked at him, and looked at one another, and seemed very unhappy indeed. The ladies on the chairs looked at Elijah Pogram through their glasses, and said audibly, 'I wish he'd speak. Why don't he speak? Oh, do ask him to speak!' And Elijah Pogram looked sometimes at the ladies and sometimes elsewhere, delivering senatorial opinions, as he was asked for them. But the great end and object of the meeting seemed to be, not to let Elijah Pogram out of the corner on any account: so there they kept him, hard and fast.

A great bustle at the door, in the course of the evening, announced the arrival of some remarkable person; and immediately afterwards an elderly gentleman, much excited, was seen to precipitate himself upon the crowd, and battle his way towards the Honourable Elijah Pogram. Martin, who had found a snug place of observation in a distant corner, where he stood with Mark beside him (for he did not so often forget him now as formerly, though he still did sometimes), thought he knew this gentleman, but had no doubt of it, when he cried as loud as he could, with his eyes starting out of his head:

'Sir, Mrs. Hominy!'

'Lord bless that woman, Mark. She has turned up again!'

'Here she comes, sir,' answered Mr. Tapley. 'Pogram knows her. A public character! Always got her eye upon her country, sir! If that there lady's husband is of my opinion, what a jolly old gentleman he must be!'

A lane was made; and Mrs. Hominy, with the aristocratic stalk, the pocket handkerchief, the clasped hands, and the classical cap, came slowly up it, in a procession of one. Mr. Pogram testified emotions of delight on seeing her, and a general hush prevailed. For it was known that when a woman like Mrs. Hominy encountered a man like Pogram, something interesting must be said.

Their first salutations were exchanged in a voice too low to reach the impatient ears of the throng; but they soon became audible, for Mrs. Hominy felt her position, and knew what was expected of her.

Mrs. H. was hard upon him at first; and put him through a rigid catechism in reference to a certain vote he had given, which she had found it necessary, as the mother of the modern Gracchi, to deprecate in a line by itself, set up expressly for the purpose in German text. But Mr. Pogram evading it by a well-timed allusion to the star-spangled banner, which, it appeared, had the remarkable peculiarity of flouting the breeze whenever it was hoisted where the wind blew, she forgave him. They now enlarged on certain questions of tariff, commerical treaty, boundary, importation and exportation, with great effect. And Mrs. Hominy not only talked, as the saying is, like a book, but actually did talk her own books, word for word.

'My! what is this?' cried Mrs. Hominy, opening a little note which was handed her by her excited gentleman-usher. 'Do tell! oh, well, now! on'y think!'

And then she read aloud, as follows:

'Two literary ladies present their compliments to the mother of the modern Gracchi, and claim her kind introduction, as their talented countrywoman, to the honourable (and distinguished) Elijah Pogram, whom the two L.L.'s have often contemplated in the speaking marble of the soul-subduing Chiggle. On a verbal intimation from the mother of the M.G., that she will comply with the request of the two L.L.'s, they will have the immediate pleasure of joining the galaxy assembled to do honour to the patriotic conduct of a Pogram. It may be another bond of union between the two L.L.'s and the mother of the M.G. to observe, that the two L.L.'s are Transcendental.'

Mrs. Hominy promptly rose, and proceeded to the door, whence she returned, after a minute's interval, with the two L.L.'s, whom she led, through the lane in the crowd, with all that stateliness of deportment which was so remarkably her own, up to the great Elijah Pogram. It was (as the shrill boy cried out in an ecstasy) quite the Last Scene from Coriolanus.

One of the L.L.'s wore a brown wig of uncommon size. Sticking on the forehead of the other, by invisible means, was a massive cameo, in size and shape like the raspberry tart which is ordinarily sold for a penny, representing on its front the Capitol at Washington.

'Miss Toppit and Miss Codger!' said Mrs. Hominy.

'Codger's the lady so often mentioned in the English newspapers, I should think, sir,' whispered Mark. 'The oldest inhabitant as never remembers anything.'

'To be presented to a Pogram,' said Miss Codger, 'by a Hominy, indeed, a thrilling moment is it in its impressiveness on what we call our feelings. But why we call them so, or why impressed they are, or if impressed they are at all, or if at all we are, or if there really is, oh gasping one! a Pogram or a Hominy, or any active principle to which we give those titles, is a topic, Spirit searching, light abandoned, much too vast to enter on, at this unlooked-for crisis.'

'Mind and matter,' said the lady in the wig, 'glide swift into the vortex of immensity. Howls the sublime, and softly sleeps the calm Ideal, in the whispering chambers of Imagination.

To hear it, sweet it is. But then, outlaughs the stern philosopher, and saith to the Grotesque, "What ho! arrest for me that Agency. Go, bring it here!" And so the vision fadeth.'

After this, they both took Mr. Pogram by the hand, and pressed it to their lips, as a patriotic palm. That homage paid, the mother of the modern Gracchi called for chairs, and the three literary ladies went to work in earnest, to bring poor Pogram out, and make him show himself in all his brilliant colours.

How Pogram got out of his depth instantly, and how the three L.L.'s were never in theirs, is a piece of history not worth recording. Suffice it, that being all four out of their depths, and all unable to swim, they splashed up words in all directions, and floundered about famously. On the whole, it was considered to have been the severest mental exercise ever heard in the National Hotel. Tears stood in the shrill boy's eyes several times; and the whole company observed that their heads ached with the effort—as well they might.

When it at last became necessary to release Elijah Pogram from the corner, and the Committee saw him safely back again to the next room, they were fervent in their admiration.

'Which,' said Mr. Buffum, 'must have vent, or it will bust. Toe you, Mr. Pogram, I am grateful. Toe-wards you, sir, I am inspired with lofty veneration, and with deep e-mo-tion. The sentiment Toe which I would propose to give ex-pression, sir, is this: "May you ever be as firm, sir, as your marble statter! May it ever be as great a terror Toe its ene-mies as you."'

There is some reason to suppose that it was rather terrible to its friends; being a statue of the Elevated or Goblin School, in which the Honourable Elijah Pogram was represented as in a very high wind, with his hair all standing on end, and his nostrils blown wide open. But Mr. Pogram thanked his friend and countryman for the aspiration to which he had given utterance, and the Committee, after another solemn shaking of hands, retired to bed, except the Doctor; who immediately repaired to the newspaper-office, and there wrote a short poem suggested by the events of the evening, beginning with fourteen stars, and headed, 'A Fragment. Suggested by witnessing the Honourable Elijah Pogram engaged in a philosophical disputation with three of Columbia's fairest daughters. By Doctor Ginery Dunkle. Of Troy.'

If Pogram was as glad to get to bed as Martin was, he must

have been well rewarded for his labours. They started off again next day (Martin and Mark previously disposing of their goods to the storekeepers of whom they had purchased them, for anything they would bring), and were fellow-travellers to within a short distance of New York. When Pogram was about to leave them he grew thoughtful, and after pondering for some time, took Martin aside.

'We air going to part, sir,' said Pogram.

'Pray don't distress yourself,' said Martin; 'we must bear it.'

'It ain't that, sir,' returned Pogram, 'not at all. But I should wish you to accept a copy of My oration.'

'Thank you,' said Martin, 'you are very good. I shall be most happy.'

'It ain't quite that, sir, neither,' resumed Pogram: 'air you bold enough to introduce a copy into your country?'

'Certainly,' said Martin. 'Why not?'

'Its sentiments air strong, sir,' hinted Pogram, darkly.

'That makes no difference,' said Martin. 'I'll take a dozen if you like.'

'No, sir,' retorted Pogram. 'Not A dozen. That is more than I require. If you are content to run the hazard, sir, here is one for your Lord Chancellor,' producing it, 'and one for Your principal Secretary of State. I should wish them to see it, sir, as expressing what my opinions air. That they may not plead ignorance at a future time. But don't get into danger, sir, on my account!'

'There is not the least danger, I assure you,' said Martin. So he put the pamphlets in his pocket, and they parted.

Mr. Bevan had written in his letter that, at a certain time, which fell out happily just then, he would be at a certain hotel in the city, anxiously expecting to see them. To this place they repaired without a moment's delay. They had the satisfaction of finding him within; and of being received by their good friend, with his own warmth and heartiness.

'I am truly sorry and ashamed,' said Martin, 'to have begged of you. But look at us. See what we are, and judge to what we are reduced!'

'So far from claiming to have done you any service,' returned the other, 'I reproach myself with having been, unwittingly, the original cause of your misfortunes. I no more supposed you would go to Eden on such representations as you received; or, indeed, that you would do anything but be dispossessed, by

Martin is much gratified by an Imposing Ceremony

(p. 554)

the readiest means, of your idea that fortunes were so easily made here; than I thought of going to Eden myself.'

'The fact is, I closed with the thing in a mad and sanguine manner,' said Martin, 'and the less said about it the better for me. Mark, here, hadn't a voice in the matter.'

'Well! But he hadn't a voice in any other matter, had he?' returned Mr. Bevan: laughing with an air that showed his understanding of Mark and Martin too.

'Not a very powerful one, I am afraid,' said Martin with a blush. 'But live and learn, Mr. Bevan! Nearly die and learn: and we learn the quicker.'

'Now,' said their friend, 'about your plans. You mean to return home at once?'

'Oh, I think so,' returned Martin hastily, for he turned pale at the thought of any other suggestion. 'That is your opinion too, I hope?'

'Unquestionably. For I don't know why you ever came here; though it's not such an unusual case, I am sorry to say, that we need go any farther into that. You don't know that the ship in which you came over with our friend General Fladdock, is in port, of course?'

'Indeed!' said Martin.

'Yes. And is advertised to sail to-morrow.'

This was tempting news, but tantalising too: for Martin knew that his getting any employment on board a ship of that class was hopeless. The money in his pocket would not pay one-fourth of the sum he had already borrowed, and if it had been enough for their passage-money, he could hardly have resolved to spend it. He explained this to Mr. Bevan, and stated what their project was.

'Why, that's as wild as Eden every bit,' returned his friend. 'You must take your passage like a Christian; at least, as like a Christian as a fore-cabin passenger can; and owe me a few more dollars than you intend. If Mark will go down to the ship and see what passengers there are, and finds that you can go in her without being actually suffocated, my advice is, go! You and I will look about us in the meantime (we won't call at the Norris's unless you like), and we will all three dine together in the afternoon.'

Martin had nothing to express but gratitude, and so it was arranged. But he went out of the room after Mark, and advised him to take their passage in the Screw, though they lay upon the bare deck; which Mr. Tapley, who needed no entreaty on the subject, readily promised to do.

When he and Martin met again, and were alone, he was in high spirits, and evidently had something to communicate, in which he gloried very much.

'I've done Mr. Bevan, sir,' said Mark.

'Done Mr. Bevan!' repeated Martin.

'The cook of the Screw went and got married yesterday, sir,' said Mr. Tapley.

Martin looked at him for farther explanation.

'And when I got on board, and the word passed that it was me,' said Mark, 'the mate he comes and asks me whether I'd engage to take this said cook's place upon the passage home. "For you're used to it," he says: "you were always a-cooking for everybody on your passage out." And so I was,' said Mark, 'although I never cooked before, I'll take my oath.'

'What did you say?' demanded Martin.

'Say!' cried Mark. 'That I'd take anything I could get. "If that's so," says the mate, "why, bring a glass of rum;" which they brought according. And my wages, sir,' said Mark in high glee, 'pays your passage; and I've put the rolling-pin in your berth to take it (it's the easy one up in the corner); and there we are, Rule Britannia, and Britons strike home!'

'There never was such a good fellow as you are!' cried Martin, seizing him by the hand. 'But what do you mean by "doing" Mr. Bevan, Mark?'

'Why, don't you see?' said Mark. 'We don't tell him, you know. We take his money, but we don't spend it, and we don't keep it. What we do is, write him a little note, explaining this engagement, and roll it up, and leave it at the bar, to be given to him after we are gone. Don't you see?'

Martin's delight in this idea was not inferior to Mark's. It was all done as he proposed. They passed a cheerful evening; slept at the hotel; left the letter as arranged; and went off to the ship betimes next morning, with such light hearts as the weight of their past miseries engendered.

'Good-bye! a hundred thousand times good-bye!' said Martin to their friend. 'How shall I remember all your kindness! How shall I ever thank you!'

'If you ever become a rich man, or a powerful one,' returned his friend, 'you shall try to make your Government more careful of its subjects when they roam abroad to live. Tell it what you know of emigration in your own case, and impress upon it how much suffering may be prevented with a little pains!'

Cheerily, lads, cheerily! Anchor weighed. Ship in full sail. Her sturdy bowsprit pointing true to England. America a cloud upon the sea behind them!

'Why, Cook! what are you thinking of so steadily?' said Martin.

'Why, I was a-thinking, sir,' returned Mark, 'that if I was a painter and was called upon to paint the American Eagle, how should I do it?'

'Paint it as like an Eagle as you could, I suppose.'

'No,' said Mark. 'That wouldn't do for me, sir. I should want to draw it like a Bat, for its short-sightedness; like a Bantam, for its bragging; like a Magpie, for its honesty; like a Peacock, for its vanity; like a Ostrich, for its putting its head in the mud, and thinking nobody sees it—'

'And like a Phœnix, for its power of springing from the ashes of its faults and vices, and soaring up anew into the sky!' said Martin. 'Well, Mark. Let us hope so.'

CHAPTER XXXV

*Arriving in England, Martin witnesses a ceremony, from which
he derives the cheering information that he has not been forgotten
in his absence*

IT was mid-day, and high water in the English port for
which the Screw was bound, when, borne in gallantly upon
the fulness of the tide, she let go her anchor in the river.

Bright as the scene was; fresh, and full of motion; airy, free,
and sparkling; it was nothing to the life and exultation in the
breasts of the two travellers, at sight of the old churches, roofs,
and darkened chimney stacks of Home. The distant roar, that
swelled up hoarsely from the busy streets, was music in their
ears; the lines of people gazing from the wharves, were friends
held dear; the canopy of smoke that overhung the town was
brighter and more beautiful to them than if the richest silks of
Persia had been waving in the air. And though the water going
on its glistening track, turned, ever and again, aside to dance
and sparkle round great ships, and heave them up; and leaped
from off the blades of oars, a shower of diving diamonds; and
wantoned with the idle boats, and swiftly passed, in many a
sportive chase, through obdurate old iron rings, set deep into
the stone-work of the quays; not even it was half so buoyant,
and so restless, as their fluttering hearts, when yearning to set
foot, once more, on native ground.

A year had passed, since those same spires and roofs had
faded from their eyes. It seemed, to them, a dozen years.
Some trifling changes, here and there, they called to mind; and
wondered that they were so few and slight. In health and fortune, prospect and resource, they came back poorer men than
they had gone away. But it was home. And though home is a
name, a word, it is a strong one; stronger than magician ever
spoke, or spirit answered to, in strongest conjuration.

Being set ashore, with very little money in their pockets, and
no definite plan of operation in their heads, they sought out
a cheap tavern, where they regaled upon a smoking steak, and
certain flowing mugs of beer, as only men just landed from the
sea can revel in the generous dainties of the earth. When they
had feasted, as two grateful-tempered giants might have done,

they stirred the fire, drew back the glowing curtain from the window, and making each a sofa for himself, by union of the great unwieldy chairs, gazed blissfully into the street.

Even the street was made a fairy street, by being half hidden in an atmosphere of steak, and strong, stout, stand-up English beer. For on the window-glass hung such a mist, that Mr. Tapley was obliged to rise and wipe it with his handkerchief, before the passengers appeared like common mortals. And even then, a spiral little cloud went curling up from their two glasses of hot grog, which nearly hid them from each other.

It was one of those unaccountable little rooms which are never seen anywhere but in a tavern, and are supposed to have got into taverns by reason of the facilities afforded to the architect for getting drunk while engaged in their construction. It had more corners in it than the brain of an obstinate man; was full of mad closets, into which nothing could be put that was not specially invented and made for that purpose; had mysterious shelvings and bulk-heads, and indications of staircases in the ceiling; and was elaborately provided with a bell that rung in the room itself, about two feet from the handle, and had no connexion whatever with any other part of the establishment. It was a little below the pavement, and abutted close upon it; so that passengers grated against the window-panes with their buttons, and scraped it with their baskets; and fearful boys suddenly coming between a thoughtful guest and the light, derided him, or put out their tongues as if he were a physician; or made white knobs on the ends of their noses by flattening the same against the glass, and vanished awfully, like spectres.

Martin and Mark sat looking at the people as they passed, debating every now and then what their first step should be.

'We want to see Miss Mary, of course,' said Mark.

'Of course,' said Martin. 'But I don't know where she is. Not having had the heart to write in our distress—you yourself thought silence most advisable—and consequently, never having heard from her since we left New York the first time, I don't know where she is, my good fellow.'

'My opinion is, sir,' returned Mark, 'that what we've got to do is to travel straight to the Dragon. There's no need for you to go there, where you're known, unless you like. You may stop ten mile short of it. I'll go on. Mrs. Lupin will tell me all the news. Mr. Pinch will give me every information that we want: and right glad Mr. Pinch will be to do it. My proposal is: To set off walking this afternoon. To stop when we are tired. To get a lift when we can. To walk when we can't. To do it at once, and do it cheap.'

'Unless we do it cheap, we shall have some difficulty in doing it at all,' said Martin, pulling out the bank, and telling it over in his hand.

'The greater reason for losing no time, sir,' replied Mark. 'Whereas, when you've seen the young lady; and know what state of mind the old gentleman's in, and all about it; then you'll know what to do next.'

'No doubt,' said Martin. 'You are quite right.'

They were raising their glasses to their lips, when their hands stopped midway, and their gaze was arrested by a figure which slowly, very slowly, and reflectively, passed the window at that moment.

Mr. Pecksniff. Placid, calm, but proud. Honestly proud. Dressed with peculiar care, smiling with even more than usual blandness, pondering on the beauties of his art with a mild abstraction from all sordid thoughts, and gently travelling across the disc, as if he were a figure in a magic lantern.

As Mr. Pecksniff passed, a person coming in the opposite direction stopped to look after him with great interest and respect, almost with veneration; and the landlord bouncing out of the house, as if he had seen him too, joined this person, and spoke to him, and shook his head gravely, and looked after Mr. Pecksniff likewise.

Martin and Mark sat staring at each other, as if they could not believe it; but there stood the landlord, and the other man still. In spite of the indignation with which this glimpse of Mr. Pecksniff had inspired him, Martin could not help laughing heartily. Neither could Mark.

'We must inquire into this!' said Martin. 'Ask the landlord in, Mark.'

Mr. Tapley retired for that purpose, and immediately returned with their large-headed host in safe convoy.

'Pray, landlord!' said Martin, 'who is that gentleman who passed just now, and whom you were looking after?'

The landlord poked the fire as if, in his desire to make the most of his answer, he had become indifferent even to the price of coals; and putting his hands in his pockets, said, after inflating himself to give still further effect to his reply:

'That, gentlemen, is the great Mr. Pecksniff! The celebrated architect, gentlemen!'

He looked from one to the other while he said it, as if he were ready to assist the first man who might be overcome by the intelligence.

'The great Mr. Pecksniff, the celebrated architect, gentlemen,' said the landlord, 'has come down here, to help to lay the first stone of a new and splendid public building.'

'Is it to be built from his designs?' asked Martin.

'The great Mr. Pecksniff, the celebrated architect, gentlemen,' returned the landlord, who seemed to have an unspeakable delight in the repetition of these words, 'carried off the First Premium, and will erect the building.'

'Who lays the stone?' asked Martin.

'Our member has come down express,' returned the landlord. 'No scrubs would do for no such a purpose. Nothing less would satisfy our Directors than our member in the House of Commons, who is returned upon the Gentlemanly Interest.'

'Which interest is that?' asked Martin.

'What, don't you know!' returned the landlord.

It was quite clear the landlord didn't. They always told him at election time, that it was the Gentlemanly side, and he immediately put on his top-boots, and voted for it.

'When does the ceremony take place?' asked Martin.

'This day,' replied the landlord. Then pulling out his watch, he added, impressively, 'almost this minute.'

Martin hastily inquired whether there was any possibility of getting in to witness it; and finding that there would be no objection to the admittance of any decent person, unless indeed the ground were full, hurried off with Mark, as hard as they could go.

They were fortunate enough to squeeze themselves into a famous corner on the ground, where they could see all that passed, without much dread of being beheld by Mr. Pecksniff in return. They were not a minute too soon, for as they were in the act of congratulating each other, a great noise was heard at some distance, and everybody looked towards the gate. Several ladies prepared their pocket handkerchiefs for waving; and a stray teacher belonging to the charity school being much cheered by mistake, was immensely groaned at when detected.

'Perhaps he has Tom Pinch with him,' Martin whispered Mr. Tapley.

'It would be rather too much of a treat for him, wouldn't it, sir?' whispered Mr. Tapley in return.

There was no time to discuss the probabilities either way, for the charity school, in clean linen, came filing in two and two, so much to the self-approval of all the people present who didn't subscribe to it, that many of them shed tears. A band of music followed, led by a conscientious drummer who never left off. Then came a great many gentlemen with wands in their hands, and bows on their breasts, whose share in the proceedings did not appear to be distinctly laid down, and who trod upon each other, and blocked up the entry for a considerable period. These were followed by the Mayor and Corporation, all clustering round the member for the Gentlemanly Interest; who had the great Mr. Pecksniff, the celebrated architect, on his right hand, and conversed with him familiarly as they came along. Then the ladies waved their handkerchiefs, and the gentlemen their hats, and the charity children shrieked, and the member for the Gentlemanly Interest bowed.

Silence being restored, the member for the Gentlemanly Interest rubbed his hands, and wagged his head, and looked about him pleasantly; and there was nothing this member did, at which some lady or other did not burst into an ecstatic waving of her pocket handkerchief. When he looked up at the stone, they said how graceful! when he peeped into the hole, they said how condescending! when he chatted with the Mayor, they said how easy! when he folded his arms they cried with one accord, how statesman-like!

Mr. Pecksniff was observed too; closely. When he talked to the Mayor, they said, Oh, really, what a courtly man he was! When he laid his hand upon the mason's shoulder, giving him directions, how pleasant his demeanour to the working classes: just the sort of man who made their toil a pleasure to them, poor dear souls!

But now a silver trowel was brought; and when the member for the Gentlemanly Interest, tucking up his coat-sleeve, did a little sleight-of-hand with the mortar, the air was rent, so loud was the applause. The workman-like manner in which he did it was amazing. No one could conceive where such a gentlemanly creature could have picked the knowledge up.

When he had made a kind of dirt-pie under the direction of the mason, they brought a little vase containing coins, the which the member for the Gentlemanly Interest jingled, as if he were going to conjure. Whereat they said how droll, how cheerful, what a flow of spirits! This put into its place, an ancient scholar read the inscription, which was in Latin: not in English: that would never do. It gave great satisfaction; especially every time there was a good long substantive in the third declension, ablative case, with an adjective to match; at which periods the assembly became very tender, and were much affected.

And now the stone was lowered down into its place, amidst the shouting of the concourse. When it was firmly fixed, the member for the Gentlemanly Interest struck upon it thrice with the handle of the trowel, as if inquiring, with a touch of humour, whether anybody was at home. Mr. Pecksniff then unrolled his Plans (prodigious plans they were), and people gathered round to look at and admire them.

Martin, who had been fretting himself—quite unnecessarily, as Mark thought—during the whole of these proceedings, could no longer restrain his impatience; but stepping forward among several others, looked straight over the shoulder of the unconscious Mr. Pecksniff, at the designs and plans he had unrolled. He returned to Mark, boiling with rage.

'Why, what's the matter, sir?' cried Mark.

'Matter! This is *my* building.'

'Your building, sir!' said Mark.

'My grammar-school. I invented it. I did it all. He has only put four windows in, the villain, and spoilt it!'

Mark could hardly believe it at first, but being assured that it was really so, actually held him to prevent his interference foolishly, until his temporary heat was passed. In the meantime, the member addressed the company on the gratifying deed which he had just performed.

He said that since he had sat in Parliament to represent the Gentlemanly Interest of that town; and he might add, the Lady Interest he hoped, besides (pocket handkerchiefs); it had been his pleasant duty to come among them, and to raise his voice on their behalf in Another Place (pocket handkerchiefs and laughter), often. But he had never come among them, and had never raised his voice, with half such pure, such deep, such unalloyed delight, as now. 'The present occasion,' he

said, 'will ever be memorable to me: not only for the reasons
I have assigned, but because it has afforded me an opportunity of becoming personally known to a gentleman—'

Here he pointed the trowel at Mr. Pecksniff, who was
greeted with vociferous cheering, and laid his hand upon his
heart.

'To a gentleman who, I am happy to believe, will reap both
distinction and profit from this field: whose fame had previously penetrated to me—as to whose ears has it not!—but
whose intellectual countenance I never had the distinguished
honour to behold until this day, and whose intellectual conversation I had never before the improving pleasure to enjoy.'

Everybody seemed very glad of this, and applauded more
than ever.

'But I hope my Honourable Friend,' said the Gentlemanly
member—of course he added "if he will allow me to call him
so," and of course Mr. Pecksniff bowed—'will give me many
opportunities of cultivating the knowledge of him; and that I
may have the extraordinary gratification of reflecting in after
time that I laid on this day two first stones, both belonging to
structures which shall last my life!'

Great cheering again. All this time, Martin was cursing
Mr. Pecksniff up hill and down dale.

'My friends!' said Mr. Pecksniff, in reply. 'My duty is to
build, not speak; to act, not talk; to deal with marble, stone, and
brick: not language. I am very much affected. God bless you!'

This address, pumped out apparently from Mr. Pecksniff's
very heart, brought the enthusiasm to its highest pitch. The
pocket handkerchiefs were waved again; the charity children
were admonished to grow up Pecksniffs, every boy among
them; the Corporation, gentlemen with wands, member for
the Gentlemanly Interest, all cheered for Mr. Pecksniff. Three
cheers for Mr. Pecksniff! Three more for Mr. Pecksniff!
Three more for Mr. Pecksniff, gentlemen, if you please! One
more, gentlemen, for Mr. Pecksniff, and let it be a good one
to finish with!

In short, Mr. Pecksniff was supposed to have done a great
work, and was very kindly, courteously, and generously rewarded. When the procession moved away, and Martin and
Mark were left almost alone upon the ground, his merits and
a desire to acknowledge them, formed the common topic. He
was only second to the Gentlemanly member.

'Compare that fellow's situation to-day with ours!' said Martin, bitterly.

'Lord bless you, sir!' cried Mark, 'what's the use? Some architects are clever at making foundations, and some architects are clever at building on 'em when they're made. But it'll all come right in the end, sir; it'll all come right!'

'And in the meantime—' began Martin.

'In the meantime, as you say, sir, we have a deal to do, and far to go. So sharp's the word, and Jolly!'

'You are the best master in the world, Mark,' said Martin, 'and I will not be a bad scholar if I can help it, I am resolved! So come! Best foot foremost, old fellow!'

CHAPTER XXXVI

Tom Pinch departs to seek his fortune. What he finds at starting

OH! what a different town Salisbury was in Tom Pinch's eyes to be sure, when the substantial Pecksniff of his heart melted away into an idle dream! He possessed the same faith in the wonderful shops, the same intensified appreciation of the mystery and wickedness of the place; made the same exalted estimate of its wealth, population, and resources; and yet it was not the old city nor anything like it. He walked into the market while they were getting breakfast ready for him at the Inn: and though it was the same market as of old, crowded by the same buyers and sellers; brisk with the same business; noisy with the same confusion of tongues and cluttering of fowls in coops; fair with the same display of rolls of butter, newly made, set forth in linen cloths of dazzling whiteness; green with the same fresh show of dewy vegetables; dainty with the same array in higglers' baskets of small shaving-glasses, laces, braces, trouser-straps, and hardware; savoury with the same unstinted show of delicate pigs' feet, and pies made precious by the pork that once had walked upon them: still it was strangely changed to Tom. For, in the centre of the market-place, he missed a statue he had set up there, as in all other places of his personal resort; and it looked cold and bare without that ornament.

The change lay no deeper than this, for Tom was far from being sage enough to know that, having been disappointed in one man, it would have been a strictly rational and eminently wise proceeding to have revenged himself upon mankind in general, by mistrusting them one and all. Indeed this piece of justice, though it is upheld by the authority of divers profound poets and honourable men, bears a nearer resemblance to the justice of that good Vizier in the Thousand-and-one Nights, who issues orders for the destruction of all the Porters in Bagdad because one of that unfortunate fraternity is supposed to have misconducted himself, than to any logical, not to say Christian system of conduct, known to the world in later times.

Tom had so long been used to steep the Pecksniff of his fancy in his tea, and spread him out upon his toast, and take him as a relish with his beer, that he made but a poor breakfast on the first morning after his expulsion. Nor did he much improve his appetite for dinner by seriously considering his own affairs, and taking counsel thereon with his friend the organist's assistant.

The organist's assistant gave it as his decided opinion that whatever Tom did, he must go to London; for there was no place like it. Which may be true in the main, though hardly, perhaps, in itself, a sufficient reason for Tom's going there.

But Tom had thought of London before, and had coupled with it thoughts of his sister, and of his old friend John Westlock, whose advice he naturally felt disposed to seek in this important crisis of his fortunes. To London, therefore, he resolved to go; and he went away to the coach-office at once, to secure his place. The coach being already full, he was obliged to postpone his departure until the next night; but even this circumstance had its bright side as well as its dark one, for though it threatened to reduce his poor purse with unexpected country-charges, it afforded him an opportunity of writing to Mrs. Lupin and appointing his box to be brought to the old finger-post at the old time; which would enable him to take that treasure with him to the metropolis, and save the expense of its carriage. 'So,' said Tom, comforting himself, 'it's very nearly as broad as it's long.'

And it cannot be denied that, when he had made up his mind to even this extent, he felt an unaccustomed sense of freedom—a vague and indistinct impression of holiday-making—which was very luxurious. He had his moments of depression and anxiety, and they were, with good reason, pretty numerous; but still, it was wonderfully pleasant to reflect that he was his own master, and could plan and scheme for himself. It was startling, thrilling, vast, difficult to understand; it was a stupendous truth, teeming with responsibility and self-distrust; but, in spite of all his cares, it gave a curious relish to the viands at the Inn, and interposed a dreamy haze between him and his prospects, in which they sometimes showed to magical advantage.

In this unsettled state of mind, Tom went once more to bed in the low four-poster, to the same immovable surprise of the effigies of the former landlord and the fat ox; and in this condition, passed the whole of the succeeding day. When the coach came round at last, with 'London' blazoned in letters of gold upon the boot, it gave Tom such a turn, that he was half disposed to run away. But he didn't do it; for he took his seat upon the box instead, and looking down upon the four greys, felt as if he were another grey himself, or, at all events, a part of the turn-out; and was quite confused by the novelty and splendour of his situation.

And really it might have confused a less modest man than Tom to find himself sitting next that coachman; for of all the swells that ever flourished a whip, professionally, he might have been elected emperor. He didn't handle his gloves like another man, but put them on—even when he was standing on the pavement, quite detached from the coach—as if the four greys were, somehow or other, at the ends of the fingers. It was the same with his hat. He did things with his hat, which nothing but an unlimited knowledge of horses and the wildest freedom of the road, could ever have made him perfect in. Valuable little parcels were brought to him with particular instructions, and he pitched them into this hat, and stuck it on again; as if the laws of gravity did not admit of such an event as its being knocked off or blown off, and nothing like an accident could befall it. The guard, too! Seventy breezy miles a day were written in his very whiskers. His manners were a canter; his conversation a round trot. He was a fast coach upon a down-hill turnpike road; he was all pace. A waggon couldn't have moved slowly, with that guard and his key-bugle on the top of it.

These were all foreshadowings of London, Tom thought, as he sat upon the box, and looked about him. Such a coachman, and such a guard, never could have existed between Salisbury and any other place. The coach was none of your steady-going, yokel coaches, but a swaggering, rakish, dissipated London coach; up all night, and lying by all day, and leading a devil of a life. It cared no more for Salisbury than if it had been a hamlet. It rattled noisily through the best streets, defied the Cathedral, took the worst corners sharpest, went cutting in everywhere, making everything get out of its way; and spun along the open country-road, blowing a lively defiance out of its key-bugle, as its last glad parting legacy.

It was a charming evening. Mild and bright. And even with the weight upon his mind which arose out of the immensity and uncertainty of London, Tom could not resist the captivating sense of rapid motion through the pleasant air. The four greys skimmed along, as if they liked it quite as well as Tom did; the bugle was in as high spirits as the greys; the coachman chimed in sometimes with his voice; the wheels hummed cheerfully in unison; the brass work on the harness was an orchestra of little bells; and thus, as they went clinking, jingling, rattling smoothly on, the whole concern, from the buckles of the leaders' coupling-reins to the handle of the hind boot, was one great instrument of music.

Yoho, past hedges, gates, and trees; past cottages and barns, and people going home from work. Yoho, past donkey-chaises, drawn aside into the ditch, and empty carts with rampant horses, whipped up at a bound upon the little watercourse, and held by struggling carters close to the five-barred gate, until the coach had passed the narrow turning in the road. Yoho, by churches dropped down by themselves in quiet nooks, with rustic burial-grounds about them, where the graves are green, and daisies sleep—for it is evening—on the bosoms of the dead. Yoho, past streams, in which the cattle cool their feet, and where the rushes grow; past paddock-fences, farms, and rick-yards; past last year's stacks, cut, slice by slice, away, and showing, in the waning light, like ruined gables, old and brown. Yoho, down the pebbly dip, and through the merry water-splash, and up at a canter to the level road again. Yoho! Yoho!

Was the box there, when they came up to the old finger-post? The box! Was Mrs. Lupin herself? Had she turned out magnificently as a hostess should, in her own chaise-cart, and was she sitting in a mahogany chair, driving her own horse Dragon (who ought to have been called Dumpling), and look-ing lovely? Did the stage-coach pull up beside her, shaving her very wheel, and even while the guard helped her man up with the trunk, did he send the glad echoes of his bugle careering down the chimneys of the distant Pecksniff, as if the coach expressed its exultation in the rescue of Tom Pinch?

'This is kind indeed!' said Tom, bending down to shake hands with her. 'I didn't mean to give you this trouble.'

'Trouble, Mr. Pinch!' cried the hostess of the Dragon.

'Well! It's a pleasure to you, I know,' said Tom, squeezing her hand heartily. 'Is there any news?'

The hostess shook her head.

'Say you saw me,' said Tom, 'and that I was very bold and cheerful, and not a bit down-hearted; and that I entreated her to be the same, for all is certain to come right at last. Good-bye!'

'You'll write when you get settled, Mr. Pinch?' said Mrs Lupin.

'When I get settled!' cried Tom, with an involuntary opening of his eyes. 'Oh, yes, I'll write when I get settled. Perhaps I had better write before, because I may find that it takes a little time to settle myself: not having too much money, and having only one friend. I shall give your love to the friend, by the way. You were always great with Mr. Westlock, you know. Good-bye!'

'Good-bye!' said Mrs. Lupin, hastily producing a basket with a long bottle sticking out of it. 'Take this. Good-bye!'

'Do you want me to carry it to London for you?' cried Tom. She was already turning the chaise-cart round.

'No, no,' said Mrs. Lupin. 'It's only a little something for refreshment on the road. Sit fast, Jack. Drive on, sir. All right! Good-bye!'

She was a quarter of a mile off, before Tom collected himself; and then he was waving his hand lustily; and so was she.

'And that's the last of the old finger-post,' thought Tom, straining his eyes, 'where I have so often stood to see this very coach go by, and where I have parted with so many companions! I used to compare this coach to some great monster that appeared at certain times to bear my friends away into the world. And now it's bearing me away, to seek my fortune, Heaven knows where and how!'

It made Tom melancholy to picture himself walking up the lane and back to Pecksniff's as of old; and being melancholy, he looked downwards at the basket on his knee, which he had for the moment forgotten.

'She is the kindest and most considerate creature in the world,' thought Tom. 'Now I *know* that she particularly told that man of hers not to look at me, on purpose to prevent my throwing him a shilling! I had it ready for him all the time, and he never once looked towards me; whereas that man naturally, (for I know him very well), would have done nothing but grin and stare. Upon my word, the kindness of people perfectly melts me.'

Here he caught the coachman's eye. The coachman winked. 'Remarkable fine woman for her time of life,' said the coachman.

'I quite agree with you,' returned Tom. 'So she is.'

'Finer than many a young 'un, I mean to say,' observed the coachman. 'Eh?'

'Than many a young one,' Tom assented.

'I don't care for 'em myself when they're too young,' remarked the coachman.

This was a matter of taste, which Tom did not feel himself called upon to discuss.

'You'll seldom find 'em possessing correct opinions about refreshment, for instance, when they're too young, you know,' said the coachman: 'a woman must have arrived at maturity, before her mind's equal to coming provided with a basket like that.'

'Perhaps you would like to know what it contains?' said Tom, smiling.

As the coachman only laughed, and as Tom was curious himself, he unpacked it, and put the articles, one by one, upon the footboard. A cold roast fowl, a packet of ham in slices, a crusty loaf, a piece of cheese, a paper of biscuits, half a dozen apples, a knife, some butter, a screw of salt, and a bottle of old sherry. There was a letter besides, which Tom put in his pocket.

The coachman was so earnest in his approval of Mrs. Lupin's provident habits, and congratulated Tom so warmly on his good fortune, that Tom felt it necessary, for the lady's sake, to explain that the basket was a strictly Platonic basket, and had merely been presented to him in the way of friendship. When he had made the statement with perfect gravity; for he felt it incumbent on him to disabuse the mind of this lax rover of any incorrect impressions on the subject; he signified that he would be happy to share the gifts with him, and proposed that they should attack the basket in a spirit of good fellowship at any time in the course of the night which the coachman's experience and knowledge of the road might suggest, as being best adapted to the purpose. From this time they chatted so pleasantly together, that although Tom knew infinitely more of unicorns than horses, the coachman informed his friend the guard, at the end of the next stage, 'that rum as the box-seat looked, he was as good a one to go, in pint of conversation, as ever he'd wish to sit by.'

Yoho, among the gathering shades; making of no account the deep reflections of the trees, but scampering on through

X

light and darkness, all the same, as if the light of London fifty miles away, were quite enough to travel by, and some to spare. Yoho, beside the village-green, where cricket-players linger yet, and every little indentation made in the fresh grass by bat or wicket, ball or player's foot, sheds out its perfume on the night. Away with four fresh horses from the Bald-faced Stag, where topers congregate about the door admiring; and the last team with traces hanging loose, go roaming off towards the pond, until observed and shouted after by a dozen throats, while volunteering boys pursue them. Now, with a clattering of hoofs and striking out of fiery sparks, across the old stone bridge, and down again into the shadowy road, and through the open gate, and far away, away, into the wold. Yoho!

Yoho, behind there, stop that bugle for a moment! Come creeping over to the front, along the coach-roof, guard, and make one at this basket! Not that we slacken in our pace the while, not we: we rather put the bits of blood upon their metal, for the greater glory of the snack. Ah! It is long since this bottle of old wine was brought into contact with the mellow breath of night, you may depend, and rare good stuff it is to wet a bugler's whistle with. Only try it. Don't be afraid of turning up your finger, Bill, another pull! Now, take your breath, and try the bugle, Bill. There's music! There's a tone! 'Over the hills and far away,' indeed. Yoho! The skittish mare is all alive to-night. Yoho! Yoho!

See the bright moon! High up before we know it: making the earth reflect the objects on its breast like water. Hedges, trees, low cottages, church steeples, blighted stumps and flourishing young slips, have all grown vain upon the sudden, and mean to contemplate their own fair images till morning. The poplars yonder rustle that their quivering leaves may see themselves upon the ground. Not so the oak; trembling does not become *him;* and he watches himself in his stout old burly steadfastness, without the motion of a twig. The moss-grown gate, ill-poised upon its creaking hinges, crippled and decayed, swings to and fro before its glass, like some fantastic dowager; while our own ghostly likeness travels on, Yoho! Yoho! through ditch and brake, upon the ploughed land and the smooth, along the steep hill-side and steeper wall, as if it were a phantom-Hunter.

Clouds too! And a mist upon the Hollow! Not a dull fog that hides it, but a light airy gauze-like mist, which in our eyes of modest admiration gives a new charm to the beauties it is spread before: as real gauze has done ere now, and would again, so please you, though we were the Pope. Yoho! Why now we travel like the Moon herself. Hiding this minute in a grove of trees; next minute in a patch of vapour; emerging now upon our broad clear course; withdrawing now, but always dashing on, our journey is a counterpart of hers. Yoho! A match against the Moon!

The beauty of the night is hardly felt, when Day comes leaping up. Yoho! Two stages, and the country roads are almost changed to a continuous street. Yoho, past market-gardens, rows of houses, villas, crescents, terraces, and squares; past waggons, coaches, carts; past early workmen, late stragglers, drunken men, and sober carriers of loads; past brick and mortar in its every shape; and in among the rattling pavements, where a jaunty-seat upon a coach is not so easy to preserve! Yoho, down countless turnings, and through countless mazy ways, until an old Inn-yard is gained, and Tom Pinch, getting down, quite stunned and giddy, is in London!

'Five minutes before the time, too!' said the driver, as he received his fee of Tom.

'Upon my word,' said Tom, 'I should not have minded very much, if we had been five hours after it; for at this early hour I don't know where to go, or what to do with myself.'

'Don't they expect you then?' inquired the driver.

'Who?' said Tom.

'Why, them,' returned the driver.

His mind was so clearly running on the assumption of Tom's having come to town to see an extensive circle of anxious relations and friends, that it would have been pretty hard work to undeceive him. Tom did not try. He cheerfully evaded the subject, and going into the Inn, fell fast asleep before a fire in one of the public rooms opening from the yard. When he awoke, the people in the house were all astir, so he washed and dressed himself; to his great refreshment after the journey; and, it being by that time eight o'clock, went forth at once to see his old friend John.

John Westlock lived in Furnival's Inn, High Holborn, which was within a quarter of an hour's walk of Tom's starting-point, but seemed a long way off, by reason of his going two or three miles out of the straight road to make a short cut. When at last he arrived outside John's door, two stories up, he stood faltering with his hand upon the knocker, and trembled from head to foot. For he was rendered very nervous by the thought of having to relate what had fallen out between himself and Pecksniff; and he had a misgiving that John would exult fearfully in the disclosure.

'But it must be made,' thought Tom, 'sooner or later; and I had better get it over.'

Rat tat.

'I am afraid that's not a London knock,' thought Tom. 'It didn't sound bold. Perhaps that's the reason why nobody answers the door.'

It is quite certain that nobody came, and that Tom stood looking at the knocker: wondering whereabouts in the neighbourhood a certain gentleman resided, who was roaring out to somebody 'Come in!' with all his might.

'Bless my soul!' thought Tom at last. 'Perhaps he lives here, and is calling to me. I never thought of that. Can I open the door from the outside, I wonder. Yes, to be sure I can.'

To be sure he could, by turning the handle: and to be sure when he did turn it the same voice came rushing out, crying 'Why don't you come in? Come in, do you hear? What are you standing there for?'—quite violently.

Tom stepped from the little passage into the room from which these sounds proceeded, and had barely caught a glimpse of a gentleman in a dressing-gown and slippers (with his boots beside him ready to put on), sitting at his breakfast with a newspaper in his hand, when the said gentleman, at the imminent hazard of oversetting his tea-table, made a plunge at Tom, and hugged him.

'Why, Tom, my boy!' cried the gentleman. 'Tom!'

'How glad I am to see you, Mr. Westlock!' said Tom Pinch, shaking both his hands, and trembling more than ever. 'How kind you are!'

'Mr. Westlock!' repeated John, 'what do you mean by that, Pinch? You have not forgotten my Christian name, I suppose?'

'No, John, no. I have not forgotten it,' said Thomas Pinch. 'Good gracious me, how kind you are!'

'I never saw such a fellow in all my life!' cried John. 'What do you mean by saying *that* over and over again? What did you expect me to be, I wonder! Here, sit down, Tom, and be

a reasonable creature. How are you, my boy? I am delighted
to see you!'

'And I am delighted to see *you*,' said Tom.

'It's mutual, of course,' returned John. 'It always was, I
hope. If I had known you had been coming, Tom, I would
have had something for breakfast. I would rather have such
a surprise than the best breakfast in the world, myself; but
yours is another case, and I have no doubt you are as hungry
as a hunter. You must make out as well as you can, Tom, and
we'll recompense ourselves at dinner-time. You take sugar, I
know: I recollect the sugar at Pecksniff's. Ha, ha, ha! How *is*
Pecksniff? When did you come to town? *Do* begin at something
or other, Tom. There are only scraps here, but they are not at
all bad. Boar's Head potted. Try it, Tom. Make a beginning
whatever you do. What an old Blade you are! I am delighted
to see you.'

While he delivered himself of these words in a state of great
commotion, John was constantly running backwards and
forwards to and from the closet, bringing out all sorts of things
in pots, scooping extraordinary quantities of tea out of the
caddy, dropping French rolls into his boots, pouring hot water
over the butter, and making a variety of similar mistakes without disconcerting himself in the least.

'There!' said John, sitting down for the fiftieth time, and
instantly starting up again to make some other addition to the
breakfast. 'Now we are as well off as we are likely to be till
dinner. And now let us have the news, Tom. Imprimis, how's
Pecksniff?'

'I don't know how he is,' was Tom's grave answer.

John Westlock put the teapot down, and looked at him, in
astonishment.

'I don't know how he is,' said Thomas Pinch; 'and, saving
that I wish him no ill, I don't care. I have left him, John. I
have left him for ever.'

'Voluntarily?'

'Why, no, for he dismissed me. But I had first found out that
I was mistaken in him; and I could not have remained with
him under any circumstances. I grieve to say that you were
right in your estimate of his character. It may be a ridiculous
weakness, John, but it has been very painful and bitter to me
to find this out, I do assure you.'

Tom had no need to direct that appealing look towards his

friend, in mild and gentle deprecation of his answering with
a laugh. John Westlock would as soon have thought of striking
him down upon the floor.

'It was all a dream of mine,' said Tom, 'and it is over. I'll
tell you how it happened, at some other time. Bear with my
folly, John. I do not, just now, like to think or speak about it.'

'I swear to you, Tom,' returned his friend, with great
earnestness of manner, after remaining silent for a few moments,
'that when I see, as I do now, how deeply you feel this, I don't
know whether to be glad or sorry that you have made the
discovery at last. I reproach myself with the thought that I
ever jested on the subject; I ought to have known better.'

'My dear friend,' said Tom, extending his hand, 'it is very
generous and gallant in you to receive me and my disclosure
in this spirit; it makes me blush to think that I should have
felt a moment's uneasiness as I came along. You can't think
what a weight is lifted off my mind,' said Tom, taking up his
knife and fork again, and looking very cheerful. 'I shall punish
the Boar's Head dreadfully.'

The host, thus reminded of his duties, instantly betook himself to piling up all kinds of irreconcilable and contradictory
viands in Tom's plate, and a very capital breakfast Tom made,
and very much the better for it Tom felt.

'That's all right,' said John, after contemplating his visitor's
proceedings with infinite satisfaction. 'Now, about our plans.
You are going to stay with me, of course. Where's your box?'

'It's at the Inn,' said Tom. 'I didn't intend——'

'Never mind what you didn't intend,' John Westlock interposed. 'What you *did* intend is more to the purpose. You
intended, in coming here, to ask my advice, did you not, Tom?'

'Certainly.'

'And to take it when I gave it to you?'

'Yes,' rejoined Tom, smiling, 'if it were good advice, which,
being yours, I have no doubt it will be.'

'Very well. Then don't be an obstinate old humbug in the
outset, Tom, or I shall shut up shop and dispense none of that
invaluable commodity. You are on a visit to me. I wish I had
an organ for you, Tom!'

'So do the gentlemen down-stairs, and the gentlemen overhead, I have no doubt,' was Tom's reply.

'Let me see. In the first place, you will wish to see your sister
this morning,' pursued his friend, 'and of course you will like

to go there alone. I'll walk part of the way with you; and see about a little business of my own, and meet you here again in the afternoon. Put that in your pocket, Tom. It's only the key of the door. If you come home first you'll want it.'

'Really,' said Tom, 'quartering one's self upon a friend in this way—'

'Why, there are two keys,' interposed John Westlock. 'I can't open the door with them both at once, can I? What a ridiculous fellow you are, Tom! Nothing particular you'd like for dinner, is there?'

'Oh dear no,' said Tom.

'Very well, then you may as well leave it to me. Have a glass of cherry brandy, Tom?'

'Not a drop! What remarkable chambers these are!' said Pinch, 'there's everything in 'em!'

'Bless your soul, Tom, nothing but a few little bachelor contrivances! the sort of impromptu arrangements that might have suggested themselves to Philip Quarll or Robinson Crusoe: that's all. What do you say? Shall we walk?'

'By all means,' cried Tom. 'As soon as you like.'

Accordingly, John Westlock took the French rolls out of his boots, and put his boots on, and dressed himself: giving Tom the paper to read in the meanwhile. When he returned, equipped for walking, he found Tom in a brown study, with the paper in his hand.

'Dreaming, Tom?'

'No,' said Mr. Pinch, 'No. I have been looking over the advertising sheet, thinking there might be something in it, which would be likely to suit me. But, as I often think, the strange thing seems to be that nobody is suited. Here are all kinds of employers wanting all sorts of servants, and all sorts of servants wanting all kinds of employers, and they never seem to come together. Here is a gentleman in a public office in a position of temporary difficulty, who wants to borrow five hundred pounds; and in the very next advertisement here is another gentleman who has got exactly that sum to lend. But he'll never lend it to him, John, you'll find! Here is a lady possessing a moderate independence, who wants to board and lodge with a quiet, cheerful family; and here is a family describing themselves in those very words, "a quiet, cheerful family," who want exactly such a lady to come and live with them. But she'll never go, John! Neither do any of these single gentlemen who want an airy bedroom, with the occasional use of a parlour, ever appear to come to terms with these other people who live in a rural situation, remarkable for its bracing atmosphere, within five minutes' walk of the Royal Exchange. Even those letters of the alphabet, who are always running away from their friends and being entreated at the tops of columns to come back, never *do* come back, if we may judge from the number of times they are asked to do it and don't. It really seems,' said Tom, relinquishing the paper with a thoughtful sigh, 'as if people had the same gratification in printing their complaints as in making them known by word of mouth; as if they found it a comfort and consolation to proclaim "I want such and such a thing, and I can't get it, and I don't expect I ever shall!"'

John Westlock laughed at the idea, and they went out together. So many years had passed since Tom was last in London, and he had known so little of it then, that his interest in all he saw was very great. He was particularly anxious, among other notorious localities, to have those streets pointed out to him which were appropriated to the slaughter of countrymen; and was quite disappointed to find, after a half-an-hour's walking, that he hadn't had his pocket picked. But on John Westlock's inventing a pickpocket for his gratification, and pointing out a highly respectable stranger as one of that fraternity, he was much delighted.

His friend accompanied him to within a short distance of Camberwell, and having put him beyond the possibility of mistaking the wealthy brass-and-copper founder's, left him to make his visit. Arriving before the great bell-handle, Tom gave it a gentle pull. The porter appeared.

'Pray does Miss Pinch live here?' said Tom.

'Miss Pinch is Governess here,' replied the porter.

At the same time he looked at Tom from head to foot, as if he would have said, 'You are a nice man, *you* are; where did *you* come from?'

'It's the same young lady,' said Tom. 'It's quite right. Is she at home?'

'I don't know, I'm sure,' rejoined the porter.

'Do you think you could have the goodness to ascertain?' said Tom. He had quite a delicacy in offering the suggestion, for the possibility of such a step did not appear to present itself to the porter's mind at all.

The fact was that the porter in answering the gate-bell had, according to usage, rung the house-bell (for it is as well to do these things in the Baronial style while you are about it), and that there the functions of his office had ceased. Being hired to open and shut the gate, and not to explain himself to strangers, he left this little incident to be developed by the footman with the tags, who, at this juncture, called out from the door steps:

'Hollo, there! wot are you up to? This way, young man!'

'Oh!' said Tom, hurrying towards him. 'I didn't observe that there was anybody else. Pray is Miss Pinch at home?'

'She's *in*,' replied the footman. As much as to say to Tom: 'But if you think she has anything to do with the proprietorship of this place you had better abandon that idea.'

'I wish to see her, if you please,' said Tom.

The footman, being a lively young man, happened to have his attention caught at that moment by the flight of a pigeon, in which he took so warm an interest that his gaze was rivetted on the bird until it was quite out of sight. He then invited Tom to come in, and showed him into a parlour.

'Hany neem?' said the young man, pausing languidly at the door.

It was a good thought: because without providing the stranger, in case he should happen to be of a warm temper, with a sufficient excuse for knocking him down, it implied this young man's estimate of his quality, and relieved his breast of the oppressive burden of rating him in secret as a nameless and obscure individual.

'Say her brother, if you please,' said Tom.

'Mother?' drawled the footman.

'Brother,' repeated Tom, slightly raising his voice. 'And if you will say, in the first instance, a gentleman, and then say her brother, I shall be obliged to you, as she does not expect me or know I am in London, and I do not wish to startle her.'

The young man's interest in Tom's observations had ceased long before this time, but he kindly waited until now; when, shutting the door, he withdrew.

'Dear me!' said Tom. 'This is very disrespectful and uncivil behaviour. I hope these are new servants here, and that Ruth is very differently treated.'

His cogitations were interrupted by the sound of voices in the adjoining room. They seemed to be engaged in high dispute, or in indignant reprimand of some offender; and gathering strength occasionally, broke out into a perfect whirlwind. It was in one of these gusts, as it appeared to Tom, that the footman announced him; for an abrupt and unnatural calm took place, and then a dead silence. He was standing before the window, wondering what domestic quarrel might have caused these sounds, and hoping Ruth had nothing to do with it, when the door opened, and his sister ran into his arms.

'Why, bless my soul!' said Tom, looking at her with great pride, when they had tenderly embraced each other, 'how altered you are, Ruth! I should scarcely have known you, my love, if I had seen you anywhere else, I declare! You are so improved,' said Tom, with inexpressible delight: 'you are so womanly; you are so—positively, you know, you are so handsome!'

'If *you* think so, Tom—'

'Oh, but everybody must think so, you know,' said Tom, gently smoothing down her hair. 'It's a matter of fact; not opinion. But what's the matter?' said Tom, looking at her more intently, 'how flushed you are! and you have been crying.'

'No, I have not, Tom.'

'Nonsense,' said her brother stoutly. 'That's a story. Don't tell me! I know better. What is it, dear? I'm not with Mr. Pecksniff now; I am going to try and settle myself in London; and if you are not happy here (as I very much fear you are not, for I begin to think you have been deceiving me with the kindest and most affectionate intention) you shall not remain here.'

Oh! Tom's blood was rising; mind that! Perhaps the Boar's Head had something to do with it, but certainly the footman had. So had the sight of his pretty sister—a great deal to do with it. Tom could bear a good deal himself, but he was proud of her, and pride is a sensitive thing. He began to think, 'there are more Pecksniffs than one, perhaps,' and by all the pins and needles that run up and down in angry veins, Tom was in a most unusual tingle all at once!

'We will talk about it, Tom,' said Ruth, giving him another kiss to pacify him. 'I am afraid I cannot stay here.'

'Cannot!' replied Tom. 'Why then, you shall not, my love. Heyday! You are not an object of charity! Upon my word!'

Tom was stopped in these exclamations by the footman,

who brought a message from his master, importing that he wished to speak with him before he went, and with Miss Pinch also.

'Show the way,' said Tom. 'I'll wait upon him at once.'

Accordingly they entered the adjoining room from which the noise of altercation had proceeded; and there they found a middle-aged gentleman, with a pompous voice and manner, and a middle-aged lady, with what may be termed an excise-able face, or one in which starch and vinegar were decidedly employed. There was likewise present that eldest pupil of Miss Pinch, whom Mrs. Todgers, on a previous occasion, had called a syrup, and who was now weeping and sobbing spite-fully.

'My brother, sir,' said Ruth Pinch, timidly presenting Tom.

'Oh!' cried the gentleman, surveying Tom attentively. 'You really are Miss Pinch's brother, I presume? You will excuse my asking. I don't observe any resemblance.'

'Miss Pinch has a brother, I know,' observed the lady.

'Miss Pinch is always talking about her brother, when she ought to be engaged upon my education,' sobbed the pupil.

'Sophia! Hold your tongue!' observed the gentleman. 'Sit down, if you please,' addressing Tom.

Tom sat down, looking from one face to another, in mute surprise.

'Remain here, if you please, Miss Pinch,' pursued the gentleman, looking slightly over his shoulder.

Tom interrupted him here, by rising to place a chair for his sister. Having done which he sat down again.

'I am glad you chance to have called to see your sister to-day, sir,' resumed the brass-and-copper founder. 'For although I do not approve, as a principle, of any young person engaged in my family in the capacity of a governess, receiving visitors, it happens in this case to be well-timed. I am sorry to inform you that we are not at all satisfied with your sister.'

'We are very much *dis*satisfied with her,' observed the lady.

'I'd never say another lesson to Miss Pinch if I was to be beat to death for it!' sobbed the pupil.

'Sophia!' cried her father. 'Hold your tongue!'

'Will you allow me to inquire what your ground of dis-satisfaction is?' asked Tom.

'Yes,' said the gentleman, 'I will. I don't recognise it as a right; but I will. Your sister has not the slightest innate power of commanding respect. It has been a constant source of difference between us. Although she has been in this family for some time, and although the young lady who is now present has almost, as it were, grown up under her tuition, that young lady has no respect for her. Miss Pinch has been perfectly unable to command my daughter's respect, or to win my daughter's confidence. Now,' said the gentleman, allowing the palm of his hand to fall gravely down upon the table: 'I maintain that there is something radically wrong in that! You, as her brother, may be disposed to deny it—'

'I beg your pardon, sir,' said Tom. 'I am not at all disposed to deny it. I am sure that there is something radically wrong: radically monstrous: in that.'

'Good Heavens!' cried the gentleman, looking round the room with dignity, 'what do I find to be the case! what results obtrude themselves upon me as flowing from this weakness of character on the part of Miss Pinch! What are my feelings as a father, when, after my desire (repeatedly expressed to Miss Pinch, as I think she will not venture to deny) that my daughter should be choice in her expressions, genteel in her deportment, as becomes her station in life, and politely distant to her inferiors in society, I find her, only this very morning, addressing Miss Pinch herself as a beggar!'

'A beggarly thing,' observed the lady, in correction.

'Which is worse,' said the gentleman, triumphantly; 'which is worse. A beggarly thing. A low, coarse, despicable expression!'

'Most despicable,' cried Tom. 'I am glad to find that there is a just appreciation of it here.'

'So just, sir,' said the gentleman, lowering his voice to be the more impressive. 'So just, that, but for my knowing Miss Pinch to be an unprotected young person, an orphan, and without friends, I would, as I assured Miss Pinch, upon my veracity and personal character, a few minutes ago, I would have severed the connexion between us at that moment and from that time.'

'Bless my soul, sir!' cried Tom, rising from his seat; for he was now unable to contain himself any longer; 'don't allow such considerations as those to influence you, pray. They don't exist, sir. She is not unprotected. She is ready to depart this instant. Ruth, my dear, get your bonnet on!'

'Oh, a pretty family!' cried the lady. 'Oh, he's her brother! There's no doubt about that!'

'As little doubt, madam,' said Tom, 'as that young lady yonder is the child of your teaching, and not my sister's. Ruth, my dear, get your bonnet on!'

'When you say, young man,' interposed the brass-and-copper founder, haughtily, 'with that impertinence which is natural to you, and which I therefore do not condescend to notice further, that the young lady, my eldest daughter, has been educated by any one but Miss Pinch, you—I needn't proceed. You comprehend me fully. I have no doubt you are used to it.'

'Sir!' cried Tom, after regarding him in silence for some little time. 'If you do not understand what I mean, I will tell you. If you do understand what I mean, I beg you not to repeat that mode of expressing yourself in answer to it. My meaning is, that no man can expect his children to respect what he degrades.'

'Ha, ha, ha!' laughed the gentleman. 'Cant! cant! The common cant!'

'The common story, sir!' said Tom; 'the story of a common mind. Your governess cannot win the confidence and respect of your children, forsooth! Let her begin by winning yours, and see what happens then.'

'Miss Pinch is getting her bonnet on, I trust, my dear?' said the gentleman.

'I trust she is,' said Tom, forestalling the reply. 'I have no doubt she is. In the meantime I address myself to you, sir. You made your statement to me, sir; you required to see me for that purpose; and I have a right to answer it. I am not loud or turbulent,' said Tom, which was quite true, 'though I can scarcely say as much for you, in your manner of addressing yourself to me. And I wish, on my sister's behalf, to state the simple truth.'

'You may state anything you like, young man,' returned the gentleman, affecting to yawn. 'My dear, Miss Pinch's money.'

'When you tell me,' resumed Tom, who was not the less indignant for keeping himself quiet, 'that my sister has no innate power of commanding the respect of your children, I must tell you it is not so; and that she has. She is as well bred, as well taught, as well qualified by nature to command respect, as any hirer of a governess you know. But when you place her at a disadvantage in reference to every servant in your house, how can you suppose, if you have the gift of common sense, that she is not in a tenfold worse position in reference to your daughters?'

'Pretty well! Upon my word,' exclaimed the gentleman, 'this is pretty well!'

'It is very ill, sir,' said Tom. 'It is very bad and mean, and wrong and cruel. Respect! I believe young people are quick enough to observe and imitate; and why or how should they respect whom no one else respects, and everybody slights? And very partial they must grow—oh, very partial!—to their studies, when they see to what a pass proficiency in those same tasks has brought their governess! Respect! Put anything the most deserving of respect before your daughters in the light in which you place her, and you will bring it down as low, no matter what it is!'

'You speak with extreme impertinence, young man,' observed the gentleman.

'I speak without passion, but with extreme indignation and contempt for such a course of treatment, and for all who practise it,' said Tom. 'Why, how can you, as an honest gentleman, profess displeasure or surprise at your daughter telling my sister she is something beggarly and humble, when you are for ever telling her the same thing yourself in fifty plain, outspeaking ways, though not in words; and when your very porter and footman make the same delicate announcement to all comers? As to your suspicion and distrust of her: even of her word: if she is not above their reach, you have no right to employ her.'

'No right!' cried the brass-and-copper founder.

'Distinctly not,' Tom answered. 'If you imagine that the payment of an annual sum of money gives it to you, you immensely exaggerate its power and value. Your money is the least part of your bargain in such a case. You may be punctual in that to half a second on the clock, and yet be Bankrupt. I have nothing more to say,' said Tom, much flushed and flustered, now that it was over, 'except to crave permission to stand in your garden until my sister is ready.'

Not waiting to obtain it, Tom walked out.

Before he had well begun to cool, his sister joined him. She was crying; and Tom could not bear that any one about the house should see her doing that.

'They will think you are sorry to go,' said Tom. 'You are not sorry to go?'

'No, Tom, no. I have been anxious to go for a very long time.'

'Very well, then! Don't cry!' said Tom.

'I am so sorry for *you*, dear,' sobbed Tom's sister.

'But you ought to be glad on my account,' said Tom. 'I shall be twice as happy with you for a companion. Hold up your head. There! Now we go out as we ought. Not blustering, you know, but firm and confident in ourselves.'

The idea of Tom and his sister blustering, under any circumstances, was a splendid absurdity. But Tom was very far from feeling it to be so, in his excitement; and passed out at the gate with such severe determination written in his face that the porter hardly knew him again.

It was not until they had walked some short distance, and Tom found himself getting cooler and more collected, that he was quite restored to himself by an inquiry from his sister, who said in her pleasant little voice:

'Where are we going, Tom?'

'Dear me!' said Tom, stopping, 'I don't know.'

'Don't you—don't you live anywhere, dear?' asked Tom's sister, looking wistfully in his face.

'No,' said Tom. 'Not at present. Not exactly. I only arrived this morning. We must have some lodgings.'

He didn't tell her that he had been going to stay with his friend John, and could on no account think of billeting two inmates upon him, of whom one was a young lady; for he knew that would make her uncomfortable, and would cause her to regard herself as being an inconvenience to him. Neither did he like to leave her anywhere while he called on John, and told him of this change in his arrangements; for he was delicate of seeming to encroach upon the generous and hospitable nature of his friend. Therefore he said again, 'We must have some lodgings, of course;' and said it as stoutly as if he had been a perfect Directory and Guide-Book to all the lodgings in London.

'Where shall we go and look for 'em?' said Tom. 'What do you think?'

Tom's sister was not much wiser on such a topic than he was. So she squeezed her little purse into his coat-pocket, and folding the little hand with which she did so on the other little hand with which she clasped his arm, said nothing.

'It ought to be a cheap neighbourhood,' said Tom, 'and not too far from London. Let me see. Should you think Islington a good place?'

'I should think it was an excellent place, Tom.'

'It used to be called Merry Islington, once upon a time,' said Tom. 'Perhaps it's merry now; if so, it's all the better. Eh?'

'If it's not too dear,' said Tom's sister.

'Of course, if it's not too dear,' assented Tom. 'Well, where *is* Islington? We can't do better than go there, I should think. Let's go.'

Tom's sister would have gone anywhere with him; so they walked off, arm in arm, as comfortably as possible. Finding, presently, that Islington was not in that neighbourhood, Tom made inquiries respecting a public conveyance thither: which they soon obtained. As they rode along they were very full of conversation indeed, Tom relating what had happened to him, and Tom's sister relating what had happened to her, and both finding a great deal more to say than time to say it in: for they had only just begun to talk, in comparison with what they had to tell each other, when they reached their journey's end.

'Now,' said Tom, 'we must first look out for some very unpretending streets, and then look out for bills in the windows.'

So they walked off again, quite as happily as if they had just stepped out of a snug little house of their own, to look for lodgings on account of somebody else. Tom's simplicity was unabated, Heaven knows; but now that he had somebody to rely upon him, he was stimulated to rely a little more upon himself, and was, in his own opinion, quite a desperate fellow.

After roaming up and down for some hours, looking at some scores of lodgings, they began to find it rather fatiguing, especially as they saw none which were at all adapted to their purpose. At length, however, in a singular little old-fashioned house, up a blind street, they discovered two small bedrooms and a triangular parlour, which promised to suit them well enough. Their desiring to take possession immediately was a suspicious circumstance, but even this was surmounted by the payment of their first week's rent, and a reference to John Westlock, Esquire, Furnival's Inn, High Holborn,

Ah! It was a goodly sight, when this important point was settled, to behold Tom and his sister trotting round to the baker's, and the butcher's, and the grocer's, with a kind of dreadful delight in the unaccustomed cares of housekeeping; taking secret counsel together as they gave their small orders, and distracted by the least suggestion on the part of the shop-keeper! When they got back to the triangular parlour, and Tom's sister, bustling to and fro, busy about a thousand pleasant nothings, stopped every now and then to give old Tom a kiss, or smile upon him, Tom rubbed his hands as if all Islington were his.

It was late in the afternoon now, though, and high time for Tom to keep his appointment. So, after agreeing with his sister that in consideration of not having dined, they would venture on the extravagance of chops for supper at nine, he walked out again to narrate these marvellous occurrences to John.

'I am quite a family man all at once,' thought Tom. 'If I can only get something to do, how comfortable Ruth and I may be! Ah, that if! But it's of no use to despond. I can but do that, when I have tried everything and failed; and even then it won't serve me much. Upon my word,' thought Tom, quickening his pace, 'I don't know what John will think has become of me. He'll begin to be afraid I have strayed into one of those streets where the countrymen are murdered; and that I have been made meat-pies of, or some such horrible thing.'

CHAPTER XXXVII

Tom Pinch, going astray, finds that he is not the only person in that predicament. He retaliates upon a fallen foe

TOM'S evil genius did not lead him into the dens of any of those preparers of cannibalic pastry, who are represented in many standard country legends as doing a lively retail business in the Metropolis; nor did it mark him out as the prey of ring-droppers, pea and thimble-riggers, duffers, touters, or any of those bloodless sharpers, who are, perhaps, a little better known to the Police. He fell into conversation with no gentleman who took him into a public-house, where there happened to be another gentleman who swore he had more money than any gentleman, and very soon proved he had more money than one gentleman by taking his away from him: neither did he fall into any other of the numerous man-traps which are set up, without notice, in the public grounds of this city. But he lost his way. He very soon did that; and in trying to find it again he lost it more and more.

Now Tom, in his guileless distrust of London, thought himself very knowing in coming to the determination that he would not ask to be directed to Furnival's Inn, if he could help it; unless, indeed, he should happen to find himself near the Mint, or the Bank of England; in which case he would step in, and ask a civil question or two, confiding in the perfect respectability of the concern. So on he went, looking up all the streets he came near, and going up half of them; and thus, by dint of not being true to Goswell Street, and filing off into Aldermanbury, and bewildering himself in Barbican, and being constant to the wrong point of the compass in London Wall, and then getting himself crosswise into Thames Street, by an instinct that would have been marvellous if he had had the least desire or reason to go there, he found himself, at last, hard by the Monument.

The Man in the Monument was quite as mysterious a being to Tom as the Man in the Moon. It immediately occurred to him that the lonely creature who held himself aloof from all mankind in that pillar like some old hermit was the very man of whom to ask his way. Cold, he might be; little sympathy he

Mr. Pinch departs to seek his Fortune
(*p. 560*)

had, perhaps, with human passion—the column seemed too tall for that; but if Truth didn't live in the base of the Monument, notwithstanding Pope's couplet about the outside of it, where in London (thought Tom) was she likely to be found!

Coming close below the pillar, it was a great encouragement to Tom to find that the Man in the Monument had simple tastes; that stony and artificial as his residence was, he still preserved some rustic recollections; that he liked plants, hung up bird-cages, was not wholly cut off from fresh groundsel, and kept young trees in tubs. The Man in the Monument, himself, was sitting outside the door—his own door: the Monument-door: what a grand idea!—and was actually yawning, as if there were no Monument to stop his mouth, and give him a perpetual interest in his own existence.

Tom was advancing towards this remarkable creature, to inquire the way to Furnival's Inn, when two people came to see the Monument. They were a gentleman and a lady; and the gentleman said, 'How much a-piece?'

The Man in the Monument replied, 'A Tanner.'

It seemed a low expression, compared with the Monument.

The gentleman put a shilling into his hand, and the Man in the Monument opened a dark little door. When the gentleman and lady had passed out of view, he shut it again, and came slowly back to his chair.

He sat down and laughed.

'They don't know what a many steps there is!' he said. 'It's worth twice the money to stop here. Oh, my eye!'

The Man in the Monument was a Cynic; a worldly man! Tom couldn't ask his way of *him*. He was prepared to put no confidence in anything he said.

'My gracious!' cried a well-known voice behind Mr. Pinch. 'Why, to be sure it is!'

At the same time he was poked in the back by a parasol. Turning round to inquire into this salute, he beheld the eldest daughter of his late patron.

'Miss Pecksniff!' said Tom.

'Why, my goodness, Mr. Pinch!' cried Cherry. 'What are you doing here?'

'I have rather wandered from my way,' said Tom. 'I—'

'I hope you have run away,' said Charity. 'It would be quite spirited and proper if you had, when my Papa so far forgets himself.'

'I have left him,' returned Tom. 'But it was perfectly under-stood on both sides. It was not done clandestinely.'

'Is he married?' asked Cherry, with a spasmodic shake of her chin.

'No, not yet,' said Tom, colouring: 'to tell you the truth, I don't think he is likely to be, if—if Miss Graham is the object of his passion.'

'Tcha, Mr. Pinch!' cried Charity, with sharp impatience, 'you're very easily deceived. You don't know the arts of which such a creature is capable. Oh! it's a wicked world.'

'You are not married?' Tom hinted, to divert the conversation.

'N—no!' said Cherry, tracing out one particular paving-stone in Monument Yard with the end of her parasol. 'I—but really it's quite impossible to explain. Won't you walk in?'

'You live here, then?' said Tom.

'Yes,' returned Miss Pecksniff, pointing with her parasol to Todgers's: 'I reside with this lady, *at present.*'

The great stress on the two last words suggested to Tom that he was expected to say something in reference to them. So he said:

'Only at present! Are you going home again, soon?'

'No, Mr. Pinch,' returned Charity. 'No, thank you. No! A mother-in-law who is younger than—I mean to say, who is as nearly as possible about the same age as one's self, would not quite suit my spirit. Not quite!' said Cherry, with a spiteful shiver.

'I thought from your saying "at present"'—Tom observed.

'Really, upon my word! I had no idea you would press me so very closely on the subject, Mr. Pinch,' said Charity, blush-ing, 'or I should not have been so foolish as to allude to—Oh really!—won't you walk in?'

Tom mentioned, to excuse himself, that he had an appoint-ment in Furnival's Inn, and that coming from Islington he had taken a few wrong turnings, and arrived at the Monument instead. Miss Pecksniff simpered very much when he asked her if she knew the way to Furnival's Inn, and at length found courage to reply:

'A gentleman who is a friend of mine, or at least who is not exactly a friend so much as a sort of acquaintance—Oh, upon my word, I hardly know what I say, Mr. Pinch; you mustn't suppose there is any engagement between us; or at least if there is, that it is at all a settled thing as yet—is going to Furnival's Inn immediately, I believe upon a little business, and I am sure he would be very glad to accompany you, so as to prevent your going wrong again. You had better walk in. You will very likely find my sister Merry here,' she said, with a curious toss of her head, and anything but an agreeable smile.

'Then, I think, I'll endeavour to find my way alone,' said Tom: 'for I fear she would not be very glad to see me. That unfortunate occurrence, in relation to which you and I had some amicable words together, in private, is not likely to have impressed her with any friendly feeling towards me. Though it really was not my fault.'

'She has never heard of that, you may depend,' said Cherry, gathering up the corners of her mouth, and nodding at Tom. 'I am far from sure that she would bear you any mighty ill will for it, if she had.'

'You don't say so?' cried Tom, who was really concerned by this insinuation.

'I say nothing,' said Charity. 'If I had not already known what shocking things treachery and deceit are in themselves, Mr. Pinch, I might perhaps have learnt it from the success they meet with—from the success they meet with.' Here she smiled as before. 'But I don't say anything. On the contrary, I should scorn it. You had better walk in!'

There was something hidden here, which piqued Tom's interest and troubled his tender heart. When, in a moment's irresolution, he looked at Charity, he could not but observe a struggle in her face between a sense of triumph and a sense of shame; nor could he but remark how, meeting even his eyes, which she cared so little for, she turned away her own, for all the splenetic defiance in her manner.

An uneasy thought entered Tom's head; a shadowy misgiving that the altered relations between himself and Pecksniff were somehow to involve an altered knowledge on his part of other people, and were to give him an insight into much of which he had had no previous suspicion. And yet he put no definite construction upon Charity's proceedings. He certainly had no idea that as he had been the audience and spectator of her mortification, she grasped with eager delight at any opportunity of reproaching her sister with his presence in *her* far deeper misery; for he knew nothing of it, and only pictured that sister as the same giddy, careless, trivial creature she always had been, with the same slight estimation of himself which she had never been at the least pains to conceal. In short, he had merely a confused impression that Miss Pecksniff was not quite sisterly or kind; and being curious to set it right, accompanied her as she desired.

The house-door being opened, she went in before Tom, requesting him to follow her; and led the way to the parlour door.

'Oh, Merry!' she said, looking in, 'I am so glad you have not gone home. Who do you think I have met in the street, and brought to see you! Mr. Pinch! There. Now you *are* surprised, I am sure!'

Not more surprised than Tom was, when he looked upon her. Not so much. Not half so much.

'Mr. Pinch has left Papa, my dear,' said Cherry, 'and his prospects are quite flourishing. I have promised that Augustus, who is going that way, shall escort him to the place he wants. Augustus, my child, where are you?'

With these words Miss Pecksniff screamed her way out of the parlour, calling on Augustus Moddle to appear; and left Tom Pinch alone with her sister.

If she had always been his kindest friend; if she had treated him through all his servitude with such consideration as was never yet received by struggling man; if she had lightened every moment of those many years, and had ever spared and never wounded him; his honest heart could not have swelled before her with a deeper pity, or a purer freedom from all base remembrance, than it did then.

'My gracious me! You are really the last person in the world I should have thought of seeing, I am sure!'

Tom was sorry to hear her speaking in her old manner. He had not expected that. Yet he did not feel it a contradiction that he should be sorry to see her so unlike her old self, and sorry at the same time to hear her speaking in her old manner. The two things seemed quite natural.

'I wonder you find any gratification in coming to see me. I can't think what put it in your head. I never had much in seeing you. There was no love lost between us, Mr. Pinch, at any time, I think.'

Her bonnet lay beside her on the sofa, and she was very busy with the ribbons as she spoke. Much too busy to be conscious of the work her fingers did.

'We never quarrelled,' said Tom.—Tom was right in that, for one person can no more quarrel without an adversary, than one person can play at chess, or fight a duel. 'I hoped you would be glad to shake hands with an old friend. Don't let us rake up bygones,' said Tom. 'If I ever offended you, forgive me.'

She looked at him for a moment; dropped her bonnet from her hands; spread them before her altered face, and burst into tears.

'Oh, Mr. Pinch!' she said, 'although I never used you well, I did believe your nature was forgiving. I did not think you could be cruel.'

She spoke as little like her old self now, for certain, as Tom could possibly have wished. But she seemed to be appealing to him reproachfully, and he did not understand her.

'I seldom showed it—never—I know that. But I had that belief in you, that if I had been asked to name the person in the world least likely to retort upon me, I would have named you, confidently.'

'Would have named me!' Tom repeated.

'Yes,' she said with energy, 'and I have often thought so.'

After a moment's reflection, Tom sat himself upon a chair beside her.

'Do you believe,' said Tom, 'oh, can you think, that what I said just now, I said with any but the true and plain intention which my words professed? I mean it, in the spirit and the letter. If I ever offended you, forgive me; I may have done so, many times. You never injured or offended me. How, then, could I possibly retort, if even I were stern and bad enough to wish to do it!'

After a little while she thanked him, through her tears and sobs, and told him she had never been at once so sorry and so comforted, since she left home. Still she wept bitterly; and it was the greater pain to Tom to see her weeping, from her standing in especial need, just then, of sympathy and tenderness.

'Come, come!' said Tom, 'you used to be as cheerful as the day was long.'

'Ah! used!' she cried, in such a tone as rent Tom's heart.

'And will be again,' said Tom.

'No, never more. No, never, never more. If you should talk with old Mr. Chuzzlewit, at any time,' she added, looking hurriedly into his face—'I sometimes thought he liked you, but suppressed it—will you promise me to tell him that you saw me here, and that I said I bore in mind the time we talked together in the churchyard?'

Tom promised that he would.

'Many times since then, when I have wished I had been carried there before that day, I have recalled his words. I wish that he should know how true they were, although the least acknowledgment to that effect has never passed my lips, and never will.'

Tom promised this, conditionally, too. He did not tell her how improbable it was that he and the old man would ever meet again, because he thought it might disturb her more.

'If he should ever know this, through your means, dear Mr. Pinch,' said Mercy, 'tell him that I sent the message, not for myself, but that he might be more forbearing and more patient, and more trustful to some other person, in some other time of need. Tell him that if he could know how my heart trembled in the balance that day, and what a very little would have turned the scale, his own would bleed with pity for me.'

'Yes, yes,' said Tom, 'I will.'

'When I appeared to him the most unworthy of his help, I was—I know I was, for I have often, often, thought about it since—the most inclined to yield to what he showed me. Oh! if he had relented but a little more; if he had thrown himself in my way for but one other quarter of an hour; if he had extended his compassion for a vain, unthinking, miserable girl, in but the least degree; he might, and I believe he would, have saved her! Tell him that I don't blame him, but am grateful for the effort that he made; but ask him for the love of God, and youth, and in merciful consideration for the struggle which an ill-advised and unawakened nature makes to hide the strength it thinks its weakness—ask him never, never, to forget this, when he deals with one again!'

Although Tom did not hold the clue to her full meaning, he could guess it pretty nearly. Touched to the quick, he took her hand and said, or meant to say, some words of consolation. She felt and understood them, whether they were spoken or no. He was not quite certain, afterwards, but that she had tried to kneel down at his feet, and bless him.

He found that he was not alone in the room when she had left it. Mrs. Todgers was there, shaking her head. Tom had never seen Mrs. Todgers, it is needless to say, but he had a perception of her being the lady of the house; and he saw some genuine compassion in her eyes, that won his good opinion.

'Ah, sir! You are an old friend, I see,' said Mrs. Todgers.

'Yes,' said Tom.

'And yet,' quoth Mrs. Todgers, shutting the door softly, 'she hasn't told you what her troubles are, I'm certain.'

Tom was struck by these words, for they were quite true. 'Indeed,' he said, 'she has not.'

'And never would,' said Mrs. Todgers, 'if you saw her daily. She never makes the least complaint to me, or utters a single word of explanation or reproach. But I know,' said Mrs. Todgers, drawing in her breath, '*I* know!'

Tom nodded sorrowfully, 'so do I.'

'I fully believe,' said Mrs. Todgers, taking her pocket-handkerchief from the flat reticule, 'that nobody can tell one half of what that poor young creature has to undergo. But though she comes here, constantly, to ease her poor full heart without his knowing it; and saying, "Mrs. Todgers, I am very low to-day; I think that I shall soon be dead," sits crying in my room until the fit is past; I know no more from her. And, I believe,' said Mrs. Todgers, putting back her handkerchief again, 'that she considers me a good friend too.'

Mrs. Todgers might have said her best friend. Commercial gentlemen and gravy had tried Mrs. Todgers's temper; the main chance—it was such a very small one in her case, that she might have been excused for looking sharp after it, lest it should entirely vanish from her sight—had taken a firm hold on Mrs. Todgers's attention. But in some odd nook in Mrs. Todgers's breast, up a great many steps, and in a corner easy to be overlooked, there was a secret door, with 'Woman' written on the spring, which, at a touch from Mercy's hand, had flown wide open, and admitted her for shelter.

When boarding-house accounts are balanced with all other ledgers, and the books of the Recording Angel are made up for ever, perhaps there may be seen an entry to thy credit, lean Mrs. Todgers, which shall make thee beautiful!

She was growing beautiful so rapidly in Tom's eyes; for he saw that she was poor, and that this good had sprung up in her from among the sordid strivings of her life; that she might have been a very Venus in a minute more, if Miss Pecksniff had not entered with her friend.

'Mr. Thomas Pinch!' said Charity, performing the cere-mony of introduction with evident pride. 'Mr. Moddle. Where's my sister?'

'Gone, Miss Pecksniff,' Mrs. Todgers answered. 'She had appointed to be home.'

'Ah!' said Charity, looking at Tom. 'Oh, dear me!'

'She's greatly altered since she's been Anoth—since she's been married, Mrs. Todgers!' observed Moddle.

'My dear Augustus!' said Miss Pecksniff, in a low voice, 'I verily believe you have said that fifty thousand times, in my hearing. What a Prose you are!'

This was succeeded by some trifling love passages, which appeared to originate with, if not to be wholly carried on by Miss Pecksniff. At any rate, Mr. Moddle was much slower in his responses than is customary with young lovers, and ex-hibited a lowness of spirits which was quite oppressive.

He did not improve at all when Tom and he were in the streets, but sighed so dismally that it was dreadful to hear him. As a means of cheering him up, Tom told him that he wished him joy.

'Joy!' cried Moddle. 'Ha, ha!'

'What an extraordinary young man!' thought Tom.

'The Scorner has not set his seal upon you. *You* care what becomes of you?' said Moddle.

Tom admitted that it was a subject in which he certainly felt some interest.

'I don't,' said Mr. Moddle. 'The Elements may have me when they please. I'm ready.'

Tom inferred from these, and other expressions of the same nature, that he was jealous. Therefore he allowed him to take his own course; which was such a gloomy one, that he felt a load removed from his mind when they parted company at the gate of Furnival's Inn.

It was now a couple of hours past John Westlock's dinner-time; and he was walking up and down the room, quite anxious for Tom's safety. The table was spread; the wine was carefully decanted; and the dinner smelt delicious.

'Why, Tom, old boy, where on earth have you been? Your box is here. Get your boots off instantly, and sit down!'

'I am sorry to say I can't stay, John,' replied Tom Pinch, who was breathless with the haste he had made in running up the stairs.

'Can't stay!'

'If you'll go on with your dinner,' said Tom, 'I'll tell you my reason the while. I mustn't eat myself, or I shall have no appetite for the chops.'

'There are no chops here, my good fellow.'

'No. But there are at Islington,' said Tom.

John Westlock was perfectly confounded by this reply, and vowed he would not touch a morsel until Tom had explained himself fully. So Tom sat down, and told him all; to which he listened with the greatest interest.

He knew Tom too well, and respected his delicacy too much, to ask him why he had taken these measures without communicating with him first. He quite concurred in the expediency of Tom's immediately returning to his sister, as he knew so little of the place in which he had left her; and good-humouredly proposed to ride back with him in a cab, in which he might convey his box. Tom's proposition that he should sup with them that night, he flatly rejected, but made an appointment with him for the morrow. 'And now, Tom,' he said, as they rode along, 'I have a question to ask you, to which I expect a manly and straightforward answer. Do you want any money? I am pretty sure you do.'

'I don't indeed,' said Tom.

'I believe you are deceiving me.'

'No. With many thanks to you, I am quite in earnest,' Tom replied. 'My sister has some money, and so have I. If I had nothing else, John, I have a five-pound note, which that good creature, Mrs. Lupin, of the Dragon, handed up to me outside the coach, in a letter, begging me to borrow it; and then drove off as hard as she could go.'

'And a blessing on every dimple in her handsome face, say I!' cried John, 'though why you should give her the preference over me, I don't know. Never mind. I bide my time, Tom.'

'And I hope you'll continue to bide it,' returned Tom, gaily. 'For I owe you more, already, in a hundred other ways, than I can ever hope to pay.'

They parted at the door of Tom's new residence. John Westlock, sitting in the cab, and, catching a glimpse of a blooming little busy creature darting out to kiss Tom and to help him with his box, would not have had the least objection to change places with him.

Well! she *was* a cheerful little thing; and had a quaint, bright quietness about her that was infinitely pleasant. Surely she was the best sauce for chops ever invented. The potatoes seemed to take a pleasure in sending up their grateful steam before her; the froth upon the pint of porter pouted to attract her notice. But it was all in vain. She saw nothing but Tom. Tom was the first and last thing in the world.

As she sat opposite to Tom at supper, fingering one of Tom's pet tunes upon the table-cloth, and smiling in his face, he had never been so happy in his life.

CHAPTER XXXVIII

Secret service

IN walking from the City with his sentimental friend, Tom Pinch had looked into the face, and brushed against the threadbare sleeve, of Mr. Nadgett, man of mystery to the Anglo-Bengalee Disinterested Loan and Life Assurance Company. Mr. Nadgett naturally passed away from Tom's remembrance as he passed out of his view; for he didn't know him, and had never heard his name.

As there are a vast number of people in the huge metropolis of England who rise up every morning not knowing where their heads will rest at night, so there are a multitude who shooting arrows over houses as their daily business, never know on whom they fall. Mr. Nadgett might have passed Tom Pinch ten thousand times; might even have been quite familiar with his face, his name, pursuits, and character; yet never once have dreamed that Tom had any interest in any act or mystery of his. Tom might have done the like by him, of course. But the same private man out of all the men alive, was in the mind of each at the same moment; was prominently connected, though in a different manner, with the day's adventures of both; and formed, when they passed each other in the street, the one absorbing topic of their thoughts.

Why Tom had Jonas Chuzzlewit in his mind requires no explanation. Why Mr. Nadgett should have had Jonas Chuzzlewit in his, is quite another thing.

But, somehow or other, that amiable and worthy orphan had become a part of the mystery of Mr. Nadgett's existence. Mr. Nadgett took an interest in his lightest proceedings; and it never flagged or wavered. He watched him in and out of the Assurance Office, where he was now formally installed as a Director; he dogged his footsteps in the streets; he stood listening when he talked; he sat in coffee-rooms entering his name in the great pocket-book, over and over again; he wrote letters to himself about him constantly; and, when he found them in his pocket, put them in the fire, with such distrust and caution that he would bend down to watch the crumpled tinder while it floated upward, as if his mind misgave him, that the mystery it had contained might come out at the chimney-pot.

And yet all this was quite a secret. Mr. Nadgett kept it to himself, and kept it close. Jonas had no more idea that Mr. Nadgett's eyes were fixed on him, than he had that he was living under the daily inspection and report of a whole order of Jesuits. Indeed Mr. Nadgett's eyes were seldom fixed on any other objects than the ground, the clock, or the fire; but every button on his coat might have been an eye: he saw so much.

The secret manner of the man disarmed suspicion in this wise; suggesting, not that he was watching any one, but that he thought some other man was watching him. He went about so stealthily, and kept himself so wrapped up in himself, that the whole object of his life appeared to be, to avoid notice and preserve his own mystery. Jonas sometimes saw him in the street, hovering in the outer office, waiting at the door for the man who never came, or slinking off with his immovable face and drooping head, and the one beaver glove dangling before him; but he would as soon have thought of the cross upon the top of St. Paul's Cathedral taking note of what he did, or slowly winding a great net about his feet, as of Nadgett's being engaged in such an occupation.

Mr. Nadgett made a mysterious change about this time in his mysterious life: for whereas he had, until now, been first seen every morning coming down Cornhill, so exactly like the Nadgett of the day before as to occasion a popular belief that he never went to bed or took his clothes off, he was now first seen in Holborn, coming out of Kingsgate Street; and it was soon discovered that he actually went every morning to a barber's shop in that street to get shaved; and that the barber's name was Sweedlepipe. He seemed to make appointments with the man who never came, to meet him at this barber's; for he would frequently take long spells of waiting in the shop, and would ask for pen and ink, and pull out his pocket-book, and be very busy over it for an hour at a time. Mrs. Gamp and Mr. Sweedlepipe had many deep discoursings on the subject of this mysterious customer; but they usually agreed that he had speculated too much and was keeping out of the way.

He must have appointed the man who never kept his word, to meet him at another new place too; for one day he was found, for the first time, by the waiter at the Mourning Coach-Horse, the House-of-call for Undertakers, down in the City there, making figures with a pipe-stem in the sawdust of a clean spittoon; and declining to call for anything, on the ground of expecting a gentleman presently. As the gentleman was not honourable enough to keep his engagement, he came again next day, with his pocket-book in such a state of distention that he was regarded in the bar as a man of large property. After that, he repeated his visits every day, and had so much writing to do, that he made nothing of emptying a capacious leaden inkstand in two sittings. Although he never talked much, still, by being there among the regular customers, he made their acquaintance; and in course of time became quite intimate with Mr. Tacker, Mr. Mould's foreman; and even with Mr. Mould himself, who openly said he was a long-headed man, a dry one, a salt fish, a deep file, a rasper; and made him the subject of many other flattering encomiums.

At the same time, too, he told the people at the Assurance Office, in his own mysterious way, that there was something wrong (secretly wrong, of course) in his liver, and that he feared he must put himself under the doctor's hands. He was delivered over to Jobling upon this representation; and though Jobling could not find out where his liver was wrong, wrong Mr. Nadgett said it was; observing that it was his own liver, and he hoped he ought to know. Accordingly, he became Mr. Jobling's patient; and detailing his symptoms in his slow and secret way, was in and out of that gentleman's room a dozen times a day.

As he pursued all these occupations at once; and all steadily; and all secretly; and never slackened in his watchfulness of everything that Mr. Jonas said and did, and left unsaid and undone; it is not improbable that they were, secretly, essential parts of some great scheme which Mr. Nadgett had on foot.

It was on the morning of this very day on which so much had happened to Tom Pinch, that Nadgett suddenly appeared before Mr. Montague's house in Pall Mall—he always made his appearance as if he had that moment come up a trap—when the clocks were striking nine. He rang the bell in a covert under-handed way, as though it were a treasonable act; and passed in at the door, the moment it was opened wide enough to receive his body. That done, he shut it immediately with his own hands.

Mr. Bailey, taking up his name without delay, returned with a request that he would follow him into his master's chamber. The chairman of the Anglo-Bengalee Disinterested Loan and

Y

Life Assurance Board was dressing, and received him as a business person who was often backwards and forwards, and was received at all times for his business' sake.

'Well, Mr. Nadgett?'

Mr. Nadgett put his hat upon the ground and coughed. The boy having withdrawn and shut the door, he went to it softly, examined the handle, and returned to within a pace or two of the chair in which Mr. Montague sat.

'Any news, Mr. Nadgett?'

'I think we have some news at last, sir.'

'I am happy to hear it. I began to fear you were off the scent, Mr. Nadgett.'

'No, sir. It grows cold occasionally. It will sometimes. We can't help that.'

'You are truth itself, Mr. Nadgett. Do you report a great success?'

'That depends upon your judgment and construction of it,' was his answer, as he put on his spectacles.

'What do you think of it yourself? Have you pleased yourself?'

Mr. Nadgett rubbed his hands slowly, stroked his chin, looked round the room, and said, 'Yes, yes, I think it's a good case. I am disposed to think it's a good case. Will you go into it at once?'

'By all means.'

Mr. Nadgett picked out a certain chair from among the rest, and having planted it in a particular spot, as carefully as if he had been going to vault over it, placed another chair in front of it: leaving room for his own legs between them. He then sat down in chair number two, and laid his pocket-book, very carefully, on chair number one. He then untied the pocket-book, and hung the string over the back of chair number one. He then drew both the chairs a little nearer Mr. Montague, and opening the pocket-book spread out its contents. Finally he selected a certain memorandum from the rest, and held it out to his employer, who, during the whole of these preliminary ceremonies, had been making violent efforts to conceal his impatience.

'I wish you wouldn't be so fond of making notes, my excellent friend,' said Tigg Montague with a ghastly smile. 'I wish you would consent to give me their purport by word of mouth.'

'I don't like word of mouth,' said Mr. Nadgett gravely. 'We never know who's listening.'

Mr. Montague was going to retort, when Nadgett handed him the paper, and said, with quiet exultation in his tone, 'We'll begin at the beginning, and take that one first, if you please, sir.'

The chairman cast his eyes upon it, coldly, and with a smile which did not render any great homage to the slow and methodical habits of his spy. But he had not read half-a-dozen lines when the expression of his face began to change, and before he had finished the perusal of the paper, it was full of grave and serious attention.

'Number Two,' said Mr. Nadgett, handing him another, and receiving back the first. 'Read Number Two, sir, if you please. There is more interest as you go on.'

Tigg Montague leaned backward in his chair, and cast upon his emissary such a look of vacant wonder (not unmingled with alarm), that Mr. Nadgett considered it necessary to repeat the request he had already twice preferred: with the view of recalling his attention to the point in hand. Profiting by the hint, Mr. Montague went on with Number Two, and afterwards with Numbers Three, and Four, and Five, and so on.

These documents were all in Mr. Nadgett's writing, and were apparently a series of memoranda, jotted down from time to time upon the backs of old letters, or any scrap of paper that came first to hand. Loose straggling scrawls they were, and of very uninviting exterior; but they had weighty purpose in them, if the chairman's face were any index to the character of their contents.

The progress of Mr. Nadgett's secret satisfaction arising out of the effect they made, kept pace with the emotions of the reader. At first, Mr. Nadgett sat with his spectacles low down upon his nose, looking over them at his employer, and nervously rubbing his hands. After a little while, he changed his posture in his chair for one of greater ease, and leisurely perused the next document he held ready, as if an occasional glance at his employer's face were now enough, and all occasion for anxiety or doubt were gone. And finally he rose and looked out of the window, where he stood with a triumphant air, until Tigg Montague had finished.

'And this is the last, Mr. Nadgett!' said that gentleman, drawing a long breath.

'That, sir, is the last.'

'You are a wonderful man, Mr. Nadgett!'

'I think it is a pretty good case,' he returned as he gathered up his papers. 'It cost some trouble, sir.'

'The trouble shall be well rewarded, Mr. Nadgett.' Nadgett bowed. 'There is a deeper impression of Somebody's Hoof here, than I had expected, Mr. Nadgett. I may congratulate myself upon your being such a good hand at a secret.'

'Oh! nothing has an interest to me that's not a secret,' replied Nadgett, as he tied the string about his pocket-book, and put it up. 'It almost takes away any pleasure I may have had in this inquiry even to make it known to you.'

'A most invaluable constitution,' Tigg retorted. 'A great gift for a gentleman employed as you are, Mr. Nadgett. Much better than discretion: though you possess that quality also in an eminent degree. I think I heard a double knock. Will you put your head out of window, and tell me whether there is anybody at the door?'

Mr. Nadgett softly raised the sash, and peered out from the very corner, as a man might who was looking down into a street from whence a brisk discharge of musketry might be expected at any moment. Drawing in his head with equal caution, he observed, not altering his voice or manner:

'Mr. Jonas Chuzzlewit!'

'I thought so,' Tigg retorted.

'Shall I go?'

'I think you had better. Stay though! No! remain here, Mr. Nadgett, if you please.'

It was remarkable how pale and flurried he had become in an instant. There was nothing to account for it. His eye had fallen on his razors; but what of them!

Mr. Chuzzlewit was announced.

'Show him up directly. Nadgett! don't you leave us alone together. Mind you don't, now! By the Lord!' he added in a whisper to himself: 'We don't know what may happen.'

Saying this, he hurriedly took up a couple of hair-brushes, and began to exercise them on his own head, as if his toilet had not been interrupted. Mr. Nadgett withdrew to the stove, in which there was a small fire for the convenience of heating curling-irons; and taking advantage of so favourable an opportunity for drying his pocket-handkerchief, produced it without loss of time. There he stood, during the whole interview, holding it before the bars, and sometimes, but not often, glancing over his shoulder.

'My dear Chuzzlewit!' cried Montague, as Jonas entered: 'you rise with the lark. Though you go to bed with the nightingale, you rise with the lark. You have superhuman energy, my dear Chuzzlewit!'

'Ecod!' said Jonas, with an air of languor and ill-humour, as he took a chair, 'I should be very glad not to get up with the lark, if I could help it. But I am a light sleeper; and it's better to be up than lying awake, counting the dismal old church-clocks, in bed.'

'A light sleeper!' cried his friend. 'Now, what is a light sleeper? I often hear the expression, but upon my life I have not the least conception what a light sleeper is.'

'Hallo!' said Jonas, 'Who's that? Oh, old what's-his-name: looking (as usual) as if he wanted to skulk up the chimney.'

'Ha, ha! I have no doubt he does.'

'Well! He's not wanted here, I suppose,' said Jonas. 'He may go, mayn't he?'

'Oh, let him stay, let him stay!' said Tigg. 'He's a mere piece of furniture. He has been making his report, and is waiting for further orders. He has been told,' said Tigg, raising his voice, 'not to lose sight of certain friends of ours, or to think that he has done with them by any means. He understands his business.'

'He need,' replied Jonas; 'for of all the precious old dummies in appearance that ever I saw, he's about the worst. He's afraid of me, I think.'

'It's my belief,' said Tigg, 'that you are Poison to him. Nadgett! give me that towel!'

He had as little occasion for a towel as Jonas had for a start. But Nadgett brought it quickly; and, having lingered for a moment, fell back upon his old post by the fire.

'You see, my dear fellow,' resumed Tigg, 'you are too——— What's the matter with your lips? How white they are!'

'I took some vinegar just now,' said Jonas. 'I had oysters for my breakfast. Where are they white?' he added, muttering an oath, and rubbing them upon his handkerchief. 'I don't believe they *are* white.'

'Now I look again, they are not,' replied his friend. 'They are coming right again.'

'Say what you were going to say,' cried Jonas angrily, 'and let my face be! As long as I can show my teeth when I want to (and I can do that pretty well), the colour of my lips is not material.'

'Quite true,' said Tigg. 'I was only going to say that you are too quick and active for our friend. He is too shy to cope with such a man as you, but does his duty well. Oh, very well! But what is a light sleeper?'

'Hang a light sleeper!' exclaimed Jonas pettishly.

'No, no,' interrupted Tigg. 'No. We'll not do that.'

'A light sleeper ain't a heavy one,' said Jonas in his sulky way; 'don't sleep much, and don't sleep well, and don't sleep sound.'

'And dreams,' said Tigg, 'and cries out in an ugly manner; and when the candle burns down in the night, is in an agony; and all that sort of thing. I see!'

They were silent for a little time. Then Jonas spoke:

'Now we've done with child's talk, I want to have a word with you. I want to have a word with you before we meet up yonder to-day. I am not satisfied with the state of affairs.'

'Not satisfied!' cried Tigg. 'The money comes in well.'

'The money comes in well enough,' retorted Jonas: 'but it don't come out well enough. It can't be got at easily enough. I haven't sufficient power; it is all in your hands. Ecod! what with one of your by-laws, and another of your by-laws, and your votes in this capacity, and your votes in that capacity, and your official rights, and your individual rights, and other people's rights who are only you again, there are no rights left for me. Everybody else's rights are my wrongs. What's the use of my having a voice if it's always drowned? I might as well be dumb, and it would be much less aggravating. I'm not a-going to stand that, you know.'

'No!' said Tigg in an insinuating tone.

'No!' returned Jonas, 'I'm not indeed. I'll play Old Goose-berry with the office, and make you glad to buy me out at a good high figure, if you try any of your tricks with me.'

'I give you my honour——' Montague began.

'Oh! confound your honour,' interrupted Jonas, who became more coarse and quarrelsome as the other remonstrated, which may have been a part of Mr. Montague's intention: 'I want a little more control over the money. You may have all the honour, if you like; I'll never bring you to book for that.

But I'm not a-going to stand it, as it is now. If you should take it into your honourable head to go abroad with the bank, I don't see much to prevent you. Well! That won't do. I've had some very good dinners here, but they'd come too dear on such terms: and therefore that won't do.'

'I am unfortunate to find you in this humour,' said Tigg, with a remarkable kind of smile: 'for I was going to propose to you—for your own advantage; solely for your own advantage—that you should venture a little more with us.'

'Was you, by G—?' said Jonas, with a short laugh.

'Yes. And to suggest,' pursued Montague, 'that surely you have friends; indeed, I know you have; who would answer our purpose admirably, and whom we should be delighted to receive.'

'How kind of you! You'd be delighted to receive 'em, would you?' said Jonas, bantering.

'I give you my sacred honour, quite transported. As your friends, observe!'

'Exactly,' said Jonas; 'as my friends, of course. You'll be very much delighted when you get 'em, I have no doubt. And it'll be all to my advantage, won't it?'

'It will be very much to your advantage,' answered Montague, poising a brush in each hand, and looking steadily upon him. 'It will be very much to your advantage, I assure you.'

'And you can tell me how,' said Jonas, 'can't you?'

'SHALL I tell you how?' returned the other.

'I think you had better,' said Jonas. 'Strange things have been done in the Assurance way before now, by strange sorts of men, and I mean to take care of myself.'

'Chuzzlewit!' replied Montague, leaning forward, with his arms upon his knees, and looking full into his face. 'Strange things have been done, and are done every day; not only in our way, but in a variety of other ways; and no one suspects them. But ours, as you say, my good friend, is a strange way; and we strangely happen, sometimes, to come into the knowledge of very strange events.'

He beckoned to Jonas to bring his chair nearer; and looking slightly round, as if to remind him of the presence of Nadgett, whispered in his ear.

From red to white; from white to red again; from red to yellow; then to a cold, dull, awful, sweat-bedabbled blue. In that short whisper, all these changes fell upon the face of Jonas

Chuzzlewit; and when at last he laid his hand upon the whisperer's mouth, appalled, lest any syllable of what he said should reach the ears of the third person present, it was as bloodless and as heavy as the hand of Death.

He drew his chair away, and sat a spectacle of terror, misery, and rage. He was afraid to speak, or look, or move, or sit still. Abject, crouching, and miserable, he was a greater degradation to the form he bore, than if he had been a loathsome wound from head to heel.

His companion leisurely resumed his dressing, and completed it, glancing sometimes with a smile at the transformation he had effected, but never speaking once.

'You'll not object,' he said, when he was quite equipped, 'to venture further with us, Chuzzlewit, my friend?'

His pale lips faintly stammered out a 'No.'

'Well said! That's like yourself. Do you know I was thinking yesterday that your father-in-law, relying on your advice as a man of great sagacity in money matters, as no doubt you are, would join us, if the thing were well presented to him. He has money?'

'Yes, he has money.'

'Shall I leave Mr. Pecksniff to you? Will you undertake for Mr. Pecksniff?'

'I'll try. I'll do my best.'

'A thousand thanks,' replied the other, clapping him upon the shoulder. 'Shall we walk down-stairs? Mr. Nadgett! Follow us, if you please.'

They went down in that order. Whatever Jonas felt in reference to Montague; whatever sense he had of being caged, and barred, and trapped, and having fallen down into a pit of deepest ruin; whatever thoughts came crowding on his mind even at that early time, of one terrible chance of escape, of one red glimmer in a sky of blackness; he no more thought that the slinking figure half-a-dozen stairs behind him was his pursuing Fate, than that the other figure at his side was his Good Angel.

CHAPTER XXXIX

Containing some further particulars of the domestic economy of the Pinches; with strange news from the City, narrowly concerning Tom

PLEASANT little Ruth! Cheerful, tidy, bustling, quiet little Ruth! No doll's house ever yielded greater delight to its young mistress, than little Ruth derived from her glorious dominion over the triangular parlour and the two small bedrooms.

To be Tom's housekeeper. What dignity! Housekeeping, upon the commonest terms, associated itself with elevated responsibilities of all sorts and kinds; but housekeeping for Tom implied the utmost complication of grave trusts and mighty charges. Well might she take the keys out of the little chiffonier which held the tea and sugar; and out of the two little damp cupboards down by the fire-place, where the very black beetles got mouldy, and had the shine taken out of their backs by envious mildew; and jingle them upon a ring before Tom's eyes when he came down to breakfast! Well might she, laughing musically, put them up in that blessed little pocket of hers with a merry pride! For it was such a grand novelty to be mistress of anything, that if she had been the most relentless and despotic of all little housekeepers, she might have pleaded just that much for her excuse, and have been honourably acquitted.

So far from being despotic, however, there was a coyness about her very way of pouring out the tea, which Tom quite revelled in. And when she asked him what he would like to have for dinner, and faltered out 'chops' as a reasonably good suggestion after their last night's successful supper, Tom grew quite facetious and rallied her desperately.

'I don't know, Tom,' said his sister, blushing, 'I am not quite confident, but I think I could make a beef-steak pudding, if I tried, Tom.'

'In the whole catalogue of cookery, there is nothing I should like so much as a beef-steak pudding!' cried Tom: slapping his leg to give the greater force to this reply.

'Yes, dear, that's excellent! But if it should happen not to come quite right the first time,' his sister faltered; 'if it should happen not to be a pudding exactly, but should turn out a stew, or a soup, or something of that sort, you'll not be vexed, Tom, will you?'

The serious way in which she looked at Tom; the way in which Tom looked at her; and the way in which she gradually broke into a merry laugh at her own expense; would have enchanted you.

'Why,' said Tom, 'this is capital. It gives us a new, and quite an uncommon interest in the dinner. We put into a lottery for a beef-steak pudding, and it is impossible to say what we may get. We may make some wonderful discovery, perhaps, and produce such a dish as never was known before.'

'I shall not be at all surprised if we do, Tom,' returned his sister, still laughing merrily, 'or if it should prove to be such a dish as we shall not feel very anxious to produce again; but the meat must come out of the saucepan at last, somehow or other, you know. We can't cook it into nothing at all; that's a great comfort. So if you like to venture, *I* will.'

'I have not the least doubt,' rejoined Tom, 'that it will come out an excellent pudding; or at all events, I am sure that I shall think it so. There is naturally something so handy and brisk about you, Ruth, that if you said you could make a bowl of faultless turtle soup, I should believe you.'

And Tom was right. She was precisely that sort of person. Nobody ought to have been able to resist her coaxing manner; and nobody had any business to try. Yet she never seemed to know it was her manner at all. That was the best of it.

Well! she washed up the breakfast cups, chatting away the whole time, and telling Tom all sorts of anecdotes about the brass-and-copper founder; put everything in its place; made the room as neat as herself;—you must not suppose its shape was half as neat as hers though, or anything like it—and brushed Tom's old hat round and round and round again, until it was as sleek as Mr. Pecksniff. Then she discovered, all in a moment, that Tom's shirt-collar was frayed at the edge; and flying up-stairs for a needle and thread, came flying down again with her thimble on, and set it right with wonderful expertness; never once sticking the needle into his face, although she was humming his pet tune from first to last, and beating time with the fingers of her left hand upon his neck-cloth. She had no sooner done this, than off she was again; and there she stood once more, as brisk and busy as a bee, tying that compact little chin of hers into an equally compact little bonnet: intent on bustling out to the butcher's, without a minute's loss of time; and inviting Tom to come and see the steak cut, with his own eyes. As to Tom, he was ready to go anywhere; so off they trotted, arm-in-arm, as nimbly as you please; saying to each other what a quiet street it was to lodge in, and how very cheap, and what an airy situation.

To see the butcher slap the steak, before he laid it on the block, and give his knife a sharpening, was to forget breakfast instantly. It was agreeable, too—it really was—to see him cut it off, so smooth and juicy. There was nothing savage in the act, although the knife was large and keen; it was a piece of art, high art; there was delicacy of touch, clearness of tone, skilful handling of the subject, fine shading. It was the triumph of mind over matter; quite.

Perhaps the greenest cabbage-leaf ever grown in a garden was wrapped about this steak, before it was delivered over to Tom. But the butcher had a sentiment for his business, and knew how to refine upon it. When he saw Tom putting the cabbage-leaf into his pocket awkwardly, he begged to be allowed to do it for him; 'for meat,' he said with some emotion, 'must be humoured, not drove.'

Back they went to the lodgings again, after they had bought some eggs, and flour, and such small matters; and Tom sat gravely down to write at one end of the parlour table, while Ruth prepared to make the pudding at the other end; for there was nobody in the house but an old woman (the landlord being a mysterious sort of man, who went out early in the morning, and was scarcely ever seen); and saving in mere household drudgery, they waited on themselves.

'What are you writing, Tom?' inquired his sister, laying her hand upon his shoulder.

'Why, you see, my dear,' said Tom, leaning back in his chair, and looking up in her face, 'I am very anxious, of course, to obtain some suitable employment; and before Mr. Westlock comes this afternoon, I think I may as well prepare a little description of myself and my qualifications; such as he could show to any friend of his.'

'You had better do the same for me, Tom, also,' said his sister, casting down her eyes. 'I should dearly like to keep house for you, and take care of you always, Tom; but we are not rich enough for that.'

'We are not rich,' returned Tom, 'certainly; and we may be

much poorer. But we will not part if we can help it. No, no: we will make up our minds, Ruth, that unless we are so very unfortunate as to render me quite sure that you would be better off away from me than with me, we will battle it out together. I am certain we shall be happier if we can battle it out together. Don't you think we shall?'

'Think, Tom!'

'Oh, tut, tut!' interposed Tom, tenderly. 'You mustn't cry.'

'No, no; I won't, Tom. But you can't afford it, dear. You can't, indeed.'

'We don't know that,' said Tom. 'How are we to know that, yet awhile, and without trying? Lord bless my soul!' Tom's energy became quite grand. 'There is no knowing what may happen, if we try hard. And I am sure we can live contentedly upon a very little—if we can only get it.'

'Yes: that I am sure we can, Tom.'

'Why, then,' said Tom, 'we must try for it. My friend, John Westlock, is a capital fellow, and very shrewd and intelligent. I'll take his advice. We'll talk it over with him—both of us together. You'll like John very much, when you come to know him, I am certain. Don't cry, don't cry. *You* make a beef-steak pudding, indeed!' said Tom, giving her a gentle push. 'Why, you haven't boldness enough for a dumpling!'

'You *will* call it a pudding, Tom. Mind! I told you not!'

'I may as well call it that, till it proves to be something else,' said Tom. 'Oh, you are going to work in earnest, are you?'

Aye, aye! That she was. And in such pleasant earnest, moreover, that Tom's attention wandered from his writing every moment. First, she tripped down-stairs into the kitchen for the flour, then for the pie-board, then for the eggs, then for the butter, then for a jug of water, then for the rolling-pin, then for a pudding-basin, then for the pepper, then for the salt; making a separate journey for everything, and laughing every time she started off afresh. When all the materials were collected, she was horrified to find she had no apron on, and so ran *up*-stairs, by way of variety, to fetch it. She didn't put it on up-stairs, but came dancing down with it in her hand; and being one of those little women to whom an apron is a most becoming little vanity, it took an immense time to arrange; having to be carefully smoothed down beneath—Oh, heaven, what a wicked little stomacher! and to be gathered up into

little plaits by the strings before it could be tied, and to be
tapped, rebuked, and wheedled, at the pockets, before it would
set right, which at last it did, and when it did—but never
mind; this is a sober chronicle. And then, there were her cuffs
to be tucked up, for fear of flour; and she had a little ring to
pull off her finger, which wouldn't come off (foolish little
ring!); and during the whole of these preparations she looked
demurely every now and then at Tom, from under her dark
eye-lashes, as if they were all a part of the pudding and indispensable to its composition.

For the life and soul of him Tom could get no further in his
writing than, 'A respectable young man, aged thirty-five,' and
this, notwithstanding the show she made of being supernaturally quiet, and going about on tiptoe, lest she should
disturb him: which only served as an additional means of
distracting his attention, and keeping it upon her

'Tom,' she said at last, in high glee. 'Tom!'

'What now?' said Tom, repeating to himself, 'aged thirty-
five!'

'Will you look here a moment, please?'

As if he hadn't been looking all the time!

'I am going to begin, Tom. Don't you wonder why I butter
the inside of the basin?' said his busy little sister.

'Not more than you do, I dare say,' replied Tom, laughing.
'For I believe you don't know anything about it.'

'What an Infidel you are, Tom! How else do you think it
would turn out easily when it was done! For a civil-engineer
and land-surveyor not to know that! My goodness, Tom!'

It was wholly out of the question to try to write. Tom lined
out 'respectable young man, aged thirty-five;' and sat looking
on, pen in hand, with one of the most loving smiles imaginable.

Such a busy little woman as she was! So full of self-impor-
tance, and trying so hard not to smile, or seem uncertain about
anything! It was a perfect treat to Tom to see her with her
brows knit, and her rosy lips pursed up, kneading away at the
crust, rolling it out, cutting it up into strips, lining the basin
with it, shaving it off fine round the rim, chopping up the
steak into small pieces, raining down pepper and salt upon
them, packing them into the basin, pouring in cold water for
gravy, and never venturing to steal a look in his direction, lest
her gravity should be disturbed; until, at last, the basin being
quite full and only wanting the top crust, she clapped her

hands all covered with paste and flour, at Tom, and burst out heartily into such a charming little laugh of triumph, that the pudding need have had no other seasoning to commend it to the taste of any reasonable man on earth.

'Where's the pudding?' said Tom. For he was cutting his jokes, Tom was.

'Where!' she answered, holding it up with both hands. 'Look at it!'

'*That* a pudding!' said Tom.

'It will be, you stupid fellow, when it's covered in,' returned his sister. Tom still pretending to look incredulous, she gave him a tap on the head with the rolling-pin, and still laughing merrily, had returned to the composition of the top crust, when she started and turned very red. Tom started, too, for following her eyes, he saw John Westlock in the room.

'Why, my goodness, John! How did *you* come in?'

'I beg pardon,' said John—'your sister's pardon especially— but I met an old lady at the street door, who requested me to enter here; and as you didn't hear me knock, and the door was open, I made bold to do so. I hardly know,' said John, with a smile, 'why any of us should be disconcerted at my having accidentally intruded upon such an agreeable domestic occupation, so very agreeably and skilfully pursued; but I must confess that *I* am. Tom, will you kindly come to my relief?'

'Mr. John Westlock,' said Tom. 'My sister.'

'I hope that, as the sister of so old a friend,' said John, laughing, 'you will have the goodness to detach your first impressions of me from my unfortunate entrance.'

'My sister is not indisposed perhaps to say the same to you on her own behalf,' retorted Tom.

John said, of course, that this was quite unnecessary, for he had been transfixed in silent admiration; and he held out his hand to Miss Pinch; who couldn't take it, however, by reason of the flour and paste upon her own. This, which might seem calculated to increase the general confusion and render matters worse, had in reality the best effect in the world, for neither of them could help laughing; and so they both found themselves on easy terms immediately.

'I am delighted to see you,' said Tom. 'Sit down.'

'I can only think of sitting down on one condition,' returned his friend: 'and that is, that your sister goes on with the pudding, as if you were still alone.'

'That I am sure she will,' said Tom. 'On one other condition, and that is, that you stay and help us to eat it.'

Poor little Ruth was seized with a palpitation of the heart when Tom committed this appalling indiscretion, for she felt that if the dish turned out a failure, she never would be able to hold up her head before John Westlock again. Quite unconscious of her state of mind, John accepted the invitation with all imaginable heartiness; and after a little more pleasantry concerning this same pudding, and the tremendous expectations he made believe to entertain of it, she blushingly resumed her occupation, and he took a chair.

'I am here much earlier than I intended, Tom; but I will tell you what brings me, and I think I can answer for your being glad to hear it. Is that anything you wish to show me?'

'Oh dear no!' cried Tom, who had forgotten the blotted scrap of paper in his hand, until this inquiry brought it to his recollection. ' "A respectable young man, aged thirty-five"— The beginning of a description of myself. That's all.'

'I don't think you will have occasion to finish it, Tom. But how is it you never told me you had friends in London?'

Tom looked at his sister with all his might; and certainly his sister looked with all her might at him.

'Friends in London!' echoed Tom.

'Ah!' said Westlock, 'to be sure.'

'Have *you* any friends in London, Ruth, my dear?' asked Tom.

'No, Tom.'

'I am very happy to hear that *I* have,' said Tom, 'but it's news to me. I never knew it. They must be capital people to keep a secret, John.'

'You shall judge for yourself,' returned the other. 'Seriously, Tom, here is the plain state of the case. As I was sitting at breakfast this morning, there comes a knock at my door.'

'On which you cried out, very loud, "Come in!"' suggested Tom.

'So I did. And the person who knocked, not being a respectable young man, aged thirty-five, from the country, came in when he was invited, instead of standing gaping and staring about him on the landing. Well! When he came in, I found he was a stranger; a grave, business-like, sedate-looking, stranger. "Mr. Westlock?" said he. "That is my name," said I. "The favour of a few words with you?" said he. "Pray be seated, sir," said I.'

Here John stopped for an instant, to glance towards the table, where Tom's sister, listening attentively, was still busy with the basin, which by this time made a noble appearance. Then he resumed:

'The pudding having taken a chair, Tom—'

'What!' cried Tom.

'Having taken a chair.'

'You said a pudding.'

'No, no,' replied John, colouring rather; 'a chair. The idea of a stranger coming into my rooms at half-past eight o'clock in the morning, and taking a pudding! Having taken a chair, Tom, a chair—amazed me by opening the conversation thus: "I believe you are acquainted, sir, with Mr. Thomas Pinch?"'

'No!' cried Tom.

'His very words, I assure you. I told him I was. Did I know where you were at present residing? Yes. In London? Yes. He had casually heard, in a roundabout way, that you had left your situation with Mr. Pecksniff. Was that the fact? Yes, it was. Did you want another? Yes, you did.'

'Certainly,' said Tom, nodding his head.

'Just what I impressed upon him. You may rest assured that I set that point beyond the possibility of any mistake, and gave him distinctly to understand that he might make up his mind about it. Very well.'

' "Then," said he, "I think I can accommodate him."'

Tom's sister stopped short.

'Lord bless me!' cried Tom. 'Ruth, my dear, "think I can accommodate him."'

'Of course I begged him,' pursued John Westlock, glancing at Tom's sister, who was not less eager in her interest than Tom himself, 'to proceed, and said that I would undertake to see you immediately. He replied that he had very little to say, being a man of few words, but such as it was, it was to the purpose: and so, indeed, it turned out: for he immediately went on to tell me that a friend of his was in want of a kind of secretary and librarian; and that although the salary was small, being only a hundred pounds a year, with neither board nor lodging, still the duties were not heavy, and there the post was. Vacant, and ready for your acceptance.'

'Good gracious me!' cried Tom; 'a hundred pounds a year! My dear John! Ruth, my love! A hundred pounds a year!'

'But the strangest part of the story,' resumed John Westlock,

Mr. Nadgett breathes, as usual, an Atmosphere of Mystery
(p. 594)

laying his hand on Tom's wrist, to bespeak his attention, and repress his ecstasies for the moment: 'the strangest part of the story, Miss Pinch, is this. I don't know this man from Adam; neither does this man know Tom.'

'He can't,' said Tom, in great perplexity, 'if he's a Londoner. I don't know any one in London.'

'And on my observing,' John resumed, still keeping his hand upon Tom's wrist, 'that I had no doubt he would excuse the freedom I took in inquiring who directed him to me; how he came to know of the change which had taken place in my friend's position; and how he came to be acquainted with my friend's peculiar fitness for such an office as he had described; he drily said that he was not at liberty to enter into any explanations.'

'Not at liberty to enter into any explanations!' repeated Tom, drawing a long breath.

' "I must be perfectly aware," he said,' John added, ' "that to any person who had ever been in Mr. Pecksniff's neighbourhood, Mr. Thomas Pinch and his acquirements were as well known as the Church steeple, or the Blue Dragon." '

'The Blue Dragon!' repeated Tom, staring alternately at his friend and his sister.

'Aye; think of that! He spoke as familiarly of the Blue Dragon, I give you my word, as if he had been Mark Tapley. I opened my eyes, I can tell you, when he did so; but I could not fancy I had ever seen the man before, although he said with a smile, "You know the Blue Dragon, Mr. Westlock; you kept it up there, once or twice, yourself." Kept it up there! So I did. You remember, Tom?'

Tom nodded with great significance, and, falling into a state of deeper perplexity than before, observed that this was the most unaccountable and extraordinary circumstance he had ever heard of in his life.

'Unaccountable?' his friend repeated. 'I became afraid of the man. Though it was broad day, and bright sunshine, I was positively afraid of him. I declare I half suspected him to be a supernatural visitor, and not a mortal, until he took out a common-place description of pocket-book, and handed me this card.'

'Mr. Fips,' said Tom, reading it aloud. 'Austin Friars. Austin Friars sounds ghostly, John.'

'Fips don't, I think,' was John's reply. 'But there he lives,

Tom, and there he expects us to call this morning. And now you know as much of this strange incident as I do, upon my honour.'

Tom's face, between his exultation in the hundred pounds a year, and his wonder at this narration, was only to be equalled by the face of his sister, on which there sat the very best expression of blooming surprise that any painter could have wished to see. What the beef-steak pudding would have come to, if it had not been by this time finished, astrology itself could hardly determine.

'Tom,' said Ruth, after a little hesitation, 'perhaps Mr. Westlock, in his friendship for you, knows more of this than he chooses to tell.'

'No, indeed!' cried John, eagerly. 'It is not so, I assure you. I wish it were. I cannot take credit to myself, Miss Pinch, for any such thing. All that I know, or, so far as I can judge, am likely to know, I have told you.'

'Couldn't you know more, if you thought proper?' said Ruth, scraping the pie-board industriously.

'No,' retorted John. 'Indeed, no. It is very ungenerous in you to be so suspicious of me, when I repose implicit faith in you. I have unbounded confidence in the pudding, Miss Pinch.'

She laughed at this, but they soon got back into a serious vein, and discussed the subject with profound gravity. Whatever else was obscure in the business, it appeared to be quite plain that Tom was offered a salary of one hundred pounds a year; and this being the main point, the surrounding obscurity rather set it off than otherwise.

Tom, being in a great flutter, wished to start for Austin Friars instantly, but they waited nearly an hour, by John's advice, before they departed. Tom made himself as spruce as he could before leaving home, and when John Westlock, through the half-opened parlour door, had glimpses of that brave little sister brushing the collar of his coat in the passage, taking up loose stitches in his gloves, and hovering lightly about and about him, touching him up here and there in the height of her quaint, little, old-fashioned tidiness, he called to mind the fancy-portraits of her on the wall of the Pecksniffian work-room, and decided with uncommon ·indignation that they were gross libels, and not half pretty enough: though, as hath been mentioned in its place, the artists always made those

Mr. Pinch and Ruth unconscious of a Visitor
(*p. 603*)

sketches beautiful, and he had drawn at least a score of them with his own hands.

'Tom,' he said, as they were walking along, 'I begin to think you must be somebody's son.'

'I suppose I am,' Tom answered in his quiet way.

'But I mean somebody's of consequence.'

'Bless your heart,' replied Tom, 'my poor father was of no consequence, nor my mother either.'

'You remember them perfectly, then?'

'Remember them? oh dear yes. My poor mother was the last. She died when Ruth was a mere baby, and then we both became a charge upon the savings of that good old grandmother I used to tell you of. You remember! Oh! There's nothing romantic in our history, John.'

'Very well,' said John in quiet despair. 'Then there is no way of accounting for my visitor of this morning. So we'll not try, Tom.'

They did try, notwithstanding, and never left off trying until they got to Austin Friars, where, in a very dark passage on the first floor, oddly situated at the back of a house, across some leads, they found a little blear-eyed glass door up in one corner, with Mr. Fips painted on it in characters which were meant to be transparent. There was also a wicked old sideboard hiding in the gloom hard by, meditating designs upon the ribs of visitors; and an old mat, worn into lattice work, which, being useless as a mat (even if anybody could have seen it, which was impossible), had for many years directed its industry into another channel, and regularly tripped up every one of Mr. Fips's clients.

Mr. Fips, hearing a violent concussion between a human hat and his office door, was apprised, by the usual means of communication, that somebody had come to call upon him, and giving that somebody admission, observed that it was 'rather dark.'

'Dark indeed,' John whispered in Tom Pinch's ear. 'Not a bad place to dispose of a countryman in, I should think, Tom.'

Tom had been already turning over in his mind the possibility of their having been tempted into that region to furnish forth a pie; but the sight of Mr. Fips, who was small and spare, and looked peaceable, and wore black shorts and powder, dispelled his doubts.

'Walk in,' said Mr. Fips.

They walked in. And a mighty yellow-jaundiced little office Mr. Fips had of it: with a great, black, sprawling splash upon the floor in one corner, as if some old clerk had cut his throat there, years ago, and had let out ink instead of blood.

'I have brought my friend Mr. Pinch, sir,' said John West-lock.

'Be pleased to sit,' said Mr. Fips.

They occupied the two chairs, and Mr. Fips took the office stool, from the stuffing whereof he drew forth a piece of horse-hair of immense length, which he put into his mouth with a great appearance of appetite.

He looked at Tom Pinch curiously, but with an entire free-dom from any such expression as could be reasonably construed into an unusual display of interest. After a short silence, during which Mr. Fips was so perfectly unembarrassed as to render it manifest that he could have broken it sooner without hesita-tion, if he had felt inclined to do so, he asked if Mr. Westlock had made his offer fully known to Mr. Pinch.

John answered in the affirmative.

'And you think it worth your while, sir, do you?' Mr. Fips inquired of Tom.

'I think it a piece of great good fortune, sir,' said Tom. 'I am exceedingly obliged to you for the offer.'

'Not to me,' said Mr. Fips. 'I act upon instructions.'

'To your friend, sir, then,' said Tom. 'To the gentleman with whom I am to engage, and whose confidence I shall endeavour to deserve. When he knows me better, sir, I hope he will not lose his good opinion of me. He will find me punctual and vigilant, and anxious to do what is right. That I think I can answer for, and so,' looking towards him, 'can Mr. Westlock.'

'Most assuredly,' said John.

Mr. Fips appeared to have some little difficulty in resuming the conversation. To relieve himself, he took up the wafer-stamp, and began stamping capital F's all over his legs.

'The fact is,' said Mr. Fips, 'that my friend is not, at this present moment, in town.'

Tom's countenance fell; for he thought this equivalent to telling him that his appearance did not answer; and that Fips must look out for somebody else.

'When do you think he will be in town, sir?' he asked.

'I can't say; it's impossible to tell. I really have no idea.

But,' said Fips, taking off a very deep impression of the wafer-stamp upon the calf of his left leg, and looking steadily at Tom, 'I don't know that it's a matter of much consequence.'

Poor Tom inclined his head deferentially, but appeared to doubt that.

'I say,' repeated Mr. Fips, 'that I don't know it's a matter of much consequence. The business lies entirely between your-self and me, Mr. Pinch. With reference to your duties, I can set you going; and with reference to your salary, I can pay it. Weekly,' said Mr. Fips, putting down the wafer-stamp, and looking at John Westlock and Tom Pinch by turns, 'weekly; in this office; at any time between the hours of four and five o'clock in the afternoon.' As Mr. Fips said this, he made up his face as if he were going to whistle. But he didn't.

'You are very good,' said Tom, whose countenance was now suffused with pleasure: 'and nothing can be more satisfactory or straightforward. My attendance will be required—'

'From half-past nine to four o'clock or so, I should say,' interrupted Mr. Fips. 'About that.'

'I did not mean the hours of attendance,' retorted Tom, 'which are light and easy, I am sure; but the place.'

'Oh, the place! The place is in the Temple.'

Tom was delighted.

'Perhaps,' said Mr. Fips, 'you would like to see the place?'

'Oh, dear!' cried Tom. 'I shall only be too glad to consider myself engaged, if you will allow me; without any further reference to the place.'

'You may consider yourself engaged, by all means,' said Mr. Fips: 'you couldn't meet me at the Temple Gate in Fleet Street, in an hour from this time, I suppose, could you?'

Certainly Tom could.

'Good,' said Mr. Fips, rising. 'Then I will show you the place; and you can begin your attendance to-morrow morning. In an hour, therefore, I shall see you. You too, Mr. Westlock? Very good. Take care how you go. It's rather dark.'

With this remark, which seemed superfluous, he shut them out upon the staircase, and they groped their way into the street again.

The interview had done so little to remove the mystery in which Tom's new engagement was involved, and had done so much to thicken it, that neither could help smiling at the puzzled looks of the other. They agreed, however, that the introduction of Tom to his new office and office companions could hardly fail to throw a light upon the subject; and therefore postponed its further consideration until after the fulfilment of the appointment they had made with Mr. Fips.

After looking at John Westlock's chambers, and devoting a few spare minutes to the Boar's Head, they issued forth again to the place of meeting. The time agreed upon had not quite come; but Mr. Fips was already at the Temple Gate, and expressed his satisfaction at their punctuality.

He led the way through sundry lanes and courts, into one more quiet and more gloomy than the rest, and, singling out a certain house, ascended a common staircase: taking from his pocket, as he went, a bunch of rusty keys. Stopping before a door upon an upper story, which had nothing but a yellow smear of paint where custom would have placed the tenant's name, he began to beat the dust out of one of these keys, very deliberately, upon the great broad hand-rail of the balustrade.

'You had better have a little plug made,' he said, looking round at Tom, after blowing a shrill whistle into the barrel of the key. 'It's the only way of preventing them from getting stopped up. You'll find the lock go the better, too, I dare say, for a little oil.'

Tom thanked him; but was too much occupied with his own speculations, and John Westlock's looks, to be very talkative. In the meantime, Mr. Fips opened the door, which yielded to his hand very unwillingly, and with a horribly discordant sound. He took the key out, when he had done so, and gave it to Tom.

'Aye, aye!' said Mr. Fips. 'The dust lies rather thick here.'

Truly, it did. Mr. Fips might have gone so far as to say, very thick. It had accumulated everywhere; lay deep on everything; and in one part, where a ray of sun shone through a crevice in the shutter and struck upon the opposite wall, it went twirling round and round, like a gigantic squirrel-cage.

Dust was the only thing in the place that had any motion about it. When their conductor admitted the light freely, and lifting up the heavy window-sash, let in the summer air, he showed the mouldering furniture, discoloured wainscoting and ceiling, rusty stove, and ashy hearth, in all their inert neglect. Close to the door there stood a candlestick, with an extinguisher upon it: as if the last man who had been there had paused, after securing a retreat, to take a parting look at the dreariness he left behind, and then had shut out light and life together, and closed the place up like a tomb.

There were two rooms on that floor; and in the first or outer one a narrow staircase, leading to two more above. These last were fitted up as bed-chambers. Neither in them, nor in the rooms below, was any scarcity of convenient furniture observable, although the fittings were of a bygone fashion; but solitude and want of use seemed to have rendered it unfit for any purposes of comfort, and to have given it a grisly, haunted air.

Movables of every kind lay strewn about, without the least attempt at order, and were intermixed with boxes, hampers, and all sorts of lumber. On all the floors were piles of books, to the amount, perhaps, of some thousands of volumes: these, still in bales: those, wrapped in paper, as they had been purchased: others scattered singly or in heaps: not one upon the shelves which lined the walls. To these Mr. Fips called Tom's attention.

'Before anything else can be done, we must have them put in order, catalogued, and ranged upon the book-shelves, Mr. Pinch. That will do to begin with, I think, sir.'

Tom rubbed his hands in the pleasant anticipation of a task so congenial to his taste, and said:

'An occupation full of interest for me, I assure you. It will occupy me, perhaps, until Mr. ——'

'Until Mr. ——' repeated Fips; as much as to ask Tom what he was stopping for.

'I forgot that you had not mentioned the gentleman's name,' said Tom.

'Oh!' cried Mr. Fips, pulling on his glove, 'didn't I? No, by-the-bye, I don't think I did. Ah! I dare say he'll be here soon. You will get on very well together, I have no doubt. I wish you success, I am sure. You won't forget to shut the door? It'll lock of itself if you slam it. Half-past nine, you know. Let us say from half-past nine to four, or half-past four, or thereabouts; one day, perhaps, a little earlier, another day, perhaps, a little later, according as you feel disposed, and as you arrange your work. Mr. Fips, Austin Friars, of course you'll remember? And you won't forget to slam the door, if you please!'

He said all this in such a comfortable, easy manner, that Tom could only rub his hands, and nod his head, and smile in acquiescence, which he was still doing, when Mr. Fips walked coolly out.

'Why, he's gone!' cried Tom.

'And what's more, Tom,' said John Westlock, seating himself upon a pile of books, and looking up at his astonished friend, 'he is evidently not coming back again: so here you are, installed. Under rather singular circumstances, Tom!'

It was such an odd affair throughout, and Tom standing there among the books with his hat in one hand and the key in the other, looked so prodigiously confounded, that his friend could not help laughing heartily. Tom himself was tickled: no less by the hilarity of his friend than by the recollection of the sudden manner in which he had been brought to a stop, in the very height of his urbane conference with Mr. Fips; so by degrees Tom burst out laughing too; and each making the other laugh more, they fairly roared.

When they had had their laugh out, which did not happen very soon, for give John an inch that way and he was sure to take several ells, being a jovial, good-tempered fellow, they looked about them more closely, groping among the lumber for any stray means of enlightenment that might turn up. But no scrap or shred of information could they find. The books were marked with a variety of owners' names, having, no doubt, been bought at sales, and collected here and there at different times; but whether any one of these names belonged to Tom's employer, and, if so, which of them, they had no means whatever of determining. It occurred to John as a very bright thought to make inquiry at the steward's office, to whom the chambers belonged, or by whom they were held; but he came back no wiser than he went, the answer being, 'Mr. Fips, of Austin Friars.'

'After all, Tom, I begin to think it lies no deeper than this. Fips is an eccentric man; has some knowledge of Pecksniff; despises him, of course; has heard or seen enough of you to know that you are the man he wants; and engages you in his own whimsical manner.'

'But why in his own whimsical manner?' asked Tom.

'Oh! why does any man entertain his own whimsical taste? Why does Mr. Fips wear shorts and powder, and Mr. Fips's next-door neighbour boots and a wig?'

Tom, being in that state of mind in which any explanation is a great relief, adopted this last one (which indeed was quite as feasible as any other) readily, and said he had no doubt of it. Nor was his faith at all shaken by his having said exactly the same thing to each suggestion of his friend's in turn, and being perfectly ready to say it again if he had any new solution to propose.

As he had not, Tom drew down the window-sash, and folded the shutter; and they left the rooms. He closed the door heavily, as Mr. Fips had desired him; tried it, found it all safe, and put the key in his pocket.

They made a pretty wide circuit in going back to Islington, as they had time to spare, and Tom was never tired of looking about him. It was well he had John Westlock for his companion, for most people would have been weary of his perpetual stoppages at shop-windows, and his frequent dashes into the crowded carriage-way at the peril of his life, to get the better view of church steeples, and other public buildings. But John was charmed to see him so much interested, and every time Tom came back with a beaming face from among the wheels of carts and hackney-coaches, wholly unconscious of the personal congratulations addressed to him by the drivers, John seemed to like him better than before.

There was no flour on Ruth's hands when she received them in the triangular parlour, but there were pleasant smiles upon her face, and a crowd of welcomes shining out of every smile, and gleaming in her bright eyes. By-the-bye, how bright they were! Looking into them for but a moment, when you took her hand, you saw, in each, such a capital miniature of yourself, representing you as such a restless, flashing, eager, brilliant little fellow—

Ah! if you could only have kept them for your own miniature! But, wicked, roving, restless, too impartial eyes, it was enough for any one to stand before them, and straightway there he danced and sparkled quite as merrily as you!

The table was already spread for dinner; and though it was spread with nothing very choice in the way of glass or linen, and with green-handled knives, and very mountebanks of two-pronged forks, which seemed to be trying how far asunder they could possibly stretch their legs without converting themselves into double the number of iron toothpicks, it wanted neither damask, silver, gold, nor china: no, nor any other garniture at all. There it was: and, being there, nothing else would have done as well.

The success of that initiative dish: that first experiment of hers in cookery: was so entire, so unalloyed and perfect, that

John Westlock and Tom agreed she must have been studying the art in secret for a long time past; and urged her to make a full confession of the fact. They were exceedingly merry over this jest, and many smart things were said concerning it; but John was not as fair in his behaviour as might have been expected, for, after luring Tom Pinch on for a long time, he suddenly went over to the enemy, and swore to everything his sister said. However, as Tom observed the same night before going to bed, it was only in joke, and John had always been famous for being polite to ladies, even when he was quite a boy. Ruth said, 'Oh! indeed!' She didn't say anything else.

It is astonishing how much three people may find to talk about. They scarcely left off talking once. And it was not all lively chat which occupied them; for when Tom related how he had seen Mr. Pecksniff's daughters, and what a change had fallen on the younger, they were very serious.

John Westlock became quite absorbed in her fortunes; asking many questions of Tom Pinch about her marriage, inquiring whether her husband was the gentleman whom Tom had brought to dine with him at Salisbury; in what degree of relationship they stood towards each other, being different persons; and taking, in short, the greatest interest in the subject. Tom then went into it at full length; he told how Martin had gone abroad, and had not been heard of for a long time; how Dragon Mark had borne him company; how Mr. Pecksniff had got the poor old doting grandfather into his power; and how he basely sought the hand of Mary Graham. But not a word said Tom of what lay hidden in his heart; his heart, so deep, and true, and full of honour, and yet with so much room for every gentle and unselfish thought: not a word.

Tom, Tom! The man in all this world most confident in his sagacity and shrewdness; the man in all this world most proud of his distrust of other men, and having most to show in gold and silver as the gains belonging to his creed; the meekest favourer of that wise doctrine, Every man for himself, and God for us all (there being high wisdom in the thought that the Eternal Majesty of Heaven ever was, or can be, on the side of selfish lust and love!); shall never find, oh, never find, be sure of that, the time come home to him, when all his wisdom is an idiot's folly, weighed against a simple heart!

Well, well, Tom, it was simple too, though simple in a different way, to be so eager touching that same theatre, of which John said, when tea was done, he had the absolute command, so far as taking parties in without the payment of a sixpence was concerned; and simpler yet, perhaps, never to suspect that when he went in first, alone, he paid the money! Simple in thee, dear Tom, to laugh and cry so heartily at such a sorry show, so poorly shown; simple, to be so happy and loquacious trudging home with Ruth; simple, to be so surprised to find that merry present of a cookery-book awaiting her in the parlour next morning, with the beef-steak-pudding-leaf turned down and blotted out. There! Let the record stand! Thy quality of soul was simple, simple; quite contemptible, Tom Pinch!

CHAPTER XL

*The Pinches make a new acquaintance, and have fresh
occasion for surprise and wonder*

THERE was a ghostly air about these uninhabited chambers
in the Temple, and attending every circumstance of Tom's
employment there, which had a strange charm in it. Every
morning when he shut his door at Islington, he turned his face
towards an atmosphere of unaccountable fascination, as surely
as he turned it to the London smoke; and from that moment
it thickened round and round him all day long, until the time
arrived for going home again, and leaving it, like a motionless
cloud, behind.

It seemed to Tom, every morning, that he approached this
ghostly mist, and became enveloped in it, by the easiest succession of degrees imaginable. Passing from the roar and rattle
of the streets into the quiet court-yards of the Temple, was
the first preparation. Every echo of his footsteps sounded to
him like a sound from the old walls and pavements, wanting
language to relate the histories of the dim, dismal rooms; to
tell him what lost documents were decaying in forgotten
corners of the shut-up cellars, from whose lattices such mouldy
sighs came breathing forth as he went past; to whisper of dark
bins of rare old wine, bricked up in vaults among the old
foundations of the Halls; or mutter in a lower tone yet darker
legends of the cross-legged knights, whose marble effigies were
in the church. With the first planting of his foot upon the
staircase of his dusty office, all these mysteries increased; until,
ascending step by step, as Tom ascended, they attained their
full growth in the solitary labours of the day.

Every day brought one recurring, never-failing source of
speculation. This employer; would he come to-day, and what
would he be like? For Tom could not stop short at Mr. Fips;
he quite believed that Mr. Fips had spoken truly, when he said
he acted for another; and what manner of man that other was,
became a full-blown flower of wonder in the garden of Tom's
fancy, which never faded or got trodden down.

At one time, he conceived that Mr. Pecksniff, repenting of
his falsehood, might, by exertion of his influence with some
third person, have devised these means of giving him employ-

ment. He found this idea so insupportable after what had taken place between that good man and himself, that he confided it to John Westlock on the very same day; informing John that he would rather ply for hire as a porter, than fall so low in his own esteem as to accept the smallest obligation from the hands of Mr. Pecksniff. But John assured him that he (Tom Pinch) was far from doing justice to the character of Mr. Pecksniff yet, if he supposed that gentleman capable of performing a generous action; and that he might make his mind quite easy on that head until he saw the sun turn green and the moon black, and at the same time distinctly perceived with the naked eye, twelve first-rate comets careering round those planets. In which unusual state of things, he said (and not before), it might become not absolutely lunatic to suspect Mr. Pecksniff of anything so monstrous. In short he laughed the idea down completely; and Tom, abandoning it, was thrown upon his beam-ends again, for some other solution.

In the meantime Tom attended to his duties daily, and made considerable progress with the books: which were already reduced to some sort of order, and made a great appearance in his fairly-written catalogue. During his business hours, he indulged himself occasionally with snatches of reading; which were often, indeed, a necessary part of his pursuit; and as he usually made bold to carry one of these goblin volumes home at night (always bringing it back again next morning, in case his strange employer should appear and ask what had become of it), he led a happy, quiet, studious kind of life, after his own heart.

But though the books were never so interesting, and never so full of novelty to Tom, they could not so enchain him, in those mysterious chambers, as to render him unconscious, for a moment, of the lightest sound. Any footstep on the flags without set him listening attentively, and when it turned into that house, and came up, up, up, the stairs, he always thought with a beating heart, 'Now I am coming face to face with him at last!' But no footstep ever passed the floor immediately below: except his own.

This mystery and loneliness engendered fancies in Tom's mind, the folly of which his common sense could readily discover, but which his common sense was quite unable to keep away, notwithstanding; that quality being with most of us, in such a case, like the old French Police—quick at detection, but very weak as a preventive power. Misgivings, undefined, absurd, inexplicable, that there was some one hiding in the inner room—walking softly overhead, peeping in through the door-chink, doing something stealthy, anywhere where he was not—came over him a hundred times a day, making it pleasant to throw up the sash, and hold communication even with the sparrows who had built in the roof and water-spout, and were twittering about the windows all day long.

He sat with the outer door wide open, at all times, that he might hear the footsteps as they entered, and turned off into the chambers on the lower floor. He formed odd prepossessions too, regarding strangers in the streets; and would say within himself of such or such a man, who struck him as having any-thing uncommon in his dress or aspect, 'I shouldn't wonder, now, if that were he!' But it never was. And though he actually turned back and followed more than one of these suspected individuals, in a singular belief that they were going to the place he was then upon his way from, he never got any other satisfaction by it, than the satisfaction of knowing it was not the case.

Mr. Fips, of Austin Friars, rather deepened than illumined the obscurity of his position; for on the first occasion of Tom's waiting on him to receive his weekly pay, he said:

'Oh! by-the-bye, Mr. Pinch, you needn't mention it, if you please!'

Tom thought he was going to tell him a secret; so he said that he wouldn't on any account, and that Mr. Fips might entirely depend upon him. But as Mr. Fips said 'Very good,' in reply, and nothing more, Tom prompted him:

'Not on any account,' repeated Tom.

Mr. Fips repeated 'Very good.'

'You were going to say'—Tom hinted.

'Oh dear no!' cried Fips. 'Not at all.'—However, seeing Tom confused, he added, 'I mean that you needn't mention any particulars about your place of employment, to people generally. You'll find it better not.'

'I have not had the pleasure of seeing my employer yet, sir,' observed Tom, putting his week's salary in his pocket.

'Haven't you?' said Fips. 'No, I don't suppose you have though.'

'I should like to thank him, and to know that what I have done so far, is done to his satisfaction,' faltered Tom.

'Quite right,' said Mr. Fips, with a yawn. 'Highly creditable. Very proper.'

Tom hastily resolved to try him on another tack.

'I shall soon have finished with the books,' he said. 'I hope that will not terminate my engagement, sir, or render me useless?'

'Oh dear no!' retorted Fips. 'Plenty to do: plen-ty to do! Be careful how you go. It's rather dark.'

This was the very utmost extent of information Tom could ever get out of *him*. So, it was dark enough in all conscience: and if Mr. Fips expressed himself with a double meaning, he had good reason for doing so.

But now a circumstance occurred, which helped to divert Tom's thoughts from even this mystery, and to divide them between it and a new channel, which was a very Nile in itself.

The way it came about was this. Having always been an early riser, and having now no organ to engage him in sweet converse every morning, it was his habit to take a long walk before going to the Temple; and naturally inclining, as a stranger, towards those parts of the town which were conspicuous for the life and animation pervading them, he became a great frequenter of the market-places, bridges, quays, and especially the steam-boat wharves; for it was very lively and fresh to see the people hurrying away upon their many schemes of business or pleasure, and it made Tom glad to think that there was that much change and freedom in the monotonous routine of city lives.

In most of these morning excursions Ruth accompanied him. As their landlord was always up and away at his business (whatever that might be, no one seemed to know) at a very early hour, the habits of the people of the house in which they lodged corresponded with their own. Thus they had often finished their breakfast, and were out in the summer air, by seven o'clock. After a two hours' stroll they parted at some convenient point: Tom going to the Temple, and his sister returning home, as methodically as you please.

Many and many a pleasant stroll they had in Covent Garden Market: snuffing up the perfume of the fruits and flowers, wondering at the magnificence of the pine-apples and melons; catching glimpses down side avenues, of rows and rows of old women, seated on inverted baskets shelling peas; looking unutterable things at the fat bundles of asparagus with

which the dainty shops were fortified as with a breastwork;
and, at the herbalists' doors, gratefully inhaling scents as of
veal-stuffing yet uncooked, dreamily mixed up with capsicums,
brown-paper, seeds: even with hints of lusty snails and fine
young curly leeches. Many and many a pleasant stroll they
had among the poultry markets, where ducks and fowls, with
necks unnaturally long, lay stretched out in pairs, ready for
cooking; where there were speckled eggs in mossy baskets,
white country sausages beyond impeachment by surviving cat
or dog, or horse or donkey, new cheeses to any wild extent,
live birds in coops and cages, looking much too big to be
natural, in consequence of those receptacles being much too
little; rabbits, alive and dead, innumerable. Many a pleasant
stroll they had among the cool, refreshing, silvery fish-stalls,
with a kind of moonlight effect about their stock-in-trade,
excepting always for the ruddy lobsters. Many a pleasant stroll
among the waggon-loads of fragrant hay, beneath which dogs
and tired waggoners lay fast asleep, oblivious of the pieman
and the public-house. But never half so good a stroll as down
among the steam-boats on a bright morning.

There they lay, alongside of each other; hard and fast for
ever, to all appearance, but designing to get out somehow, and
quite confident of doing it; and in that faith shoals of passengers, and heaps of luggage, were proceeding hurriedly on
board. Little steam-boats dashed up and down the stream
incessantly. Tiers upon tiers of vessels, scores of masts, laby-
rinths of tackle, idle sails, splashing oars, gliding row-boats,
lumbering barges, sunken piles, with ugly lodgings for the
water-rat within their mud-discoloured nooks; church steeples,
warehouses, house-roofs, arches, bridges, men and women,
children, casks, cranes, boxes, horses, coaches, idlers, and
hard-labourers: there they were, all jumbled up together,
any summer morning, far beyond Tom's power of separation.

In the midst of all this turmoil, there was an incessant roar
from every packet's funnel, which quite expressed and carried
out the uppermost emotion of the scene. They all appeared
to be perspiring and bothering themselves, exactly as their
passengers did; they never left off fretting and chafing, in their
own hoarse manner, once; but were always panting out,
without any stops, 'Come along do make haste I'm very
nervous come along oh good gracious we shall never get there
how late you are do make haste I'm off directly come along!'

Even when they had left off, and had got safely out into the current, on the smallest provocation they began again: for the bravest packet of them all, being stopped by some entanglement in the river, would immediately begin to fume and pant afresh, 'Oh here's a stoppage what's the matter do go on there I'm in a hurry it's done on purpose did you ever oh my goodness *do* go on here!' and so, in a state of mind bordering on distraction, would be last seen drifting slowly through the mist into the summer light beyond, that made it red.

Tom's ship, however; or, at least, the packet-boat in which Tom and his sister took the greatest interest on one particular occasion; was not off yet, by any means; but was at the height of its disorder. The press of passengers was very great; another steam-boat lay on each side of her; the gangways were choked up; distracted women, obviously bound for Gravesend, but turning a deaf ear to all representations that this particular vessel was about to sail for Antwerp, persisted in secreting baskets of refreshments behind bulkheads and water-casks, and under seats; and very great confusion prevailed.

It was so amusing, that Tom, with Ruth upon his arm, stood looking down from the wharf, as nearly regardless as it was in the nature of flesh and blood to be, of an elderly lady behind him, who had brought a large umbrella with her, and didn't know what to do with it. This tremendous instrument had a hooked handle; and its vicinity was first made known to him by a painful pressure on the windpipe, consequent upon its having caught him round the throat. Soon after disengaging himself with perfect good humour, he had a sensation of the ferule in his back; immediately afterwards, of the hook entangling his ankles; then of the umbrella generally, wandering about his hat, and flapping at it like a great bird; and, lastly, of a poke or thrust below the ribs, which gave him such exceeding anguish, that he could not refrain from turning round to offer a mild remonstrance.

Upon his turning round, he found the owner of the umbrella struggling on tip-toe, with a countenance expressive of violent animosity, to look down upon the steam-boats; from which he inferred that she had attacked him, standing in the front row, by design, and as her natural enemy.

'What a very ill-natured person you must be!' said Tom.

The lady cried out fiercely, 'Where's the pelisse!' meaning the constabulary—and went on to say, shaking the handle of the umbrella at Tom, that but for them fellers never being in the way when they was wanted, she'd have given him in charge, she would.

'If they greased their whiskers less, and minded the duties which they're paid so heavy for, a little more,' she observed, 'no one needn't be drove mad by scrouding so!'

She had been grievously knocked about, no doubt, for her bonnet was bent into the shape of a cocked hat. Being a fat little woman, too, she was in a state of great exhaustion and intense heat. Instead of pursuing the altercation, therefore, Tom civilly inquired what boat she wanted to go on board of?

'I suppose,' returned the lady, 'as nobody but yourself can want to look at a steam package, without wanting to go a-boarding of it, can they! Booby!'

'Which one do you want to look at then?' said Tom. 'We'll make room for you if we can. Don't be so ill-tempered.'

'No blessed creetur as ever I was with in trying times,' returned the lady, somewhat softened, 'and they're a many in their numbers, ever brought it as a charge again myself that I was anythin' but mild and equal in my spirits. Never mind a-contradicting of me, if you seems to feel it does you good, ma'am, I often says, for well you know that Sairey may be trusted not to give it back again. But I will not denige that I am worrited and wexed this day, and with good reagion, Lord forbid!'

By this time, Mrs. Gamp (for it was no other than that experienced practitioner) had, with Tom's assistance, squeezed and worked herself into a small corner between Ruth and the rail; where, after breathing very hard for some little time, and performing a short series of dangerous evolutions with her umbrella, she managed to establish herself pretty comfortably.

'And which of all them smoking monsters is the Ankworks boat, I wonder. Goodness me!' cried Mrs. Gamp.

'What boat did you want?' asked Ruth.

'The Ankworks package,' Mrs. Gamp replied. 'I will not deceive you, my sweet. Why should I?'

'That is the Antwerp packet in the middle,' said Ruth.

'And I wish it was in Jonadge's belly, I do,' cried Mrs. Gamp; appearing to confound the prophet with the whale in this miraculous aspiration.

Ruth said nothing in reply; but, as Mrs. Gamp, laying her

chin against the cool iron of the rail, continued to look intently at the Antwerp boat, and every now and then to give a little groan, she inquired whether any child of hers was going abroad that morning? Or perhaps her husband, she said kindly.

'Which shows,' said Mrs. Gamp, casting up her eyes, 'what a little way you've travelled into this wale of life, my dear young creetur! As a good friend of mine has frequent made remark to me, which her name, my love, is Harris, Mrs. Harris through the square and up the steps a-turnin' round by the tobacker shop, "Oh, Sairey, Sairey, little do we know wot lays afore us!" "Mrs. Harris, ma'am," I says, "not much, it's true, but more than you suppoge. Our calciations, ma'am," I says, "respectin' wot the number of a family will be, comes most times within one, and oftener than you would suppoge, exact." "Sairey," says Mrs. Harris, in a awful way, "Tell me wot is my indiwidgle number." "No, Mrs. Harris," I says to her, "ex-cuge me, if you please. My own," I says, "has fallen out of three-pair backs, and had damp doorsteps settled on their lungs, and one was turned up smilin' in a bedstead, un-beknown. Therefore, ma'am," I says, "seek not to proticipate, but take 'em as they come and as they go." Mine,' said Mrs. Gamp, 'mine is all gone, my dear young chick. And as to husbands, there's a wooden leg gone likeways home to its account, which in its constancy of walkin' into wine vaults, and never comin' out again 'till fetched by force, was quite as weak as flesh, if not weaker.'

When she had delivered this oration, Mrs. Gamp leaned her chin upon the cool iron again; and looking intently at the Antwerp packet, shook her head and groaned.

'I wouldn't,' said Mrs. Gamp, 'I wouldn't be a man and have such a think upon my mind!—but nobody as owned the name of man, could do it!'

Tom and his sister glanced at each other; and Ruth, after a moment's hesitation, asked Mrs. Gamp what troubled her so much.

'My dear,' returned that lady, dropping her voice, 'you are single, ain't you?'

Ruth laughed, blushed, and said 'Yes.'

'Worse luck,' proceeded Mrs. Gamp, 'for all parties! But others is married, and in the marriage state; and there is a dear young creetur a-comin' down this mornin' to that very package, which is no more fit to trust herself to sea, than nothin' is!'

She paused here to look over the deck of the packet in question, and on the steps leading down to it, and on the gangways. Seeming to have thus assured herself that the object of her commiseration had not yet arrived, she raised her eyes gradually up to the top of the escape-pipe, and indignantly apostrophised the vessel:

'Oh, drat you!' said Mrs. Gamp, shaking her umbrella at it, 'you're a nice spluttering nisy monster for a delicate young creetur to go and be a passinger by; ain't you! *You* never do no harm in that way, do you? With your hammering, and roaring, and hissing, and lamp-iling, you brute! Them confugion steamers,' said Mrs. Gamp, shaking her umbrella again, 'has done more to throw us out of our reg'lar work and bring ewents on at times when nobody counted on 'em (especially them screeching railroad ones), than all the other frights that ever was took. I have heerd of one young man, a guard upon a railway, only three years opened—well does Mrs. Harris know him, which indeed he is her own relation by her sister's marriage with a master sawyer—as is godfather at this present time to six-and-twenty blessed little strangers, equally unexpected, and all on 'um named after the Ingeins as was the cause. Ugh!' said Mrs. Gamp, resuming her apostrophe, 'one might easy know you was a man's inwention, from your disregardlessness of the weakness of our naturs, so one might, you brute!'

It would not have been unnatural to suppose, from the first part of Mrs. Gamp's lamentations, that she was connected with the stage-coaching or post-horsing trade. She had no means of judging of the effect of her concluding remarks upon her young companion; for she interrupted herself at this point, and exclaimed:

'There she identically goes! Poor sweet young creetur, there she goes, like a lamb to the sacrifige! If there's any illness when that wessel gets to sea,' said Mrs. Gamp, prophetically, 'it's murder, and I'm the witness for the persecution.'

She was so very earnest on the subject, that Tom's sister (being as kind as Tom himself) could not help saying something to her in reply.

'Pray, which is the lady,' she inquired, 'in whom you are so much interested?'

'There!' groaned Mrs. Gamp. 'There she goes! A-crossin'' the little wooden bridge at this minute. She's a-slippin' on a bit of orange-peel!' tightly clutching her umbrella. 'What a turn it give me!'

'Do you mean the lady who is with that man wrapped up from head to foot in a large cloak, so that his face is almost hidden?'

'Well he may hide it!' Mrs. Gamp replied. 'He's good call to be ashamed of himself. Did you see him a-jerking of her wrist, then?'

'He seems to be hasty with her, indeed.'

'Now he's a-taking of her down into the close cabin!' said Mrs. Gamp, impatiently. 'What's the man about! The deuce is in him, I think. Why can't he leave her in the open air?'

He did not, whatever his reason was, but led her quickly down and disappeared himself, without loosening his cloak, or pausing on the crowded deck one moment longer than was necessary to clear their way to that part of the vessel.

Tom had not heard this little dialogue; for his attention had been engaged in an unexpected manner. A hand upon his sleeve had caused him to look round, just when Mrs. Gamp concluded her apostrophe to the steam-engine; and on his right arm, Ruth being on his left, he found their landlord: to his great surprise.

He was not so much surprised at the man's being there, as at his having got close to him so quietly and swiftly; for another person had been at his elbow one instant before; and he had not in the meantime been conscious of any change or pressure in the knot of people among whom he stood. He and Ruth had frequently remarked how noiselessly this landlord of theirs came into and went out of his own house; but Tom was not the less amazed to see him at his elbow now.

'I beg your pardon, Mr. Pinch,' he said in his ear. 'I am rather infirm, and out of breath, and my eyes are not very good. I am not as young as I was, sir. You don't see a gentleman in a large cloak down yonder, with a lady on his arm; a lady in a veil and a black shawl; do you?'

If *he* did not, it was curious that in speaking he should have singled out from all the crowd the very people whom he described: and should have glanced hastily from them to Tom, as if he were burning to direct his wandering eyes.

'A gentleman in a large cloak!' said Tom, 'and a lady in a black shawl! Let me see!'

'Yes, yes!' replied the other, with keen impatience. 'A gentleman muffled up from head to foot—strangely muffled up for such a morning as this—like an invalid, with his hand to his face at this minute, perhaps. No, no, no! not there,' he added, following Tom's gaze; 'the other way; in that direction; down yonder.' Again he indicated, but this time in his hurry, with his outstretched finger, the very spot on which the progress of these persons was checked at that moment.

'There are so many people, and so much motion, and so many objects,' said Tom, 'that I find it difficult to—no, I really don't see a gentleman in a large cloak, and a lady in a black shawl. There's a lady in a red shawl over there!'

'No, no, no!' cried his landlord, pointing eagerly again, 'not there. The other way: the other way. Look at the cabin steps. To the left. They must be near the cabin steps. Do you see the cabin steps? There's the bell ringing already! *Do* you see the steps?'

'Stay!' said Tom, 'you're right. Look! there they go now. Is that the gentleman you mean? Descending at this minute, with the folds of a great cloak trailing down after him?'

'The very man!' returned the other, not looking at what Tom pointed out, however, but at Tom's own face. 'Will you do me a kindness, sir, a great kindness? Will you put that letter in his hand? Only give him that! He expects it. I am charged to do it by my employers, but I am late in finding him, and, not being as young as I have been, should never be able to make my way on board and off the deck again in time. Will you pardon my boldness, and do me that great kindness?'

His hands shook, and his face bespoke the utmost interest and agitation, as he pressed the letter upon Tom, and pointed to its destination, like the Tempter in some grim old carving.

To hesitate in the performance of a good-natured or compassionate office was not in Tom's way. He took the letter; whispered Ruth to wait till he returned, which would be immediately; and ran down the steps with all the expedition he could make. There were so many people going down, so many others coming up, such heavy goods in course of transit to and fro, such a ringing of bells, blowing-off of steam, and shouting of men's voices, that he had much ado to force his way, or keep in mind to which boat he was going. But he reached the right one with good speed, and going down the cabin-stairs immediately, descried the object of his search standing at the upper end of the saloon, with his back towards him, reading some notice which was hung against the wall. As Tom advanced to give him the letter, he started, hearing footsteps, and turned round.

What was Tom's astonishment to find in him the man with whom he had had the conflict in the field—poor Mercy's husband. Jonas!

Tom understood him to say, what the devil did he want; but it was not easy to make out what he said; he spoke so indistinctly.

'I want nothing with you for myself,' said Tom; 'I was asked, a moment since, to give you this letter. You were pointed out to me, but I didn't know you in your strange dress. Take it!'

He did so, opened it, and read the writing on the inside. The contents were evidently very brief; not more perhaps than one line; but they struck upon him like a stone from a sling. He reeled back as he read.

His emotion was so different from any Tom had ever seen before, that he stopped involuntarily. Momentary as his state of indecision was, the bell ceased while he stood there, and a hoarse voice calling down the steps, inquired if there was any one to go ashore?

'Yes,' cried Jonas, 'I—I am coming. Give me time. Where's that woman! Come back; come back here.'

He threw open another door as he spoke, and dragged, rather than led, her forth. She was pale and frightened, and amazed to see her old acquaintance; but had no time to speak, for they were making a great stir above; and Jonas drew her rapidly towards the deck.

'Where are we going? What is the matter?'

'We are going back,' said Jonas. 'I have changed my mind. I can't go. Don't question me, or I shall be the death of you, or some one else. Stop there! Stop! We're for the shore. Do you hear? We're for the shore!'

He turned, even in the madness of his hurry, and scowling darkly back at Tom, shook his clenched hand at him. There are not many human faces capable of the expression with which he accompanied that gesture.

He dragged her up, and Tom followed them. Across the deck, over the side, along the crazy plank, and up the steps, he dragged her fiercely; not bestowing any look on her, but

gazing upwards all the while among the faces on the wharf.
Suddenly he turned again, and said to Tom with a tremendous
oath:

'Where is he?'

Before Tom, in his indignation and amazement, could
return an answer to a question he so little understood, a gentleman approached Tom behind, and saluted Jonas Chuzzlewit
by name. He was a gentleman of foreign appearance, with a
black moustache and whiskers; and addressed him with a
polite composure, strangely different from his own distracted
and desperate manner.

'Chuzzlewit, my good fellow!' said the gentleman, raising
his hat in compliment to Mrs. Chuzzlewit, 'I ask your pardon
twenty thousand times. I am most unwilling to interfere
between you and a domestic trip of this nature (always so very
charming and refreshing, I know, although I have not the
happiness to be a domestic man myself, which is the great
infelicity of my existence): but the bee-hive, my dear friend,
the bee-hive—will you introduce me?'

'This is Mr. Montague,' said Jonas, whom the words
appeared to choke.

'The most unhappy and most penitent of men, Mrs. Chuzzlewit,' pursued that gentleman, 'for having been the means of
spoiling this excursion; but as I tell my friend, the bee-hive,
the bee-hive. You projected a short little continental trip, my
dear friend, of course?'

Jonas maintained a dogged silence.

'May I die,' cried Montague, 'but I am shocked! Upon my
soul I am shocked. But that confounded bee-hive of ours in the
city must be paramount to every other consideration, when
there is honey to be made; and that is my best excuse. Here is
a very singular old female dropping curtseys on my right,' said
Montague, breaking off in his discourse, and looking at Mrs.
Gamp, 'who is not a friend of mine. Does anybody know
her?'

'Ah! Well they knows me, bless their precious hearts!' said
Mrs. Gamp, 'not forgettin' your own merry one, sir, and long
may it be so! Wishin' as every one' (she delivered this in the
form of a toast or sentiment) 'was as merry, and as handsome-
lookin', as a little bird has whispered me a certain gent is,
which I will not name for fear I give offence where none is doo!
My precious lady,' here she stopped short in her merriment,

for she had until now affected to be vastly entertained, 'you're too pale by half!'

'*You* are here too, are you?' muttered Jonas. 'Ecod, there are enough of you.'

'I hope, sir,' returned Mrs. Gamp, dropping an indignant curtsey, 'as no bones is broke by me and Mrs. Harris a-walkin' down upon a public wharf. Which was the very words she says to me (although they was the last I ever had to speak) was these: "Sairey," she says, "is it a public wharf?" "Mrs. Harris," I makes answer, "can you doubt it? You have know'd me now, ma'am, eight and thirty year; and did you ever know me go, or wish to go, where I was not made welcome, say the words." "No, Sairey," Mrs. Harris says, "contrairy quite." And well she knows it too. I am but a poor woman, but I've been sought arter, sir, though you may not think it. I've been knocked up at all hours of the night, and warned out by a many landlords, in consequence of being mistook for Fire. I goes out workin' for my bread, 'tis true, but I maintains my indepency, with your kind leave, and which I will till death. I has my feelins as a woman, sir, and I have been a mother likeways; but touch a pipkin as belongs to me, or make the least remarks on what I eats or drinks, and though you was the favouritest young for'ard hussy of a servant-gal as ever come into a house, either you leaves the place, or me. My earnins is not great, sir, but I will not be impoged upon. Bless the babe, and save the mother, is my mortar, sir; but I makes so free as add to that, Don't try no impogician with the Nuss, for she will not abear it!'

Mrs. Gamp concluded by drawing her shawl tightly over herself with both hands, and, as usual, referring to Mrs. Harris for full corroboration of these particulars. She had that peculiar trembling of the head which, in ladies of her excitable nature, may be taken as a sure indication of their breaking out again very shortly; when Jonas made a timely interposition.

'As you *are* here,' he said, 'you had better see to her, and take her home. I am otherwise engaged.' He said nothing more; but looked at Montague as if to give him notice that he was ready to attend him.

'I am sorry to take you away,' said Montague.

Jonas gave him a sinister look, which long lived in Tom's memory, and which he often recalled afterwards.

'I am, upon my life,' said Montague. 'Why did you make it necessary?'

With the same dark glance as before, Jonas replied, after a moment's silence:

'The necessity is none of my making. You have brought it about yourself.'

He said nothing more. He said even this as if he were bound, and in the other's power, but had a sullen and suppressed devil within him, which he could not quite resist. His very gait, as they walked away together, was like that of a fettered man; but, striving to work out at his clenched hands, knitted brows, and fast-set lips, was the same imprisoned devil still.

They got into a handsome cabriolet which was waiting for them, and drove away.

The whole of this extraordinary scene had passed so rapidly, and the tumult which prevailed around was so unconscious of any impression from it, that, although Tom had been one of the chief actors, it was like a dream. No one had noticed him after they had left the packet. He had stood behind Jonas, and so near him, that he could not help hearing all that passed. He had stood there, with his sister on his arm, expecting and hoping to have an opportunity of explaining his strange share in this yet stranger business. But Jonas had not raised his eyes from the ground; no one else had even looked towards him; and before he could resolve on any course of action, they were all gone.

He gazed round for his landlord. But he had done that more than once already, and no such man was to be seen. He was still pursuing this search with his eyes, when he saw a hand beckoning to him from a hackney-coach; and hurrying towards it, found it was Merry's. She addressed him hurriedly, but bent out of the window, that she might not be overheard by her companion, Mrs. Gamp.

'What is it?' she said, 'Good Heaven, what is it? Why did he tell me last night to prepare for a long journey, and why have you brought us back like criminals? Dear Mr. Pinch!' she clasped her hands distractedly, 'be merciful to us. Whatever this dreadful secret is, be merciful, and God will bless you!'

'If any power of mercy lay with me,' cried Tom, 'trust me, you shouldn't ask in vain. But I am far more ignorant and weak than you.'

She withdrew into the coach again, and he saw the hand waving towards him for a moment; but whether in reproach-fulness or incredulity, or misery, or grief, or sad adieu, or what else, he could not, being so hurried, understand. *She* was gone now; and Ruth and he were left to walk away, and wonder.

Had Mr. Nadgett appointed the man who never came, to meet him upon London Bridge that morning? He was certainly looking over the parapet, and down upon the steam-boat-wharf at that moment. It could not have been for pleasure; he never took pleasure. No. He must have had some business there.

CHAPTER XLI

Mr. Jonas and his friend, arriving at a pleasant understanding,
set forth upon an enterprise

THE office of the Anglo-Bengalee Disinterested Loan and
Life Assurance Company being near at hand, and Mr.
Montague driving Jonas straight there, they had very little
way to go. But the journey might have been one of several
hours' duration, without provoking a remark from either: for
it was clear that Jonas did not mean to break the silence which
prevailed between them, and that it was not, as yet, his dear
friend's cue to tempt him into conversation.

He had thrown aside his cloak, as having now no motive for
concealment, and with that garment huddled on his knees, sat
as far removed from his companion as the limited space in such
a carriage would allow. There was a striking difference in his
manner, compared with what it had been, within a few minutes,
when Tom encountered him so unexpectedly on board the
packet, or when the ugly change had fallen on him in Mr.
Montague's dressing-room. He had the aspect of a man found
out and held at bay; of being baffled, hunted, and beset; but
there was now a dawning and increasing purpose in his face,
which changed it very much. It was gloomy, distrustful,
lowering; pale with anger and defeat; it still was humbled,
abject, cowardly, and mean; but, let the conflict go on as it
would, there was one strong purpose wrestling with every
emotion of his mind, and casting the whole series down as they
arose.

Not prepossessing in appearance at the best of times, it may
be readily supposed that he was not so now. He had left deep
marks of his front teeth in his nether lip; and those tokens of
the agitation he had lately undergone improved his looks as
little as the heavy corrugations in his forehead. But he was self-
possessed now; unnaturally self-possessed, indeed, as men quite
otherwise than brave are known to be in desperate extremities;
and when the carriage stopped, he waited for no invitation,
but leapt hardily out, and went up-stairs.

The chairman followed him; and closing the board-room
door as soon as they had entered, threw himself upon a sofa.

Jonas stood before the window, looking down into the street; and leaned against the sash, resting his head upon his arms.

'This is not handsome, Chuzzlewit!' said Montague at length. 'Not handsome, upon my soul!'

'What would you have me do?' he answered, looking round abruptly; 'what do you expect?'

'Confidence, my good fellow. Some confidence!' said Montague, in an injured tone.

'Ecod! You show great confidence in me,' retorted Jonas. 'Don't you?'

'Do I not?' said his companion, raising his head, and looking at him, but he had turned again. 'Do I not? Have I not confided to you the easy schemes I have formed for our advantage; *our* advantage, mind; not mine alone; and what is my return? Attempted flight!'

'How do you know that? Who said I meant to fly?'

'Who said? Come, come. A foreign boat, my friend, an early hour, a figure wrapped up for disguise! Who said? If you didn't mean to jilt me, why were you there? If you didn't mean to jilt me, why did you come back?'

'I came back,' said Jonas, 'to avoid disturbance.'

'You were wise,' rejoined his friend.

Jonas stood quite silent; still looking down into the street, and resting his head upon his arms.

'Now, Chuzzlewit,' said Montague, 'notwithstanding what has passed I will be plain with you. Are you attending to me there? I only see your back.'

'*I* hear you. Go on!'

'I say that notwithstanding what has passed, I will be plain with you.'

'You said that before. And I have told you once I heard you say it. Go on.'

'You are a little chafed, but I can make allowance for that, and am, fortunately, myself in the very best of tempers. Now, let us see how circumstances stand. A day or two ago, I mentioned to you, my dear fellow, that I thought I had discovered——'

'Will you hold your tongue?' said Jonas, looking fiercely round, and glancing at the door.

'Well, well!' said Montague. 'Judicious! Quite correct! My discoveries being published, would be like many other men's discoveries in this honest world; of no further use to me.

You see, Chuzzlewit, how ingenuous and frank I am in showing you the weakness of my own position! To return. I make,
or think I make, a certain discovery, which I take an early
opportunity of mentioning in your ear, in that spirit of confidence which I really hoped did prevail between us, and was
reciprocated by you. Perhaps there is something in it; perhaps
there is nothing. I have my knowledge and opinion on the
subject. You have yours. We will not discuss the question. But,
my good fellow, you have been weak; what I wish to point out
to you is, that you have been weak. I may desire to turn this
little incident to my account (indeed, I do—I'll not deny it),
but my account does not lie in probing it, or using it against
you.'

'What do you call using it against me?' asked Jonas, who
had not yet changed his attitude.

'Oh!' said Montague, with a laugh. 'We'll not enter into
that.'

'Using it to make a beggar of me. Is that the use you mean?'

'No.'

'Ecod,' muttered Jonas, bitterly. 'That's the use in which
your account *does* lie. You speak the truth there.'

'I wish you to venture (it's a very safe venture) a little more
with us, certainly, and to keep quiet,' said Montague. 'You
promised me you would; and you must. I say it plainly,
Chuzzlewit, you must. Reason the matter. If you don't, my
secret is worthless to me; and being so, it may as well become
the public property as mine: better, for I shall gain some
credit, bringing it to light. I want you, besides, to act as a
decoy in a case I have already told you of. You don't mind
that, I know. You care nothing for the man (you care nothing
for any man; you are too sharp; so am I, I hope); and could
bear any loss of his with pious fortitude. Ha, ha, ha! You have
tried to escape from the first consequence. You cannot escape
it, I assure you. I have shown you that to-day. Now, I am not
a moral man, you know. I am not the least in the world
affected by anything you may have done; by any little indiscretion you may have committed; but I wish to profit by it if
I can; and to a man of your intelligence I make that free confession. I am not at all singular in that infirmity. Everybody
profits by the indiscretion of his neighbour; and the people in
the best repute, the most. Why do you give me this trouble?
It must come to a friendly agreement, or an unfriendly crash.

It must. If the former, you are very little hurt. If the latter—well! you know best what is likely to happen then.'

Jonas left the window, and walked up close to him. He did not look him in the face; it was not his habit to do that; but he kept his eyes towards him—on his breast, or thereabouts—and was at great pains to speak slowly and distinctly in reply. Just as a man in a state of conscious drunkenness might be.

'Lying is of no use now,' he said. 'I *did* think of getting away this morning, and making better terms with you from a distance.'

'To be sure! To be sure!' replied Montague. 'Nothing more natural. I foresaw that, and provided against it. But I am afraid I am interrupting you.'

'How the devil,' pursued Jonas, with a still greater effort, 'you made choice of your messenger, and where you found him, I'll not ask you. I owed him one good turn before to-day. If you are so careless of men in general, as you said you were just now, you are quite indifferent to what becomes of such a crop-tailed cur as that, and will leave me to settle my account with him in my own manner.'

If he had raised his eyes to his companion's face, he would have seen that Montague was evidently unable to comprehend his meaning. But continuing to stand before him, with his furtive gaze directed as before, and pausing here only to moisten his dry lips with his tongue, the fact was lost upon him. It might have struck a close observer that this fixed and steady glance of Jonas's was a part of the alteration which had taken place in his demeanour. He kept it rivetted on one spot, with which his thoughts had manifestly nothing to do; like as a juggler walking on a cord or wire to any dangerous end, holds some object in his sight to steady him, and never wanders from it, lest he trip.

Montague was quick in his rejoinder, though he made it at a venture. There was no difference of opinion between him and his friend on *that* point. Not the least.

'Your great discovery,' Jonas proceeded, with a savage sneer that got the better of him for the moment, 'may be true, and may be false. Whichever it is, I dare say I'm no worse than other men.'

'Not a bit,' said Tigg. 'Not a bit. We're all alike—or nearly so.'

'I want to know this,' Jonas went on to say; 'is it your own? You'll not wonder at my asking the question.'

'My own!' repeated Montague.

'Aye!' returned the other, gruffly. 'Is it known to anybody else? Come! Don't waver about that.'

'No!' said Montague, without the smallest hesitation. 'What would it be worth, do you think, unless I had the keeping of it?'

Now, for the first time, Jonas looked at him. After a pause, he put out his hand, and said, with a laugh:

'Come! make things easy to me, and I'm yours. I don't know that I may not be better off here, after all, than if I had gone away this morning. But here I am, and here I'll stay now. Take your oath!'

He cleared his throat, for he was speaking hoarsely, and said in a lighter tone:

'Shall I go to Pecksniff? When? Say when!'

'Immediately!' cried Montague. 'He cannot be enticed too soon.'

'Ecod!' cried Jonas, with a wild laugh. 'There's some fun in catching that old hypocrite. I hate him. Shall I go to-night?'

'Aye! This,' said Montague, ecstatically, 'is like business! We understand each other now! To-night, my good fellow, by all means.'

'Come with me,' cried Jonas. 'We must make a dash: go down in state, and carry documents, for he's a deep file to deal with, and must be drawn on with an artful hand, or he'll not follow. I know him. As I can't take your lodgings or your dinners down, I must take you. Will you come to-night?'

His friend appeared to hesitate; and neither to have anticipated this proposal, nor to relish it very much.

'We can concert our plans upon the road,' said Jonas. 'We must not go direct to him, but cross over from some other place, and turn out of our way to see him. I may not want to introduce you, but I must have you on the spot. I know the man, I tell you.'

'But what if the man knows me?' said Montague, shrugging his shoulders.

'He know!' cried Jonas. 'Don't you run that risk with fifty men a day! Would your father know you? Did I know you? Ecod! you were another figure when I saw you first. Ha, ha, ha! I see the rents and patches now! No false hair then, no black dye! You were another sort of joker in those days, you were! You even spoke different then. You've acted the gentleman so seriously since, that you've taken in yourself. If he should know you, what does it matter? Such a change is a proof of your success. You know that, or you would not have made yourself known to me. Will you come?'

'My good fellow,' said Montague, still hesitating, 'I can trust you alone.'

'Trust me! Ecod, you may trust me now, far enough. I'll try to go away no more—no more!' He stopped, and added in a more sober tone, 'I can't get on without you. Will you come?'

'I will,' said Montague, 'if that's your opinion.' And they shook hands upon it.

The boisterous manner which Jonas had exhibited during the latter part of this conversation, and which had gone on rapidly increasing with almost every word he had spoken; from the time when he looked his honourable friend in the face until now; did not now subside, but, remaining at its height, abided by him. Most unusual with him at any period; most inconsistent with his temper and constitution; especially unnatural it would appear in one so darkly circumstanced; it abided by him. It was not like the effect of wine, or any ardent drink, for he was perfectly coherent. It even made him proof against the usual influence of such means of excitement; for, although he drank deeply several times that day, with no reserve or caution, he remained exactly the same man, and his spirits neither rose nor fell in the least observable degree.

Deciding, after some discussion, to travel at night, in order that the day's business might not be broken in upon, they took counsel together in reference to the means. Mr. Montague being of opinion that four horses were advisable, at all events for the first stage, as throwing a great deal of dust into people's eyes, in more senses than one, a travelling chariot and four lay under orders for nine o'clock. Jonas did not go home: observing, that his being obliged to leave town on business in so great a hurry, would be a good excuse for having turned back so unexpectedly in the morning. So he wrote a note for his portmanteau, and sent it by a messenger, who duly brought his luggage back, with a short note from that other piece of luggage, his wife, expressive of her wish to be allowed to come and see him for a moment. To this request he sent for answer, 'she had better;' and one such threatening affirmative being sufficient, in defiance of the English grammar, to express a negative, she kept away.

Mr. Montague being much engaged in the course of the day,

Jonas bestowed his spirits chiefly on the doctor, with whom he lunched in the medical officer's own room. On his way thither, encountering Mr. Nadgett in the outer room, he bantered that stealthy gentleman on always appearing anxious to avoid him, and inquired if he were afraid of him. Mr. Nadgett slyly answered, 'No, but he believed it must be his way, as he had been charged with much the same kind of thing before.'

Mr. Montague was listening to, or, to speak with greater elegance, he overheard, this dialogue. As soon as Jonas was gone he beckoned Nadgett to him with the feather of his pen, and whispered in his ear,

'Who gave him my letter this morning?'

'My lodger, sir,' said Nadgett, behind the palm of his hand.

'How came that about?'

'I found him on the wharf, sir. Being so much hurried, and you not arrived, it was necessary to do something. It fortunately occurred to me, that if I gave it him myself I could be of no further use. I should have been blown upon immediately.'

'Mr. Nadgett, you are a jewel,' said Montague, patting him on the back. 'What's your lodger's name?'

'Pinch, sir. Thomas Pinch.'

Montague reflected for a little while, and then asked:

'From the country, do you know?'

'From Wiltshire, sir, he told me.'

They parted without another word. To see Mr Nadgett's bow when Montague and he next met, and to see Mr. Montague acknowledge it, anybody might have undertaken to swear that they had never spoken to each other confidentially in all their lives.

In the meanwhile, Mr. Jonas and the doctor made themselves very comfortable up-stairs, over a bottle of the old Madeira and some sandwiches; for the doctor having been already invited to dine below, at six o'clock, preferred a light repast for lunch. It was advisable, he said, in two points of view: First, as being healthy in itself. Secondly, as being the better preparation for dinner.

'And you are bound for all our sakes to take particular care of your digestion, Mr. Chuzzlewit, my dear sir,' said the doctor, smacking his lips after a glass of wine; 'for depend upon it, it is worth preserving. It must be in admirable condition, sir; perfect chronometer-work. Otherwise your spirits could not be so remarkable. Your bosom's lord sits lightly on its throne,

Mysterious Installation of Mr. Pinch
(p. 614)

Mr. Chuzzlewit, as what's-his-name says in the play. I wish he said it in a play which did anything like common justice to our profession, by-the-bye. There is an apothecary in that drama, sir, which is a low thing; vulgar, sir; out of nature altogether.'

Mr. Jobling pulled out his shirt-frill of fine linen, as though he would have said, 'This is what I call nature in a medical man, sir;' and looked at Jonas for an observation.

Jonas not being in a condition to pursue the subject, took up a case of lancets that was lying on the table, and opened it.

'Ah!' said the doctor, leaning back in his chair, 'I always take 'em out of my pocket before I eat. My pockets are rather tight. Ha, ha, ha!'

Jonas had opened one of the shining little instruments; and was scrutinising it with a look as sharp and eager as its own bright edge.

'Good steel, doctor. Good steel. Eh?'

'Ye-es,' replied the doctor, with the faltering modesty of ownership. 'One might open a vein pretty dexterously with that, Mr. Chuzzlewit.'

'It has opened a good many in its time, I suppose?' said Jonas, looking at it with a growing interest.

'Not a few, my dear sir, not a few. It has been engaged in a —in a pretty good practice, I believe I may say,' replied the doctor, coughing as if the matter-of-fact were so very dry and literal that he couldn't help it. 'In a pretty good practice,' repeated the doctor, putting another glass of wine to his lips.

'Now, could you cut a man's throat with such a thing as this?' demanded Jonas.

'Oh certainly, certainly, if you took him in the right place,' returned the doctor. 'It all depends upon that.'

'Where you have your hand now, hey?' cried Jonas, bending forward to look at it.

'Yes,' said the doctor; 'that's the jugular.'

Jonas, in his vivacity, made a sudden sawing in the air, so close behind the doctor's jugular that he turned quite red. Then Jonas (in the same strange spirit of vivacity) burst into a loud discordant laugh.

'No, no,' said the doctor, shaking his head: 'edge-tools, edge-tools; never play with 'em. A very remarkable instance of the skilful use of edge-tools, by the way, occurs to me at this moment. It was a case of murder. I am afraid it was a case of murder, committed by a member of our profession; it was so artistically done.'

'Aye!' said Jonas. 'How was that?'

'Why, sir,' returned Jobling, 'the thing lies in a nutshell. A certain gentleman was found, one morning, in an obscure street, lying in an angle of a doorway—I should rather say, leaning, in an upright position, in the angle of a doorway, and supported consequently *by* the doorway. Upon his waistcoat there was one solitary drop of blood. He was dead and cold; and had been murdered, sir.'

'Only one drop of blood!' said Jonas.

'Sir, that man,' replied the doctor, 'had been stabbed to the heart. Had been stabbed to the heart with such dexterity, sir, that he had died instantly, and had bled internally. It was supposed that a medical friend of his (to whom suspicion attached) had engaged him in conversation on some pretence; had taken him, very likely, by the button in a conversational manner; had examined his ground at leisure with his other hand; had marked the exact spot; drawn out the instrument, whatever it was, when he was quite prepared; and——'

'And done the trick,' suggested Jonas.

'Exactly so,' replied the doctor. 'It was quite an operation in its way, and very neat. The medical friend never turned up; and, as I tell you, he had the credit of it. Whether he did it or not I can't say. But, having had the honour to be called in with two or three of my professional brethren on the occasion, and having assisted to make a careful examination of the wound, I have no hesitation in saying that it would have reflected credit on any medical man; and that in an unprofessional person it could not but be considered, either as an extraordinary work of art, or the result of a still more extraordinary, happy, and favourable conjunction of circumstances.'

His hearer was so much interested in this case, that the doctor went on to elucidate it with the assistance of his own finger and thumb and waistcoat; and at Jonas's request, he took the further trouble of going into a corner of the room, and alternately representing the murdered man and the murderer; which he did with great effect. The bottle being emptied and the story done, Jonas was in precisely the same boisterous and unusual state as when they had sat down. If, as Jobling theorised, his good digestion were the cause, he must have been a very ostrich.

At dinner it was just the same; and after dinner too; though wine was drunk in abundance, and various rich meats eaten. At nine o'clock it was still the same. There being a lamp in the carriage, he swore they would take a pack of cards, and a bottle of wine: and with these things under his cloak, went down to the door.

'Out of the way, Tom Thumb, and get to bed!'

This was the salutation he bestowed on Mr. Bailey, who, booted and wrapped up, stood at the carriage-door to help him in.

'To bed, sir! I'm a-going, too,' said Bailey.

He alighted quickly, and walked back into the hall, where Montague was lighting a cigar: conducting Mr. Bailey with him, by the collar.

'You are not a-going to take this monkey of a boy, are you?'

'Yes,' said Montague.

He gave the boy a shake, and threw him roughly aside. There was more of his familiar self in the action, than in any-thing he had done that day; but he broke out laughing im-mediately afterwards, and making a thrust at the doctor with his hand, in imitation of his representation of the medical friend, went out to the carriage again, and took his seat. His companion followed immediately. Mr. Bailey climbed into the rumble.

'It will be a stormy night!' exclaimed the doctor, as they started.

CHAPTER XLII

Continuation of the enterprise of Mr. Jonas and his friend

THE Doctor's prognostication in reference to the weather was speedily verified. Although the weather was not a patient of his, and no third party had required him to give an opinion on the case, the quick fulfilment of his prophecy may be taken as an instance of his professional tact; for, unless the threatening aspect of the night had been perfectly plain and unmistakable, Mr. Jobling would never have compromised his reputation by delivering any sentiments on the subject. He used this principle in Medicine with too much success to be unmindful of it in his commonest transactions.

It was one of those hot, silent nights, when people sit at windows listening for the thunder which they know will shortly break; when they recall dismal tales of hurricanes and earthquakes; and of lonely travellers on open plains, and lonely ships at sea, struck by lightning. Lightning flashed and quivered on the black horizon even now; and hollow murmurings were in the wind, as though it had been blowing where the thunder rolled, and still was charged with its exhausted echoes. But the storm, though gathering swiftly, had not yet come up; and the prevailing stillness was the more solemn, from the dull intelligence that seemed to hover in the air, of noise and conflict afar off.

It was very dark; but in the murky sky there were masses of cloud which shone with a lurid light, like monstrous heaps of copper that had been heated in a furnace, and were growing cold. These had been advancing steadily and slowly, but they were now motionless, or nearly so. As the carriage clattered round the corners of the streets, it passed at every one a knot of persons who had come there—many from their houses close at hand, without hats—to look up at that quarter of the sky. And now a very few large drops of rain began to fall, and thunder rumbled in the distance.

Jonas sat in a corner of the carriage with his bottle resting on his knee, and gripped as tightly in his hand as if he would have ground its neck to powder if he could. Instinctively attracted by the night, he had laid aside the pack of cards upon the cushion: and with the same involuntary impulse, so intelligible to both of them as not to occasion a remark on either side, his companion had extinguished the lamp. The front glasses were down; and they sat looking silently out upon the gloomy scene before them.

They were clear of London, or as clear of it as travellers can be whose way lies on the Western Road, within a stage of that enormous city. Occasionally they encountered a foot-passenger, hurrying to the nearest place of shelter; or some unwieldy cart proceeding onward at a heavy trot, with the same end in view. Little clusters of such vehicles were gathered round the stable-yard or baiting-place of every wayside tavern; while their drivers watched the weather from the doors and open windows, or made merry within. Everywhere the people were disposed to bear each other company rather than sit alone; so that groups of watchful faces seemed to be looking out upon the night *and them* from almost every house they passed.

It may appear strange that this should have disturbed Jonas, or rendered him uneasy: but it did. After muttering to himself, and often changing his position, he drew up the blind on his side of the carriage, and turned his shoulder sulkily towards it. But he neither looked at his companion, nor broke the silence which prevailed between them, and which had fallen so suddenly upon himself, by addressing a word to him.

The thunder rolled, the lightning flashed; the rain poured down like Heaven's wrath. Surrounded at one moment by intolerable light, and at the next by pitchy darkness, they still pressed forward on their journey. Even when they arrived at the end of the stage, and might have tarried, they did not; but ordered horses out immediately. Nor had this any reference to some five minutes' lull, which at that time seemed to promise a cessation of the storm. They held their course as if they were impelled and driven by its fury. Although they had not ex-changed a dozen words, and might have tarried very well, they seemed to feel, by joint consent, that onward they must go.

Louder and louder the deep thunder rolled, as through the myriad halls of some vast temple in the sky; fiercer and brighter became the lightning; more and more heavily the rain poured down. The horses (they were travelling now with a single pair) plunged and started from the rills of quivering fire that seemed to wind along the ground before them; but there these two men sat, and forward they went as if they were led on by an invisible attraction.

The eye, partaking of the quickness of the flashing light, saw in its every gleam a multitude of objects which it could not see at steady noon in fifty times that period. Bells in steeples, with the rope and wheel that moved them; ragged nests of birds in cornices and nooks; faces full of consternation in the tilted waggons that came tearing past: their frightened teams ringing out a warning which the thunder drowned; harrows and ploughs left out in fields; miles upon miles of hedge-divided country, with the distant fringe of trees as obvious as the scarecrow in the beanfield close at hand; in a trembling, vivid, flickering instant, everything was clear and plain: then came a flush of red into the yellow light; a change to blue; a brightness so intense that there was nothing else but light; and then the deepest and profoundest darkness.

The lightning being very crooked and very dazzling may have presented or assisted a curious optical illusion, which suddenly rose before the startled eyes of Montague in the carriage, and as rapidly disappeared. He thought he saw Jonas with his hand lifted, and the bottle clenched in it like a hammer, making as if he would aim a blow at his head. At the same time he observed (or so believed) an expression in his face: a combination of the unnatural excitement he had shown all day, with a wild hatred and fear: which might have rendered a wolf a less terrible companion.

He uttered an involuntary exclamation, and called to the driver, who brought his horses to a stop with all speed.

It could hardly have been as he supposed, for although he had not taken his eyes off his companion, and had not seen him move, he sat reclining in his corner as before.

'What's the matter?' said Jonas. 'Is that your general way of waking out of your sleep?'

'I could swear,' returned the other, 'that I have not closed my eyes!'

'When you have sworn it,' said Jonas, composedly, 'we had better go on again, if you have only stopped for that.'

He uncorked the bottle with the help of his teeth; and putting it to his lips, took a long draught.

'I wish we had never started on this journey. This is not,' said Montague, recoiling instinctively, and speaking in a voice that betrayed his agitation: 'this is not a night to travel in.'

'Ecod! you're right there,' returned Jonas: 'and we shouldn't be out in it but for you. If you hadn't kept me waiting all day, we might have been at Salisbury by this time; snug abed and fast asleep. What are we stopping for?'

His companion put his head out of window for a moment, and drawing it in again, observed (as if that were his cause of anxiety), that the boy was drenched to the skin.

'Serve him right,' said Jonas. 'I'm glad of it. What the devil are we stopping for? Are you going to spread him out to dry?'

'I have half a mind to take him inside,' observed the other with some hesitation.

'Oh! thankee!' said Jonas. 'We don't want any damp boys here; especially a young imp like him. Let him be where he is. He ain't afraid of a little thunder and lightning, I dare say; whoever else is. Go on, driver. We had better have *him* inside perhaps,' he muttered with a laugh; 'and the horses!'

'Don't go too fast,' cried Montague to the postillion; 'and take care how you go. You were nearly in the ditch when I called to you.'

This was not true; and Jonas bluntly said so, as they moved forward again. Montague took little or no heed of what he said, but repeated that it was not a night for travelling, and showed himself, both then and afterwards, unusually anxious.

From this time Jonas recovered his former spirits, if such a term may be employed to express the state in which he had left the city. He had his bottle often at his mouth; roared out snatches of songs, without the least regard to time or tune or voice, or anything but loud discordance; and urged his silent friend to be merry with him.

'You're the best company in the world, my good fellow,' said Montague with an effort, 'and in general irresistible; but to-night—do you hear it?'

'Ecod! I hear and see it too,' cried Jonas, shading his eyes, for the moment, from the lightning which was flashing, not in any one direction, but all around them. 'What of that? It don't change you, nor me, nor our affairs. Chorus, chorus.

It may lighten and storm,
Till it hunt the red worm
From the grass where the gibbet is driven;
But it can't hurt the dead,
And it won't save the head
That is doom'd to be rifled and riven.

That must be a precious old song,' he added with an oath, as he stopped short in a kind of wonder at himself. 'I haven't heard it since I was a boy, and how it comes into my head now, unless the lightning put it there, I don't know. "Can't hurt the dead"! No, no. "And won't save the head"! No, no. No! Ha, ha, ha!'

His mirth was of such a savage and extraordinary character, and was, in an inexplicable way, at once so suited to the night, and yet such a coarse intrusion on its terrors, that his fellow-traveller, always a coward, shrunk from him in positive fear. Instead of Jonas being his tool and instrument, their places seemed to be reversed. But there was reason for this too, Montague thought; since the sense of his debasement might naturally inspire such a man with the wish to assert a noisy independence, and in that licence to forget his real condition. Being quick enough, in reference to such subjects of contemplation, he was not long in taking this argument into account, and giving it its full weight. But still, he felt a vague sense of alarm, and was depressed and uneasy.

He was certain he had not been asleep; but his eyes might have deceived him; for, looking at Jonas now in any interval of darkness, he could represent his figure to himself in any attitude his state of mind suggested. On the other hand, he knew full well that Jonas had no reason to love him; and even taking the piece of pantomime which had so impressed his mind to be a real gesture, and not the working of his fancy, the most that could be said of it was, that it was quite in keeping with the rest of his diabolical fun, and had the same impotent expression of truth in it. 'If he could kill me with a wish,' thought the swindler, 'I should not live long.'

He resolved that when he should have had his use of Jonas, he would restrain him with an iron curb: in the meantime, that he could not do better than leave him to take his own way, and preserve his own peculiar description of good-humour, after his own uncommon manner. It was no great sacrifice to bear with him: 'for when all is got that can be got,' thought Montague, 'I shall decamp across the water, and have the laugh on my side—and the gains.'

Such were his reflections from hour to hour; his state of mind being one in which the same thoughts constantly present themselves over and over again in wearisome repetition; while Jonas, who appeared to have dismissed reflection altogether, entertained himself as before. They agreed that they would go to Salisbury, and would cross to Mr. Pecksniff's in

Mr. Jonas exhibits his Presence of Mind

the morning; and at the prospect of deluding that worthy gentleman, the spirits of his amiable son-in-law became more boisterous than ever.

As the night wore on, the thunder died away, but still rolled gloomily and mournfully in the distance. The lightning too, though now comparatively harmless, was yet bright and frequent. The rain was quite as violent as it had ever been.

It was their ill-fortune, at about the time of dawn and in the last stage of their journey, to have a restive pair of horses. These animals had been greatly terrified in their stable by the tempest; and coming out into the dreary interval between night and morning, when the glare of the lightning was yet unsubdued by day, and the various objects in their view were presented in indistinct and exaggerated shapes which they would not have worn by night, they gradually became less and less capable of control; until, taking a sudden fright at something by the roadside, they dashed off wildly down a steep hill, flung the driver from his saddle, drew the carriage to the brink of a ditch, stumbled headlong down, and threw it crashing over.

The travellers had opened the carriage door, and had either jumped or fallen out. Jonas was the first to stagger to his feet. He felt sick and weak, and very giddy, and reeling to a five-barred gate, stood holding by it: looking drowsily about as the whole landscape swam before his eyes. But, by degrees, he grew more conscious, and presently observed that Montague was lying senseless in the road, within a few feet of the horses.

In an instant, as if his own faint body were suddenly animated by a demon, he ran to the horses' heads; and pulling at their bridles with all his force, set them struggling and plunging with such mad violence as brought their hoofs at every effort nearer to the skull of the prostrate man; and must have led in half a minute to his brains being dashed out on the highway.

As he did this, he fought and contended with them like a man possessed: making them wilder by his cries.

'Whoop!' cried Jonas. 'Whoop! again! another! A little more, a little more! Up, ye devils! Hillo!'

As he heard the driver, who had risen and was hurrying up, crying to him to desist, his violence increased.

'Hillo! Hillo!' cried Jonas.

'For God's sake!' cried the driver. 'The gentleman—in the road—he'll be killed!'

The same shouts and the same struggles were his only answer. But the man darting in at the peril of his own life, saved Montague's, by dragging him through the mire and water out of the reach of present harm. That done, he ran to Jonas; and with the aid of his knife they very shortly disengaged the horses from the broken chariot, and got them, cut and bleeding, on their legs again. The postillion and Jonas had now leisure to look at each other, which they had not had yet.

'Presence of mind, presence of mind!' cried Jonas, throwing up his hands wildly. 'What would you have done without me?'

'The other gentleman would have done badly without *me*,' returned the man, shaking his head. 'You should have moved him first. I gave him up for dead.'

'Presence of mind, you croaker, presence of mind!' cried Jonas, with a harsh loud laugh. 'Was he struck, do you think?'

They both turned to look at him. Jonas muttered something to himself, when he saw him sitting up beneath the hedge, looking vacantly round.

'What's the matter?' asked Montague. 'Is anybody hurt?'

'Ecod!' said Jonas, 'it don't seem so. There are no bones broke, after all.'

They raised him, and he tried to walk. He was a good deal shaken, and trembled very much. But with the exception of a few cuts and bruises this was all the damage he had sustained.

'Cuts and bruises, eh?' said Jonas. 'We've all got them. Only cuts and bruises, eh?'

'I wouldn't have given sixpence for the gentleman's head in half-a-dozen seconds more, for all he's only cut and bruised,' observed the post-boy. 'If ever you're in an accident of this sort again, sir; which I hope you won't be; never you pull at the bridle of a horse that's down, when there's a man's head in the way. That can't be done twice without there being a dead man in the case; it would have ended in that, this time, as sure as ever you were born, if I hadn't come up just when I did.'

Jonas replied by advising him with a curse to hold his tongue, and to go somewhere, whither he was not very likely to go of his own accord. But Montague, who had listened eagerly to every word, himself diverted the subject, by exclaiming: 'Where's the boy?'

'Ecod! I forgot that monkey,' said Jonas. 'What's become of him?' A very brief search settled that question. The unfortunate Mr. Bailey had been thrown sheer over the hedge or the five-barred gate; and was lying in the neighbouring field, to all appearance dead.

'When I said to-night, that I wished I had never started on this journey,' cried his master, 'I knew it was an ill-fated one. Look at this boy!'

'Is that all?' growled Jonas. 'If you call *that* a sign of it—'

'Why, what should I call a sign of it?' asked Montague, hurriedly. 'What do you mean?'

'I mean,' said Jonas, stooping down over the body, 'that I never heard you were his father, or had any particular reason to care much about him. Halloa. Hold up here!'

But the boy was past holding up, or being held up, or giving any other sign of life than a faint and fitful beating of the heart. After some discussion the driver mounted the horse which had been least injured, and took the lad in his arms as well as he could; while Montague and Jonas, leading the other horse, and carrying a trunk between them, walked by his side towards Salisbury.

'You'd get there in a few minutes, and be able to send assistance to meet us, if you went forward, post-boy,' said Jonas. 'Trot on!'

'No, no,' cried Montague; 'we'll keep together.'

'Why, what a chicken you are! You are not afraid of being robbed; are you?' said Jonas.

'I am not afraid of anything,' replied the other, whose looks and manner were in flat contradiction to his words. 'But we'll keep together.'

'You were mighty anxious about the boy, a minute ago,' said Jonas. 'I suppose you know that he may die in the meantime?'

'Aye, aye. I know. But we'll keep together.'

As it was clear that he was not to be moved from this determination, Jonas made no other rejoinder than such as his face expressed; and they proceeded in company. They had three or four good miles to travel; and the way was not made easier by the state of the road, the burden by which they were embarrassed, or their own stiff and sore condition. After a sufficiently long and painful walk, they arrived at the Inn; and having knocked the people up (it being yet very early in the morning), sent out messengers to see to the carriage and its contents, and roused a surgeon from his bed to tend the chief sufferer. All the service he could render, he rendered promptly and skilfully. But he gave it as his opinion that the boy was labouring under a severe concussion of the brain, and that Mr. Bailey's mortal course was run.

If Montague's strong interest in the announcement could have been considered as unselfish in any degree, it might have been a redeeming trait in a character that had no such lineaments to spare. But it was not difficult to see that, for some unexpressed reason best appreciated by himself, he attached a strange value to the company and presence of this mere child. When, after receiving some assistance from the surgeon himself, he retired to the bedroom prepared for him, and it was broad day, his mind was still dwelling on this theme.

'I would rather have lost,' he said, 'a thousand pounds than lost the boy just now. But I'll return home alone. I am resolved upon that. Chuzzlewit shall go forward first, and I will follow in my own time. I'll have no more of this,' he added, wiping his damp forehead. 'Twenty-four hours of this would turn my hair grey!'

After examining his chamber, and looking under the bed, and in the cupboards, and even behind the curtains, with unusual caution (although it was, as has been said, broad day), he double-locked the door by which he had entered, and retired to rest. There was another door in the room, but it was locked on the outer side; and with what place it communicated he knew not.

His fears or evil conscience reproduced this door in all his dreams. He dreamed that a dreadful secret was connected with it: a secret which he knew, and yet did not know, for although he was heavily responsible for it, and a party to it, he was harassed even in his vision by a distracting uncertainty in reference to its import. Incoherently entwined with this dream was another, which represented it as the hiding-place of an enemy, a shadow, a phantom; and made it the business of his life to keep the terrible creature closed up, and prevent it from forcing its way in upon him. With this view Nadgett, and he, and a strange man with a bloody smear upon his head (who told him that he had been his playfellow, and told him, too, the real name of an old schoolmate, forgotten until then), worked with iron plates and nails to make the door secure; but though they worked never so hard, it was all in vain, for the nails broke, or changed to soft twigs, or what was worse, to worms, between their fingers; the wood of the door splintered and crumbled, so that even nails would not remain in it; and the iron plates curled up like hot paper. All this time the creature on the other side—whether it was in the shape of man, or beast, he neither knew nor sought to know—was gaining on them. But his greatest terror was when the man with the bloody smear upon his head demanded of him if he knew this creature's name, and said that he would whisper it. At this the dreamer fell upon his knees, his whole blood thrilling with inexplicable fear, and held his ears. But looking at the speaker's lips, he saw that they formed the utterance of the letter 'J;' and crying out aloud that the secret was discovered, and they were all lost, he awoke.

Awoke to find Jonas standing at his bedside watching him. And that very door wide open.

As their eyes met, Jonas retreated a few paces, and Montague sprang out of bed.

'Heyday!' said Jonas. 'You're all alive this morning.'

'Alive!' the other stammered, as he pulled the bell-rope violently: 'What are you doing here?'

'It's your room to be sure,' said Jonas; 'but I'm almost inclined to ask you what *you* are doing here? My room is on the other side of that door. No one told me last night not to open it. I thought it led into a passage, and was coming out to order breakfast. There's—there's no bell in my room.'

Montague had in the meantime admitted the man with his hot water and boots, who hearing this, said, yes, there was; and passed into the adjoining room to point it out, at the head of the bed.

'I couldn't find it, then,' said Jonas: 'it's all the same. Shall I order breakfast?'

Montague answered in the affirmative. When Jonas had retired, whistling, through his own room, he opened the door of communication, to take out the key and fasten it on the inner side. But it was taken out already.

He dragged a table against the door, and sat down to collect himself, as if his dreams still had some influence upon his mind.

'An evil journey,' he repeated several times. 'An evil journey. But I'll travel home alone. I'll have no more of this.'

His presentiment, or superstition, that it was an evil journey, did not at all deter him from doing the evil for which the journey was undertaken. With this in view, he dressed himself more carefully than usual to make a favourable impression on Mr. Pecksniff: and, reassured by his own appearance, the beauty of the morning, and the flashing of the wet boughs outside his window in the merry sunshine, was soon sufficiently inspirited to swear a few round oaths, and hum the fag-end of a song.

But he still muttered to himself at intervals, for all that: 'I'll travel home alone!'

CHAPTER XLIII

Has an influence on the fortunes of several people. Mr. Pecksniff is exhibited in the plenitude of power, and wields the same with fortitude and magnanimity

ON the night of the storm, Mrs. Lupin, hostess of the Blue Dragon, sat by herself in her little bar. Her solitary condition, or the bad weather, or both united, made Mrs. Lupin thoughtful, not to say sorrowful. As she sat with her chin upon her hand, looking out through a low back lattice, rendered dim in the brightest daytime by clustering vine-leaves, she shook her head very often, and said, 'Dear me! Ah, dear, dear me!'

It was a melancholy time, even in the snugness of the Dragon bar. The rich expanse of corn-field, pasture-land, green slope, and gentle undulation, with its sparkling brooks, its many hedgerows, and its clumps of beautiful trees, was black and dreary, from the diamond panes of the lattice away to the far horizon, where the thunder seemed to roll along the hills. The heavy rain beat down the tender branches of vine and jessamine, and trampled on them in its fury; and when the lightning gleamed it showed the tearful leaves shivering and cowering together at the window, and tapping at it urgently, as if beseeching to be sheltered from the dismal night.

As a mark of respect for the lightning, Mrs. Lupin had removed her candle to the chimney-piece. Her basket of needlework stood unheeded at her elbow; her supper, spread on a round table not far off, was untasted; and the knives had been removed for fear of attraction. She had sat for a long time with her chin upon her hand, saying to herself at intervals, 'Dear me! Ah, dear, dear me!'

She was on the eve of saying so, once more, when the latch of the house-door (closed to keep the rain out), rattled on its well-worn catch, and a traveller came in, who, shutting it after him, and walking straight up to the half-door of the bar, said, rather gruffly:

'A pint of the best old beer here.'

He had some reason to be gruff, for if he had passed the day in a waterfall, he could scarcely have been wetter than he was.

He was wrapped up to the eyes in a rough blue sailor's coat, and had an oil-skin hat on, from the capacious brim of which the rain fell trickling down upon his breast, and back, and shoulders. Judging from a certain liveliness of chin—he had so pulled down his hat, and pulled up his collar to defend himself from the weather, that she could only see his chin, and even across that he drew the wet sleeve of his shaggy coat, as she looked at him—Mrs. Lupin set him down for a good-natured fellow, too.

'A bad night!' observed the hostess cheerfully.

The traveller shook himself like a Newfoundland dog, and said it was, rather.

'There's a fire in the kitchen,' said Mrs. Lupin, 'and very good company there. Hadn't you better go and dry yourself?'

'No, thankee,' said the man, glancing towards the kitchen as he spoke; he seemed to know the way.

'It's enough to give you your death of cold,' observed the hostess.

'I don't take my death easy,' returned the traveller; 'or I should most likely have took it afore to-night. Your health, ma'am!'

Mrs. Lupin thanked him; but in the act of lifting the tankard to his mouth, he changed his mind, and put it down again. Throwing his body back, and looking about him stiffly, as a man does who is wrapped up, and has his hat low down over his eyes, he said,

'What do you call this house? Not the Dragon, do you?'

Mrs. Lupin complacently made answer, 'Yes, the Dragon.'

'Why, then, you've got a sort of a relation of mine here, ma'am,' said the traveller: 'a young man of the name of Tapley. What! Mark, my boy!' apostrophising the premises, 'have I come upon you at last, old buck!'

This was touching Mrs. Lupin on a tender point. She turned to trim the candle on the chimney-piece, and said, with her back towards the traveller:

'Nobody should be made more welcome at the Dragon, master, than any one who brought me news of Mark. But it's many and many a long day and month since he left here and England. And whether he's alive or dead, poor fellow, Heaven above us only knows!'

She shook her head, and her voice trembled; her hand must have done so too, for the light required a deal of trimming.

'Where did he go, ma'am?' asked the traveller, in a gentler voice.

'He went,' said Mrs. Lupin, with increased distress, 'to America. He was always tender-hearted and kind, and perhaps at this moment may be lying in prison under sentence of death, for taking pity on some miserable black, and helping the poor runaway creetur to escape. How could he ever go to America! Why didn't he go to some of those countries where the savages eat each other fairly, and give an equal chance to every one!'

Quite subdued by this time, Mrs. Lupin sobbed, and was retiring to a chair to give her grief free vent, when the traveller caught her in his arms, and she uttered a glad cry of recognition.

'Yes, I will!' cried Mark, 'another—one more—twenty more! You didn't know me in that hat and coat? I thought you would have known me anywheres! Ten more!'

'So I should have known you, if I could have seen you; but I couldn't, and you spoke so gruff. I didn't think you could speak gruff to me, Mark, at first coming back.'

'Fifteen more!' said Mr. Tapley. 'How handsome and how young you look! Six more! The last half-dozen warn't a fair one, and must be done over again. Lord bless you, what a treat it is to see you! One more! Well, I never was so jolly. Just a few more, on account of there not being any credit in it!'

When Mr. Tapley stopped in these calculations in simple addition, he did it, not because he was at all tired of the exercise, but because he was out of breath. The pause reminded him of other duties.

'Mr. Martin Chuzzlewit's outside,' he said. 'I left him under the cart-shed, while I came on to see if there was anybody here. We want to keep quiet to-night, till we know the news from you, and what it's best for us to do.'

'There's not a soul in the house, except the kitchen company,' returned the hostess. 'If they were to know you had come back, Mark, they'd have a bonfire in the street, late as it is.'

'But they mustn't know it to-night, my precious soul,' said Mark: 'so have the house shut, and the kitchen fire made up; and when it's all ready, put a light in the winder, and we'll come in. One more! I long to hear about old friends. You'll tell me all about 'em, won't you: Mr. Pinch, and the butcher's dog down the street, and the terrier over the way, and the wheelwright's, and every one of 'em. When I first caught sight of the church to-night, I thought the steeple would have choked me, I did. One more! Won't you? Not a very little one to finish off with?'

'You have had plenty, I am sure,' said the hostess. 'Go along with your foreign manners!'

'That ain't foreign, bless you!' cried Mark. 'Native as oysters, that is! One more, because it's native! As a mark of respect for the land we live in! This don't count as between you and me, you understand,' said Mr. Tapley. 'I ain't a-kissing you now, you'll observe. I have been among the patriots: I'm a-kissin' my country.'

It would have been very unreasonable to complain of the exhibition of his patriotism with which he followed up this explanation, that it was at all lukewarm or indifferent. When he had given full expression to his nationality, he hurried off to Martin; while Mrs. Lupin, in a state of great agitation and excitement, prepared for their reception.

The company soon came tumbling out: insisting to each other that the Dragon clock was half an hour too fast, and that the thunder must have affected it. Impatient, wet, and weary though they were, Martin and Mark were overjoyed to see these old faces, and watched them with delighted interest as they departed from the house, and passed close by them.

'There's the old tailor, Mark!' whispered Martin.

'There he goes, sir! A little bandier than he was, I think, sir, ain't he? His figure's so far altered, as it seems to me, that you might wheel a rather larger barrow between his legs as he walks, than you could have done conveniently when we know'd him. There's Sam a-coming out, sir.'

'Ah, to be sure!' cried Martin: 'Sam, the hostler. I wonder whether that horse of Pecksniff's is alive still?'

'Not a doubt on it, sir,' returned Mark. 'That's a description of animal, sir, as will go on in a bony way peculiar to himself for a long time, and get into the newspapers at last under the title of 'Sing'lar Tenacity of Life in a Quadruped.' As if he had ever been alive in all his life, worth mentioning! There's the clerk, sir,—wery drunk, as usual.'

'I see him!' said Martin, laughing. 'But, my life, how wet you are, Mark!'

'*I* am! What do you consider yourself, sir?'

'Oh, not half as bad,' said his fellow-traveller, with an air of great vexation. 'I told you not to keep on the windy side, Mark, but to let us change and change about. The rain has been beating on you ever since it began.'

'You don't know how it pleases me, sir,' said Mark, after a short silence: 'if I may make so bold as say so, to hear you a-going on in that there uncommon considerate way of yours; which I don't mean to attend to, never, but which, ever since that time when I was floored in Eden, you have showed.'

'Ah, Mark!' sighed Martin, 'the less we say of that the better. Do I see the light yonder?'

'That's the light!' cried Mark. 'Lord bless her, what briskness she possesses! Now for it, sir. Neat wines, good beds, and first-rate entertainment for man or beast.'

The kitchen fire burnt clear and red, the table was spread out, the kettle boiled; the slippers were there, the boot-jack too, sheets of ham were there, cooking on the gridiron; half-a-dozen eggs were there, poaching in the frying-pan; a plethoric cherry-brandy bottle was there, winking at a foaming jug of beer upon the table; rare provisions were there, dangling from the rafters as if you had only to open your mouth, and something exquisitely ripe and good would be glad of the excuse for tumbling into it. Mrs. Lupin, who for their sakes had dislodged the very cook, high priestess of the temple, with her own genial hands was dressing their repast.

It was impossible to help it—a ghost must have hugged her. The Atlantic Ocean and the Red Sea being, in that respect, all one, Martin hugged her instantly. Mr. Tapley (as if the idea were quite novel, and had never occurred to him before), followed, with much gravity, on the same side.

'Little did I ever think,' said Mrs. Lupin, adjusting her cap and laughing heartily; yes, and blushing too; 'often as I have said that Mr. Pecksniff's young gentlemen were the life and soul of the Dragon, and that without them it would be too dull to live in—little did I ever think, I am sure, that any one of them would ever make so free as you, Mr. Martin! And still less that I shouldn't be angry with him, but should be glad with all my heart to be the first to welcome him home from America, with Mark Tapley for his—'

'For his friend, Mrs. Lupin,' interposed Martin.

'For his friend,' said the hostess, evidently gratified by this distinction, but at the same time admonishing Mr. Tapley with a fork to remain at a respectful distance. 'Little did I ever think that! But still less, that I should ever have the changes to relate that I shall have to tell you of, when you have done your supper!'

'Good Heaven!' cried Martin, changing colour, 'what changes?'

'*She*,' said the hostess, 'is quite well, and now at Mr. Pecksniff's. Don't be at all alarmed about her. She is everything you could wish. It 's of no use mincing matters, or making secrets, is it?' added Mrs. Lupin. 'I know all about it, you see!'

'My good creature,' returned Martin, 'you are exactly the person who ought to know all about it. I am delighted to think you *do* know all about it. But what changes do you hint at? Has any death occurred?'

'No, no!' said the hostess. 'Not so bad as that. But I declare now that I will not be drawn into saying another word till you have had your supper. If you ask me fifty questions in the meantime, I won't answer one.'

She was so positive, that there was nothing for it but to get the supper over as quickly as possible; and as they had been walking a great many miles, and had fasted since the middle of the day, they did no great violence to their own inclinations in falling on it tooth and nail. It took rather longer to get through than might have been expected; for, half-a-dozen times, when they thought they had finished, Mrs. Lupin exposed the fallacy of that impression triumphantly. But at last, in the course of time and nature, they gave in. Then, sitting with their slippered feet stretched out upon the kitchen hearth (which was wonderfully comforting, for the night had grown by this time raw and chilly), and looking with involuntary admiration at their dimpled, buxom, blooming hostess, as the firelight sparkled in her eyes and glimmered in her raven hair, they composed themselves to listen to her news.

Many were the exclamations of surprise which interrupted her, when she told them of the separation between Mr. Pecksniff and his daughters, and between the same good gentleman and Mr. Pinch. But these were nothing to the indignant demonstrations of Martin, when she related, as the common talk of the neighbourhood, what entire possession he had obtained over the mind and person of old Mr. Chuzzlewit, and what high honour he designed for Mary. On receipt of this intelligence, Martin's slippers flew off in a twinkling, and he began pulling on his wet boots with that indefinite intention of going somewhere instantly, and doing something to somebody, which is the first safety-valve of a hot temper.

'He!' said Martin, 'smooth-tongued villain that he is! He! Give me that other boot, Mark!'

'Where was you a-thinking of going to, sir?' inquired Mr. Tapley, drying the sole at the fire, and looking coolly at it as he spoke, as if it were a slice of toast.

'Where!' repeated Martin. 'You don't suppose I am going to remain here, do you?'

The imperturbable Mark confessed that he did.

'You do!' retorted Martin angrily. 'I am much obliged to you. What do you take me for?'

'I take you for what you are, sir,' said Mark; 'and, consequently, am quite sure that whatever you do will be right and sensible. The boot, sir.'

Martin darted an impatient look at him, without taking it, and walked rapidly up and down the kitchen several times, with one boot and a stocking on. But, mindful of his Eden resolution, he had already gained many victories over himself when Mark was in the case, and he resolved to conquer now. So he came back to the boot-jack, laid his hand on Mark's shoulder to steady himself, pulled the boot off, picked up his slippers, put them on, and sat down again. He could not help thrusting his hands to the very bottom of his pockets, and muttering at intervals, 'Pecksniff too! That fellow! Upon my soul! In-deed! What next?' and so forth: nor could he help occasionally shaking his fist at the chimney, with a very threatening countenance: but this did not last long; and he heard Mrs. Lupin out, if not with composure, at all events in silence.

'As to Mr. Pecksniff himself,' observed the hostess in conclusion, spreading out the skirts of her gown with both hands, and nodding her head a great many times as she did so, 'I don't know what to say. Somebody must have poisoned his mind, or influenced him in some extraordinary way. I cannot believe that such a noble-spoken gentleman would go and do wrong of his own accord!'

A noble-spoken gentleman! How many people are there in the world, who, for no better reason, uphold their Pecksniffs to the last, and abandon virtuous men, when Pecksniffs breathe upon them!

'As to Mr. Pinch,' pursued the landlady, 'if ever there was a dear, good, pleasant, worthy soul alive, Pinch, and no other, is his name. But how do we know that old Mr. Chuzzlewit himself was not the cause of difference arising between him and Mr. Pecksniff? No one but themselves can tell: for Mr. Pinch has a proud spirit, though he has such a quiet way; and when he left us, and was so sorry to go, he scorned to make his story good, even to me.'

'Poor old Tom!' said Martin, in a tone that sounded like remorse.

'It's a comfort to know,' resumed the landlady, 'that he has his sister living with him, and is doing well. Only yesterday he sent me back, by post, a little'—here the colour came into her cheeks—'a little trifle I was bold enough to lend him when he went away: saying, with many thanks, that he had good employment, and didn't want it. It was the same note; he hadn't broken it. I never thought I could have been so little pleased to see a bank-note come back to me, as I was to see that.'

'Kindly said, and heartily!' said Martin. 'Is it not, Mark?'

'She can't say anything as does not possess them qualities,' returned Mr. Tapley; 'which as much belong to the Dragon as its licence. And now that we have got quite cool and fresh, to the subject again, sir: what will you do? If you're not proud, and can make up your mind to go through with what you spoke of, coming along, that's the course for you to take. If you started wrong with your grandfather (which, you'll excuse my taking the liberty of saying, appears to have been the case), up with you, sir, and tell him so, and make an appeal to his affections. Don't stand out. He's a great deal older than you, and if he was hasty, you was hasty too. Give way, sir, give way.'

The eloquence of Mr. Tapley was not without its effect on Martin, but he still hesitated, and expressed his reason thus:

'That's all very true, and perfectly correct, Mark; and if it were a mere question of humbling myself before *him*, I would not consider it twice. But don't you see, that being wholly under this hypocrite's government, and having (if what we hear be true) no mind or will of his own, I throw myself, in fact, not at his feet, but at the feet of Mr. Pecksniff? And when I am rejected and spurned away,' said Martin, turning crimson at the thought, 'it is not by him: my own blood stirred against me: but Mr. Pecksniff—Pecksniff, Mark!'

'Well, but we know beforehand,' returned the politic Mr. Tapley, 'that Pecksniff is a wagabond, a scoundrel, and a willain.'

'A most pernicious villain!' said Martin.

'A most pernicious willain. We know that beforehand, sir; and, consequently, it's no shame to be defeated by Pecksniff. Blow Pecksniff!' cried Mr. Tapley, in the fervour of his eloquence. 'Who's he! It's not in the natur of Pecksniff to shame *us*, unless he agreed with us, or done us a service; and, in case he offered any outdacity of that description, we could express our sentiments in the English language, I hope. Pecksniff!' repeated Mr. Tapley, with ineffable disdain. 'What's Pecksniff, who's Pecksniff, where's Pecksniff, that he's to be so much considered? We're not a-calculating for ourselves;' he laid uncommon emphasis on the last syllable of that word, and looked full in Martin's face; 'we're making a effort for a young lady likewise as has undergone her share; and whatever little hope we have, this here Pecksniff is not to stand in its way, I expect. I never heard of any act of Parliament as was made by Pecksniff. Pecksniff! Why, I wouldn't see the man myself; I wouldn't hear him; I wouldn't choose to know he was in company. I'd scrape my shoes on the scraper of the door, and call that Pecksniff, if you liked; but I wouldn't condescend no further.'

The amazement of Mrs. Lupin, and indeed of Mr. Tapley himself for that matter, at this impassioned flow of language, was immense. But Martin, after looking thoughtfully at the fire for a short time, said:

'You are right, Mark. Right or wrong, it shall be done. I'll do it.'

'One word more, sir,' returned Mark. 'Only think of him so far as not to give him a handle against you. Don't you do anything secret that he can report before you get there. Don't you even see Miss Mary in the morning, but let this here dear friend of ours;' Mr. Tapley bestowed a smile upon the hostess; 'prepare her for what's a-going to happen, and carry any little message as may be agreeable. She knows how. Don't you?' Mrs. Lupin laughed and tossed her head. 'Then you go in, bold and free as a gentleman should. "I haven't done nothing under-handed," says you. "I haven't been a-skulking about the premises, here I am, for-give me, I ask your pardon, God Bless You!"'

Martin smiled, but felt that it was good advice notwith-standing, and resolved to act upon it. When they had ascertained from Mrs. Lupin that Pecksniff had already returned from the great ceremonial at which they had beheld him in his glory; and when they had fully arranged the order of their proceedings; they went to bed, intent upon the morrow.

In pursuance of their project as agreed upon at this discussion, Mr. Tapley issued forth next morning, after breakfast, charged with a letter from Martin to his grandfather, requesting leave to wait upon him for a few minutes. And postponing as he went along the congratulations of his numerous friends until a more convenient season, he soon arrived at Mr. Pecksniff's house. At that gentleman's door; with a face so immovable that it would have been next to an impossibility for the most acute physiognomist to determine what he was thinking about, or whether he was thinking at all: he straightway knocked.

A person of Mr. Tapley's observation could not long remain insensible to the fact that Mr. Pecksniff was making the end of his nose very blunt against the glass of the parlour window, in an angular attempt to discover who had knocked at the door. Nor was Mr. Tapley slow to baffle this movement on the part of the enemy, by perching himself on the top step, and presenting the crown of his hat in that direction. But possibly Mr. Pecksniff had already seen him, for Mark soon heard his shoes creaking, as he advanced to open the door with his own hands.

Mr. Pecksniff was as cheerful as ever, and sang a little song in the passage.

'How d'ye do, sir?' said Mark.

'Oh!' cried Mr. Pecksniff. 'Tapley, I believe? The Prodigal returned! We don't want any beer, my friend.'

'Thankee, sir,' said Mark. 'I couldn't accommodate you if you did. A letter, sir. Wait for an answer.'

'For me?' cried Mr. Pecksniff. 'And an answer, eh?'

'Not for you I think, sir,' said Mark, pointing out the direction. 'Chuzzlewit, I believe the name is, sir.'

'Oh!' returned Mr. Pecksniff. 'Thank you. Yes. Who's it from, my good young man?'

'The gentleman it comes from wrote his name inside, sir,' returned Mr. Tapley with extreme politeness. 'I see him a-signing of it at the end, while I was a-waitin'.'

'And he said he wanted an answer, did he?' asked Mr. Pecksniff in his most persuasive manner.

Mark replied in the affirmative.

'He shall have an answer. Certainly,' said Mr. Pecksniff, tearing the letter into small pieces, as mildly as if that were the most flattering attention a correspondent could receive. 'Have the goodness to give him that, with my compliments, if you please. Good morning!' Whereupon he handed Mark the scraps; retired; and shut the door.

Mark thought it prudent to subdue his personal emotions, and return to Martin at the Dragon. They were not unprepared for such a reception, and suffered an hour or so to elapse before making another attempt. When this interval had gone by, they returned to Mr. Pecksniff's house in company. Martin knocked this time, while Mr. Tapley prepared himself to keep the door open with his foot and shoulder, when anybody came, and by that means secure an enforced parley. But this precaution was needless, for the servant-girl appeared almost immediately. Brushing quickly past her as he had resolved in such a case to do, Martin (closely followed by his faithful ally) opened the door of that parlour in which he knew a visitor was most likely to be found; passed at once into the room; and stood, without a word of notice or announcement, in the presence of his grandfather.

Mr. Pecksniff also was in the room; and Mary. In the swift instant of their mutual recognition, Martin saw the old man droop his grey head, and hide his face in his hands.

It smote him to the heart. In his most selfish and most careless day, this lingering remnant of the old man's ancient love, this buttress of a ruined tower he had built up in the time gone by, with so much pride and hope, would have caused a pang in Martin's heart. But now, changed for the better in his worst respect; looking through an altered medium on his former friend, the guardian of his childhood, so broken and bowed down; resentment, sullenness, self-confidence, and pride, were all swept away, before the starting tears upon the withered cheeks. He could not bear to see them. He could not bear to think they fell at sight of him. He could not bear to view reflected in them, the reproachful and irrevocable Past.

He hurriedly advanced to seize the old man's hand in his, when Mr. Pecksniff interposed himself between them.

'No, young man!' said Mr. Pecksniff, striking himself upon

the breast, and stretching out his other arm towards his guest as if it were a wing to shelter him. 'No, sir. None of that. Strike here, sir, here! Launch your arrows at me, sir, if you'll have the goodness; not at Him!'

'Grandfather!' cried Martin. 'Hear me! I implore you, let me speak!'

'Would you, sir? Would you?' said Mr. Pecksniff, dodging about, so as to keep himself always between them. 'Is it not enough, sir, that you come into my house like a thief in the night, or I should rather say, for we can never be too particular on the subject of Truth, like a thief in the day-time: bringing your dissolute companions with you, to plant themselves with their backs against the insides of parlour doors, and prevent the entrance or issuing forth of any of my household;' Mark had taken up this position, and held it quite unmoved; 'but would you also strike at venerable Virtue? Would you? Know that it is not defenceless. I will be its shield, young man. Assail me. Come on, sir. Fire away!'

'Pecksniff,' said the old man, in a feeble voice. 'Calm yourself. Be quiet.'

'I can't be calm,' cried Mr. Pecksniff, 'and I won't be quiet. My benefactor and my friend! Shall even my house be no refuge for your hoary pillow!'

'Stand aside!' said the old man, stretching out his hand; 'and let me see what it is I used to love so dearly.'

'It is right that you should see it, my friend,' said Mr. Pecksniff. 'It is well that you should see it, my noble sir. It is desirable that you should contemplate it in its true proportions. Behold it! There it is, sir. There it is!'

Martin could hardly be a mortal man, and not express in his face something of the anger and disdain with which Mr. Pecksniff inspired him. But beyond this he evinced no knowledge whatever of that gentleman's presence or existence. True, he had once, and that at first, glanced at him involuntarily, and with supreme contempt; but for any other heed he took of him, there might have been nothing in his place save empty air.

As Mr. Pecksniff withdrew from between them, agreeably to the wish just now expressed (which he did during the delivery of the observations last recorded), old Martin, who had taken Mary Graham's hand in his, and whispered kindly to her, as telling her she had no cause to be alarmed, gently pushed her from him, behind his chair; and looked steadily at his grandson.

'And that,' he said, 'is he. Ah! that is he! Say what you wish to say. But come no nearer.'

'His sense of justice is so fine,' said Mr. Pecksniff, 'that he will hear even him, although he knows beforehand that nothing can come of it. Ingenuous mind!' Mr. Pecksniff did not address himself immediately to any person in saying this, but assuming the position of the Chorus in a Greek Tragedy, delivered his opinion as a commentary on the proceedings.

'Grandfather!' said Martin, with great earnestness. 'From a painful journey, from a hard life, from a sick-bed, from privation and distress, from gloom and disappointment, from almost hoplessness and despair, I have come back to you.'

'Rovers of this sort,' observed Mr. Pecksniff, as Chorus, 'very commonly come back when they find they don't meet with the success they expected in their marauding ravages.'

'But for this faithful man,' said Martin, turning towards Mark, 'whom I first knew in this place, and who went away with me voluntarily, as a servant, but has been, throughout, my zealous and devoted friend; but for him, I must have died abroad. Far from home, far from any help or consolation: far from the probability even of my wretched fate being ever known to any one who cared to hear it—oh that you would let me say, of being known to you!'

The old man looked at Mr. Pecksniff. Mr. Pecksniff looked at him. 'Did you speak, my worthy sir?' said Mr. Pecksniff, with a smile. The old man answered in the negative. 'I know what you thought,' said Mr. Pecksniff, with another smile. 'Let him go on, my friend. The development of self-interest in the human mind is always a curious study. Let him go on, sir.'

'Go on!' observed the old man; in a mechanical obedience, it appeared, to Mr. Pecksniff's suggestion.

'I have been so wretched and so poor,' said Martin, 'that I am indebted to the charitable help of a stranger, in a land of strangers, for the means of returning here. All this tells against me in your mind, I know. I have given you cause to think I have been driven here wholly by want, and have not been led on, in any degree, by affection or regret. When I parted from you, Grandfather, I deserved that suspicion, but I do not now. I do not now.'

The Chorus put its hand in its waistcoat, and smiled. 'Let him go on, my worthy sir,' it said. 'I know what you are thinking of, but don't express it prematurely.'

Old Martin raised his eyes to Mr. Pecksniff's face, and appearing to derive renewed instruction from his looks and words, said, once again:

'Go on!'

'I have little more to say,' returned Martin. 'And as I say it now, with little or no hope, Grandfather; whatever dawn of hope I had on entering the room; believe it to be true. At least, believe it to be true.'

'Beautiful Truth!' exclaimed the Chorus, looking upward. 'How is your name profaned by vicious persons! You don't live in a well, my holy principle, but on the lips of false mankind. It is hard to bear with mankind, dear sir,'—addressing the elder Mr. Chuzzlewit; 'but let us do so meekly. It is our duty so to do. Let us be among the Few who do their duty. If,' pursued the Chorus, soaring up into a lofty flight, 'as the poet informs us, England expects Every man to do his duty, England is the most sanguine country on the face of the earth, and will find itself continually disappointed.'

'Upon that subject,' said Martin, looking calmly at the old man as he spoke, but glancing once at Mary, whose face was now buried in her hands, upon the back of his easy-chair: 'upon that subject, which first occasioned a division between us, my mind and heart are incapable of change. Whatever influence they have undergone, since that unhappy time, has not been one to weaken but to strengthen me. I cannot profess sorrow for that, nor irresolution in that, nor shame in that. Nor would you wish me, I know. But that I might have trusted to your love, if I had thrown myself manfully upon it; that I might have won you over with ease, if I had been more yielding and more considerate; that I should have best remembered myself in forgetting myself, and recollecting you; reflection, solitude, and misery, have taught me. I came resolved to say this, and to ask your forgiveness: not so much in hope for the future, as in regret for the past: for all that I would ask of you is, that you would aid me to live. Help me to get honest work to do, and I would do it. My condition places me at the disadvantage of seeming to have only my selfish ends to serve, but try if that be so or not. Try if I be self-willed, obdurate, and haughty, as I was; or have been disciplined in a rough school. Let the voice of nature and association plead between us, Grandfather; and do not, for one fault, however thankless, quite reject me!'

As he ceased, the grey head of the old man drooped again; and he concealed his face behind his outspread fingers.

'My dear sir,' cried Mr. Pecksniff, bending over him, 'you must not give way to this. It is very natural, and very amiable, but you must not allow the shameless conduct of one whom you long ago cast off, to move you so far. Rouse yourself. Think,' said Pecksniff, 'think of Me, my friend.'

'I will,' returned old Martin, looking up into his face. 'You recall me to myself. I will.'

'Why, what,' said Mr. Pecksniff, sitting down beside him in a chair which he drew up for the purpose, and tapping him playfully on the arm, 'what is the matter with my strong-minded compatriot, if I may venture to take the liberty of calling him by that endearing expression? Shall I have to scold my coadjutor, or to reason with an intellect like his? I think not.'

'No, no. There is no occasion,' said the old man. 'A momentary feeling. Nothing more.'

'Indignation,' observed Mr. Pecksniff, '*will* bring the scalding tear into the honest eye, I know;' he wiped his own elaborately. 'But we have higher duties to perform than that. Rouse yourself, Mr. Chuzzlewit. Shall I give expression to your thoughts, my friend?'

'Yes,' said old Martin, leaning back in his chair, and looking at him, half in vacancy and half in admiration, as if he were fascinated by the man. 'Speak for me, Pecksniff. Thank you. You are true to me. Thank you!'

'Do not unman me, sir,' said Mr. Pecksniff, shaking his hand vigorously, 'or I shall be unequal to the task. It is not agreeable to my feelings, my good sir, to address the person who is now before us, for when I ejected him from this house, after hearing of his unnatural conduct from your lips, I renounced communication with him for ever. But you desire it; and that is sufficient. Young man! The door is immediately behind the companion of your infamy. Blush if you can; begone without a blush, if you can't.'

Martin looked as steadily at his grandfather as if there had been a dead silence all this time. The old man looked no less steadily at Mr. Pecksniff.

'When I ordered you to leave this house upon the last occasion of your being dismissed from it with disgrace,' said Mr. Pecksniff: 'when, stung and stimulated beyond endurance by your shameless conduct to this extraordinarily noble-minded individual, I exclaimed "Go forth!" I told you that I wept for your depravity. Do not suppose that the tear which stands in my eye at this moment, is shed for you. It is shed for him, sir. It is shed for him.'

Here Mr. Pecksniff, accidentally dropping the tear in question on a bald part of Mr. Chuzzlewit's head, wiped the place with his pocket-handkerchief, and begged pardon.

'It is shed for him, sir, whom you seek to make the victim of your arts,' said Mr. Pecksniff: 'whom you seek to plunder, to deceive, and to mislead. It is shed in sympathy with him, and admiration of him; not in pity for him, for happily he knows what you are. You shall not wrong him further, sir, in any way,' said Mr. Pecksniff, quite transported with enthusiasm, 'while I have life. You may bestride my senseless corse, sir. That is very likely. I can imagine a mind like yours deriving great satisfaction from any measure of that kind. But while I continue to be called upon to exist, sir, you must strike at him through me. Aye!' said Mr. Pecksniff, shaking his head at Martin with indignant jocularity; 'and in such a cause you will find me, my young sir, an Ugly Customer!'

Still Martin looked steadily and mildly at his grandfather. 'Will you give me no answer,' he said, at length, 'not a word?'

'You hear what has been said,' replied the old man, without averting his eyes from the face of Mr. Pecksniff: who nodded encouragingly.

'I have not heard your voice. I have not heard your spirit,' returned Martin.

'Tell him again,' said the old man, still gazing up in Mr. Pecksniff's face.

'I only hear,' replied Martin, strong in his purpose from the first, and stronger in it as he felt how Pecksniff winced and shrunk beneath his contempt; 'I only hear what you say to me, grandfather.'

Perhaps it was well for Mr. Pecksniff that his venerable friend found in his (Mr. Pecksniff's) features an exclusive and engrossing object of contemplation, for if his eyes had gone astray, and he had compared young Martin's bearing with that of his zealous defender, the latter disinterested gentleman would scarcely have shown to greater advantage than on the memorable afternoon when he took Tom Pinch's last receipt in full of all demands. One really might have thought there was some quality in Mr. Pecksniff—an emanation from the brightness and purity within him perhaps—which set off and adorned his foes: they looked so gallant and so manly beside him.

'Not a word?' said Martin, for the second time.

'I remember that I have a word to say, Pecksniff,' observed the old man. 'But a word. You spoke of being indebted to the charitable help of some stranger for the means of returning to England. Who is he? And what help in money did he render you?'

Although he asked this question of Martin, he did not look towards him, but kept his eyes on Mr. Pecksniff as before. It appeared to have become a habit with him, both in a literal and figurative sense, to look to Mr. Pecksniff alone.

Martin took out his pencil, tore a leaf from his pocket-book, and hastily wrote down the particulars of his debt to Mr. Bevan. The old man stretched out his hand for the paper, and took it; but his eyes did not wander from Mr. Pecksniff's face.

'It would be a poor pride and a false humility,' said Martin, in a low voice, 'to say, I do not wish that to be paid, or that I have any present hope of being able to pay it. But I never felt my poverty so deeply as I feel it now.'

'Read it to me, Pecksniff,' said the old man.

Mr. Pecksniff, after approaching the perusal of the paper as if it were a manuscript confession of a murder, complied.

'I think, Pecksniff,' said old Martin, 'I could wish that to be discharged. I should not like the lender, who was abroad; who had no opportunity of making inquiry, and who did (as he thought) a kind action; to suffer.'

'An honourable sentiment, my dear sir. Your own entirely. But a dangerous precedent,' said Mr. Pecksniff, 'permit me to suggest.'

'It shall not be a precedent,' returned the old man. 'It is the only recognition of him. But we will talk of it again. You shall advise me. There is nothing else?'

'Nothing else,' said Mr. Pecksniff buoyantly, 'but for you to recover this intrusion—this cowardly and indefensible outrage on your feelings—with all possible dispatch, and smile again.'

'You have nothing more to say?' inquired the old man, laying his hand with unusual earnestness on Mr. Pecksniff's sleeve.

Mr. Pecksniff would not say what rose to his lips. For reproaches, he observed, were useless.

'You have nothing at all to urge? You are sure of that? If you have, no matter what it is, speak freely. I will oppose nothing that you ask of me,' said the old man.

The tears rose in such abundance to Mr. Pecksniff's eyes at this proof of unlimited confidence on the part of his friend, that he was fain to clasp the bridge of his nose convulsively before he could at all compose himself. When he had the power of utterance again, he said, with great emotion, that he hoped he should live to deserve this; and added, that he had no other observation whatever to make.

For a few moments the old man sat looking at him, with that blank and motionless expression which is not uncommon in the faces of those whose faculties are on the wane, in age. But he rose up firmly too, and walked towards the door, from which Mark withdrew to make way for him.

The obsequious Mr. Pecksniff proffered his arm. The old man took it. Turning at the door, he said to Martin, waving him off with his hand.

'You have heard him. Go away. It is all over. Go!'

Mr. Pecksniff murmured certain cheering expressions of sympathy and encouragement as they retired; and Martin, awakening from the stupor into which the closing portion of this scene had plunged him, to the opportunity afforded by their departure, caught the innocent cause of all in his embrace, and pressed her to his heart.

'Dear girl!' said Martin. 'He has not changed you. Why, what an impotent and harmless knave the fellow is!'

'You have restrained yourself so nobly! You have borne so much!'

'Restrained myself!' cried Martin, cheerfully. 'You were by, and were unchanged, I knew. What more advantage did I want? The sight of me was such a bitterness to the dog, that I had my triumph in his being forced to endure it. But tell me, love—for the few hasty words we can exchange now are precious—what is this which has been rumoured to me? Is it true that you are persecuted by this knave's addresses?'

'I was, dear Martin, and to some extent am now; but my

chief source of unhappiness has been anxiety for you. Why did you leave us in such terrible suspense?'

'Sickness, distance; the dread of hinting at our real condition, the impossibility of concealing it except in perfect silence; the knowledge that the truth would have pained you infinitely more than uncertainty and doubt,' said Martin, hurriedly; as indeed everything else was done and said, in those few hurried moments, 'were the causes of my writing only once. But Pecksniff? You needn't fear to tell me the whole tale: for you saw me with him face to face, hearing him speak, and not taking him by the throat: what is the history of his pursuit of you? Is it known to my grandfather?'

'Yes.'

'And he assists him in it?'

'No,' she answered eagerly.

'Thank Heaven!' cried Martin, 'that it leaves his mind unclouded in that one respect!'

'I do not think,' said Mary, 'it was known to him at first. When this man had sufficiently prepared his mind, he revealed it to him by degrees. I think so, but I only know it from my own impression: not from anything they told me. Then he spoke to me alone.'

'My grandfather did?' said Martin.

'Yes—spoke to me alone, and told me—'

'What the hound had said,' cried Martin. 'Don't repeat it.'

'And said I knew well what qualities he possessed; that he was moderately rich; in good repute; and high in his favour and confidence. But seeing me very much distressed, he said that he would not control or force my inclinations, but would content himself with telling me the fact. He would not pain me by dwelling on it, or reverting to it: nor has he ever done so since, but has truly kept his word.'

'The man himself?—' asked Martin.

'He has had few opportunities of pursuing his suit. I have never walked out alone, or remained alone an instant in his presence. Dear Martin, I must tell you,' she continued, 'that the kindness of your grandfather to me remains unchanged. I am his companion still. An indescribable tenderness and compassion seem to have mingled themselves with his old regard; and if I were his only child, I could not have a gentler father. What former fancy or old habit survives in this, when his heart has turned so cold to you, is a mystery I cannot penetrate; but it has been, and it is, a happiness to me, that I remained true to him; that if he should wake from his delusion, even at the point of death, I am here, love, to recall you to his thoughts.'

Martin looked with admiration on her glowing face, and pressed his lips to hers.

'I have sometimes heard, and read,' she said, 'that those whose powers had been enfeebled long ago, and whose lives had faded, as it were, into a dream, have been known to rouse themselves before death, and inquire for familiar faces once very dear to them; but forgotten, unrecognised, hated even, in the meantime. Think, if with his old impressions of this man, he should suddenly resume his former self, and find in him his only friend!'

'I would not urge you to abandon him, dearest,' said Martin, 'though I could count the years we are to wear out asunder. But the influence this fellow exercises over him has steadily increased, I fear.'

She could not help admitting that. Steadily, imperceptibly, and surely, until now it was paramount and supreme. She herself had none; and yet he treated her with more affection than at any previous time. Martin thought the inconsistency a part of his weakness and decay.

'Does the influence extend to fear?' said Martin. 'Is he timid of asserting his own opinion in the presence of this infatuation? I fancied so just now.'

'I have thought so, often. Often when we are sitting alone, almost as we used to do, and I have been reading a favourite book to him, or he has been talking quite cheerfully, I have observed that the entrance of Mr. Pecksniff has changed his whole demeanour. He has broken off immediately, and become what you have seen to-day. When we first came here he had his impetuous outbreaks, in which it was not easy for Mr. Pecksniff with his utmost plausibility to appease him. But these have long since dwindled away. He defers to him in everything, and has no opinion upon any question, but that which is forced upon him by this treacherous man.'

Such was the account; rapidly furnished in whispers, and interrupted, brief as it was, by many false alarms of Mr. Pecksniff's return; which Martin received of his grandfather's decline, and of that good gentleman's ascendancy. He heard

Mr. Pecksniff announces himself as the Shield of Virtue

(*p. 666*)

of Tom Pinch too, and Jonas too, with not a little about himself into the bargain; for though lovers are remarkable for leaving a great deal unsaid on all occasions, and very properly desiring to come back and say it, they are remarkable also for a wonderful power of condensation; and can, in one way or other, give utterance to more language—eloquent language—in any given short space of time, than all the six hundred and fifty-eight members in the Commons House of Parliament of the United Kingdom of Great Britain and Ireland; who are strong lovers, no doubt, but of their country only, which makes all the difference; for in a passion of that kind (which is not always returned), it is the custom to use as many words as possible, and express nothing whatever.

A caution from Mr. Tapley; a hasty interchange of farewells, and of something else which the proverb says must not be told of afterwards; a white hand held out to Mr. Tapley himself, which he kissed with the devotion of a knight-errant; more farewells, more something else's; a parting word from Martin that he would write from London and would do great things there yet (Heaven knows what, but he quite believed it); and Mark and he stood on the outside of the Pecksniffian halls.

'A short interview after such an absence!' said Martin, sorrowfully. 'But we are well out of the house. We might have placed ourselves in a false position by remaining there, even so long, Mark.'

'I don't know about ourselves, sir,' he returned; 'but somebody else would have got into a false position, if he had happened to come back again, while we was there. I had the door all ready, sir. If Pecksniff had showed his head, or had only so much as listened behind it, I would have caught him like a walnut. He's the sort of man,' added Mr. Tapley, musing, 'as would squeeze soft, I know.'

A person who was evidently going to Mr. Pecksniff's house, passed them at this moment. He raised his eyes at the mention of the architect's name; and when he had gone on a few yards, stopped, and gazed at them. Mr. Tapley, also, looked over his shoulder, and so did Martin; for the stranger, as he passed, had looked very sharply at them.

'Who may that be, I wonder!' said Martin. 'The face seems familiar to me, but I don't know the man.'

'He seems to have a amiable desire that his face should be tolerable familiar to us,' said Mr. Tapley, 'for he's a-staring pretty hard. He'd better not waste his beauty, for he ain't got much to spare.'

Coming in sight of the Dragon, they saw a travelling carriage at the door.

'And a Salisbury carriage, eh!' said Mr. Tapley. 'That's what he came in, depend upon it. What's in the wind now? A new pupil, I shouldn't wonder. P'raps it's a order for another grammar-school, of the same pattern as the last.'

Before they could enter at the door, Mrs. Lupin came running out; and beckoning them to the carriage showed them a portmanteau with the name of CHUZZLEWIT upon it.

'Miss Pecksniff's husband that was,' said the good woman to Martin. 'I didn't know what terms you might be on, and was quite in a worry till you came back.'

'He and I have never interchanged a word yet,' observed Martin; 'and as I have no wish to be better or worse acquainted with him, I will not put myself in his way. We passed him on the road, I have no doubt. I am glad he timed his coming as he did. Upon my word! Miss Pecksniff's husband travels gaily!'

'A very fine-looking gentleman with him—in the best room now,' whispered Mrs. Lupin, glancing up at the window as they went into the house. 'He has ordered everything that can be got for dinner; and has the glossiest moustaches and whiskers ever you saw.'

'Has he?' cried Martin, 'why then we'll endeavour to avoid him too, in the hope that our self-denial may be strong enough for the sacrifice. It is only for a few hours,' said Martin, dropping wearily into a chair behind the little screen in the bar. 'Our visit has met with no success, my dear Mrs. Lupin, and I must go to London.'

'Dear, dear!' cried the hostess.

'Yes. One foul wind no more makes a winter, than one swallow makes a summer. I'll try it again. Tom Pinch has succeeded. With his advice to guide me, I may do the same. I took Tom under my protection once, God save the mark!' said Martin, with a melancholy smile; 'and promised I would make his fortune. Perhaps Tom will take me under *his* protection now, and teach me how to earn my bread.'

CHAPTER XLIV

Further continuation of the enterprise of Mr. Jonas and his friend

IT was a special quality, among the many admirable qualities possessed by Mr. Pecksniff, that the more he was found out, the more hypocrisy he practised. Let him be discomfited in one quarter, and he refreshed and recompensed himself by carrying the war into another. If his workings and windings were detected by A, so much the greater reason was there for practising without loss of time on B, if it were only to keep his hand in. He had never been such a saintly and improving spectacle to all about him, as after his detection by Thomas Pinch. He had scarcely ever been at once so tender in his humanity, and so dignified and exalted in his virtue, as when young Martin's scorn was fresh and hot upon him.

Having this large stock of superfluous sentiment and morality on hand which must positively be cleared off at any sacrifice, Mr. Pecksniff no sooner heard his son-in-law announced, than he regarded him as a kind of wholesale or general order, to be immediately executed. Descending, therefore, swiftly to the parlour, and clasping the young man in his arms, he exclaimed, with looks and gestures that denoted the perturbation of his spirit:

'Jonas. My child! She is well! There is nothing the matter?'

'What, you're at it again, are you?' replied his son-in-law. 'Even with me? Get away with you, will you?'

'Tell me she is well then,' said Mr. Pecksniff. 'Tell me she is well, my boy!'

'She's well enough,' retorted Jonas, disengaging himself. 'There's nothing the matter with *her*.'

'There is nothing the matter with her!' cried Mr. Pecksniff, sitting down in the nearest chair, and rubbing up his hair. 'Fie upon my weakness! I cannot help it, Jonas. Thank you. I am better now. How is my other child; my eldest; my Cherry-werrychigo?' said Mr. Pecksniff, inventing a playful little name for her, in the restored lightness of his heart.

'She's much about the same as usual,' returned Jonas. 'She sticks pretty close to the vinegar-bottle. You know she's got a sweetheart, I suppose?'

'I have heard of it,' said Mr. Pecksniff, 'from headquarters; from my child herself. I will not deny that it moved me to contemplate the loss of my remaining daughter, Jonas—I am afraid we parents are selfish, I am afraid we are—but it has ever been the study of my life to qualify them for the domestic hearth; and it is a sphere which Cherry will adorn.'

'She need adorn some sphere or other,' observed the son-in-law, 'for she ain't very ornamental in general.'

'My girls are now provided for,' said Mr. Pecksniff. 'They are now happily provided for, and I have not laboured in vain!'

This is exactly what Mr. Pecksniff would have said, if one of his daughters had drawn a prize of thirty thousand pounds in the lottery, or if the other had picked up a valuable purse in the street, which nobody appeared to claim. In either of these cases he would have invoked a patriarchal blessing on the fortunate head, with great solemnity, and would have taken immense credit to himself, as having meant it from the infant's cradle.

'Suppose we talk about something else, now,' observed Jonas, drily; 'just for a change. Are you quite agreeable?'

'Quite,' said Mr. Pecksniff. 'Ah, you wag, you naughty wag! You laugh at poor old fond papa. Well! He deserves it. And he don't mind it either, for his feelings are their own reward. You have come to stay with me, Jonas?'

'No. I've got a friend with me,' said Jonas.

'Bring your friend!' cried Mr. Pecksniff, in a gush of hospitality. 'Bring any number of your friends!'

'This ain't the sort of man to be brought,' said Jonas, contemptuously. 'I think I see myself "bringing" him to your house, for a treat! Thank'ee all the same; but he's a little too near the top of the tree for that, Pecksniff.'

The good man pricked up his ears; his interest was awakened. A position near the top of the tree was greatness, virtue, goodness, sense, genius; or, it should rather be said, a dispensation from all, and in itself something immeasurably better than all; with Mr. Pecksniff. A man who was able to look down upon Mr. Pecksniff could not be looked up at, by that gentleman, with too great an amount of deference, or from a position of too much humility. So it always is with great spirits.

'I'll tell you what you may do, if you like,' said Jonas: 'you may come and dine with us at the Dragon. We were forced to come down to Salisbury last night, on some business, and I got him to bring me over here this morning, in his carriage; at least, not his own carriage, for we had a breakdown in the night, but one we hired instead; it's all the same. Mind what you're about, you know. He's not used to all sorts; he only mixes with the best!'

'Some young nobleman who has been borrowing money of you at good interest, eh?' said Mr. Pecksniff, shaking his forefinger facetiously. 'I shall be delighted to know the gay sprig.'

'Borrowing!' echoed Jonas. 'Borrowing! When you're a twentieth part as rich as he is, you may shut up shop! We should be pretty well off if we could buy his furniture, and plate, and pictures, by clubbing together. A likely man to borrow: Mr. Montague! Why, since I was lucky enough (come! and I'll say, sharp enough, too) to get a share in the Assurance Office that he's President of, I've made—never mind what I've made,' said Jonas, seeming to recover all at once his usual caution. 'You know me pretty well, and I don't blab about such things. But, Ecod, I've made a trifle.'

'Really, my dear Jonas,' cried Mr. Pecksniff, with much warmth, 'a gentleman like this should receive some attention. Would he like to see the church? Or if he has a taste for the fine arts—which I have no doubt he has, from the description you give of his circumstances—I can send him down a few portfolios. Salisbury Cathedral, my dear Jonas,' said Mr. Pecksniff; the mention of the portfolios and his anxiety to display himself to advantage, suggesting his usual phraseology in that regard; 'is an edifice replete with venerable associations, and strikingly suggestive of the loftiest emotions. It is here we contemplate the work of bygone ages. It is here we listen to the swelling organ, as we stroll through the reverberating aisles. We have drawings of this celebrated structure from the North, from the South, from the East, from the West, from the South-East, from the Nor'-West——'

During this digression, and indeed during the whole dialogue, Jonas had been rocking on his chair, with his hands in his pockets, and his head thrown cunningly on one side. He looked at Mr. Pecksniff now with such shrewd meaning twinkling in his eyes, that Mr. Pecksniff stopped, and asked him what he was going to say.

'Ecod!' he answered. 'Pecksniff, if I knew how you meant to leave your money, I could put you in the way of doubling it in no time. It wouldn't be bad to keep a chance like this snug in the family. But you're such a deep one!'

'Jonas!' cried Mr. Pecksniff, much affected, 'I am not a diplomatical character: my heart is in my hand. By far the greater part of the inconsiderable savings I have accumulated in the course of—I hope—a not dishonourable or useless career, is already given, devised, and bequeathed (correct me, my dear Jonas, if I am technically wrong), with expressions of confidence, which I will not repeat; and in securities which it is unnecessary to mention; to a person whom I cannot, whom I will not, whom I need not, name.' Here he gave the hand of his son-in-law a fervent squeeze, as if he would have added, 'God bless you; be very careful of it when you get it!'

Mr. Jonas only shook his head and laughed, and, seeming to think better of what he had had in his mind, said, 'No. He would keep his own counsel.' But as he observed that he would take a walk, Mr. Pecksniff insisted on accompanying him, remarking that he could leave a card for Mr. Montague, as they went along, by way of gentleman-usher to himself at dinner-time. Which he did.

In the course of their walk, Mr. Jonas affected to maintain that close reserve which had operated as a timely check upon him during the foregoing dialogue. And as he made no attempt to conciliate Mr. Pecksniff, but, on the contrary, was more boorish and rude to him than usual, that gentleman, so far from suspecting his real design, laid himself out to be attacked with advantage. For it is in the nature of a knave to think the tools with which he works indispensable to knavery; and knowing what he would do himself in such a case, Mr. Pecksniff argued, 'if this young man wanted anything of me for his own ends, he would be polite and deferential.'

The more Jonas repelled him in his hints and inquiries, the more solicitous, therefore, Mr. Pecksniff became to be initiated into the golden mysteries at which he had obscurely glanced. Why should there be cold and worldly secrets, he observed, between relations? What was life without confidence? If the chosen husband of his daughter, the man to whom he had delivered her with so much pride and hope, such bounding and such beaming joy: if he were not a green spot in the barren waste of life, where was that Oasis to be found?

Little did Mr. Pecksniff think on what a very green spot he planted one foot at that moment! Little did he foresee when he said, 'All is but dust!' how very shortly he would come down with his own!

Inch by inch, in his grudging and ill-conditioned way; sustained to the life, for the hope of making Mr. Pecksniff suffer in that tender place, the pocket, where Jonas smarted so terribly himself, gave him an additional and malicious interest in the wiles he was set on to practise: inch by inch, and bit by bit, Jonas rather allowed the dazzling prospects of the Anglo-Bengalee establishment to escape him, than paraded them before his greedy listener. And in the same niggardly spirit, he left Mr. Pecksniff to infer, if he chose (which he *did* choose, of course), that a consciousness of not having any great natural gifts of speech and manner himself, rendered him desirous to have the credit of introducing to Mr. Montague some one who was well endowed in those respects, and so atone for his own deficiencies. Otherwise, he muttered discontentedly, he would have seen his beloved father-in-law 'far enough off,' before he would have taken him into his confidence.

Primed in this artful manner, Mr. Pecksniff presented himself at dinner-time in such a state of suavity, benevolence, cheerfulness, politeness, and cordiality, as even he had perhaps never attained before. The frankness of the country gentleman, the refinement of the artist, the good-humoured allowance of the man of the world; philanthropy, forbearance, piety, toleration, all blended together in a flexible adaptability to anything and everything; were expressed in Mr. Pecksniff, as he shook hands with the great speculator and capitalist.

'Welcome, respected sir,' said Mr. Pecksniff, 'to our humble village! We are a simple people: primitive clods, Mr. Montague; but we can appreciate the honour of your visit, as my dear son-in-law can testify. It is very strange,' said Mr. Pecksniff, pressing his hand almost reverentially, 'but I seem to know you. That towering forehead, my dear Jonas,' said Mr. Pecksniff aside, 'and those clustering masses of rich hair— I must have seen you, my dear sir, in the sparkling throng.'

Nothing was more probable, they all agreed.

'I could have wished,' said Mr. Pecksniff, 'to have had the honour of introducing you to an elderly inmate of our house: to the uncle of our friend. Mr. Chuzzlewit, sir, would have been proud indeed to have taken you by the hand.'

'Is the gentleman here now?' asked Montague, turning deeply red.

'He is,' said Mr. Pecksniff.

'You said nothing about that, Chuzzlewit.'

'I didn't suppose you'd care to hear of it,' returned Jonas. 'You wouldn't care to know him, I can promise you.'

'Jonas! my dear Jonas!' remonstrated Mr Pecksniff. 'Really!'

'Oh! it's all very well for you to speak up for him,' said Jonas. 'You have nailed him. You'll get a fortune by him.'

'Oho! Is the wind in that quarter?' cried Montague. 'Ha, ha, ha!' and here they all laughed—especially Mr. Pecksniff.

'No, no!' said that gentleman, clapping his son-in-law playfully upon the shoulder. 'You must not believe all that my young relative says, Mr. Montague. You may believe him in official business, and trust him in official business, but you must not attach importance to his flights of fancy.'

'Upon my life, Mr. Pecksniff,' cried Montague, 'I attach the greatest importance to that last observation of his. I trust and hope it's true. Money cannot be turned and turned again quickly enough in the ordinary course, Mr. Pecksniff. There is nothing like building our fortune on the weaknesses of mankind.'

'Oh fie! Oh fie, for shame!' cried Mr. Pecksniff. But they all laughed again—especially Mr. Pecksniff.

'I give you my honour that *we* do it,' said Montague.

'Oh fie, fie!' cried Mr. Pecksniff. 'You are very pleasant. That I am sure you don't! That I am sure you don't! How *can* you, you know?'

Again they all laughed in concert; and again Mr. Pecksniff laughed especially.

This was very agreeable indeed. It was confidential, easy, straightforward: and still left Mr. Pecksniff in the position of being in a gentle way the Mentor of the party. The greatest achievements in the article of cookery that the Dragon had ever performed, were set before them; the oldest and best wines in the Dragon's cellar saw the light on that occasion; a thousand bubbles, indicative of the wealth and station of Mr. Montague in the depths of his pursuits, were constantly rising to the surface of the conversation; and they were as frank and merry as three honest men could be. Mr. Pecksniff thought it a pity (he said so) that Mr. Montague should think lightly of mankind and their weaknesses. He was anxious upon this subject; his mind ran upon it; in one way or another he was constantly coming back to it; he must make a convert of him, he said. And as often as Mr. Montague repeated his sentiment about building fortunes on the weaknesses of mankind, and added frankly, '*We* do it!' just as often Mr. Pecksniff repeated 'Oh fie! Oh fie, for shame! I am sure you don't. How *can* you, you know?' laying a greater stress each time on those last words.

The frequent repetition of this playful inquiry on the part of Mr. Pecksniff, led at last to playful answers on the part of Mr. Montague; but after some little sharp-shooting on both sides, Mr. Pecksniff became grave, almost to tears; observing that if Mr. Montague would give him leave, he would drink the health of his young kinsman, Mr. Jonas; congratulating him upon the valuable and distinguished friendship he had formed, but envying him, he would confess, his usefulness to his fellow-creatures. For, if he understood the objects of that Institution with which he was newly and advantageously connected—knowing them but imperfectly—they were calculated to do Good; and for his (Mr. Pecksniff's) part, if he could in any way promote them, he thought he would be able to lay his head upon his pillow every night, with an absolute certainty of going to sleep at once.

The transition from this accidental remark (for it was quite accidental, and had fallen from Mr. Pecksniff in the openness of his soul), to the discussion of the subject as a matter of business, was easy. Books, papers, statements, tables, calculations of various kinds, were soon spread out before them; and as they were all framed with one object, it is not surprising that they should all have tended to one end. But still, whenever Montague enlarged upon the profits of the office, and said that as long as there were gulls upon the wing it must succeed, Mr. Pecksniff mildly said 'Oh fie!'—and might indeed have remonstrated with him, but that he knew he was joking. Mr. Pecksniff did know he was joking; because he said so.

There never had been before, and there never would be again, such an opportunity for the investment of a considerable sum (the rate of advantage increased in proportion to the amount invested), as at that moment. The only time that had at all approached it, was the time when Jonas had come into the concern; which made him ill-natured now, and inclined him to pick out a doubt in this place, and a flaw in that, and grumblingly to advise Mr. Pecksniff to think better of it. The sum which would complete the proprietorship in this snug concern, was nearly equal to Mr. Pecksniff's whole hoard: not counting Mr. Chuzzlewit, that is to say, whom he looked upon as money in the Bank, the possession of which inclined him the more to make a dash with his own private sprats for the capture of such a whale as Mr. Montague described. The returns began almost immediately, and were immense. The end of it was, that Mr. Pecksniff agreed to become the last partner and proprietor in the Anglo-Bengalee, and made an appointment to dine with Mr. Montague, at Salisbury, on the next day but one, then and there to complete the negotiation.

It took so long to bring the subject to this head, that it was nearly midnight when they parted. When Mr. Pecksniff walked down-stairs to the door, he found Mrs. Lupin standing there, looking out.

'Ah, my good friend!' he said: 'not a-bed yet! Contemplating the stars, Mrs. Lupin?'

'It's a beautiful starlight night, sir.'

'A beautiful starlight night,' said Mr. Pecksniff, looking up. 'Behold the planets, how they shine! Behold the——those two persons who were here this morning have left your house, I hope, Mrs. Lupin?'

'Yes, sir. They are gone.'

'I am glad to hear it,' said Mr. Pecksniff. 'Behold the wonders of the firmament, Mrs. Lupin! How glorious is the scene! When I look up at those shining orbs, I think that each of them is winking to the other to take notice of the vanity of men's pursuits. My fellow-men!' cried Mr. Pecksniff, shaking his head in pity; 'you are much mistaken; my wormy relatives, you are much deceived! The stars are perfectly contented (I suppose so) in their several spheres. Why are not you? Oh! do not strive and struggle to enrich yourselves, or to get the better of each other, my deluded friends, but look up there, with me!'

Mrs. Lupin shook her head, and heaved a sigh. It was very affecting.

'Look up there, with me!' repeated Mr. Pecksniff, stretching out his hand; 'with me, an humble individual who is also an Insect like yourselves. Can silver, gold, or precious stones, sparkle like those constellations! I think not. Then do not thirst for silver, gold, or precious stones; but look up there, with me!'

With those words, the good man patted Mrs. Lupin's hand between his own, as if he would have added 'think of this, my good woman!' and walked away in a sort of ecstasy or rapture, with his hat under his arm.

Jonas sat in the attitude in which Mr. Pecksniff had left him, gazing moodily at his friend: who, surrounded by a heap of documents, was writing something on an oblong slip of paper.

'You mean to wait at Salisbury over the day after to-morrow, do you, then?' said Jonas.

'You heard our appointment,' returned Montague, without raising his eyes. 'In any case I should have waited to see after the boy.'

They appeared to have changed places again; Montague being in high spirits; Jonas gloomy and lowering.

'You don't want me, I suppose?' said Jonas.

'I want you to put your name here,' he returned, glancing at him with a smile, 'as soon as I have filled up the stamp. I may as well have your note of hand for that extra capital. That's all I want. If you wish to go home, I can manage Mr. Pecksniff now, alone. There is a perfect understanding between us.'

Jonas sat scowling at him as he wrote, in silence. When he had finished his writing, and had dried it on the blotting paper in his travelling-desk; he looked up, and tossed the pen towards him.

'What, not a day's grace, not a day's trust, eh?' said Jonas, bitterly. 'Not after the pains I have taken with to-night's work?'

'To-night's work was a part of our bargain,' replied Montague; 'and so was this.'

'You drive a hard bargain,' said Jonas, advancing to the table. 'You know best. Give it here!'

Montague gave him the paper. After pausing as if he could not make up his mind to put his name to it, Jonas dipped his pen hastily in the nearest inkstand, and began to write. But he had scarcely marked the paper when he started back, in a panic.

'Why, what the devil's this?' he said. 'It's bloody!'

He had dipped the pen, as another moment showed, into red ink. But he attached a strange degree of importance to the mistake. He asked how it had come there, who had brought it, why it had been brought; and looked at Montague, at first, as if he thought he had put a trick upon him. Even when he used a different pen, and the right ink, he made some scratches on another paper first, as half-believing they would turn red also.

'Black enough, this time,' he said, handing the note to Montague. 'Good-bye.'

'Going now! How do you mean to get away from here?'

'I shall cross early in the morning to the high road, before you are out of bed; and catch the day-coach, going up. Good-bye!'

'You are in a hurry!'

'I have Something to do,' said Jonas. 'Good-bye!'

His friend looked after him as he went out, in surprise, which gradually gave place to an air of satisfaction and relief.

'It happens all the better. It brings about what I wanted, without any difficulty. I shall travel home alone.'

CHAPTER XLV

In which Tom Pinch and his sister take a little pleasure; but quite in a domestic way, and with no ceremony about it

TOM PINCH and his sister having to part, for the dispatch of the morning's business, immediately after the dispersion of the other actors in the scene upon the Wharf with which the reader has been already made acquainted, had no opportunity of discussing the subject at that time. But Tom, in his solitary office, and Ruth, in the triangular parlour, thought about nothing else all day; and, when their hour of meeting in the afternoon approached, they were very full of it, to be sure.

There was a little plot between them, that Tom should always come out of the Temple by one way; and that was past the fountain. Coming through Fountain Court, he was just to glance down the steps leading into Garden Court, and to look once all round him; and if Ruth had come to meet him, there he would see her; not sauntering, you understand (on account of the clerks), but coming briskly up, with the best little laugh upon her face that ever played in opposition to the fountain, and beat it all to nothing. For, fifty to one, Tom had been looking for her in the wrong direction, and had quite given her up, while she had been tripping towards him from the first: jingling that little reticule of hers (with all the keys in it) to attract his wandering observation.

Whether there was life enough left in the slow vegetation of Fountain Court for the smoky shrubs to have any consciousness of the brightest and purest-hearted little woman in the world, is a question for gardeners, and those who are learned in the loves of plants. But, that it was a good thing for that same paved yard to have such a delicate little figure flitting through it; that it passed like a smile from the grimy old houses, and the worn flagstones, and left them duller, darker, sterner than before; there is no sort of doubt. The Temple fountain might have leaped up twenty feet to greet the spring of hopeful maidenhood, that in her person stole on, sparkling, through the dry and dusty channels of the Law; the chirping sparrows, bred in Temple chinks and crannies, might have held their peace to listen to imaginary skylarks, as so fresh a little creature passed; the dingy boughs, unused to droop, otherwise than in their puny growth, might have bent down in a kindred grace-fulness to shed their benedictions on her graceful head; old love letters, shut up in iron boxes in the neighbouring offices, and made of no account among the heaps of family papers into which they had strayed, and of which, in their degeneracy, they formed a part, might have stirred and fluttered with a moment's recollection of their ancient tenderness, as she went lightly by. Anything might have happened that did not happen, and never will, for the love of Ruth.

Something happened, too, upon the afternoon of which the history treats. Not for her love. Oh no! quite by accident, and without the least reference to her at all.

Either she was a little too soon, or Tom was a little too late—she was so precise in general, that she timed it to half a minute—but no Tom was there. Well! But was anybody else there, that she blushed so deeply, after looking round, and tripped off down the steps with such unusual expedition?

Why, the fact is, that Mr. Westlock was passing at that moment. The Temple is a public thoroughfare; they may write up on the gates that it is not, but so long as the gates are left open it is, and will be; and Mr. Westlock had as good a right to be there as anybody else. But why did she run away, then? Not being ill dressed, for she was much too neat for that, why did she run away? The brown hair that had fallen down beneath her bonnet, and had one impertinent imp of a false flower clinging to it, boastful of its licence before all men, *that* could not have been the cause, for it looked charming. Oh! foolish, panting, frightened little heart, why did she run away!

Merrily the tiny fountain played, and merrily the dimples sparkled on its sunny face. John Westlock hurried after her. Softly the whispering water broke and fell; and roguishly the dimples twinkled, as he stole upon her footsteps.

Oh, foolish, panting, timid little heart, why did she feign to be unconscious of his coming! Why wish herself so far away, yet be so flutteringly happy there!

'I felt sure it was you,' said John, when he overtook her in the sanctuary of Garden Court. 'I knew I couldn't be mis-taken.'

She was *so* surprised.

'You are waiting for your brother,' said John. 'Let me bear you company.'

So light was the touch of the coy little hand, that he glanced down to assure himself he had it on his arm. But his glance, stopping for an instant at the bright eyes, forgot its first design, and went no farther.

They walked up and down three or four times, speaking about Tom and his mysterious employment. Now that was a very natural and innocent subject, surely. Then why, whenever Ruth lifted up her eyes, did she let them fall again immediately, and seek the uncongenial pavement of the court? They were not such eyes as shun the light; they were not such eyes as require to be hoarded to enhance their value. They were much too precious and too genuine to stand in need of arts like those. Somebody must have been looking at them!

They found out Tom, though, quickly enough. This pair of eyes descried him in the distance, the moment he appeared. He was staring about him, as usual, in all directions but the right one; and was as obstinate in not looking towards them, as if he had intended it. As it was plain that, being left to himself, he would walk away home, John Westlock darted off to stop him.

This made the approach of poor little Ruth, by herself, one of the most embarrassing of circumstances. There was Tom, manifesting extreme surprise (he had no presence of mind, that Tom, on small occasions); there was John, making as light of it as he could, but explaining at the same time with most unnecessary elaboration; and here was she, coming towards them, with both of them looking at her, conscious of blushing to a terrible extent, but trying to throw up her eyebrows carelessly, and pout her rosy lips, as if she were the coolest and most unconcerned of little women.

Merrily the fountain plashed and plashed, until the dimples, merging into one another, swelled into a general smile, that covered the whole surface of the basin.

'What an extraordinary meeting!' said Tom. 'I should never have dreamed of seeing you two together here.'

'Quite accidental,' John was heard to murmur.

'Exactly,' cried Tom; 'that's what I mean, you know. If it wasn't accidental, there would be nothing remarkable in it.'

'To be sure,' said John.

'Such an out-of-the-way place for you to have met in,' pursued Tom, quite delighted. 'Such an unlikely spot!'

John rather disputed that. On the contrary, he considered it a very likely spot, indeed. He was constantly passing to and

fro there, he said. He shouldn't wonder if it were to happen
again. His only wonder was, that it had never happened before.

By this time Ruth had got round on the farther side of her
brother, and had taken his arm. She was squeezing it now, as
much as to say, 'Are you going to stop here all day, you dear
old blundering Tom?'

Tom answered the squeeze as if it had been a speech. 'John,'
he said, 'if you'll give my sister your arm, we'll take her
between us, and walk on. I have a curious circumstance to
relate to you. Our meeting could not have happened better.'

Merrily the fountain leaped and danced, and merrily the
smiling dimples twinkled and expanded more and more, until
they broke into a laugh against the basin's rim, and vanished.

'Tom,' said his friend, as they turned into the noisy street,
'I have a proposition to make. It is, that you and your sister—
if she will so far honour a poor bachelor's dwelling—give me
a great pleasure, and come and dine with me.'

'What, to-day?' cried Tom.

'Yes, to-day. It's close by, you know. Pray, Miss Pinch,
insist upon it. It will be very disinterested, for I have nothing
to give you.'

'Oh! you must not believe that, Ruth,' said Tom. 'He is the
most tremendous fellow, in his housekeeping, that I ever
heard of, for a single man. He ought to be Lord Mayor. Well!
what do you say? Shall we go?'

'If you please, Tom,' rejoined his dutiful little sister.

'But I mean,' said Tom, regarding her with smiling admiration: 'is there anything you ought to wear, and haven't got?
I am sure I don't know, John: she may not be able to take her
bonnet off, for anything I can tell.'

There was a great deal of laughing at this, and there were
divers compliments from John Westlock—not compliments
he said at least (and really he was right), but good, plain,
honest truths, which no one could deny. Ruth laughed, and
all that, but she made no objection; so it was an engagement.

'If I had known it a little sooner,' said John, 'I would have
tried another pudding. Not in rivalry; but merely to exalt that
famous one. I wouldn't on any account have had it made with
suet.'

'Why not?' asked Tom.

'Because that cookery-book advises suet,' said John Westlock; 'and ours was made with flour and eggs.'

'Oh good gracious!' cried Tom. 'Ours was made with flour and eggs, was it? Ha, ha, ha! A beefsteak pudding made with flour and eggs! Why anybody knows better than that. I know better than that! Ha, ha, ha!'

It is unnecessary to say that Tom had been present at the making of the pudding, and had been a devoted believer in it all through. But he was so delighted to have this joke against his busy little sister, and was tickled to that degree at having found her out, that he stopped in Temple Bar to laugh; and it was no more to Tom, that he was anathematised and knocked about by the surly passengers, than it would have been to a post; for he continued to exclaim with unabated good humour, 'flour and eggs! A beefsteak pudding made with flour and eggs!' until John Westlock and his sister fairly ran away from him, and left him to have his laugh out by himself; which he had; and then came dodging across the crowded street to them, with such sweet temper and tenderness (it was quite a tender joke of Tom's) beaming in his face, God bless it, that it might have purified the air, though Temple Bar had been, as in the golden days gone by, embellished with a row of rotting human heads.

There are snug chambers in those Inns where the bachelors live, and, for the desolate fellows they pretend to be, it is quite surprising how well they get on. John was very pathetic on the subject of his dreary life, and the deplorable makeshifts and apologetic contrivances it involved; but he really seemed to make himself pretty comfortable. His rooms were the perfection of neatness and convenience at any rate; and if he were anything but comfortable, the fault was certainly not theirs.

He had no sooner ushered Tom and his sister into his best room (where there was a beautiful little vase of fresh flowers on the table, all ready for Ruth.—Just as if he had expected her, Tom said), than seizing his hat, he bustled out again, in his most energetically bustling way; and presently came hurrying back, as they saw through the half-opened door, attended by a fiery-faced matron attired in a crunched bonnet, with particularly long strings to it hanging down her back; in conjunction with whom he instantly began to lay the cloth for dinner, polishing up the wine-glasses with his own hands, brightening the silver top of the pepper-castor on his coat-sleeve, drawing corks and filling decanters, with a skill and expedition that were quite dazzling. And as if, in the course of this rubbing and polishing, he had rubbed an enchanted lamp or a magic ring, obedient to which there were twenty thousand supernatural slaves at least, suddenly there appeared a being in a white waistcoat, carrying under his arm a napkin, and attended by another being with an oblong box upon his head, from which a banquet, piping hot, was taken out and set upon the table.

Salmon, lamb, peas, innocent young potatoes, a cool salad, sliced cucumber, a tender duckling, and a tart—all there. They all came at the right time. Where they came from, didn't appear; but the oblong box was constantly going and coming, and making its arrival known to the man in the white waistcoat by bumping modestly against the outside of the door; for, after its first appearance, it entered the room no more. He was never surprised, this man; he never seemed to wonder at the extraordinary things he found in the box; but took them out with a face expressive of a steady purpose and impenetrable character, and put them on the table. He was a kind man; gentle in his manners, and much interested in what they ate and drank. He was a learned man, and knew the flavour of John Westlock's private sauces, which he softly and feelingly described, as he handed the little bottles round. He was a grave man, and a noiseless; for dinner being done, and wine and fruit arranged upon the board, he vanished, box and all, like something that had never been.

'Didn't I say he was a tremendous fellow in his housekeeping?' cried Tom. 'Bless my soul! It's wonderful.'

'Ah, Miss Pinch,' said John. 'This is the bright side of the life we lead in such a place. It would be a dismal life, indeed, if it didn't brighten up to-day.'

'Don't believe a word he says,' cried Tom. 'He lives here like a monarch, and wouldn't change his mode of life for any consideration. He only pretends to grumble.'

No, John really did not appear to pretend; for he was uncommonly earnest in his desire to have it understood that he was as dull, solitary, and uncomfortable on ordinary occasions as an unfortunate young man could, in reason, be. It was a wretched life, he said, a miserable life. He thought of getting rid of the chambers as soon as possible; and meant, in fact, to put a bill up very shortly.

'Well!' said Tom Pinch, 'I don't know where you can go,

John, to be more comfortable. That's all I can say. What do *you* say, Ruth?'

Ruth trifled with the cherries on her plate, and said that she thought Mr. Westlock ought to be quite happy, and that she had no doubt he was.

Ah, foolish, panting, frightened little heart, how timidly she said it!

'But you are forgetting what you had to tell, Tom: what occurred this morning,' she added in the same breath.

'So I am,' said Tom. 'We have been so talkative on other topics, that I declare I have not had time to think of it. I'll tell it you at once, John, in case I should forget it altogether.'

On Tom's relating what had passed upon the wharf, his friend was very much surprised, and took such a great interest in the narrative as Tom could not quite understand. He believed he knew the old lady whose acquaintance they had made, he said; and that he might venture to say, from their description of her, that her name was Gamp. But of what nature the communication could have been which Tom had borne so unexpectedly; why its delivery had been entrusted to him; how it happened that the parties were involved together; and what secret lay at the bottom of the whole affair; perplexed him very much. Tom had been sure of his taking some interest in the matter; but was not prepared for the strong interest he showed. It held John Westlock to the subject even after Ruth had left the room; and evidently made him anxious to pursue it further than as a mere subject of conversation.

'I shall remonstrate with my landlord, of course,' said Tom: 'though he is a very singular secret sort of man, and not likely to afford me much satisfaction; even if he knew what was in the letter.'

'Which you may swear he did,' John interposed.

'You think so?'

'I am certain of it.'

'Well!' said Tom, 'I shall remonstrate with him when I see him (he goes in and out in a strange way, but I will try to catch him to-morrow morning), on his having asked me to execute such an unpleasant commission. And I have been thinking, John, that if I went down to Mrs. What's-her-name's in the City, where I was before, you know—Mrs. Todgers's— to-morrow morning, I might find poor Mercy Pecksniff there, perhaps, and be able to explain to her how I came to have any hand in the business.'

'You are perfectly right, Tom,' returned his friend, after a short interval of reflection. 'You cannot do better. It is quite clear to me that whatever the business is, there is little good in it; and it is so desirable for you to disentangle yourself from any appearance of wilful connexion with it, that I would counsel you to see her husband, if you can, and wash your hands of it by a plain statement of the facts. I have a misgiving that there is something dark at work here, Tom. I will tell you why, at another time: when I have made an inquiry or two myself.'

All this sounded very mysterious to Tom Pinch. But as he knew he could rely upon his friend, he resolved to follow this advice.

Ah, but it would have been a good thing to have had a coat of invisibility, wherein to have watched little Ruth, when she was left to herself in John Westlock's chambers, and John and her brother were talking thus, over their wine! The gentle way in which she tried to get up a little conversation with the fiery-faced matron in the crunched bonnet, who was waiting to attend her; after making a desperate rally in regard of her dress, and attiring herself in a washed-out yellow gown with sprigs of the same upon it, so that it looked like a tesselated work of pats of butter. That would have been pleasant. The grim and griffin-like inflexibility with which the fiery-faced matron repelled these engaging advances, as proceeding from a hostile and dangerous power, who could have no business there, unless it were to deprive her of a customer, or suggest what became of the self-consuming tea and sugar, and other general trifles. That would have been agreeable. The bashful, winning, glorious curiosity, with which little Ruth, when fiery-face was gone, peeped into the books and nick-nacks that were lying about, and had a particular interest in some delicate paper-matches on the chimney-piece: wondering who could have made them. That would have been worth seeing. The faltering hand with which she tied those flowers together; with which, almost blushing at her own fair self as imaged in the glass, she arranged them in her breast, and looking at them with her head aside, now half resolved to take them out again, now half resolved to leave them where they were. That would have been delightful!

John seemed to think it all delightful: for coming in with Tom to tea, he took his seat beside her like a man enchanted. And when the tea-service had been removed, and Tom, sitting down at the piano, became absorbed in some of his old organ tunes, he was still beside her at the open window, looking out upon the twilight.

There is little enough to see in Furnival's Inn. It is a shady, quiet place, echoing to the footsteps of the stragglers who have business there; and rather monotonous and gloomy on summer evenings. What gave it such a charm to them, that they remained at the window as unconscious of the flight of time as Tom himself, the dreamer, while the melodies which had so often soothed his spirit were hovering again about him! What power infused into the fading light, the gathering darkness; the stars that here and there appeared; the evening air, the City's hum and stir, the very chiming of the old church clocks; such exquisite enthralment, that the divinest regions of the earth spread out before their eyes could not have held them captive in a stronger chain?

The shadows deepened, deepened, and the room became quite dark. Still Tom's fingers wandered over the keys of the piano; and still the window had its pair of tenants.

At length, her hand upon his shoulder, and her breath upon his forehead, roused Tom from his reverie.

'Dear me!' he cried, desisting with a start. 'I am afraid I have been very inconsiderate and unpolite.'

Tom little thought how much consideration and politeness he had shown!

'Sing something to us, my dear,' said Tom. 'Let us hear your voice. Come!'

John Westlock added his entreaties with such earnestness that a flinty heart alone could have resisted them. Hers was not a flinty heart. O dear no! Quite another thing.

So down she sat, and in a pleasant voice began to sing the ballads Tom loved well. Old rhyming stories, with here and there a pause for a few simple chords, such as a harper might have sounded in the ancient time while looking upward for the current of some half-remembered legend; words of old poets, wedded to such measures that the strain of music might have been the poet's breath, giving utterance and expression to his thoughts; and now a melody so joyous and light-hearted, that the singer seemed incapable of sadness, until in her incon-

stancy (oh wicked little singer!) she relapsed, and broke the
listeners' hearts again: these were the simple means she used
to please them. And that these simple means prevailed, and
she *did* please them, let the still darkened chamber, and its
long-deferred illumination witness.

The candles came at last, and it was time for moving homeward. Cutting paper carefully, and rolling it about the stalks
of those same flowers, occasioned some delay; but even this
was done in time, and Ruth was ready.

'Good night!' said Tom. 'A memorable and delightful visit,
John! Good night!'

John thought he would walk with them.

'No, no. Don't!' said Tom. 'What nonsense! We can get
home very well alone. I couldn't think of taking you out.'

But John said he would rather.

'Are you sure you would rather?' said Tom. 'I am afraid you
only say so out of politeness.'

John being quite sure, gave his arm to Ruth, and led her out.
Fiery-face, who was again in attendance, acknowledged her
departure with so cold a curtsey that it was hardly visible; and
cut Tom dead.

Their host was bent on walking the whole distance, and
would not listen to Tom's dissuasions. Happy time, happy
walk, happy parting, happy dreams! But there are some sweet
day-dreams, so there are, that put the visions of the night to
shame.

Busily the Temple fountain murmured in the moonlight,
while Ruth lay sleeping, with her flowers beside her; and John
Westlock sketched a portrait—whose?—from memory.

CHAPTER XLVI

In which Miss Pecksniff makes love, Mr. Jonas makes wrath,
Mrs. Gamp makes tea, and Mr. Chuffey makes business

ON the next day's official duties coming to a close, Tom
hurried home without losing any time by the way; and
after dinner and a short rest, sallied out again, accompanied
by Ruth, to pay his projected visit to Todgers's. Tom took
Ruth with him, not only because it was a great pleasure to him
to have her for his companion whenever he could, but because
he wished her to cherish and comfort poor Merry; which she,
for her own part (having heard the wretched history of that
young wife from Tom), was all eagerness to do.

'She was so glad to see me,' said Tom, 'that I am sure she
will be glad to see you. Your sympathy is certain to be much
more delicate and acceptable than mine.'

'I am very far from being certain of that, Tom,' she replied;
'and indeed you do yourself an injustice. Indeed you do. But
I hope she may like me, Tom.'

'Oh, she is sure to do that!' cried Tom, confidently.

'What a number of friends I should have, if everybody was
of your way of thinking. Shouldn't I, Tom, dear?' said his
little sister, pinching him upon the cheek.

Tom laughed, and said that with reference to this particular
case he had no doubt at all of finding a disciple in Merry. 'For
you women,' said Tom, 'you women, my dear, are so kind, and
in your kindness have such nice perception; you know so well
how to be affectionate and full of solicitude without appearing
to be; your gentleness of feeling is like your touch: so light and
easy, that the one enables you to deal with wounds of the mind
as tenderly as the other enables you to deal with wounds of the
body. You are such——'

'My goodness, Tom!' his sister interposed. 'You ought to
fall in love immediately.'

Tom put this observation off good humouredly, but somewhat gravely too; and they were soon very chatty again on
some other subject.

As they were passing through a street in the City, not very
far from Mrs. Todgers's place of residence, Ruth checked Tom

before the window of a large Upholstery and Furniture Warehouse, to call his attention to something very magnificent and
ingenious, displayed there to the best advantage, for the
admiration and temptation of the public. Tom had hazarded
some most erroneous and extravagantly wrong guess in relation
to the price of this article, and had joined his sister in laughing
heartily at his mistake, when he pressed her arm in his, and
pointed to two persons at a little distance, who were looking in
at the same window with a deep interest in the chests of
drawers and tables.

'Hush!' Tom whispered. 'Miss Pecksniff, and the young
gentleman to whom she is going to be married.'

'Why does he look as if he was going to be buried, Tom?'
inquired his little sister.

'Why, he is naturally a dismal young gentleman, I believe,'
said Tom: 'but he is very civil and inoffensive.'

'I suppose they are furnishing their house,' whispered Ruth.

'Yes, I suppose they are,' replied Tom. 'We had better avoid
speaking to them.'

They could not very well avoid looking at them, however,
especially as some obstruction on the pavement, at a little
distance, happened to detain them where they were for a few
moments. Miss Pecksniff had quite the air of having taken the
unhappy Moddle captive, and brought him up to the contemplation of the furniture like a lamb to the altar. He offered
no resistance, but was perfectly resigned and quiet. The
melancholy depicted in the turn of his languishing head, and
in his dejected attitude, was extreme; and though there was
a full-sized four-post bedstead in the window, such a tear stood
trembling in his eye, as seemed to blot it out.

'Augustus, my love,' said Miss Pecksniff, 'ask the price of
the eight rosewood chairs, and the loo table.'

'Perhaps they are ordered already,' said Augustus. 'Perhaps
they are Another's.'

'They can make more like them, if they are,' rejoined Miss
Pecksniff.

'No, no, they can't,' said Moddle. 'It's impossible!'

He appeared, for the moment, to be quite overwhelmed and
stupefied by the prospect of his approaching happiness; but
recovering, entered the shop. He returned immediately: saying
in a tone of despair:

'Twenty-four pound ten!'

Miss Pecksniff, turning to receive this announcement, became conscious of the observation of Tom Pinch and his sister.

'Oh, really!' cried Miss Pecksniff, glancing about her, as if for some convenient means of sinking into the earth. 'Upon my word, I—there never was such a—to think that one should be so very—Mr. Augustus Moddle, Miss Pinch!'

Miss Pecksniff was quite gracious to Miss Pinch in this triumphant introduction; exceedingly gracious. She was more than gracious; she was kind and cordial. Whether the recollection of the old service Tom had rendered her in knocking Mr. Jonas on the head had wrought this change in her opinions; or whether her separation from her parent had reconciled her to all human-kind, or to all that increasing portion of human-kind which was not friendly to him; or whether the delight of having some new female acquaintance to whom to communicate her interesting prospects was paramount to every other consideration; cordial and kind Miss Pecksniff was. And twice Miss Pecksniff kissed Miss Pinch upon the cheek.

'Augustus—Mr. Pinch, you know. My dear girl!' said Miss Pecksniff, aside. 'I never was so ashamed in my life.'

Ruth begged her not to think of it.

'I mind your brother less than anybody else,' simpered Miss Pecksniff. 'But the indelicacy of meeting any gentleman under such circumstances! Augustus, my child, did you——'

Here Miss Pecksniff whispered in his ear. The suffering Moddle repeated:

'Twenty-four pound ten!'

'Oh, you silly man! I don't mean them,' said Miss Pecksniff. 'I am speaking of the——'

Here she whispered him again.

'If it's the same patterned chintz as that in the window; thirty-two, twelve, six,' said Moddle, with a sigh. 'And very dear.'

Miss Pecksniff stopped him from giving any further explanation by laying her hand upon his lips, and betraying a soft embarrassment. She then asked Tom Pinch which way he was going.

'I was going to see if I could find your sister,' answered Tom, 'to whom I wished to say a few words. We were going to Mrs. Todgers's, where I had the pleasure of seeing her before.'

'It's of no use your going on, then,' said Cherry, 'for we have not long left there; and I know she is not at home. But I'll take you to my sister's house, if you please. Augustus—Mr. Moddle,

I mean—and myself, are on our way to tea there, now. You needn't think of *him*,' she added, nodding her head, as she observed some hesitation on Tom's part. 'He is not at home.'

'Are you sure?' asked Tom.

'Oh, I am quite sure of that. I don't want any *more* revenge,' said Miss Pecksniff, expressively. 'But, really, I must beg you two gentlemen to walk on, and allow me to follow with Miss Pinch. My dear, I never was so taken by surprise!'

In furtherance of this bashful arrangement, Moddle gave his arm to Tom; and Miss Pecksniff linked her own in Ruth's.

'Of course, my love,' said Miss Pecksniff, 'it would be useless for me to disguise, after what you have seen, that I am about to be united to the gentleman who is walking with your brother. It would be in vain to conceal it. What do you think of him? Pray, let me have your candid opinion.'

Ruth intimated that, as far as she could judge, he was a very eligible swain.

'I am curious to know,' said Miss Pecksniff, with loquacious frankness, 'whether you have observed, or fancied, in this very short space of time, that he is of a rather melancholy turn?'

'So very short a time,' Ruth pleaded.

'No, no; but don't let that interfere with your answer,' returned Miss Pecksniff. 'I am curious to hear what you say.'

Ruth acknowledged that he had impressed her at first sight as looking 'rather low.'

'No, really?' said Miss Pecksniff. 'Well! that is quite remarkable! Everybody says the same. Mrs. Todgers says the same; and Augustus informs me that it is quite a joke among the gentlemen in the house. Indeed, but for the positive commands I have laid upon him, I believe it would have been the occasion of loaded fire-arms being resorted to more than once. What do you think is the cause of his appearance of depression?'

Ruth thought of several things; such as his digestion, his tailor, his mother, and the like. But hesitating to give utterance to any one of them, she refrained from expressing an opinion.

'My dear,' said Miss Pecksniff; 'I shouldn't wish it to be known, but I don't mind mentioning it to you, having known your brother for so many years—I refused Augustus three times. He is of a most amiable and sensitive nature; always ready to shed tears if you look at him, which is extremely charming; and he has never recovered the effect of that cruelty. For it *was* cruel,' said Miss Pecksniff, with a self-convicting candour that might have adorned the diadem of her own papa. 'There is no doubt of it. I look back upon my conduct now with blushes. I always liked him. I felt that he was not to me what the crowd of young men who had made proposals had been, but something very different. Then what right had I to refuse him three times?'

'It was a severe trial of his fidelity, no doubt,' said Ruth.

'My dear,' returned Miss Pecksniff. 'It was wrong. But such is the caprice and thoughtlessness of our sex! Let me be a warning to you. Don't try the feelings of any one who makes you an offer, as I have tried the feelings of Augustus; but if you ever feel towards a person as I really felt towards him, at the very time when I was driving him to distraction, let that feeling find expression, if that person throws himself at your feet, as Augustus Moddle did at mine. Think,' said Miss Pecksniff, 'what my feelings would have been, if I had goaded him to suicide, and it had got into the papers!'

Ruth observed that she would have been full of remorse, no doubt.

'Remorse!' cried Miss Pecksniff, in a sort of snug and comfortable penitence. 'What my remorse is at this moment, even after making reparation by accepting him, it would be impossible to tell you! Looking back upon my giddy self, my dear, now that I am sobered down and made thoughtful, by treading on the very brink of matrimony; and contemplating myself as I was when I was like what you are now; I shudder. I shudder. What is the consequence of my past conduct? Until Augustus leads me to the altar he is not sure of me. I have blighted and withered the affections of his heart to that extent that he is not sure of me. I see that preying on his mind and feeding on his vitals. What are the reproaches of my conscience, when I see this in the man I love!'

Ruth endeavoured to express some sense of her unbounded and flattering confidence; and presumed that she was going to be married soon.

'Very soon indeed,' returned Miss Pecksniff. 'As soon as our house is ready. We are furnishing now as fast as we can.'

In the same vein of confidence Miss Pecksniff ran through a general inventory of the articles that were already bought, with the articles that remained to be purchased; what garments she intended to be married in, and where the ceremony was to be performed; and gave Miss Pinch, in short (as she told her), early and exclusive information on all points of interest connected with the event.

While this was going forward in the rear, Tom and Mr. Moddle walked on, arm in arm, in the front, in a state of profound silence, which Tom at last broke: after thinking for a long time what he could say that should refer to an indifferent topic, in respect of which he might rely, with some degree of certainty, on Mr. Moddle's bosom being unruffled.

'I wonder,' said Tom, 'that in these crowded streets the foot-passengers are not oftener run over.'

Mr. Moddle, with a dark look, replied:

'The drivers won't do it.'

'Do you mean?' Tom began—

'That there are some men,' interrupted Moddle, with a hollow laugh, 'who can't get run over. They live a charmed life. Coal waggons recoil from them, and even cabs refuse to run them down. Ah!' said Augustus, marking Tom's astonishment. 'There are such men. One of 'em is a friend of mine.'

'Upon my word and honour,' thought Tom, 'this young gentleman is in a state of mind which is very serious indeed!' Abandoning all idea of conversation, he did not venture to say another word; but he was careful to keep a tight hold upon Augustus's arm, lest he should fly into the road, and making another and a more successful attempt, should get up a private little Juggernaut before the eyes of his betrothed. Tom was so afraid of his committing this rash act, that he had scarcely ever experienced such mental relief as when they arrived in safety at Mrs. Jonas Chuzzlewit's house.

'Walk up, pray, Mr. Pinch,' said Miss Pecksniff: for Tom halted, irresolutely, at the door.

'I am doubtful whether I should be welcome,' replied Tom, 'or, I ought rather to say, I have no doubt about it. I will send up a message, I think.'

'But what nonsense that is!' returned Miss Pecksniff, speaking apart to Tom. 'He is not at home, I am certain; I know he is not; and Merry hasn't the least idea that you ever——'

'No,' interrupted Tom. 'Nor would I have her know it, on any account. I am not so proud of that scuffle, I assure you.'

'Ah, but then you are so modest, you see,' returned Miss Pecksniff, with a smile. 'But pray walk up. If you don't wish her to know it, and do wish to speak to her, pray walk up. Pray walk up, Miss Pinch. Don't stand here.'

Mr. Moddle is led to the Contemplation of his Destiny
(*p. 698*)

Tom still hesitated; for he felt that he was in an awkward position. But Cherry passing him at this juncture, and leading his sister up-stairs, and the house-door being at the same time shut behind them, he followed without quite knowing whether it was well or ill-judged so to do.

'Merry, my darling!' said the fair Miss Pecksniff, opening the door of the usual sitting-room. 'Here are Mr. Pinch and his sister come to see you! I thought we should find you here, Mrs. Todgers! How do you do, Mrs. Gamp? And how do you do, Mr. Chuffey, though it's of no use asking you the question, I am well aware.'

Honouring each of these parties, as she severally addressed them, with an acid smile, Miss Charity presented Mr. Moddle.

'I believe you have seen *him* before,' she pleasantly observed. 'Augustus, my sweet child, bring me a chair.'

The sweet child did as he was told; and was then about to retire into a corner to mourn in secret, when Miss Charity, calling him in an audible whisper 'a little pet,' gave him leave to come and sit beside her. It is to be hoped, for the general cheerfulness of mankind, that such a doleful little pet was never seen as Mr. Moddle looked when he complied. So despondent was his temper, that he showed no outward thrill of ecstasy when Miss Pecksniff placed her lily hand in his, and concealed this mark of her favour from the vulgar gaze by covering it with a corner of her shawl. Indeed, he was infinitely more rueful then than he had been before; and, sitting uncomfortably upright in his chair, surveyed the company with watery eyes, which seemed to say, without the aid of language, 'Oh, good gracious! look here! Won't some kind Christian help me!'

But the ecstasies of Mrs. Gamp were sufficient to have furnished forth a score of young lovers: and they were chiefly awakened by the sight of Tom Pinch and his sister. Mrs. Gamp was a lady of that happy temperament which can be ecstatic without any other stimulating cause than a general desire to establish a large and profitable connexion. She added daily so many strings to her bow, that she made a perfect harp of it; and upon that instrument she now began to perform an extemporaneous concerto.

'Why, goodness me!' she said, 'Mrs. Chuzzlewit! To think as I should see beneath this blessed ouse, which well I know it, Miss Pecksniff, my sweet young lady, to be a ouse as there is not a many like, worse luck, and wishin' it ware not so, which then this tearful walley would be changed into a flowerin' guardian, Mr. Chuffey; to think as I should see beneath this indiwidgle roof, identically comin', Mr. Pinch (I take the liberty, though almost unbeknown), and do assure you of it, sir, the smilinest and sweetest face as ever, Mrs. Chuzzlewit, I see, exceptin' yourn, my dear good lady, and *your* good lady's too, sir, Mr. Moddle, if I may make so bold as speak so plain of what is plain enough to them as needn't look through mill-stones, Mrs. Todgers, to find out wot is wrote upon the wall behind. Which no offence is meant, ladies and gentlemen; none bein' took, I hope. To think as I should see that smilinest and sweetest face which me and another friend of mine, took notige of among the packages down London Bridge, in this promiscuous place, is a surprige in-deed!'

Having contrived, in this happy manner, to invest every member of her audience with an individual share and imme-diate personal interest in her address, Mrs. Gamp dropped several curtseys to Ruth, and smilingly shaking her head a great many times, pursued the thread of her discourse:

'Now, ain't we rich in beauty this here joyful arternoon, I'm sure. I knows a lady, which her name, I'll not deceive you, Mrs. Chuzzlewit, is Harris, her husband's brother bein' six foot three, and marked with a mad bull in Wellington boots upon his left arm, on account of his precious mother havin' been worrited by one into a shoemaker's shop, when in a sitiwation which blessed is the man as has his quiver full of sech, as many times I've said to Gamp when words has roge betwixt us on account of the expense—and often have I said to Mrs. Harris, "Oh, Mrs. Harris, ma'am! your countenance is quite a angel's!" Which, but for Pimples, it would be, "No, Sairey Gamp," says she, "you best of hard-working and industrious creeturs as ever was underpaid at any price, which underpaid you are, quite diff'rent. Harris had it done afore marriage at ten and six," she says, "and wore it faithful next his heart 'till the colour run, when the money was declined to be give back, and no arrangement could be come to. But he never said it was a angel's, Sairey, wotever he might have thought." If Mrs. Harris's husband was here now,' said Mrs. Gamp, looking round, and chuckling as she dropped a general curtsey, 'he'd speak out plain, he would, and his dear wife would be the last to blame him! For if ever a woman lived as

Mrs. Gamp makes Tea
(p. 706)

know'd not wot it was to form a wish to pizon them as had good looks, and had no reagion give her by the best of husbands. Mrs. Harris is that ev'nly dispogician!'

With these words the worthy woman, who appeared to have dropped in to take tea as a delicate little attention, rather than to have any engagement on the premises in an official capacity, crossed to Mr. Chuffey, who was seated in the same corner as of old, and shook him by the shoulder.

'Rouge yourself, and look up! Come!' said Mrs. Gamp. 'Here's company, Mr. Chuffey.'

'I am sorry for it,' cried the old man, looking humbly round the room. 'I know I'm in the way. I ask pardon, but I've nowhere else to go to. Where is she?'

Merry went to him.

'Ah!' said the old man, patting her on the cheek. 'Here she is. Here she is! She's never hard on poor old Chuffey. Poor old Chuff!'

As she took her seat upon a low chair by the old man's side, and put herself within the reach of his hand, she looked up once at Tom. It was a sad look that she cast upon him, though there was a faint smile trembling on her face. It was a speaking look, and Tom knew what it said. 'You see how misery has changed me. I can feel for a dependant *now*, and set some value on his attachment.'

'Aye, aye!' cried Chuffey in a soothing tone. 'Aye, aye, aye! Never mind him. It's hard to bear, but never mind him. He'll die one day. There are three hundred and sixty-five days in the year—three hundred and sixty-six in leap year—and he may die on any one of 'em.'

'You're a wearing old soul, and that's the sacred truth,' said Mrs. Gamp, contemplating him from a little distance with anything but favour, as he continued to mutter to himself. 'It's a pity that you don't know wot you say, for you'd tire your own patience out if you did, and fret yourself into a happy releage for all as knows you.'

'His son,' murmured the old man, lifting up his hand. 'His son!'

'Well, I'm sure!' said Mrs. Gamp, 'you're a-settlin' of it, Mr. Chuffey. To your satigefaction, sir, I hope. But I wouldn't lay a new pin-cushion on it myself, sir, though you *are* so well informed. Drat the old creetur, he's a-layin' down the law tolerable confident, too! A deal he knows of sons! Or darters

C C

either! Suppose you was to favour us with some remarks on
twins, sir, *would* you be so good!'

The bitter and indignant sarcasm which Mrs. Gamp conveyed into these taunts was altogether lost on the unconscious
Chuffey, who appeared to be as little cognizant of their
delivery as of his having given Mrs. Gamp offence. But that
high-minded woman being sensitively alive to any invasion of
her professional province, and imagining that Mr. Chuffey had
given utterance to some prediction on the subject of sons,
which ought to have emanated in the first instance from herself as the only lawful authority, or which should at least have
been on no account proclaimed without her sanction and
concurrence, was not so easily appeased. She continued to
sidle at Mr. Chuffey with looks of sharp hostility, and to defy
him with many other ironical remarks, uttered in that low key
which commonly denotes suppressed indignation; until the
entrance of the tea-board, and a request from Mrs. Jonas that
she would make tea at a side-table for the party that had
unexpectedly assembled, restored her to herself. She smiled
again, and entered on her ministration with her own particular
urbanity.

'And quite a family it is to make tea for,' said Mrs. Gamp;
'and wot a happiness to do it! My good young 'ooman'—to
the servant-girl—'p'raps somebody would like to try a new-
laid egg or two, not biled too hard. Likeways, a few rounds o'
buttered toast, first cuttin' off the crust, in consequence of
tender teeth, and not too many of 'em; which Gamp himself,
Mrs. Chuzzlewit, at one blow, being in liquor, struck out four,
two single and two double, as was took by Mrs. Harris for a
keepsake, and is carried in her pocket at this present hour,
along with two cramp-bones, a bit o' ginger, and a grater like
a blessed infant's shoe, in tin, with a little heel to put the nut-
meg in: as many times I've seen and said, and used for caudle
when required, within the month.'

As the privileges of the side-table—besides including the
small prerogatives of sitting next the toast, and taking two
cups of tea to other people's one, and always taking them at
a crisis, that is to say, before putting fresh water into the teapot, and after it had been standing for some time—also com-
prehended a full view of the company, and an opportunity of
addressing them as from a rostrum, Mrs. Gamp discharged the
functions entrusted to her with extreme good-humour and

affability. Sometimes resting her saucer on the palm of her outspread hand, and supporting her elbow on the table, she stopped between her sips of tea to favour the circle with a smile, a wink, a roll of the head, or some other mark of notice; and at those periods her countenance was lighted up with a degree of intelligence and vivacity, which it was almost impossible to separate from the benignant influence of distilled waters.

But for Mrs. Gamp, it would have been a curiously silent party. Miss Pecksniff only spoke to her Augustus, and to him in whispers. Augustus spoke to nobody, but sighed for every one, and occasionally gave himself such a sounding slap upon the forehead as would make Mrs. Todgers, who was rather nervous, start in her chair with an involuntary exclamation. Mrs. Todgers was occupied in knitting, and seldom spoke. Poor Merry held the hand of cheerful little Ruth between her own, and listening with evident pleasure to all she said, but rarely speaking herself, sometimes smiled, and sometimes kissed her on the cheek, and sometimes turned aside to hide the tears that trembled in her eyes. Tom felt this change in her so much, and was so glad to see how tenderly Ruth dealt with her, and how she knew and answered to it, that he had not the heart to make any movement towards their departure, although he had long since given utterance to all he came to say.

The old clerk, subsiding into his usual state, remained profoundly silent, while the rest of the little assembly were thus occupied, intent upon the dreams, whatever they might be, which hardly seemed to stir the surface of his sluggish thoughts. The bent of these dull fancies combining probably with the silent feasting that was going on about him, and some struggling recollection of the last approach to revelry he had witnessed, suggested a strange question to his mind. He looked round upon a sudden, and said,

'Who's lying dead up-stairs?'

'No one,' said Merry, turning to him. 'What is the matter? We are all here.'

'All here!' cried the old man. 'All here! Where is he then—my old master, Mr. Chuzzlewit, who had the only son? Where is he?'

'Hush! Hush!' said Merry, speaking kindly to him. 'That happened long ago. Don't you recollect?'

'Recollect!' rejoined the old man, with a cry of grief. 'As if I could forget! As if I ever could forget!'

He put his hand up to his face for a moment; and then repeated, turning round exactly as before

'Who's lying dead up-stairs?'

'No one!' said Merry.

At first he gazed angrily upon her, as upon a stranger who endeavoured to deceive him; but peering into her face, and seeing that it was indeed she, he shook his head in sorrowful compassion.

'You think not. But they don't tell you. No, no, poor thing! They don't tell you. Who are these, and why are they merry-making here, if there is no one dead? Foul play! Go see who it is!'

She made a sign to them not to speak to him, which indeed they had little inclination to do; and remained silent herself. So did he for a short time; but then he repeated the same question with an eagerness that had a peculiar terror in it.

'There's some one dead,' he said, 'or dying; and I want to know who it is. Go see, go see! Where's Jonas?'

'In the country,' she replied.

The old man gazed at her as if he doubted what she said, or had not heard her; and, rising from his chair, walked across the room and up-stairs, whispering as he went, 'Foul play!' They heard his footsteps overhead, going up into that corner of the room in which the bed stood (it was there old Anthony had died); and then they heard him coming down again immediately. His fancy was not so strong or wild that it pictured to him anything in the deserted bed-chamber which was not there; for he returned much calmer, and appeared to have satisfied himself.

'They don't tell you,' he said to Merry in his quavering voice, as he sat down again, and patted her upon the head. 'They don't tell me either; but I'll watch, I'll watch. They shall not hurt you; don't be frightened. When you have sat up watching, I have sat up watching too. Aye, aye, I have!' he piped out, clenching his weak, shrivelled hand. 'Many a night I have been ready!'

He said this with such trembling gaps and pauses in his want of breath, and said it in his jealous secrecy so closely in her ear, that little or nothing of it was understood by the visitors. But they had heard and seen enough of the old man to be disquieted, and to have left their seats and gathered about him; thereby affording Mrs. Gamp, whose professional coolness was not so easily disturbed, an eligible opportunity for concentrating the whole resources of her powerful mind and appetite upon the toast and butter, tea and eggs. She had brought them to bear upon those viands with such vigour that her face was in the highest state of inflammation, when she now (there being nothing left to eat or drink) saw fit to interpose.

'Why, highty tighty, sir!' cried Mrs. Gamp, 'is these your manners? You want a pitcher of cold water throw'd over you to bring you round; that's my belief; and if you was under Betsey Prig you'd have it, too, I do assure you, Mr. Chuffey. Spanish Flies is the only thing to draw this nonsense out of you, and if anybody wanted to do you a kindness, they'd clap a blister of 'em on your head, and put a mustard poultige on your back. Who's dead, indeed! It wouldn't be no grievous loss if some one was, I think!'

'He's quiet now, Mrs. Gamp,' said Merry. 'Don't disturb him.'

'Oh, bother the old wictim, Mrs. Chuzzlewit,' replied that zealous lady, 'I ain't no patience with him. You give him his own way too much by half. A worritin' wexagious creetur!'

No doubt with the view of carrying out the precepts she enforced, and 'bothering the old wictim' in practice as well as in theory, Mrs. Gamp took him by the collar of his coat, and gave him some dozen or two of hearty shakes backward and forward in his chair; that exercise being considered by the disciples of the Prig school of nursing (who are very numerous among professional ladies) as exceedingly conducive to repose, and highly beneficial to the performance of the nervous functions. Its effect in this instance was to render the patient so giddy and addle-headed, that he could say nothing more; which Mrs. Gamp regarded as the triumph of her art.

'There!' she said, loosening the old man's cravat, in consequence of his being rather black in the face, after this scientific treatment. 'Now, I hope, you're easy in your mind. If you should turn at all faint we can soon rewive you, sir, I promige you. Bite a person's thumbs, or turn their fingers the wrong way,' said Mrs. Gamp, smiling with the consciousness of at once imparting pleasure and instruction to her auditors, 'and they comes to, wonderful, Lord bless you!'

As this excellent woman had been formally entrusted with

the care of Mr. Chuffey on a previous occasion, neither Mrs. Jonas nor anybody else had the resolution to interfere directly with her mode of treatment: though all present (Tom Pinch and his sister especially) appeared to be disposed to differ from her views. For such is the rash boldness of the uninitiated, that they will frequently set up some monstrous abstract principle, such as humanity, or tenderness, or the like idle folly, in obstinate defiance of all precedent and usage; and will even venture to maintain the same against the persons who have made the precedents and established the usage, and who must therefore be the best and most impartial judges of the subject.

'Ah, Mr. Pinch!' said Miss Pecksniff. 'It all comes of this unfortunate marriage. If my sister had not been so precipitate, and had not united herself to a Wretch, there would have been no Mr. Chuffey in the house.'

'Hush!' cried Tom. 'She'll hear you.'

'I should be very sorry if she did hear me, Mr. Pinch,' said Cherry, raising her voice a little: 'for it is not in my nature to add to the uneasiness of any person: far less of my own sister. *I* know what a sister's duties are, Mr. Pinch, and I hope I always showed it in my practice. Augustus, my dear child, find my pocket-handkerchief, and give it to me.'

Augustus obeyed, and took Mrs. Todgers aside to pour his griefs into her friendly bosom.

'I am sure, Mr. Pinch,' said Charity, looking after her betrothed and glancing at her sister, 'that I ought to be very grateful for the blessings I enjoy, and those which are yet in store for me. When I contrast Augustus'—here she was modest and embarrassed—'who, I don't mind saying to you, is all softness, mildness, and devotion, with the detestable man who is my sister's husband; and when I think, Mr. Pinch, that in the dispensations of this world, our cases might have been reversed; I have much to be thankful for, indeed, and much to make me humble and contented.'

Contented she might have been, but humble she assuredly was not. Her face and manner experienced something so widely different from humility, that Tom could not help understanding and despising the base motives that were working in her breast. He turned away, and said to Ruth, that it was time for them to go.

'I will write to your husband,' said Tom to Merry, 'and explain to him, as I would have done if I had met him here, that if he has sustained any inconvenience through my means, it is not my fault: a postman not being more innocent of the news he brings, than I was when I handed him that letter.'

'I thank you!' said Merry. 'It may do some good.'

She parted tenderly from Ruth, who with her brother was in the act of leaving the room, when a key was heard in the lock of the door below, and immediately afterwards a quick footstep in the passage. Tom stopped, and looked at Merry.

It was Jonas, she said timidly.

'I had better not meet him on the stairs, perhaps,' said Tom, drawing his sister's arm through his, and coming back a step or two. 'I'll wait for him here, a moment.'

He had scarcely said it when the door opened, and Jonas entered. His wife came forward to receive him; but he put her aside with his hand, and said in a surly tone:

'I didn't know you'd got a party.'

As he looked, at the same time, either by accident or design, towards Miss Pecksniff; and as Miss Pecksniff was only too delighted to quarrel with him, she instantly resented it.

'Oh dear!' she said, rising. 'Pray don't let us intrude upon your domestic happiness! That would be a pity. We have taken tea here, sir, in your absence; but if you will have the goodness to send us a note of the expense, receipted, we shall be happy to pay it. Augustus, my love, we will go, if you please. Mrs. Todgers, unless you wish to remain here, we shall be happy to take you with us. It would be a pity, indeed, to spoil the bliss which this gentleman always brings with him: especially into his own home.'

'Charity! Charity!' remonstrated her sister, in such a heart-felt tone that she might have been imploring her to show the cardinal virtue whose name she bore.

'Merry, my dear, I am much obliged to you for your advice,' returned Miss Pecksniff, with a stately scorn: by the way, she had not been offered any: 'but *I* am not his slave——'

'No, nor wouldn't have been if you could,' interrupted Jonas. 'We know all about it.'

'*What* did you say, sir?' cried Miss Pecksniff, sharply.

'Didn't you hear?' retorted Jonas, lounging down upon a chair. 'I am not a-going to say it again. If you like to stay, you may stay. If you like to go, you may go. But if you stay, please to be civil.'

'Beast!' cried Miss Pecksniff, sweeping past him. 'Augustus!

He is beneath your notice!' Augustus had been making some faint and sickly demonstration of shaking his fist. 'Come away, child,' screamed Miss Pecksniff, 'I command you!'

The scream was elicited from her by Augustus manifesting an intention to return and grapple with him. But Miss Pecksniff giving the fiery youth a pull, and Mrs. Todgers giving him a push, they all three tumbled out of the room together, to the music of Miss Pecksniff's shrill remonstrances.

All this time Jonas had seen nothing of Tom and his sister; for they were almost behind the door when he opened it, and he had sat down with his back towards them, and had purposely kept his eyes upon the opposite side of the street during his altercation with Miss Pecksniff, in order that his seeming carelessness might increase the exasperation of that wronged young damsel. His wife now faltered out that Tom had been waiting to see him; and Tom advanced.

The instant he presented himself, Jonas got up from his chair, and swearing a great oath, caught it in his grasp, as if he would have felled Tom to the ground with it. As he most unquestionably would have done, but that his very passion and surprise made him irresolute, and gave Tom, in his calmness, an opportunity of being heard.

'You have no cause to be violent, sir,' said Tom. 'Though what I wish to say relates to your own affairs, I know nothing of them, and desire to know nothing of them.'

Jonas was too enraged to speak. He held the door open; and stamping his foot upon the ground, motioned Tom away.

'As you cannot suppose,' said Tom, 'that I am here with any view of conciliating you or pleasing myself, I am quite indifferent to your reception of me, or your dismissal of me. Hear what I have to say, if you are not a madman! I gave you a letter the other day, when you were about to go abroad.'

'You Thief, you did!' retorted Jonas. 'I'll pay you for the carriage of it one day, and settle an old score besides. I will!'

'Tut, tut,' said Tom, 'you needn't waste words or threats. I wish you to understand—plainly because I would rather keep clear of you and everything that concerns you: not because I have the least apprehension of your doing me any injury: which would be weak indeed—that I am no party to the contents of that letter. That I know nothing of it. That I was not even aware that it was to be delivered to you; and that I had it from——'

'By the Lord!' cried Jonas, fiercely catching up the chair, 'I'll knock your brains out, if you speak another word.'

Tom, nevertheless, persisting in his intention, and opening his lips to speak again, Jonas set upon him like a savage; and in the quickness and ferocity of his attack would have surely done him some grievous injury, defenceless as he was, and embarrassed by having his frightened sister clinging to his arm, if Merry had not run between them, crying to Tom for the love of Heaven to leave the house. The agony of this poor creature, the terror of his sister, the impossibility of making himself audible, and the equal impossibility of bearing up against Mrs. Gamp, who threw herself upon him like a feather-bed, and forced him backwards down the stairs by the mere oppression of her dead weight, prevailed. Tom shook the dust of that house off his feet, without having mentioned Nadgett's name.

If the name could have passed his lips; if Jonas, in the insolence of his vile nature, had never roused him to do that old act of manliness, for which (and not for his last offence) he hated him with such malignity; if Jonas could have learned, as then he could and would have learned, through Tom's means, what unsuspected spy there was upon him; he would have been saved from the commission of a Guilty Deed, then drawing on towards its black accomplishment. But the fatality was of his own working; the pit was of his own digging; the gloom that gathered round him was the shadow of his own life.

His wife had closed the door, and thrown herself before it, on the ground, upon her knees. She held up her hands to him now, and besought him not to be harsh with her, for she had interposed in fear of bloodshed.

'So, so!' said Jonas, looking down upon her, as he fetched his breath. 'These are your friends, are they, when I am away? You plot and tamper with this sort of people, do you?'

'No, indeed! I have no knowledge of these secrets, and no clue to their meaning. I have never seen him since I left home but once—but twice—before to-day.'

'Oh!' sneered Jonas, catching at this correction. 'But once, but twice, eh? Which do you mean? Twice and once perhaps. Three times! How many more, you lying jade?'

As he made an angry motion with his hand, she shrunk down hastily. A suggestive action! Full of a cruel truth!

'How many more times?' he repeated.

'No more. The other morning, and to-day, and once besides.'

He was about to retort upon her, when the clock struck. He started, stopped, and listened: appearing to revert to some engagement, or to some other subject, a secret within his own breast, recalled to him by this record of the progress of the hours.

'Don't lie there! Get up!'

Having helped her to rise, or rather hauled her up by the arm, he went on to say:

'Listen to me, young lady; and don't whine when you have no occasion, or I may make some for you. If I find him in my house again, or find that you have seen him in anybody else's house, you'll repent it. If you are not deaf and dumb to every-thing that concerns me, unless you have my leave to hear and speak, you'll repent it. If you don't obey exactly what I order, you'll repent it. Now, attend. What's the time?'

'It struck Eight a minute ago.'

He looked towards her intently; and said, with a laboured distinctness, as if he had got the words off by heart:

'I have been travelling day and night, and am tired. I have lost some money, and that don't improve me. Put my supper in the little off-room below, and have the truckle-bed made. I shall sleep there to-night, and maybe to-morrow night; and if I can sleep all day to-morrow, so much the better, for I've got trouble to sleep off, if I can. Keep the house quiet, and don't call me. Mind! Don't call me. Don't let anybody call me. Let me lie there.'

She said it should be done. Was that all?

'All what? You must be prying and questioning!' he angrily retorted. 'What more do you want to know?'

'I want to know nothing, Jonas, but what you tell me. All hope of confidence between us has long deserted me!'

'Ecod, I should hope so!' he muttered.

'But if you will tell me what you wish, I will be obedient and will try to please you. I make no merit of that, for I have no friend in my father or my sister, but am quite alone. I am very humble and submissive. You told me you would break my spirit, and you have done so. Do not break my heart too!'

She ventured, as she said these words, to lay her hand upon his shoulder. He suffered it to rest there, in his exultation; and the whole mean, abject, sordid, pitiful soul of the man, looked at her, for the moment, through his wicked eyes.

For the moment only: for, with the same hurried return to something within himself, he bade her, in a surly tone, show her obedience by executing his commands without delay. When she had withdrawn, he paced up and down the room several times; but always with his right hand clenched, as if it held something; which it did not, being empty. When he was tired of this, he threw himself into a chair, and thoughtfully turned up the sleeve of his right arm, as if he were rather musing about its strength than examining it; but, even then, he kept the hand clenched.

He was brooding in this chair, with his eyes cast down upon the ground, when Mrs. Gamp came in to tell him that the little room was ready. Not being quite sure of her reception after interfering in the quarrel, Mrs. Gamp, as a means of interesting and propitiating her patron, affected a deep solicitude in Mr. Chuffey.

'How is he now, sir?' she said.

'Who?' cried Jonas, raising his head, and staring at her.

'To be sure!' returned the matron with a smile and a curtsey. 'What am I thinking of! You wasn't here, sir, when he was took so strange. I never see a poor dear creetur took so strange in all my life, except a patient much about the same age, as I once nussed, which his calling was the custom-'us, and his name was Mrs. Harris's own father, as pleasant a singer, Mr. Chuzzlewit, as ever you heerd, with a voice like a Jew's-harp in the bass notes, that it took six men to hold at sech times, foaming frightful.'

'Chuffey, eh?' said Jonas carelessly, seeing that she went up to the old clerk, and looked at him. 'Ha!'

'The creetur's head's so hot,' said Mrs. Gamp, 'that you might heat a flat-iron at it. And no wonder I am sure, considerin' the things he said!'

'Said!' cried Jonas. 'What did he say?'

Mrs. Gamp laid her hand upon her heart, to put some check upon its palpitations, and turning up her eyes replied in a faint voice:

'The awfullest things, Mr. Chuzzlewit, as ever I heerd! Which Mrs. Harris's father never spoke a word when took so, some does and some don't, except sayin' when he come round, "Where is Sairey Gamp?" But raly, sir, when Mr. Chuffey comes to ask who's lyin' dead up-stairs, and——'

'Who's lying dead up-stairs!' repeated Jonas, standing aghast.

Mrs. Gamp nodded, made as if she were swallowing, and went on.

'Who's lying dead up-stairs; such was his Bible language; and where was Mr. Chuzzlewit as had the only son; and when he goes up-stairs a-looking in the beds and wandering about the rooms, and comes down again a-whisperin' softly to his-self about foul play and that; it give me sech a turn, I don't deny it, Mr. Chuzzlewit, that I never could have kep myself up but for a little drain of spirits, which I seldom touches, but could always wish to know where to find, if so dispoged, never knowin' wot may happen next, the world bein' so uncertain.'

'Why, the old fool's mad!' cried Jonas, much disturbed.

'That's my opinion, sir,' said Mrs. Gamp, 'and I will not deceive you. I believe as Mr. Chuffey, sir, rekwires attention (if I may make so bold), and should not have his liberty to wex and worrit your sweet lady as he doos.'

'Why, who minds what he says?' retorted Jonas.

'Still he is worritin', sir,' said Mrs. Gamp. 'No one don't mind him, but he *is* a ill conwenience.'

'Ecod you're right,' said Jonas, looking doubtfully at the subject of this conversation. 'I have half a mind to shut him up.'

Mrs. Gamp rubbed her hands, and smiled, and shook her head, and sniffed expressively, as scenting a job.

'Could you—could you take care of such an idiot, now, in some spare room up-stairs?' asked Jonas.

'Me and a friend of mine, one off, one on, could do it, Mr. Chuzzlewit,' replied the nurse; 'our charges not bein' high, but wishin' they was lower, and allowance made considerin' not strangers. Me and Betsy Prig, sir, would undertake Mr. Chuffey reasonable,' said Mrs. Gamp, looking at him with her head on one side, as if he had been a piece of goods, for which she was driving a bargain; 'and give every satigefaction. Betsey Prig has nussed a many lunacies, and well she knows their ways, which puttin' 'em right close afore the fire, when fractious, is the certainest and most compoging.'

While Mrs. Gamp discoursed to this effect, Jonas was walking up and down the room again: glancing covertly at the old clerk, as he did so. He now made a stop, and said:

'I must look after him, I suppose, or I may have him doing some mischief. What say you?'

'Nothin' more likely!' Mrs. Gamp replied. 'As well I have experienged, I do assure you, sir.'

'Well! Look after him for the present, and—let me see—three days from this time let the other woman come here, and we'll see if we can make a bargain of it. About nine or ten o'clock at night, say. Keep your eye upon him in the meanwhile, and don't talk about it. He's as mad as a March hare!'

'Madder!' cried Mrs. Gamp. 'A deal madder!'

'See to him, then: take care that he does no harm; and recollect what I have told you.'

Leaving Mrs. Gamp in the act of repeating all she had been told, and of producing in support of her memory and trustworthiness, many commendations selected from among the most remarkable opinions of the celebrated Mrs. Harris, he descended to the little room prepared for him, and pulling off his coat and his boots, put them outside the door before he locked it. In locking it, he was careful so to adjust the key as to baffle any curious person who might try to peep in through the key-hole; and when he had taken these precautions, he sat down to his supper.

'Mr. Chuff,' he muttered, 'it'll be pretty easy to be even with *you*. It's of no use doing things by halves, and as long as I stop here, I'll take good care of you. When I'm off you may say what you please. But it's a d—d strange thing,' he added, pushing away his untouched plate, and striding moodily to and fro, 'that his drivellings should have taken this turn just now.'

After pacing the little room from end to end several times, he sat down in another chair.

'I say just now, but for anything I know, he may have been carrying on the same game all along. Old dog! He shall be gagged!'

He paced the room again in the same restless and unsteady way; and then sat down upon the bedstead, leaning his chin upon his hand, and looking at the table. When he had looked at it for a long time, he remembered his supper; and resuming the chair he had first occupied, began to eat with great rapacity: not like a hungry man, but as if he were determined to do it. He drank too, roundly; sometimes stopping in the middle of a draught to walk, and change his seat and walk again, and dart back to the table and fall to, in a ravenous hurry, as before.

It was now growing dark. As the gloom of evening, deepening into night, came on, another dark shade emerging from within him seemed to overspread his face, and slowly change it. Slowly, slowly; darker and darker; more and more haggard; creeping over him by little and little; until it was black night within him and without.

The room in which he had shut himself up, was on the ground floor, at the back of the house. It was lighted by a dirty skylight, and had a door in the wall, opening into a narrow covered passage or blind-alley, very little frequented after five or six o'clock in the evening, and not in much use as a thoroughfare at any hour. But it had an outlet in a neighbouring street.

The ground on which this chamber stood had, at one time, not within his recollection, been a yard; and had been converted to its present purpose for use as an office. But the occasion for it died with the man who built it; and saving that it had sometimes served as an apology for a spare bedroom, and that the old clerk had once held it (but that was years ago) as his recognised apartment, it had been little troubled by Anthony Chuzzlewit and Son. It was a blotched, stained, mouldering room, like a vault; and there were water-pipes running through it, which at unexpected times in the night, when other things were quiet, clicked and gurgled suddenly, as if they were choking.

The door into the court had not been open for a long, long time; but the key had always hung in one place, and there it hung now. He was prepared for its being rusty; for he had a little bottle of oil in his pocket and the feather of a pen, with which he lubricated the key, and the lock too, carefully. All this while he had been without his coat, and had nothing on his feet but his stockings. He now got softly into bed in the same state, and tossed from side to side to tumble it. In his restless condition that was easily done.

When he arose, he took from his portmanteau, which he had caused to be carried into that place when he came home, a pair of clumsy shoes, and put them on his feet; also a pair of leather leggings, such as countrymen are used to wear, with straps to fasten them to the waistband. In these he dressed himself at leisure. Lastly, he took out a common frock of coarse dark jean, which he drew over his own underclothing; and a felt hat—he had purposely left his own up-stairs. He then sat himself down by the door, with the key in his hand, waiting.

He had no light; the time was dreary, long, and awful. The ringers were practising in a neighbouring church, and the

clashing of the bells was almost maddening. Curse the clamouring bells, they seemed to know that he was listening at the
door, and to proclaim it in a crowd of voices to all the town!
Would they never be still?

They ceased at last, and then the silence was so new and
terrible that it seemed the prelude to some dreadful noise.
Footsteps in the court! Two men. He fell back from the door
on tiptoe, as if they could have seen him through its wooden
panels.

They passed on, talking (he could make out) about a
skeleton which had been dug up yesterday, in some work of
excavation near at hand, and was supposed to be that of a
murdered man. 'So murder is not always found out, you see,'
they said to one another as they turned the corner.

Hush!

He put the key into the lock, and turned it. The door resisted for a while, but soon came stiffly open; mingling with
the sense of fever in his mouth, a taste of rust, and dust, and
earth, and rotting wood. He looked out; passed out; locked it
after him.

All was clear and quiet, as he fled away.

CHAPTER XLVII

Conclusion of the enterprise of Mr. Jonas and his friend

DID no men passing through the dim streets shrink without knowing why, when he came stealing up behind them? As he glided on, had no child in its sleep an indistinct perception of a guilty shadow falling on its bed, that troubled its innocent rest? Did no dog howl, and strive to break its rattling chain, that it might tear him; no burrowing rat, scenting the work he had in hand, essay to gnaw a passage after him, that it might hold a greedy revel at the feast of his providing? When he looked back, across his shoulder, was it to see if his quick footsteps still fell dry upon the dusty pavement, or were already moist and clogged with the red mire that stained the naked feet of Cain!

He shaped his course for the main western road, and soon reached it: riding a part of the way, then alighting and walking on again. He travelled for a considerable distance upon the roof of a stage-coach, which came up while he was afoot; and when it turned out of his road, bribed the driver of a return post-chaise to take him on with him; and then made across the country at a run, and saved a mile or two before he struck again into the road. At last, as his plan was, he came up with a certain lumbering, slow, night-coach, which stopped wherever it could, and was stopping then at a public-house, while the guard and coachman ate and drank within.

He bargained for a seat outside this coach, and took it. And he quitted it no more until it was within a few miles of its destination, but occupied the same place all night.

All night! It is a common fancy that nature seems to sleep by night. It is a false fancy, as who should know better than he?

The fishes slumbered in the cold, bright, glistening streams and rivers, perhaps; and the birds roosted on the branches of the trees; and in their stalls and pastures beasts were quiet; and human creatures slept. But what of that, when the solemn night was watching, when it never winked, when its darkness watched no less than its light! The stately trees, the moon and shining stars, the softly-stirring wind, the over-shadowed lane, the broad, bright country-side, they all kept watch. There was not a blade of growing grass or corn, but watched; and the quieter it was, the more intent and fixed its watch upon him seemed to be.

And yet he slept. Riding on among those sentinels of God, he slept, and did not change the purpose of his journey. If he forgot it in his troubled dreams, it came up steadily, and woke him. But it never woke him to remorse, or to abandonment of his design.

He dreamed at one time that he was lying calmly in his bed, thinking of a moonlight night and the noise of wheels, when the old clerk put his head in at the door, and beckoned him. At this signal he arose immediately: being already dressed in the clothes he actually wore at that time: and accompanied him into a strange city, where the names of the streets were written on the walls in characters quite new to him; which gave him no surprise or uneasiness, for he remembered in his dream to have been there before. Although these streets were very precipitous, insomuch that to get from one to another it was necessary to descend great heights by ladders that were too short, and ropes that moved deep bells, and swung and swayed as they were clung to, the danger gave him little emotion beyond the first thrill of terror: his anxieties being concentrated on his dress, which was quite unfitted for some festival that was about to be holden there, and in which he had come to take a part. Already, great crowds began to fill the streets, and in one direction myriads of people came rushing down an interminable perspective, strewing flowers and making way for others on white horses, when a terrible figure started from the throng, and cried out that it was the Last Day for all the world. The cry being spread, there was a wild hurrying on to Judgment; and the press became so great that he and his companion (who was constantly changing, and was never the same man two minutes together, though he never saw one man come or another go) stood aside in a porch, fearfully surveying the multitude; in which there were many faces that he knew, and many that he did not know, but dreamed he did; when all at once a struggling head rose up among the rest—livid and deadly, but the same as he had known it—and denounced him as having appointed that direful day to happen. They closed together. As he strove to free the hand in which he held a club, and strike the blow he had so often thought of, he started to the knowledge of his waking purpose and the rising of the sun.

The sun was welcome to him. There were life and motion, and a world astir, to divide the attention of Day. It was the eye of Night: of wakeful, watchful, silent, and attentive Night, with so much leisure for the observation of his wicked thoughts: that he dreaded most. There is no glare in the night. Even Glory shows to small advantage in the night, upon a crowded battle-field. How then shows Glory's blood-relation, bastard Murder!

Aye! He made no compromise, and held no secret with himself now. Murder. He had come to do it.

'Let me get down here,' he said.

'Short of the town, eh!' observed the coachman.

'I may get down where I please, I suppose?'

'You got up to please yourself, and may get down to please yourself. It won't break our hearts to lose you, and it wouldn't have broken 'em if we'd never found you. Be a little quicker. That's all.'

The guard had alighted, and was waiting in the road to take his money. In the jealousy and distrust of what he contemplated, he thought this man looked at him with more than common curiosity.

'What are you staring at?' said Jonas.

'Not a handsome man,' returned the guard. 'If you want your fortune told, I'll tell you a bit of it. You won't be drowned. That's a consolation for you.'

Before he could retort or turn away, the coachman put an end to the dialogue by giving him a cut with his whip, and bid him get out for a surly dog. The guard jumped up to his seat at the same moment, and they drove off, laughing; leaving him to stand in the road and shake his fist at them. He was not displeased though, on second thoughts, to have been taken for an ill-conditioned common country fellow; but rather congratulated himself upon it as a proof that he was well disguised.

Wandering into a copse by the road-side—but not in that place: two or three miles off—he tore out from a fence a thick, hard, knotted stake; and, sitting down beneath a hayrick, spent some time in shaping it, in peeling off the bark, and fashioning its jagged head with his knife.

The day passed on. Noon, afternoon, evening. Sunset.

At that serene and peaceful time two men, riding in a gig, came out of the city by a road not much frequented. It was the day on which Mr. Pecksniff had agreed to dine with Montague. He had kept his appointment, and was now going home. His host was riding with him for a short distance; meaning to return by a pleasant track, which Mr. Pecksniff had engaged to show him, through some fields. Jonas knew their plans. He had hung about the inn-yard while they were at dinner and had heard their orders given.

They were loud and merry in their conversation, and might have been heard at some distance: far above the sound of their carriage wheels or horses' hoofs. They came on noisily, to where a stile and footpath indicated their point of separation. Here they stopped.

'It's too soon. Much too soon,' said Mr. Pecksniff. 'But this is the place, my dear sir. Keep the path, and go straight through the little wood you'll come to. The path is narrower there, but you can't miss it. When shall I see you again? Soon I hope?'

'I hope so,' replied Montague.

'Good night!'

'Good night. And a pleasant ride!'

So long as Mr. Pecksniff was in sight, and turned his head at intervals to salute him, Montague stood in the road smiling, and waving his hand. But when his new partner had disappeared, and this show was no longer necessary, he sat down on the stile with looks so altered, that he might have grown ten years older in the meantime.

He was flushed with wine, but not gay. His scheme had succeeded, but he showed no triumph. The effort of sustaining his difficult part before his late companion had fatigued him, perhaps, or it may be that the evening whispered to his conscience, or it may be (as it *has* been) that a shadowy veil was dropping round him, closing out all thoughts but the presentiment and vague foreknowledge of impending doom.

If there be fluids, as we know there are, which, conscious of a coming wind, or rain, or frost, will shrink and strive to hide themselves in their glass arteries; may not that subtle liquor of the blood perceive, by properties within itself, that hands are raised to waste and spill it; and in the veins of men run cold and dull as his did, in that hour!

So cold, although the air was warm: so dull, although the sky was bright: that he rose up shivering from his seat, and hastily resumed his walk. He checked himself as hastily:

undecided whether to pursue the footpath, which was lonely and retired, or to go back by the road.

He took the footpath.

The glory of the departing sun was on his face. The music of the birds was in his ears. Sweet wild flowers bloomed about him. Thatched roofs of poor men's homes were in the distance; and an old grey spire, surmounted by a Cross, rose up between him and the coming night.

He had never read the lesson which these things conveyed; he had ever mocked and turned away from it; but, before going down into a hollow place, he looked round, once, upon the evening prospect, sorrowfully. Then he went down, down, down, into the dell.

It brought him to the wood; a close, thick, shadowy wood, through which the path went winding on, dwindling away into a slender sheep-track. He paused before entering; for the stillness of this spot almost daunted him.

The last rays of the sun were shining in, aslant, making a path of golden light along the stems and branches in its range, which, even as he looked, began to die away, yielding gently to the twilight that came creeping on. It was so very quiet that the soft and stealthy moss about the trunks of some old trees, seemed to have grown out of the silence, and to be its proper offspring. Those other trees which were subdued by blasts of wind in winter time, had not quite tumbled down, but being caught by others, lay all bare and scathed across their leafy arms, as if unwilling to disturb the general repose by the crash of their fall. Vistas of silence opened everywhere, into the heart and innermost recesses of the wood; beginning with the likeness of an aisle, a cloister, or a ruin open to the sky; then tangling off into a deep green rustling mystery, through which gnarled trunks, and twisted boughs, and ivy-covered stems, and trembling leaves, and bark-stripped bodies of old trees stretched out at length, were faintly seen in beautiful confusion.

As the sunlight died away, and evening fell upon the wood, he entered it. Moving, here and there, a bramble or a drooping bough which stretched across his path, he slowly disappeared. At intervals a narrow opening showed him passing on, or the sharp cracking of some tender branch denoted where he went; then he was seen or heard no more.

Never more beheld by mortal eye or heard by mortal ear: one man excepted. That man, parting the leaves and branches on the other side, near where the path emerged again, came leaping out soon afterwards.

What had he left within the wood, that he sprang out of it as if it were a hell!

The body of a murdered man. In one thick solitary spot, it lay among the last year's leaves of oak and beech, just as it had fallen headlong down. Sopping and soaking in among the leaves that formed its pillow; oozing down into the boggy ground, as if to cover itself from human sight; forcing its way between and through the curling leaves, as if those senseless things rejected and forswore it, and were coiled up in abhorrence; went a dark, dark stain that dyed the whole summer night from earth to heaven.

The doer of this deed came leaping from the wood so fiercely, that he cast into the air a shower of fragments of young boughs, torn away in his passage, and fell with violence upon the grass. But he quickly gained his feet again, and keeping underneath a hedge with his body bent, went running on towards the road. The road once reached, he fell into a rapid walk, and set on towards London.

And he was not sorry for what he had done. He was frightened when he thought of it—when did he not think of it!—but he was not sorry. He had had a terror and dread of the wood when he was in it; but being out of it, and having committed the crime, his fears were now diverted, strangely, to the dark room he had left shut up at home. He had a greater horror, infinitely greater, of that room than of the wood. Now that he was on his return to it, it seemed beyond comparison more dismal and more dreadful than the wood. His hideous secret was shut up in the room, and all its terrors were there; to his thinking it was not in the wood at all.

He walked on for ten miles; and then stopped at an ale-house for a coach, which he knew would pass through, on its way to London, before long; and which he also knew was not the coach he had travelled down by, for it came from another place. He sat down outside the door here, on a bench, beside a man who was smoking his pipe. Having called for some beer, and drunk, he offered it to this companion, who thanked him, and took a draught. He could not help thinking that, if the man had known all, he might scarcely have relished drinking out of the same cup with him.

'A fine night, master!' said this person. 'And a rare sunset.'

'I didn't see it,' was his hasty answer.

'Didn't see it?' returned the man.

'How the devil could I see it, if I was asleep?'

'Asleep! Aye, aye.' The man appeared surprised by his un-expected irritability, and saying no more, smoked his pipe in silence. They had not sat very long, when there was a knocking within.

'What's that?' cried Jonas.

'Can't say, I'm sure,' replied the man.

He made no further inquiry, for the last question had escaped him, in spite of himself. But he was thinking, at the moment, of the closed-up room; of the possibility of their knocking at the door on some special occasion; of their being alarmed at receiving no answer; of their bursting it open; of their finding the room empty; of their fastening the door into the court, and rendering it impossible for him to get into the house without showing himself in the garb he wore; which would lead to rumour, rumour to detection, detection to death. At that instant, as if by some design and order of cir-cumstances, the knocking had come.

It still continued; like a warning echo of the dread reality he had conjured up. As he could not sit and hear it, he paid for his beer and walked on again. And having slunk about, in places unknown to him, all day; and being out at night, in a lonely road, in an unusual dress, and in that wandering and unsettled frame of mind; he stopped more than once to look about him, hoping he might be in a dream.

Still he was not sorry. No. He had hated the man too much, and had been bent, too desperately and too long, on setting himself free. If the thing could have come over again, he would have done it again. His malignant and revengeful passions were not so easily laid. There was no more penitence or remorse with-in him now than there had been while the deed was brewing.

Dread and fear were upon him, to an extent he had never counted on, and could not manage in the least degree. He was so horribly afraid of that infernal room at home. This made him, in a gloomy, murderous, mad way, not only fearful *for* himself, but *of* himself; for being, as it were, a part of the room: a something supposed to be there, yet missing from it: he invested himself with its mysterious terrors; and when he pictured in his mind the ugly chamber, false and quiet, false and quiet, through the dark hours of two nights; and the tumbled bed, and he not in it, though believed to be; he became in a manner his own ghost and phantom, and was at once the haunting spirit and the haunted man.

When the coach came up, which it soon did, he got a place outside, and was carried briskly onward towards home. Now, in taking his seat among the people behind, who were chiefly country people, he conceived a fear that they knew of the murder, and would tell him that the body had been found; which, considering the time and place of the commission of the crime, were events almost impossible to have happened yet, as he very well knew. But although he did know it, and had therefore no reason to regard their ignorance as anything but the natural sequence to the facts, still this very ignorance of theirs encouraged him. So far encouraged him, that he began to believe the body never would be found, and began to speculate on that probability. Setting off from this point, and measuring time by the rapid hurry of his guilty thoughts, and what had gone before the bloodshed, and the troops of incoherent and disordered images of which he was the constant prey; he came by daylight to regard the murder as an old murder, and to think himself comparatively safe, because it had not been discovered yet. Yet! When the sun which looked into the wood, and gilded with its rising light a dead man's face, had seen that man alive, and sought to win him to a thought of Heaven, on its going down last night!

But here were London streets again. Hush!

It was but five o'clock. He had time enough to reach his own house unobserved, and before there were many people in the streets, if nothing had happened so far, tending to his discovery. He slipped down from the coach without troubling the driver to stop his horses: and hurrying across the road, and in and out of every by-way that lay near his course, at length approached his own dwelling. He used additional caution in his immediate neighbourhood; halting first to look all down the street before him; then gliding swiftly through that one, and stopping to survey the next; and so on.

The passage-way was empty when his murderer's face looked into it. He stole on to the door on tiptoe, as if he dreaded to disturb his own imaginary rest.

He listened. Not a sound. As he turned the key with a trembling hand, and pushed the door softly open with his knee, a monstrous fear beset his mind.

What if the murdered man were there before him!

He cast a fearful glance all round. But there was nothing there.

He went in, locked the door, drew the key through and through the dust and damp in the fire-place to sully it again, and hung it up as of old. He took off his disguise, tied it up in a bundle ready for carrying away and sinking in the river before night, and locked it up in a cupboard. These precautions taken, he undressed and went to bed.

The raging thirst, the fire that burnt within him as he lay beneath the clothes, the augmented horror of the room when they shut it out from his view; the agony of listening, in which he paid enforced regard to every sound, and thought the most unlikely one the prelude to that knocking which should bring the news; the starts with which he left his couch, and looking in the glass, imagined that his deed was broadly written in his face, and lying down and burying himself once more beneath the blankets, heard his own heart beating Murder, Murder, Murder, in the bed; what words can paint tremendous truths like these!

The morning advanced. There were footsteps in the house. He heard the blinds drawn up, and shutters opened; and now and then a stealthy tread outside his own door. He tried to call out, more than once, but his mouth was dry as if it had been filled with sand. At last he sat up in his bed, and cried:

'Who's there!'

It was his wife.

He asked her what it was o'clock? Nine.

'Did—did no one knock at my door yesterday?' he faltered. 'Something disturbed me; but unless you had knocked the door down, you would have got no notice from me.'

'No one,' she replied. That was well. He had waited, almost breathless, for her answer. It was a relief to him, if anything could be.

'Mr. Nadgett wanted to see you,' she said, 'but I told him you were tired, and had requested not to be disturbed. He said it was of little consequence, and went away. As I was opening my window to let in the cool air, I saw him passing through the street this morning, very early; but he hasn't been again.'

Passing through the street that morning? Very early! Jonas trembled at the thought of having had a narrow chance of seeing him himself: even him, who had no object but to avoid people, and sneak on unobserved, and keep his own secrets: and who saw nothing.

He called to her to get his breakfast ready, and prepared to go up-stairs: attiring himself in the clothes he had taken off when he came into that room, which had been, ever since, outside the door. In his secret dread of meeting the household for the first time, after what he had done, he lingered at the door on slight pretexts that they might see him without looking in his face; and left it ajar while he dressed; and called out to have the windows opened, and the pavement watered, that they might become accustomed to his voice. Even when he had put off the time, by one means or other, so that he had seen or spoken to them all, he could not muster courage for a long while to go in among them, but stood at his own door listening to the murmur of their distant conversation.

He could not stop there for ever, and so joined them. His last glance at the glass had seen a tell-tale face, but that might have been because of his anxious looking in it. He dared not look at them to see if they observed him, but he thought them very silent.

And whatsoever guard he kept upon himself, he could not help listening, and showing that he listened. Whether he attended to their talk, or tried to think of other things, or talked himself, or held his peace, or resolutely counted the dull tickings of a hoarse clock at his back, he always lapsed, as if a spell were on him, into eager listening. For he knew it must come; and his present punishment, and torture, and distraction, were, to listen for its coming.

Hush!

CHAPTER XLVIII

Bears tidings of Martin, and of Mark, as well as of a third person not quite unknown to the reader. Exhibits filial piety in an ugly aspect; and casts a doubtful ray of light upon a very dark place

TOM PINCH and Ruth were sitting at their early break-fast, with the window open, and a row of the freshest little plants ranged before it on the inside by Ruth's own hands; and Ruth had fastened a sprig of geranium in Tom's button-hole, to make him very smart and summer-like for the day (it was obliged to be fastened in, or that dear old Tom was certain to lose it); and people were crying flowers up and down the street; and a blundering bee, who had got himself in between the two sashes of the window, was bruising his head against the glass, endeavouring to force himself out into the fine morning, and considering himself enchanted because he couldn't do it; and the morning was as fine a morning as ever was seen; and the fragrant air was kissing Ruth and rustling about Tom, as if it said, 'How are you, my dears: I came all this way on purpose to salute you;' and it was one of those glad times when we form, or ought to form, the wish that every one on earth were able to be happy, and catching glimpses of the summer of the heart, to feel the beauty of the summer of the year.

It was even a pleasanter breakfast than usual; and it was always a pleasant one. For little Ruth had now two pupils to attend, each three times a week, and each two hours at a time; and besides this, she had painted some screens and card-racks, and, unknown to Tom (was there ever anything so delightful!) had walked into a certain shop which dealt in such articles, after often peeping through the window; and had taken courage to ask the mistress of that shop whether she would buy them. And the mistress had not only bought them, but had ordered more; and that very morning Ruth had made con-fession of these facts to Tom, and had handed him the money in a little purse she had worked expressly for the purpose. They had been in a flutter about this, and perhaps had shed a happy tear or two for anything the history knows to the contrary; but it was all over now; and a brighter face than Tom's, or a brighter face than Ruth's, the bright sun had not looked on, since he went to bed last night.

'My dear girl,' said Tom, coming so abruptly on the subject, that he interrupted himself in the act of cutting a slice of bread, and left the knife sticking in the loaf, 'what a queer fellow our landlord is! I don't believe he has been home once since he got me into that unsatisfactory scrape. I begin to think he will never come home again. What a mysterious life that man does lead, to be sure!'

'Very strange. Is it not, Tom!'

'Really,' said Tom, 'I hope it is only strange. I hope there may be nothing wrong in it. Sometimes I begin to be doubtful of that. I must have an explanation with him,' said Tom, shaking his head as if this were a most tremendous threat, 'when I can catch him!'

A short double knock at the door put Tom's menacing looks to flight, and awakened an expression of surprise instead.

'Heyday!' said Tom. 'An early hour for visitors! It must be John, I suppose.'

'I—I—don't think it was his knock, Tom,' observed his little sister.

'No?' said Tom. 'It surely can't be my employer suddenly arrived in town; directed here by Mr. Fips; and come for the key of the office. It's somebody inquiring for me, I declare! Come in, if you please!'

But when the person came in, Tom Pinch, instead of saying, 'Did you wish to speak with me, sir?' or, 'My name is Pinch, sir; what is your business, may I ask?' or addressing him in any such distant terms; cried out, 'Good gracious Heaven!' and seized him by both hands, with the liveliest manifestations of astonishment and pleasure.

The visitor was not less moved than Tom himself, and they shook hands a great many times, without another word being spoken on either side. Tom was the first to find his voice.

'Mark Tapley, too!' said Tom, running towards the door, and shaking hands with somebody else. 'My dear Mark, come in. How are you, Mark? He don't look a day older than he used to do at the Dragon. How *are* you, Mark?'

'Uncommonly jolly, sir, thank'ee,' returned Mr. Tapley, all smiles and bows. 'I hope I see you well, sir.'

'Good gracious me!' cried Tom, patting him tenderly on the back. 'How delightful it is to hear his old voice again! My dear

Martin, sit down. My sister, Martin. Mr. Chuzzlewit, my love. Mark Tapley from the Dragon, my dear. Good gracious me, what a surprise this is! Sit down. Lord bless me!'

Tom was in such a state of excitement that he couldn't keep himself still for a moment, but was constantly running between Mark and Martin, shaking hands with them alternately, and presenting them over and over again to his sister.

'I remember the day we parted, Martin, as well as if it were yesterday,' said Tom. 'What a day it was! and what a passion you were in! And don't you remember my overtaking you in the road that morning, Mark, when I was going to Salisbury in the gig to fetch him, and you were looking out for a situation? And don't you recollect the dinner we had at Salisbury, Martin, with John Westlock, eh? Good gracious me! Ruth, my dear, Mr. Chuzzlewit. Mark Tapley, my love, from the Dragon. More cups and saucers, if you please. Bless my soul, how glad I am to see you both!'

And then Tom (as John Westlock had done on his arrival) ran off to the loaf to cut some bread and butter for them; and before he had spread a single slice, remembered something else, and came running back again to tell it; and then he shook hands with them again; and then he introduced his sister again; and then he did everything he had done already all over again; and then he did everything he had done already all over again; and nothing Tom could do, and nothing Tom could say, was half sufficient to express his joy at their safe return.

Mr. Tapley was the first to resume his composure. In a very short space of time he was discovered to have somehow installed himself in office as waiter, or attendant upon the party; a fact which was first suggested to them by his temporary absence in the kitchen, and speedy return with a kettle of boiling water, from which he replenished the tea-pot with a self-possession that was quite his own.

'Sit down, and take your breakfast, Mark,' said Tom. 'Make him sit down and take his breakfast, Martin.'

'Oh! I gave him up, long ago, as incorrigible,' Martin replied. 'He takes his own way, Tom. You would excuse him, Miss Pinch, if you knew his value.'

'She knows it, bless you!' said Tom. 'I have told her all about Mark Tapley. Have I not, Ruth?'

'Yes, Tom.'

'Not all,' returned Martin, in a low voice. 'The best of Mark

Tapley is only known to one man, Tom; and but for Mark he would hardly be alive to tell it.'

'Mark!' said Tom Pinch, energetically: 'if you don't sit down this minute, I'll swear at you!'

'Well, sir,' returned Mr. Tapley, 'sooner than you should do that, I'll com-ply. It's a considerable invasion of a man's jollity to be made so partickler welcome, but a Werb is a word as signifies to be, to do, or to suffer (which is all the grammar, and enough too, as ever I wos taught); and if there's a Werb alive, I'm it. For I'm always a-bein', sometimes a-doin', and continually a-sufferin'.'

'Not jolly yet?' asked Tom, with a smile.

'Why, I was rather so, over the water, sir,' returned Mr. Tapley; 'and not entirely without credit. But Human Natur' is in a conspiracy again' me; I can't get on. I shall have to leave it in my will, sir, to be wrote upon my tomb: "He was a man as might have come out strong if he could have got a chance. But it was denied him."'

Mr. Tapley took this occasion of looking about him with a grin, and subsequently attacking the breakfast, with an appetite not at all expressive of blighted hopes, or insurmountable despondency.

In the meanwhile, Martin drew his chair a little nearer to Tom and his sister, and related to them what had passed at Mr. Pecksniff's house; adding in few words a general summary of the distresses and disappointments he had undergone since he left England.

'For your faithful stewardship in the trust I left with you, Tom,' he said, 'and for all your goodness and disinterestedness, I can never thank you enough. When I add Mary's thanks to mine——'

Ah, Tom! The blood retreated from his cheeks, and came rushing back, so violently, that it was pain to feel it; ease though, ease, compared with the aching of his wounded heart.

'When I add Mary's thanks to mine,' said Martin, 'I have made the only poor acknowledgment it is in our power to offer; but if you knew how much we feel, Tom, you would set some store by it, I am sure.'

And if they had known how much Tom felt—but that no human creature ever knew—they would have set some store by him. Indeed they would.

Tom changed the topic of discourse. He was sorry he could

not pursue it, as it gave Martin pleasure; but he was unable, at that moment. No drop of envy or bitterness was in his soul; but he could not master the firm utterance of her name.

He inquired what Martin's projects were.

'No longer to make your fortune, Tom,' said Martin, 'but to try to live. I tried that once in London, Tom; and failed. If you will give me the benefit of your advice and friendly counsel, I may succeed better under your guidance. I will do anything, Tom, anything, to gain a livelihood by my own exertions. My hopes do not soar above that, now.'

High-hearted, noble Tom! Sorry to find the pride of his old companion humbled, and to hear him speaking in this altered strain, at once, at once, he drove from his breast the inability to contend with its deep emotions, and spoke out bravely.

'Your hopes do not soar above that!' cried Tom. 'Yes they do. How can you talk so! They soar up to the time when you will be happy with her, Martin. They soar up to the time when you will be able to claim her, Martin. They soar up to the time when you will not be able to believe that you were ever cast down in spirit, or poor in pocket, Martin. Advice, and friendly counsel! Why, of course. But you shall have better advice and counsel (though you cannot have more friendly) than mine. You shall consult John Westlock. We'll go there immediately. It is yet so early that I shall have time to take you to his chambers before I go to business; they are in my way; and I can leave you there, to talk over your affairs with him. So come along. Come along. I am a man of occupation now, you know,' said Tom, with his pleasantest smile; 'and have no time to lose. Your hopes don't soar higher than that? I dare say they don't. *I* know you, pretty well. They'll be soaring out of sight soon, Martin, and leaving all the rest of us leagues behind.'

'Aye! But I may be a little changed,' said Martin, 'since you knew me pretty well, Tom.'

'What nonsense!' exclaimed Tom. 'Why should you be changed? You talk as if you were an old man. I never heard such a fellow! Come to John Westlock's, come. Come along, Mark Tapley. It's Mark's doing, I have no doubt; and it serves you right for having such a grumbler for your companion.'

'There's no credit to be got through being jolly with *you*, Mr. Pinch, anyways,' said Mark, with his face all wrinkled up with grins. 'A parish doctor might be jolly with you. There's nothing short of goin' to the U-nited States for a second trip, as would make it at all creditable to be jolly, arter seein' you again!'

Tom laughed, and taking leave of his sister, hurried Mark and Martin out into the street, and away to John Westlock's by the nearest road; for his hour of business was very near at hand, and he prided himself on always being exact to his time.

John Westlock was at home, but, strange to say, was rather embarrassed to see them; and when Tom was about to go into the room where he was breakfasting, said he had a stranger there. It appeared to be a mysterious stranger, for John shut that door as he said it, and led them into the next room.

He was very much delighted, though, to see Mark Tapley; and received Martin with his own frank courtesy. But Martin felt that he did not inspire John Westlock with any unusual interest; and twice or thrice observed that he looked at Tom Pinch doubtfully; not to say compassionately. He thought, and blushed to think, that he knew the cause of this.

'I apprehend you are engaged,' said Martin, when Tom had announced the purport of their visit. 'If you will allow me to come again at your own time, I shall be glad to do so.'

'I *am* engaged,' replied John, with some reluctance; 'but the matter on which I am engaged is one, to say the truth, more immediately demanding your knowledge than mine.'

'Indeed!' cried Martin.

'It relates to a member of your family, and is of a serious nature. If you will have the kindness to remain here, it will be a satisfaction to me to have it privately communicated to you, in order that you may judge of its importance for yourself.'

'And in the meantime,' said Tom, 'I must really take myself off, without any further ceremony.'

'Is your business so very particular,' asked Martin, 'that you cannot remain with us for half an hour? I wish you could. What *is* your business, Tom?'

It was Tom's turn to be embarrassed now: but he plainly said, after a little hesitation:

'Why, I am not at liberty to say what it is, Martin: though I hope soon to be in a condition to do so, and am aware of no other reason to prevent my doing so now, than the request of my employer. It's an awkward position to be placed in,' said Tom, with an uneasy sense of seeming to doubt his friend, 'as I feel every day; but I really cannot help it, can I, John?'

John Westlock replied in the negative; and Martin, expressing himself perfectly satisfied, begged them not to say another
word: though he could not help wondering very much what
curious office Tom held, and why he was so secret, and embarrassed, and unlike himself, in reference to it. Nor could he
help reverting to it, in his own mind, several times after Tom
went away, which he did as soon as this conversation was
ended, taking Mr. Tapley with him, who, as he laughingly
said, might accompany him as far as Fleet Street without
injury.

'And what do _you_ mean to do, Mark?' asked Tom, as they
walked on together.

'Mean to do, sir?' returned Mr. Tapley.

'Aye. What course of life do you mean to pursue?'

'Well, sir,' said Mr. Tapley. 'The fact is, that I have been
a-thinking rather of the matrimonial line, sir.'

'You don't say so, Mark!' cried Tom.

'Yes, sir. I've been a-turnin' of it over.'

'And who is the lady, Mark?'

'The which, sir?' said Mr. Tapley.

'The lady. Come! You know what I said,' replied Tom,
laughing, 'as well as I do!'

Mr. Tapley suppressed his own inclination to laugh; and
with one of his most whimsically-twisted looks, replied,

'You couldn't guess, I suppose, Mr. Pinch?'

'How is it possible?' said Tom. 'I don't know any of your
flames, Mark. Except Mrs. Lupin, indeed.'

'Well, sir!' retorted Mr. Tapley. 'And supposing it was her!'

Tom stopping in the street to look at him, Mr. Tapley for
a moment presented to his view an utterly stolid and expres-
sionless face: a perfect dead wall of countenance. But opening
window after window in it with astonishing rapidity, and
lighting them all up as for a general illumination, he repeated:

'Supposin', for the sake of argument, as it was her, sir!'

'Why, I thought such a connexion wouldn't suit you, Mark,
on any terms!' cried Tom.

'Well, sir, I used to think so myself, once,' said Mark. 'But
I ain't so clear about it now. A dear, sweet creetur, sir!'

'A dear, sweet creature? To be sure she is,' cried Tom. 'But
she always was a dear sweet creature, was she not?'

'_Was_ she not!' assented Mr. Tapley.

'Then why on earth didn't you marry her at first, Mark,

Mrs. Gamp proposes a Toast
(p. 753)

instead of wandering abroad, and losing all this time, and leaving her alone by herself, liable to be courted by other people?'

'Why, sir,' retorted Mr. Tapley, in a spirit of unbounded confidence, 'I'll tell you how it come about. You know me, Mr. Pinch, sir; there ain't a gentleman alive as knows me better. You're acquainted with my constitution, and you're acquainted with my weakness. My constitution is, to be jolly; and my weakness is, to wish to find a credit in it. Wery good, sir. In this state of mind, I gets a notion in my head that she looks on me with a eye of—with what you may call a favour-able sort of a eye in fact,' said Mr. Tapley, with modest hesita-tion.

'No doubt,' replied Tom. 'We knew that perfectly well when we spoke on this subject long ago; before you left the Dragon.'

Mr. Tapley nodded assent. 'Well, sir! But bein' at that time full of hopeful wisions, I arrives at the conclusion that no credit is to be got out of such a way of life as that, where everything agreeable would be ready to one's hand. Lookin' on the bright side of human life in short, one of my hopeful wisions is, that there's a deal of misery a-waitin' for me; in the midst of which I may come out tolerable strong, and be jolly under circumstances as reflects some credit. I goes into the world, sir, wery boyant, and I tries this. I goes aboard ship first, and wery soon dis-covers (by the ease with which I'm jolly, mind you) as there's no credit to be got *there*. I might have took warning by this, and gave it up; but I didn't. I gets to the U-nited States; and then I *do* begin, I won't deny it, to feel some little credit in sustaining my spirits. What follows? Jest as I'm a-beginning to come out, and am a-treadin' on the werge, my master deceives me.'

'Deceives you!' cried Tom.

'Swindles me,' retorted Mr. Tapley, with a beaming face. 'Turns his back on ev'rything as made his service a creditable one, and leaves me, high and dry, without a leg to stand upon. In which state I returns home. Wery good. Then all my hope-ful wisions bein' crushed; and findin' that there ain't no credit for me nowhere; I abandons myself to despair, and says, "Let me do that as has the least credit in it of all; marry a dear, sweet creetur, as is wery fond of me: me bein', at the same time, wery fond of her: lead a happy life, and struggle no more again' the blight which settles on my prospects."'

'If your philosophy, Mark,' said Tom, who laughed heartily at this speech, 'be the oddest I ever heard of, it is not the least wise. Mrs. Lupin has said "yes," of course?'

'Why, no, sir,' replied Mr. Tapley; 'she hasn't gone so far as that yet. Which I attribute principally to my not havin' asked her. But we was wery agreeable together—comfortable, I may say—the night I come home. It 's all right, sir.'

'Well!' said Tom, stopping at the Temple Gate. 'I wish you joy, Mark, with all my heart. I shall see you again to-day, I dare say. Good-bye for the present.'

'Good-bye, sir! Good-bye, Mr. Pinch!' he added, by way of soliloquy, as he stood looking after him: 'Although you *are* a damper to a honourable ambition. You little think it, but you was the first to dash my hopes. Pecksniff would have built me up for life, but your sweet temper pulled me down. Good-bye, Mr. Pinch!'

While these confidences were interchanged between Tom Pinch and Mark, Martin and John Westlock were very differently engaged. They were no sooner left alone together than Martin said, with an effort he could not disguise:

'Mr. Westlock, we have met only once before, but you have known Tom a long while, and that seems to render you familiar to me. I cannot talk freely with you on any subject unless I relieve my mind of what oppresses it just now. I see with pain that you so far mistrust me that you think me likely to impose on Tom's regardlessness of himself, or on his kind nature, or some of his good qualities.'

'I had no intention,' replied John, 'of conveying any such impression to you, and am exceedingly sorry to have done so.'

'But you entertain it?' said Martin.

'You ask me so pointedly and directly,' returned the other, 'that I cannot deny the having accustomed myself to regard you as one who, not in wantonness but in mere thoughtlessness of character, did not sufficiently consider his nature and did not quite treat it as it deserves to be treated. It is much easier to slight than to appreciate Tom Pinch.'

This was not said warmly, but was energetically spoken too; for there was no subject in the world (but one) on which the speaker felt so strongly.

'I grew into the knowledge of Tom,' he pursued, 'as I grew towards manhood; and I have learned to love him as something infinitely better than myself. I did not think that you understood him when we met before. I did not think that you greatly cared to understand him. The instances of this which I observed in you were, like my opportunities for observation, very trivial—and were very harmless, I dare say. But they were not agreeable to me, and they forced themselves upon me; for I was not upon the watch for them, believe me. You will say,' added John, with a smile, as he subsided into more of his accustomed manner, 'that I am not by any means agreeable to you. I can only assure you, in reply, that I would not have originated this topic on any account.'

'I originated it,' said Martin; 'and so far from having any complaint to make against you, highly esteem the friendship you entertain for Tom, and the very many proofs you have given him of it. Why should I endeavour to conceal from you:' he coloured deeply though: 'that I neither understood him nor cared to understand him when I was his companion; and that I am very truly sorry for it now!'

It was so sincerely said, at once so modestly and manfully, that John offered him his hand as if he had not done so before; and Martin giving his in the same open spirit, all constraint between the young men vanished.

'Now pray,' said John, 'when I tire your patience very much in what I am going to say, recollect that it has an end to it, and that the end is the point of the story.'

With this preface, he related all the circumstances connected with his having presided over the illness and slow recovery of the patient at the Bull; and tacked on to the skirts of that narrative Tom's own account of the business on the wharf. Martin was not a little puzzled when he came to an end, for the two stories seemed to have no connexion with each other, and to leave him, as the phrase is, all abroad.

'If you will excuse me for one moment,' said John, rising, 'I will beg you almost immediately to come into the next room.'

Upon that, he left Martin to himself, in a state of considerable astonishment; and soon came back again to fulfil his promise. Accompanying him into the next room, Martin found there a third person; no doubt the stranger of whom his host had spoken when Tom Pinch introduced him.

He was a young man; with deep black hair and eyes. He was gaunt and pale; and evidently had not long recovered from a severe illness. He stood as Martin entered, but sat again at John's desire. His eyes were cast downward; and but for one glance at them both, half in humiliation and half in entreaty, he kept them so, and sat quite still and silent.

'This person's name is Lewsome,' said John Westlock, 'whom I have mentioned to you as having been seized with an illness at the Inn near here, and undergone so much. He has had a very hard time of it, ever since he began to recover; but, as you see, he is now doing well.'

As he did not move or speak, and John Westlock made a pause, Martin, not knowing what to say, said that he was glad to hear it.

'The short statement that I wish you to hear from his own lips, Mr. Chuzzlewit,' John pursued: looking attentively at him, and not at Martin: 'he made to me for the first time yesterday, and repeated to me this morning, without the least variation of any essential particular. I have already told you that he informed me before he was removed from the Inn, that he had a secret to disclose to me which lay heavy on his mind. But, fluctuating between sickness and health, and between his desire to relieve himself of it, and his dread of involving himself by revealing it, he has, until yesterday, avoided the disclosure. I never pressed him for it (having no idea of its weight or import, or of my right to do so), until within a few days past; when, understanding from him, on his own voluntary avowal, in a letter from the country, that it related to a person whose name was Jonas Chuzzlewit; and thinking that it might throw some light on that little mystery which made Tom anxious now and then; I urged the point upon him, and heard his statement, as you will now, from his own lips. It is due to him to say, that in the apprehension of death, he committed it to writing sometime since, and folded it in a sealed paper, addressed to me: which he could not resolve, however, to place of his own act in my hands. He has the paper in his breast, I believe, at this moment.'

The young man touched it hastily; in corroboration of the fact.

'It will be well to leave that in our charge, perhaps,' said John. 'But do not mind it now.'

As he said this, he held up his hand to bespeak Martin's attention. It was already fixed upon the man before him, who, after a short silence said, in a low, weak, hollow voice:

'What relation was Mr. Anthony Chuzzlewit, who—'

'—Who died—to me?' said Martin. 'He was my grandfather's brother.'

'I fear he was made away with. Murdered!'

'My God!' said Martin. 'By whom?'

The young man, Lewsome, looked up in his face, and casting down his eyes again, replied:

'I fear, by me.'

'By you?' cried Martin.

'Not by my act, but I fear by my means.'

'Speak out!' said Martin, 'and speak the truth.'

'I fear this *is* the truth.'

Martin was about to interrupt him again, but John Westlock saying softly, 'Let him tell his story in his own way,' Lewsome went on thus:

'I have been bred a surgeon, and for the last few years have served a general practitioner in the City, as his assistant. While I was in his employment I became acquainted with Jonas Chuzzlewit. He is the principal in this deed.'

'What do you mean?' demanded Martin, sternly. 'Do you know he is the son of the old man of whom you have spoken?'

'I do,' he answered.

He remained silent for some moments, when he resumed at the point where he had left off.

'I have reason to know it; for I have often heard him wish his old father dead, and complain of his being wearisome to him, and a drag upon him. He was in the habit of doing so, at a place of meeting we had—three or four of us—at night. There was no good in the place, you may suppose, when you hear that he was the chief of the party. I wish I had died myself, and never seen it!'

He stopped again; and again resumed as before.

'We met to drink and game; not for large sums, but for sums that were large to us. He generally won. Whether or no, he lent money at interest to those who lost; and in this way, though I think we all secretly hated him, he came to be the master of us. To propitiate him, we made a jest of his father: it began with his debtors; I was one: and we used to toast a quicker journey to the old man, and a swift inheritance to the young one.'

He paused again.

'One night he came there in a very bad humour. He had been greatly tried, he said, by the old man that day. He and I were alone together: and he angrily told me, that the old man was in his second childhood; that he was weak, imbecile, and drivelling; as unbearable to himself as he was to other people; and that it would be a charity to put him out of the way. He swore that he had often thought of mixing something with the stuff he took for his cough, which should help him to die easily. People were sometimes smothered who were bitten by mad dogs, he said; and why not help these lingering old men out of their troubles too? He looked full at me as he said so, and I looked full at him; but it went no farther that night.'

He stopped once more, and was silent for so long an interval that John Westlock said 'Go on.' Martin had never removed his eyes from his face, but was so absorbed in horror and astonishment that he could not speak.

'It may have been a week after that, or it may have been less, or more—the matter was in my mind all the time, but I cannot recollect the time, as I should any other period—when he spoke to me again. We were alone then, too; being there before the usual hour of assembling. There was no appointment between us; but I think I went there to meet him, and I know he came there to meet me. He was there first. He was reading a newspaper when I went in, and nodded to me without looking up, or leaving off reading. I sat down opposite and close to him. He said, immediately, that he wanted me to get him some of two sorts of drugs. One that was instantaneous in its effect; of which he wanted very little. One that was slow, and not suspicious in appearance; of which he wanted more. While he was speaking to me he still read the newspaper. He said "Drugs," and never used any other word. Neither did I.'

'This all agrees with what I have heard before,' observed John Westlock.

'I asked him what he wanted the drugs for? He said for no harm; to physic cats; what did it matter to me? I was going out to a distant colony (I had recently got the appointment, which, as Mr. Westlock knows, I have since lost by my sickness, and which was my only hope of salvation from ruin), and what did it matter to me? He could get them without my aid at half a hundred places, but not so easily as he could get them of me. This was true. He might not want them at all, he said, and he had no present idea of using them; but he wished to have them by him. All this time he still read the newspaper. We talked about the price. He was to forgive me a small debt—I was quite in his power—and to pay me five pounds; and there the matter dropped, through others coming in. But, next night, under exactly similar circumstances, I gave him the drugs, on his saying I was a fool to think that he should ever use them for any harm; and he gave me the money. We have never met since. I only know that the poor old father died soon afterwards, just as he would have died from this cause: and that I have undergone, and suffer now, intolerable misery. Nothing,' he added, stretching out his hands, 'can paint my misery! It is well deserved, but nothing can paint it.'

With that he hung his head, and said no more. Wasted and wretched, he was not a creature upon whom to heap reproaches that were unavailing

'Let him remain at hand,' said Martin, turning from him; 'but out of sight, in Heaven's name!'

'He will remain here,' John whispered. 'Come with me!' Softly turning the key upon him as they went out, he conducted Martin into the adjoining room, in which they had been before.

Martin was so amazed, so shocked, and confounded by what he had heard, that it was some time before he could reduce it to any order in his mind, or could sufficiently comprehend the bearing of one part upon another, to take in all the details at one view. When he, at length, had the whole narrative clearly before him, John Westlock went on to point out the great probability of the guilt of Jonas being known to other people, who traded in it for their own benefit, and who were, by such means, able to exert that control over him which Tom Pinch had accidentally witnessed, and unconsciously assisted. This appeared so plain, that they agreed upon it without difficulty; but instead of deriving the least assistance from this source, they found that it embarrassed them the more.

They knew nothing of the real parties who possessed this power. The only person before them was Tom's landlord. They had no right to question Tom's landlord, even if they could find him, which, according to Tom's account, it would not be easy to do. And granting that they did question him, and he answered (which was taking a good deal for granted), he had only to say, with reference to the adventure on the wharf, that he had been sent from such and such a place to summon Jonas back on urgent business, and there was an end of it.

Besides, there was the great difficulty and responsibility of moving at all in the matter. Lewsome's story might be false; in his wretched state it might be greatly heightened by a diseased brain; or admitting it to be entirely true, the old man might have died a natural death. Mr. Pecksniff had been there at the time; as Tom immediately remembered, when he came back in the afternoon, and shared their counsels; and there had been no secrecy about it. Martin's grandfather was of right the person to decide upon the course that should be taken; but to get at his views would be impossible, for Mr. Pecksniff's views were certain to be his. And the nature of Mr. Pecksniff's views in reference to his own son-in-law might be easily reckoned upon.

Apart from these considerations, Martin could not endure the thought of seeming to grasp at this unnatural charge against his relative, and using it as a stepping-stone to his grandfather's favour. But that he would seem to do so, if he presented himself before his grandfather in Mr. Pecksniff's house again, for the purpose of declaring it; and that Mr. Pecksniff, of all men, would represent his conduct in that despicable light, he perfectly well knew. On the other hand, to be in possession of such a statement, and take no measures of further inquiry in reference to it, was tantamount to being a partner in the guilt it professed to disclose.

In a word, they were wholly unable to discover any outlet from this maze of difficulty, which did not lie through some perplexed and entangled thicket. And although Mr. Tapley was promptly taken into their confidence; and the fertile imagination of that gentleman suggested many bold expedients, which, to do him justice, he was quite ready to carry into instant operation on his own personal responsibility; still 'bating the general zeal of Mr. Tapley's nature, nothing was made particularly clearer by these offers of service.

It was in this position of affairs that Tom's account of the strange behaviour of the decayed clerk, on the night of the tea-party, became of great moment, and finally convinced them that to arrive at a more accurate knowledge of the workings of that old man's mind and memory, would be to take a most important stride in their pursuit of the truth. So, having first satisfied themselves that no communication had ever taken place between Lewsome and Mr. Chuffey (which would have accounted at once for any suspicions the latter might entertain), they unanimously resolved that the old clerk was the man they wanted.

But, like the unanimous resolution of a public meeting, which will oftentimes declare that this or that grievance is not to be borne a moment longer, which is nevertheless borne for a century or two afterwards, without any modification, they only reached in this the conclusion that they were all of one mind. For it was one thing to want Mr. Chuffey, and another thing to get at him; and to do that without alarming him, or without alarming Jonas, or without being discomfited by the difficulty of striking, in an instrument so out of tune and so unused, the note they sought, was an end as far from their reach as ever.

The question then became, who of those about the old clerk had had most influence with him that night? Tom said his young mistress clearly. But Tom and all of them shrunk from the thought of entrapping her, and making her the innocent means of bringing retribution on her cruel husband. Was there nobody else? Why yes. In a very different way, Tom said, he was influenced by Mrs. Gamp, the nurse: who had once had the control of him, as he understood, for some time.

They caught at this immediately. Here was a new way out, developed in a quarter until then overlooked. John Westlock knew Mrs. Gamp; he had given her employment; he was acquainted with her place of residence: for that good lady had obligingly furnished him, at parting, with a pack of her professional cards for general distribution. It was decided that Mrs. Gamp should be approached with caution, but approached without delay; and that the depths of that discreet matron's knowledge of Mr. Chuffey, and means of bringing them, or one of them, into communication with him, should be carefully sounded.

On this service, Martin and John Westlock determined to proceed that night; waiting on Mrs. Gamp first, at her lodgings; and taking their chance of finding her in the repose of private life, or of having to seek her out, elsewhere, in the exercise of her professional duties. Tom returned home, that he might lose no opportunity of having an interview with Nadgett, by being absent in the event of his reappearance. And Mr. Tapley remained (by his own particular desire) for the time being in Furnival's Inn, to look after Lewsome; who might safely have been left to himself, however, for any thought he seemed to entertain of giving them the slip.

Before they parted on their several errands, they caused him

to read aloud, in the presence of them all, the paper which
he had about him, and the declaration he had attached to it,
which was to the effect that he had written it voluntarily, in
the fear of death and in the torture of his mind. And when he
had done so, they all signed it, and taking it from him, of his
free will, locked it in a place of safety.

Martin also wrote, by John's advice, a letter to the trustees
of the famous Grammar School, boldly claiming the successful
design as his, and charging Mr. Pecksniff with the fraud he had
committed. In this proceeding also, John was hotly interested:
observing with his usual irreverence, that Mr. Pecksniff had
been a successful rascal all his life through, and that it would
be a lasting source of happiness to him (John) if he could help
to do him justice in the smallest particular.

A busy day! But Martin had no lodgings yet; so when these
matters were disposed of, he excused himself from dining with
John Westlock and was fain to wander out alone, and look
for some. He succeeded, after great trouble, in engaging two
garrets for himself and Mark, situated in a court in the Strand,
not far from Temple Bar. Their luggage, which was waiting for
them at a coach-office, he conveyed to this new place of refuge;
and it was with a glow of satisfaction, which as a selfish man
he never could have known and never had, that, thinking how
much pains and trouble he had saved Mark, and how pleased
and astonished Mark would be, he afterwards walked up and
down, in the Temple, eating a meat-pie for his dinner.

CHAPTER XLIX

*In which Mrs. Harris, assisted by a teapot, is the cause of
a division between friends*

MRS. GAMP'S apartment in Kingsgate Street, High Holborn, wore, metaphorically speaking, a robe of state. It
was swept and garnished for the reception of a visitor. That
visitor was Betsey Prig: Mrs. Prig, of Bartlemy's: or as some
said Barklemy's, or as some said Bardlemy's; for by all these
endearing and familiar appellations, had the hospital of Saint
Bartholomew become a household word among the sisterhood
which Betsey Prig adorned.

Mrs. Gamp's apartment was not a spacious one, but, to a
contented mind, a closet is a palace; and the first-floor front
at Mr. Sweedlepipe's may have been, in the imagination of
Mrs. Gamp, a stately pile. If it were not exactly that, to restless
intellects, it at least comprised as much accommodation as any
person, not sanguine to insanity, could have looked for in a
room of its dimensions. For only keep the bedstead always in
your mind; and you were safe. That was the grand secret.
Remembering the bedstead, you might even stoop to look
under the little round table for anything you had dropped,
without hurting yourself much against the chest of drawers, or
qualifying as a patient of Saint Bartholomew, by falling into
the fire.

Visitors were much assisted in their cautious efforts to preserve an unflagging recollection of this piece of furniture, by
its size: which was great. It was not a turn-up bedstead, nor
yet a French bedstead, nor yet a four-post bedstead, but what
is poetically called a tent: the sacking whereof was low and
bulgy, insomuch that Mrs. Gamp's box would not go under it,
but stopped half-way, in a manner which, while it did violence
to the reason, likewise endangered the legs of a stranger. The
frame too, which would have supported the canopy and hangings if there had been any, was ornamented with divers pippins
carved in timber, which on the slightest provocation, and
frequently on none at all, came tumbling down; harassing the
peaceful guest with inexplicable terrors.

The bed itself was decorated with a patchwork quilt of great antiquity; and at the upper end, upon the side nearest to the door, hung a scanty curtain of blue check, which prevented the Zephyrs that were abroad in Kingsgate Street, from visiting Mrs. Gamp's head too roughly. Some rusty gowns and other articles of that lady's wardrobe depended from the posts; and these had so adapted themselves by long usage to her figure, that more than one impatient husband coming in precipitately, at about the time of twilight, had been for an instant stricken dumb by the supposed discovery that Mrs. Gamp had hanged herself. One gentleman, coming on the usual hasty errand, had said indeed, that they looked like guardian angels 'watching of her in her sleep.' But that, as Mrs. Gamp said, 'was his first;' and he never repeated the sentiment, though he often repeated his visit.

The chairs in Mrs. Gamp's apartment were extremely large and broad-backed, which was more than a sufficient reason for there being but two in number. They were both elbow-chairs, of ancient mahogany; and were chiefly valuable for the slippery nature of their seats, which had been originally horse-hair, but were now covered with a shiny substance of a bluish tint, from which the visitor began to slide away with a dismayed countenance, immediately after sitting down. What Mrs. Gamp wanted in chairs she made up in bandboxes; of which she had a great collection, devoted to the reception of various miscellaneous valuables, which were not, however, as well protected as the good woman, by a pleasant fiction, seemed to think: for, though every bandbox had a carefully closed lid, not one among them had a bottom: owing to which cause the property within was merely, as it were, extinguished. The chest of drawers having been originally made to stand upon the top of another chest, had a dwarfish, elfin look, alone; but in regard of its security it had a great advantage over the bandboxes, for as all the handles had been long ago pulled off, it was very difficult to get at its contents. This indeed was only to be done by one or two devices; either by tilting the whole structure forward until all the drawers fell out together, or by opening them singly with knives, like oysters.

Mrs. Gamp stored all her household matters in a little cupboard by the fire-place; beginning below the surface (as in nature) with the coals, and mounting gradually upwards to the spirits, which, from motives of delicacy, she kept in a teapot. The chimney-piece was ornamented with a small

almanack, marked here and there in Mrs. Gamp's own hand
with a memorandum of the date at which some lady was
expected to fall due. It was also embellished with three profiles:
one, in colours, of Mrs. Gamp herself in early life; one, in
bronze, of a lady in feathers, supposed to be Mrs. Harris, as
she appeared when dressed for a ball; and one, in black, of
Mr. Gamp, deceased. The last was a full length, in order that
the likeness might be rendered more obvious and forcible by
the introduction of the wooden leg.

A pair of bellows, a pair of pattens, a toasting-fork, a kettle,
a pap-boat, a spoon for the administration of medicine to the
refractory, and lastly, Mrs. Gamp's umbrella, which as something of great price and rarity, was displayed with particular
ostentation, completed the decorations of the chimney-piece
and adjacent wall. Towards these objects Mrs. Gamp raised
her eyes in satisfaction when she had arranged the tea-board,
and had concluded her arrangements for the reception of
Betsey Prig, even unto the setting forth of two pounds of New-
castle salmon, intensely pickled.

'There! Now drat you, Betsey, don't be long!' said Mrs.
Gamp, apostrophising her absent friend. 'For I can't abear to
wait, I do assure you. To wotever place I goes, I sticks to this
one mortar, "I'm easy pleased; it is but little as I wants; but
I must have that little of the best, and to the minute when the
clock strikes, else we do not part as I could wish, but bearin'
malice in our arts."'

Her own preparations were of the best, for they compre-
hended a delicate new loaf, a plate of fresh butter, a basin of
fine white sugar, and other arrangements on the same scale.
Even the snuff with which she now refreshed herself, was so
choice in quality that she took a second pinch.

'There's the little bell a-ringing now,' said Mrs. Gamp,
hurrying to the stair-head and looking over. 'Betsey Prig, my—
why it's that there disapintin' Sweedlepipes, I do believe.'

'Yes, it's me,' said the barber in a faint voice: 'I've just
come in.'

'You're always a-comin' in, I think,' muttered Mrs. Gamp
to herself, 'except wen you're a-goin' out. I ha'n't no patience
with that man!'

'Mrs. Gamp,' said the barber. 'I say! Mrs. Gamp!'

'Well,' cried Mrs. Gamp, impatiently, as she descended the
stairs. 'What is it? Is the Thames a-fire, and cooking its own

fish, Mr. Sweedlepipes? Why wot's the man gone and been a-doin' of to himself? He's as white as chalk!'

She added the latter clause of inquiry, when she got downstairs, and found him seated in the shaving-chair, pale and disconsolate.

'You recollect,' said Poll. 'You recollect young—'

'Not young Wilkins!' cried Mrs. Gamp. 'Don't say young Wilkins, wotever you do. If young Wilkins's wife is took—'

'It isn't anybody's wife,' exclaimed the little barber. 'Bailey, young Bailey!'

'Why, wot do you mean to say that chit's been a-doin' of?' retorted Mrs. Gamp, sharply. 'Stuff and nonsense, Mr. Sweedlepipes!'

'He hasn't been a-doing anything!' exclaimed poor Poll, quite desperate. 'What do you catch me up so short for, when you see me put out to that extent that I can hardly speak? He'll never do anything again. He's done for. He's killed. The first time I ever see that boy,' said Poll, 'I charged him too much for a red-poll. I asked him three-halfpence for a penny one, because I was afraid he'd beat me down. But he didn't. And now he's dead; and if you was to crowd all the steam-engines and electric fluids that ever was, into this shop, and set 'em every one to work their hardest, they couldn't square the account, though it's only a ha'penny!'

Mr. Sweedlepipe turned aside to the towel, and wiped his eyes with it.

'And what a clever boy he was!' he said. 'What a surprising young chap he was! How he talked! and what a deal he know'd! Shaved in this very chair he was; only for fun; it was all his fun; he was full of it. Ah! to think that he'll never be shaved in earnest! The birds might every one have died, and welcome,' cried the little barber, looking round him at the cages, and again applying to the towel, 'sooner than I'd have heard this news!'

'How did you ever come to hear it?' said Mrs. Gamp. 'Who told you?'

'I went out,' returned the little barber, 'into the City, to meet a sporting gent upon the Stock Exchange, that wanted a few slow pigeons to practise at; and when I'd done with him, I went to get a little drop of beer, and there I heard everybody a-talking about it. It's in the papers.'

'You are in a nice state of confugion, Mr. Sweedlepipes, you are!' said Mrs. Gamp, shaking her head; 'and my opinion is, as half-a-dudgeon fresh young lively leeches on your temples, wouldn't be too much to clear your mind, which so I tell you. Wot were they a-talkin' on, and wot was in the papers?'

'All about it!' cried the barber. 'What else do you suppose? Him and his master were upset on a journey, and he was carried to Salisbury, and was breathing his last when the account came away. He never spoke afterwards. Not a single word. That's the worst of it to me; but that ain't all. His master can't be found. The other manager of their office in the city: Crimple, David Crimple: has gone off with the money, and is advertised for, with a reward, upon the walls. Mr. Montague, poor young Bailey's master (what a boy he was!) is advertised for, too. Some say he's slipped off, to join his friend abroad; some say he mayn't have got away yet; and they're looking for him high and low. Their office is a smash; a swindle altogether. But what's a Life Assurance Office to a Life! And what a Life Young Bailey's was!'

'He was born into a wale,' said Mrs. Gamp, with philosophical coolness; 'and he lived in a wale; and he must take the consequences of sech a sitiwation. But don't you hear nothink of Mr. Chuzzlewit in all this?'

'No,' said Poll, 'nothing to speak of. His name wasn't printed as one of the board, though some people say it was just going to be. Some believe he was took in, and some believe he was one of the takers-in; but however that may be, they can't prove nothing against him. This morning he went up of his own accord afore the Lord Mayor or some of them City big-wigs, and complained that he'd been swindled, and that these two persons had gone off and cheated him, and that he had just found out that Montague's name wasn't even Montague, but something else. And they do say that he looked like Death, owing to his losses. But, Lord forgive me,' cried the barber, coming back again to the subject of his individual grief, 'what's his looks to me! He might have died and welcome, fifty times, and not been such a loss as Bailey!'

At this juncture the little bell rang, and the deep voice of Mrs. Prig struck into the conversation.

'Oh! You're a-talkin' about it, are you!' observed that lady. 'Well, I hope you've got it over, for I ain't interested in it myself.'

'My precious Betsey,' said Mrs. Gamp, 'how late you are!'

The worthy Mrs. Prig replied, with some asperity, 'that if perwerse people went off dead, when they was least expected, it warn't no fault of her'n. And further, 'that it was quite aggrawation enough to be made late when one was dropping for one's tea, without hearing on it again.'

Mrs. Gamp, deriving from this exhibition of repartee some clue to the state of Mrs. Prig's feelings, instantly conducted her up-stairs: deeming that the sight of pickled salmon might work a softening change.

But Betsey Prig expected pickled salmon. It was obvious that she did; for her first words, after glancing at the table, were: 'I know'd she wouldn't have a cowcumber!'

Mrs. Gamp changed colour, and sat down upon the bedstead.

'Lord bless you, Betsey Prig, your words is true. I quite forgot it!'

Mrs. Prig, looking steadfastly at her friend, put her hand in her pocket, and with an air of surly triumph drew forth either the oldest of lettuces or youngest of cabbages, but at any rate, a green vegetable of an expansive nature, and of such magnificent proportions that she was obliged to shut it up like an umbrella before she could pull it out. She also produced a handful of mustard and cress, a trifle of the herb called dandelion, three bunches of radishes, an onion rather larger than an average turnip, three substantial slices of beetroot, and a short prong or antler of celery; the whole of this garden-stuff having been publicly exhibited, but a short time before, as a twopenny salad, and purchased by Mrs. Prig on condition that the vendor could get it all into her pocket. Which had been happily accomplished, in High Holborn, to the breathless interest of a hackney-coach stand. And she laid so little stress on this surprising forethought, that she did not even smile, but returning her pocket into its accustomed sphere, merely recommended that these productions of nature should be sliced up, for immediate consumption, in plenty of vinegar.

'And don't go a-droppin' none of your snuff in it,' said Mrs. Prig. 'In gruel, barley-water, apple-tea, mutton-broth, and that, it don't signify. It stimilates a patient. But I don't relish it myself.'

'Why, Betsey Prig!' cried Mrs. Gamp, 'how *can* you talk so!'

'Why, ain't your patients, wotever their diseases is, always a-sneezin' their wery heads off, along of your snuff?' said Mrs. Prig.

'And wot if they are!' said Mrs. Gamp.

'Nothing if they are,' said Mrs. Prig. 'But don't deny it, Sairah.'

'Who deniges of it?' Mrs. Gamp inquired.

Mrs. Prig returned no answer.

'Who deniges of it, Betsey?' Mrs. Gamp inquired again. Then Mrs. Gamp, by reversing the question, imparted a deeper and more awful character of solemnity to the same. 'Betsey, who deniges of it?'

It was the nearest possible approach to a very decided difference of opinion between these ladies; but Mrs. Prig's impatience for the meal being greater at the moment than her impatience of contradiction, she replied, for the present, 'Nobody, if you don't, Sairah,' and prepared herself for tea. For a quarrel can be taken up at any time, but a limited quantity of salmon cannot.

Her toilet was simple. She had merely to 'chuck' her bonnet and shawl upon the bed; give her hair two pulls, one upon the right side and one upon the left, as if she were ringing a couple of bells; and all was done. The tea was already made, Mrs. Gamp was not long over the salad, and they were soon at the height of their repast.

The temper of both parties was improved, for the time being, by the enjoyments of the table. When the meal came to a termination (which it was pretty long in doing), and Mrs. Gamp having cleared away, produced the teapot from the top-shelf, simultaneously with a couple of wine-glasses, they were quite amiable.

'Betsey,' said Mrs. Gamp, filling her own glass, and passing the teapot, 'I will now propoge a toast. My frequent pardner, Betsey Prig!'

'Which, altering the name to Sairah Gamp; I drink,' said Mrs. Prig, 'with love and tenderness.'

From this moment symptoms of inflammation began to lurk in the nose of each lady; and perhaps, notwithstanding all appearances to the contrary, in the temper also.

'Now, Sairah,' said Mrs. Prig, 'joining business with pleasure, wot is this case in which you wants me?'

Mrs. Gamp betraying in her face some intention of returning an evasive answer, Betsey added:

'*Is* it Mrs. Harris?'

'No, Betsey Prig, it ain't,' was Mrs. Gamp's reply.

'Well!' said Mrs. Prig, with a short laugh. 'I'm glad of that, at any rate.'

'Why should you be glad of that, Betsey?' Mrs. Gamp retorted, warmly. 'She is unbeknown to you except by hearsay, why should you be glad? If you have anythink to say contrairy to the character of Mrs. Harris, which well I knows behind her back, afore her face, or anywheres, is not to be impeaged, out with it, Betsey. I have know'd that sweetest and best of women,' said Mrs. Gamp, shaking her head, and shedding tears, 'ever since afore her First, which Mr. Harris who was dreadful timid went and stopped his ears in a empty dog-kennel, and never took his hands away or come out once till he was showed the baby, wen bein' took with fits, the doctor collared him and laid him on his back upon the airy stones, and she was told to ease her mind, his owls was organs. And I have know'd her, Betsey Prig, when he has hurt her feelin' art by sayin' of his Ninth that it was one too many, if not two, while that dear innocent was cooin' in his face, which thrive it did though bandy, but I have know'd as you had occagion to be glad, Betsey, on accounts of Mrs. Harris not requiring you. Require she never will, depend upon it, for her constant words in sickness is, and will be, "Send for Sairey!"'

During this touching address, Mrs. Prig adroitly feigning to be the victim of that absence of mind which has its origin in excessive attention to one topic, helped herself from the teapot without appearing to observe it. Mrs. Gamp observed it, however, and came to a premature close in consequence.

'Well, it ain't her, it seems,' said Mrs. Prig, coldly: 'who is it then?'

'You have heerd me mention, Betsey,' Mrs. Gamp replied, after glancing in an expressive and marked manner at the teapot, 'a person as I took care on at the time as you and me was pardners off and on, in that there fever at the Bull?'

'Old Snuffey,' Mrs. Prig observed.

Sarah Gamp looked at her with an eye of fire, for she saw in this mistake of Mrs. Prig, another wilful and malignant stab at that same weakness or custom of hers, an ungenerous allusion to which, on the part of Betsey, had first disturbed their harmony that evening. And she saw it still more clearly, when, politely but firmly correcting that lady by the distinct enunciation of the word 'Chuffey,' Mrs. Prig received the correction with a diabolical laugh.

The best among us have their failings, and it must be conceded of Mrs. Prig, that if there were a blemish in the goodness of her disposition, it was a habit she had of not bestowing all its sharp and acid properties upon her patients (as a thoroughly amiable woman would have done), but of keeping a considerable remainder for the service of her friends. Highly pickled salmon, and lettuces chopped up in vinegar, may, as viands possessing some acidity of their own, have encouraged and increased this failing in Mrs. Prig; and every application to the teapot certainly did; for it was often remarked of her by her friends, that she was most contradictory when most elevated. It is certain that her countenance became about this time derisive and defiant, and that she sat with her arms folded, and one eye shut up, in a somewhat offensive, because obtrusively intelligent, manner.

Mrs. Gamp observing this, felt it the more necessary that Mrs. Prig should know her place, and be made sensible of her exact station in society, as well as of her obligations to herself. She therefore assumed an air of greater patronage and importance, as she went on to answer Mrs. Prig a little more in detail.

'Mr. Chuffey, Betsey,' said Mrs. Gamp, 'is weak in his mind. Excuge me if I makes remark, that he may neither be so weak as people thinks, nor people may not think he is so weak as they pretends, and what I knows, I knows; and what you don't, you don't; so do not ask me, Betsey. But Mr. Chuffey's friends has made propojals for his bein' took care on, and has said to me, "Mrs. Gamp, *will* you undertake it? We couldn't think," they says, "of trusting him to nobody but you, for, Sairey, you are gold as has passed the furnage. Will you undertake it, at your own price, day and night, and by your own self?" "No," I says, "I will not. Do not reckon on it. There is," I says, "but one creetur in the world as I would undertake on sech terms, and her name is Harris. But," I says, "I am acquainted with a friend, whose name is Betsey Prig, that I can recommend, and will assist me. Betsey," I. says, "is always to be trusted, under me, and will be guided as I could desire."'

Here Mrs. Prig, without any abatement of her offensive manner, again counterfeited abstraction of mind, and stretched out her hand to the teapot. It was more than Mrs. Gamp could bear. She stopped the hand of Mrs. Prig with her own, and said, with great feeling:

'No, Betsey! Drink fair, wotever you do!'

Mrs. Prig, thus baffled, threw herself back in her chair, and closing the same eye more emphatically, and folding her arms tighter, suffered her head to roll slowly from side to side, while she surveyed her friend with a contemptuous smile.

Mrs. Gamp resumed:

'Mrs. Harris, Betsey—'

'Bother Mrs. Harris!' said Betsey Prig.

Mrs. Gamp looked at her with amazement, incredulity, and indignation; when Mrs. Prig, shutting her eye still closer, and folding her arms still tighter, uttered these memorable and tremendous words:

'I don't believe there's no sich a person!'

After the utterance of which expressions, she leaned forward, and snapped her fingers once, twice, thrice; each time nearer to the face of Mrs. Gamp, and then rose to put on her bonnet, as one who felt that there was now a gulf between them, which nothing could ever bridge across.

The shock of this blow was so violent and sudden, that Mrs. Gamp sat staring at nothing with uplifted eyes, and her mouth open as if she were gasping for breath, until Betsey Prig had put on her bonnet and her shawl, and was gathering the latter about her throat. Then Mrs. Gamp rose—morally and physically rose—and denounced her.

'What!' said Mrs. Gamp, 'you bage creetur, have I know'd Mrs. Harris five and thirty year, to be told at last that there ain't no sech a person livin'! Have I stood her friend in all her troubles, great and small, for it to come at last to sech a end as this, which her own sweet picter hanging up afore you all the time, to shame your Bragian words! But well you mayn't believe there's no sech a creetur, for she wouldn't demean herself to look at you, and often has she said, when I have made mention of your name, which, to my sinful sorrow, I have done, "What, Sairey Gamp! debage yourself to *her*!" Go along with you!'

'I'm a-goin', ma'am, ain't I?' said Mrs. Prig, stopping as she said it.

'You had better, ma'am,' said Mrs. Gamp.

'Do you know who you're talking to, ma'am?' inquired her visitor.

'Aperiently,' said Mrs. Gamp, surveying her with scorn from head to foot, 'to Betsey Prig. Aperiently so. *I* know her. No one better. Go along with you!'

'And *you* was a-goin' to take me under you!' cried Mrs. Prig, surveying Mrs. Gamp from head to foot in her turn. '*You* was, was you? Oh, how kind! Why, deuce take your imperence,' said Mrs. Prig, with a rapid change from banter to ferocity, 'what do you mean?'

'Go along with you!' said Mrs. Gamp. 'I blush for you.'

'You had better blush a little for yourself, while you *are* about it!' said Mrs. Prig. 'You and your Chuffeys! What, the poor old creetur isn't mad enough, isn't he? Aha!'

'He'd very soon be mad enough, if you had anything to do with him,' said Mrs. Gamp.

'And that's what I was wanted for, is it?' cried Mrs. Prig, triumphantly. 'Yes. But you'll find yourself deceived. I won't go near him. We shall see how you get on without me. I won't have nothink to do with him.'

'You never spoke a truer word than that!' said Mrs. Gamp. 'Go along with you!'

She was prevented from witnessing the actual retirement of Mrs. Prig from the room, notwithstanding the great desire she had expressed to behold it, by that lady, in her angry withdrawal, coming into contact with the bedstead, and bringing down the previously mentioned pippins; three or four of which came rattling on the head of Mrs. Gamp so smartly, that when she recovered from this wooden showerbath, Mrs. Prig was gone.

She had the satisfaction, however, of hearing the deep voice of Betsey, proclaiming her injuries and her determination to have nothing to do with Mr. Chuffey, down the stairs, and along the passage, and even out in Kingsgate Street. Likewise of seeing in her own apartment, in the place of Mrs. Prig, Mr. Sweedlepipe and two gentlemen.

'Why, bless my life!' exclaimed the little barber, 'what's amiss? The noise you ladies have been making, Mrs. Gamp! Why, these two gentlemen have been standing on the stairs, outside the door, nearly all the time, trying to make you hear, while you were pelting away, hammer and tongs! It'll be the death of the little bullfinch in the shop, that draws his own water. In his fright, he's been a-straining himself all to bits, drawing more water than he could drink in a twelvemonth. He must have thought it was Fire!"

Mrs. Gamp had in the meanwhile sunk into her chair, from whence, turning up her overflowing eyes, and clasping her hands, she delivered the following lamentation:

'Oh, Mr. Sweedlepipes, which Mr. Westlock also, if my eyes do not deceive, and a friend not havin' the pleasure of bein' beknown, wot I have took from Betsey Prig this blessed night, no mortial creetur knows! If she had abuged me, bein' in liquor, which I thought I smelt her wen she come, but could not so believe, not bein' used myself'—Mrs. Gamp, by the way, was pretty far gone, and the fragrance of the teapot was strong in the room—'I could have bore it with a thankful art. But the words she spoke of Mrs. Harris, lambs could not forgive. No, Betsey!' said Mrs. Gamp, in a violent burst of feeling, 'nor worms forget!'

The little barber scratched his head, and shook it, and looked at the teapot, and gradually got out of the room. John Westlock, taking a chair, sat down on one side of Mrs. Gamp. Martin, taking the foot of the bed, supported her on the other.

'You wonder what we want, I dare say,' observed John. 'I'll tell you presently, when you have recovered. It's not pressing, for a few minutes or so. How do you find yourself? Better?'

Mrs. Gamp shed more tears, shook her head and feebly pronounced Mrs. Harris's name.

'Have a little—' John was at a loss what to call it.

'Tea,' suggested Martin.

'It ain't tea,' said Mrs. Gamp.

'Physic of some sort, I suppose,' cried John. 'Have a little.'

Mrs. Gamp was prevailed upon to take a glassful. 'On condition,' she passionately observed, 'as Betsey never has another stroke of work from me.'

'Certainly not,' said John. 'She shall never help to nurse *me*.'

'To think,' said Mrs. Gamp, 'as she should ever have helped to nuss that friend of yourn, and been so near of hearing things that—Ah!'

John looked at Martin.

'Yes,' he said. 'That was a narrow escape, Mrs. Gamp.'

'Narrer, in-deed!' she returned. 'It was only my having the night, and hearin' of him in his wanderings; and her the day, that saved it. Wot would she have said and done, if she had know'd what *I* know; that perfeejus wretch! Yet, oh good gracious me!' cried Mrs. Gamp, trampling on the floor, in the absence of Mrs. Prig, 'that I should hear from that same woman's lips what I have heerd her speak of Mrs. Harris!'

'Never mind,' said John. 'You know it is not true.'

'Isn't true!' cried Mrs. Gamp. 'True! Don't I know as that dear woman is expecting of me at this minnit, Mr. Westlock, and is a-lookin' out of window down the street, with little Tommy Harris in her arms, as calls me his own Gammy, and truly calls, for bless the mottled little legs of that there precious child (like Canterbury Brawn his own dear father says, which so they are) his own I have been, ever since I found him, Mr. Westlock, with his small red worsted shoe a-gurglin' in his throat, where he had put it in his play, a chick, wile they was leavin' of him on the floor a-lookin' for it through the ouse and him a-choakin' sweetly in the parlour! Oh, Betsey Prig, what wickedness you've showed this night, but never shall you darken Sairey's doors agen, you twining serpiant!'

'You were always so kind to her, too!' said John, consolingly.

'That's the cutting part.. That's where it hurts me, Mr. Westlock,' Mrs. Gamp replied; holding out her glass unconsciously, while Martin filled it.

'Chosen to help you with Mr. Lewsome!' said John. 'Chosen to help you with Mr. Chuffey!'

'Chose once, but chose no more,' cried Mrs. Gamp. 'No pardnership with Betsey Prig agen, sir!'

'No, no,' said John. 'That would never do.'

'I don't know as it ever would have done, sir,' Mrs. Gamp replied, with the solemnity peculiar to a certain stage of intoxication. 'Now that the marks,' by which Mrs. Gamp is supposed to have meant mask, 'is off that creetur's face, I do not think it ever would have done. There are reagions in families for keeping things a secret, Mr. Westlock, and havin' only them about you as you knows you can repoge in. Who could repoge in Betsey Prig, arter her words of Mrs. Harris, setting in that chair afore my eyes!'

'Quite true,' said John; 'quite. I hope you have time to find another assistant, Mrs. Gamp?'

Between her indignation and the teapot, her powers of comprehending what was said to her began to fail. She looked at John with tearful eyes, and murmuring the well-remembered name which Mrs. Prig had challenged—as if it were a talisman against all earthly sorrows—seemed to wander in her mind.

'I hope,' repeated John, 'that you have time to find another assistant?'

'Which short it is, indeed,' cried Mrs. Gamp, turning up her languid eyes, and clasping Mr. Westlock's wrist with matronly affection. 'To-morrow evenin', sir, I waits upon his friends. Mr. Chuzzlewit apinted it from nine to ten.'

'From nine to ten,' said John, with a significant glance at Martin; 'and then Mr. Chuffey retires into safe keeping, does he?'

'He needs to be kep safe, I do assure you,' Mrs. Gamp replied, with a mysterious air. 'Other people besides me has had a happy deliverance from Betsey Prig. I little know'd that woman. She'd have let it out!'

'Let *him* out, you mean,' said John.

'Do I!' retorted Mrs. Gamp. 'Oh!'

The severely ironical character of this reply was strengthened by a very slow nod, and a still slower drawing down of the corners of Mrs. Gamp's mouth. She added with extreme stateliness of manner, after indulging in a short doze:

'But I am a-keepin' of you gentlemen, and time is precious.'

Mingling with that delusion of the teapot which inspired her with the belief that they wanted her to go somewhere immediately, a shrewd avoidance of any further reference to the topics into which she had lately strayed, Mrs. Gamp rose; and putting away the teapot in its accustomed place, and locking the cupboard with much gravity, proceeded to attire herself for a professional visit.

This preparation was easily made, as it required nothing more than the snuffy black bonnet, the snuffy black shawl, the pattens, and the indispensable umbrella, without which neither a lying-in nor a laying-out could by any possibility be attempted. When Mrs. Gamp had invested herself with these appendages she returned to her chair, and sitting down again, declared herself quite ready.

'It's a appiness to know as one can benefit the poor sweet creetur,' she observed, 'I'm sure. It isn't all as can. The torters Betsey Prig inflicts is frightful!'

Closing her eyes as she made this remark, in the acuteness of her commiseration for Betsey's patients, she forgot to open them again until she dropped a patten. Her nap was also broken at intervals, like the fabled slumbers of Friar Bacon, by the dropping of the other patten, and of the umbrella. But when she had got rid of those incumbrances, her sleep was peaceful.

The two young men looked at each other, ludicrously enough; and Martin stifling his disposition to laugh, whispered in John Westlock's ear,

'What shall we do now?'

'Stay here,' he replied.

Mrs. Gamp was heard to murmur 'Mrs. Harris' in her sleep.

'Rely upon it,' whispered John, looking cautiously towards her, 'that you shall question this old clerk, though you go as Mrs. Harris herself. We know quite enough to carry her our own way now, at all events; thanks to this quarrel, which confirms the old saying that when rogues fall out, honest people get what they want. Let Jonas Chuzzlewit look to himself; and let her sleep as long as she likes. We shall gain our end in good time.'

CHAPTER L

*Surprises Tom Pinch very much, and shows how certain
confidences passed between him and his sister*

IT was the next evening; and Tom and his sister were sitting
together before tea, talking, in their usual quiet way, about
a great many things, but not at all about Lewsome's story or
anything connected with it; for John Westlock—really John,
for so young a man, was one of the most considerate fellows in
the world—had particularly advised Tom not to mention it to
his sister just yet, in case it should disquiet her. 'And I wouldn't,
Tom,' he said, with a little hesitation, 'I wouldn't have a
shadow on her happy face, or an uneasy thought in her gentle
heart, for all the wealth and honours of the universe!' Really
John was uncommonly kind; extraordinarily kind. If he had
been her father, Tom said, he could not have taken a greater
interest in her.

But although Tom and his sister were extremely conversational, they were less lively, and less cheerful, than usual. Tom
had no idea that this originated with Ruth, but took it for
granted that he was rather dull himself. In truth he was; for
the lightest cloud upon the Heaven of her quiet mind, cast its
shadow upon Tom.

And there was a cloud on little Ruth that evening. Yes,
indeed. When Tom was looking in another direction, her
bright eyes, stealing on towards his face, would sparkle still
more brightly than their custom was, and then grow dim.
When Tom was silent, looking out upon the summer weather,
she would sometimes make a hasty movement, as if she were
about to throw herself upon his neck; then check the impulse,
and when he looked round, show a laughing face, and speak
to him very merrily; when she had anything to give Tom, or
had any excuse for coming near him, she would flutter about
him, and lay her bashful hand upon his shoulder, and not be
willing to withdraw it; and would show by all such means that
there was something on her heart which in her great love she
longed to say to him, but had not the courage to utter.

So they were sitting, she with her work before her, but not
working, and Tom with his book beside him, but not reading,
when Martin knocked at the door. Anticipating who it was,

Tom went to open it: and he and Martin came back into the room together. Tom looked surprised, for in answer to his cordial greeting Martin had hardly spoken a word.

Ruth also saw that there was something strange in the manner of their visitor, and raised her eyes inquiringly to Tom's face, as if she were seeking an explanation there. Tom shook his head, and made the same mute appeal to Martin.

Martin did not sit down, but walked up to the window, and stood there looking out. He turned round after a few moments to speak, but hastily averted his head again, without doing so.

'What has happened, Martin?' Tom anxiously inquired. 'My dear fellow, what bad news do you bring?'

'Oh, Tom!' replied Martin, in a tone of deep reproach. 'To hear you feign that interest in anything that happens to me, hurts me even more than your ungenerous dealing.'

'My ungenerous dealing! Martin! My—' Tom could say no more.

'How could you, Tom, how could you suffer me to thank you so fervently and sincerely for your friendship; and not tell me, like a man, that you had deserted me! Was it true, Tom! Was it honest! Was it worthy of what you used to be: of what I am sure you used to be: to tempt me, when you had turned against me, into pouring out my heart! Oh, Tom!'

His tone was one of such strong injury and yet of so much grief for the loss of a friend he had trusted in; it expressed such high past love for Tom, and so much sorrow and compassion for his supposed unworthiness; that Tom, for a moment, put his hand before his face, and had no more power of justifying himself, than if he had been a monster of deceit and falsehood.

'I protest, as I must die,' said Martin, 'that I grieve over the loss of what I thought you; and have no anger in the recollection of my own injuries. It is only at such a time, and after such a discovery, that we know the full measure of our old regard for the subject of it. I swear, little as I showed it; little as I know I showed it; that when I had the least consideration for you, Tom, I loved you like a brother.'

Tom was composed by this time, and might have been the Spirit of Truth, in a homely dress—it very often wears a homely dress, thank God!—when he replied to him.

'Martin,' he said, 'I don't know what is in your mind, or who has abused it, or by what extraordinary means. But the means are false. There is no truth whatever in the impression under which you labour. It is a delusion from first to last; and I warn you that you will deeply regret the wrong you do me. I can honestly say that I have been true to you, and to myself. You will be very sorry for this. Indeed, you will be very sorry for it, Martin.'

'I *am* sorry,' returned Martin, shaking his head. 'I think I never knew what it was to be sorry in my heart, until now.'

'At least,' said Tom, 'if I had always been what you charge me with being now, and had never had a place in your regard, but had always been despised by you, and had always deserved it, you should tell me in what you have found me to be treacherous; and on what grounds you proceed. I do not intreat you, therefore, to give me that satisfaction as a favour, Martin, but I ask it of you as a right.'

'My own eyes are my witnesses,' returned Martin. 'Am I to believe them?'

'No,' said Tom, calmly. 'Not if they accuse me.'

'Your own words. Your own manner,' pursued Martin. 'Am I to believe *them?*'

'No,' replied Tom, calmly. 'Not if they accuse me. But they never have accused me. Whoever has perverted them to such a purpose, has wronged me almost as cruelly;' his calmness rather failed him here; 'as you have done.'

'I came here,' said Martin; 'and I appeal to your good sister to hear me—'

'Not to her,' interrupted Tom. 'Pray, do not appeal to her. She will never believe you.'

He drew her arm through his own, as he said it.

'*I* believe it, Tom!'

'No, no,' cried Tom, 'of course not. I said so. Why, tut, tut, tut. What a silly little thing you are!'

'I never meant,' said Martin, hastily, 'to appeal to you against your brother. Do not think me so unmanly and unkind. I merely appealed to you to hear my declaration, that I came here for no purpose of reproach—I have not one reproach to vent—but in deep regret. You could not know in what bitterness of regret, unless you knew how often I have thought of Tom; how long in almost hopeless circumstances, I have looked forward to the better estimation of his friendship; and how steadfastly I have believed and trusted in him.'

'Tut, tut,' said Tom, stopping her as she was about to speak.

'He is mistaken. He is deceived. Why should you mind? He is sure to be set right at last.'

'Heaven bless the day that sets me right!' cried Martin, 'if it could ever come!'

'Amen!' said Tom. 'And it will!'

Martin paused, and then said in a still milder voice:

'You have chosen for yourself, Tom, and will be relieved by our parting. It is not an angry one. There is no anger on my side—'

'There is none on mine,' said Tom.

'—It is merely what you have brought about, and worked to bring about. I say again, you have chosen for yourself. You have made the choice that might have been expected in most people situated as you are, but which I did not expect in you. For that, perhaps, I should blame my own judgment more than you. There is wealth and favour worth having, on one side; and there is the worthless friendship of an abandoned, struggling fellow, on the other. You were free to make your election, and you made it; and the choice was not difficult. But those who have not the courage to resist such temptations, should have the courage to avow what they have yielded to them; and I *do* blame you for this, Tom: that you received me with a show of warmth, encouraged me to be frank and plain-spoken, tempted me to confide in you, and professed that you were able to be mine; when you had sold yourself to others. I do not believe,' said Martin, with emotion: 'hear me say it from my heart; I *cannot* believe, Tom, now that I am standing face to face with you, that it would have been in your nature to do me any serious harm, even though I had not discovered, by chance, in whose employment you were. But I should have encumbered you; I should have led you into more double-dealing; I should have hazarded your retaining the favour for which you have paid so high a price, bartering away your former self; and it is best for both of us that I have found out what you so much desired to keep secret.'

'Be just,' said Tom; who had not removed his mild gaze from Martin's face since the commencement of this last address; 'be just even in your injustice, Martin. You forget. You have not yet told me what your accusation is!'

'Why should I?' returned Martin, waving his hand, and moving towards the door. 'You could not know it the better for my dwelling on it, and though it would be really none the

worse, it might seem to me to be. No, Tom. Bygones shall be
bygones between us. I can take leave of you at this moment,
and in this place: in which you are so amiable and so good: as
heartily, if not as cheerfully, as ever I have done since we first
met. All good go with you, Tom!—I—'

'You leave me so? You can leave me so, can you?' said
Tom.

'I—you—you have chosen for yourself, Tom! I—I hope it
was a rash choice,' Martin faltered. 'I think it was. I am sure
it was! Good-bye!'

And he was gone.

Tom led his little sister to her chair, and sat down in his own.
He took his book, and read, or seemed to read. Presently he
said aloud: turning a leaf as he spoke: 'He will be very sorry
for this.' And a tear stole down his face, and dropped upon the
page.

Ruth nestled down beside him on her knees, and clasped her
arms about his neck.

'No, Tom! No, no! Be comforted! Dear Tom!'

'I am quite—comforted,' said Tom. 'It will be set right.'

'Such a cruel, bad return!' cried Ruth.

'No, no,' said Tom. 'He believes it. I cannot imagine why.
But it will be set right.'

More closely yet, she nestled down about him; and wept as
if her heart would break.

'Don't. Don't,' said Tom. 'Why do you hide your face, my
dear!'

Then in a burst of tears, it all broke out at last.

'Oh Tom, dear Tom, I know your secret heart. I have found
it out; you couldn't hide the truth from me. Why didn't you
tell me? I am sure I could have made you happier, if you had!
You love her, Tom, so dearly!'

Tom made a motion with his hand as if he would have put
his sister hurriedly away; but it clasped upon hers, and all
his little history was written in the action. All its pathetic
eloquence was in the silent touch.

'In spite of that,' said Ruth, 'you have been so faithful and
so good, dear; in spite of that, you have been so true and self-
denying, and have struggled with yourself; in spite of that, you
have been so gentle, and so kind, and even-tempered, that I
have never seen you give a hasty look, or heard you say one
irritable word. In spite of all, you have been so cruelly mis-

taken. Oh Tom, dear Tom, will *this* be set right too! Will it, Tom? Will you always have this sorrow in your breast; you who deserve to be so happy; or is there any hope?'

And still she hid her face from Tom, and clasped him round the neck, and wept for him, and poured out all her woman's heart and soul in the relief and pain of this disclosure.

It was not very long before she and Tom were sitting side by side, and she was looking with an earnest quietness in Tom's face. Then Tom spoke to her thus: cheerily, though gravely.

'I am very glad, my dear, that this has passed between us. Not because it assures me of your tender affection (for I was well assured of that before), but because it relieves my mind of a great weight.'

Tom's eyes glistened when he spoke of her affection; and he kissed her on the cheek.

'My dear girl,' said Tom: 'with whatever feeling I regard her;' they seemed to avoid the name by mutual consent; 'I have long ago—I am sure I may say from the very first—looked upon it as a dream. As something that might possibly have happened under very different circumstances, but which can never be. Now, tell me. What would you have set right?'

She gave Tom such a significant little look, that he was obliged to take it for an answer whether he would or no; and to go on.

'By her own choice and free consent, my love, she is betrothed to Martin; and was, long before either of them knew of my existence. You would have her betrothed to me?'

'Yes,' she said directly.

'Yes,' rejoined Tom, 'but that might be setting it wrong, instead of right. Do you think,' said Tom, with a grave smile, 'that even if she had never seen him, it is very likely she would have fallen in love with Me?'

'Why not, dear Tom?'

Tom shook his head, and smiled again.

'You think of me, Ruth,' said Tom, 'and it is very natural that you should, as if I were a character in a book; and you make it a sort of poetical justice that I should, by some impossible means or other, come, at last, to marry the person I love. But there is a much higher justice than poetical justice, my dear, and it does not order events upon the same principle. Accordingly, people who read about heroes in books, and choose to make heroes of themselves out of books, consider it

E e

a very fine thing to be discontented and gloomy, and misan-
thropical, and perhaps a little blasphemous, because they
cannot have everything ordered for their individual accommodation. Would you like me to become one of that sort of
people?'

'No, Tom. But still I know,' she added timidly, 'that this
is a sorrow to you in your own better way.'

Tom thought of disputing the position. But it would have
been mere folly, and he gave it up.

'My dear,' said Tom, 'I will repay your affection with the
Truth, and all the Truth. It is a sorrow to me. I have proved
it to be so sometimes, though I have always striven against it.
But somebody who is precious to you may die, and you may
dream that you are in heaven with the departed spirit, and you
may find it a sorrow to wake to the life on earth, which is no
harder to be borne than when you fell asleep. It is sorrowful to
me to contemplate my dream, which I always knew was a
dream, even when it first presented itself; but the realities
about me are not to blame. They are the same as they were.
My sister, my sweet companion, who makes this place so dear,
is she less devoted to me, Ruth, than she would have been, if
this vision had never troubled me? My old friend John, who
might so easily have treated me with coldness and neglect, is he
less cordial to me? The world about me, is there less good in
that? Are my words to be harsh and my looks to be sour, and
is my heart to grow cold, because there has fallen in my way
a good and beautiful creature, who but for the selfish regret
that I cannot call her my own, would, like all other good and
beautiful creatures, make me happier and better! No, my dear
sister. No,' said Tom stoutly. 'Remembering all my means of
happiness, I hardly dare to call this lurking something a
sorrow; but whatever name it may justly bear, I thank Heaven
that it renders me more sensible of affection and attachment,
and softens me in fifty ways. Not less happy. Not less happy,
Ruth!'

She could not speak to him, but she loved him, as he well
deserved. Even as he deserved, she loved him.

'She will open Martin's eyes,' said Tom, with a glow of pride,
'and that (which is indeed wrong) will be set right. Nothing
will persuade her, I know, that I have betrayed him. It will be
set right through her, and he will be very sorry for it. Our
secret, Ruth, is our own, and lives and dies with us. I don't

Mr. Pinch is amazed by an Unexpected Apparition
(p. 771)

believe I ever could have told it you,' said Tom, with a smile, 'but how glad I am to think you have found it out!'

They had never taken such a pleasant walk as they took that night. Tom told her all so freely and so simply, and was so desirous to return her tenderness with his fullest confidence, that they prolonged it far beyond their usual hour, and sat up late when they came home. And when they parted for the night there was such a tranquil, beautiful expression in Tom's face, that she could not bear to shut it out, but going back on tiptoe to his chamber-door, looked in and stood there till he saw her, and then embracing him again, withdrew. And in her prayers and in her sleep—good times to be remembered with such fervour, Tom!—his name was uppermost.

When he was left alone, Tom pondered very much on this discovery of hers, and greatly wondered what had led her to it. 'Because,' thought Tom, 'I have been so very careful. It was foolish and unnecessary in me, as I clearly see now, when I am so relieved by her knowing it; but I have been so very careful to conceal it from her. Of course I knew that she was intelligent and quick, and for that reason was more upon my guard; but I was not in the least prepared for this. I am sure her discovery has been sudden too. Dear me!' said Tom. 'It's a most singular instance of penetration!'

Tom could not get it out of his head. There it was, when his head was on his pillow.

'How she trembled when she began to tell me she knew it!' thought Tom, recalling all the little incidents and circumstances; 'and how her face flushed! But that was natural! Oh, quite natural! That needs no accounting for.'

Tom little thought how natural it was. Tom little knew that there was that in Ruth's own heart, but newly set there, which had helped her to the reading of his mystery. Ah, Tom! He didn't understand the whispers of the Temple Fountain, though he passed it every day.

Who so lively and cheerful as busy Ruth next morning! Her early tap at Tom's door, and her light foot outside, would have been music to him though she had not spoken. But she said it was the brightest morning ever seen; and so it was; and if it had been otherwise, she would have made it so to Tom.

She was ready with his neat breakfast when he went downstairs, and had her bonnet ready for the early walk, and was so full of news, that Tom was lost in wonder. She might have been up all night, collecting it for his entertainment. There was Mr. Nadgett not come home yet, and there was bread down a penny a loaf, and there was twice as much strength in this tea as in the last, and the milkwoman's husband had come out of the hospital cured, and the curly-headed child over the way had been lost all yesterday, and she was going to make all sorts of preserves in a desperate hurry, and there happened to be a saucepan in the house which was the very saucepan for the purpose; and she knew all about the last book Tom had brought home, all through, though it was a teazer to read; and she had so much to tell him that she had finished breakfast first. Then she had her little bonnet on, and the tea and sugar locked up, and the keys in her reticule, and the flower, as usual, in Tom's coat, and was in all respects quite ready to accompany him, before Tom knew she had begun to prepare. And in short, as Tom said, with a confidence in his own assertion which amounted to a defiance of the public in general, there never was such a little woman.

She made Tom talkative. It was impossible to resist her. She put such enticing questions to him; about books, and about dates of churches, and about organs, and about the Temple, and about all kinds of things. Indeed, she lightened the way (and Tom's heart with it) to that degree, that the Temple looked quite blank and solitary when he parted from her at the gate.

'No Mr. Fips's friend to-day, I suppose,' thought Tom, as he ascended the stairs.

Not yet, at any rate, for the door was closed as usual, and Tom opened it with his key. He had got the books into perfect order now, and had mended the torn leaves, and had pasted up the broken backs, and substituted neat labels for the worn-out letterings. It looked a different place, it was so orderly and neat. Tom felt some pride in contemplating the change he had wrought, though there was no one to approve or disapprove of it.

He was at present occupied in making a fair copy of his draught of the catalogue; on which, as there was no hurry, he was painfully concentrating all the ingenious and laborious neatness he had ever expended on map or plan in Mr. Pecksniff's workroom. It was a very marvel of a catalogue; for Tom sometimes thought he was really getting his money too easily, and he had determined within himself that this document should take a little of his superfluous leisure out of him.

So with pens and ruler, and compasses and india-rubber, and pencil, and black ink, and red ink, Tom worked away all the morning. He thought a good deal about Martin, and their interview of yesterday, and would have been far easier in his mind if he could have resolved to confide it to his friend John, and to have taken his opinion on the subject. But besides that he knew what John's boiling indignation would be, he bethought himself that he was helping Martin now in a matter of great moment, and that to deprive the latter of his assistance at such a crisis of affairs, would be to inflict a serious injury upon him.

'So I'll keep it to myself,' said Tom, with a sigh. 'I'll keep it to myself.'

And to work he went again, more assiduously than ever, with the pens, and the ruler, and the india-rubber, and the pencil, and the black ink, and the red ink, that he might forget it.

He had laboured away for another hour or more, when he heard a footstep in the entry, down below.

'Ah!' said Tom, looking towards the door; 'time was, not long ago either, when that would have set me wondering and expecting. But I have left off now.'

The footstep came on, up the stairs.

'Thirty-six, thirty-seven, thirty-eight,' said Tom, counting. 'Now you'll stop. Nobody ever comes past the thirty-eighth stair.'

The person did stop, certainly, but only to take breath; for up the footstep came again. Forty, forty-one, forty-two, and so on.

The door stood open. As the tread advanced, Tom looked impatiently and eagerly towards it. When a figure came upon the landing, and arriving in the doorway, stopped and gazed at him, he rose up from his chair, and half believed he saw a spirit.

Old Martin Chuzzlewit! The same whom he had left at Mr. Pecksniff's, weak and sinking!

The same? No, not the same, for this old man, though old, was strong, and leaned upon his stick with a vigorous hand, while with the other he signed to Tom to make no noise. One glance at the resolute face, the watchful eye, the vigorous hand upon the staff, the triumphant purpose in the figure, and such a light broke in on Tom as blinded him.

'You have expected me,' said Martin, 'a long time.'

'I was told that my employer would arrive soon,' said Tom; 'but—'

'I know. You were ignorant who he was. It was my desire. I am glad it has been so well observed. I intended to have been with you much sooner. I thought the time had come. I thought I could know no more, and no worse, of him, than I did on that day when I saw you last. But I was wrong.'

He had by this time come up to Tom, and now he grasped his hand.

'I have lived in his house, Pinch, and had him fawning on me days and weeks and months. You know it. I have suffered him to treat me like his tool and instrument. You know it; you have seen me there. I have undergone ten thousand times as much as I could have endured if I had been the miserable weak old man he took me for. You know it. I have seen him offer love to Mary. You know it; who better—who better, my true heart! I have had his base soul bare before me, day by day, and have not betrayed myself once. I never could have undergone such torture but for looking forward to this time.'

He stopped, even in the passion of his speech; if that can be called passion which was so resolute and steady; to press Tom's hand again. Then he said, in great excitement:

'Close the door, close the door. He will not be long after me, but may come too soon. The time now drawing on,' said the old man, hurriedly: his eyes and whole face brightening as he spoke: 'will make amends for all. I wouldn't have him die or hang himself, for millions of golden pieces! Close the door!'

Tom did so, hardly knowing yet whether he was awake or in a dream.

CHAPTER LI

Sheds new and brighter light upon the very dark place; and contains the sequel of the enterprise of Mr. Jonas and his friend

THE night had now come, when the old clerk was to be delivered over to his keepers. In the midst of his guilty distractions, Jonas had not forgotten it.

It was a part of his guilty state of mind to remember it; for on his persistence in the scheme depended one of his precautions for his own safety. A hint, a word, from the old man, uttered at such a moment in attentive ears, might fire the train of suspicion, and destroy him. His watchfulness of every avenue by which the discovery of his guilt might be approached, sharpened with his sense of the danger by which he was encompassed. With murder on his soul, and its innumerable alarms and terrors dragging at him night and day, he would have repeated the crime, if he had seen a path of safety stretching out beyond. It was in his punishment; it was in his guilty condition. The very deed which his fears rendered insupportable, his fears would have impelled him to commit again.

But keeping the old man close, according to his design, would serve his turn. His purpose was to escape, when the first alarm and wonder had subsided: and when he could make the attempt without awakening instant suspicion. In the meanwhile these women would keep him quiet; and if the talking humour came upon him, would not be easily startled. He knew their trade.

Nor had he spoken idly when he said the old man should be gagged. He had resolved to ensure his silence; and he looked to the end, not the means. He had been rough and rude and cruel to the old man all his life; and violence was natural to his mind in connexion with him. 'He shall be gagged if he speaks, and pinioned if he writes,' said Jonas, looking at him; for they sat alone together. 'He is mad enough for that; I'll go through with it!'

Hush!

Still listening! To every sound. He had listened ever since, and it had not come yet. The exposure of the Assurance office;

the flight of Crimple and Bullamy with the plunder, and among
the rest, as he feared, with his own bill, which he had not found
in the pocket-book of the murdered man, and which with
Mr. Pecksniff's money had probably been remitted to one of
other of those trusty friends for safe deposit at the banker's;
his immense losses, and peril of being still called to account as
a partner in the broken firm; all these things rose in his mind
at one time and always, but he could not contemplate them.
He was aware of their presence, and of the rage, discomfiture,
and despair, they brought along with them; but he thought—
of his own controlling power and direction he thought—of the
one dread question only. When they would find the body in
the wood.

He tried—he had never left off trying—not to forget it was
there, for that was impossible, but to forget to weary himself
by drawing vivid pictures of it in his fancy: by going softly
about it and about it among the leaves, approaching it nearer
and nearer through a gap in the boughs, and startling the very
flies that were thickly sprinkled all over it, like heaps of dried
currants. His mind was fixed and fastened on the discovery,
for intelligence of which he listened intently to every cry and
shout; listened when any one came in or went out; watched
from the window the people who passed up and down the
street; mistrusted his own looks and words. And the more his
thoughts were set upon the discovery, the stronger was the
fascination which attracted them to the thing itself: lying
alone in the wood. He was for ever showing and presenting
it, as it were, to every creature whom he saw. 'Look here!
Do you know of this? Is it found? Do you suspect *me?*' If he
had been condemned to bear the body in his arms, and lay it
down for recognition at the feet of every one he met, it could
not have been more constantly with him, or a cause of more
monotonous and dismal occupation than it was in this state of
his mind.

Still he was not sorry. It was no contrition or remorse for
what he had done that moved him; it was nothing but alarm
for his own security. The vague consciousness he possessed of
having wrecked his fortune in the murderous venture, intensified his hatred and revenge, and made him set the greater
store by what he had gained. The man was dead; nothing
could undo that. He felt a triumph yet, in the reflection.

He had kept a jealous watch on Chuffey ever since the deed;

seldom leaving him but on compulsion, and then for as short intervals as possible. They were alone together now. It was twilight, and the appointed time drew near at hand. Jonas walked up and down the room. The old man sat in his accustomed corner.

The slightest circumstance was matter of disquiet to the murderer, and he was made uneasy at this time by the absence of his wife, who had left home early in the afternoon, and had not returned yet. No tenderness for her was at the bottom of this; but he had a misgiving that she might have been waylaid, and tempted into saying something that would criminate him when the news came. For anything he knew, she might have knocked at the door of his room, while he was away, and discovered his plot. Confound her, it was like her pale face to be wandering up and down the house! Where was she now?

'She went to her good friend, Mrs. Todgers,' said the old man, when he asked the question with an angry oath.

Aye! To be sure! Always stealing away into the company of that woman. She was no friend of his. Who could tell what devil's mischief they might hatch together! Let her be fetched home directly.

The old man, muttering some words softly, rose as if he would have gone himself, but Jonas thrust him back into his chair with an impatient imprecation, and sent a servant-girl to fetch her. When he had charged her with her errand he walked to and fro again, and never stopped till she came back, which she did pretty soon: the way being short, and the woman having made good haste.

Well! Where was she? Had she come?

No. She had left there, full three hours.

'Left there! Alone?'

The messenger had not asked; taking that for granted.

'Curse you for a fool. Bring candles!'

She had scarcely left the room when the old clerk, who had been unusually observant of him ever since he had asked about his wife, came suddenly upon him.

'Give her up!' cried the old man. 'Come! Give her up to me! Tell me what you have done with her. Quick! I have made no promises on that score. Tell me what you have done with her.'

He laid his hands upon his collar as he spoke, and grasped it· tightly too.

'You shall not leave me!' cried the old man. 'I am strong enough to cry out to the neighbours, and I will, unless you give her up. Give her up to me!'

Jonas was so dismayed and conscience-stricken, that he had not even hardihood enough to unclench the old man's hands with his own; but stood looking at him as well as he could in the darkness, without moving a finger. It was as much as he could do to ask him what he meant.

'I will know what you have done with her!' retorted Chuffey. 'If you hurt a hair of her head, you shall answer it. Poor thing! Poor thing! Where is she?'

'Why, you old madman!' said Jonas, in a low voice, and with trembling lips. 'What Bedlam fit has come upon you now?'

'It is enough to make me mad, seeing what I have seen in this house!' cried Chuffey. 'Where is my dear old master! Where is his only son that I have nursed upon my knee, a child! Where is she, she who was the last; she that I've seen pining day by day, and heard weeping in the dead of night! She was the last, the last of all my friends! Heaven help me, she was the very last!'

Seeing that the tears were stealing down his face, Jonas mustered courage to unclench his hands, and push him off before he answered:

'Did you hear me ask for her? Did you hear me send for her? How can I give you up what I haven't got, idiot! Ecod, I'd give her up to you and welcome, if I could; and a precious pair you'd be!'

'If she has come to any harm,' cried Chuffey, 'mind! I'm old and silly; but I have my memory sometimes; and if she has come to any harm—'

'Devil take you,' interrupted Jonas, but in a suppressed voice still; 'what harm do you suppose she has come to? I know no more where she is than you do; I wish I did. Wait till she comes home, and see; she can't be long. Will that content you?'

'Mind!' exclaimed the old man. 'Not a hair of her head! not a hair of her head ill-used! I won't bear it. I—I—have borne it too long, Jonas. I am silent, but I—I—I can speak. I—I—I can speak—' he stammered, as he crept back to his chair, and turned a threatening, though a feeble, look upon him.

'You can speak, can you!' thought Jonas. 'So, so, we'll stop your speaking. It's well I knew of this in good time. Prevention is better than cure.'

He had made a poor show of playing the bully and evincing a desire to conciliate at the same time, but was so afraid of the old man that great drops had started out upon his brow; and they stood there yet. His unusual tone of voice and agitated manner had sufficiently expressed his fear; but his face would have done so now, without that aid, as he again walked to and fro, glancing at him by the candle-light.

He stopped at the window to think. An opposite shop was lighted up; and the tradesman and a customer were reading some printed bill together across the counter. The sight brought him back, instantly, to the occupation he had forgotten. 'Look here! Do you know of this? Is it found? Do you suspect *me?*'

A hand upon the door. 'What's that!'

'A pleasant evenin',' said the voice of Mrs. Gamp, 'though warm, which, bless you, Mr. Chuzzlewit, we must expect when cowcumbers is three for twopence. How does Mr. Chuffey find his self to-night, sir?'

Mrs. Gamp kept particularly close to the door in saying this, and curtseyed more than usual. She did not appear to be quite so much at her ease as she generally was.

'Get him to his room,' said Jonas, walking up to her, and speaking in her ear. 'He has been raving to-night—stark mad. Don't talk while he's here, but come down again.'

'Poor sweet dear!' cried Mrs. Gamp, with uncommon tenderness. 'He's all of a tremble.'

'Well he may be,' said Jonas, 'after the mad fit he has had. Get him up-stairs.'

She was by this time assisting him to rise.

'There's my blessed old chick!' cried Mrs. Gamp, in a tone that was at once soothing and encouraging. 'There's my darlin' Mr. Chuffey! Now come up to your own room, sir, and lay down on your bed a bit; for you're a-shakin' all over, as if your precious jints was hung upon wires. That's a good creetur! Come with Sairey!'

'Is she come home?' inquired the old man.

'She'll be here directly minnit,' returned Mrs. Gamp. 'Come with Sairey, Mr. Chuffey. Come with your own Sairey!'

The good woman had no reference to any female in the world in promising this speedy advent of the person for whom Mr. Chuffey inquired, but merely threw it out as a means of pacifying the old man. It had its effect, for he permitted her to lead him away: and they quitted the room together.

Jonas looked out of the window again. They were still read-ing the printed paper in the shop opposite, and a third man had joined in the perusal. What could it be, to interest them so?

A dispute or discussion seemed to arise among them, for they all looked up from their reading together, and one of the three, who had been glancing over the shoulder of another, stepped back to explain or illustrate some action by his gestures.

Horror! How like the blow he had struck in the wood!

It beat him from the window as if it had lighted on himself. As he staggered into a chair he thought of the change in Mrs. Gamp, exhibited in her new-born tenderness to her charge. Was that because it was found?—because she knew of it?—because she suspected him?

'Mr. Chuffey is a-lyin' down,' said Mrs. Gamp, returning, 'and much good may it do him, Mr. Chuzzlewit, which harm it can't and good it may, be joyful!'

'Sit down,' said Jonas, hoarsely, 'and let us get this business done. Where is the other woman?'

'The other person's with him now,' she answered.

'That's right,' said Jonas. 'He is not fit to be left to himself. Why, he fastened on me to-night; here, upon my coat; like a savage dog. Old as he is, and feeble as he is usually, I had some trouble to shake him off. You—Hush!—It's nothing. You told me the other woman's name. I forget it.'

'I mentioned Betsey Prig,' said Mrs. Gamp.

'She is to be trusted, is she?'

'That she ain't!' said Mrs. Gamp; 'nor have I brought her, Mr. Chuzzlewit. I've brought another, which engages to give every satigefaction.'

'What is her name?' asked Jonas.

Mrs. Gamp looked at him in an odd way without returning any answer, but appeared to understand the question too.

'What is her name?' repeated Jonas.

'Her name,' said Mrs. Gamp, 'is Harris.'

It was extraordinary how much effort it cost Mrs. Gamp to pronounce the name she was commonly so ready with. She made some three or four gasps before she could get it out; and, when she had uttered it, pressed her hand upon her side, and turned up her eyes, as if she were going to faint away. But, knowing her to labour under a complication of internal disorders, which rendered a few drops of spirits indispensable at certain times to her existence, and which came on very strong when that remedy was not at hand, Jonas merely supposed her to be the victim of one of these attacks.

'Well!' he said, hastily, for he felt how incapable he was of confining his wandering attention to the subject. 'You and she have arranged to take care of him, have you?'

Mrs. Gamp replied in the affirmative, and softly discharged herself of her familiar phrase, 'Turn and turn about; one off, one on.' But she spoke so tremulously that she felt called upon to add, 'which fiddle-strings is weakness to expredge my nerves this night!'

Jonas stopped to listen. Then said, hurriedly:

'We shall not quarrel about terms. Let them be the same as they were before. Keep him close, and keep him quiet. He must be restrained. He has got it in his head to-night that my wife's dead, and has been attacking me as if I had killed her. It's—it's common with mad people to take the worst fancies of those they like best. Isn't it?'

Mrs. Gamp assented with a short groan.

'Keep him close, then, or in one of his fits he'll be doing me a mischief. And don't trust him at any time; for when he seems most rational, he's wildest in his talk. But that you know already. Let me see the other.'

'The t'other person, sir?' said Mrs. Gamp.

'Aye! Go you to him and send the other. Quick! I'm busy.'

Mrs. Gamp took two or three backward steps towards the door, and stopped there.

'It is your wishes, Mr. Chuzzlewit,' she said, in a sort of quavering croak, 'to see the t'other person. Is it?'

But the ghastly change in Jonas told her that the other person was already seen. Before she could look round towards the door, she was put aside by old Martin's hand; and Chuffey and John Westlock entered with him.

'Let no one leave the house,' said Martin. 'This man is my brother's son. Ill-met, ill-trained, ill-begotten. If he moves from the spot on which he stands, or speaks a word above his breath to any person here, open the window, and call for help!'

'What right have you to give such directions in this house?' asked Jonas faintly.

'The right of your wrong-doing. Come in there!'

An irrepressible exclamation burst from the lips of Jonas, as

Lewsome entered at the door. It was not a groan, or a shriek, or a word, but was wholly unlike any sound that had ever fallen on the ears of those who heard it, while at the same time it was the most sharp and terrible expression of what was working in his guilty breast, that nature could have invented.

He had done murder for this! He had girdled himself about with perils, agonies of mind, innumerable fears, for this! He had hidden his secret in the wood; pressed and stamped it down into the bloody ground; and here it started up when least expected, miles upon miles away; known to many; proclaiming itself from the lips of an old man who had renewed his strength and vigour as by a miracle, to give it voice against him!

He leaned his hand on the back of a chair, and looked at them. It was in vain to try to do so scornfully, or with his usual insolence. He required the chair for his support. But he made a struggle for it.

'I know that fellow,' he said, fetching his breath at every word, and pointing his trembling finger towards Lewsome. 'He's the greatest liar alive. What's his last tale? Ha, ha! You're rare fellows, too! Why, that uncle of mine is childish; he's even a greater child than his brother, my father, was, in his old age; or than Chuffey is. What the devil do you mean,' he added, looking fiercely at John Westlock and Mark Tapley (the latter had entered with Lewsome), 'by coming here, and bringing two idiots and a knave with you to take my house by storm? Hallo, there! Open the door! Turn these strangers out!'

'I tell you what,' cried Mr. Tapley, coming forward, 'if it wasn't for your name, I'd drag you through the streets of my own accord, and single-handed, I would! Ah, I would! Don't try and look bold at me. You can't do it! Now go on, sir,' this was to old Martin. 'Bring the murderin' wagabond upon his knees! If he wants noise, he shall have enough of it; for as sure as he's a shiverin' from head to foot, I'll raise a uproar at this winder that shall bring half London in. Go on, sir! Let him try me once, and see whether I'm a man of my word or not.'

With that, Mark folded his arms, and took his seat upon the window-ledge, with an air of general preparation for anything, which seemed to imply that he was equally ready to jump out himself, or to throw Jonas out, upon receiving the slightest hint that it would be agreeable to the company.

Old Martin turned to Lewsome:

'This is the man,' he said, extending his hand towards Jonas. 'Is it?'

'You need do no more than look at him to be sure of that, or of the truth of what I have said,' was the reply. 'He is my witness.'

'Oh, brother!' cried old Martin, clasping his hands and lifting up his eyes. 'Oh, brother, brother! Were we strangers half our lives that you might breed a wretch like this, and I make life a desert by withering every flower that grew about me! Is it the natural end of your precepts and mine, that this should be the creature of your rearing, training, teaching, hoarding, striving for: and I the means of bringing him to punishment, when nothing can repair the wasted past!'

He sat down upon a chair as he spoke, and turning away his face, was silent for a few moments. Then with recovered energy he proceeded:

'But the accursed harvest of our mistaken lives shall be trodden down. It is not too late for that. You are confronted with this man, yon monster there; not to be spared, but to be dealt with justly. Hear what he says! Reply, be silent, contradict, repeat, defy, do what you please. My course will be the same. Go on! And you,' he said to Chuffey, 'for the love of your old friend, speak out, good fellow!'

'I have been silent for his love!' cried the old man. 'He urged me to it. He made me promise it upon his dying bed. I never would have spoken, but for your finding out so much. I have thought about it ever since: I couldn't help that: and sometimes I have had it all before me in a dream: but in the daytime, not in sleep. Is there such a kind of dream?' said Chuffey, looking anxiously in old Martin's face.

As Martin made him an encouraging reply, he listened attentively to his voice, and smiled.

'Ah, aye!' he cried. 'He often spoke to me like that. We were at school together, he and I. I couldn't turn against his son, you know—his only son, Mr. Chuzzlewit!'

'I would to Heaven you had been his son!' said Martin.

'You speak so like my dear old master,' cried the old man with a childish delight, 'that I almost think I hear him. I can hear you quite as well as I used to hear him. It makes me young again. He never spoke unkindly to me, and I always understood him. I could always see him too, though my sight was dim. Well, well! He's dead, he's dead. He was very good to me, my dear old master!'

He shook his head mournfully over the brother's hand. At this moment Mark, who had been glancing out of the window, left the room.

'I couldn't turn against his only son, you know,' said Chuffey. 'He has nearly driven me to do it sometimes; he very nearly did to-night. Ah!' cried the old man, with a sudden recollection of the cause. 'Where is she? She's not come home!'

'Do you mean his wife?' said Mr. Chuzzlewit.

'Yes.'

'I have removed her. She is in my care, and will be spared the present knowledge of what is passing here. She has known misery enough, without that addition.'

Jonas heard this with a sinking heart. He knew that they were on his heels, and felt that they were resolute to run him to destruction. Inch by inch the ground beneath him was sliding from his feet; faster and faster the encircling ruin contracted and contracted towards himself, its wicked centre, until it should close in and crush him.

And now he heard the voice of his accomplice stating to his face, with every circumstance of time and place and incident; and openly proclaiming, with no reserve, suppression, passion, or concealment; all the truth. The truth, which nothing would keep down; which blood would not smother, and earth would not hide; the truth, whose terrible inspiration seemed to change dotards into strong men; and on whose avenging wings, one whom he had supposed to be at the extremest corner of the earth came swooping down upon him.

He tried to deny it, but his tongue would not move. He conceived some desperate thought of rushing away, and tearing through the streets; but his limbs would as little answer to his will as his stark, stiff, staring face. All this time the voice went slowly on, denouncing him. It was as if every drop of blood in the wood had found a voice to jeer him with.

When it ceased, another voice took up the tale, but strangely: for the old clerk, who had watched, and listened to the whole, and had wrung his hands from time to time, as if he knew its truth and could confirm it, broke in with these words:

'No, no, no! you're wrong; you're wrong—all wrong together! Have patience, for the truth is only known to me!'

'How can that be,' said his old master's brother, 'after what you have heard? Besides, you said just now, above-stairs, when I told you of the accusation against him, that you knew he was his father's murderer.'

'Aye, yes! and so he was!' cried Chuffey, wildly. 'But not as you suppose—not as you suppose. Stay! Give me a moment's time. I have it all here—all here! It was foul, foul, cruel, bad; but not as you suppose. Stay, stay!'

He put his hands up to his head, as if it throbbed or pained him. After looking about him in a wandering and vacant manner for some moments, his eyes rested upon Jonas, when they kindled up with sudden recollection and intelligence.

'Yes!' cried old Chuffey, 'yes! That's how it was. It's all upon me now. He—he got up from his bed before he died, to be sure, to say that he forgave him; and he came down with me into this room; and when he saw him—his only son, the son he loved—his speech forsook him: he had no speech for what he knew—and no one understood him except me. But I did— I did!'

Old Martin regarded him in amazement; so did his companions. Mrs. Gamp, who had said nothing yet; but had kept two-thirds of herself behind the door, ready for escape, and one-third in the room, ready for siding with the strongest party; came a little further in and remarked, with a sob, that Mr. Chuffey was 'the sweetest old creetur goin'.'

'He bought the stuff,' said Chuffey, stretching out his arm towards Jonas, while an unwonted fire shone in his eye, and lightened up his face; 'he bought the stuff, no doubt, as you have heard, and brought it home. He mixed the stuff—look at him!—with some sweetmeat in a jar, exactly as the medicine for his father's cough was mixed, and put it in a drawer; in that drawer yonder in the desk; he knows which drawer I mean! He kept it there locked up. But his courage failed him, or his heart was touched—my God! I hope it was his heart! He was his only son!—and he did not put it in the usual place, where my old master would have taken it twenty times a day.'

The trembling figure of the old man shook with the strong emotions that possessed him. But, with the same light in his eye, and with his arm outstretched, and with his grey hair stirring on his head, he seemed to grow in size, and was like a man inspired. Jonas shrunk from looking at him, and cowered down into the chair by which he had held. It seemed as if this tremendous Truth could make the dumb speak.

'I know it every word now!' cried Chuffey. 'Every word! He put it in that drawer, as I have said. He went so often there, and was so secret, that his father took notice of it; and when he was out, had it opened. We were there together, and we found the mixture—Mr. Chuzzlewit and I. He took it into his possession, and made light of it at the time; but in the night he came to my bedside, weeping, and told me that his own son had it in his mind to poison him. "Oh, Chuff," he said, "oh, dear old Chuff! a voice came into my room to-night, and told me that this crime began with me. It began when I taught him to be too covetous of what I have to leave, and made the expectation of it his great business!" Those were his words; aye, they are his very words! If he was a hard man now and then, it was for his only son. He loved his only son, and he was always good to me!'

Jonas listened with increased attention. Hope was breaking in upon him.

' "He shall not weary for my death, Chuff:" that was what he said next,' pursued the old clerk, as he wiped his eyes; 'that was what he said next, crying like a little child: "He shall not weary for my death, Chuff. He shall have it now; he shall marry where he has a fancy, Chuff, although it don't please me; and you and I will go away and live upon a little. I always loved him; perhaps he'll love *me* then. It's a dreadful thing to have my own child thirsting for my death. But I might have known it. I have sown, and I must reap. He shall believe that I am taking this; and when I see that he is sorry, and has all he wants, I'll tell him that I found it out, and I'll forgive him. He'll make a better man of his own son, and be a better man himself, perhaps, Chuff!"'

Poor Chuffey paused to dry his eyes again. Old Martin's face was hidden in his hands. Jonas listened still more keenly, and his breast heaved like a swollen water, but with hope. With growing hope.

'My dear old master made believe next day,' said Chuffey, 'that he had opened the drawer by mistake with a key from the bunch, which happened to fit it (we had one made and hung upon it); and that he had been surprised to find his fresh supply of cough medicine in such a place, but supposed it had been put there in a hurry when the drawer stood open. We burnt it; but his son believed that he was taking it—he knows he did. Once Mr. Chuzzlewit to try him took heart to say it had a strange taste; and he got up directly, and went out.'

Jonas gave a short, dry cough; and, changing his position for an easier one, folded his arms without looking at them, though they could now see his face.

'Mr. Chuzzlewit wrote to her father; I mean the father of the poor thing who's his wife;' said Chuffey; 'and got him to come up: intending to hasten on the marriage. But his mind, like mine, went a little wrong through grief, and then his heart broke. He sank and altered from the time when he came to me in the night; and never held up his head again. It was only a few days, but he had never changed so much in twice the years. "Spare him, Chuff!" he said, before he died. They were the only words he could speak. "Spare him, Chuff!" I promised him I would. I've tried to do it. He's his only son.'

In his recollection of the last scene in his old friend's life, poor Chuffey's voice, which had grown weaker and weaker, quite deserted him. Making a motion with his hand, as if he would have said that Anthony had taken it, and had died with it in his, he retreated to the corner where he usually concealed his sorrows; and was silent.

Jonas could look at his company now, and vauntingly too. 'Well!' he said, after a pause. 'Are you satisfied? Or have you any more of your plots to broach? Why that fellow, Lewsome, can invent 'em for you by the score. Is this all? Have you nothing else?'

Old Martin looked at him steadily.

'Whether you are what you seemed to be at Pecksniff's, or are something else and a mountebank, I don't know and I don't care,' said Jonas, looking downward with a smile, 'but I don't want you here. You were here so often when your brother was alive, and were always so fond of him (your dear, dear brother, and you would have been cuffing one another before this, ecod!), that I am not surprised at your being attached to the place; but the place is not attached to you, and you can't leave it too soon, though you may leave it too late. And for my wife, old man, send her home straight, or it will be the worse for her. Ha, ha! You carry it with a high hand too! But it isn't hanging yet for a man to keep a penn'orth of poison for his own purposes, and have it taken from him by two old crazy jolter-heads who go and act a play about it. Ha, ha! Do you see the door?'

His base triumph, struggling with his cowardice, and shame, and guilt, was so detestable, that they turned away from him, as if he were some obscene and filthy animal, repugnant to the sight. And here that last black crime was busy with him too; working within him to his perdition. But for that, the old clerk's story might have touched him, though never so lightly; but for that, the sudden removal of so great a load might have brought about some wholesome change even in him. With that deed done, however; with that unnecessary wasteful danger haunting him; despair was in his very triumph and relief; wild, ungovernable, raging despair, for the uselessness of the peril into which he had plunged; despair that hardened him and maddened him, and set his teeth a-grinding in a moment of his exultation.

'My good friend!' said old Martin, laying his hand on Chuffey's sleeve. 'This is no place for you to remain in. Come with me.'

'Just his old way!' cried Chuffey, looking up into his face. 'I almost believe it's Mr. Chuzzlewit alive again. Yes! Take me with you! Stay, though, stay.'

'For what?' asked old Martin.

'I can't leave her, poor thing!' said Chuffey. 'She has been very good to me. I can't leave her, Mr. Chuzzlewit. Thank you kindly. I'll remain here. I hav'n't long to remain; it's no great matter.'

As he meekly shook his poor, grey head, and thanked old Martin in these words, Mrs. Gamp, now entirely in the room, was affected to tears.

'The mercy as it is!' she said, 'as sech a dear, good, reverend creetur never got into the clutches of Betsey Prig, which but for me he would have done, undoubted, facts bein' stubborn and not easy drove!'

'You heard me speak to you just now, old man,' said Jonas to his uncle. 'I'll have no more tampering with my people, man or woman. Do you see the door?'

'Do *you* see the door?' returned the voice of Mark, coming from that direction. 'Look at it!'

He looked, and his gaze was nailed there. Fatal, ill-omened, blighted threshold, cursed by his father's footsteps in his dying hour, cursed by his young wife's sorrowing tread, cursed by the daily shadow of the old clerk's figure, cursed by the crossing of his murderer's feet—what men were standing in the doorway!

Nadgett foremost.

Hark! It came on, roaring like a sea! Hawkers burst into the street, crying it up and down; windows were thrown open that the inhabitants might hear it; people stopped to listen in the road and on the pavement; the bells, the same bells, began to ring: tumbling over one another in a dance of boisterous joy at the discovery (that was the sound they had in his distempered thoughts), and making their airy playground rock.

'That is the man,' said Nadgett. 'By the window!'

Three others came in, laid hands upon him, and secured him. It was so quickly done, that he had not lost sight of the informer's face for an instant when his wrists were manacled together.

'Murder,' said Nadgett, looking round on the astonished group. 'Let no one interfere.'

The sounding street repeated Murder; barbarous and dreadful Murder; Murder, Murder, Murder. Rolling on from house to house, and echoing from stone to stone, until the voices died away into the distant hum, which seemed to mutter the same word!

They all stood silent: listening, and gazing in each other's faces, as the noise passed on.

Old Martin was the first to speak. 'What terrible history is this?' he demanded.

'Ask *him*,' said Nadgett. 'You're his friend, sir. He can tell you, if he will. He knows more of it than I do, though I know much.'

'How do you know much?'

'I have not been watching him so long for nothing,' returned Nadgett. 'I never watched a man so close as I have watched him.'

Another of the phantom forms of this terrific Truth! Another of the many shapes in which it started up about him, out of vacancy. This man, of all men in the world, a spy upon him; this man, changing his identity: casting off his shrinking, purblind, unobservant character, and springing up into a watchful enemy! The dead man might have come out of his grave, and not confounded and appalled him more.

The game was up. The race was at an end; the rope was woven for his neck. If, by a miracle, he could escape from this strait, he had but to turn his face another way, no matter where, and there would rise some new avenger front to front with him; some infant in an hour grown old, or old man in an hour grown young, or blind man with his sight restored, or deaf man with his hearing given him. There was no chance. He sank down in a heap against the wall, and never hoped again from that moment.

'I am not his friend, although I have the dishonour to be his relative,' said Mr. Chuzzlewit. 'You may speak to me. Where have you watched, and what have you seen?'

'I have watched in many places,' returned Nadgett, 'night and day. I have watched him lately, almost without rest or relief;' his anxious face and bloodshot eyes confirmed it. 'I little thought to what my watching was to lead. As little as he did when he slipped out in the night, dressed in those clothes which he afterwards sunk in a bundle at London Bridge!'

Jonas moved upon the ground like a man in bodily torture. He uttered a suppressed groan, as if he had been wounded by some cruel weapon; and plucked at the iron band upon his wrists, as though (his hands being free) he would have torn himself.

'Steady, kinsman!' said the chief officer of the party. 'Don't be violent.'

'Whom do you call kinsman?' asked old Martin sternly.

'You,' said the man, 'among others.'

Martin turned his scrutinising gaze upon him. He was sitting lazily across a chair with his arms resting on the back; eating nuts, and throwing the shells out of window as he cracked them; which he still continued to do while speaking.

'Aye,' he said, with a sulky nod. 'You may deny your nephews till you die, but Chevy Slyme is Chevy Slyme still, all the world over. Perhaps even you may feel it some disgrace to your own blood to be employed in this way. I'm to be bought off.'

'At every turn!' cried Martin. 'Self, self, self. Every one among them for himself!'

'You had better save one or two among them the trouble then, and be for them as well as *your*self,' replied his nephew. 'Look here at me! Can you see the man of your family who has more talent in his little finger than all the rest in their united brains, dressed as a police officer without being ashamed? I took up with this trade on purpose to shame you. I didn't think I should have to make a capture in the family, though.'

'If your debauchery, and that of your chosen friends, has

really brought you to this level,' returned the old man, 'keep it. You are living honestly, I hope, and that's something.'

'Don't be hard upon my chosen friends,' returned Slyme, 'for they were sometimes your chosen friends too. Don't say you never employed my friend Tigg, for I know better. We quarrelled upon it.'

'I hired the fellow,' retorted Mr. Chuzzlewit, 'and I paid him.'

'It's well you paid him,' said his nephew, 'for it would be too late to do so now. He has given his receipt in full—or had it forced from him rather.'

The old man looked at him as if he were curious to know what he meant, but scorned to prolong the conversation.

'I have always expected that he and I would be brought together again in the course of business,' said Slyme, taking a fresh handful of nuts from his pocket; 'but I thought he would be wanted for some swindling job; it never entered my head that I should hold a warrant for the apprehension of his murderer.'

'*His* murderer!' cried Mr. Chuzzlewit, looking from one to another.

'His or Mr. Montague's,' said Nadgett. 'They are the same, I am told. I accuse him yonder of the murder of Mr. Montague, who was found last night, killed, in a wood. You will ask me why I accuse him, as you have already asked me how I know so much. I'll tell you. It can't remain a secret long.'

The ruling passion of the man expressed itself even then, in the tone of regret in which he deplored the approaching publicity of what he knew.

'I told you I had watched him,' he proceeded. 'I was instructed to do so by Mr. Montague, in whose employment I have been for some time. We had our suspicions of him; and you know what they pointed at, for you have been discussing it since we have been waiting here, outside the room. If you care to hear now it's all over, in what our suspicions began, I'll tell you plainly: in a quarrel (it first came to our ears through a hint of his own) between him and another office in which his father's life was insured, and which had so much doubt and distrust upon the subject, that he compounded with them, and took half the money; and was glad to do it. Bit by bit, I ferreted out more circumstances against him, and not a few. It required a little patience, but it's my calling. I found the nurse—here she is to confirm me; I found the doctor, I found the undertaker, I found the undertaker's man. I found out how the old gentleman there, Mr. Chuffey, had behaved at the funeral; and I found out what this man,' touching Lewsome on the arm, 'had talked about in his fever. I found out how he conducted himself before his father's death, and how since, and how at the time; and writing it all down, and putting it carefully together, made case enough for Mr. Montague to tax him with the crime, which (as he himself believed until to-night) he had committed. I was by when this was done. You see him now. He is only worse than he was then.'

Oh, miserable, miserable fool! oh, insupportable, excruciating torture! To find alive and active—a party to it all—the brain and right-hand of the secret he had thought to crush! In whom, though he had walled the murdered man up, by enchantment in a rock, the story would have lived and walked abroad! He tried to stop his ears with his fettered arms, that he might shut out the rest.

As he crouched upon the floor, they drew away from him as if a pestilence were in his breath. They fell off, one by one, from that part of the room, leaving him alone upon the ground. Even those who had him in their keeping shunned him, and (with the exception of Slyme, who was still occupied with his nuts) kept apart.

'From that garret-window opposite,' said Nadgett, pointing across the narrow street, 'I have watched this house and him for days and nights. From that garret-window opposite I saw him return home, alone, from a journey on which he had set out with Mr. Montague. That was my token that Mr. Montague's end was gained; and I might rest easy on my watch, though I was not to leave it until he dismissed me. But, standing at the door opposite, after dark that same night, I saw a countryman steal out of this house, by a side-door in the court, who had never entered it. I knew his walk, and that it was himself, disguised. I followed him immediately. I lost him on the western road, still travelling westward.'

Jonas looked up at him for an instant, and muttered an oath.

'I could not comprehend what this meant,' said Nadgett: 'but, having seen so much, I resolved to see it out, and through. And I did. Learning, on inquiry at his house from his wife, that he was supposed to be sleeping in the room from which I had seen him go out, and that he had given strict orders not to be disturbed, I knew that he was coming back; and for his coming back I watched. I kept my watch in the street—in doorways, and such places—all that night; at the same window, all next day; and when night came on again, in the street once more. For I knew he would come back, as he had gone out, when this part of the town was empty. He did. Early in the morning, the same countryman came creeping, creeping, creeping home.'

'Look sharp!' interposed Slyme, who had now finished his nuts. 'This is quite irregular, Mr. Nadgett.'

'I kept at the window all day,' said Nadgett, without heeding him. 'I think I never closed my eyes. At night, I saw him come out with a bundle. I followed him again. He went down the steps at London Bridge, and sunk it in the river. I now began to entertain some serious fears, and made a communication to the Police, which caused that bundle to be—'

'To be fished up,' interrupted Slyme. 'Be alive, Mr. Nadgett.'

'It contained the dress I had seen him wear,' said Nadgett; 'stained with clay, and spotted with blood. Information of the murder was received in town last night. The wearer of that dress is already known to have been seen near the place; to have been lurking in that neighbourhood; and to have alighted from a coach coming from that part of the country, at a time exactly tallying with the very minute when I saw him returning home. The warrant has been out, and these officers have been with me, some hours. We chose our time; and seeing you come in, and seeing this person at the window—'

'Beckoned to him,' said Mark, taking up the thread of the narrative, on hearing this allusion to himself, 'to open the door; which he did with a deal of pleasure.'

'That's all at present,' said Nadgett, putting up his great pocket-book, which from mere habit he had produced when he began his revelation, and had kept in his hand all the time; 'but there is plenty more to come. You asked me for the facts, so far I have related them, and need not detain these gentlemen any longer. Are you ready, Mr. Slyme?'

'And something more,' replied that worthy, rising. 'If you walk round to the office, we shall be there as soon as you. Tom! Get a coach!'

The officer to whom he spoke departed for that purpose. Old Martin lingered for a few moments, as if he would have addressed some words to Jonas; but looking round, and seeing him still seated on the floor, rocking himself in a savage manner to and fro, took Chuffey's arm, and slowly followed Nadgett out. John Westlock and Mark Tapley accompanied them. Mrs. Gamp had tottered out first, for the better display of her feelings, in a kind of walking swoon; for Mrs. Gamp performed swoons of different sorts, upon a moderate notice, as Mr. Mould did Funerals.

'Ha!' muttered Slyme, looking after them. 'Upon my soul! As insensible of being disgraced by having such a nephew as myself, in such a situation, as he was of my being an honour and a credit to the family! That's the return I get for having humbled my spirit—such a spirit as mine—to earn a livelihood, is it?'

He got up from his chair, and kicked it away indignantly.

'And such a livelihood too! When there are hundreds of men, not fit to hold a candle to me, rolling in carriages and living on their fortunes. Upon my soul it's a nice world!'

His eyes encountered Jonas, who looked earnestly towards him, and moved his lips as if he were whispering.

'Eh?' said Slyme.

Jonas glanced at the attendant whose back was towards him, and made a clumsy motion with his bound hands towards the door.

'Humph!' said Slyme, thoughtfully. 'I couldn't hope to disgrace him into anything when you have shot so far ahead of me though. I forgot that.'

Jonas repeated the same look and gesture.

'Jack!' said Slyme.

'Hallo!' returned his man.

'Go down to the door, ready for the coach. Call out when it comes. I'd rather have you there. Now then,' he added, turning hastily to Jonas, when the man was gone. 'What's the matter?'

Jonas essayed to rise.

'Stop a bit,' said Slyme. 'It's not so easy when your wrists are tight together. Now then! Up! What is it?'

'Put your hand in my pocket. Here! The breast pocket, on the left!' said Jonas.

He did so; and drew out a purse.

'There's a hundred pound in it,' said Jonas, whose words were almost unintelligible; as his face, in its pallor and agony, was scarcely human.

Slyme looked at him; gave it into his hands; and shook his head.

'I can't. I daren't. I couldn't if I dared. Those fellows below—'

'Escape's impossible,' said Jonas. 'I know it. One hundred pound for only five minutes in the next room!'

'What to do?' he asked.

The face of his prisoner as he advanced to whisper in his ear, made him recoil involuntarily. But he stopped and listened to him. The words were few, but his own face changed as he heard them.

'I have it about me,' said Jonas, putting his hands to his throat, as though whatever he referred to were hidden in his neckerchief. 'How should you know of it? How could you know? A hundred pound for only five minutes in the next room! The time's passing. Speak!'

'It would be more—more creditable to the family,' observed Slyme, with trembling lips. 'I wish you hadn't told me half so much. Less would have served your purpose. You might have kept it to yourself.'

'A hundred pound for only five minutes in the next room! Speak!' cried Jonas, desperately.

He took the purse. Jonas, with a wild unsteady step, retreated to the door in the glass partition.

'Stop!' cried Slyme, catching at his skirts. 'I don't know about this. Yet it must end so at last. Are you guilty?'

'Yes!' said Jonas.

'Are the proofs as they were told just now?'

'Yes!' said Jonas.

'Will you—will you engage to say a—a Prayer, now, or something of that sort?' faltered Slyme.

Jonas broke from him without replying, and closed the door between them.

Slyme listened at the keyhole. After that, he crept away on tip-toe, as far off as he could; and looked awfully towards the place. He was roused by the arrival of the coach, and their letting down the steps.

'He's getting a few things together,' he said, leaning out of window, and speaking to the two men below, who stood in the full light of a street-lamp. 'Keep your eye upon the back, one of you, for form's sake.'

One of the men withdrew into the court. The other, seating

himself on the steps of the coach, remained in conversation with Slyme at the window: who perhaps had risen to be his superior, in virtue of his old propensity (one so much lauded by the murdered man) of being always round the corner. A useful habit in his present calling.

'Where is he?' asked the man.

Slyme looked into the room for an instant and gave his head a jerk, as much as to say, 'Close at hand. I see him.'

'He's booked,' observed the man.

'Through,' said Slyme.

They looked at each other, and up and down the street. The man on the coach-steps took his hat off, and put it on again, and whistled a little.

'I say! He's taking his time!' he remonstrated.

'I allowed him five minutes,' said Slyme. 'Time's more than up, though. I'll bring him down.'

He withdrew from the window accordingly, and walked on tiptoe to the door in the partition. He listened. There was not a sound within. He set the candles near it, that they might shine through the glass.

It was not easy, he found, to make up his mind to the opening of the door. But he flung it wide open suddenly, and with a noise; then retreated. After peeping in and listening again, he entered.

He started back as his eyes met those of Jonas, standing in an angle of the wall, and staring at him. His neckerchief was off; his face was ashy pale.

'You're too soon,' said Jonas, with an abject whimper. 'I've not had time. I have not been able to do it. I—five minutes more—two minutes more!—Only one!'

Slyme gave him no reply, but thrusting the purse upon him and forcing it back into his pocket, called up his men.

He whined, and cried, and cursed, and entreated them, and struggled, and submitted, in the same breath, and had no power to stand. They got him away and into the coach, where they put him on a seat; but he soon fell moaning down among the straw at the bottom, and lay there.

The two men were with him; Slyme being on the box with the driver; and they let him lie. Happening to pass a fruiterer's on their way; the door of which was open, though the shop was by this time shut; one of them remarked how faint the peaches smelt.

The other assented at the moment, but presently stooped down in quick alarm, and looked at the prisoner.

'Stop the coach! He has poisoned himself! The smell comes from this bottle in his hand!'

The hand had shut upon it tight. With that rigidity of grasp with which no living man, in the full strength and energy of life, can clutch a prize he has won.

They dragged him out into the dark street; but jury, judge, and hangman, could have done no more, and could do nothing now. Dead, dead, dead.

CHAPTER LII

In which the tables are turned completely upside down

OLD MARTIN'S cherished projects, so long hidden in his own breast, so frequently in danger of abrupt disclosure through the bursting forth of the indignation he had hoarded up during his residence with Mr. Pecksniff, were retarded, but not beyond a few hours, by the occurrences just now related. Stunned as he had been at first by the intelligence conveyed to him through Tom Pinch and John Westlock, of the supposed manner of his brother's death; overwhelmed as he was by the subsequent narratives of Chuffey and Nadgett, and the forging of that chain of circumstances ending in the death of Jonas, of which catastrophe he was immediately informed; scattered as his purposes and hopes were for the moment, by the crowding in of all these incidents between him and his end; still their very intensity and the tumult of their assemblage nerved him to the rapid and unyielding execution of his scheme. In every single circumstance, whether it were cruel, cowardly, or false, he saw the flowering of the same pregnant seed. Self; grasping, eager, narrow-ranging, over-reaching self; with its long train of suspicions, lusts, deceits, and all their growing consequences; was the root of the vile tree. Mr. Pecksniff had so presented his character before the old man's eyes, that he—the good, the tolerant, enduring Pecksniff—had become the incarnation of all selfishness and treachery; and the more odious the shapes in which those vices ranged themselves before him now, the sterner consolation he had in his design of setting Mr. Pecksniff right, and Mr. Pecksniff's victims too.

To this work he brought, not only the energy and determination natural to his character (which, as the reader may have observed in the beginning of his or her acquaintance with this gentleman, was remarkable for the strong development of those qualities), but all the forced and unnaturally nurtured energy consequent upon their long suppression. And these two tides of resolution setting into one and sweeping on, became so strong and vigorous, that, to prevent themselves from being carried away before it, Heaven knows where, was as much as John Westlock and Mark Tapley together (though they were tolerably energetic too) could manage to effect.

He had sent for John Westlock immediately on his arrival; and John, under the conduct of Tom Pinch, had waited on him. Having a lively recollection of Mr. Tapley, he had caused that gentleman's attendance to be secured, through John's means, without delay; and thus, as we have seen, they had all repaired together to the City. But his grandson he had refused to see until to-morrow, when Mr. Tapley was instructed to summon him to the Temple at ten o'clock in the forenoon. Tom he would not allow to be employed in anything, lest he should be wrongfully suspected; but he was a party to all their proceedings, and was with them until late at night—until after they knew of the death of Jonas; when he went home to tell all these wonders to little Ruth, and to prepare her for accompanying him to the Temple in the morning, agreeably to Mr. Chuzzlewit's particular injunction.

It was characteristic of old Martin, and his looking on to something which he had distinctly before him, that he communicated to them nothing of his intentions, beyond such hints of reprisal on Mr. Pecksniff as they gathered from the game he had played in that gentleman's house, and the brightening of his eyes whenever his name was mentioned. Even to John Westlock, in whom he was evidently disposed to place great confidence (which may indeed be said of every one of them), he gave no explanation whatever. He merely requested him to return in the morning; and with this for their utmost satisfaction, they left him, when the night was far advanced, alone.

The events of such a day might have worn out the body and spirit of a much younger man than he, but he sat in deep and painful meditation until the morning was bright. Nor did he even then seek any prolonged repose, but merely slumbered in his chair, until seven o'clock, when Mr. Tapley had appointed to come to him by his desire: and came—as fresh and clean and cheerful as the morning itself.

'You are punctual,' said Mr. Chuzzlewit, opening the door to him in reply to his light knock, which had roused him instantly.

'My wishes, sir,' replied Mr. Tapley, whose mind would appear from the context to have been running on the matrimonial service, 'is to love, honour, and obey. The clock's a-striking now, sir.'

'Come in!'

F f

'Thank'ee, sir,' rejoined Mr. Tapley, 'what could I do for you first, sir?'

'You gave my message to Martin?' said the old man, bending his eyes upon him.

'I did, sir,' returned Mark; 'and you never see a gentleman more surprised in all your born days than he was.'

'What more did you tell him?' Mr. Chuzzlewit inquired.

'Why, sir,' said Mr. Tapley, smiling, 'I should have liked to tell him a deal more, but not being able, sir, I didn't tell it him.'

'You told him all you knew?'

'But it was precious little, sir,' retorted Mr. Tapley. 'There was very little respectin' you that I was able to tell him, sir. I only mentioned my opinion that Mr. Pecksniff would find himself deceived, sir, and that you would find yourself deceived, and that he would find himself deceived, sir.'

'In what?' asked Mr. Chuzzlewit.

'Meaning him, sir?'

'Meaning both him and me.'

'Well, sir,' said Mr. Tapley. 'In your old opinions of each other. As to him, sir, and his opinions, I know he's a altered man. I know it. I know'd it long afore he spoke to you t'other day, and I must say it. Nobody don't know half as much of him as I do. Nobody can't. There was always a deal of good in him, but a little of it got crusted over, somehow. I can't say who rolled the paste of that 'ere crust myself, but——'

'Go on,' said Martin. 'Why do you stop?'

'But it—well! I beg your pardon, but I think it may have been you, sir. Unintentional I think it may have been you. I don't believe that neither of you gave the other quite a fair chance. There! Now I've got rid on it,' said Mr. Tapley in a fit of desperation: 'I can't go a-carryin' it about in my own mind, bustin' myself with it; yesterday was quite long enough. It's out now. I can't help it. I'm sorry for it. Don't wisit it on him, sir, that's all.'

It was clear that Mark expected to be ordered out immediately, and was quite prepared to go.

'So you think,' said Martin, 'that his old faults are, in some degree, of my creation, do you?'

'Well, sir,' retorted Mr. Tapley, 'I'm wery sorry, but I can't unsay it. It's hardly fair of you, sir, to make a ignorant man conwict himself in this way, but I do think so. I am as respect-ful disposed to you, sir, as a man can be; but I do think so.'

The light of a faint smile seemed to break through the dull steadiness of Martin's face, as he looked attentively at him, without replying.

'Yet you are an ignorant man, you say,' he observed after a long pause.

'Wery much so,' Mr. Tapley replied.

'And I a learned, well-instructed man, you think?'

'Likewise wery much so,' Mr. Tapley answered.

The old man, with his chin resting on his hand, paced the room twice or thrice before he added:

'You have left him this morning?'

'Come straight from him now, sir.'

'For what: does he suppose?'

'He don't know what to suppose, sir, no more than myself. I told him jest wot passed yesterday, sir, and that you had said to me, "Can you be here by seven in the morning?" and that you had said to him, through me, "Can you be here by ten in the morning?" and that I had said "Yes" to both. That's all, sir.'

His frankness was so genuine that it plainly *was* all.

'Perhaps,' said Martin, 'he may think you are going to desert him, and to serve me?'

'I have served him in that sort of way, sir,' replied Mark, without the loss of any atom of his self-possession; 'and we have been that sort of companions in misfortune, that my opinion is, he don't believe a word on it. No more than you do, sir.'

'Will you help me to dress? and get me some breakfast from the hotel?' asked Martin.

'With pleasure, sir,' said Mark.

'And by-and-bye,' pursued Martin, 'remaining in the room, as I wish you to do, will you attend to the door yonder—give admission to visitors, I mean, when they knock?'

'Certainly, sir,' said Mr. Tapley.

'You will not find it necessary to express surprise at their appearance,' Martin suggested.

'Oh dear no, sir!' said Mr. Tapley, 'not at all.'

Although he pledged himself to this with perfect confidence, he was in a state of unbounded astonishment even now. Martin appeared to observe it, and to have some sense of the ludicrous bearing of Mr. Tapley under these perplexing circumstances; for in spite of the composure of his voice and the gravity of his face, the same indistinct light flickered on the latter several times. Mark bestirred himself, however, to execute the offices with which he was entrusted; and soon lost all tendency to any outward expression of his surprise, in the occupation of being brisk and busy.

But when he had put Mr. Chuzzlewit's clothes in good order for dressing, and when that gentleman was dressed and sitting at his breakfast, Mr. Tapley's feelings of wonder began to return upon him with great violence; and, standing beside the old man with a napkin under his arm (it was as natural and easy a joke to Mark to be a butler in the Temple, as it had been to volunteer as cook on board the Screw), he found it difficult to resist the temptation of casting sidelong glances at him very often. Nay, he found it impossible; and accordingly yielded to this impulse so often, that Martin caught him in the fact some fifty times. The extraordinary things Mr. Tapley did with his own face when any of these detections occurred; the sudden occasions he had to rub his eyes or his nose or his chin; the look of wisdom with which he immediately plunged into the deepest thought, or became intensely interested in the habits and customs of the flies upon the ceiling, or the sparrows out of doors; or the overwhelming politeness with which he endeavoured to hide his confusion by handing the muffin; may not unreasonably be assumed to have exercised the utmost power of feature that even Martin Chuzzlewit the elder possessed.

But he sat perfectly quiet and took his breakfast at his leisure, or made a show of doing so, for he scarcely ate or drank, and frequently lapsed into long intervals of musing. When he had finished, Mark sat down to his breakfast at the same table; and Mr. Chuzzlewit, quite silent still, walked up and down the room.

Mark cleared away in due course, and set a chair out for him, in which, as the time drew on towards ten o'clock, he took his seat, leaning his hands upon his stick, and clenching them upon the handle, and resting his chin on them again. All his impatience and abstraction of manner had vanished now; and as he sat there, looking, with his keen eyes, steadily towards the door, Mark could not help thinking what a firm, square, powerful face it was; or exulting in the thought that Mr. Pecksniff, after playing a pretty long game of bowls with its owner, seemed to be at last in a very fair way of coming in for a rubber or two.

*Warm Reception of Mr. Pecksniff by his Venerable
Friend*
(p. 803)

Mark's uncertainty in respect of what was going to be done or said, and by whom to whom, would have excited him in itself. But knowing for a certainty besides, that young Martin was coming, and in a very few minutes must arrive, he found it by no means easy to remain quiet and silent. But, excepting that he occasionally coughed in a hollow and unnatural manner to relieve himself, he behaved with great decorum through the longest ten minutes he had ever known.

A knock at the door. Mr. Westlock. Mr. Tapley, in admitting him, raised his eyebrows to the highest possible pitch, implying thereby that he considered himself in an unsatisfactory position. Mr. Chuzzlewit received him very courteously.

Mark waited at the door for Tom Pinch and his sister, who were coming up the stairs. The old man went to meet them; took their hands in his; and kissed her on the cheek. As this looked promising, Mr. Tapley smiled benignantly.

Mr. Chuzzlewit had resumed his chair before young Martin, who was close behind them, entered. The old man, scarcely looking at him, pointed to a distant seat. This was less encouraging; and Mr. Tapley's spirits fell again.

He was quickly summoned to the door by another knock. He did not start, or cry, or tumble down, at sight of Miss Graham and Mrs. Lupin, but he drew a very long breath, and came back perfectly resigned, looking on them and on the rest with an expression which seemed to say, that nothing could surprise him any more; and that he was rather glad to have done with that sensation for ever.

The old man received Mary no less tenderly than he had received Tom Pinch's sister. A look of friendly recognition passed between himself and Mrs. Lupin, which implied the existence of a perfect understanding between them. It engendered no astonishment in Mr. Tapley; for, as he afterwards observed, he had retired from the business, and sold off the stock.

Not the least curious feature in this assemblage was, that everybody present was so much surprised and embarrassed by the sight of everybody else, that nobody ventured to speak. Mr. Chuzzlewit alone broke silence.

'Set the door open, Mark!' he said; 'and come here.' Mark obeyed.

The last appointed footstep sounded now upon the stairs.

They all knew it. It was Mr. Pecksniff's; and Mr. Pecksniff was in a hurry too, for he came bounding up with such uncommon expedition that he stumbled twice or thrice.

'Where is my venerable friend?' he cried upon the upper landing; and then with open arms came darting in.

Old Martin merely looked at him; but Mr. Pecksniff started back as if he had received the charge of an electric battery.

'My venerable friend is well?' cried Mr. Pecksniff.

'Quite well.'

It seemed to reassure the anxious inquirer. He clasped his hands, and, looking upwards with a pious joy, silently expressed his gratitude. He then looked round on the assembled group, and shook his head reproachfully. For such a man severely, quite severely.

'Oh, vermin!' said Mr. Pecksniff. 'Oh, bloodsuckers! Is it not enough that you have embittered the existence of an individual, wholly unparalleled in the biographical records of amiable persons; but must you now, even now, when he has made his election, and reposed his trust in a Numble, but at least sincere and disinterested relative; must you now, vermin and swarmers (I regret to make use of these strong expressions, my dear sir, but there are times when honest indignation will not be controlled), must you now, vermin and swarmers (for I WILL repeat it), taking advantage of his unprotected state, assemble round him from all quarters, as wolves and vultures, and other animals of the feathered tribe assemble round—I will not say round carrion or a carcass, for Mr. Chuzzlewit is quite the contrary—but round their prey—their prey—to rifle and despoil; gorging their voracious maws, and staining their offensive beaks, with every description of carnivorous enjoyment!'

As he stopped to fetch his breath, he waved them off, in a solemn manner, with his hand.

'Horde of unnatural plunderers and robbers!' he continued; 'leave him! leave him, I say! Begone! Abscond! You had better be off! Wander over the face of the earth, young sirs, like vagabonds as you are, and do not presume to remain in a spot which is hallowed by the grey hairs of the patriarchal gentleman to whose tottering limbs I have the honour to act as an unworthy, but I hope an unassuming, prop and staff. And you, my tender sir,' said Mr. Pecksniff, addressing himself in a tone of gentle remonstrance to the old man, 'how could you ever leave me, though even for this short period! You have absented yourself, I do not doubt, upon some act of kindness to me; bless you for it: but you must not do it; you must not be so venturesome. I should really be angry with you if I could, my friend!'

He advanced with outstretched arms to take the old man's hand. But he had not seen how the hand clasped and clutched the stick within its grasp. As he came smiling on, and got within his reach, old Martin, with his burning indignation crowded into one vehement burst, and flashing out of every line and wrinkle in his face, rose up, and struck him down upon the ground.

With such a well-directed nervous blow, that down he went, as heavily and true as if the charge of a Life-Guardsman had tumbled him out of a saddle. And whether he was stunned by the shock, or only confused by the wonder and novelty of this warm reception, he did not offer to get up again; but lay there, looking about him with a disconcerted meekness in his face so enormously ridiculous, that neither Mark Tapley nor John Westlock could repress a smile, though both were actively interposing to prevent a repetition of the blow; which the old man's gleaming eyes and vigorous attitude seemed to render one of the most probable events in the world.

'Drag him away! Take him out of my reach!' said Martin; 'or I can't help it. The strong restraint I have put upon my hands has been enough to palsy them. I am not master of myself while he is within their range. Drag him away!'

Seeing that he still did not rise, Mr. Tapley, without any compromise about it, actually did drag him away, and stick him up on the floor, with his back against the opposite wall.

'Hear me, rascal!' said Mr. Chuzzlewit. 'I have summoned you here to witness your own work. I have summoned you here to witness it, because I know it will be gall and wormwood to you! I have summoned you here to witness it, because I know the sight of everybody here must be a dagger in your mean, false heart! What! do you know me as I am, at last!'

Mr. Pecksniff had cause to stare at him, for the triumph in his face and speech and figure was a sight to stare at.

'Look there!' said the old man, pointing at him, and appealing to the rest. 'Look there! And then—come hither, my dear Martin—look here! here! here!' At every repetition of the word he pressed his grandson closer to his breast.

'The passion I felt, Martin, when I dared not do this,' he said, 'was in the blow I struck just now. Why did we ever part! How could we ever part! How could you ever fly from me to him!'

Martin was about to answer, but he stopped him, and went on.

'The fault was mine no less than yours. Mark has told me so to-day, and I have known it long; though not so long as I might have done. Mary, my love, come here.'

As she trembled and was very pale, he sat her in his own chair, and stood beside it with her hand in his; and Martin standing by him.

'The curse of our house,' said the old man, looking kindly down upon her, 'has been the love of self; has ever been the love of self. How often have I said so, when I never knew that I had wrought it upon others!'

He drew one hand through Martin's arm, and standing so, between them, proceeded thus:

'You all know how I bred this orphan up, to tend me. None of you can know by what degrees I have come to regard her as a daughter; for she has won upon me, by her self-forgetfulness, her tenderness, her patience, all the goodness of her nature, when Heaven is her witness that I took but little pains to draw it forth. It blossomed without cultivation, and it ripened without heat. I cannot find it in my heart to say that I am sorry for it now, or yonder fellow might be holding up his head.'

Mr. Pecksniff put his hand into his waistcoat, and slightly shook that part of him to which allusion had been made: as if to signify that it was still uppermost.

'There is a kind of selfishness,' said Martin: 'I have learned it in my own experience of my own breast: which is constantly upon the watch for selfishness in others; and holding others at a distance by suspicions and distrusts, wonders why they don't approach, and don't confide, and calls that selfishness in them. Thus I once doubted those about me—not without reason in the beginning—and thus I once doubted you, Martin.'

'Not without reason,' Martin answered; 'either.'

'Listen, hypocrite! Listen, smooth-tongued, servile, crawling knave!' said Martin. 'Listen, you shallow dog. What! When I was seeking him, you had already spread your nets; you were already fishing for him, were ye? When I lay ill in this good woman's house, and your meek spirit pleaded for my grandson, you had already caught him, had ye? Counting on the restora-

tion of the love you knew I bore him, you designed him for one
of your two daughters, did ye? Or failing that, you traded in
him as a speculation which at any rate should blind me with
the lustre of your charity, and found a claim upon me! Why,
even then I knew you, and I told you so. Did I tell you that I
knew you, even then?'

'I am not angry, sir,' said Mr. Pecksniff, softly. 'I can bear
a great deal from you. I will never contradict you, Mr. Chuzzlewit.'

'Observe!' said Martin, looking round. 'I put myself in that
man's hands on terms as mean and base, and as degrading to
himself as I could render them in words. I stated them at
length to him, before his own children, syllable by syllable, as
coarsely as I could, and with as much offence, and with as
plain an exposition of my contempt, as words—not looks and
manner merely—could convey. If I had only called the angry
blood into his face, I would have wavered in my purpose. If I
had only stung him into being a man for a minute I would have
abandoned it. If he had offered me one word of remonstrance,
in favour of the grandson whom he supposed I had disinherited; if he had pleaded with me, though never so faintly,
against my appeal to him to abandon him to misery and cast
him from his house; I think I could have borne with him for
ever afterwards. But not a word, not a word. Pandering to the
worst of human passions was the office of his nature; and faithfully he did his work!'

'I am not angry,' observed Mr. Pecksniff. 'I am hurt, Mr.
Chuzzlewit: wounded in my feelings: but I am not angry, my
good sir.'

Mr. Chuzzlewit resumed.

'Once resolved to try him, I was resolute to pursue the trial
to the end; but while I was bent on fathoming the depth of his
duplicity, I made a sacred compact with myself that I would
give him credit on the other side for any latent spark of goodness, honour, forbearance—any virtue—that might glimmer
in him. From first to last there has been no such thing. Not
once. He cannot say I have not given him opportunity. He
cannot say I have ever led him on. He cannot say I have not
left him freely to himself in all things; or that I have not been
a passive instrument in his hands, which he might have used
for good as easily as evil. Or if he can, he Lies! And that's his
nature too.'

'Mr. Chuzzlewit,' interrupted Pecksniff, shedding tears. 'I am not angry, sir. I cannot be angry with you. But did you never, my dear sir, express a desire that the unnatural young man who by his wicked arts has estranged your good opinion from me, for the time being: only for the time being: that your grandson, Mr. Chuzzlewit, should be dismissed my house? Recollect yourself, my Christian friend.'

'I have said so, have I not?' retorted the old man, sternly. 'I could not tell how far your specious hypocrisy had deceived him, knave; and knew no better way of opening his eyes than by presenting you before him in your own servile character. Yes. I did express that desire. And you leaped to meet it; and you met it; and turning in an instant on the hand you had licked and beslavered, as only such hounds can, you strengthened, and confirmed, and justified me in my scheme.'

Mr. Pecksniff made a bow; a submissive, not to say a grovelling and an abject bow. If he had been complimented on his practice of the loftiest virtues, he never could have bowed as he bowed then.

'The wretched man who has been murdered,' Mr. Chuzzlewit went on to say; 'then passing by the name of——'

'Tigg,' suggested Mark.

'Of Tigg—brought begging messages to me on behalf of a friend of his, and an unworthy relative of mine; and finding him a man well enough suited to my purpose, I employed him to glean some news of you, Martin, for me. It was from him I learned that you had taken up your abode with yonder fellow. It was he, who meeting you here, in town, one evening —you remember where?'

'At the pawnbroker's shop,' said Martin.

'Yes; watched you to your lodging, and enabled me to send you a Bank note.'

'I little thought,' said Martin, greatly moved, 'that it had come from you. I little thought that you were interested in my fate. If I had——'

'If you had,' returned the old man, sorrowfully, 'you would have shown less knowledge of me as I seemed to be, and as I really was. I hoped to bring you back, Martin, penitent and humbled. I hoped to distress you into coming back to me. Much as I loved you, I had that to acknowledge which I could not reconcile it to myself to avow, then, unless you made submission to me first. Thus it was I lost you. If I have had, indirectly, any act or part in the fate of that unhappy man, by putting means, however small, within his reach; Heaven forgive me! I might have known, perhaps, that he would misuse money; that it was ill-bestowed upon him; and that sown by his hands it could engender mischief only. But I never thought of him at that time as having the disposition or ability to be a serious impostor, or otherwise than as a thoughtless, idle-humoured, dissipated spendthrift, sinning more against himself than others, and frequenting low haunts and indulging vicious tastes, to his own ruin only.'

'Beggin' your pardon, sir,' said Mr. Tapley, who had Mrs. Lupin on his arm by this time, quite agreeably: 'if I may make so bold as say so, my opinion is, as you was quite correct, and that he turned out perfectly nat'ral for all that. There's a surprisin' number of men, sir, who as long as they've only got their own shoes and stockings to depend upon, will walk down-hill, along the gutters quiet enough, and by themselves, and not do much harm. But set any on 'em up with a coach and horses, sir; and it's wonderful what a knowledge of drivin' he'll show, and how he'll fill his wehicle with passengers, and start off in the middle of the road, neck or nothing, to the Devil! Bless your heart, sir, there's ever so many Tiggs a-passin' this here Temple-gate any hour in the day, that only want a chance to turn out full-blown Montagues every one!'

'Your ignorance, as you call it, Mark,' said Mr. Chuzzlewit, 'is wiser than some men's enlightenment, and mine among them. You are right; not for the first time to-day. Now hear me out, my dears. And hear me, you, who, if what I have been told be accurately stated, are Bankrupt in pocket no less than in good name! And when you have heard me, leave this place, and poison my sight no more!'

Mr. Pecksniff laid his hand upon his breast, and bowed again.

'The penance I have done in his house,' said Mr. Chuzzle-wit, 'has carried this reflection with it constantly, above all others. That if it had pleased Heaven to visit such infirmity on my old age as really had reduced me to the state in which I feigned to be, I should have brought its misery upon myself. Oh you whose wealth, like mine, has been a source of continual unhappiness, leading you to distrust the nearest and dearest, and to dig yourself a living grave of suspicion and reserve; take heed that, having cast off all whom you might have bound to you, and tenderly, you do not become in your decay the instrument of such a man as this, and waken in another world to the knowledge of such wrong as would embitter Heaven itself, if wrong or you could ever reach it!'

And then he told them how he had sometimes thought, in the beginning, that love might grow up between Mary and Martin; and how he had pleased his fancy with the picture of observing it when it was new, and taking them to task, apart, in counterfeited doubt, and then confessing to them that it had been an object dear to his heart; and by his sympathy with them, and generous provision for their young fortunes, establishing a claim on their affection and regard which nothing should wither, and which should surround his old age with means of happiness. How in the first dawn of this design, and when the pleasure of such a scheme for the happiness of others was new and indistinct within him, Martin had come to tell him that he had already chosen for himself; knowing that he, the old man, had some faint project on that head, but ignorant whom it concerned. How it was little comfort to him to know that Martin had chosen Her, because the grace of his design was lost, and because finding that she had returned his love, he tortured himself with the reflection that they, so young, to whom he had been so kind a benefactor, were already like the world, and bent on their own selfish, stealthy ends. How in the bitterness of this impression, and of his past experience, he had reproached Martin so harshly (forgetting that he had never invited his confidence on such a point, and confounding what he had meant to do with what he had done), that high words sprung up between them, and they separated in wrath. How he loved him still, and hoped he would return. How on the night of his illness at the Dragon, he had secretly written tenderly of him, and made him his heir, and sanctioned his marriage with Mary; and how, after his interview with Mr. Pecksniff, he had distrusted him again, and burnt the paper to ashes, and had lain down in his bed distracted by suspicions, doubts, and regrets.

And then he told them how, resolved to probe this Pecksniff, and to prove the constancy and truth of Mary (to himself no less than Martin), he had conceived and entered on his plan; and how, beneath her gentleness and patience, he had softened more and more; still more and more beneath the goodness and simplicity, the honour and the manly faith of Tom. And when he spoke of Tom, he said God bless him; and the tears were in his eyes; for he said that Tom, mistrusted and disliked by him at first, had come like summer rain upon his heart; and had disposed it to believe in better things. And Martin took him by the hand, and Mary too, and John, his old friend, stoutly too: and Mark, and Mrs. Lupin, and his sister, little Ruth. And peace of mind, deep, tranquil peace of mind was on Tom Pinch.

The old man then related how nobly Mr. Pecksniff had performed the duty in which he stood indebted to society, in the matter of Tom's dismissal; and how, having often heard disparagement of Mr. Westlock from Pecksniffian lips, and knowing him to be a friend to Tom, he had used, through his confidential agent and solicitor, that little artifice which had kept him in readiness to receive his unknown friend in London. And he called on Mr. Pecksniff (by the name of Scoundrel) to remember that there again he had not trapped him to do evil, but that he had done it of his own free will and agency; nay, that he had cautioned him against it. And once again he called on Mr. Pecksniff (by the name of Hangdog) to remember that when Martin coming home at last, an altered man, had sued for the forgiveness which awaited him, he, Pecksniff, had rejected him in language of his own, and had remorselessly stepped in between him and the least touch of natural tenderness. 'For which,' said the old man, 'if the bending of my finger would remove a halter from your neck, I wouldn't bend it!'

'Martin,' he added, 'your rival has not been a dangerous one, but Mrs. Lupin here has played duenna for some weeks; not so much to watch your love as to watch her lover. For that Ghoul'—his fertility in finding names for Mr. Pecksniff was astonishing—'would have crawled into her daily walks otherwise, and polluted the fresh air. What's this? Her hand is trembling strangely. See if you can hold it.'

Hold it! If he clasped it half as tightly as he did her waist.——Well, well!

But it was good in him that even then, in his high fortune and happiness, with her lips nearly printed on his own, and her proud young beauty in his close embrace, he had a hand still left to stretch out to Tom Pinch.

'Oh, Tom! Dear Tom! I saw you, accidentally, coming here Forgive me!'

'Forgive!' cried Tom. 'I'll never forgive you as long as I live, Martin, if you say another syllable about it. Joy to you both! Joy, my dear fellow, fifty thousand times.'

Joy! There is not a blessing on earth that Tom did not wish them. There is not a blessing on earth that Tom would not have bestowed upon them, if he could.

'I beg your pardon, sir,' said Mr. Tapley, stepping forward, 'but you was mentionin', just now, a lady of the name of Lupin, sir.'

'I was,' returned old Martin.

'Yes, sir. It's a pretty name, sir?'

'A very good name,' said Martin.

'It seems a'most a pity to change such a name into Tapley. Don't it, sir?' said Mark.

'That depends upon the lady. What is *her* opinion?'

'Why, sir,' said Mr. Tapley, retiring, with a bow, towards the buxom hostess, 'her opinion is as the name ain't a change for the better, but the indiwidual may be, and therefore, if nobody ain't acquainted with no jest cause or impediment, et cetrer, the Blue Dragon will be con-werted into the Jolly Tapley. A sign of my own inwention, sir. Wery new, con-wivial, and expressive!'

The whole of these proceedings were so agreeable to Mr. Pecksniff, that he stood with his eyes fixed upon the floor and his hands clasping one another alternately, as if a host of penal sentences were being passed upon him. Not only did his figure appear to have shrunk, but his discomfiture seemed to have ex-tended itself even to his dress. His clothes seemed to have grown shabbier, his linen to have turned yellow, his hair to have become lank and frowsy; his very boots looked villanous and dim, as if their gloss had departed with his own.

Feeling, rather than seeing, that the old man now pointed to the door, he raised his eyes, picked up his hat, and thus addressed him:

'Mr. Chuzzlewit, sir! you have partaken of my hospitality.'

'And paid for it,' he observed.

'Thank you. That savours,' said Mr. Pecksniff, taking out his pocket-handkerchief, 'of your old familiar frankness. You have paid for it. I was about to make the remark. You have deceived me, sir. Thank you again. I am glad of it. To see you in the possession of your health and faculties on any terms, is, in itself, a sufficient recompense. To have been deceived implies a trusting nature. Mine is a trusting nature. I am thankful for it. I would rather have a trusting nature, do you know, sir, than a doubting one!'

Here Mr. Pecksniff, with a sad smile, bowed, and wiped his eyes.

'There is hardly any person present, Mr. Chuzzlewit,' said Pecksniff, 'by whom I have *not* been deceived. I have forgiven those persons on the spot. That was my duty; and, of course, I have done it. Whether it was worthy of you to partake of my hospitality, and to act the part you did act in my house, that, sir, is a question which I leave to your own conscience. And your conscience does not acquit you. No, sir, no!'

Pronouncing these last words in a loud and solemn voice, Mr. Pecksniff was not so absolutely lost in his own fervour as to be unmindful of the expediency of getting a little nearer to the door.

'I have been struck this day,' said Mr. Pecksniff, 'with a walking-stick (which I have every reason to believe has knobs upon it), on that delicate and exquisite portion of the human anatomy—the brain. Several blows have been inflicted, sir, without a walking-stick, upon that tenderer portion of my frame—my heart. You have mentioned, sir, my being bankrupt in my purse. Yes, sir, I am. By an unfortunate speculation, combined with treachery, I find myself reduced to poverty; at a time, sir, when the child of my bosom is widowed, and affliction and disgrace are in my family.'

Here Mr. Pecksniff wiped his eyes again, and gave himself two or three little knocks upon the breast, as if he were answering two or three other little knocks from within, given by the tinkling hammer of his conscience, to express 'Cheer up, my boy!'

'I know the human mind, although I trust it. That is my weakness. Do I not know, sir;' here he became exceedingly plaintive, and was observed to glance towards Tom Pinch; 'that my misfortunes bring this treatment on me? Do I not know, sir, that but for them I never should have heard what I have heard to-day? Do I not know that in the silence and the solitude of night, a little voice will whisper in your ear, Mr. Chuzzlewit, "This was not well. This was not well, sir!" Think of this, sir (if you will have the goodness), remote from the impulses of passion, and apart from the specialities, if I may use that strong remark, of prejudice. And if you ever contemplate the silent tomb, sir, which you will excuse me for entertaining some doubt of your doing, after the conduct into which you have allowed yourself to be betrayed this day; if you ever contemplate the silent tomb, sir, think of me. If you find yourself approaching to the silent tomb, sir, think of me. If you should wish to have anything inscribed upon your silent tomb, sir, let it be, that I—ah, my remorseful sir! that I—the humble individual who has now the honour of reproaching you, forgave you. That I forgave you when my injuries were fresh, and when my bosom was newly wrung. It may be bitterness to you to hear it now, sir, but you will live to seek a consolation in it. May you find a consolation in it when you want it, sir! Good morning!'

With this sublime address, Mr. Pecksniff departed. But the effect of his departure was much impaired by his being immediately afterwards run against, and nearly knocked down, by a monstrously-excited little man in velveteen shorts and a very tall hat; who came bursting up the stairs, and straight into the chambers of Mr. Chuzzlewit, as if he were deranged.

'Is there anybody here that knows him?' cried the little man. 'Is there anybody here that knows him? Oh, my stars, is there anybody here that knows him?'

They looked at each other for an explanation; but nobody knew anything more than that here was an excited little man with a very tall hat on, running in and out of the room as hard as he could go; making his single pair of bright blue stockings appear at least a dozen; and constantly repeating in a shrill voice, '*Is* there anybody here that knows him?'

'If your brains is not turned topjy turjey, Mr. Sweedlepipes!' exclaimed another voice, 'hold that there nige of yourn, I beg you, sir.'

At the same time Mrs. Gamp was seen in the doorway; out of breath from coming up so many stairs, and panting fearfully; but dropping curtseys to the last.

'Excuge the weakness of the man,' said Mrs. Gamp, eyeing Mr. Sweedlepipe with great indignation; 'and well I might expect it, as I should have know'd, and wishin' he was drownded in the Thames afore I had brought him here, which not a blessed hour ago he nearly shaved the noge off from the father of as lovely a family as ever, Mr. Chuzzlewit, was born three sets of twins, and would have done it, only he see it a-goin' in the glass, and dodged the rager. And never, Mr. Sweedlepipes, I do assure you, sir, did I so well know what a misfortun it was to be acquainted with you, as now I do, which so I say, sir, and I don't deceive you!'

'I ask your pardon, ladies and gentlemen all,' cried the little barber, taking off his hat, 'and yours too, Mrs. Gamp. But—but,' he added this half laughing and half crying, '*Is* there anybody here that knows him?'

As the barber said these words, a something in top-boots, with its head bandaged up, staggered into the room, and began going round and round and round, apparently under the impression that it was walking straight forward.

'Look at him!' cried the excited little barber. 'Here he is! That'll soon wear off, and then he'll be all right again. He's no more dead than I am. He's all alive and hearty. Ain't you, Bailey?'

'R—r—reether so, Poll!' replied that gentleman.

'Look here!' cried the little barber, laughing and crying in the same breath. 'When I steady him he comes all right. There! He's all right now. Nothing's the matter with him now, except that he's a little shook and rather giddy; is there, Bailey?'

'R—r—reether shook, Poll—reether so!' said Mr. Bailey. 'What, my lovely Sairey! There you air!'

'What a boy he is!' cried the tender-hearted Poll, actually sobbing over him. 'I never see sech a boy! It's all his fun. He's full of it. He shall go into the business along with me. I am determined he shall. We'll make it Sweedlepipe and Bailey. He shall have the sporting branch (what a one he'll be for the matches!) and me the shavin'. I'll make over the birds to him as soon as ever he's well enough. He shall have the little bullfinch in the shop, and all. He's sech a boy! I ask your pardon, ladies and gentlemen, but I thought there might be some one here that know'd him!'

Mrs. Gamp had observed, not without jealousy and scorn, that a favourable impression appeared to exist in behalf of Mr. Sweedlepipe and his young friend; and that she had fallen rather into the background in consequence. She now struggled to the front, therefore, and stated her business.

'Which, Mr. Chuzzlewit,' she said, 'is well beknown to Mrs. Harris as has one sweet infant (though she *do* not wish it known) in her own family by the mother's side, kep in spirits in a bottle; and that sweet babe she see at Greenwich Fair, a-travelling in company with the pink-eyed lady, Prooshan dwarf, and livin' skelinton, which judge her feelins when the barrel organ played, and she was showed her own dear sister's child, the same not bein' expected from the outside picter, where it was painted quite contrairy in a livin' state, a many sizes larger, and performing beautiful upon the Arp, which never did that dear child know or do: since breathe it never did, to speak on, in this wale! And Mrs. Harris, Mr. Chuzzlewit, has knowed me many year, and can give you information that the lady which is widdered can't do better and may do worse, than let me wait upon her, which I hope to do. Permittin' the sweet faces as I see afore me.'

'Oh!' said Mr. Chuzzlewit. 'Is that your business? Was this good person paid for the trouble we gave her?'

'I paid her, sir,' returned Mark Tapley; 'liberal.'

'The young man's words is true,' said Mrs. Gamp, 'and thank you kindly.'

'Then here we will close our acquaintance, Mrs. Gamp,' retorted Mr. Chuzzlewit. 'And Mr. Sweedlepipe—is that your name?'

'That is my name, sir,' replied Poll, accepting with a profusion of gratitude, some chinking pieces which the old man slipped into his hand.

'Mr. Sweedlepipe, take as much care of your lady-lodger as you can, and give her a word or two of good advice now and then. Such,' said old Martin, looking gravely at the astonished Mrs. Gamp, 'as hinting at the expediency of a little less liquor, and a little more humanity, and a little less regard for herself, and a little more regard for her patients, and perhaps a trifle of additional honesty. Or when Mrs. Gamp gets into trouble, Mr. Sweedlepipe, it had better not be at a time when I am near enough to the Old Bailey to volunteer myself as a witness to her character. Endeavour to impress that upon her at your leisure, if you please.'

Mrs. Gamp clasped her hands, turned up her eyes until they were quite invisible, threw back her bonnet for the admission of fresh air to her heated brow; and in the act of saying faintly —'Less liquor!—Sairey Gamp—Bottle on the chimney-piece, and let me put my lips to it, when I am so dispoged!'—fell into one of the walking swoons; in which pitiable state she was conducted forth by Mr. Sweedlepipe, who, between his two patients, the swooning Mrs. Gamp and the revolving Bailey, had enough to do, poor fellow.

The old man looked about him, with a smile, until his eyes rested on Tom Pinch's sister; when he smiled the more.

'We will all dine here together,' he said; 'and as you and Mary have enough to talk of, Martin, you shall keep house for us until the afternoon, with Mr. and Mrs. Tapley. I must see your lodgings in the meanwhile, Tom.'

Tom was quite delighted. So was Ruth. She would go with them.

'Thank you, my love,' said Mr. Chuzzlewit. 'But I am afraid I must take Tom a little out of the way, on business. Suppose you go on first, my dear?'

Pretty little Ruth was equally delighted to do that.

'But not alone,' said Martin, 'not alone. Mr. Westlock, I dare say, will escort you.'

Why, of course he would: what else had Mr. Westlock in his mind? How dull these old men are!

'You are sure you have no engagement?' he persisted.

Engagement! As if he could have any engagement!

So they went off arm-in-arm. When Tom and Mr. Chuzzlewit went off arm-in-arm a few minutes after them, the latter was still smiling: and really, for a gentleman of his habits, in rather a knowing manner.

CHAPTER LIII

What John Westlock said to Tom Pinch's sister; what Tom Pinch's sister said to John Westlock; what Tom Pinch said to both of them; and how they all passed the remainder of the day

BRILLIANTLY the Temple Fountain sparkled in the sun, and laughingly its liquid music played, and merrily the idle drops of water danced and danced, and peeping out in sport among the trees, plunged lightly down to hide themselves, as little Ruth and her companion came towards it.

And why they came towards the Fountain at all is a mystery; for they had no business there. It was not in their way. It was quite out of their way. They had no more to do with the Fountain, bless you, than they had with—with Love, or any out-of-the-way thing of that sort.

It was all very well for Tom and his sister to make appointments by the Fountain, but that was quite another affair. Because, of course, when she had to wait a minute or two, it would have been very awkward for her to have had to wait in any but a tolerably quiet spot; but that was as quiet a spot, everything considered, as they could choose. But when she had John Westlock to take care of her, and was going home with her arm in his (home being in a different direction altogether), their coming anywhere near that Fountain was quite extraordinary.

However, there they found themselves. And another extraordinary part of the matter was, that they seemed to have come there, by a silent understanding. Yet when they got there, they were a little confused by being there, which was the strangest part of all; because there is nothing naturally confusing in a Fountain. We all know that.

What a good old place it was! John said. With quite an earnest affection for it.

'A pleasant place indeed,' said little Ruth. 'So shady!'

Oh wicked little Ruth!

They came to a stop when John began to praise it. The day was exquisite; and stopping at all, it was quite natural— nothing could be more so—that they should glance down Garden Court; because Garden Court ends in the Garden, and the Garden ends in the River, and that glimpse is very bright and fresh and shining on a summer's day. Then, oh little Ruth, why not look boldly at it! Why fit that tiny precious, blessed little foot into the cracked corner of an insensible old flagstone in the pavement; and be so very anxious to adjust it to a nicety!

If the Fiery-faced matron in the crunched bonnet could have seen them as they walked away, how many years' purchase might Fiery Face have been disposed to take for her situation in Furnival's Inn as laundress to Mr. Westlock!

They went away, but not through London's streets! Through some enchanted city, where the pavements were of air; where all the rough sounds of a stirring town were softened into gentle music; where everything was happy; where there was no distance, and no time. There were two good-tempered burly draymen letting down big butts of beer into a cellar, somewhere; and when John helped her—almost lifted her—the lightest, easiest, neatest thing you ever saw—across the rope, they said he owed them a good turn for giving him the chance. Celestial draymen!

Green pastures in the summer tide, deep-littered strawyards in the winter, no stint of corn and clover, ever, to that noble horse who *would* dance on the pavement with a gig behind him, and who frightened her, and made her clasp his arm with both hands (both hands: meeting one upon the other so endearingly!), and caused her to implore him to take refuge in the pastry-cook's; and afterwards to peep out at the door so shrinkingly; and then: looking at him with those eyes: to ask him was he sure—now was he sure—they might go safely on! Oh for a string of rampant horses! For a lion, for a bear, for a mad bull, for anything to bring the little hands together on his arm, again!

They talked, of course. They talked of Tom, and all these changes, and the attachment Mr. Chuzzlewit had conceived for him, and the bright prospects he had in such a friend, and a great deal more to the same purpose. The more they talked, the more afraid this fluttering little Ruth became of any pause; and sooner than have a pause she would say the same things over again; and if she hadn't courage or presence of mind enough for that (to say the truth she very seldom had), she was ten thousand times more charming and irresistible than she had been before.

'Martin will be married very soon now, I suppose?' said John.

She supposed he would. Never did a bewitching little woman suppose anything in such a faint voice as Ruth supposed that.

But seeing that another of those alarming pauses was approaching, she remarked that he would have a beautiful wife. Didn't Mr. Westlock think so?

'Ye—yes,' said John; 'oh, yes.'

She feared he was rather hard to please—he spoke so coldly.

'Rather say already pleased,' said John. 'I have scarcely seen her. I had no care to see her. I had no eyes for *her*, this morning.'

Oh, good gracious!

It was well they had reached their destination. She never could have gone any further. It would have been impossible to walk in such a tremble.

Tom had not come in. They entered the triangular parlour together, and alone. Fiery Face, Fiery Face, how many years' purchase *now!*

She sat down on the little sofa, and untied her bonnet-strings. He sat down by her side, and very near her: very, very near her. Oh, rapid, swelling, bursting little heart, you knew that it would come to this, and hoped it would. Why beat so wildly, heart!

'Dear Ruth! Sweet Ruth! If I had loved you less, I could have told you that I loved you, long ago. I have loved you from the first. There never was a creature in the world more truly loved than you, dear Ruth, by me!'

She clasped her little hands before her face. The gushing tears of joy, and pride, and hope, and innocent affection, would not be restrained. Fresh from her full young heart they came to answer him.

'My dear love! If this is—I almost dare to hope it is, now— not painful or distressing to you, you make me happier than I can tell, or you imagine. Darling Ruth! My own good, gentle, winning Ruth! I hope I know the value of your heart, I hope I know the worth of your angel nature. Let me try and show you that I do; and you will make me happier, Ruth——'

'Not happier,' she sobbed, 'than you make me. No one can be happier, John, than you make me!'

Fiery Face, provide yourself! The usual wages or the usual

warning. It's all over, Fiery Face. We needn't trouble you
any further.

The little hands could meet each other now, without a
rampant horse to urge them. There was no occasion for lions,
bears, or mad bulls. It could all be done, and infinitely better,
without their assistance. No burly drayman or big butts of
beer, were wanted for apologies. No apology at all was wanted.
The soft light touch fell coyly, but quite naturally, upon the
lover's shoulder; the delicate waist, the drooping head, the
blushing cheek, the beautiful eyes, the exquisite mouth itself,
were all as natural as possible. If all the horses in Araby had
run away at once, they couldn't have improved upon it.

They soon began to talk of Tom again.

'I hope he will be glad to hear of it!' said John, with sparkling eyes.

Ruth drew the little hands a little tighter when he said it,
and looked up seriously into his face.

'I am never to leave him, *am* I, dear? I could never leave
Tom. I am sure you know that.'

'Do you think I would ask you?' he returned, with a—well!
Never mind with what.

'I am sure you never would,' she answered, the bright tears
standing in her eyes.

'And I will swear it, Ruth, my darling, if you please. Leave
Tom! That would be a strange beginning. Leave Tom, dear!
If Tom and we be not inseparable, and Tom (God bless him)
have not all honour and all love in our home, my little wife,
may that home never be! And that's a strong oath, Ruth.'

Shall it be recorded how she thanked him? Yes, it shall. In
all simplicity and innocence and purity of heart, yet with a
timid, graceful, half-determined hesitation, she set a little rosy
seal upon the vow, whose colour was reflected in her face, and
flashed up to the braiding of her dark brown hair.

'Tom will be so happy, and so proud, and glad,' she said,
clasping her little hands. 'But so surprised! I am sure he had
never thought of such a thing.'

Of course John asked her immediately—because you know
they were in that foolish state when great allowances must be
made—when *she* had begun to think of such a thing, and this
made a little diversion in their talk; a charming diversion to
them, but not so interesting to us; at the end of which, they
came back to Tom again.

'Ah! dear Tom!' said Ruth. 'I suppose I ought to tell you everything now. I should have no secrets from you. Should I, John, love?'

It is of no use saying how that preposterous John answered her, because he answered in a manner which is untranslatable on paper, though highly satisfactory in itself. But what he conveyed was, No no no, sweet Ruth; or something to that effect.

Then she told him Tom's great secret; not exactly saying how she had found it out, but leaving him to understand it if he liked; and John was sadly grieved to hear it, and was full of sympathy and sorrow. But they would try, he said, only the more, on this account, to make him happy, and to beguile him with his favourite pursuits. And then, in all the confidence of such a time, he told her how he had a capital opportunity of establishing himself in his old profession in the country; and how he had been thinking, in the event of that happiness coming upon him which had actually come—there was another slight diversion here—how he had been thinking that it would afford occupation to Tom, and enable them to live together in the easiest manner, without any sense of dependence on Tom's part; and to be as happy as the day was long. And Ruth receiving this with joy, they went on catering for Tom to that extent that they had already purchased him a select library and built him an organ, on which he was performing with the greatest satisfaction: when they heard him knocking at the door.

Though she longed to tell him what had happened, poor little Ruth was greatly agitated by his arrival; the more so because she knew that Mr. Chuzzlewit was with him. So she said, all in a tremble:

'What shall I do, dear John! I can't bear that he should hear it from any one but me, and I could not tell him, unless we were alone.'

'Do, my love,' said John, 'whatever is natural to you on the impulse of the moment, and I am sure it will be right.'

He had hardly time to say thus much, and Ruth had hardly time to—just to get a little farther off upon the sofa, when Tom and Mr. Chuzzlewit came in. Mr. Chuzzlewit came first, and Tom was a few seconds behind him.

Now Ruth had hastily resolved that she would beckon Tom up-stairs after a short time, and would tell him in his little bedroom. But when she saw his dear old face come in, her heart was so touched that she ran into his arms, and laid her head down on his breast, and sobbed out, 'Bless me, Tom! My dearest brother!'

Tom looked up, in surprise, and saw John Westlock close beside him, holding out his hand.

'John!' cried Tom. 'John!'

'Dear Tom,' said his friend, 'give me your hand. We are brothers, Tom.'

Tom wrung it with all his force, embraced his sister fervently, and put her in John Westlock's arms.

'Don't speak to me, John. Heaven is very good to us. I——' Tom could find no further utterance, but left the room; and Ruth went after him.

And when they came back, which they did by-and-bye, she looked more beautiful, and Tom more good and true (if that were possible) than ever. And though Tom could not speak upon the subject even now; being yet too newly glad: he put both his hands in both of John's with emphasis sufficient for the best speech ever spoken.

'I am glad you chose to-day,' said Mr. Chuzzlewit to John; with the same knowing smile as when they had left him. 'I thought you would. I hoped Tom and I lingered behind a discreet time. It's so long since I had any practical knowledge of these subjects, that I have been anxious, I assure you.'

'Your knowledge is still pretty accurate, sir,' returned John, laughing, 'if it led you to foresee what would happen to-day.'

'Why, I am not sure, Mr. Westlock,' said the old man, 'that any great spirit of prophecy was needed, after seeing you and Ruth together. Come hither, pretty one. See what Tom and I purchased this morning, while you were dealing in exchange with that young merchant there.'

The old man's way of seating her beside him, and humouring his voice as if she were a child, was whimsical enough, but full of tenderness, and not ill adapted, somehow, to little Ruth.

'See here!' he said, taking a case from his pocket, 'what a beautiful necklace. Ah! How it glitters! Earrings, too, and bracelets, and a zone for your waist. This set is yours, and Mary has another like it. Tom couldn't understand why I wanted two. What a short-sighted Tom! Earrings and bracelets, and a zone for your waist! Ah! beautiful! Let us see how brave they look. Ask Mr. Westlock to clasp them on.'

It was the prettiest thing to see her holding out her round, white arm; and John (oh deep, deep John!) pretending that the bracelet was very hard to fasten; it was the prettiest thing to see her girding on the precious little zone, and yet obliged to have assistance because her fingers were in such terrible perplexity; it was the prettiest thing to see her so confused and bashful, with the smiles and blushes playing brightly on her face, like the sparkling light upon the jewels; it was the prettiest thing that you would see, in the common experiences of a twelvemonth, rely upon it.

'The set of jewels and the wearer are so well matched,' said the old man, 'that I don't know which becomes the other most. Mr. Westlock could tell me, I have no doubt, but I'll not ask him, for he is bribed. Health to wear them, my dear, and happiness to make you forgetful of them, except as a remembrance from a loving friend!'

He patted her upon the cheek, and said to Tom:

'I must play the part of a father here, Tom, also. There are not many fathers who marry two such daughters on the same day: but we will overlook the improbability for the gratification of an old man's fancy. I may claim that much indulgence,' he added, 'for I have gratified few fancies enough in my life tending to the happiness of others, Heaven knows!'

These various proceedings had occupied so much time, and they fell into such a pleasant conversation now, that it was within a quarter of an hour of the time appointed for dinner before any of them thought about it. A hackney-coach soon carried them to the Temple, however; and there they found everything prepared for their reception.

Mr. Tapley having been furnished with unlimited credentials relative to the ordering of dinner, had so exerted himself for the honour of the party, that a prodigious banquet was served, under the joint direction of himself and his Intended. Mr. Chuzzlewit would have had them of the party, and Martin urgently seconded his wish, but Mark could by no means be persuaded to sit down at table; observing, that in having the honour of attending to their comforts, he felt himself, indeed, the landlord of the Jolly Tapley, and could almost delude himself into the belief that the entertainment was actually being held under the Jolly Tapley's roof.

For the better encouragement of himself in this fable, Mr. Tapley took it upon him to issue divers general directions to the waiters from the hotel, relative to the disposal of the dishes and so forth; and as they were usually in direct opposition to all precedent, and were always issued in his most facetious form of thought and speech, they occasioned great merriment among those attendants; in which Mr. Tapley participated, with an infinite enjoyment of his own humour. He likewise entertained them with short anecdotes of his travels, appropriate to the occasion; and now and then with some comic passage or other between himself and Mrs. Lupin; so that explosive laughs were constantly issuing from the side-board, and from the backs of chairs; and the head-waiter (who wore powder, and knee-smalls, and was usually a grave man) got to be a bright scarlet in the face, and broke his waistcoat-strings audibly.

Young Martin sat at the head of the table, and Tom Pinch at the foot; and if there were a genial face at that board, it was Tom's. They all took their tone from Tom. Everybody drank to him, everybody looked to him, everybody thought of him, everybody loved him. If he so much as laid down his knife and fork, somebody put out a hand to shake with him. Martin and Mary had taken him aside before dinner, and spoken to him so heartily of the time to come: laying such fervent stress upon the trust they had in his completion of their felicity, by his society and closest friendship: that Tom was positively moved to tears. He couldn't bear it. His heart was full, he said, of happiness. And so it was. Tom spoke the honest truth. It was. Large as thy heart was, dear Tom Pinch, it had no room that day for anything but happiness and sympathy!

And there was Fips, old Fips of Austin Friars, present at the dinner, and turning out to be the jolliest old dog that ever did violence to his convivial sentiments by shutting himself up in a dark office. 'Where is he?' said Fips, when he came in. And then he pounced on Tom, and told him that he wanted to relieve himself of all his old constraint: and in the first place shook him by one hand, and in the second place shook him by the other, and in the third place nudged him in the waistcoat, and in the fourth place said, 'How *are* you?' and in a great many other places did a great many other things to show his friendliness and joy. And he sang songs, did Fips; and made speeches, did Fips; and knocked off his wine pretty hand-somely, did Fips; and in short, he showed himself a perfect Trump, did Fips, in all respects.

But ah! the happiness of strolling home at night—obstinate little Ruth, she wouldn't hear of riding!—as they had done on that dear night, from Furnival's Inn! The happiness of being able to talk about it, and to confide their happiness to each other! The happiness of stating all their little plans to Tom, and seeing his bright face grow brighter as they spoke!

When they reached home, Tom left John and his sister in the parlour, and went up-stairs into his own room, under pretence of seeking a book. And Tom actually winked to himself when he got up-stairs: he thought it such a deep thing to have done.

'They like to be by themselves, of course,' said Tom; 'and I came away so naturally, that I have no doubt they are expecting me, every moment, to return. That's capital!'

But he had not sat reading very long, when he heard a tap at his door.

'May I come in?' said John.

'Oh, surely!' Tom replied.

'Don't leave us, Tom. Don't sit by yourself. We want to make you merry; not melancholy.'

'My dear friend,' said Tom, with a cheerful smile.

'Brother, Tom. Brother.'

'My dear brother,' said Tom; 'there is no danger of my being melancholy, how can I be melancholy, when I know that you and Ruth are so blest in each other! I think I can find my tongue to-night, John,' he added, after a moment's pause. 'But I never can tell you what unutterable joy this day has given me. It would be unjust to you to speak of your having chosen a portionless girl, for I feel that you know her worth; I am sure you know her worth. Nor will it diminish in your estimation, John, which money might.'

'Which money would, Tom,' he returned. 'Her worth! Oh, who could see her here, and not love her! Who could know her, Tom, and not honour her! Who could ever stand possessed of such a heart as hers, and grow indifferent to the treasure! Who could feel the rapture that I feel to-day, and love as I love her, Tom, without knowing something of her worth! Your joy unutterable! No, no, Tom. It's mine, it's mine.'

'No, no, John,' said Tom. 'It's mine, it's mine.'

Their friendly contention was brought to a close by little Ruth herself, who came peeping in at the door. And oh, the look, the glorious, half-proud, half-timid look she gave Tom, when her lover drew her to his side! As much as to say, 'Yes, indeed, Tom, he will do it. But then he has a right, you know. Because I *am* fond of him, Tom.'

As to Tom, he was perfectly delighted. He could have sat and looked at them, just as they were, for hours.

'I have told Tom, love, as we agreed, that we are not going to permit him to run away, and that we cannot possibly allow it. The loss of one person, and such a person as Tom, too, out of our small household of three, is not to be endured; and so I have told him. Whether he is considerate, or whether he is only selfish, I don't know. But he needn't be considerate, for he is not the least restraint upon us. Is he, dearest Ruth?'

Well! He really did not seem to be any particular restraint upon them. Judging from what ensued.

Was it folly in Tom to be so pleased by their remembrance of him at such a time? Was their graceful love a folly, were their dear caresses follies, was their lengthened parting folly? Was it folly in him to watch her window from the street, and rate its scantiest gleam of light above all diamonds; folly in her to breathe his name upon her knees, and pour out her pure heart before that Being, from whom such hearts and such affections come?

If these be follies, then Fiery Face go on and prosper! If they be not, then Fiery Face avaunt! But set the crunched bonnet at some other single gentleman, in any case, for one is lost to thee for ever!

CHAPTER LIV

Gives the author great concern. For it is the last in the book

TODGERS'S was in high feather, and mighty preparations for a late breakfast were astir in its commercial bowers. The blissful morning had arrived when Miss Pecksniff was to be united in holy matrimony to Augustus.

Miss Pecksniff was in a frame of mind equally becoming to herself and the occasion. She was full of clemency and conciliation. She had laid in several chaldrons of live coals, and was prepared to heap them on the heads of her enemies. She bore no spite nor malice in her heart. Not the least.

Quarrels, Miss Pecksniff said, were dreadful things in families; and though she never could forgive her dear papa, she was willing to receive her other relations. They had been separated, she observed, too long. It was enough to call down a judgment upon the family. She believed the death of Jonas *was* a judgment on them for their internal dissensions. And Miss Pecksniff was confirmed in this belief, by the lightness with which the visitation had fallen on herself.

By way of doing sacrifice—not in triumph; not, of course, in triumph, but in humiliation of spirit—this amiable young person wrote, therefore, to her kinswoman of the strong mind, and informed her that her nuptials would take place on such a day. That she had been much hurt by the unnatural conduct of herself and daughters, and hoped they might not have suffered in their consciences. That being desirous to forgive her enemies, and make her peace with the world before entering into the most solemn of covenants with the most devoted of men, she now held out the hand of friendship. That if the strong-minded woman took that hand, in the temper in which it was extended to her, she, Miss Pecksniff, did invite her to be present at the ceremony of her marriage, and did furthermore invite the three red-nosed spinsters, her daughters (but Miss Pecksniff did not particularise their noses), to attend as bridesmaids.

The strong-minded woman returned for answer, that herself and daughters were, as regarded their consciences, in the enjoyment of robust health, which she knew Miss Pecksniff would be glad to hear. That she had received Miss Pecksniff's note with unalloyed delight, because she never had attached the least importance to the paltry and insignificant jealousies with which herself and circle had been assailed; otherwise than as she found them, in the contemplation, a harmless source of innocent mirth. That she would joyfully attend Miss Pecksniff's bridal; and that her three dear daughters would be happy to assist on so interesting, and *so very unexpected*—which the strong-minded woman underlined—*so very unexpected* an occasion.

On the receipt of this gracious reply, Miss Pecksniff extended her forgiveness and her invitations to Mr. and Mrs. Spottletoe; to Mr. George Chuzzlewit the bachelor cousin; to the solitary female who usually had the tooth-ache; and to the hairy young gentleman with the outline of a face; surviving remnants of the party that had once assembled in Mr. Pecksniff's parlour. After which Miss Pecksniff remarked, that there was a sweetness in doing our duty, which neutralised the bitter in our cups.

The wedding guests had not yet assembled, and indeed it was so early that Miss Pecksniff herself was in the act of dressing at her leisure, when a carriage stopped near the Monument; and Mark, dismounting from the rumble, assisted Mr. Chuzzlewit to alight. The carriage remained in waiting; so did Mr. Tapley. Mr. Chuzzlewit betook himself to Todgers's.

He was shown, by the degenerate successor of Mr. Bailey, into the dining-parlour; where—for his visit was expected—Mrs. Todgers immediately appeared.

'You are dressed, I see, for the wedding,' he said.

Mrs. Todgers, who was greatly flurried by the preparations, replied in the affirmative.

'It goes against my wishes to have it in progress just now, I assure you, sir,' said Mrs. Todgers; 'but Miss Pecksniff's mind was set upon it, and it really is time that Miss Pecksniff was married. That cannot be denied, sir.'

'No,' said Mr. Chuzzlewit, 'assuredly not. Her sister takes no part in the proceedings?'

'Oh dear, no, sir. Poor thing!' said Mrs. Todgers, shaking her head, and dropping her voice. 'Since she has known the worst, she has never left my room; the next room.'

'Is she prepared to see me?' he inquired.

'Quite prepared, sir.'

'Then let us lose no time.'

Mrs. Todgers conducted him into the little back chamber commanding the prospect of the cistern; and there, sadly different from when it had first been her lodging, sat poor Merry, in mourning weeds. The room looked very dark and sorrowful; and so did she; but she had one friend beside her, faithful to the last. Old Chuffey.

When Mr. Chuzzlewit sat down at her side, she took his hand and put it to her lips. She was in great grief. He too was agitated; for he had not seen her since their parting in the churchyard.

'I judged you hastily,' he said, in a low voice. 'I fear I judged you cruelly. Let me know that I have your forgiveness.'

She kissed his hand again; and retaining it in hers, thanked him, in a broken voice, for all his kindness to her since.

'Tom Pinch,' said Martin, 'has faithfully related to me all that you desired him to convey; at a time when he deemed it very improbable that he would ever have an opportunity of delivering your message. Believe me, that if I ever deal again with an ill-advised and unawakened nature, hiding the strength it thinks its weakness, I will have long and merciful consideration for it.'

'You had for me; even for me,' she answered. 'I quite believe it. I said the words you have repeated, when my distress was very sharp and hard to bear; I say them now for others; but I cannot urge them for myself. You spoke to me after you had seen and watched me day by day. There was great consideration in that. You might have spoken, perhaps, more kindly; you might have tried to invite my confidence by greater gentleness; but the end would have been the same.'

He shook his head in doubt, and not without some inward self-reproach.

'How can I hope,' she said, 'that your interposition would have prevailed with me, when I know how obdurate I was! I never thought at all; dear Mr. Chuzzlewit, I never thought at all; I had no thought, no heart, no care to find one; at that time. It has grown out of my trouble. I have felt it in my trouble. I wouldn't recall my trouble, such as it is and has been—and it is light in comparison with trials which hundreds of good people suffer every day, I know—I wouldn't recall it to-morrow, if I could. It has been my friend, for without it no one could have changed me; nothing could have changed me.

Do not mistrust me because of these tears; I cannot help them. I am grateful for it, in my soul. Indeed I am!'

'Indeed she is!' said Mrs. Todgers. 'I believe it, sir.'

'And so do I!' said Mr. Chuzzlewit. 'Now, attend to me, my dear. Your late husband's estate, if not wasted by the confession of a large debt to the broken office (which document, being useless to the runaways, has been sent over to England by them: not so much for the sake of the creditors as for the gratification of their dislike to him, whom they suppose to be still living), will be seized upon by law; for it is not exempt, as I learn, from the claims of those who have suffered by the fraud in which he was engaged. Your father's property was all, or nearly all, embarked in the same transaction. If there be any left, it will be seized on in like manner. There is no home *there*.'

'I couldn't return to him,' she said, with an instinctive reference to his having forced her marriage on. 'I could not return to him!'

'I know it,' Mr. Chuzzlewit resumed; 'and I am here because I know it. Come with me! From all who are about me, you are certain (I have ascertained it) of a generous welcome. But until your health is re-established, and you are sufficiently composed to bear that welcome, you shall have your abode in any quiet retreat of your own choosing, near London; not so far removed but that this kind-hearted lady may still visit you as often as she pleases. You have suffered much; but you are young, and have a brighter and a better future stretching out before you. Come with me. Your sister is careless of you, I know. She hurries on and publishes her marriage, in a spirit which (to say no more of it) is barely decent, is unsisterly, and bad. Leave the house before her guests arrive. She means to give you pain. Spare her the offence, and come with me!'

Mrs. Todgers, though most unwilling to part with her, added her persuasions. Even poor old Chuffey (of course included in the project) added his. She hurriedly attired herself, and was ready to depart, when Miss Pecksniff dashed into the room.

Miss Pecksniff dashed in so suddenly, that she was placed in an embarrassing position. For though she had completed her bridal toilette as to her head, on which she wore a bridal bonnet with orange flowers, she had not completed it as to her skirts, which displayed no choicer decoration than a dimity bedgown. She had dashed in, in fact, about half-way through,

to console her sister in her affliction with a sight of the aforesaid bonnet: and being quite unconscious of the presence of a
visitor, until she found Mr. Chuzzlewit standing face to face
with her, her surprise was an uncomfortable one.

'So, young lady!' said the old man, eyeing her with strong
disfavour. 'You are to be married to-day!'

'Yes, sir,' returned Miss Pecksniff, modestly. 'I am. I—my
dress is rather—really, Mrs. Todgers!'

'Your delicacy,' said old Martin, 'is troubled, I perceive.
I am not surprised to find it so. You have chosen the period of
your marriage unfortunately.'

'I beg your pardon, Mr. Chuzzlewit,' retorted Cherry; very
red and angry in a moment: 'but if you have anything to say
on that subject, I must beg to refer you to Augustus. You will
scarcely think it manly, I hope, to force an argument on me,
when Augustus is at all times ready to discuss it with you. I
have nothing to do with any deceptions that may have been
practised on my parent,' said Miss Pecksniff, pointedly; 'and
as I wish to be on good terms with everybody at such a time,
I should have been glad if you would have favoured us with
your company at breakfast. But I will not ask you as it is:
seeing that you have been prepossessed and set against me in
another quarter. I hope I have my natural affections for
another quarter, and my natural pity for another quarter; but
I cannot always submit to be subservient to it, Mr. Chuzzlewit.
That would be a little too much. I trust I have more respect
for myself, as well as for the man who claims me as his Bride.'

'Your sister, meeting—as I think: not as she says, for she
has said nothing about it—with little consideration from you,
is going away with me,' said Mr. Chuzzlewit.

'I am very happy to find that she has some good fortune at
last,' returned Miss Pecksniff, tossing her head. 'I congratulate
her, I am sure. I am not surprised that this event should be
painful to her—painful to her—but I can't help that, Mr.
Chuzzlewit. It's not my fault.'

'Come, Miss Pecksniff!' said the old man, quietly. 'I should
like to see a better parting between you. I should like to see
a better parting on your side, in such circumstances. It would
make me your friend. You may want a friend one day or other.'

'Every relation of life, Mr. Chuzzlewit, begging your pardon:
and every friend in life:' returned Miss Pecksniff, with dignity,
'is now bound up and cemented in Augustus. So long as

Augustus is my own, I cannot want a friend. When you speak
of friends, sir, I must beg, once for all, to refer you to Augustus.
That is my impression of the religious ceremony in which I am
so soon to take a part at that altar to which Augustus will conduct me. I bear no malice at any time, much less in a moment
of triumph, towards any one; much less towards my sister. On
the contrary, I congratulate her. If you didn't hear me say so,
I am not to blame. And as I owe it to Augustus, to be punctual
on an occasion when he may naturally be supposed to be—
to be impatient—really, Mrs. Todgers!—I must beg your
leave, sir, to retire.'

After these words the bridal bonnet disappeared; with as
much state as the dimity bedgown left in it.

Old Martin gave his arm to the younger sister without
speaking; and led her out. Mrs. Todgers, with her holiday
garments fluttering in the wind, accompanied them to the
carriage, clung round Merry's neck at parting, and ran back
to her own dingy house, crying the whole way. She had a lean
lank body, Mrs. Todgers, but a well-conditioned soul within.
Perhaps the Good Samaritan was lean and lank, and found it
hard to live. Who knows!

Mr. Chuzzlewit followed her so closely with his eyes, that,
until she had shut her own door, they did not encounter
Mr. Tapley's face.

'Why, Mark!' he said, as soon as he observed it, 'what's the
matter?'

'The wonderfullest ewent, sir!' returned Mark, pumping at
his voice in a most laborious manner, and hardly able to
articulate with all his efforts. 'A coincidence as never was
equalled! I'm blessed if here ain't two old neighbours of ourn,
sir!'

'What neighbours?' cried old Martin, looking out of window.
'Where?'

'I was a-walkin' up and down not five yards from this spot,'
said Mr. Tapley, breathless, 'and they come upon me like their
own ghosts, as I thought they was! It's the wonderfullest
ewent that ever happened. Bring a feather, somebody, and
knock me down with it!'

'What do you mean!' exclaimed old Martin, quite as much
excited by the spectacle of Mark's excitement as that strange
person was himself. 'Neighbours, where?'

'Here, sir!' replied Mr. Tapley. 'Here in the city of London!

Here upon these very stones! Here they are, sir! Don't I know
'em? Lord love their welcome faces, don't I know 'em!'

With which ejaculations Mr. Tapley not only pointed to a
decent-looking man and woman standing by, but commenced
embracing them alternately, over and over again, in Monument Yard.

'Neighbours, WHERE?' old Martin shouted: almost maddened by his ineffectual efforts to get out at the coach-door.

'Neighbours in America! Neighbours in Eden!' cried Mark.
'Neighbours in the swamp, neighbours in the bush, neighbours
in the fever. Didn't she nurse us! Didn't he help us! Shouldn't
we both have died without 'em! Hav'n't they come a-strugglin'
back, without a single child for their consolation! And talk to
me of neighbours!'

Away he went again, in a perfectly wild state, hugging them,
and skipping round them, and cutting in between them, as if
he were performing some frantic and outlandish dance.

Mr. Chuzzlewit no sooner gathered who these people were,
than he burst open the coach-door somehow or other, and
came tumbling out among them; and as if the lunacy of Mr.
Tapley were contagious, he immediately began to shake hands
too, and exhibit every demonstration of the liveliest joy.

'Get up, behind!' he said. 'Get up in the rumble. Come
along with me! Go you on the box, Mark. Home! Home!'

'Home!' cried Mr. Tapley, seizing the old man's hand in a
burst of enthusiasm. 'Exactly my opinion, sir. Home for ever!
Excuse the liberty, sir, I can't help it. Success to the Jolly
Tapley! There's nothin' in the house they shan't have for the
askin' for, except a bill. Home to be sure! Hurrah!'

Home they rolled accordingly, when he had got the old man
in again, as fast as they could go; Mark abating nothing of his
fervour by the way, but allowing it to vent itself as unre-
strainedly as if he had been on Salisbury Plain.

And now the wedding party began to assemble at Todgers's.
Mr. Jinkins, the only boarder invited, was on the ground first.
He wore a white favour in his button-hole, and a bran new
extra super double-milled blue saxony dress coat (that was its
description in the bill), with a variety of tortuous embellish-
ments about the pockets, invented by the artist to do honour
to the day. The miserable Augustus no longer felt strongly
even on the subject of Jinkins. He hadn't strength of mind
enough to do it. 'Let him come!' he had said, in answer to

Miss Pecksniff, when she urged the point. 'Let him come! He has ever been my rock ahead through life. 'Tis meet he should be there. Ha, ha! Oh, yes! let Jinkins come!'

Jinkins had come with all the pleasure in life; and there he was. For some few minutes he had no companion but the breakfast, which was set forth in the drawing-room, with unusual taste and ceremony. But Mrs. Todgers soon joined him; and the bachelor cousin, the hairy young gentleman, and Mr. and Mrs. Spottletoe, arrived in quick succession.

Mr. Spottletoe honoured Jinkins with an encouraging bow. 'Glad to know you, sir,' he said. 'Give you joy!' Under the impression that Jinkins was the happy man.

Mr. Jinkins explained. He was merely doing the honours for his friend Moddle, who had ceased to reside in the house, and had not yet arrived.

'Not arrived, sir!' exclaimed Spottletoe, in a great heat.

'Not yet,' said Mr. Jinkins.

'Upon my soul!' cried Spottletoe. 'He begins well! Upon my life and honour this young man begins well! But I should very much like to know how it is that every one who comes into contact with this family is guilty of some gross insult to it. Death! Not arrived yet. Not here to receive us!'

The nephew with the outline of a countenance, suggested that perhaps he had ordered a new pair of boots, and they hadn't come home.

'Don't talk to me of Boots, sir!' retorted Spottletoe, with immense indignation. 'He is bound to come here in his slippers then; he is bound to come here barefoot. Don't offer such a wretched and evasive plea to me on behalf of your friend, as Boots, sir.'

'He is not *my* friend,' said the nephew. 'I never saw him.'

'Very well, sir,' returned the fiery Spottletoe. 'Then don't talk to me!'

The door was thrown open at this juncture, and Miss Pecksniff entered, tottering, and supported by her three bridesmaids. The strong-minded woman brought up the rear; having waited outside until now, for the purpose of spoiling the effect.

'How do you do, ma'am!' said Spottletoe to the strong-minded woman in a tone of defiance. 'I believe you see Mrs. Spottletoe, ma'am?'

The strong-minded woman with an air of great interest in

Mrs. Spottletoe's health, regretted that she was not more easily seen. Nature erring, in that lady's case, upon the slim side.

'Mrs. Spottletoe is at least more easily seen than the bride-groom, ma'am,' returned that lady's husband. 'That is, unless he has confined his attentions to any particular part or branch of this family, which would be quite in keeping with its usual proceedings.'

'If you allude to me, sir——' the strong-minded woman began.

'Pray,' interposed Miss Pecksniff, 'do not allow Augustus, at this awful moment of his life and mine, to be the means of disturbing that harmony which it is ever Augustus's and my wish to maintain. Augustus has not been introduced to any of my relations now present. He preferred not.'

'Why, then, I venture to assert,' cried Mr. Spottletoe, 'that the man who aspires to join this family, and "prefers not" to be introduced to its members, is an impertinent Puppy. That is my opinion of *him!*'

The strong-minded woman remarked with great suavity, that she was afraid he must be. Her three daughters observed aloud that it was 'shameful!'

'You do not know Augustus,' said Miss Pecksniff, tearfully, 'indeed you do not know him. Augustus is all mildness and humility. Wait till you see Augustus, and I am sure he will conciliate your affections.'

'The question arises,' said Spottletoe, folding his arms: 'How long we are to wait. I am not accustomed to wait; that's the fact. And I want to know how long we are expected to wait.'

'Mrs. Todgers!' said Charity, 'Mr. Jinkins! I am afraid there must be some mistake. I think Augustus must have gone straight to the Altar!'

As such a thing was possible, and the church was close at hand, Mr. Jinkins ran off to see: accompanied by Mr. George Chuzzlewit the bachelor cousin, who preferred anything to the aggravation of sitting near the breakfast, without being able to eat it. But they came back with no other tidings than a familiar message from the clerk, importing that if they wanted to be married that morning they had better look sharp, as the curate wasn't going to wait there all day.

The bride was now alarmed; seriously alarmed. Good Heavens, what could have happened! Augustus! Dear Augustus!

*The Nuptials of Miss Pecksniff receive
a Temporary Check*
(*p. 835*)

Mr. Jinkins volunteered to take a cab, and seek him at the newly-furnished house. The strong-minded woman administered comfort to Miss Pecksniff. 'It was a specimen of what she had to expect. It would do her good. It would dispel the romance of the affair.' The red-nosed daughters also administered the kindest comfort. 'Perhaps he'd come,' they said. The sketchy nephew hinted that he might have fallen off a bridge. The wrath of Mr. Spottletoe resisted all the entreaties of his wife. Everybody spoke at once, and Miss Pecksniff, with clasped hands, sought consolation everywhere and found it nowhere, when Jinkins, having met the postman at the door, came back with a letter: which he put into her hand.

Miss Pecksniff opened it; glanced at it; uttered a piercing shriek; threw it down upon the ground; and fainted away.

They picked it up; and crowding round, and looking over one another's shoulders, read, in the words and dashes following, this communication:

'OFF GRAVESEND.
"CLIPPER SCHOONER, CUPID.
'*Wednesday night.*

'EVER-INJURED MISS PECKSNIFF,

'Ere this reaches you, the undersigned will be—if not a corpse—on the way to Van Dieman's Land. Send not in pursuit. I never will be taken alive!

'The burden—300 tons per register—forgive, if in my distraction, I allude to the ship—on my mind—has been truly dreadful. Frequently—when you have sought to soothe my brow with kisses—has self-destruction flashed across me. Frequently—incredible as it may seem—have I abandoned the idea.

'I love another. She is Another's. Everything appears to be somebody else's. Nothing in the world is mine—not even my Situation—which I have forfeited—by my rash conduct—in running away.

'If you ever loved me, hear my last appeal! The last appeal of a miserable and blighted exile. Forward the inclosed—it is the key of my desk—to the office—by hand. Please address to Bobbs and Cholberry—I mean to Chobbs and Bolberry—but my mind is totally unhinged. I left a penknife—with a buckhorn handle—in your work-box. It will repay the messenger. May it make him happier than ever it did me!

'Oh, Miss Pecksniff, why didn't you leave me alone! Was it

not cruel, *cruel!* Oh, my goodness, have you not been a witness of my feelings—have you not seen them flowing from my eyes—did you not, yourself, reproach me with weeping more than usual on that dreadful night when last we met—in that house—where I once was peaceful—though blighted—in the society of Mrs. Todgers!

'But it was written—in the Talmud—that you should involve yourself in the inscrutable and gloomy Fate which it is my mission to accomplish, and which wreathes itself—e'en now—about my—temples. I will not reproach, for I have wronged you. May the Furniture make some amends!

'Farewell! Be the proud bride of a ducal coronet, and forget me! Long may it be before you know the anguish with which I now subscribe myself—amid the tempestuous howlings of the—sailors,

'Unalterably, never yours,
'Augustus.'

They thought as little of Miss Pecksniff, while they greedily perused this letter, as if she were the very last person on earth whom it concerned. But Miss Pecksniff really had fainted away. The bitterness of her mortification; the bitterness of having summoned witnesses, and such witnesses, to behold it; the bitterness of knowing that the strong-minded woman and the red-nosed daughters towered triumphant in this hour of their anticipated overthrow; was too much to be borne. Miss Pecksniff had fainted away in earnest.

———————

What sounds are these that fall so grandly on the ear! What darkening room is this!

And that mild figure seated at an organ, who is he! Ah Tom, dear Tom, old friend!

Thy head is prematurely grey, though Time has passed between thee and our old association, Tom. But, in those sounds with which it is thy wont to bear the twilight company, the music of thy heart speaks out: the story of thy life relates itself.

Thy life is tranquil, calm, and happy, Tom. In the soft strain which ever and again comes stealing back upon the ear, the memory of thine old love may find a voice perhaps; but it is a pleasant, softened, whispering memory, like that in which we sometimes hold the dead, and does not pain or grieve thee, God be thanked!

Touch the notes lightly, Tom, as lightly as thou wilt, but never will thine hand fall half so lightly on that Instrument as on the head of thine old tyrant brought down very, very low; and never will it make as hollow a response to any touch of thine, as he does always.

For a drunken, squalid, begging-letter-writing man, called Pecksniff (with a shrewish daughter), haunts thee, Tom; and when he makes appeals to thee for cash, reminds thee that he built thy fortunes better than his own; and when he spends it, entertains the alehouse company with tales of thine ingratitude and his munificence towards thee once upon a time; and then he shows his elbows worn in holes, and puts his soleless shoes up on a bench, and begs his auditors look there, while thou art comfortably housed and clothed. All known to thee, and yet all borne with, Tom!

So, with a smile upon thy face, thou passest gently to another measure—to a quicker and more joyful one—and little feet are used to dance about thee at the sound, and bright young eyes to glance up into thine. And there is one slight creature, Tom—her child; not Ruth's—whom thine eyes follow in the romp and dance: who, wondering sometimes to see thee look so thoughtful, runs to climb up on thy knee, and put her cheek to thine: who loves thee, Tom, above the rest, if that can be: and falling sick once, chose thee for her nurse, and never knew impatience, Tom, when Thou wert by her side.

Thou glidest now, into a graver air; an air devoted to old friends and bygone times; and in thy lingering touch upon the keys, and the rich swelling of the mellow harmony, they rise before thee. The spirit of that old man dead, who delighted to anticipate thy wants, and never ceased to honour thee, is there, among the rest: repeating, with a face composed and calm, the words he said to thee upon his bed, and blessing thee!

And coming from a garden, Tom, bestrewn with flowers by children's hands, thy sister, little Ruth, as light of foot and heart as in old days, sits down beside thee. From the Present, and the Past, with which she is so tenderly entwined in all thy thoughts, thy strain soars onward to the Future. As it resounds within thee and without, the noble music, rolling round ye both, shuts out the grosser prospect of an earthly parting, and uplifts ye both to Heaven!

THE END

POSTSCRIPT

AT a Public Dinner given to me on Saturday the 18th of April, 1868, in the City of New York, by two hundred representatives of the Press of the United States of America, I made the following observations among others:

'So much of my voice has lately been heard in the land, that I might have been contented with troubling you no further from my present standing-point, were it not a duty with which I henceforth charge myself, not only here but on every suitable occasion, whatsoever and wheresoever, to express my high and grateful sense of my second reception in America, and to bear my honest testimony to the national generosity and magnanimity. Also, to declare how astounded I have been by the amazing changes I have seen around me on every side,— changes moral, changes physical, changes in the amount of land subdued and peopled, changes in the rise of vast new cities, changes in the growth of older cities almost out of recognition, changes in the graces and amenities of life, changes in the Press, without whose advancement no advancement can take place anywhere. Nor am I, believe me, so arrogant as to suppose that in five and twenty years there have been no changes in me, and that I had nothing to learn and no extreme impressions to correct when I was here first. And this brings me to a point on which I have, ever since I landed in the United States last November, observed a strict silence, though sometimes tempted to break it, but in reference to which I will, with your good leave, take you into my confidence now. Even the Press, being human, may be sometimes mistaken or misinformed, and I rather think that I have in one or two rare instances observed its information to be not strictly accurate with reference to myself. Indeed, I have, now and again, been more surprised by printed news that I have read of myself, than by any printed news that I have ever read in my present state of existence. Thus, the vigour and perseverance with which I have for some months past been collecting materials for, and hammering away at, a new book on America has much astonished me; seeing that all that time my declaration has been perfectly well known to my publishers on both sides of the Atlantic, that no consideration on earth would induce me to write one. But what I have intended, what I have resolved upon (and this is the confidence I seek to place in you) is, on my return to England, in my own person, in my own Journal, to bear, for the behoof of my countrymen, such testimony to the gigantic changes in this country as I have hinted at to-night. Also, to record that wherever I have been, in the smallest places equally with the largest, I have been received with unsurpassable politeness, delicacy, sweet temper, hospitality, consideration, and with unsurpassable respect for the privacy daily enforced upon me by the nature of my avocation here and the state of my health. This testimony, so long as I live, and so long as my descendants have any legal right in my books, I shall cause to be republished, as an appendix to every copy of those two books of mine in which I have referred to America. And this I will do and cause to be done, not in mere love and thankfulness, but because I regard it as an act of plain justice and honour.'

I said these words with the greatest earnestness that I could lay upon them, and I repeat them in print here with equal earnestness. So long as this book shall last, I hope that they will form a part of it, and will be fairly read as inseparable from my experiences and impressions of America.

CHARLES DICKENS.

May, 1868.

APPENDIX

MONTAGUE TIGG'S LIFE ASSURANCE COMPANY[1]

Dickens, like Tennyson, both men of journalistic minds, was for ever looking round at the world he was living in (I do not mean the world of his current novel but his own world). He knew what was going on. At the time *Martin Chuzzlewit* was in the writing there was sitting a Select Committee formed in 1841 to examine into fraudulent promotions of Companies and among the most flagrant examples were some of the mushroom Assurance Companies. The Select Committee sat under the chairmanship of Mr. Gladstone, and the mark of Mr. Gladstone is on the Report.

From disclosures made to the Select Committee, and particularly with regard to a Company called West Middlesex General Annuity Assurance Company, Dickens got his idea of the bogus Life Assurance Company. He used it to bring together Montague Tigg—now Tigg Montague—Jonas Chuzzlewit and Nadgett. Montague found out that Jonas thought that he had murdered his father and so got Jonas so completely into his power that his only possible way out was the murder of Montague. That is the main plot of the book and the working out of it with the discovery of Jonas as the murderer of Montague is among Dickens's most skilful pieces of construction and, to my thinking, the most powerful of all his murder stories.

It will be remembered that the 'Anglo-Bengalee Disinterested Loan and Life Assurance Company started into existence one morning not as an Infant Institution but as a Grown-up Company running along at a great pace and doing business right and left'. That had been Montague's idea. He had said to one of his tools 'provided we did it on a sufficiently large scale we could furnish an office and make a show without any money at all'. Many readers of *Martin Chuzzlewit*, including for a long time myself, have wondered how Montague got the cash to pay for the lease and the fine furniture, the porter Bullamy ('by your leave there by your leave') and all the rest of it, for they must have been paid for in cash. The answer is this. It was a time of speculative boom. Anyone could form what was called a Company, but was in fact a partnership, could state as the capital any figure he liked (the capital of Montague's Anglo-Bengalee was 'a figure of two and as many oughts after it as the printer could get into the same line') and issue a prospectus stating as much or as little as he thought fit to state. And on the basis of such a prospectus the Company would issue scrip or, later, transfers in blank, and these pieces of paper, almost as in the times of the South Sea Bubble, could be sold to

[1] I have been greatly assisted in this note on Insurance by Mr. Harold Raynes, an Actuary and the author of *A History of British Insurance*.

gambling speculators by brokers at constantly rising prices. The pieces of paper were, in the case of the Anglo-Bengalee, worthless, for the only 'amenable' asset of the company was property in Bengal which Montague said he owned. This Montague described to one of his tools who was 'tickled into fits' as a 'devilish fine property to be amenable to any claims; the preserve of tigers alone is worth a mint of money'. Montague chose a Life Assurance company because large sums could be collected as premiums for life assurance or the purchase price of annuities with no legal obligation to reserve the amounts required for the future obligations on the death of the assured or the survival of the annuitant. And, it will be remembered, Montague told Jonas once, when he was being lured into the partnership, 'once a couple of unlucky deaths had brought us down to a grand piano; but my dear fellow we got over it; we granted a great many new policies that week (liberal allowance to solicitors by the by) and got over it in no time. Whenever they should chance to fall in heavily as you very justly say they may one of these days, then—"Bolt".' Immediately on the discovery of the murder of Montague the Anglo-Bengalee came to a complete smash with nothing for anybody.

C. R.